PENGUIN BOOKS
LÉLIA

Born in Elbeuf, France, in 1885, André
Maurois was educated in Rouen, where he
came under the influence of the great
humanist and teacher Alain, and at the
University of Caen. He went on to direct
his family's textile factory and to serve as
an interpreter with British forces during
World War I. His first book, *The Silence of
Colonel Bramble* (1918), was a novel affectionately satirizing English military life.
Ariel (1923), a biography of Percy Bysshe
Shelley, was followed by lives of Benjamin
Disraeli, Lord Byron, Voltaire, Marcel
Proust, Victor Hugo, Honoré de Balzac, and
others. These works established and confirmed Maurois's reputation as a master of
the *vie romancée*—biography combining
scrupulous accuracy with colorful narrative
art. Maurois is also the author of histories of
England and of the United States, of literary
and philosophical essays, and of fantasies
and stories for children. In 1938 he was
elected to the French Academy. He died in
Paris in 1967.

LÉLIA

THE LIFE OF GEORGE SAND

ANDRÉ
MAUROIS

Translated from the French by Gerard Hopkins

PENGUIN BOOKS

TO JULIEN CAIN
A TRIBUTE OF AFFECTION AND GRATITUDE

Penguin Books Ltd, Harmondsworth,
Middlesex, England
Penguin Books, 625 Madison Avenue,
New York, New York 10022, U.S.A.
Penguin Books Australia Ltd, Ringwood,
Victoria, Australia
Penguin Books Canada Limited, 2801 John Street,
Markham, Ontario, Canada L3R 1B4
Penguin Books (N.Z.) Ltd, 182–190 Wairau Road,
Auckland 10, New Zealand

First published in Great Britain by Jonathan Cape 1953
First published in the United States of America
by Harper and Row 1953
This edition reprinted by arrangement with Harper & Row, Publishers
Published in Penguin Books 1977
Reprinted 1978, 1980

LIBRARY OF CONGRESS CATALOGING IN PUBLICATION DATA
Maurois, André, 1885–1967.
Lélia: the life of George Sand.
Reprint of the 1953 ed. published by Harper, New York.
Bibliography: p. 575.
Includes index.
1. Sand, George, pseud. of Mme. Dudevant, 1804–1876—
Biography. 2. Authors, French—Biography. I. Title.
PQ2412.M313   1977   843'.8 [B]   76–29029
ISBN 0 14 00.4354 3

Printed in the United States of America by
Offset Paperback Mfrs., Inc., Dallas, Pennsylvania
Set in Linotype Times Roman

CONTENTS

AUTHOR'S PREFACE

WHY GEORGE Sand? Temperamental, as well as emotional, friendships are born of chance meetings and interlocking relationships. A friend whom we admire introduces us to his friends, and they, in their turn, win our affection because of qualities which they share with him. I reached George Sand by way of Marcel Proust and Alain. George Sand's novels were the first grownup books that Marcel Proust received as presents from his mother and his grandmother. When he was ill they read aloud to him from *La Petite Fadette* or *François le Champi*. Later, when he had grown to be a good judge of style, he came to share their liking for that smooth-flowing prose which, like the language of Tolstoy's novels, 'is ever redolent of goodness of heart and moral distinction'. Alain, for his part, always spoke of Sand with respect: 'That great woman', he would say, and the tone of his voice would make it clear that for him the great woman was also a very great man. To these sponsors must be added the masters who were her contemporaries. It is not, for us, without significance that she inspired both Chopin and Musset; that Delacroix had a studio in her house; that Balzac turned to 'George Sand, the best of pals' when he was seeking a subject for one of the finest of his books—*Béatrix;* that Flaubert addressed her as 'my dear master', and wept at the news of her death; that Dostoievsky saw in her a writer who was 'well nigh unique, for vigour of mind and talent'. This accumulated evidence explains why I wanted to study a woman who, for the greater part of her life, was a powerful spiritual influence, and who, today, is far too seldom read.

'Too seldom read?'—some will say: 'That is because she is unreadable.' To hold such a view is to be guilty of a grave error. That many of her novels were written to 'keep the top boiling' is true enough; but we have only to turn to her *Histoire de ma Vie*, to her *Correspondance*, to her *Lettres un voyageur*, to her *Jouranux intimes*, to realize that, as a

7

writer, she can rank with the greatest. What author was
even more fertile of invention? She was 'the voice of her sex
at a time when that voice was seldom heard'. She spoke of
music as well as Stendhal ever did, and better than Balzac
or Hugo. She described the life of French country-people
with a sweep that was sometimes idyllic, sometimes epic.
She felt, and expressed, a sincere love of 'The People' long
before universal suffrage had imposed that attitude upon the
reading public. 'I am not', she said, 'of those patient ones
who take injustice with an unmoved face.' She was the first
woman to deal, as she did in *Lélia,* with those problems of
the senses which only now are being frankly probed.
Finally, in her best period, she was the very embodiment of
the novel, and the opening pages of *Consuelo* remain
among the finest examples of controlled narrative in the
whole of our literature.

All this provides, I hope, a sufficient answer to the
question 'Why Sand?' But there still remained the difficulty
of breathing new life into a story which is usually regarded
as over-familiar. Why, if so many have told it already, go to
all the trouble of telling it again? To that question there are
two answers. The first is, that I was fortunate enough to
discover a number of documents which have enabled me to
give much needed prominence to George Sand's youth and
maturity, and to place in their true perspective a great many
episodes which have become the commonplaces of popular
knowledge. The second is, that most of those who have
written about George Sand have been only too obviously
hostile to her personality and her ideas. It has been too long
the fashion to adopt an attitude of irony and condemnation
in dealing with her. It has been my good fortune, or my
weakness, to develop a great affection for her. Once, when
writing of another woman, Marie Dorval, she used the
following words: 'Her nature is lovely, generous and tender: her intelligence is outstanding: her life has been full of
loose ends and wretchedness . . . and for that, Marie Dorval, I love and respect you the more!' The comment is no
less applicable to the woman who made it. George Sand,
too, was by nature generous: her life, too, was filled with
loose ends and wretchedness. Genius, for all who manifest
it, is an exigent and dangerous companion; for a woman
more than for most. In love, the clash of two geniuses is
productive of a rain of brilliant sparks. I have made no
attempt to conceal her 'loose ends'. To what purpose should
I lie? But I hope that I have set her genius in a bright light,

and led the reader, as I myself have been led, to feel respect for 'this great woman', and to accord to her in the history of literature the honourable place which is hers by right.

I owe more of thanks than can ever adequately be expressed to Madame Aurore Lauth-Sand, who has made free of all her treasures, has told me all she can remember, and has left me absolute freedom to treat the subject as I felt it must be treated. Marcel Bouteron, curator of the Spoelberch de Lovenjoul Collection, has shown the greatest friendliness and generosity in giving me access to all his records, in particular to several groups of letters, Dorval—Sand . . . Balzac—Sand . . . Madame d'Agoult—Sand, of which, till now, little or nothing had been known. Monsieur Julien Cain, Director-General of the Bibliothèque Nationale, Monsieur Jean Porcher, Keeper of the Department of Manuscripts, Monsieur Jacques Suffel, and Monsieur Marcel Thomas, have placed at my disposal much unpublished material—George Sand's *Diaries* from 1852 until her death, her correspondence with the younger Dumas, and the important letters which she wrote to Dr. Emile Regnault, only a small part of which had been used previously by Madame Marie-Louise Pailleron, and Miss Mabel Silver. Monsieur Henri Goüin has allowed me to see the extremely interesting letters which passed between Madame Sand and his grandfather, Edouard Rodrigues. Madame Bonnier de la Chapelle has shown me a number of unprinted letters to Hetzel, the publisher. Monsieur Henri Martineau and Monsieur Alfred Dupont have supplied many useful documents. Madame Jacques Lion brought me into personal contact with the Comte de Grandsagne who, though he could not show me the letters written by George Sand to his great uncle—which were destroyed by the latter's son—did tell me what the tradition in his family had been about them, and about the love-affair to which they referred. Finally, I must express my gratitude to Madame Jacques Suffel who compiled the Index to this long book.

It has been, for many long years, my pleasant duty, in the opening pages of my various volumes on History or Biography, to thank my wife for the immense labours she has undertaken in the matter of research and copying. Never has my debt to her been greater than it is in connection with the present work. She has sorted and classified mountains of letters, records and miscellaneous documents. She has made five separate copies of this extensive manuscript in its successive versions. She has prepared an edition, soon to appear, of the George Sand—Marie Dorval correspondence, as well as of the letters from Sand to Augustine Brault, Charles Marchal, and others, of which she possesses the originals. For all this work, pursued in common, and with a shared enthusiasm, I wish to express my deep sense of obligation.

If, in spite of all the care I have taken, the labour I have exerted, and the friendly help I have received, mistakes can still be found, the responsibility is mine, and I can do no more than ask the reader's indulgence. I have done my best to give shape and order to all that is at present known of a great life. But the progress of research is rich in surprises. It may well be that future scholars will come on sources which I have missed. If any of them can improve on my achievement, I shall be the first to rejoice.

A. M.

PART ONE

AURORE DUPIN

Come to think of it, old man, a woman's a queer fish—
something of all sorts in her—so much that one never
comes to the end.

Paul Claudel

THE STORY of George Sand is that of a woman who by
birth belonged to the borderline between two social classes,
and by education to a small world in which the rationalism
of the eighteenth century rubbed shoulders with the
romanticism of the nineteenth. While still a child she lost
her father, tried to fill his place with a mother whom she
adored, and, consequently, developed a masculine attitude
strengthened by the boyish upbringing which she received at
the hands of a somewhat eccentric tutor who encouraged
her to wear a man's clothes. At seventeen, she found herself
independent and mistress of a great estate and a fine house,
at Nohant. For the rest of her life she strove, unconsciously,
to recreate the free paradise of her childhood, with the
result that she could never submit to a master, and
demanded of love what she found in motherhood—a
chance to protect others who were weaker than herself.
Impatient of all masculine authority, she fought a battle for
the emancipation of women, and sought to win for them the
right to dispose freely of their bodies and their hearts. In
this way she came to exercise a wide and beneficial
influence upon the manners of her time. She was at first a
Catholic, remained, all her life long, a Christian, and
believed herself to be in some sort of mystical communion
with her God. While in no way deviating from her Christian
faith, she became a Socialist as a result of the natural
generosity of her mind and feelings. In 1848 she was mixed
up in a revolutionary movement, and, after its failure,
managed to retain her prestige while remaining true to her
theories. Though in her private, as well as in her public, life
she flouted all the conventions, she kept the respect of her
contemporaries by reason of her genius, her achievements

and her courage. At long last, all passion spent, she succeeded in rebuilding, in the home of her childhood, the paradise which she had lost, and found in a serene old age, marked by unceasing activity and a matriarchal dominance, the happiness which she had vainly sought in passion.

I

KINGS AND SOLDIERS:
MOTHERS-SUPERIOR AND ACTRESSES

IT IS always rash to attempt to explain any person's character in terms of heredity. Some ancestral quirk may suddenly reappear in the fifteenth generation. Not seldom a man of talent will have children of but mediocre ability. Sometimes a lawyer's family will produce a Voltaire. Nevertheless, nobody reading the record of George Sand's forbears but must feel that she was marked out for a strange and lofty career. Many families can count in their genealogy at least one, and sometimes two or three, outstanding individuals, but in her background *everyone* had been extraordinary. She came of a line in which there had been an intermingling of kings and mothers-superior, of great soldiers and ladies of the theatre. All the women had been named Aurore—as in the fairy-tales. They had all had sons and lovers, and had been fonder of the sons than of the lovers. Natural children had rained down like hail, but had been recognized, promoted and royally raised. The men had been anarchists, devastatingly attractive, tender-hearted, and cruel. 'To this robust and uncouth race,' said Maurras, 'George owed something of her physical make-up, her earthiness, her impudent challenging of life, and what I can only call her gluttony of desire.'[1] Her family history held elements of the *comédie galante*, and something, too, of the *Arabian Nights*.

The Koenigsmarks, of German-Swedish stock, had won a name in the days when a soldier of fortune could move from Court to Court, and become Commander-in-Chief of the very armies against which, a short time previously, he had been fighting. They had first appeared upon the

[1] CHARLES MAURRAS: *Les Amants de Venise*, p. 9.

European stage during the Thirty-Years' War. The founder
of their fortunes had been a certain Field-Marshal Jean
Christophe de Koenigsmark, a hardened trooper, a thieving
rogue of a fellow, at once both shrewd and brutal. All the
men of the clan who came after him had been heroes,
adventurers, and fatal to women. The women had been
saints or adorable sinners. Among them had figured, at the
end of the seventeenth century, an Aurore de Koenigsmark.
She was a creature of rare beauty, and sister to that Philippe
de Koenigsmark whom the Elector of Hanover—the future
George I of England—had had murdered, out of jealousy,
in 1694. Inquiries had been set on foot as a result of this
murder, and in the course of them she had made the
acquaintance of Frédéric-Augustus, Elector of Saxony who,
later, became King of Poland. With her great, dark, velvety
eyes, her wit—which was wholly French—and her brilliant
gaiety, she was quite irresistible. Augustus of Saxony loved
her in his rather coarse way. For him one woman was as
good as another, provided she were elegant and consenting.
He was completely insensitive to her qualities of delicacy
and distinction. He had a child by her. This child, who was
born in 1696, was baptized by the name of Maurice, and
created Comte de Saxe.

All intimacy between the lovers had ceased even before
Aurore's lying-in, and was never again renewed. Abandoned by Frédéric, she showed her brilliant and aggressive
spirit by taking refuge in the Protestant Abbey of Quedlim-
bourg, which, to the horror of the Mother-Superior, she
proceeded to turn into a cross between the Hôtel de Ram-
bouillet and a Court of Love. During her residence there
she gave a reception for Peter the Great which long
remained famous, in the course of which she appeared in the
character of a Muse to recite a French poem written by
herself. On that occasion she charmed not only the
Tsarevitch, but the Lady Abbess, a deaf and very old lady,
who mistook the Muse for a Saint. Aurore sang Italian airs,
accompanying herself on the harpsichord. The Queen of
Sweden called her 'my Swedish nightingale'. She travelled
post from Dresden to Vienna, from Berlin to Stockholm,
and died in 1728, ruined by her indulgence in jewellery,
dresses and perfumery—and also by her son whom she
loved tenderly, and for whom she was violently ambitious.

This son, Maurice de Saxe, had his mother's beauty of
feature and height of forehead. He was by nature loyal,

frank and affectionate. Like many natural children he was inclined to indulge in a mood of sentimental melancholy, and would passionately kiss the twin lockets containing the portraits of his father and his mother. From a very early age he showed a marked disposition for the profession of arms. His father had him trained in a hard school. By his orders Maurice was compelled to live on a diet of bread and broth. He was made to cross Europe on foot, carrying his equipment. At thirteen he was promoted Ensign on the field of battle, and eloped with a girl of his own age whom he had got with child. He had inherited his father's gift of promiscuity. His 'affairs' with the Princesse de Conti, with Adrienne Lecouvreur, with Madame Favart and the Duchesse de Bouillon, were the talk of Paris. As the son of a King he long let his mind dwell on the possibilities of kingship from a morbid desire to obliterate the memory of his bastardy. He tried to get himself elected Duke of Courland. His mother, Aurore de Koenigsmark, and his mistress, Adrienne Lecouvreur, sold their jewels to help him. He was on the point of marrying the widow of the late Duke, Anna Ivanovna, the future Tsarina of all the Russias, and was within sight of his goal, when he was imprudent enough to introduce a young mistress into the Palace. The incident was discovered, and away went all his cloudy dreams of grandeur. Love had cost him a crown.

But it was an age in which glory and love were easy bedfellows. As is generally known, Maurice de Saxe eventually took service under the King of France, whose relative he became when he brought about a marriage between his niece, Marie-Joseph de Saxe, and the Dauphin. She was the mother of Louis XVI, Louis XVIII and Charles X. Though no king himself, he belonged to a family of kings. As a Protestant, he had need of this marriage in order to assure his own position in a Catholic realm. He conducted the necessary negotiations as he fought his battles, 'match lit and drums beating', and, in his furtherance of the intrigue, wrote a series of charming and madly ill-spelt letters. Illiterate soldier though he was, he had a weakness for ideas, and composed a volume of *Rêveries* or *Mémoires sur l' Art de Guerre*, in which his views were trenchantly and lucidly expressed:

Axiom: The more dead, the fewer enemies. *Consequence:* Kill, but don't get killed.—Twelve soldiers to capture a

small outpost?—what an idea! Not that it matters, if it
happens that the twelve are lieutenants-general . . . It
needs more cleverness than is generally supposed to draw
up a bad plan of battle: but one has got to be able to
change it into a good one at a moment's notice: nothing
so disconcerts the enemy. He expects one thing, and takes
steps to meet it. He attacks—and finds no one there to
fight.[1]

That is a true forecast of Torres Vedras. In these same
Rêveries, he showed himself to be a true child of the
Century of Enlightenment. He was curious in matters of
reform, and, having laid down the law for the better
destruction of the human species, set himself to show the
way to its propagation. 'Marriages should be for five years
only, after which time they should be renewable only on the
grant of a special dispensation, unless at least one child has
been born during that period.' . . . It is somewhat
remarkable that such an idea should have occurred to the
great-grandfather of George Sand.

He was a lucky commander in the field, and deserved his
luck. He became a Marshal of France. Throughout his
career of conquest, he never lost his love of women, and
they gave him theirs in return. 'It is a matter of common
knowledge,' wrote Marmontel, 'that for all his nobility and
pride of spirit, the Maréchal de Saxe had the habits of a
debauchee. From taste as much as from policy he liked an
atmosphere of gaiety to prevail in his armies, saying that
Frenchmen never fought so well as when they were led with
a laughing flourish, and that what they most feared in war
was boredom . . .'[2] He kept permanently 'on the strength' a
company of actresses, obedient to his whims. Each evening
there was a performance, and an announcement of the next
day's battle was made from the stage.

> Demain nous donnerons Relâche,
> Quoique le directeur s'en fâche;
> Vous voir comblerait nos désirs.
> On doit tout céder à la gloire.

[1] MAURICE, COMTE DE SAXE: *Lettres et Documents
inédits*, pp. 342-55.
[2] GASTON MAUGRAS: *Les Demoiselles de Verrières*, p.
28.

Nous ne songeons qu'à vous plaire,
Vous ne songez qu'à la victoire.[1]

'Maurice's reputation for gallantry was known far and wide,' and when Monsieur and Madame Rinteau, a middle-class couple living in Paris, and destined to become the ancestors of Monsieur and Madame Cardinal, decided, in 1745, that it might be no bad thing to turn to account the extraordinary beauty of their two daughters, Marie and Geneviève, it was of him that they thought. Marie was seventeen years old, Geneviève nearly fifteen. The zealous efforts of their admirable parents were amply rewarded. Marie found favour, for several years, in the Marshal's eyes. He set her up in a house in Paris, where the two sisters came to be known as 'les demoiselles de Verrières'. In 1748 she bore him a daughter, Marie-Aurore, who inherited her parents' good looks. That was all, however, that she did inherit. Marie de Verrières, who was no more addicted to virtue than other great ladies of her day, fell successively into the arms of the son of Monsieur d'Epinay—a Farmer-General—and of Marmontel, the writer, who had been entrusted with the task of teaching her diction. On his return from a journey into Saxony, the Marshal 'learned not only of the lessons in elocution which his protégée had been taking, but also of the use to which she had been turning them'. He had a strong sense of what was due to him, and, when he died in 1750, it was found that both mother and daughter had been cut out of his will. The only heirlooms which Marie de Verrières was able to leave to the girl consisted of a snuff-box given by the King to his Marshal after the Battle of Fontenoy, a seal, and a portrait of Aurore de Koenigsmark.

'La Demoiselle Aurore, natural child and only daughter of the Maréchal de Saxe,' presented a humble petition to Madame la Dauphine, the hero's niece, in which she begged to be granted a pension. In the margin there is the following comment: *The King grants to Mademoiselle Aurore an*

[1] GASTON MAUGRAS: *Les Demoiselles de Verrières*, p. 30. This might (very roughly) be rendered as follows: We shall not be playing as usual tomorrow,/ Much to the management's anger and sorrow;/ We want nothing more than to see you alive./ Yours not to reason why, yours but to do and die./ To please you and charm you we all of us strive/ And to fight and to conquer we know that you'll try.

*allowance of eight hundred livres for such time as she shall
remain in a Convent to be named by Madame la
Dauphine.*'[1] The choice fell on the Religious House of the
Ladies of Saint-Cyr, and there the young girl received the
education of a lady of quality. In 1766 the Dauphine, being
unable to hand her back to her mother, wished to find a
suitable husband for her. The fact, however, that she was a
natural child of unknown parentage frightened off all the
acceptable suitors. Aurore suffered sorely under this
humiliation, and, in a second petition, addressed, this time,
to the Parlement, asked that the following words should be
inserted after her name in the official register: *natural
daughter of Maurice, Comte de Saxe, Marshal-General in
the Armies of France, and of Marie Rinteau.*[2]

The Parlement gave its approval to this act of posthumous recognition, and a suitable husband was found.
Everything written by George Sand in her *Histoire de ma
Vie* about the first marriage of her ancestress, and repeated
by successive biographers, is wholly fictional and bears no
relation to the facts. Aurore is there described as having
married a certain Comte de Horn, one of Louis XV's
bastards. It is further stated that this marriage was never
consummated, and lasted for only three weeks, at the end of
which time the husband was killed in a duel. There is not a
word of truth in all this. The man in question was, in fact,
an Infantry Captain of forty-four, called Antoine de Horne.
On the occasion of her daughter's marriage Marie de
Verrières gave a magnificent reception at her country
'retreat' in the village of Auteuil,[3] at which Aurore made
the acquaintance of her half-brother, the Chevalier de
Beaumont, the son of one of Maurice de Saxe's successors
in her mother's favours.

When Horne married, he was appointed King's Lieutenant at Sélestat, in other words, Commandant of a small
town. Five months, however, elapsed before he set off for
Alsace. When, at length, the King's Lieutenant and his
wife did arrive, they were certainly not received, as Sand
describes, with a beating of drums, nor were the keys of the
town presented to them on a golden tray. Nevertheless,

---

[1] Ministère de la Guerre, archives administratives: *Dossier
du maréchal de Saxe.*

[2] Archives nationales: *Parlement* X i A 4533, May 15th,
1766.

[3] Now, No. 45 rue d'Auteuil.

'they were both of them filled with feelings of gaiety and hope'. They reached Sélestat on a Monday. Next morning, Monsieur de Horne 'complained of a tightness in the chest', and, in spite of bleedings, was dead by Friday.[1] The young widow once more flung herself at the feet of Louis XV, with a request that she should be continued in her husband's employment. But the suggestion was absurd. How could a woman be appointed military governor of a town? To make matters worse, Aurore lost her protectress, the Dauphine, who died in 1767. She took refuge in a Convent, where she did her best to compose a really effective petition:

> *Aurore de Horne to the Duc de Choiseul, Minister for War.* I am the daughter of the Maréchal de Saxe, and have been so recognized by the Parlement of Paris. Death deprived me of my father at a very early age ... I feel sure that the Minister who directs the War Office with so much wisdom, benevolence and distinction ... will not permit the daughter of the Maréchal de Saxe to languish in poverty. ...[2]

But the Duke remained deaf to her appeal. After Choiseul's fall three years later, she again addressed herself to the new Minister: 'I am the daughter of the Maréchal de Saxe, and have been so recognized by the Parlement of Paris ... Finding it impossible to pay for my keep in the Convent where I had taken refuge, I have been compelled to leave it.'[3] This was true. She had betaken herself to the house of Marie de Verrières who was living at that time with her sister Geneviève, in a handsome establishment in the Chaussée d'Antin, where the two of them kept house on the liberality of their protectors. There the Demoiselles de Verrières maintained a high style of living, saw much of good society, and gave theatrical entertainments. Monsieur d'Epinay was one of their 'regulars', thus giving a fine example of 'illegitimate constancy'. Aurore's mother, though now a woman in her ripe maturity, had lost none of her beauty. Among her lovers had been several men of cultivated mind, such as Marmontel and the poet Colardeau. Anyone reading her letters today cannot but be struck by the clear-cut quality of their style and the strength of intelligence which they express.

[1] Ministère de la Guerre: *Dossier de Horne* (Antoine).

[2] Ministère de la Guerre: *Dossier du Maréchal de Saxe*, April 1768.

[3] Ibid., November 1772.

Monsieur d'Epinay, the Farmer-General, had grounds of complaint against his wife. The celebrated Madame d'Epinay, the friend of Rousseau, Diderot and Grimm, was, at this time, carrying on an 'affair' with another financial operator, Claude Dupin de Francueil. He was an excellent musician, and, having offered to give Madame d'Epinay lessons in composition, very soon transformed them into lessons in love. The only revenge which d'Epinay allowed himself to take was to introduce his rival into the Verrières circle where, since he promptly fell in love with the younger sister, Geneviève, Dupin de Francueil found his punishment unexpectedly sweet. He saw, in these new surroundings, a great deal of his mistress's niece, Aurore de Horne, and was soon charmed by her education and her talents. The young widow who, at Saint-Cyr, had been brought up in the tradition of Madame de Maintenon, combined the gifts of a great lady, an accomplished actress and a perfect musician. In the private theatre of the house in the Chaussée d'Antin, where performances were given under direction of the critic, La Harpe, she appeared as Colette in the *Devin de Village*, and, later, in Operas by Grétry and Sedaine. She had a sure and subtle taste in music, and preferred above all other composers the old Italian masters, Porpora, Hasse and Pergolesi. Not unnaturally she was much courted, but, having more of sense than sensibility, never yielded to the temptations offered by the free-mannered society in which she found herself. But of the protection afforded by a deep-rooted faith, she knew nothing. Voltaire's deism was her only form of religion.

She was a woman of great strength of mind, clear-sighted, and imbued with the ideals of pride and self-respect. With coquetry she would have nothing to do, being too highly gifted to feel the need of a technique of provocation which offended her sense of dignity. She passed through a period of great licentiousness, and lived in a corrupt society, without losing so much as a feather from her wings. Condemned by a strange freak of destiny never to know passion in marriage, she managed to solve the great problem of how to live remote from emotional storms, and never became the victim of ill-natured gossip or slander. . . .[1]

[1] GEORGE SAND: *Histoire de ma Vie*. Volume I, p. 39.

Her two greatest friends were Buffon, who was a frequent attendant at the Verrières 'Salon', and the pleasing Dupin de Francueil, whom she called *Papa*. This Monsieur Dupin (or du Pin) was the representative of the Farmer-General in the Province of Berry, where he also had an interest in a cloth-mill at Chateauroux. All things considered, he was a man of substance.

Aurore de Horne was outstanding at a time when many women dazzled their contemporaries with their culture. The following letter to an adorer gives some idea of her charm:

> . . . You, too, sir, show a desire to instruct me in philosophy, but I would have you know that I have ever been, from my earliest years, a follower of Plato . . . Should you feel some aversion to believing what I say, because of my appearance and my age, then you must overcome it, as I, for my part, have had to overcome a certain feeling of self-respect in admitting it. I am infinitely sensible to the emotion of friendship, to which I can yield without reserve, since, however far I may set its limits, they are for ever clearly before my eyes. But I fear anything that might make me blind, and ever dread the doing of too much or not enough . . . I have always lived with persons considerably my elders, and have insensibly placed myself on a level with them. My youth was of no long duration, and, from that being so, I may have lost something of enjoyment, though I have gained much in reason. . . .[1]

In 1775, Marie de Verrières died at the age of forty-seven, passing away as quietly as she had lived. Monsieur d'Epinay, who had been her lover for twenty-five years, deeply mourned the loss—but continued to keep house with the surviving sister. Aurore, feeling that life with her aunt might be difficult, retired once more into a Convent. There, her old friend, Dupin de Francueil paid her frequent visits, and in spite of his age found favour in her eyes. In 1778 he asked her hand in marriage, and was accepted. Marie-Aurore was thirty, Dupin de Francueil, sixty-two. She had been a widow for fifteen years and had learned wisdom.

They were very happy. Much later, when she was an old lady, Madame Dupin spoke as follows to her granddaughter, Aurore, who was no other than George Sand:

[1] Catalogue of the Etienne Charavay Sale of manuscripts, May 14th, 1888.

An old man is capable of greater love than a young one, and it is impossible not to feel love for somebody who loves one with perfect devotion. I used to call him 'my old husband' and 'papa'. He liked me to do so, and ever addressed me as his daughter, even in public. But no one was really old in those days! It was the Revolution that brought old age into the world. Up to the day of his death, my dear, your grandfather was handsome, elegant, well cared-for, gracious, sweet-smelling, lively, kindly, affectionate and easy-tempered. As a young man he was too attractive to have rested content with so uneventful an existence, and I should, as likely as not, have known less of happiness with him. I might have had too many rivals. I am quite sure that what I had of him was the best part of his life, and that never did a young man make a young woman so happy as I was in our marriage. We were never parted for a moment, and, so long as he was there, I never knew a moment's boredom. He was a living encyclopaedia of ideas, information, and talents, and for me ever remained an inexhaustible storehouse of delight. He had the secret of pleasing others when he was himself pleased. We used to spend the days making music together. He was an excellent performer on the violin, and always made his instruments himself, because he had a knowledge of the craft, just as he had of clock-making and architecture, or turning on the lathe, or painting. He could construct locks and paint pictures. He knew about decoration and the preparing of food. He could write poetry, compose music, and do carpentry. He was a beautiful embroiderer. I know nothing that he could not do. It was a misfortune that he squandered his estate in the satisfaction of his many tastes, and in making experiments. I was dazzled by his brilliance, and we ruined ourselves quite delightfully. In the evenings, when we were not at some reception, he would sit by my side, drawing, while I was busy with my tatting. Sometimes we would read to one another, turn and turn about, or charming friends would call on us, and keep his wit and wisdom on the stretch in conversation. I had many young women as acquaintances who had made brilliant marriages, but they never ceased to say how much they envied me my old husband.

Ah! in those days, people knew how to live, and how to die! . . . No one allowed himself to be dictated to by sickness. If a man had the gout, he walked, just the same, and without pulling faces. It was part of one's education never to show when one was suffering. Business preoccupations, which are the ruin of home-life, and make the mind muddy, were then unknown. A man would meet ruin without flinching, like those gamblers who can lose without showing either anxiety or resentment. There were those who would have themselves carried, more dead than alive, to a shooting party, and people held that it was far preferable to die at a play or a ball than in bed between lighted candles, with a lot of nasty men in black praying over them. We were philosophers in those days. We made no exhibition of austerity. We had to put up with it at times, but we did not make a showy virtue of it. Those of us who behaved rationally, did so because we wished to, not because we wanted to display our prudishness or priggery. We enjoyed life, and when the moment came for us to leave it we had no wish to spoil the pleasure that others took in living. When my old husband bade me farewell he made me promise to live long and happily. To show so generous a heart was a sure way to be truly mourned . . .[1]

In their life together, Monsieur and Madame Dupin cultivated the arts of literature and music. Both admired Rousseau and received him as a friend. They spent a great part of their lives at Châteauroux, where official duties demanded their presence, and lived in princely style at the old Château Raoul. They spent a fortune on music, spongers and charities. When Monsieur Dupin died in 1788, his affairs, both private and public, were in a state of terrible confusion. After all the debts had been paid, Madame Dupin was left with a yearly income of seventy-five thousand livres. That was what she called being 'ruined'.

[1] GEORGE SAND: *Histoire de ma Vie*. Volume I, pp. 43-4.

II

THE REVOLUTION AND THE EMPIRE

A REVOLUTION separates the inhabitants of a country into three main groups: those who cannot help but be whole-hearted revolutionaries; those who cannot help but be on the other side, and those whose sympathies fall between the two, because, though bound by tradition and sympathy to the threatened class, they have, nevertheless, certain grievances against it. It was to this third group that Madame Dupin de Francueil belonged. Through her royal connections, her education and her fortune, she was an aristocrat. On the other hand, she had never ceased to smart under the stigma of a double bastardy. She was touched in her pride, and held that there had been a lack of generosity in the way the Court had behaved to her. In her mother's house, as in her husband's, she had mingled freely with the philosophers of the day, and with several of the contributors to the *Encyclopaedia*. She had a deep veneration for Voltaire and Rousseau, and she hated the members of the Queen's circle. She regarded the early days of the Revolution as an opportunity to be revenged upon her enemies. They were, too, the triumphant vindication of theories in which she had always believed.

After she had been left a widow, she settled with the boy Maurice, who was eleven years old in 1789, in the rue du Roi de Sicile. With them went the boy's tutor, the 'Abbé' Deschartres. The latter, who had never been ordained, found it wiser to discard his 'bands' and to become the 'Citizen Deschartres'. He was an odd creature, a man with a well-stored mind, a handsome presence, and the temperament of a pedant and a purist, who carried self-satisfaction to extravagant lengths. But he was brave to the point of recklessness, and admirably unselfish: in fact, he had 'every good quality and a character that was nothing short of intolerable'. His pupil Maurice Dupin, who yielded to none in nobility of feeling, developed a deep affection for the ridiculous, yet sublime, individual who had been put in charge of

24

his education. Maurice was as pretty as a girl. He had the fatal charm of the Koenigsmark family, their velvety eyes, their love of music and poetry, their natural sense of style. Mother and son adored one another. When Mirabeau's revolution became Danton's revolution, Madame Dupin fell out of love with it. She was foolish enough to subscribe sixty-five thousand livres to a fund which had been raised for the emigré princess. She had no wish to leave France, but thought it advisable to move from Paris. The Province of Berry, where once she had been happy, seemed likely to offer a secure refuge. Consequently, on August 23rd, 1793, she bought from the Comtes de Serennes—whose property had not been sequestrated—the estate of Nohant, lying between Châteauroux and La Châtre, for the sum of thirty thousand livres. There had once been at Nohant a feudal castle, built by a certain 'Charles de Villalumini, Squire at arms', in the fourteenth century. Of this nothing now remained but a single tower, noisy with the cooing of doves. A large house in the style of Louis XVI had replaced the ancient structure, a simple but commodious place which stood 'in the middle of a rural community, and was about as ostentatious as a village dwelling'. The main entrance faced the *Place* of the little country town, with its old and shady elms.

Madame Dupin was on the point of withdrawing into the peaceful solitude of this countryside when, as the result of an entirely unforeseen blow, she found herself suddenly in a position of great danger.

While still in Paris she had left the apartment which she had first taken, and gone to live in the rue de Bondy, hoping thereby 'to remain obscure and forgotten in the stress and tumult of the times'.[1] Her landlord was an old fellow called Ammonin, who had been a body-servant in the employment of the Comte d'Artois. With his help she managed to conceal a silver dinner-service and some jewellery 'behind a large birdcage in the dressing-room, between the panelling and the masonry'. On 5th Frimaire (November 25th), 1793, an individual called Villard informed the Revolutionary Committee (of the Bonconseil Section) of the whereabouts of this hiding-place, the use of which was strictly against the

---

[1] Cf. CH. GAILLY DE TAURINES: *Adventuriers et Femmes de Qualité. La Fille du Maréchal de Saxe* (Hachette, Paris, 1907).

law.[1] The place was searched, and the Citizeness Dupin
arrested. She was imprisoned in the Convent of the English
Augustinians, in the rue des Fossés-Saint-Victor which had
been turned into a 'house of detention for English women'.
This was a terrible shock for her son and for Deschartres,
not only because it involved separation, but, more particularly, because they had every reason to fear for her safety.
The Terror, at that time, was at its height, and Deschartres happened to know that a number of extremely
compromising papers, including the Comte d'Artois's
acknowledgment of the money she had 'lent', were in the
secret hiding-place to which the Comité de Sûreté Général
had affixed its seal. With Maurice's help he managed to get
into the house at night, break the seal, and burn the
dangerous documents. So high a degree of courage and
devotion more than counterbalanced any silliness in his
character. In the midst of all these happenings Maurice
matured rapidly. The hard lessons of his youth combined to
produce a man of 'honesty, courage and simple goodness
well above the ordinary'.

The Citizen Deschartres and, more especially, the young
Citizen Dupin, set themselves, not without success, to win
over the members of the Bonconseil Section to the side of
the imprisoned woman, who, for her part, well schooled in
the drawing up of petitions, addressed a powerful plea
to the Comité de Sûreté Générale:

> Citizens of the Republic, do not, I beg of you, harden
> your hearts to the sorrows of a mother who has been torn
> from her son, from the child whom she has brought up,
> and who has never, till now, been left without a mother's
> care; a young man trained by her to the service of his
> country . . . When the Tyrant attempted to save himself
> by a shameful flight, a certain citizen then living in the
> house which I occupy asked me whether I had no fears
> for my goods and chattels, and said that if I would
> entrust him with my silver dinner-service he would hide it
> in a sure place where no harm could come to it. I did as
> he suggested. Since then I have made no use of it,
> thinking it improper, in these hard times to draw at-
> tention to such criminal luxury . . . My behaviour in all
> circumstances, from the very first day of the Revolution,

[1] Archives nationales. Comité de Sûreté Générale (Dossier
Ammonin).

and my concern for the general good, should, surely, have set me above suspicion. Furthermore, permit me to say that no single one of my relatives, near or distant, has taken refuge in emigration. Three years ago I might myself have gone abroad, taking with me all the property which, at that time, was wholly in my control. But I had too independent a spirit to consent to breathe the corrupt air of slavery. . . .[1]

Then came Thermidor. The Citizeness Dupin was released from prison, and even obtained a 'Certificate of Civic Dependability', on the recommendation of Antoine, one of her former footmen, who had been among the conquerors of the Bastille. In October 1794, she was able to take up residence at Nohant, with her son. All that remained of her once great fortune, now sadly reduced by the collapse of the Assignats, and numerous forced loans, was an annual income of fifteen thousand livres. She spent four years in completing Maurice's education, assisted by Deschartres. It was necessary to decide what profession he should adopt. His own choice was for a military career, but from this she did her best to dissuade him. Ever since the Terror Madame Dupin had shown herself to be markedly hostile to the excesses of the Revolution, though not to its principles. She was still loyal to her earlier feelings of devotion to Voltaire and Rousseau, but she would have preferred to see Maurice in the service of a moderate Monarch, with the hope of having his merits rewarded. In Paris, Barras was king. Nothing, fundamentally, had changed. As always, the honest man trudged the streets while the scoundrel rode in his carriage. The only difference was that 'the scoundrels were not the same'.

That comment came from Maurice who, in the mood of scepticism which inevitably follows on the heels of social crises, found a bitter pleasure in seeing gorged revolutionaries coming to terms with fops in order to save their skins —and their purses. He could always find comfort in his violin for not being one of those who had made a personal fortune from the régime. It was happiness enough to shine as a member of an amateur orchestra at La Châtre. During 1798, in the close companionship of thirty or so young people of both sexes, the Duvernets, the Latouches, the

---

[1] Archives nationales. Comité de Sûreté Générale. Agenda of the Meeting of the 21st Frimaire (December 11th), 1793.

Papets, the Fleurys, he engaged much in private theatricals 'for which he showed a natural talent which was quite
irresistible'. But inaction weighed heavily upon him. In vain
did his mother tell him that by taking service as a soldier of the Republic he would be risking his life for a bad
cause. His own view was that any cause is good which
involves fighting for one's country. He knew that his mother
was a great deal more patriotic than she would admit, and
had the details of Jemmapes and Valmy at her finger tips no
less surely than those of Fontenoy, Raucoux and Lawfeld.
'What!' said she, 'serve as a simple private in the ranks?'
But La Tour d'Auvergne, the bravest soldier in all France,
to whom he was presented, spoke differently. 'Can it be that
the grandson of the Maréchal de Saxe is afraid of facing
fire?—surely not!' He enlisted as a volunteer.

Those were the days when Frenchmen dreamed of
carrying liberty to Europe, and of making themselves
universally beloved in the process. Maurice Dupin, at
Cologne, achieved conquests of a different kind—and told
his mother all about his love affairs. Virtuous though she
was—from temperament rather than principle—she had
remained at heart a woman of the eighteenth century, and
found it easy to forgive a man for being dissolute, provided
he showed a certain style in his love-making. Maurice, true
to the family tradition had, before leaving Nohant, got with
child one of the young servant-girls. Madame Dupin took
charge of her little illegitimate grandson, Hippolyte, who,
since he had not been acknowledged, went by his mother's
name of Châtiron. The child was put out to nurse with a
peasant woman who lived not far from Nohant. Madame
Dupin sent news of him to Maurice.

Nohant: 6th Brumaire, Year VIII: The *Little House* is
well and of a monstrous size. He has a charming laugh. I
spend my time fussing over him. It is wonderful how
soon he has grown to know me. . . .[1]

Maurice's letters were lively, and touched with poetic
feeling. If he went to the theatre, and heard a song his
mother used to sing, he wrote: 'In a flash I was back with
you, in the little pearl-grey boudoir of the rue du Roi de
Sicile! It is extraordinary how music sends one back into
memories of the past—and it is the same with smells. When

[1] GEORGE SAND: *Histoire de ma Vie.* Volume I, p. 338.

I sniff your letter, it is as though I were in your room at Nohant, and my heart misses a beat at the thought that I am going to see you open that inlaid desk which smells so good!'[1]

Madame Dupin longed for peace, her son for war, so that he might become an officer. 'If I distinguish myself in action, I might be promoted on the field. What happiness! What glory!'

In 1800, at Milan, Maurice Dupin, now an aide-de-camp, resplendent with yellow plume and scarlet, gold-fringed sash, met, in his general's room, an extremely pretty, laughing and charming girl who was filling the autumn of the old warrior's years with sunshine. Her name was Antoinette-Sophie-Victoire Delaborde.

I give all three of her Christian names because, in the course of her restless life, she has used each in succession . . . When she was a child she was usually addressed as Antoinette, because it was the name of the Queen of France. During the successful wars of the Empire, Victoire naturally prevailed. After their marriage, my father always called her Sophie. . . .[2]

Sophie-Victoire Delaborde was the daughter of a professional bird-fancier who had once kept an 'Estaminet' specializing in billiards. He later took to selling canaries and goldfinches on the Paris Quays. She had had a stormy childhood because her family was poor, and the times were bad.

My mother [wrote George Sand] was one of the world's gypsies, spiritual heir of a degraded and vagabond race. At one time she was a dancer, or, rather, something lower than a dancer, in one of the most disreputable of the Paris theatres, but a rich man rescued her from this abject condition, only to impose upon her one more abject still. She was thirty when my father first fell in with her, and living in a whirl of wild indiscipline. But he had a big heart, and realized that the beautiful creature had still a capacity for love. . . .[3]

[1] GEORGE SAND: *Histoire de ma Vie.* Volume I, p. 241.
[2] Ibid., Volume I, p. 409.
[3] Unpublished letter from George Sand to Charles Poncy (December 23rd, 1843). Spoelberch de Lovenjoul Collection: Group E. 921, folio 70.

Sophie-Victoire had had a child by a former lover, a girl called Caroline who went with her when she threw in her lot with the Army of Italy. Scorning all considerations of seniority, Sophie abandoned the General in favour of the Lieutenant, whom she enchanted by her mingled passion and tenderness. In his dealings with the ladies of La Châtre and the Mothers-Superior of Germany, he had already had a taste of sentimental devotion, but now this charming, wanton woman revealed to him the secrets of romantic passion. To his mother he confided the full extent of his happiness: 'How good it is to be loved!—to have a fond mother, good friends, a handsome mistress, a share of glory, fine horses, and enemies to fight!' It might be Stendhal's Fabrice speaking. This new attachment showed no signs of weakening on either side, and Madame Dupin became extremely uneasy. Disciple of Rousseau though she was, she preferred the cynicism of *Les Liaisons Dangereuses* to the ecstasies of *La Nouvelle Héloïse*. Sexually frustrated as the result of her scrupulous temperament, she had made of her son the object of a jealous and passionate affection. When, in 1801, Maurice returned to Nohant, he set up his mistress at the Tête Noire Inn at La Châtre. Deschartres had never been in love, and therefore understood nothing of the heats of passion. Out of devotion to the young man's mother, he conceived the idea of driving her son's mistress from the neighbourhood. A number of violent scenes took place at the inn. Sophie-Victoire lacked neither high spirits nor presence of mind. She jumped down the tiresome creature's throat, and Maurice would have used physical violence, had he not remembered how devoted and courageous Deschartres had been at the time of the Terror. This attempt on the tutor's part, however, made it quite clear that Madame Dupin was going in daily fear of a marriage, the idea of which, until then, the two lovers had not so much as dared to entertain. And, 'since it always happens that one gives form and substance to the dangers upon which one broods to excess, the dread of the possibility became an accurate forecast of the future'.[1]

Maurice Dupin to his mother, May 1802: Tell Deschartres from me that his pedantic attitude, his small-shopkeeper's mentality, and his eunuch's views on passion, would make him an admirable consultant for

[1] GEORGE SAND: *Histoire de ma Vie*. Volume I, p. 433.

Monsieur de Pourceaugnac alike in matters of morality and in those relating to his bodily ailments. . . .[1]

After this legitimate outburst, Maurice fell into his mother's arms, and even into his tutor's. The three were far too fond of one another to keep a quarrel going for long. All the same, he remained faithful to his mistress. Though Madame Dupin de Francueil still made a great show of being superior to aristocratic prejudice, she continued to take the view that misalliances inevitably produce misunderstandings. Her son, however, with a soldier's simple good sense, refused to see that there was any question of a misalliance.

Maurice Dupin to his mother: Prairial, Year Nine (May 1801): Do let us be reasonable, mamma. Why should my liking for this or that woman be regarded as an insult to you or as a danger to myself? Why should you worry yourself sick, or shed tears, over this business? . . . I am no longer a child but a man, and perfectly well able to make up my own mind about where my affections lie. I am quite willing to admit that there do exist women who, to talk like Deschartres, are *strumpets* and *creatures*. But I neither like them nor seek them out . . . Such degrading epithets, however, can never be applied to a woman of heart. Love purifies everything. Love can ennoble the most abject of beings, and, still more, those whose only crime is that they had the misfortune to be flung into the world without moral support, without money and without anyone to advise them. Why should a defenceless woman be condemned?[2]

Meanwhile, France was changing. Bonaparte was flowering into Napoleon. Maurice was at Charleville with General Dupont, and these two republicans had little liking for the 'Master'. Dupont said that one never knew how to tackle him, that when he was in one of his moods he was impossible. Promotion was now a matter of backstairs intrigue. Things were very different from what they had been in the days of Marengo. 'This is what happens when a man gets supreme power . . . You didn't bring me up, mother dear, to be a courtier, and I am not the sort of man

[1] Ibid., Volume I, p. 434.
[2] GEORGE SAND: *Histoire de ma Vie*. Volume I, p. 471.

to hang about the anterooms of the great . . .' She had not
brought him up to be either a courtier or a cadger. All the
same, she wished that he might have been successful in his
profession, and rather less faithful in love. Logic was not
this charming woman's strong suit.

In 1804, Sophie-Victoire joined Captain Dupin in camp
at Boulogne. She was with child, and, realizing that her time
was drawing close, wanted to return to Paris. She did so,
and Maurice followed her. On 16th Prairial, Year XII, they
were secretly married at the Mairie of the Second
Arrondissement, in order to assure legitimacy of the child.
The young wife was all a-quiver with happiness. She had
long set her heart upon this union, though she had never
really believed in its possibility. Up to the very last moment
she had been willing to withdraw, because she realized that
her lover, overcome by terror and remorse, dared not tell
his mother of what they were planning to do. Immediately
after the ceremony, Maurice left for Nohant, 'fully
intending to make a complete confession'. But he could not
do it. Scarcely had he begun to speak that Madame Dupin
dissolved in tears, and, 'in a mood of tender perfidy' said to
him, 'there is somebody you love more than me, and that
means that you no longer love me at all! . . . If only I had
died, like so many others, in '93, I should never, then, have
had a rival in your affections!'[1] Maurice kept his secret to
himself.

On July 1st, 1804, the first year of the Empire, while
Sophie-Victoire, in Paris, was dancing a quadrille, dressed
in a pretty rose-coloured costume, and Maurice was
improvising on a Cremona violin, she suddenly felt unwell
and went into the next room. A moment later, her sister
Lucie cried out: 'Come quick, Maurice, you've got a
daughter!' 'She shall be called Aurore,' he said, 'after my
poor mother, who is not here to give her a blessing, though
she will live to bless her in days to come.' Aunt Lucie, who
was a woman of experience, declared: 'She was born to the
sound of music and with the colour of roses about her. That
means that she will be happy and fortunate.' The father
of this third Aurore was twenty-six years old, the mother,
thirty.

It was no longer possible to keep anything secret. On
learning of the marriage, Madame Dupin de Francueil did
her best to have it annulled. But she was opposed by the

[1] Ibid., Volume II, p. 72.

firm determination of her son, who said to her, in a style worthy of Rousseau: 'Do not reproach me for being what you have made me.' Since the ceremony had not taken place in church, Sophie-Victoire did not consider herself to have been really married. Consequently she could not hold herself to be guilty of rebellion against her husband's mother, and failed to understand why she should have incurred the resentment of that 'proud and aristocratic lady'. Admittedly, since the marriage was an accomplished fact, Madame Dupin de Francueil's embittered obstinacy was both cruel and useless. But she was passionately attached to this only son of hers. She had planned a brilliant future for him, and could not bear to see him living in an attic with a 'trollop' for wife. He was forbidden to mention Sophie in her presence, and she obstinately refused to see the girl. A scene worthy of Greuze had to be contrived in order to trick her into taking her granddaughter on her lap. But as soon as she saw the dark, velvety, Koenigsmark eyes, she could hold out no longer. 'Poor mite, this is none of her doing! Who was it brought her?'—'Your son in person, madame; he is waiting below.' Maurice rushed upstairs, with tears streaming down his cheeks, and embraced his mother. Emotion is an act of policy. It makes it possible to admit an error without seeming ridiculous.

Some time later the religious ceremony was carried out in the presence of Madame Dupin. But relations with her daughter-in-law remained difficult. All that was best in Sophie-Victoire expressed itself in a sense of pride. She was conscious to her finger-tips that she belonged to the 'People', and thought herself to be 'possessed of more true nobility than all the patricians and nobility in the world'.[1] There was nothing of the wheedler about her, and she was too sensitive, too genuinely reserved, to run the risk of being cold-shouldered. Only in domesticity was she completely happy, and her husband shared her views on this point. 'From them', said Sand, 'I inherited that profound sense of unsociability which has always made the great world intolerable to me, and a *home* essential . . .'[2] They also bequeathed to her their horror of a society which, by its prejudices, had caused them much unhappiness.

[1] GEORGE SAND: *Histoire de ma Vie*. Volume II, p. 117.
[2] Ibid., Volume II, p. 118.

III

AURORE'S CHILDHOOD

. . . When my mother set off for Italy, I was sent to
Chaillot to be weaned. For the next two or three years
Clotilde and I lived there in the house of a good, kind
woman. On Sundays we were taken into Paris on a
donkey's back, each of us in a panier along with cabbages
and carrots for the market. . . .[1]

CLOTILDE MARECHAL was the little Aurore Dupin's
first cousin, and Aunt Lucie's daughter. Since Maurice's
family refused to have anything to do with the child, she was
intimate for the first four years of her life only with her
mother's relatives. Her father, a serving soldier of the
Empire, was nothing more to her than a flashing, gold-laced
apparition who dashed in, between campaigns, to give her a
kiss. It was not until much later that she read Maurice
Dupin's letters, and realized how deeply fond she was of
him. It was a matter for joy to her, then, to discover in this
vanished father of hers a warrior and a rebel, a man who
held nobility of birth to be an illusion and poverty a useful
lesson. She was proud to think that she resembled him. 'My
nature is a reflection of his, dim no doubt, but fairly
complete . . . Had I been a boy, and had I lived twenty years
earlier, I know, and feel in my bones, that I should have
behaved in all circumstances precisely as he did.'

From her earliest childhood she developed a passion for
her mother. Sophie-Victoire had a sharp tongue and a hasty
temper, but her charm, her gaiety, and a sort of natural
poetry which marked her attitude to life, carried all before
them. Though completely uneducated, she possessed a
'magic key' which could open the mind of her small
daughter to that sense of the beautiful which, though
untrained, was deeply embedded in her own heart. 'That's

[1] GEORGE SAND: *Voyage en Auvergne et en Espagne*,
1825, a work published posthumously in the Literary Supplement of the *Figaro*, August 4th and 11th, 1888.

pretty,' she would say: 'look!'—and her instinct, bred in the
Paris streets, rarely led her astray. All day long she would
cook, knit and sew in their attic in the rue de la Grange-
Batelière. She would perch Aurore on an unlit foot-warmer,
hemmed in by four chairs, and give her picture-books to
look at filled with scenes from mythology and the gospel
stories. These she explained with a simple-minded shrewdness. She told the child fairy-tales, made her recite fables,
and, at night, say her prayers. It was not difficult to keep
her amused. She could sit for hours on her foot-warmer, as
on a tripod, her eyes fixed in a stare, her mouth half open,
telling herself stories, or listening to a neighbour playing on
the flute. All her life long she remembered, with a stab of
nostalgic longing, those days of tender affection, magic and
poverty.

In 1808, Colonel Dupin was serving in Madrid as
Murat's aide-de-camp. He had made his peace with
Napoleon, though he still held it against the Emperor that
he should have a weakness for flatterers unworthy of so
great a man. In spite of everything, however, he loved him.
'He does not frighten me in the least,' said Colonel Dupin,
'and that makes me feel quite certain that he is far superior
to the picture he likes to paint of himself.' Sophie-Victoire
was wildly jealous. She was terrified to think what effect the
beautiful Spanish women might be having on her husband.
Consequently, though already eight months pregnant, she
joined him, taking their daughter with her. The journey
through a hostile countryside was rough and difficult. All
that Aurore remembered of it was Godoy's palace in
Madrid, and a diminutive aide-de-camp's uniform which
she put on to amuse Murat.

Maurice Dupin to his mother: June 12th, 1808: Sophie
was brought to bed this morning of a strapping boy . . .
Aurore is vastly well, and I shall pack myself and the lot
of them into a barouche which I have recently acquired.
Then, we shall set off on the road to Nohant . . . The
prospect, mother dear, fills me with joy. . . .[1]

He expected immense happiness from this first meeting in
the family home, and felt sure that they would find an
affectionate welcome. But the journey back was beset with
difficulties. They had to drive across battlefields littered with

[1] GEORGE SAND: *Histoire de ma Vie.* Volume II, p. 208.

corpses. The children suffered from fever and insufficient food. They picked up lice in dirty inns, and caught the itch. Aurore was an inert, hot, bundle of misery. She did not recover consciousness until they drove into the courtyard at Nohant. She was received by her grandmother, whom she scarcely knew, and stared with amazement at the pink and white face, the crimpled fair wig, and the little round cap with its stiff lace cockade. Madame Dupin de Francueil was hospitable and masterful. She packed off her daughter-in-law to get some rest, and carried Aurore into her own room. There, she laid her on the bed shaped like a hearse, with great plumes of feathers at each corner, and lace-trimmed pillows. Never had the child seen anything so lovely, and she thought she must be in heaven.

The children were 'deloused' and generally cleaned up by their grandmother. Deschartres, wearing knee-breeches and white stockings, examined them in his capacity as a medical man. Aurore made a quick recovery, but the baby died. A few days later, Maurice, who had brought back from Spain a magnificent and mettlesome charger called *Leopardo,* was killed. He had been thrown on to a heap of stones just as he was leaving La Châtre after dark, to ride back to Nohant. what a tragedy—and what a misfortune, too, that, as a result of sheer chance, two women so different in temperament and background, should now have been forced into so close an intimacy: 'one of them (the grandmother), pink and white, fair, serious, calm, and dignified, with all the self-confidence of a great lady and the open-handedness of a patroness; the other (her daughter-in-law), dark-haired and pale, hot-blooded, awkward, always shy in fashionable company, and always prone to outbursts of temper: jealous and passionate, angry and weak, a sad mixture of qualities both good and bad. . . .'[1]

The grandmother studied the mother with curiosity, trying to understand why it was that Maurice had loved her so dearly. It was not long before she solved the problem. Sophie-Victoire was an artist to her finger-tips. She could write a good letter, though she did not know the first thing about spelling, could sing delightfully, though she had never studied music, draw, though she had never been taught. There was something fairylike, too, about the way she could cut out the most exquisite dresses, trim hats, or mend a broken harpsichord. There was nothing she would not

[1] GEORGE SAND: *Histoire de ma Vie.* Volume II, p. 243.

attempt, and in everything to which she turned her hand she succeeded . . . But she had a horror of things that served no purpose, and would mutter that they were no better than a lot of toys for an 'old countess'.[1] She had a sparkling gift for criticism, bringing to it the glibness of the Paris guttersnipe. It is easy to see why her daughter, Aurore, found such an endless source of amusement in her 'incisive and picturesque' comments.

Though, when apart, mother and grandmother had no great liking for one another, they could not help but get on well together at close quarters, because each had the powerful weapon of charm. Whenever quarrels did break out, Aurore sided with her mother, regardless of the fact that she was constantly nagging and smacking her. She would not have put up with one hundredth part of such rough handling from her grandmother. She realized that the 'old countesses' of the district treated her mother with contempt, and felt the need to play a man's part in protecting her. Realizing the depths of despair in which her husband's death had plunged the young widow, the child tried to make up for the loss by an extravagant devotion. Very soon she learned to read, and lived in the world of Perrault and Madame d'Aulnoy. Among her companions was Hippolyte Châtiron, the child of the 'little house', her half-brother, a great, hulking, unmannerly boy, whom she, nevertheless, found amusing. He pretended that he had been a dog in a former existence, and he certainly had retained a cur's uncouthness. Then there were the children of the village, Ursule, Pierrot, Rosette, Sylvain, with whom she enjoyed the freedom of the lovely park, and imbibed that passionate love of the soil which she never lost.

'I already adored the poetry of country things', she said, 'and have never ceased to do so.' She loved the great, slow-moving oxen with their hanging heads, the hay-wains, the village merrymakings and peasant weddings, and listening to old tales told by the spinners at the fire. She took part in the work of the farm, tending the lambs, feeding the chickens. Her mother encouraged her in these activities, and played with her in her own little patch of garden, building grottoes of cockle-shells, and tiny waterfalls for her delight. It worried her grandmother to see the child learning 'country manners'. She had grown fond of her, and already foresaw that she would grow up to be an intelligent woman.

[1] *Ibid.*, Volume II, p. 245.

Without altogether meaning to, she got into the habit of
calling her 'Maurice', and would refer to her in conversation as 'my son'. In this way, mother and grandmother were
responsible for making her regret that she was not a boy.
Aurore longed to protect her mother. Madame Dupin
wanted to bring back her son from the grave.

Madame Dupin de Francueil was anxious to wean her
granddaughter from the 'bird-fancier' side of her past, in
order that she might grow up to be worthy of her Nohant
heritage. Aurore knew that the 'old countesses' were
watching her with critical eyes. One of them, Madame
Pardaillan, always called her 'my poor child', and used to
say: 'You must be a good girl, because you will have a great
deal to forgive.' On every side she heard references to the
difficult future which her father's misalliance had prepared
for her. Her grandmother's dearest wish was to see her grow
into a woman 'of gracious appearance, attentive to the
details of her person, and of an elegant style'.

My grandmother believed that deportment must be
learned, that there was a right way of walking, of sitting
down, of curtseying, of picking up a glove, of holding a
fork, and handing a plate—a whole code of behaviour, in
fact, which a child must be taught at a very early age to
imitate, in order that it might become second nature to
her. My mother thought it all very silly, and I am inclined
to hold that she was right. . . .[1]

The disagreement between the two women extended to
the sphere of religion. Aurore's mother had the emotional
belief of the simple-minded. She was a French woman of
her period, and, though she did not realize it, interpreted
her faith by the standards of poetic feeling which were already on the way to becoming romantic. Her grandmother,
on the other hand, belonged to the eighteenth century. She
accepted the abstract tenets of the philosophers. She 'held
Jesus Christ', she said, 'in high esteem'. She saw to it that her
grandson, Hippolyte, took his First Communion, but was
equally insistent that the ceremony should be conducted by
the good old curé of Saint-Chartier, the Abbé de Mont-
peyrous. Aurore, who yearned after the marvellous, was
devoted to her mother's religion, and was sad when her

[1] GEORGE SAND: *Histoire de ma Vie*. Volume II, p. 330.

grandmother, in the name of reason, mocked at the miracles which were so dear to her.

> I read of the wonders of the Jewish and the Pagan antiquity with an equal pleasure. I wanted nothing better than to believe in them. From time to time, my grandmother would make a short, sharp appeal to my reason, and I must confess that I entirely failed, in her eyes, to justify my faith. I took revenge, however, in the rather mild grief which I felt on such occasions, by refusing to deny it in my heart. . . .[1]

It was inevitable that the two Dupin ladies should part. The grandmother would not hear of receiving Caroline-Delaborde under her roof, that half-sister of Aurore who had been born before Maurice had appeared upon the scene. The mother, for her part, refused to abandon a child who had no one in the world to turn to but herself. The decision before Sophie-Victoire was a difficult one. What she had to determine was whether Aurore would be happier at Nohant than with herself. The child begged and pleaded, but her mother could not feel sure that she had the right to deprive her of a brilliant upbringing, and an income of fifteen thousand livres a year. Besides, they would see one another every winter in Paris. Aurore felt as though she were being torn in pieces. 'My mother and my grandmother were quarrelling over the fragments of my heart.' Her passion for her mother appeared to her in the agonizing light of a forbidden love. She thought of herself as bound hand and foot, and delivered over to the mercies of a world which Sophie-Victoire had taught her to despise. She cried a great deal.

Nevertheless, after her mother had gone she enjoyed complete freedom at Nohant. Deschartres instructed her in Latin and the natural sciences. Her grandmother made of her an accomplished musician, and taught her to appreciate the treasures of her own literary taste. Aurore read the *Iliad* and *Gerusalemme Liberata*. She wrote descriptions of country life which contained the seeds of her future vocation. But what really mattered was that, like mankind in general, she was in quest of a religion, and that nobody could point her along the way to one. In her books she could

[1] GEORGE SAND: *Histoire de ma Vie*. Volume II. p. 365.

find only Jupiter and Jehovah. She longed for some more
human God. Though she had been confirmed, no one ever
spoke to her of Christ. She needed to love and to understand: 'Why am I here?—Why should this world exist?
—Why should there be evil men?—Why should there be
old countesses?' The adult projects these questions on to
the world's screen, where they take the form of Myths. But
children need to feel that they are upheld by some magic
power. Aurore created for herself a private god, a being all
sweetness and goodness. She called him *Corambé*. In the
secret depths of a little wood she built him an altar of moss
and shells, and thither she would go, not to sacrifice, but to
liberate birds and beetles. The trouble was that before she
could liberate them she must make them prisoner, and that
caused her much suffering. From which it may be seen that
Corambé-ism, like all religions, had its mysteries.

The Empire was moving to its fall. Marie-Aurore de Saxe
wasted no tears on it, but Sophie-Victoire Delaborde shared
with the 'old sweats' a fervid faith in Napoleon. This created
yet one more subject of disagreement between the two
ladies. When her grandmother took Aurore to Paris, the girl
was overjoyed to find again in her mother's diminutive
apartment the remembered settings of her childhood, the
vases filled with paper flowers, the foot-warmer on which
she had sat and dreamed her earliest dreams. But these visits
were doled out to her with a niggardly hand. She was
forbidden to play with her half-sister Caroline, and
whenever this happened there were scenes and tears. 'Just
you be patient for a while,' her mother said, 'I am going to
open a dress-shop, and then I will take you back, and you
can help me.' This mirage, in which even Sophie-Victoire
herself only half believed, filled Aurore with enthusiasm,
and she took to hiding away odds and ends of trinkets so
that one day she might sell them and run away from
Nohant. Her grandmother's maid, Mademoiselle Julie, a
dried-up stick of a woman who thoroughly disliked the
child, discovered the innocent plot. 'So you want to go back
to your slum, do you?' she said contemptuously—and went
off to tell what she had found to Madame Dupin de
Francueil, who had just had a slight stroke.

The scene which followed was deplorable. The old lady
made her granddaughter kneel beside her bed, and
proceeded to tell the story of her own life, of her son's life,
and, finally, of her daughter-in-law's life, whose past and
present immoralities she painted in lurid colours. This she

did without pity or kindliness. In fairness to Aurore's
mother she should have said something of the causes which
had produced her many misfortunes, should have explained
how she had been left lonely and poor at the age of
fourteen, should at least have mentioned the corrupt and
wealthy libertines who are always ready to tempt the
hungry and debauch the innocent, should have made some
reference to the heartlessness of a self-righteous society.
Most of all, she should have explained to the child that
Maurice Dupin had been truly and faithfully loved for eight
years. But the poor old woman, spurred on by hatred and
by what she took to be her duty, was not sparing of words.
Sophie-Victoire she said was a 'lost woman', and Aurore a
'blind child, trembling on the brink of destruction'.

This revelation produced a violent crisis. Aurore neglected
her studies and became a rebel. 'My child,' said her grandmother, 'you have lost what common sense you ever had
. . . I have therefore decided to place you in a Convent,
and I shall take you to Paris in order to carry out my
intention.' Aurore rejoiced at the prospect. She hoped that
in Paris she would see her mother again, and that in a
Convent she would find a new way of life. She entered it
without the slightest sense of regret, and without any feeling
of repugnance.

IV

THE DEVIL AMONG THE NUNS

It is with faith as with love: one finds it when one least
expects to.   *George Sand*

THE CONVENT of the *Dames Augustines Anglaises,* an
English Community established in Paris when Cromwell
was engaged in persecuting the Catholics, succeeded in
slowly smoothing away the rough edges of the ardent,
mannerless tomboy who had been the product of country
ways and family quarrels. On her way through Paris she
had been to see her mother. She had greeted her 'darling
mamma' with her accustomed emotional warmth, and a

passionate wish to see in her all those virtues for which an unjust world refused to give her credit. She had found a woman who, apparently, regarded her with complete indifference, whose new life of freedom was filled with strange faces and new interests, and who approved of the Convent project in words which wounded her deeply.

The point of capital importance was that Aurore, during the decisive years of her childhood, had developed for her mad, attractive mother feelings of devotion which nothing could ever destroy. Much later, she wrote: 'Oh, my dear, dear mother, why is it that you do not love me, while I love you so truly?' She was to learn, because the lesson was necessary, how to do without her indifferent parent, how no longer to consult her. But reject her entirely, she could not. She always retained her liking for those rather vulgar high spirits. If, all through her life, Sand took pleasure in shocking 'Society', if, in every revolution, she always began by thinking the 'People' in the right, the reason was that she had never ceased to remember with emotion Sophie-Victoire's garret. Naturally enough she tried to rationalize her attitude, but the misery of having been severed from the greatest love that she had ever known took pride of place in her heart, and long determined her outlook.

At the age of fourteen she was sick of being an 'apple of discord' between two beings of whom she wanted to be equally fond. The Convent took on for her the appearance of a marvellous oasis in a cruel world. The House had remained extremely English. The 'Mothers' all came from England, and she fell into their habits—which she never lost—of talking English, of drinking tea, and sometimes even of thinking in English. The 'Mothers' had good, if somewhat distant, manners. Their establishment was as highly thought of in the Faubourg-Saint-Germain as the Sacré-Coeur or the Abbaye, and Aurore had for company the daughters of some of the noblest families in France. The Professed nuns and girl boarders all alike wore the habit of fine purple serge. The building, which was almost like a large village, was covered in vine and jasmin. The only men who ever entered it were the two chaplains, the Abbé de Villèle, and the Abbé de Prémord. Here are some of the 'resolutions' drawn up for the girls by the Abbé de Prémord, and copied out by Aurore Dupin.

Every day I will get up at a fixed hour . . . giving to sleep only the time necessary to keep me in health, and never lying in bed from laziness. I will be scrupulous in avoiding vain dreamings and aimless thoughts, and will never indulge in any imaginings which might bring a blush to my cheeks were anyone to know what was going on in the intimacies of my heart. I will carefully avoid ever being alone with persons of the other sex, and will never permit them the least familiarity, no matter what their age or condition. If any proposal should be made to me, no matter how honourable, I will at once inform my parents. I will take care always to be sweet-tempered and considerate to those who serve me, but will never permit them to be familiar with me: nor will I ever confide in them my sorrows or my joys. . . .[1]

So far as Aurore was concerned, warnings against persons 'of the other sex' were unnecessary. She never thought about men. The young girls at the Convent, she decided, fell into three groups: the 'Sensibles', who were pious and sweet-tempered: the 'Devils', who were rebellious and amusing, and, between these two, the 'Stupids' who formed an inert and fluid mass like the sodden substratum of any public assembly. During her first year 'Dupin' was one of the Devils, always ready to make one in mad expeditions across the roofs or through the cellars. Her friends nicknamed her *Calepin* because she was for ever jotting things down in a notebook, or *Some Bread*—the English translation of *du pain*. The nuns knew her as *Madcap,* or *Mischievous,* because she was always in trouble. The other girls were very fond of her. At first they had thought her apathetic and silent, an expanse of 'still water'. She would withdraw into gloomy privacies of thought occasioned by her reflections upon the strange family situation in which she found herself. But experience showed that she was always ready to enjoy the gaiety of others, and when things got difficult was always dependable, and at times even heroic. She was the person to be with when it was a question of 'looking for the victim' (imprisoned in some subterranean dungeon)—a favourite adventure-game at the Convent.

The 'Devils' had a way of scrawling the covers of their books—the *Spelling Book, The Garden of the Soul*—with the initials of their 'best friends' (ISFA was the talismanic

[1] Unpublished. Spoelberch de Lovenjoul Collection: Group E. 946, ff. 10-14.

word for 'Dupin'—meaning Isabelle, Sophie, Fanelly, Anna)—and with mock confessions:

> Alas! dear Father Villèle, I have very often covered myself with ink-stains, snuffed candles with my fingers, and suffered from indigestion as a result of *gorging*, as they say in the great world where I was a-brought up . . . I have scandalized the young *ladies* in the class-room by reason of my lack of personal cleanliness . . . I have slept during catechism, and snored at Mass . . . This week I made at least fifteen howlers in French, and thirty in English. I scorched my shoes at the stove, and stank out the whole form. *Mea culpa, mea culpa, mea maxima culpa.* . . .[1]

On the fly-leaf of one of her English books she inscribed the following odd, childish and aggressive sentiments:

> This worthy and interesting volume belongs to my noble self: DUPIN, in other words, the illustrious Marquis de Sainte-Lucy, Generalissimo of the French Army of the Convent, a great fighter, an accomplished officer, an intrepid soldier crowned on the field of battle with oak-leaves and laurel, defender of the Oriflamme.
>
> Anna de Wismes is a little darling. Isabella Clifford is charming.
>
> Down with the English! Death to the English dogs! Long Live France! I do not like Wellington.
>
> Interesting sillies, dear little snotties, I miss you terribly: all the same, I am delighted to think that I am no longer in the infant class. Good night.
>
> The House of the English Ladies, 1818.[2]

This first year as a boarder was, for Aurore, a time of ingenuousness, courage and revolt. She had become one of the 'Devils' because 'a sort of emotional despair had driven her to seek intoxication in her own mischievous activities'.[3] It often happens that unhappy children, because of a sense of grievance and resentment, become difficult children. Aurore was not at this time, nor could she have been, an orthodox Catholic, for she had been brought up by a tutor

---

1 GEORGE SAND: *Histoire de ma Vie.* Volume III, p. 131.
2 Unpublished. Madam Aurore Lauth-Sand's Collection.
3 GEORGE SAND: *Histoire de ma Vie.* Volume III, p. 84.

THE DEVIL AMONG THE NUNS

who had never been ordained, and a grandmother who belonged to the tradition of Voltaire. She followed the religious discipline from necessity and a sense of seemliness. She had never once, since her confirmation, felt the least desire to take Communion. She believed in God, and in the Life Everlasting, but there was nothing of fear in her faith, and she felt that she might receive the benison of Grace on her death-bed, and so be saved. All that was best in her found expression in her tender feelings of devotion to her friends, and in her very real love of the arts. She could play the harp, she had a genuine gift for drawing, and she scribbled both blank verse and prose. When she became a 'Senior', and had a 'cell' of her own, her description of it showed considerable talent.

My room is on the first floor as one comes down the stairs. It is neither round nor square, and six very short paces will measure its extent. It is close to the eaves, and within sound of the nightly concert of the cats. My bed, innocent of curtains, is in the widest part, that is to say, next to the wall . . . I say *innocent of curtains,* but it is wrong of me to complain, because I have no need of them. The beams and the sloping roof are immediately above my head, and so low that I bump against them each morning when I get up. My window, composed of four small panes, looks out onto an expanse of tiled roofs . . . The wall-paper was once yellow—or so I am told. However that may be, I find in it a source of constant interest, for it is scribbled all over with names, mottoes, verses, all sorts of foolishness, reflections, and dates—the relics of former occupants. Whoever has this room after me will find much to amuse her, for I am determined to leave behind me, for her to decipher, whole novels and poems, as well as a number of intriguing drawings scratched with a knife on the stone sill outside the window. . . .[1]

It was the custom for several of the Ladies to have one girl in particular among the boarders over whom they watched with maternal solicitude. In her second year Aurore developed a longing to be 'adopted' in this way by

[1] This passage is quoted by Samuel Rocheblave in an article entitled 'George Sand avant George Sand', which appeared in the *Revue de Paris* for May 15th, 1898.

the best, the most charming, the most intelligent of the
nuns, Madame Mary-Alicia. This Mother Alicia was very
beautiful. The goodness of her heart was reflected in a pair
of wide blue eyes framed in dark lashes, 'mirrors of purity'.
Neither wimple nor habit could disguise the gracefulness of
her figure, and she had a lovely voice. Aurore grew to have
a childish passion for her, and, taking her courage in both
hands, asked to become her adopted little girl. 'You?' said
Madame Alicia, 'the worst Devil in the place?' But Aurore
insisted. 'Please give me a chance. Who knows, perhaps I
may improve, just so as to please you . . .' Madame Alicia
gave way, and the girl, seeking in this admirable woman
what she had in vain hoped to find in her own mother, and
even in her grandmother, became the victim of an intense
and painful devotion. Her friends noticed a great change in
her. *'You are low-spirited today,* Dupin; *what's the matter!'*[1] She felt the need of somebody to worship, of somebody in whom she might find perfection, of somebody to
whom she might dedicate her heart, a second Corambé,
and this imagined somebody had taken on the grave, calm
features of Mary-Alicia.

She set herself to read the *Lives of the Saints.* The
courage and stoicism of the martyrs struck some deep chord
in her nature. In the Chapel of the Convent there was a
picture by Titian representing Christ in the Garden of
Olives.

As I turned the pages of the *Lives of the Saints,* I let my
eyes wander more and more to this picture. The time was
summer, and the setting sun did not touch it during our
hours of prayer. But the object contemplated was now
more necessary to my inward than to my outer eye. As I
knelt there, mechanically interrogating those vast, vague
masses, I would try to find a meaning in Christ's agony,
to probe the secret of that deliberately endured and
lacerating torment. I began, in an uncertain sort of way,
to be aware of something far greater and more profound
than anything I had been taught, of some deep sadness in
myself, as though I were indeed being torn with pity and
with a sense of suffering such as, till then, I had never
known. . . .[2]

[1] GEORGE SAND: *Histoire de ma Vie.* Volume III, pp.
150-1.
[2] GEORGE SAND: *Histoire de ma Vie.* Volume III, p. 179.

There was another picture, too, less beautiful than the Titian, which showed Saint Augustine under the fig tree, and a miraculous shaft of light on which were written the famous words: '*Tolle, lege*', which the son of Saint Monica had heard issuing from the leaves.

This *Tolle, lege* led Aurore Dupin to re-read the Gospels, but a memory of Voltairean mockeries put her on her guard. 'Reading of the agony and death of Jesus, I remained quite cold.' Was she, then, to remain a 'Devil' all her life long? She was now fifteen years old, and a young girl's vague and solemn sense of expectation had taken the place, in her, of the earlier and untamed exuberance of childhood. One evening, as she sadly paced the cloisters, watching, as though they had been ghosts, those fervent women passing back and forth, 'who were stealing furtively to lay their hearts in penitence at the feet of the God of Love', it occurred to her to study their behaviour at closer quarters. She entered the Chapel. The charm of the interior, wrapped at this hour in darkness, took hold upon her spirit. The only light in the nave came from the single silver sanctuary lamp. One of the great windows was open, and through it drifted the mingled scents of jasmine and honeysuckle:

One star lost in the immensity of the night, was, as it were, framed in the glazed tracery, and seemed to be watching me fixedly. The whole place breathed a calm, a loveliness, a composure and a mystery such as I had never dreamed. The birds were singing . . . I was shaken in some strange way to the very roots of my being. I felt dizzy, and then I seemed to hear the murmur of a voice, saying—*Tolle, lege* . . . The tears gushed from my eyes. At that moment I felt that I loved God truly . . . It was as though some obstacle, till then invincible, which had stood between the ardour of my spirit and this burning centre of ineffable adoration, had suddenly melted away. . . .[1]

Always her religion was to take this mystical form, was to appear to her in the guise of a direct communication with the Divine Will within her. In faith, as in love, a woman

[1] Ibid., Volume III.

delights 'to gather into her heart the flood of passion which
drives upon her from above, to be its slave'.[1] Thereafter, all
sense of spiritual resistance ceased. 'My heart once
captured, I deliberately, and with a sort of frantic joy,
showed reason the door. I accepted everything, I believed
everything without a struggle, without any consciousness
of suffering, without regret, and without false shame. How
could I blush for what I had learned to adore?'[2]

Being, as she was, a creature of extremes, she took this
conversion for a vocation, and formed the project of
entering the Order. But it was typical that she should think
of doing so as a lay sister charged with such humble tasks as
sweeping out the rooms, and tending the sick. There may, in
her nature, have been elements of both saint and sinner, but
her saintliness was of the kind that finds its exercise in
household chores. 'Our Lord', Saint Teresa had said, 'walks
among the kitchen crocks.' 'I will be a lay sister', thought
Aurore, 'a servant bowed down with fatigue, a sweeper of
gravestones, a scavenger, anything . . . provided only that
God shall see my suffering, and His love be my sole reward.
. . .[3]

Her confessor, the Abbé de Prémord, a wise old Jesuit,
laid down for her a rule of high thinking and healthy living.
He felt moved when she sought him out for the purpose of
making a general confession and to achieve her peace with
Heaven, but he did not encourage his young penitent in a
form of mysticism which tended to break down the barrier
between man and God. The prudent Abbé had no wish that
she should become so deeply absorbed in dreamy longing
for a better world as to forget her duty of making the best of
this one. 'I truly believe', wrote Sand at the age of fifty, 'that
but for him I should now be either mad or a professed
Religious.' For the young girl's devotion had become a
passion. 'I felt my complete inner identification with the
Divine as a miracle. I literally burned, like Saint Teresa. I
could no longer sleep, no longer eat. I walked without being
conscious of the movements of my body. . . .'[4] The Abbé de
Prémord found it blameworthy that she should exhaust
herself like a guttering lamp in the pursuit of a self-

[1] SIMONE DE BEAUVOIR: *Le Deuxième Sexe*. Volume II,
p. 508.

[2] Ibid., Volume III, p. 207.

[3] Ibid., Volume III, pp. 195-6.

[4] GEORGE SAND: *Histoire de ma Vie*. Volume III, p. 188.

satisfying mysticism, instead of assuming her human responsibilities. 'You are growing', he said, 'into a sad, gloomy ecstatic. Your companions no longer recognize you . . . Take care! If you continue in this way, you will breed in others a fear and a hatred of piety . . . Your grandmother writes that we are turning you into a fanatic . . . Though you may not realize it, there is a deal of pride in what you take to be humility, and in the morbid scrupulosity which now obsesses you. I enjoin upon you as a penance that you shal return to the innocent pleasures and pastimes suited to your age. . . .'[1]

She obeyed. Her thoughts became calmer. After six months of mortification and brooding, she suddenly came down to earth. She arranged private theatricals in which she took part, wrote out for performance the whole of *Le Bourgeois Gentilhomme,* which she had read at Nohant, became the life and soul of the Convent, and an object of infatuation to nuns and pupils alike. But, in her heart of hearts, she still clung to her vocation, and, as she wrote later, would almost certainly have taken the veil, had not her grandmother, now much enfeebled and deeply worried by the extravagant emotionalism of her granddaughter, sent for her to Nohant. 'My child, it is necessary that I find a husband for you quickly, for I shall soon be gone.'[2] The old lady believed that her death was not far off, and spoke of it with philosophic calm. But she would die in despair, she said, if she thought that she was leaving Aurore at the mercy of an unworthy mother. And so it came about that the girl was compelled to leave the Convent which she had come to regard as a Paradise.

She went back to the world full of apprehension and with her mind made up to return to the refuge of the cloister as soon as she could do so without endangering her grandmother's life. She was indebted to the English Convent for many, and happy, changes in herself. The noble courtesy of the nuns, the lessons of the professor of deportment, had given her charming manners which, all through her life, brought an air of distinction to her most daring eccentricities. Above all, she had acquired a new seriousness, a new depth of character. Her grandmother had brought her up in the graces of the eighteenth century: Nohant had taught her the poetry of Nature: her new faith had instruct-

1 Ibid., Volume III, p. 232.
2 GEORGE SAND: *Histoire de ma Vie.* Volume III, p. 252.

ed her in the love of something other than herself. 'The
exaltations of devotion have this one great effect, at least,
upon the character—they kill self-love, or, if they merely
deaden it, they undoubtedly purge it of much meanness and
of many trivial preoccupations. . . .'[1] Just as many of the
English poets have owed the vigour of their images to a
constant reading of the Old Testament, so, too, was Aurore
Dupin led unconsciously to transplant into the texture of her
prose the grave benevolence of Madame Alicia and the
sublime simplicity of the Gospels.

V

THE HEIRESS OF NOHANT

AFTER LEAVING the Convent, she spent some days in
Paris with her grandmother. Her besetting fear was a forced
marriage. Was she about to endure the fate of the young
women in Molière's plays? Was she to be handed over to an
old greybeard, with the words: 'My child, either you must
say yes, or deal me a mortal blow'? But on this point she
was quickly reassured. An old friend of her grandmother,
Madame de Pontcarré, had a 'match' up her sleeve. Aurore
decided that he must be ugly even before she had seen him.
Madame de Pontcarré told her not to be a little goose, and
that he was excessively good looking. The project, however,
was dropped. Very soon, Mademoiselle Julie was packing
her trunks for the journey to Nohant, and Aurore heard her
grandmother say: 'She is so young that we must allow her a
year's respite.' She had hoped that her mother would come
to Nohant to celebrate her return, but she found her in a
hard, defiant mood. 'I shall certainly never cross the
threshold of that house so long as my mother-in-law is
alive!' Deeply imbued with Christian charity, Aurore
begged the two ladies to be mutually forgiving. Having
failed in her efforts, she next offered humbly to stay with
her mother, but was snubbed for her pains. 'We shall be
together again sooner than *some people* think!' was the

[1] Ibid., Volume III, p. 214.

terrible Sophie-Victoire's answer to the suggestion. Aurore
found this allusion to her grandmother's approaching death
extremely painful. 'Your mother is a woman completely
lacking in education'—was Madame Dupin de Francueil's
contribution to the discussion: 'she loves her children as a
bird its young . . . So soon as they can use their wings, she
flies away to another tree, and pecks at them if they come
near.' Sainte-Aurore realized that she was powerless to
modify so much mutual hatred, and left for Berry with her
grandmother.

The great blue travelling-coach set them down at Nohant
in the spring of 1820. The trees were in leaf, the
nightingales were singing, and they could hear in the
distance the solemn age-old chanting of the ploughmen at
their work. The sight of the old house moved Aurore
deeply, but she still thought with nostalgic regret of the
Convent bell and Madame Alicia. On the window of her
room she wrote with a pencil, in English, an elegiac passage
which can still be seen:

Written at Nohant, upon my window, at the setting of the
sun, 1820: Go, fading sun! Hide thy pale beams behind
the distant trees. Nightly Vesperus is coming to announce
the close of the day. Evening descends to bring
melancholy on the landscape. With thy return, beautiful
light, Nature will find again mirth and beauty, but joy
will never comfort my soul. . . .[1]

Such gloom was in the fashion of the day. Actually,
Aurore thoroughly enjoyed her almost complete freedom.
The ancient mistress of Nohant seemed to have shrunk
since she had had her stroke. She still appeared at meals, an
upright, gracious figure, wrapped in her own quiet thoughts,
with a touch of rouge on her cheeks, and diamonds in her
ears. But she was quietly fading away. Except for an occasional outburst of senile anger, she took next to no part
in the life of the house. The Restoration, and the influences
of the new age, had softened her Voltairean outlook, but
she still clung to the philosophy of the eighteenth century,
and had many a friendly discussion with her granddaughter
who, though she did not know it, was a true disciple of
Chateaubriand.

[1] Quoted by Wladimir Karénine, in *George Sand*. Volume III,
p. 100.

It was with some surprise that she heard herself addressed as 'mademoiselle' by the friends of her childhood—Franchon, Ursule Josse and Marie Aucante. She learned for the first time how lonely the life of a great landowner can be, and missed the communal existence of the Convent. Even her brother Hippolyte, when he came home on leave, was intimidated by the sight of this young girl in her pink gingham dress. He was now Sergeant in a Hussar regiment, and perched Aurore on top of a horse, with a few simple instructions: 'What it all comes down to is, to fall or not to fall. Keep your seat, hang on to the mane, if you must, but don't let go of the reins, and don't fall off . . .' She rode Colette, a raw-boned mare with an easy action, who seemed able to guess exactly what was wanted of her. Aurore and Colette became inseparable. At the end of a week, they were jumping hedges and ditches together. The 'still water' of the Convent was a great deal more adventurous than the hussar.

To a friend of Convent days, Emilie de Wismes, daughter of the Prefect of Angers, who had already made her entry into the great world, she wrote, describing her life in the country: *'Who can be writing to me?* . . . says Emilie, all curiosity . . . Well, my dear, cast your mind back and try to remember your old schoolfellow . . .' She did not inform her correspondent that the handsome cavalryman from Saumur was her own natural brother. He became transformed into Hippolyte *de* Châtiron, a friend who was teaching her to ride English-fashion. She was studying Italian and music with Madame de Pontcarré and her daughter Pauline.

There are always two or three pieces of sheet-music on the piano, and duets and romances lying about on all the chairs. We think of you, all the same, and wish that you were here to take turns with Madame de Pontcarré, who accompanies us with great skill. We've put on a play—I was *Colin*, Pauline, *Lucette*—a lot of high-falutin sentiment which made us want to laugh. But it went off very well . . . We danced the *bourrée* . . .[1]

A certain Monsieur de Lacoux, a 'rather *precious* country neighbour', lent them a harp and read *Gerusalemme liberata* with them:

I spend my days lolling in a chair with a book in my hand, or busy with my drawing, while Hippolyte reads to me—or else sets everything at sixes and sevens in my room, and breaks the furniture. When that happens, I begin by giving him a good scolding, and end by behaving no less childishly myself. Grandmamma complains that we give her a splitting headache, but follows up her lecture by joining in the laughter . . . *Addio, cara amica; io ti abbracio teneramente e ti amo con sincerita.* . . .

January 1821: Hippolyte is gone, and we are now completely alone. I shorten the day by getting up late. Then I breakfast, after which I chat with grandmamma, sometimes for two or three hours at a stretch. Then I go to my room again and busy myself in all sorts of ways— playing on the harp and the guitar, warming myself by the fire, spitting on the red-hot embers, writing in the ash with the tongs, and chewing over old memories. Dinnertime comes, and I go downstairs. Afterwards, while Monsieur Deschartres plays at cards with grandmamma—he was once my father's tutor, and then Hippolyte's—I once more retire, and spend my time jotting down a few ideas in a green-covered notebook which is now pretty nearly filled. . . .[1]

The 'chats' with her grandmother had become by this time intimate and affectionate. Madame Dupin de Francueil, in spite of the effects of her illness, was still, in her lucid moments, a woman of high distinction. The quality of her upbringing, her natural fineness of character, and her courage in real crises, combined to make her a personality. She could be extremely tiresome and overbearing in her ordinary day to day dealings, but Aurore had learned to ignore her more irritating moods. Their roles were now reversed, and it was the granddaughter who showed herself forbearing and maternal. The old lady, realizing that the girl would soon be married, set no check upon her tongue. Though she had lived through a period of great social licence, she had never had a lover.

I was for ever telling those of my women friends who urged me to take a lover, that the ingratitude, the

[1] Ibid.

selfishness, and the beastliness of men, made me feel that
I wanted to have nothing to do with them. When I spoke
in this way, they would laugh in my face, and say that
not all men were like my old husband, and that they had
little ways with them that quite made up for their faults
and their vices . . . When I heard them talk so coarsely, I
felt quite ashamed to be a woman. . . .[1]

I have never claimed to be made of different stuff from
the rest of the human race. Now that I have ceased to
belong to any sex, I am pretty certain that, in my young
days, I was much like other women. If I did not develop
along quite the same lines, the reason was that I had
never met a man whom I could love with sufficient
passion to make it possible for me to throw a cloak of
poetry over the animal facts of life.[2]

These disillusioned references to the 'animal facts of life'
were not likely to reconcile the girl to the idea of marriage.
She was becoming increasingly aware, from such scraps of
talk between the 'old countesses' as she overheard, that she
was a rich heiress, but, because of her deplorable mother,
and the general atmosphere of illegitimacy with which she
was surrounded, not what a young man with a future would
regard as a good match. Those who sought her hand were
not young. There was a fifty-year-old General of the
Empire, with a great sabre scar across his face, and there
was a Baron de Laborde, another army officer, and a
widower of forty. He got a relation to write to one of their
Nohant neighbours, the Vicomtesse de Montlevic as
follows:

Madame: you have given me to understand that there is,
living close to you in the country, a highly eligible young
lady, a Mademoiselle Dupin, who is to have, eventually
—if my memory is not at fault—an income of from
twenty to twenty-five thousand livres . . . Monsieur le
Baron de Laborde, my first cousin, is making, at the moment, between eight and nine thousand livres. . . . He has
already proved himself to be a good husband, and is, in
every respect, a most excellent gentleman. Though he is

[1] GEORGE SAND: *Le Secrétaire intime*, p. 203.
[2] GEORGE SAND: *Le Secrétaire intime*, p. 212. George
Sand herself admitted that the portrait she drew in this book of
an old lady, was based upon memories of her own grandmother.

forty years of age, there is nothing in his appearance
which need be deemed repellent by a young woman . . . I
should add that there was no child by his former
marriage. . . .[1]

This sort of bargaining would have sickened Aurore.
Madame de Montlevic replied, giving all necessary details,
genealogical as well as financial, about her 'young neighbour, who is the child of a *most* unsuitable marriage'.

Aurore, whom I have seen several times this year, is dark-
haired, with a pleasing face and a good figure. She has a
lively wit, and is well educated. She is an accomplished
musician and can sing and play both on the harp and the
piano. She knows how to draw, is a good dancer, can ride
and shoot. Her manners, no matter what she is doing, are
those of a young woman of the *highest* quality . . . Her
fortune, of which at any moment now, she may become
complete mistress, is commonly supposed to amount to
between eighteen and twenty thousand livres a year. . . .

This marriage did not take place, nor any other. Aurore
Dupin was not in the position of most of the young women
of her period. She was not tormented by the demands of her
awakening senses; she did not need to escape from the
slavery of a family existence, nor from a fear of life. Unlike
them, she was not in pursuit of some Prince Charming who
might rescue her, nor of some master who might direct her
in the way that she should go. She was the reigning queen of
Nohant. She lived free and happy in the company of her
grandmother. She still believed herself to have a vocation
for the cloister. Old Deschartres, who was now Mayor of
Nohant, took her out shooting, and advised her to dress like
a man when after hares—a suggestion which she was only
too glad to adopt. Clad in a loose blouse, or in coat and
trousers, she felt stronger, felt as though she were acquiring
a degree of virility. Such behaviour, she thought, gave her
prestige in the eyes of her girl friends.

[1] This letter is quoted by Pierre Salomon and Jean Mallion in
an article published in the November (1949) number of the
Bulletin des Bibliophiles et des Bibliothécaires: pp. 512-18,
entitled 'Un Marriage manqué de George Sand'.

Aurore Dupin to Emilie de Wismes: May 1821: I am sure
you have never been out in a man's heavy shooting-coat,
with a cap on your head and a gun on your shoulder, and
tramped over ploughland to trouble the peace of some
wretched hare, only to find nothing and to return home
with no more to show than a few miserable sparrows.
That is what I do, and the fate of the said sparrows
reduces my sentimental maid to tears! . . . You have
never, I am certain, been broken in to the hard discipline
of a hussar's life, as I have, by Hippolyte. If I say that I
am frightened of horses when he is giving me a riding-
lesson, he seeks to reassure me by giving the huge animal
on which I am mounted a touch of the whip, and makes
him, as my grandmother says, walk on his hind-legs. . . .[1]

Deschartres instructed her in the management of the
estate. Later, for political reasons, she pretended that she
took no interest in her possessions. Actually, she remained
all her life a countrywoman of the Berry who, even in her
generosities, counted every penny. It has been said of
Byron—another romantic—that his dominant characteris-
tic was solid good sense. It will be seen that Aurore Dupin,
once she had outlived her passions, shared this trait. She
always longed to recapture that sense of masculine
independence for which Nohant and Deschartres had given
her a taste. Nor did she ever loose the shrewd, practical
outlook which she had learned from her contact with the
realities of the soil, and the work which it entails. Thought,
when too free, never, no matter how much it may try, gets
very far. Like a bird, it needs to feel the resistence of the
medium in which it moves. Only a life of activity can reveal
the limits which the human spirit must impose upon itself.
When Madame Dupin de Francueil, after a second
stroke, took to her bed for good, Deschartres surrendered
all his authority into the hands of the young girl. He insisted that she should keep the household accounts, and treated her as a grown woman. It was the best way in which to
ensure her development. The 'Great Man' (for so she called
him with affectionate irony) was doctor and chemist for the
whole village. He even undertook a certain amount of
surgery. It was his wish that Aurore should learn to help
him. In this way she became accustomed to the sight of

[1] Letter published in the *Revue de Paris,* November 1911, p.
24.

blood and of human suffering. Her pity was canalized to practical ends. Never, after those early experiences, did she feel any disgust for the human body. She always spoke of its functions without the slightest sign of inhibition, bravely, and with a professional detachment. In after years many of her lovers rated her for lack of modesty. The calm practicality of the trained nurse has a way of nonplussing and disappointing the debauchee.

But her social contacts were not confined to Deschartres. She saw a good deal of the young men of La Châtre. She would frequently ride into the little town with its narrow streets 'winding between crazy, moss-encrusted gables'. In the low houses, behind nail-studded doors, in family mansions screened by wrought-iron railings, she made the acquaintance of the sons of her father's old friends—of Charles Duvernet, of Fleury—the 'giant', of little Gustave Papet, who was considerably her junior in age. In particular, she saw much of one man who was training to be a doctor, Stéphane Ajasson de Grandsagne. He was extremely good-looking, not wholly unlike one of those emaciated Grandees whom Greco loved to paint. He came of a noble and very ancient family, but, as a result of having nine brothers and sisters, was poor, since he had inherited only a tiny share of the ancestral patrimony. Deschartres, who was interested in this combination of good birth and studiousness, had introduced him to Aurore with the suggestion that she might take lessons from him in anatomy and osteology. With this end in view, she hung a skeleton in her room, and there the young man, overjoyed at the prospect, gave lessons to his charming pupil. Aurore, at this time, had a profusion of black hair. Her eyes were Andalusian, her complexion the colour of 'Spanish snuff', and she had the most supple figure imaginable. As was only to be expected, the 'professor' was soon head over heels in love with her. But she repelled his advances, saying that people of their sort should be more concerned with 'Malebranche and his like' than with insipid gallantries. In point of fact, she would gladly have married him, but she knew that neither the Comte de Grandsagne, nor Madame Dupin de Francueil, would give their consent. The former was too 'class conscious', and would have been appalled at the idea of his son marrying the daughter of Sophie-Victoire, while the old lady would have objected strongly, on the ground that Stéphane had no fortune of his own, and was generally held to be a 'thoroughly undesirable young man'. Aurore, not, as yet, being of age, could not challenge the opposition of her family. In a very short time, Stéphane had ceased writing to her, except in terms of a 'cold and peremptory frankness'. She continued to dress like a man, and this gave rise to a number of comic mistakes. It happened, on one occasion, that when she had stopped in front of a gothic castle with the object of making a sketch, a young serving wench came out and started to make eyes at the 'young gentleman'. *Aurore Dupin to Emilie de Wismes, July 1821:* 'She gave me a number of sidelong glances, the meaning of which was only too obvious, while I, with the most gallant manner in the world, worked like a nigger in an effort to respond to her advances with a series of most fetching bows to which she was by no means averse. . . .'[1]

Her proclivity for riding after dark, for sporting a man's cap, blue blouse and trousers, for leaving pieces of skeleton scattered over the furniture, made her seem altogether too 'romantic' not to shock the respectable Berry folk. The curé of La Châtre, Aurore's confessor, got wind of the scandalous gossip which was making the rounds, and asked her whether she was not 'beginning to be in love'? Accustomed to the more delicate methods of the Abbé de Prémond, who would never have put such a question to her, she was deeply wounded in her pride, and gave up going to confession. The views of the people of La Châtre left her cold. 'Let them bray,' she said, and said no more. Her mother in Paris had heard something of the tittle-tattle, and wrote sharply to her. Aurore's reply shows that she possessed a natural talent for writing. It says what it has to say forcefully, and with admirable good sense:

Aurore to Sophie-Victoire Dupin: November 18th, 1821: I have read with care, and with the deepest feelings of respect, the letter which you were so very good as to write to me. I should not have permitted myself to say a word in my own defence, were it not for the fact that you have commanded me to do so without delay . . . You tell me that Monsieur Deschartres is much to blame for letting me have my own way. I must take the liberty of pointing out that Monsieur Deschartres neither has, nor could have, any authority over my actions. He is free to advise me as a friend, but no more. You have been told

[1] Letter published in the *Revue de Paris*, November 15th, 1911, p. 326.

by Monsieur de Grandsagne that I am by nature a
fighter. To give credit to such an assertion, you must
dear mother, be labouring under the delusion that
Monsieur de Grandsagne has a thorough knowledge of
my character. I do not myself consider that there is
sufficient intimacy between us to make it possible for him
to know anything at all about either my good or my bad
qualities . . . If he told you that he had given me lessons
in my own room, he was speaking no more than the
truth. But where, if not in my room, should I receive visitors? My grandmother is ill and sleeps badly. It seems to
me that she would be much disturbed if I entertained
elsewhere . . . You would like me, when I go walking, to
lean on the arm of my maid, or of one of the other
servants. The only reason for my doing any such thing
would be to save myself from falling. Leading-strings
were necessary to me when I was a child . . . but I am
now seventeen, and have learned to walk by myself. . . .[1]

She was still fond of her mother, but any show of respect
for her was purely formal.

In spite of the firmness of her language, she was still
feeling lost and rudderless. There was no longer a confessor
to whom she might appeal for guidance. She could not go to
the old curé of Saint-Chartier, the Abbé de Montpeyroux: 'I
was on too intimate, too familiar, terms with him.' On
Sundays she always took her midday meal with him
between Mass and Vespers, and he carried her back with
him, riding pillion, to Nohant, where he dined and spent the
evening. 'Aurore is a child whom I have always loved', he
said: and she, 'If he were sixty years younger, I could twist
him round my little finger!'[2] An old friend, completely
under one's thumb, can scarcely be regarded as an adequate
director of conscience. She must seek for truth unaided,
with a paralysed grandmother for company. Deschartres, 'a
mass of contradictions, a man crammed with information,
but lacking in any trace of common sense' had disappointed
her.[3] The Abbé de Prémord was far away. During her time
at the Convent the *Imitation* had been her bedside reading,
but the *Imitation* 'is a book for the enclosed life, a mortal

[1] This letter is quoted by Louise Vincent in *George Sand et le
Berry*, pp. 53-5.
[2] GEORGE SAND: *Correspondance*. Volume I, p. 18.
[3] Ibid., Volume VI, p. 248.

danger for those who have not been able to break with
human society'. The young mistress of Nohant had been
flung violently back into the world. Her position imposed
certain duties on her. She dressed abscesses and compound-
ed drugs; under the guidance of the handsome Ajasson de
Grandsagne she had discovered the sciences. She longed for
a form of Christianity adapted to the needs of her period,
and made the acquaintance of Chateaubriand. Thanks to the
Génie du Christianisme, her devotion took on a fresh lustre
from the golden glow of romantic poetry.

Gerson? Chateaubriand? could it be that the Church
contained within itself two contradictory truths? Something
else, too, there was, to cause her doubt and anguish. Her
grandmother was in danger of death. Ought she to make
that clear? Ought she try to convert her? Or ought she to let
her die in peace? She wrote to the Abbé de Prémord, who
replied, advising her to say nothing. 'To tell your
grandmother that she is in danger would be tantamount to
killing her. Your instinct is a true one, to keep silent and to
pray God to give her His help directly . . . Never fear when
your heart tells you what to do. *The heart can never be
wrong.*'[1] Sand underlined this sentence; for many years it
was another piece of the tolerant Jesuit's advice: 'the poets
are always religious. Do not fear the philosophers: they are
powerless against the Faith.'[2] Reassured, she cried to her
unquiet spirit: 'Forward! forward!'

She ranged widely through the records of human
thought. She would go to her room at ten o'clock each
night, and stay there reading, often until three in the
morning. The contradictions which had set the minds of
great men at odds, tormented her, and she tried 'to bring
into a common focus, a universal harmony, those many
lights of different colours which flickered about her, like the
flutter of flames on the hearth, and the light of the moon, in
a room . . . Intoxicated by her love of poetry, she had
believed at first that she could refute the philosophers
without difficulty: but she came to love them, and to see
God as greater than He had formerly seemed . . .'[3]
Chateaubriand, instead of confirming her in her catholicism
as she had hoped he would, had opened before her feet the

[1] GEORGE SAND: *Histoire de ma Vie.* Volume III, pp.
293-4.

[2] GEORGE SAND: *Histoire de ma Vie.* Volume III, p. 300.

[3] GEORGE SAND: *Impressions et Souvenirs,* p. 129.

'abyss of questioning'. She turned from the *Génie du Christianisme* to the *Imitation*. She re-read it in the copy given her by Mother Mary-Alicia. On the fly-leaf, the beloved hand of the woman she so deeply venerated had written the name of Aurore Dupin. The experience of this renewed study terrified her. If Gerson were right, then, she must renounce nature, family and reason. The choice must be between Heaven and Earth, and for her, it must be Earth. To this Chateaubriand replied: 'It is in the beauty of the Earth, of Nature and of Love, and there alone, that you will find that power of Life in which God is glorified . . .' Gerson had said: 'We are of the earth, earthy; we are but dust . . .' Chateaubriand, 'We are flame and light.' The *Imitation* laid it down that we should question nothing, the *Génie du Christianisme* that we should question everything.

> I was in much perplexity. With Colette galloping beneath me, I was all Chateaubriand. As I sat in the light of my lamp, I was all Gerson, and reproached myself at nightfall for the thoughts I had had in the morning.[1]

Chateaubriand, who had called to the aid of Christianity 'the enchantments of the mind and the special pleading of the heart', carried her by storm. Then she attacked Mably, Locke, Condillac, Montesquieu, Bacon, Bossuet, Aristotle, Leibnitz, Pascal, Montaigne, and the poets—Dante, Virgil, Shakespeare—higgledy-piggledy, and in no sort of order. She thought Leibnitz the greatest of them all, because she understood nothing of what he said. What did she care about Monads, Pre-established Harmony, and the rest of his subtleties? She was strengthened in her faith by the knowledge that this man of sublime intellect, even he, had dedicated himself to the adoration of the Divine Wisdom. 'Love God through understanding, and understand Him through love: make oneself believe what one cannot understand, but make oneself understand the better to believe:—in those axioms is comprised the sum-total of Leibnitz . . .'[2] When Deschartres tried to teach her philosophy, she threw the book at his head: 'All this is killing me, Great Man! It is all too long-winded. I am in a hurry to love God.'

Thirst for knowledge?—yes, but, still more urgent, the

[1] GEORGE SAND: *Histoire de ma Vie*. Volume III, p. 293.
[2] GEORGE SAND: *Histoire de ma Vie*. Volume IV, p. 306.

need to love. It was at this time that she made the
acquaintance of Rousseau: *Emile,* the profession of faith of
le vicaire savoyard. He let the light into her mind and
provided just the food she craved. His language took hold of
her like fine music, and swept her off her feet. 'I ranked him
with Mozart: everything was made clear to me!' She had
many things in common with him—sensibility, the desire for sincerity, the love of Nature. It was from him she
learned to mingle the vocabulary of virtue with the urgent
promptings of the heart. Leibnitz and Rousseau, the
difficult philosopher and the beloved companion, remained
her lifelong masters. But if we are really to understand her,
we must make room for a third name, and take note that,
from now on, she read much in Franklin. It is remarkable
that the slightly platitudinous note which sounds through
his practical wisdom, far from repelling, actually attracted,
her.

Was she still a Catholic? Later, when she came to write
the story of her life, she answered that question: 'I do not
think so.' In those words she voiced the plea of the mature
woman who, having broken with her Church, wished to
persuade herself that she was, nevertheless, faithful to the
visions of her youth. In 1821, Aurore still admitted her
allegiance to Mother Alicia and the Abbé de Prémord. All
the same, she was convinced that she had found true
Christianity in Rousseau, in the man who had preached the
doctrine of absolute equality, of absolute brotherhood.
Love and Sacrifice. In those two commandments, it seemed
to her, lay the lesson of Jesus Christ. She believed in God;
she believed in the immortality of the soul, in Providence,
and, first and foremost, in Love. But, without clearly
realizing it, she was an 'Immanentist'. She no longer
believed in a personal and transcendent Deity who watched
from a great distance the struggles of Humanity. 'I had
rather believe that God did not exist at all, than believe Him
indifferent.'[1] There were times when, in the throes of
mental torment she became an atheist for twenty-four
hours, but the fit never lasted long, because she felt the
divine presence in all things.

If everything is divine, even matter: if everything is
superhuman, even man—then God is in all things. I can
see and touch Him. I can feel that He is unique because I

[1] GEORGE SAND: *Impressions et Souvenirs,* p. 132.

love Him, because I have always known and felt Him,
because he is within me in a degree proportionate to my
own littleness. That does not mean that I *am* God, but
that I come from Him, and that to Him I shall return.
. . .[1]

In short, she returned, as on the day of that *Tolle, lege,* to
her faith in a superhuman alliance between her soul and
God. Rousseau enchanted her, because he provided 'inexhaustible nourishment for that emotion of the heart
which is continual divine rapture'.

We should try to see in imagination this fervent, dreamy
young woman, half tomboy and half mystic, as she was
when she galloped through the countryside, charmed by the
changing scene, by the herds she met with on her way, by
the gentle splashing of water beneath her horse's hoofs, or in
her room at night-time when, after throwing a log on the fire
(for she was always chilly), she saw through the window the
tall, motionless pines, and the moon, almost at the full,
shining in a cloudless sky. She was a very remarkable
person: a poet—though she did not know it, a philosopher—
because that was what she wanted to be, 'tortured by
thoughts of the divine', hungry for heroism and sacrifice. At
sixteen, she had hidden sheets of paper under her pillow; for
she was just beginning to write. Take, for instance, her
portrait of the 'Just Man' . . . 'The Just Man has, strictly
speaking, no sex: he is man or he is woman according to the
Will of God: but the code by which he lives is always the
same, whether he be a General or the mother of a family.'[2]
. . . It is worth noting this desire of hers for the equality of
the sexes. . . .

The Just Man has no fortune, nor is his house full of
slaves. Those who serve on him are his friends, if they
are worthy so to be. His roof belongs to the vagabond, his
purse and his clothing to all in want, his time and his
learning to those who seek them . . . The Just Man is
before all things sincere, and it is that which enables him
to exert a sublime strength, for the world is nothing but a
lie, swindling or vanity, treason or prejudice. . . .[3]

[1] GEORGE SAND: *Impressions et Souvenirs*, p. 136.
[2] GEORGE SAND: *Lettres d'un Voyageur*, p. 115.
[3] Ibid., p. 116.

She said, too: 'The Just Man is proud but not vain.' That was a sufficiently accurate portrait of what *she* wanted to be. Proud?—beyond all doubt. She felt herself to be strong: she despised the opinions of the mob: she recognized in herself, with pleasure, her father's contempt for convention, and her grandmother's sturdy intelligence. Deschartres preached prudence, and reminded her of the sacred words: *'Woe to that man by whom the offence cometh.'* But he preached to deaf ears. What the world calls offence, she said, is not what Christ meant by offence. Prudence?— 'Seeing that a man's own conscience is the sole judge, I consider myself as one completely free to be lacking in prudence should it please me to endure all the blame and all the persecution which is the lot of those who take upon themselves dangerous and difficult duties . . .'[1] She had been brought up as a boy, and her ambitions were those of a man. She had been educated as a Christian, and it was her hope to attain to the condition of the 'Just Man'.

This curious declaration of my *rights of man,* as I called it in the days when I was scarcely more than a school-girl; this innocent mixture of heresies and religious banalities, did, surely, all the same contain a system of fixed ideas, a plan for living, a choice between possible resolutions, a tendency towards a character deliberately chosen and sought out with fervour of faith. These beliefs go some way to explain the illusions of my adolescence. Right in the centre of feelings recently dictated by the Gospel, there was a sort of rebellious resistance which, in its turn, was dictated by a growing pride, by an innate obstinacy: a vague dream of human greatness, mingled with the more serious ambition of the Christian. . . .[2]

[1] GEORGE SAND: *Histoire de ma Vie.* Volume III, p. 345.
[2] GEORGE SAND: *Lettres d'un Voyageur,* p. 117.

VI

A YOUNG WOMAN DISCOVERS
THE WORLD

THE SURPRISING degree of liberty enjoyed by Aurore
Dupin, remarkable in the case of a 'young person' of 1821,
and productive of great self-confidence, derived from
conditions which, by their very nature, were unstable.
Aurore was living under the authority of her grandmother,
and her grandmother had ceased to have any authority. She
was answerable to Deschartres alone, and the poor fellow
was mad about her. Unfortunately, Madame Dupin de
Francueil's condition deteriorated towards the end of the
year. She had lost her memory, dozed continually, but never
slept. Aurore watched by her every second night, and spent
those hours reading *René* and *Lara,* as a result of which she
developed a disposition to melancholy. Her mind dwelt
sometimes on suicide, sometimes on the cloister, never on
marriage. Stéphane, the one young man in whom she had
taken an interest, had turned to atheism and materialism—
and that 'formed a great gulf between us.'

It will be remembered how the Abbé de Prémord had
dissuaded her from bringing pressure upon her grandmother
to perform her religious duties:

> Pray unceasingly, hope, and, in whatever manner your
> poor grandmother may meet her end, put your reliance
> upon the infinite wisdom and mercy of God. Rest assured
> that your sole duty is to continue to surround her with
> your loving care. With the evidence of your love before
> her eyes, of your modesty, and, if I may put it, of the
> *discretion* of your faith, she may, perhaps, be moved by a
> desire to show her gratitude and fulfil your most secret
> desire, and therefore, of her own accord, make her act of
> submission. . . .[1]

[1] GEORGE SAND: *Histoire de ma Vie.* Volume III, p. 294.

The event bore out what her wise and kindly director had
hoped might happen. The Archbishop of Arles, who was in
some sort a relation, being the natural son of grandpapa
Dupin and Madame d'Epinay, moved by a sense of
gratitude for the kindness she had shown in the old days
towards her husband's bastard, came to see her with the
intention of saving her soul. 'I know perfectly well,' he said,
'that what I am about to say will make you laugh. You do
not believe that you will be damned for not doing what I
shall ask you to do, but *I* believe it, and I should like to
think that you will give me this one small pleasure.'

To her granddaughter's great surprise, the old lady
consented. 'Say no more. I am well assured that I am about
to die, and I understand, too, your present scruples. I know
that if I die without making my peace with *that lot*, either
you will blame yourself, or they will blame you. I do not
choose that because of me your heart should be at odds
with your conscience, or that, when I am gone, you should
be in difficulties with your friends. I feel convinced that I
am guilty neither of cowardice nor of hypocrisy if I adhere
to practices which, when the moment comes for me to say
farewell to those I love, do, at least, offer an example of
good manners. Be easy in your mind. I know what I am
doing.'[1] She then sent for her good old curé of Saint-
Chartier, and expressed a wish that Aurore should be
present at her confession, which she made with frankness
and a high nobility of spirit. The old Abbé, speaking with
his peasant's brogue, said: 'My dear sister, we be all of us
pardoned, seeing as how the good God do love us, and do
know as how if us repents 'tis along on us a'loving of 'un.'

The Archbishop, the servants and all the farm-hands
were present when the Last Sacrament was administered.

She died on Christmas day, 1821. Her last words were for
Aurore: 'You are losing your best friend.' Lying there with
her fresh pink complexion, and wearing her lace cap, she
looked very beautiful, perfectly calm, extremely dominant,
and, more than ever, the daughter of the Maréchal de Saxe.
Deschartres, whose grief was painful to witness, conceived
a romantic and macabre idea. In the course of having the
family vault prepared to receive another coffin, he had
opened the one containing the remains of Aurore's father,
and had insisted on taking the young woman, on a night of

icy cold, to the little private cemetery which lay beneath the trees of the Park. Maurice Dupin's head had become detached from the skeleton. Deschartres lifted it from the coffin, and made Aurore kiss it. So moved was she, and in so high a state of exaltation, that the act seemed to her to be perfectly natural.

'You are losing your best friend,' her grandmother had said. She was losing, too, her only defence against spite and covetousness. A young woman of seventeen, and a great heiress (she now owned the Hôtel de Narbonne in Paris as well as the Nohant estate in Berry, and a good deal of liquid capital as well) might well tempt fortune-hunters. Her grandmother, in her wisdom, had appointed as Guardian Comte René de Villeneuve, her husband's grandson.[1] Aurore was to live with him at Chenonceaux, where Madame de Villeneuve would introduce her, together with her own daughter, Emma (the future Comtesse de La Roche-Aymon), to all the right people. She had always said: 'I could not go back to living in a city. I should die of boredom,' and, in this way, she would remain permanently in the country . . . this plan was perfectly agreeable to the Count and Countess, who did, however, make one stipulation, namely, that their young cousin should break entirely with her mother's 'awful set', and should forget that her father had contracted a 'garrison marriage'. Monsieur de Villeneuve came immediately to Nohant. Aurore found him delightful. He was gay and charming, and knew thousands of lines of poetry by heart. It gave her great pleasure to think that he was to be her guardian.

But she was reckoning without her mother's violent temperament. No sooner did Sophie-Victoire learn that her mother-in-law was dead, than she immediately set out for the country, taking Aunt Lucie Maréchal with her. At last she was free to go to Nohant! Aurore received her with every show of affection, and their first exchanges of endearment were exuberant. But Madame Maurice Dupin could not control the surge of unhappy memories, and was very soon voicing her hatred of the dead woman. This flow of abominable invective appalled her daughter who, strong in her resolutions of sanctity, forced herself to listen to it

[1] When Dupin de Francueil married Aurore de Saxe, he was a widower with one daughter of his first marriage. This daughter had married the Comte de Villeneuve, who owned the Château de Chenonceaux.

with silent respect. 'You are taking quite the wrong line,' said her aunt, 'you should rage and storm back.' But Aurore's principles made it impossible for her to follow this advice. The reading of the will served to pour oil upon the flaming temper of the middle-aged Fury. *She* was her daughter's legal and natural guardian, she said, and would never surrender her rights.

Aurore submitted without a murmur—not that she still felt any of her old passion for her mother. The sight and sound of so much hatred filled her with horror. She obeyed because obedience was her duty. She hoped that Sophie-Victoire would at least either send her back to the English Convent or would leave her at Nohant. Instead, she was whisked off to Paris. Before leaving she gave Deschartres a full *discharge* in all matters touching his administration of the estate, though the poor 'Great Man', who had no head for business, was in arrears on his rent-roll to the tune of eighteen thousand francs. To the fury of her mother and legal guardian, Aurore swore that she had received this sum, and secretly felt sure that God would pardon her the lie.

Once in Paris, she was abandoned by the Comte and Comtesse de Villeneuve. Feeling that they belonged to a different world from that of the 'adventuress', they would neither endure her insults nor share Aurore with her. Their estrangement made the girl cry. She had made up her mind to love them. But how could she 'tread her filial duty under foot'?—how seem to be admitting the existence of a 'system of caste and natural inequality'? This generous attitude resulted in her being handed over, defenceless, to the tyrannical control of her mother, who, with her 'change of life' upon her, was in a condition bordering on insanity, excessively suspicious, and only partially responsible for her actions. She could not resign herself to growing old, and constantly demanded violent emotional excitement. She swore that she would 'get the better of' her daughter's 'artfulness', snatched the book out of her hand when she was trying to read, and accused her of being vicious and wanton. When she was in a good mood she could once again be charming, but such fine intervals were of rare occurrence. 'It is true,' she said, in her calmer moments, 'that I can put everybody's back up when I try . . . I can't help it . . . my thoughts run away with me.'

In the spring of 1822, she was within measurable distance

of going completely mad. She wanted to force Aurore into a marriage the very idea of which the girl detested.

Aurore's Journal: I never abandoned my attitude of calm superiority. My face was drawn and haggard, my health undermined . . . but my determination remained as firm as a wall of bronze . . . For some time past I had been threatened with seclusion. I said nothing to this except 'You wouldn't be so cruel!' They tried to frighten me by taking me to the very threshold of the prison . . . Several nuns came to meet us at the gate. We were led through a number of dark and tortuous passages. Finally, they opened the door of one of the cells, I can compare it with nothing save, perhaps, one of the cells described in Gresset's *La Chartreuse.*

'You asked to go to a Convent,' I was told: 'and hoped that if you returned to the one in which you were educated, and in which you picked up all your wicked notions, you would enjoy a greater degree of freedom. Oh, they would have had you back, right enough. They would have overlooked your faults, excused your behaviour, and concealed your goings on. Here you will be looked after a great deal better. The Community has been told all about you, and will be armed against your wheedling words. You had better make up your mind to the fact that you will spend the remaining three and a half years of your minority in this cell. It is no use your thinking that you can invoke the law. No one will listen to your complaints, and neither you nor your friends will know the name of the whereabouts of your retreat. . . .'

And then, perhaps because my mother felt ashamed at taking so despotic a course, perhaps because she really was afraid of the law, perhaps because she had meant only to frighten me—she abandoned the scheme altogether. . . .[1]

What a lesson for a simple-minded girl, who had thought herself so strong and so powerful in the days when she had queened it at Nohant! She had discovered that a minor was, quite literally, a slave. She was ill. Her stomach had become contracted as a result of the furious anger which she had

[1] GEORGE SAND: *Le Roman d'Aurore Dudevant et d'Aurélien de Sèze*, pp. 40-2.

kept to herself. She refused all food. She hoped that she
would starve to death. Fortunately, Sophie-Victoire grew
tired of the struggle. In April 1822, she took Aurore to stay
for a few days at the house of an ex-Colonel of Chasseurs, a
former army friend of Maurice Dupin, called James
Roettiers du Pelssis.

James and Angèle Roettiers du Plessis (forty and twenty-
seven years old respectively) lived on their estate not far
from Melun. Both were good-natured and frank-hearted
people. They were bringing up a family of five children in a
huge park where Aurore, who could never be happy for
long without grass and flowers around her, renewed her
contact, if not with the poetry of Nohant, at least with
country scenes and country employments. They had been
there only for one day when Sophie-Victoire grew bored,
and decided to leave. She changed her quarters as readily as
she changed the colour of her hair. Madame du Plessis,
seeing that Aurore was depressed at the idea of returning to
Paris, offered to keep her for a week. The girl's mother
accepted the invitation, perhaps with the thought at the
back of her mind that she might, in this way, compromise
her inflexible daughter. She had noticed that a great many
officers visited the house, and that life there was free and
easy.

The du Plessis couple became very fond of Aurore. In a
short while she was the boon companion of their children,
and a source of much happiness to the family. Her mother
seemed to have forgotten her completely. They kept her
with them for several months, found her in clothes (for she
had no wardrobe of her own), and treated her as though she
had been their daughter. She adored her 'father James', and
her 'mother *Angel*'. The country air restored her appetite.
The sight of so happy a family reconciled her to the thought
of marriage. There was another reason why she should feel
the need of a protector. As has already been mentioned,
there were a great many young military men at Plessis, to
whom her mother had not hesitated to describe her as 'a
very original, and, to say no worse, irresponsible young
woman'. Consequently she was the object of a good many
pressing attentions. 'Madame *Angel*, for all her goodness
and generosity, was not sufficiently serious-minded to
protect me from the dangers to which I was exposed.'[1] To

[1] GEORGE SAND: *Le Roman d'Aurore Dudevant et
d'Aurélien de Sèze*, p. 145.

make matters worse, her own lively, gay and rather scatter-brained behaviour appeared to encourage advances which, in fact, annoyed her intensely.

She brooded sadly over the difficult situation of a young woman in society who has no man to protect her. Then one evening in Paris, when she was eating ices with the Du Plessis outside the Café Tortoni, Angèle suddenly said to her husband: 'Look! there's Casimir!' A slim, elegant young man, with a gay expression and a military bearing, came up to their table, shook hands, and answered the eager questions which they put to him about his father, Colonel the Baron Dudevant, a man much beloved and respected by the family. He inquired in a low voice who the young lady might be, and remembered that his father had been a friend of Colonel Dupin. Aurore, too, asked about the young man. He was the natural, but acknowledged, son of a Baron of the Empire and a servant girl, Augustine Soulès. His family enjoyed an income of between seventy and eighty-four thousand livres, and owned an estate at Guillery, in the Gascon country. A few days later, Casimir Dudevant paid a visit to Plessis, and joined like a big boy in the children's games. He seemed to take a particular interest in Aurore's plight, and gave her some good advice.

In you, so good, so honest, so disinterested, I found the protector for whom I had been looking. You never spoke to me of love. You never thought about my fortune, but tried, with wise advice, to open my eyes to the dangers by which I was threatened. I was grateful for your friendship and soon was looking on you as a brother. I went for walks with you, and in your company spent many hours. We played together like children, and never once did any thought of love or marriage come to spoil our innocent affection. It was at this time that I wrote to my brother: 'I have a comrade here of whom I am very fond, with whom I laugh, and go out jumping, as I do with you.' I need not say, for it is already known to you, that it was the friends we had in common who were responsible for setting us thinking about marriage. They were for ever offering me a choice of husbands: there was P. . . . whom I could not endure, and C. . . . whom I found odious. Many others were wealthier than you. But you were good, and that, for me, is the only true recommendation of any man. Seeing you, as I did, every day, I came to know you better and better. I appreciated

your good qualities, and nobody could have been more
deeply attached to you than I was. . . .'[1]

She was perfectly sincere. In her green notebook she
wrote: 'Unbelievable happiness' and 'Inexpressible delight'.
It was wonderful to have at last a friend on whom she could
rely. She did not think him handsome. Casimir's nose was
rather long. Nevertheless, she passed many happy hours in
his company. As any young woman would have done, who
was isolated and defenceless, she developed a strong liking
for 'this mirror of all manliness'. She was pleased with her
new suitor because he asked her to marry him without first
making any official approach to her relations. Furthermore,
she felt quite certain that he was not seeking her for the
sake of her money. He would one day have more than she
had, though actually the financial situation was a good deal
more complicated than she knew. Casimir was an only son,
but he was a natural child, and, as such, had no legal claim
to his father's estate. The latter gave him no more than sixty
thousand francs as a marriage settlement, and left everything to the Baronne Dudevant to hold in trust for him.
Casimir Dudevant did, however, as a bachelor, enjoy the position of son of the house. By marrying Aurore he would
change all this for a somewhat reduced standard of living at
Nohant. Nobody could accuse him of marrying for money.

Needless to say, the suspicious Sophie-Victoire could not
let slip so admirable an opportunity for a display of her
power. She was charmed by the good looks and distinguished air of the old Colonel. 'I said yes,' she told her
daughter, 'but in such a way as to make it possible for me to
change my mind. I don't yet know whether I care for the
son. He certainly is not handsome, and I should have liked a
handsome son-in-law to give me his arm.' A fortnight later,
she dropped like a bomb on Plessis. She claimed to have
made the discovery that Casimir was an adventurer who
had once been a café waiter! From whom could she have
collected such a pack of nonsense? Aurore came to the
conclusion that she had dreamed it all. Next, her mother
demanded a settlement in trust on the bridegroom's side, an
arrangement which Aurore found highly offensive to
Casimir. The whole question of the match was again re-
opened, again settled, again broken. And so things went on

[1] GEORGE SAND: *Le Roman d'Aurore Dudevant et
d'Aurélien de Sèze,* pp. 145-6.

until the autumn. Madame Dupin could not reconcile herself to the length of Casimir's nose, and was as critical of him to her daughter as she could contrive to be. But, at last, on September 10th, 1822, the wedding did take place.

Husband and wife left for Nohant, where Deschartres joyfully welcomed them.

PART TWO

MADAME DUDEVANT

Desire is far inferior to love, and, maybe,
does not even point the way to it.

Alain

I

A PICTURE OF MARRIED LIFE

IT WAS strange to find herself back at Nohant, and sharing with a man Madame Dupin de Francueil's great hearse-shaped bed with plumes at each of its four corners. But Aurore was determined to find happiness in marriage. 'I was, at that time,' she wrote later, 'completely innocent.' She was, indeed, and still saturated in the moral atmosphere of her Convent.

> *Aurore Dudevant to Emilie de Wismes:* I hold it necessary that in marriage one of the partners must entirely surrender all thought of self, and sacrifice not only the will, but the mind, seeing life through the eyes of the other, loving what he loves, etc. . . . What agony, then, what bitterness to find oneself united to somebody one detests . . . but, on the other hand, what a source of inexhaustible happiness springs from obeying the dictates of love. When that is so, every privation is but a pleasure the more, for then one is offering a sacrifice at once to God and to married love, is both doing one's duty and finding one's delight . . . To attain to such an experience, to ensure that the honeymoon shall never end, it is necessary not only to love one's husband, but to do so with a deep intensity. Until I gave my heart to Casimir, I, like you, had entertained a very poor opinion of marriage, and if all that is now changed, I can speak only for myself. . . .[1]

Are we to believe that in writing thus she was being altogether sincere? Would any young woman confess to an unmarried girl that she had been disappointed? The truth of the matter is that Aurore was not herself quite certain of the state of her own mind. She had been married in September. Early in October she realized that she was with child, and

[1] Spoelberch de Lovenjoul Collection: Group E. 911, ff. 34-6.

entered on that period of blissful torpor which inevitably
accompanies all normal cases of pregnancy. No husband,
unless he be a monster, can fail to show kindness and
consideration to the woman who is about to give him an
heir. During that winter of 1922-23, Casimir was prodigal
of attentions. He charged Caron, his agent in Paris, with
endless little commissions for Aurore. She expressed a wish
to have Béranger's Songs: 'Do not fail to send them, for she
who wants them is a woman big with child, and woe to you
if she is not satisfied.' She felt a longing for sweets: 'This
taste of hers has become a veritable craving, and, if you do
not satisfy it, she is more than likely to lay all the blame on
you. My advice to you, therefore, is to turn yourself into a
candied lemon-tree. . . .'[1]

From these extracts it will be seen that Monsieur
Dudevant's sense of humour was on the heavy side, and
somewhat crude. This, however, did not worry his wife.
Crude jokes amused her, provided they were not 'smutty'.
Her condition made her mentally lazy, and she felt no
regret at abandoning, for the time being, all serious reading
and all participation in intellectual activities. Out of doors it
snowed without ceasing, and Casimir, who loved shooting,
spent every day in the fields and woods. Aurore lived in a
world of dreams, all agog to feel the first stirrings of the
child within her, and occupying herself with sewing away at
baby garments. She had never before turned her hand to
dressmaking, and threw herself into the task with a
passionate intensity, astonished to find how easy it was, and
how much 'mastery and inventiveness' there could be in the
handling of a pair of scissors. All her life long needlework
was to prove irresistibly attractive to her, and a sure refuge
in times of emotional unrest.

Old Deschartres, unfailingly clad in a dress-coat of
cornflower blue with gold buttons, lived with the young
couple. Casimir, in the kindness of his heart, allowed him to
run the house and grounds, though he was looking forward
with no little impatience to the day when the 'Great Man'
should see fit to retire. Under the supervision of Aurore's
old tutor the estate was not very productive, and the sums
received from it rarely, if ever, exceeded fifteen thousand
francs. Of this sum Aurore gave her mother three thousand
francs a year, and made herself responsible for a number of

[1] Ibid., Group E. 869, ff. 1 and 3.

pensions to former members of the household. The balance
was only just sufficient to allow husband and wife to live in
a very modest style. Nevertheless the winter 'passed like a
flash', except for six weeks which, under orders from
Deschartres, Aurore was compelled to spend in bed, doing
nothing. Such a thing had never happened to her before.
Her bed was covered with a green counterpane, great pine
branches were fastened to the four posts, and in this
woodland setting she lived, surrounded by finches, robins
and sparrows. The bird-fancier's granddaughter found
much delight in this poetic company.

When her time was approaching, she left for Paris with
her husband, and settled into a furnished suite in the Hôtel
de Florence, rue Neuve-des-Mathurins. There, on June
30th, 1823, without any complication, Maurice Dudevant
was born. He was a large and lively baby. Deschartres,
recently retired, came to see the son and heir. Very stiff,
very much starched, he carefully unwrapped the child and
examined him all over 'just to see whether there was
anything to criticize in his appearance'. Then he took his
leave with a display of dryness which was only skin-deep.
The young mother, carried away by delight in the arrival of
a son, decided to feed the child herself. Of this determination Sophie-Victoire thoroughly approved. *Madame Maurice Dupin to Madame Dudevant:* 'So, you want to suckle
your baby. That is admirable. It is Nature's way, and your
decision does you credit . . .' All the same, she was labouring
under a sense of grievance, for her son-in-law, dreading the
influence of so brazen and immoral a woman, sought to
keep her from her daughter. 'Why should I be held at arm's
length? Had I never produced the mother, he would never
have been able to get on her this replica of himself. . . .'[1]

As a result of Deschartres's retirement, the management
of Nohant had now devolved upon Casimir. It was
necessary, therefore that the young couple should spend the
autumn and winter in the country. The new master, as is the
way of new masters, changed everything. There was more
discipline in the domestic staff, and abuses were fewer. The
garden paths were more carefully weeded and better looked
after. Casimir had the old horses sold, the old dogs shot.
'Nohant was improved, but at the cost of everything being
turned upside down.' These alterations filled the heiress of
Nohant with an inexplicable melancholy. In the raked and

1 Spoelberch de Lovenjoul Collection: Group E. 868, f. 270.

tended grounds she could no longer find 'the dark, abandoned corners where she had dreamed away her youth. After all, it was *her* home, and it went hard with her that she should have no voice in its administration. Had she been freed from the family leading-strings merely to become her husband's slave? She discovered that the law was hard on women. They could not do the least thing without marital authority. A wife's adultery was punishable with imprisonment; a husband's was treated with toleration. Aurore, as a young girl, had looked to marriage to give her that sense of certainty and peace which is to be found in religious faith. The highly-spiced conversation of Casimir and his boon-companions of the local squirearchy was enough to prove to her that such a mystical attitude to love was not one with which they were familiar.

Her period of torpor was now ended, and she turned once again, with pleasure, to her books.

Aurore Dudevant to Emilie de Wismers: I live very much alone, if anyone can be said to be alone who spends her days in close contact with an adored husband. While he is out shooting, I occupy my time in working, playing with my little Maurice, and reading. At the moment, I am re-reading the *Essays* of Montaigne, my favourite author ... Dear Casimir is the most active of men, and it is only with difficulty that I can get two hours with a book of an evening. Still, I have read somewhere that mutual love is best assured where there is *similarity of principles combined with difference in tastes*. . . . [1]

If difference in tastes is a true guarantee of married happiness, she would have been a contented woman, indeed! She tried to interest her husband in the books she was reading, but from boredom or sleepiness, he let them drop from his hands. She talked to him about poetry and ethics: he had never even heard of the authors she mentioned, and looked on as a romantic halfwit. When she described her emotions, her quickened heartbeats, her religious ecstasies, he merely shrugged and remarked that such exalted fantasies were 'the natural consequences of a bilious temperament, complicated in her case by certain nervous symptoms'. She did her best to make him enjoy music, but the sound of the piano sent him running from

[1] Ibid., Group E. 911, ff. 39 and 43.

the room. He liked nothing but shooting, drinking and local
politics.

It sometimes happens that the shared delights of the body
will bind two people together even when mutual sympathy
of heart and brain is absent. '*So shall my nights console
them for their days.*' But here, too, Aurore had suffered a
terrible disappointment. Her reading had prepared her for
the sentimental side of love: its physical manifestations had
shocked, without satisfying, her. Pleasure in passion is, for
the woman, a function of the imagination. She needs, more
especially when the experience is fresh and new, to feel
herself beloved, and also to admire her partner. A man of
Casimir's type—he was both egotistical and sensual—
expects the docile mistress of his home to become
immediately transformed, within the curtained darkness of
the marriage bed, into an ecstatic lover. This was not, and
could not be, the case with her. 'Marriage,' she said, 'is
pleasing only in anticipation.' Casimir found her cold. 'You
resist my approaches'—he told her: 'your senses seem proof
against all attempts of mine to rouse them.'[1]

There were quarrels, but they did not last. She could still
value her husband for his solid qualities. He was honourable, capable of affection, and an admirable father. Husband
and wife were good comrades, and signed their letters
jointly, 'the Two Casimirs'. When Casimir was away without her, he sent her letters filled with tender sentiments.
These, in his absence, had still the power to transform the
earthy husband into that bodiless lover of whom, in the old
days, the still unawakened girl had dreamed.

> *Casimir to Aurore:* I have just got up, and my first
> thought is for my darling . . . Goodbye, my angel. I press
> you to my heart, and kiss each of your lovely cheeks a
> million times to make up for the tiny tears which fall
> from your beloved eyes. . . .
>   You upbraid me, Sweet, for not having written to you
> from Paris. The fact is, I had not a single moment to
> myself, as I explained in the letter which I sent from
> Châteauroux. I am deeply afflicted by the knowledge that
> my absence has caused you so much sorrow. I would
> have you realize that I share it most sincerely, and that

[1] GEORGE SAND: *Le Roman d'Aurore Dudevant et
d'Aurélien de Sèze*, p. 18.

when I get home I shall be so much on my best behaviour that I shall make up to you for all that you have suffered, truly I will, my Angel . . . Why cannot you amuse yourself, my Angel? . . . I count every moment, every minute, that I spend away from you. Goodbye, my dearest dear. I press you to my heart, and the poor little baby, too. . . .[1]

The Two Casimirs spent the evenings at Nohant in playing at piquet. The winnings went to swell a little fund which they were building up in order to buy some *foie gras* at Chevet's. Alternatively, Aurore would ask Caron to send 'four small boxes of coral powder for the teeth, one bottle of attar of roses, another of rum, for Casimir, and three and a half yards of double-width silk, so that I can make a seamless apron—also some jars of apricots preserved in brandy—and a guitar'.[2]

All this would seem to fit in with the kind of life led by any well-to-do country family. But one morning in the spring of 1824 as they were breakfasting, Aurore felt suddenly 'choked by tears'. Casimir flew into a rage. There had been no recent disagreement sufficiently serious to account for so sharp a crisis of despair. She begged his pardon, said that she was frequently surprised by these miserable moods, and admitted that she was probably a thoroughly unbalanced woman. The most likely reason, said Casimir, was that she found the house, filled as it was with memories of her grandmother, decidedly depressing. He did not much care for it himself. They arranged to spend some time, as paying-guests, with their friends at Plessis.

There, with youth and gaiety around them, with frequent private theatricals, and a host of young girls, Aurore recovered her spirits. She shone, and Casimir, because the men of the company expressed admiration of his wife, began to show signs of jealousy. It must be admitted that Aurore, for all her innocence, was a born coquette. Her fine eyes and her talents as a 'live wire' turned more than one head. Of this she was well aware, and the knowledge pleased her. Her husband, from being at first uneasy, became aggressive. One day, when she was acting the child,

[1] Spoelberch de Lovenjoul Collection: Group E. 868, ff. 195 and 197.
[2] Ibid. Group E. 869, ff. 38 and 89.

and scattering handfuls of sand, a few grains fell into the
coffee-cups. He told her to stop, but she defied him, and
scattered some more. This public disregard of marital
authority touched him on the raw, and he gave her a not
very hard slap. At the moment this incident seemed to
produce no very great impression on her. When her
husband left to make a tour of inspection at Nohant, she
wrote to him as fondly as ever.

Aurore to Casimir, August 1st, 1824: How sad I am, my
Angel and dear darling, at having to write, instead of
being able to talk, to you. And this is only the first day of
our separation. How long it will seem, and how lonely I
feel! I do hope that you will not often be away from me.
Your absence makes me miserable, and I shall never get
used to it. I don't know what I shall do this evening, so
tired and worn-out do I feel from having cried so much.
But don't worry too badly, darling. I will do my best not
to make myself ill, or our little pet, either. But I cannot
endure many days like this one. I cry when I think of the
moment of our parting . . . Oh God! how I wish it were
Saturday, and you back! . . . Good night, beloved, good
night, my sweet. I am just off to my great big lonely
bed, where I shall lie and cry my eyes out. . . .

Le Plessis: Thursday, August 18th, 1824: Now that my
darling is not here to protect my slumbers, I find that Bibi
wakens me . . . When you are back, I shall sleep in your
arms like a log. Your son is quite moon-struck . . . Never has being away from you made me feel so miserable,
and never have I more wanted, or needed, to be with
you again, and in your arms. Besides, I want you to be
back for the Saint-Louis Ball. I have made all sorts
of magnificent preparations, in other words, a quite delicious dress cut from the material that Caron sent. But
I am very much afraid, seeing that you are not due to
start till Monday, that you will arrive on Wednesday,
tired out, and not much in the mood for dancing.
Perhaps it might be better for your sake not to leave
Nohant until Tuesday. Think over the suggestion, my
Angel . . . Goodbye, angel and dear darling, my life. I
love you, I adore you. I kiss you with all my heart, and
press you in my arms a thousand times. . . .

June 1825: Eleven o'clock at night. I am in bed, but you
are not with me . . . I was cold last night, and that is what
made me unwell. I can't wait until Friday. . . .[1]

It would be foolish to take everything she wrote quite
literally. Madame Dudevant's tone was in part deliberately
assumed in order to flatter her lord and master. In truth,
they both, by this time, had grown to dread being left
together in unbroken intimacy at Nohant. But this they did
not openly admit, and, by tacit agreement, avoided any
discussion of the matter. She made an effort to see things
with her husband's eyes, and success in this meant that she
had to do considerable violence to her own feelings.
Consequently she became thoroughly out of love with
herself, and with everything. Where should they live? Their
income was too small to make Paris possible. They rented a
small house at Ormesson. This melancholy countryside of
gardens and tall trees has a character all its own, and
Aurore was happy there, leaving it with regret after Casimir
had had a quarrel with the gardener. She suffered a return
of intense, overwhelming, and quite inexplicable depression,
as a result of which she went to see her former confessor,
the Abbé de Prémord.

She found him greatly changed. His voice had become so
weak that she could scarcely hear him when he spoke.
Nevertheless, he summoned back his gentle eloquence in an
effort to console her. 'He showed me that the mood of
melancholy to which I had surrendered is one of the most
dangerous of all conditions for the human soul, because it
exposes it to evil influences and disposes it to weakness.
How happy I should have been to follow his advice, and
recapture my former gaiety and courage! . . .'[2]

But it was not in the Abbé de Prémord's power to give
her back these things. The old Jesuit was too intelligent, too
tolerant, too human to be able to cure an evil which he
understood only too well. Aurore was starving for some
form of absolute faith. Earthly life having refused her what
she had thought it had to give, there was nothing now she
wanted but to take refuge in the certainties of her early
years. The Abbé advised her to make a retreat in the
Convent where she had been brought up. The Mother-

---

[1] Spoelberch de Lovenjoul Collection: Group E. 868, ff. 15-
17 and f. 21.

[2] Spoelberch de Lovenjoul Collection: Group E. 868, f. 32.

Superior, Madame Eugénie, consented to receive her.
Casimir gave his permission. 'My husband was not at all
religious, but thought it a very good thing that I should be.'
No doubt he hoped that a faith which he did not share
might calm his wife and give him the chance of a peaceful
life. The nuns were kind, and overflowing with maternal
solicitude. Aurore went each day to kneel in the Chapel
where once she had heard the voice of God. Had she not
been wrong to choose the world? It had brought her no
happiness. 'You have a charming child,' said good Mother
Alicia, 'and that is all you need for happiness in this world.
Life is short.'[1] Life, thought Aurore, may be short for nuns,
but it is long for those whose feelings and ardent longings
turn each day to misery and weariness. She admitted that
she was troubled by metaphysical doubts. 'Bah!' said
Mother Alicia, speaking of her: 'deep down in herself she
loves God, and He knows it.' In a short while Aurore was
once again caught up in the marvellous peace of the
cloister. She was tempted to prolong her stay. But it had
turned cold: she felt chilled, and the news that her child was
ill made it necessary for her to return home. Small things
determine great decisions.

II

PLATONIC SENTIMENT

'MOTHERHOOD HOLDS inexpressible delight, but
whether in love or in marriage, it must be bought at a price
which I would never advise anybody to incur.' This price
was the gift of the body. The very idea of physical union
filled Aurore with horror. Later, she was sufficiently
courageous to describe her feelings during the first months
of her marriage. When, in 1843, her brother Hippolyte
married off his daughter Léontine, Aurore put him on his
guard against a danger of which she had only too good
reason to be aware.

1 GEORGE SAND: *Histoire de ma Vie*. Volume III, p. 450.

See to it that your son-in-law does not brutalize your daughter on the first night of marriage, for many physical troubles, and much of the distress which many women experience in childbirth, are due to precisely that cause in cases where the wife is constitutionally delicate. Men do not know that what is fun for them is hell for us. Tell him, therefore, to be considerate, and to wait until such time as his wife, under his instruction, may gradually attain to understanding, and be able to respond to his passion. Nothing is more frightful than the terror, the suffering, and the disgust occasioned in a poor young thing as the result of being violated by a brute. *We bring them up as saints, only to dispose of them as fillies.*[1]

Aurore had spent her girlhood dreaming of love as a sublime experience *à la* Rousseau. She found it impossible to descend to the level of a man's crude appetites. The marriage bed is a rough school, in which the romantic soul feels itself to be lost and outraged. Casimir was in the highest degree uncomplicated. To him, love seemed a perfectly simple affair. He had had the ordinary experiences of a normal and far from straitlaced bachelor, and had hoped that he would, without difficulty, provoke in his wife pleasurable sensations similar to those which he found it so easy to enjoy . . . In this he failed, though for a long while he did not know it. Aurore reconciled herself to providing a pleasure in which she had no part or parcel. But when, coarse and careless, he succumbed to sleep, she would lie awake for most of the night in tears. 'The desire for physical delight became for her something like the punishment of Tantalus. The reviving and refreshing water lapped all about her, but she could not quench her thirst. The sweet fruit hung upon the branch, but her hands could not reach it. The pangs of hunger tormented her, but she could not satisfy them. Love alone can give life its true savour, but, somehow, she could not taste it, though she would have given anything to do so.'[2]

Other women, thus circumstanced, have solved the difficulty by taking a lover. Aurore was full of affection for her husband. She desired to procure his happiness, to serve him, to mingle their two lives. But he seemed to attach no importance to the treasures of which she was so lavish.

[1] Spoelberch de Lovenjoul Collection: Group E. 921, f. 11.
[2] LOUISE VINCENT: *George Sand et l'Amour*, P. 114.

At nineteen, freed from all real anxieties and troubles,
married to a man of excellent qualities and mother of a
fine child, surrounded by everything calculated to flatter
my tastes, I yet lived a life of utter boredom. This mood
of mine can be easily explained. There is a period in the
life of every woman when she needs to love, and to love
exclusively. When she is in that state of mind, it needs
must be that her every action is concentrated upon the
beloved object. She values her charms and her talents
only insofar as they give delight to him. You never
noticed mine. Such knowledge as I had was wasted, since
you did not share it. I did not put all this into words, even
to myself, but I felt it. I pressed you in my arms, I was
loved by you, and yet, something, I knew not what, was
lacking to my happiness. . . .[1]

This was what she longed to say but dared not do so until
after the occurrence of a small domestic crisis.

Pregnancy, childbirth and churching had served to
retard the necessary explanation. The return to Nohant in
1825 made it quite clear that her life was to be no happier
in the future than it had been in the past. She complained
of palpitations and headaches. She coughed continually, and
believed herself to be consumptive. Casimir, by this time
thoroughly exasperated, and realizing that her troubles were
largely imaginary, said, in so many words, that she was
being 'stupid, idiotic'. A sad item of news completely
overwhelmed her. Her old friend, Deschartres, had died in
Paris . . . This man of theories, a dogmatist in all things and
excessively self-assured, had embarked upon a course of
speculation, in addition to which he had lent considerable
sums of money to people about whom he knew little.
Ruined, and too proud to complain, he chose a stoic's
death. Sophie-Victoire, who had always hated him, was
delighted. 'So Deschartres has gone at last!' Aurore, now
that she had lost her 'Great Man', felt more than ever an
orphan. Who was there left for her to call a friend? Her
brother Hippolyte?—he was out of the same mould as
Casimir, loved good living, and was interested in nothing
but wine and women. He had made a far better marriage
than anyone had expected, with a Mademoiselle Emilie de

[1] GEORGE SAND: *Le Roman d'Aurore Dudevant et
d'Aurélien de Sèze*, pp. 148-9.

Villeneuve, and was now living at the Château de
Montgivray, not far from Nohant. He was a friendly
neighbour, 'but drunkenness was to swallow up all that
charming intelligence'. As to Sophie-Victoire, she rarely
wrote at all, except to complain—or boast.

> *Madame Maurice Dupin to Aurore Dudevant:* You were
> married, my dear daughter, on the anniversary of your
> father's funeral, and on his name-day, the feast of Saint-
> Maurice, you rejoiced, though I do not believe that your
> mother, who is far from happy, was for a moment in
> your thoughts. Try, some day, to be a better wife, a good
> sister and mother, even though you may be lacking in the
> qualities of a good daughter. . . .
>
> What a hateful fault is jealousy! Fortunately, it is no
> longer one of mine. All the same, its absence does not
> make for gaiety in me, though I should be by no means
> averse to a little gaiety just now. I only hope that I don't
> get carried away by one of my whims—Heavens! what
> am I saying!—at my age, too! You had better start
> preaching to your mother, Aurore. See what the mere
> talk of marriage will do! . . .
>
> *January 6th, 1824:* I have received one quarter's
> instalment of my allowance, four pages of nonsense
> which made me laugh, and your New Year's letter which
> gave me much pleasure. Address me in future as follows:
> Madame de Nohant-Dupin; *Hôtel de la Mayenne,* rue
> Duphot, 6. . . .[1]

The daughter of the people had chosen a name worthy of
an 'old countess'! In the condition of inner solitude which
was that of her present way of life, Aurore found a peculiar
pleasure in entertaining two friends of her Convent days,
and their father: Jane and Aimée Bazouin. The two girls
were to go in June to Cauterets. Casimir wanted to spend
the summer with his father at Guillery. It was agreed that
the Dudevants should make a short stay in the Pyrenees
before travelling to Gascony . . . 'Farewell, Nohant,' wrote
Aurore, 'perhaps I shall never see thee again.' She believed
that she was dying, though, in fact, she was suffering from
no disease more severe than an intense craving for love.

[1] Unpublished. Spoelberch de Lovenjoul Collection: Group
E. 868, ff. 280-1, 272 and 278.

Casimir tried, at times, though clumsily, to console her; but
he had, too, moments of ill-humour and impatience. On
their way through Périgueux he treated his wife to a most
unjust and violent scene, as a result of which she walked for
a long while through the ancient streets, and shed many
bitter tears. At last they came in sight of the black
mountains of marble and slate. They skirted a precipice
down which roared a mountain torrent. 'To me it seemed
both horrid and delicious.'

At Cauterets she fell into the arms of Jane and Aimée.
They were living in furnished rooms of a quite primitive
simplicity, the rent of which was exorbitant. Next day
Casimir started off for a shooting trip in the mountains. 'He
killed chamois and eagles. He got up at two in the morning,
and returned at nightfall. This, at the time, was a great
grievance to his wife. It did not seem to occur to him that a
time might come when it would be her source of happiness
. . .'[1] . . . The wind of rebellion blew about Cauterets.
Aurore had struck up a friendship with a young woman
from Bordeaux, Zoé Leroy, who became her confidant, and,
for that reason, her husband's mortal enemy. Madame
Dudevant made the following entry in her Journal:
'Marriage is a wonderful state for lovers, and a useful state
for saints . . . Marriage is the ultimate goal of love. When
love ceases, or is absent from the beginning, all that remains
is sacrifice . . . All very well for those who understand
sacrifice . . . There is probably no middle way between the
strength of the great-hearted, and that convenient negative
attitude in which the poor-spirited find refuge—or, rather,
there is a middle way, and its name is despair. . . .'[2]

There was one more way—childishness. She was so very
young. She found pleasure in everything—in running,
climbing, riding. 'I have been so little spoiled since I made
my entry into this world! I have never had a mother or a
sister to dry my tears!'[3] When a young woman with fine
eyes seeks out a twin soul, she always finds it. In the case
of Aurore Dudevant, the twin soul went by the name of
Aurélien de Sèze. He was a Junior at the Bordeaux Bar, and
twenty-six years old. He was noble-minded, with a taste for

[1] GEORGE SAND: *Histoire de ma Vie.* Volume IV, p. 13.

[2] Ibid. Volume IV, pp. 13-14.

[3] Letter from Aurore to Zoé, quoted in *Le Roman d'Aurore
Dudevant et d'Aurélien de Sèze*, p. 2.

poetry. He was staying in the Pyrenees with his fiancée's family, but fell a victim to Aurore's charms, to her gipsy beauty, to her large, questioning, supplicating eyes, to her intelligence and educated tastes, and also to that deep melancholy in her which wore the mask of exuberance. She was under orders to follow in the train of her chamois-hunting, eagle-shooting husband, and, from time to time, would join him at Luz or Bagnères. Aurélien de Sèze accompanied her on her trips among the snowfields, the torrents and the haunts of bears. He gave her the support of his arm on tracks which skirted deep mountain chasms. Aimée Bazouin scolded her for making these trips without her husband. 'I could see no harm in it, since it was he who had taken the initiative, I who followed where he wished to go ... Aimée could not understand that one might wish to find diversion for the mind, that one might want to forget ... forget what?—she would say to me ... and what answer could I make except to say—everything, and most of all, myself—. . . .'[1]

From the very first moment, Aurélien de Sèze fell in love with her. Who would not have done? When he became confiding, Aurore tried to send him back to his fiancée, but he declared that he had no feelings for her—that, pretty though she might be, she had no mind.[2]

> *Aurélien de Sèze to Aurore Dudevant:* What I love in you are the qualities of your mind: your soul, your talents, your perfect simplicity, your superior intellect, the wide range of your knowledge ... Even were you ugly I should still love you. . . .[3]

She repulsed him at first with a show of determination, for she wished to remain loyal. But the discovery that beneath the exterior of a pleasant man of the world there lurked a romantic and sensitive heart, touched her deeply.

> *Aurore Dudevant to Aurélien de Sèze, November 10th, 1825:* Oh, God! how happy we were in each other's

[1] GEORGE SAND: *Histoire de ma Vie*. Volume IV, pp. 14 and 15.

[2] GEORGE SAND: *Preface to Le Roman d'Aurore d'Aurélien de Sèze*, p. viii.

[3] Spoelberch de Lovenjoul Collection: Group E. 902, f. 24.

company, how well we undetstood one another! What
charm for me our talks together had, even when they
were of a quite general nature, touching on a variety of
out-of-the-way topics. With what delight I listened to you
telling me of many trivial things, for it seemed to me
that in your mouth they took on a peculiar interest. Nobody talks as you do: nobody has your special tone, your
voice, your laugh, your turn of fancy, your way of seeing things, your way of expressing what is in your mind
—nobody but you. How you filled me with delight,
Aurélien, that day when we were walking with Zoé, at
Médouze, and you said: 'Not only am I happy, but
contented, too. Not only do you ravish my heart: you
please me, you *suit* me. . . .'[1]

He asked for nothing more than the intimacy of
friendship.

Such pleasure did I find in listening to him that I felt he
was dearer to me than, so far, I had ventured to admit
even to myself. I feared for my peace of mind, but so
pure did his feelings seem, so pure were mine, that I
could not think that we were guilty. . . .[2]

One day, when they were in a boat together on the Lac
de Gaube, he spoke of love. 'What is virtue, as you
understand it, but convention and mere prejudice?'[3] She
remembered how her mother and her Aunt Lucie had used
to say: 'All that is very unimportant.' What if they had been
right? . . . With the point of his penknife he carved three
initials on the woodwork of the boat—AUR, saying, as he
did so, that their two names began in the same way. She
would not yet admit that she loved him, and pretended to be
angry. But her heart was beating with happiness. Aurélien,
however, took pretence for reality. Feeling himself repulsed,
he spent three days without speaking a word to her. She was
in despair. To Zoé Leroy she confessed that should Aurélien
find it impossible to remain her friend and brother, should
he demand more, then 'she must sacrifice herself'. God

1 GEORGE SAND: *Le Roman/ d'Aurore Dudevant et
d'Aurélien de Sèze*, p. 83.
2 Ibid., p. 155.
3 Ibid., p. 55.

would pardon her. Aurélien left for Gavarnie. She dragged
Casimir thither. He felt vaguely uneasy, and grumbled at
her whims. But how shall one stop a woman who is hot for
love?

One night, at a ball, she managed to spend an hour alone
with Monsieur de Sèze. He explained his feelings. He had
no wish to be a seducer. It had been wrong in him to run
after a married woman. He would try to forget her. But like
so many women, she wanted to eat her cake and have it.
She offered him an affectionate friendship. The night was
warm and lovely. The corner where they sat was dark. He
took her in his arms.

Had I yielded to that first impulse, then, no doubt, we
should have been guilty. What man is there who, alone in
the darkness, with a woman whose love for him he
knows, can quiet his senses and still their urgency?
Tearing myself from his embrace, I begged him to let me
go back. He tried, in vain, to reassure me, to swear that
he was honourable. I insisted on leaving the place where
we were sitting, and he obeyed me without a murmur.[1]

As they climbed the steep path, he put his arm about her
and, at the moment of their parting, 'imprinted a burning
kiss upon my neck'.[2]

She took to her heels and, a little further on, met Casimir.
'You spoke harshly to me. No doubt I deserved it, but your
words sent a pang to my heart. Had I not felt how necessary
it was that I should remain calm, I believe that the terror
with which you inspired me would have caused me to faint
. . .'[3] So seeming guileless is the heart when first it strays.

It was at the grotto of Lourdes, where the precipice falls
sheer, that he said goodbye to me. Our imaginations were
struck by the horrid wildness of the spot. 'Here,' he said
'where Nature is at her most sublime, I wish, in bidding
you farewell, to swear most solemnly that I will love you
all my life as I would love a mother or a sister, and to
show you the same respect that I would show to them.'

[1] GEORGE SAND: *Le Roman d'Aurore Dudevant et
d'Aurélien de Sèze*, p. 160.

[2] Ibid., p. 89.

[3] Ibid., p. 161.

He pressed me to his heart, and that was the utmost
liberty he ever took with me. . . .[1]

She left in a daze of happiness. 'Oh, Pyrenees, how can
either of us ever forget you? . . .' At last she had found a
great and comely soul, a strong mind and a just man, a man
whom she could take for guide and model. Her husband
hurried her away to Guillery, to the house of the Baron
Dudevant where they were to spend several months. It was
a small Gascon manor with a tiled roof. The main front,
with its stretch of five windows, was prolonged at either end
by low wings. This 'shooting-box', in spite of its owner's
wealth, was furnished in a far simpler style than Nohant.
The young couple were given two rooms on the ground
floor, and on winter nights the wolves prowled outside the
doors. At first Aurore found nothing but ugliness in this
countryside of sand and pines and cork-oaks smothered in
lichen. The Gascons of the neighbourhood were decent
folk, less cultivated than those of Berry, but 'infinitely
kinder than the people at home'. She got on well with her
parents-in-law who gorged her with stuffed fowls, *foie gras*
and truffles, to the great detriment of her liver, which had
never been of the strongest.

As for her heart, it was in Bordeaux. She felt torn in two.
Casimir, because he had been afraid of losing her, was
sympathetic, affectionate and kind. She reproached herself
for having changed towards him. 'I love Aurélien more,' she
reflected, 'but my love for Casimir is finer.' Later, she
described to her husband what she had been feeling at that
time. 'The need to hide from you with scrupulous care what
was happening in my heart, made me horribly unhappy.
Your caresses were sheer agony to me. I feared that if I
returned them I should be acting dishonourably, and you
thought me cold . . .'[2] She longed to fall upon her knees
before him, to kiss his hands, to beg him to forgive her. By
doing so, she would have recovered her peace of mind, but
at the cost of making him miserable. Must she, then, break
with her 'friend'? Whatever she did, she must drive either
Casimir or Aurélien to despair. She was experiencing those
torments of conscience in which a woman finds bitter-
sweet delight.

[1] Ibid., p. 163.
[2] GEORGE SAND: *Le Roman d'Aurore Dudevant et
d'Aurélien de Sèze*, p. 164.

In October, the Dudevants were invited by Zoé to La Brède. On their way thither they passed through Bordeaux. Aurélien called on them at their hotel. She tried to take advantage of Casimir's momentary absence from the room to make Aurélien understand the necessity of a rupture. The interview became highly emotional. Seized by a sudden weakness, she leaned upon Aurélien for support, and her husband, unexpectedly returning, found her with her cheek pressed to her friend's shoulder. She was new to such situations, and the possessor of a sensitive conscience. Flinging herself at Casimir's feet, she begged him to have mercy, and then fainted dead away. The poor fellow was ill equipped to deal with dramatic crises of this kind, and was at his wit's end to know what to do. He did not wish to provoke a scandal, because he was fearful of public opinion. 'It seemed to me,' she said, 'that he was divided between the necessity of believing me and the uncomfortable feeling that he was being deceived.'[1]

For Aurore, who was still imbued with the virtues of piety and loyalty, the situation was indeed frightful. Innocent though she was, she was suffering under a sense of guilt. 'My husband's anger, but still more his pain, the thought that I might never see you again . . . I clenched my teeth: my eyes were blinded with tears: I felt that I was dying . . .'[2] Casimir, for his part, was no less bewildered. 'Nobody,' he said at last, 'must know of what has happened—that must be our chief concern.'—'Are you still afraid?—then look me in the eyes!' she cried. 'True, they are incapable of concealment, but when I came upon you suddenly, as I did, you bore the marks of guilt and corruption. I read in your face at once my shame and my misery.' 'Say, rather, *my* repentance, *my* despair. Your honour is dearer to me than life, and never . . .' 'I believe it, I believe *you,* for I cannot persuade myself to think that you have learned the tricks of treachery. . . .'[3]

Next day an excursion to La Brède with Aurélien and Zoé Leroy took place as planned. There, and in the evening, too, as they left the Grand Theatre at Bordeaux, the passionate friends were able to exchange a few words. Steeped as they were in *La Princesse de Clèves* and *La*

[1] Ibid., p. 19.

[2] Ibid., p. 35.

[3] GEORGE SAND: *Le Roman d'Aurore Dudevant et d'Aurélien de Sèze*, p. 16.

Nouvelle Héloïse, they both fervently believed in the
nobility of a *ménage à trois,* provided all lies were banished
from the relationship. The die was cast. They would be as
brother and sister. They would love one another, but no
carnal bond should exist between them. In that way
Casimir's honour would be safe. 'This winter we must
combine our efforts to make him happy and tranquil. He
has shown us so much generosity and kindness that we must
not fail to communicate to him our own sense of peace of
mind. . . .'[1]

In this way there opened for Aurore a period of high and
splendid sentiments. After her return to Guillery she
corresponded with Aurélien, using Zoé as a go-between.
With him in view she kept a Journal in which she set down
her memories of childhood, not without a touch of snob-
bery, and catalogued her conquests, for, at Guillery, the
local squires paid her court, and even the curé Candelotte,
who, with many blushes, slipped verses into her hand. Over
and over again she read such letters as reached her from
Aurélien. Love-letters have the power to enable us to live
again the happy hours which they evoke, and make of
absence a more perfect and a sweeter presence. Aurore felt
that she could re-read his without scruple or remorse. She
had accepted the sacrifice of happiness. The lovers of
Cauterets would never cease to love, but never would they
belong to one another. They drank themselves drunk on
sublimity.

Never were they absent from one another in thought.
Whatever she might be doing—galloping across the heathy
wastes on her mare, Colette, or listening to the legends of
the Gascon countryside, or going to bed—he was always
with her in imagination. He shared all her thoughts. At last
she had found a man who was capable of loving without
selfishness, with modesty and delicacy. All about her there
reigned an intolerable gaiety. Her lecherous Gascon
neighbours talked of love with outspoken lust and bawdiness. They made it a point of honour to despise finè sentiments. 'The poor fools have no notion either of purity or
constancy!'[2] How grateful she was to Aurélien for having
helped her to tread the narrow path of virtue!—though she
admitted to herself that, had he been rather more exigent,
she would have left it rather than lose him.

1 Ibid., p. 20.
2 Ibid., p. 91.

There is no man in the world, not one, who can for ever stay content with the possession merely of a woman's heart. Aurélian, I am sure, feels certain that, in the long run, he will win. If he has shown that he knows how to wait, it is because he is convinced that he will eventually get what he wants. If I must give it to him, I shall die: if I refuse, I shall lose his heart. . . .[1]

But it was he who swore to respect her. 'It is you, Aurélien, who urges me to resist, who tells me not to be afraid of hurting you . . . Oh, my Angel!'[2]

Faced by conduct so angelic, she found her thoughts playing with eternity. 'There is a better world, Aurélien; you do believe that, don't you?' Since mortal dust was capable of so much love, God would give it life everlasting. 'He will unite us for ever in a world of peace, where tenderness will be freed from guilt, and bliss will never end. . . .'[3]

But would they be able to see one another again in this present life? That depended on Casimir. Since he had their word of honour to love chastely, ought he not to let them meet and correspond? 'You are great-hearted, Casimir; you are noble, you are generous—you have proved it, and I know it to be true.'[4]

Acting on Aurélien's advice, she wrote a *Confession* which ran to eighteen pages:

What a terrible situation I am in! When I feel moved to repent, to surrender to emotion, something, I know not what, holds me back, compelling me to substitute persuasive, but Oh! how cold, reasoning for the heart's eloquence. How can I define that which checks my impulse, which freezes my powers of expression? It is not, I am sure, a lack of sensibility, but, rather, a movement of pride which I deliberately assume. Sometimes I feel it as a noble sentiment, sometimes I regret it as the prompting of mere human pride . . . You have often asked me to explain, to confess, but I never could make up my mind to do so. The reason has lain not only in a feeling of

[1] GEORGE SAND: *Le Roman d'Aurore Dudevant et d'Aurélien de Sèze*, p. 34.

[2] Ibid., p. 36.

[3] Ibid., p. 88.

[4] Ibid., p. 144.

embarrassment at admitting my faults, but rather in a fear
lest I should wound you. I should have had to wield the
knife ruthlessly, to enter into details which would have
pained, and, maybe, angered you. More than that, I
should have had to tell you that you were, to some extent,
to blame for what has happened to me. Blame is, perhaps,
not the word. Your intentions, where I am concerned,
have always been admirable. You have always been so
good, so generous, so attentive, so obliging, and yet,
unknown to yourself, you have been guilty of involuntary
wrong-doing . . . You have been, if I may say so, the
innocent cause of all my restlessness. . . .[1]

She went on to tell him the story of her life, to explain
how sad it had been, how wholly stripped by their marriage
of all that might have made it beautiful. She had given up
her music, because the sound of the piano sent him
hastening from the room.

When we talked together, especially when we spoke of
literature, poetry or moral philosophy, you knew nothing
of the authors whom I mentioned. You treated my
ideas as the fantastic aberrations of a romantic mind. I
gave up discussing them, and began to be deeply pained
by the thought that we could never have any tastes in
common. . . .[2]

She admitted that he had been very good to her, that he
had spent thirty thousand gold francs—the half of his
marriage settlement—in order to satisfy his wife's whims.
He had loved her, held her in his arms, but always the deep
communion of two souls had been absent. This lack had
ended for her in tears and feelings of disgust. Then, after
this prologue, she proceeded to recount—as she believed,
sincerely—her adventure with Aurélien, and described how
deeply touched the latter had been by the nobility of
Casimir's behaviour.

'Aurore', he had said, 'I will never say a word to you
which he might not overhear, of which he could not
approve. We will combine our efforts for his happiness.

[1] Ibid., p. 141-3.
[2] GEORGE SAND: *Le Roman d'Aurore Dudevant et
d'Aurélien de Sèze*, p. 177.

That shall be our most dear concern. If ever an evil thought enters either of our minds, we must drive it out with horror. If we feel tempted to turn back into the past, we must remember what he said to you: *"You are free now to deceive me yet again, for I trust you absolutely."* How could we possibly abuse a confidence so complete? Aurore, I feel inclined to chide you for not having sufficiently loved your husband. You have never spoken to me of him. I never suspected that he could show such greatness of soul. I love him with all my heart.' . . . I smiled with pleasure. 'You know him now,' I answered: 'I, too, know him, and I love him. I have a deep affection for him, and I repent my errors.' . . .[1]

Everything, henceforward, would be easy. Now that Casimir, in his angelic goodness, knew Aurélien better, he would love him as a brother.

What an absurd project, the cold-hearted will say, those who, in their tiny sphere, can conceive no great, no splendid, thought—how false, romantic and impossible. For all who think as they do, that must be how it appears. But for us, my dear Casimir, my dear, dear friend, it is very difficult. Listen to me, understand me, and ponder my words, when I say that you have never been taught to take account of your own feelings. They are deep in your heart, for Heaven has set them there. Your mind has not been cultivated, but your soul has remained as God made it, worthy in all respects of mine. Till now, I have undervalued you. I thought you incapable of understanding me. Time was when I should never have ventured to write you a letter such as this. I should have been terrified lest, after reading it, you might say: *My poor wife has lost her senses.* But now I can open my heart to you, and take pleasure in so doing. I can make you read what is written there. I feel sure that you understand me, and approve of what I am doing. . . .[2]

So sure, indeed, did she feel, that she had drawn up a set of conditions for the future conduct of their married life.

[1] Ibid., pp. 142-3.
[2] GEORGE SAND: *Le Roman d'Aurore Dudevant et d'Aurélien de Sèze*, pp. 176-7.

ARTICLE THE FIRST: We will not go to Bordeaux
this Winter. The wounds are too recent. and I feel
that such a visit would lay too heavy a load upon
your trust . . . We will go wherever you wish, and the
planning of our Winter shall be altogether in your hands,
whether in Paris or at Nohant. Tell me what you want,
and I will obey without the slightest feeling of regret.

ARTICLE 2: I promise and swear that I will never write
secretly to Aurélien. But you must give me leave to send
him one letter a month . . . You shall read all his letters to
me, and all my answers. Here and now, before God, I
undertake never to conceal from you one single line.

ARTICLE 3: If we go to Paris we will take lessons in
languages together. You can educate yourself and share
my interests. That will give me the greatest possible
pleasure. While I draw or work, you will read aloud to
me, and our days will pass deliciously . . . I do not
demand that you shall like music. I will not bore you
with it more than I can help, and will indulge in it only
when you are out walking.

ARTICLE 5: If we spend the Winter at Nohant, we will
read together many of the useful works which are in the
library and quite unknown to you. You shall give me an
account of them, and we will then discuss what you have
read. You will let me share your thoughts, and I will
share mine. All our intellectual occupations, all our
pleasures, shall be pursued in common.

ARTICLE 6: There must be no bickering, no anger on
your part, and no vexation on mine. If you lose your
temper, I shall not conceal my distress. But I shall speak
softly, and you will soon recover your equanimity. When
we talk of the past it must be without bitterness, without
sharpness, without mutual distrust. Now that you know
everything, why should you feel distrustful? Now that we
are happy, why should we regret what has happened? Has
it not brought us together? Has it not made you more
dear to me than ever? Without it I should never have
known your worth, and you would not have known
what to do to make me happy.

ARTICLE 7: We shall be happy, and at peace, having banished all regrets, all bitterness. We shall be rivals in the struggle for perfection.

LAST ARTICLE: Some other year, if circumstances permit, we will pass the Winter in Bordeaux, if that seems possible to you. If not, we will put it off until a later date. But you will let me look forward to it happening some time or other.

This is my plan. Read it carefully, think about it, and let me have your answer. I do not think that it will wound you. I shall await your decision with anxiety, but, from now on, I shall live in hope.[1]

When Casimir read this surprising effusion, he was torn between several emotions—a desire not to disappoint his wife, a feeling of remorse at having made her so unhappy, and a dread of appearing ridiculous. To his half-brother-in-law, whom he saw at Châteauroux, he made a number of embittered confidences after a dinner at which wine had been plentiful. Hippolyte was a cynical realist. Sublimity was not his strong suit. He wrote a letter to Aurore full of chiding and reproach. In her reply, she jumped down his throat.

You treat me with contempt. I have, you say, all the faults of a bad wife. Who told you so? Certainly not Casimir. If the whole world combined to say he did, I still should not believe it. . . .[2]

Brothers and sisters judge one another with a far more cruel lucidity than husbands and wives. Hippolyte felt much sympathy for his brother-in-law, who was also his boon companion. He blamed Aurore for making Casimir ill and unhappy, and advised the latter to take a strong line. But Casimir would not listen to the amiable boozer. He, too, was caught up in an ecstasy of romance. He wanted to rise on stepping stones of his dead self to higher things. He longed to behave in such a way that his wife should not have to blush for him. Suffering spurs the mind to

[1] GEORGE SAND: *Le Roman d'Aurore Dudevant et d'Aurélien de Sèze*, pp. 182-5.
[2] Ibid., p. 133.

wakefulness. Unhappiness opens the way to sensibility.
Anguish gives wings to the heart. The Eternal Husband felt
suddenly an urge to sacrifice.

Casimir to Aurore, November 13th, 1825: I find it
impossible, my Angel, to tell you all the dreams that
came to me last night. I can recount only two of them,
or, rather, the second, which followed hard on the heels
of the first. I was with my father, though where I do not
know. 'Casimir' he said to me, 'why are you sad?—Are
you afflicted with sorrows?'—'No, indeed,' I replied, 'but
I am weary of life, and fain would die.' 'Good, my friend,
very good indeed, that is a fine sentiment'—he exclaimed
—'one that sets fire to the imagination, expands the
soul, and makes you capable of great and generous actions.' He spoke to me long on this subject. At last I said
to him—'Farewell, father, farewell.' Then I left him to
go whither I know not. Then I found myself at a dinner
in Paris, where were all the friends we had met in various watering-places and in Paris. I entered the dining-
room and saw Stanislas.[1] You were there beside him,
stretched on a board, pale, scarcely recognizable, and at
the point of death . . . I felt as though the whole world
had abandoned me. I was grievously sick. It was as though
my brain were all at odds with itself, as though my eyes
were blindfolded. There was a staleness in my mind, I
could not think . . . Whence came all these gloomy
ideas I do not know . . . What I most regret are the days
when you grumbled at me. You cried, my sweet kitten. I
seemed offended, but in my heart I was happy. You loved
me then, my dear, you often told me so. Grumble at me as
you used to do . . . I avoid my room like the plague. No
sooner do I enter it than I feel a heavy weight upon my
heart. There is no one to feel compassion for my anguish,
no heart to understand me. Mankind is naught but pride
and envy! I must stop now. I have climbed too high. I
fear lest I may fall. . . .[2]

At Nohant he borrowed Pascal's *Pensées* from the
library, and loyally tried to read them, as his wife had made

[1] Stanislas Ajasson de Grandsagne, one of Stéphane's
brothers.
[2] Spoelberch de Lovenjoul Collection: Group E. 868, ff. 217-
19.

him promise to do. 'I am filled with an infinite regret that laziness has prevented me from reading what, so far as I can see, elevates the mind, and teaches one to think and reason correctly. . . .'[1]

Each letter that he wrote to Guillery was filled with protestations of love. Aurore's many successes and conquests had the effect of making him feel inferior to her. The things he had heard about her at Bordeaux had surprised him, and awakened his sense of pride. 'You enjoy a brilliant reputation here. People speak only about your extraordinary powers of intellect . . . You may imagine how proud I feel . . . I positively strut . . .'[2] He would return with a supply of books, with an English dictionary. 'I have given up shooting. No more will I go out alone. I am going to spend my life at your side . . .' The trouble is that in married life good resolutions come, almost always, after events have rendered them useless.

Casimir had not been 'deceived', but he had lost his wife's respect. His poor, affectionate, pathetic, clumsy letters were compared, somewhat ironically, with Aurélien's productions. At Guillery, Aurore behaved to him with graciousness but also with no little degree of condescension. One day at the table when he had made some rather lumbering joke, she leaned across and said in a voice sufficiently loud to be heard by everyone: 'My poor Casimir, you really are remarkably stupid! Never mind, I love you as you are!' What is really unforgivable in marriage is not adultery, but repudiation.

The roles of husband and wife had now been reversed. It was Casimir's turn to be remote and gloomy. Happiness had restored Aurore's health. Disgusted, as a result of her conjugal experiences, with 'love in its natural and complete state', she had hoped to find salvation in a great Platonic passion. Fearing, however, lest that word might sound forbidding in the male ear, she had encouraged Aurélien to believe that what she had in mind was a quiet and saintly friendship. Only in her dreams did she give herself to him. 'I shut myself away in a world of secret and egotistical delights, and refused to let the object of my strange love have any share in the refined pleasures of my imagination . . .' When her husband, trustful as ever (in February 1826) agreed to take her on a visit to Bordeaux, she saw Aurélien

---

1 Ibid. E. 868, f. 214.
2 Ibid., E. 868, f. 214.

once again. No doubt she was the most ravishing of coquettes, for she managed to hold him in thrall for a very long time. 'I loved the delicious pain which resulted for me from this secret struggle.' The spectacle of a lover's frustration was as pleasing to her as the act of possession was painful. She realized to the full the power she exercised over her 'friend', and knew that a glance, a pressure of the fingers, could set his heart racing.

. It was while she was being fêted in Bordeaux that one day Casimir, with a pale face, hurried round to Zoé Leroy's house, to break a piece of news that he had just heard, and exclaimed, 'He is dead'. Aurore thought that he was referring to her son, and dropped to her knees. 'No, no!' said Zoé, 'he means your father-in-law!' . . . 'There is something savage in a mother's feelings. I was caught up in a sudden spasm of joy, but it was only momentary. I was sincerely fond of the old gentleman, and soon dissolved in tears . . .'[1] The young couple left at once for Guillery. An attack of gout had mounted to the Colonel's heart, and carried him off. Daughter-in-law embraced mother-in-law with a gush of emotion, but found her cold, icy. The Baronne Dudevant had admirable manners, but neither charm nor tenderness. She had seen to it that her husband's will should ensure her a life interest in his fortune, as, indeed, she was legally entitled to do, Casimir having been born out of wedlock. Though very rich, she surrendered not one penny of his father's estate to her stepson. There was nothing to be done but to break free, once and for all, from this 'sterile, bitter, fate', and Aurore set off for Nohant with Casimir, strong in the determination, in spite of all that had happened, to make it their permanent home. Policy is ruled by economics—even the policy of the heart. *Aurore to Caron:* 'We are pretty hard hit this year, having put in hand the building of some new barns—at a ruinous cost, and having got nothing whatever in the way of money from the family inheritance. . . .'[2]

[1] GEORGE SAND: *Histoire de ma Vie.* Volume IV, pp. 37-8.
[2] Spoelberch de Lovenjoul Collection: Group E. 869, f. 38.

THE FIRST STEP

NOHANT: THE little village square, shaded by age-old elms: the courtyard with its acacias and lilacs: the gravel paths: the arbours: the great bedroom on the ground-floor: the songs of birds: the divine country smells.

> *Aurore Dudevant to Zoé Leroy:* It is a real delight to be home again, under my own roof, with my own people, my animals and my furniture . . . The whole place is charged for me with memories . . . Wherever I turn, I am reminded of my whole life. This was the air I needed, dear friend, and you can imagine with what satisfaction I breathe it. . . .[1]

Satisfaction?—perhaps. Certainly it gave her pleasure to see her old servants once again, to practise, as in the old days, the arts of druggist, and, to some extent, of doctor, when the peasant-folk were ill, to compound ointments and cordials, to apply poultices, and carry out bleedings, to play in the garden with her little son who, since he could not pronounce Aurore, called her 'Mummy Aulo', to sit in the moonlight listening to 'those miniature frogs which, though they have but one note, each utter it on a different tone, and collect at night in the corner of a field, to sing their song to the moon'.[2]

But in this murmurous and flower-set Nohant, not everything was as it should be. Fond though she was of her Berrichon country folk, she found them less live-witted than the Gascons. Many of them drank to excess in an attempt to escape from their natural sluggishness. Her brother, Hippolyte, now settled in the Château de Montgivray, close by, was often so drunk that he could not stand, and Casimir

[1] GEORGE SAND: *Le Roman d'Aurore Dudevant et d'Aurélien de Sèze*, p. 187.

[2] Ibid., p. 192.

took to imitating him, in the hope, no doubt, of dissipating his melancholy. Despite their mutual assurances to the contrary, all was not well between husband and wife. Estate business was a constant source of conflict. When Casimir was absent Aurore was left in charge—as, for instance, during the harvest of 1826. But she would have liked to reign unchallenged over the little kingdom which, after all, was hers. The Prince Consort allowed her to do so for a year, but the experiment was a lamentable failure. He had arranged for her to draw the necessary sums of money up to ten thousand francs. In the event, she got through fourteen thousand, and was then relieved of her responsibility. All this was a cause of great bitterness. She still wrote regularly to Aurélien (Casimir sometimes delivered the letters, when he went to Bordeaux), and the absent recipient was constantly in her mind, both night and day.

> There was a distant friend, with whom I was continuously in correspondence, to whom I confided all my thoughts, all my dreams, all my humble virtues, all my Platonic enthusiasms—an admirable man by any standard, but whom I adored with more perfections than any human being could possess, one who appeared before me in the flesh perhaps for a few days, sometimes only a few hours, in the space of a year, who, since he was as romantic to me as I was to myself, never disturbed my religious faith nor troubled my conscience. In him I found the sole support for my troubled heart, the sole consolation for my life of exile in the world of realities. . . .[1]

Gifts were exchanged between Bordeaux and Nohant. She knitted him a purse, and made for him a pair of embroidered braces. He sent her a Basque béret, and a number of books. Aurélien's letters were not so much tender as playful and grave in turn. Since he might not speak of love, he sent her dissertations on politics, and (for he was a monarchist) did all he could to shake the hereditary Bonapartist sympathies, and instinctive liberalism, of Maurice Dupin's daughter. She wrote oftener than he did, and sometimes reproached him for his silence. He complained that her letters were too short. The truth was that, in spite of several visits which she made to Bordeaux, with

[1] GEORGE SAND: *Histoire de ma Vie.* Volume IV, p. 52.

the consent of the magnanimous Casimir, this love without love was entering into a decline.

Politics, which formed a barrier between the passionate friends, served, for a while at least, to bring husband and wife together. Casimir, like Aurore, was a liberal. The two of them combined to support an Opposition candidate in La Châtre, one Duris-Dufresne, a republican, 'a man of Roman virtues, of pleasing and benevolent temperament, who retained in his appearance something of the elegance of the Directoire, with his small wig, his earrings, his mobile, sensitive features. He was, in short, a companionable Jacobin'[1]—and gifted with great delicacy of feeling. To make their support effective, the Dudevants moved to La Châtre, where they rented a house and gave dinners and balls. There Aurore found again many of the friends of her childhood. At first her husband was mistrustful of them, but later tolerated them because they shared his ideas: there was the fair-haired Charles Duvernet—'a young man with a melancholy cast of mind': there was the huge Fleury, known as 'The Gaul'—'a man with enormous hands, a terrifying beard, and awe-inspiring eye:—a left-over from the age of fossils, a primitive': there was the witty Alexis Dutheil, a pock-marked lawyer, a brilliant, lively talker who consoled Aurore when she had the spleen: finally there was the poetic Jules Néraud, nicknamed 'The Madagascan', on the strength of a single visit to Madagascar—a disciple, as was Madame Dudevant, of Rousseau and of Chateaubriand.

This hare-brained company would roam the country roads, the woods, and the streets of the town by moonlight, disturbing the sleep of the good burgesses, spying on amorous couples, invading working-class balls to dance the 'bourrée'. Sometimes, while Casimir was snoring, Aurore would slip away from Nohant, with her brother, under the cover of darkness, and gallop to La Châtre to sing a serenade under Dutheil's window. Or, she would set out at dawn with Néraud—who was a naturalist—to study plants, minerals and insects. One autumn they specialized in mushrooms, another, in mosses and lichens. The spirit of Rousseau hovered above the botanizing pair. Naturally enough the companions of her games and studies all fell in love with the personable young woman in blouse and trousers who treated them as comrades. Dutheil was married—but that did not prevent him from laying siege to

[1] Ibid., Volume IV, p. 45.

her, without success. 'The Madagascan', also married, and
without a tooth in his head, took a chance, and was
repulsed. To Casimir the 'cruel fair', in joking mood,
repeated all the declarations she received—'since my heart
is not susceptible to the emotion of love, I feel nothing for
him or for anybody'. All the same, she did admit to 'The
Madagascan' that 'there was someone else'—which did not
prevent Madame Néraud from writing her a letter 'full of
nonsense', charging her with 'hypocrisy, coquetry, and
every other fault ending in "y". . . .'

It cannot be denied that she was finding increasing
pleasure in awakening desires which she had no intention of
satisfying. The squires of the neighbourhood and the
burgesses of La Châtre found fault with her provocative
manners and undisciplined ways. Had she not had the
impertinence to bring together at the same ball members of
the first, the second and the third social circles of the town?
Had she not urged the Sous-Préfet, Monsieur de Périgny, to
invite the local music-master and his wife? 'Just like
Madame Dudevant', people said when some new indiscretion was brought to their notice. She was perfectly well
aware of what was being said, and chose to regard the 'na-
tives' as stupid and ill-natured, all the more so since the reactionary little town was by no means in a position to cast
stones: 'the men spent their evenings at the Inn, getting
drunk and indulging in every description of debauchery,
while as to the women, even the best of them were incurably
trivial'.[1]

With such examples before her eyes, and such unjust
criticism in her ears, it was only natural that a young
woman who, until then, for all her imprudence, had been
strictly chaste, should find herself being gradually pushed
down the slope which leads to license. Aurélien's letters,
now few and far between, and increasingly less tender in
tone, offered but a poor defence against temptation:

> The absent being—I might almost call him the 'invisible'
> —of whom I had made the third keystone of my life
> (God, Him, and Me) was growing tired of constantly
> striving upwards to the sublimities of love . . . His
> passions needed a more nourishing diet than that provided
> by passionate friendship and occasional letters . . . I felt

[1] Laisnel de La Salle, quoted by Louise Vincent in *George
Sand et le Berry*, p. 103.

that I was becoming a terrible drag on him, or, at best, that I was now no more to him than a source of intellectual amusement . . . For a long time to come, I went on loving him in silence and dejection of spirits . . . As soon as I had chosen the road I meant to follow, there were, on his part, neither explanations nor reproaches. . . .[1]

What road? Her mind was still not made up. In 1827, while she was travelling in the Auvergne, she kept a Journal which, though never published, shows considerable gifts of style.

What shall I do? It is raining. Never have I so longed to go out walking. I am feeling whimsical today. I play at being the 'lovely female'—though there is not much of the female about me, and still less of the lovely. How good life was ten years ago . . . Suppose I write to somebody—to my mother, for instance . . . Oh, mother mine, what have I done to you? Why do you not love me? Truly, I am good, as you very well know. I have my violent moods, and they are terrible. I have a hundred faults, but, deep down, I am good . . . Poor mother, you are frivolous, but not bad-hearted: no, that you certainly are not—only odd . . . What about indulging in a little self-pity? What about telling myself the story of my life? Yes, that is a good idea—I will set to and write my Memoirs. . . .[2]

There follows a rough sketch of what was later to become *l'Histoire de ma Vie*. This young woman of twenty-three indulged in an anticipatory picture of old age:

My heart [she concluded on a note of sadness], remained unsullied as a mirror. It was ardent, it was sincere, but it was blind. It could not be tarnished, but it could be broken. I left for the Pyrenees . . . What's that I hear?—dinner already? . . .[3]

[1] GEORGE SAND: *Histoire de ma Vie*. Volume IV, p. 58.

[2] GEORGE SAND: *Voyage en Auvergne et en Espagne*, published in the Literary Supplement of the *Figaro*, August 4th, 1888.

[3] Ibid.

This first attempt was brought up short by the dinner gong.

In this Journal of hers there was talent, there was humour, there was despair. She had entirely given up any attempt to achieve the moral regeneration of her husband. As to Casimir, wretched in the knowledge that he had lost her, incapable of winning her back and suffering from a sense of inferiority, he had now taken to drinking in good earnest. She felt that Aurélien was slipping away from her. He had given his pledged word to respect Aurore, but not to refrain from taking his pleasures elsewhere. With his own hands he overturned the pedestal on which she had tried to place him.

> *Aurélien to Aurore:* You carry within yourself an *ideal* of reason, an *ideal* of wisdom. You body forth in imagination a being who shall fit these ideals, and, when you have created him, when you have *created him yourself*, you say—'He is'—this, that or the other . . . No, I have *not* got settled and rational ideas on everything under the sun. Must I admit it? Must I smash the idol at a single blow?—I have not, and I say it to my shame, got settled ideas on anything at all. . . .[1]

Was it, then, impossible to keep a man *without* the carnal bond? She was beginning to think so. To be beloved, yet not to give herself: to be, at one and the same time, both *femme fatale* and amazon, irreproachable wife and adored mistress—a beautiful dream, perhaps, but entirely divorced from life as it is.

She had rediscovered that same Stéphane Ajasson de Grandsagne from whom, as a young girl in days gone by, she had learned the elements of sentimental anatomy in her room at Nohant. He was now more learned than ever, and his face, framed in a fringe of beard, was as handsome as ever though prematurely aged. 'He is still waging with death a bitter battle over what remains of his youth. But the enemy has set its mark upon him, and I feel sure that his days are numbered. Part consumptive, part mad, he has come to spend his convalescence here.'[2] She was profoundly touched by the sight of his hollow cheeks, wild eyes and

[1] GEORGE SAND: *Le Roman d'Aurore Dudevant et d'Aurélien de Sèze*, p. 208.

[2] Spoelberch de Lovenjoul Collection: Group E. 905, f. 196.

stooping figure. Everything about him attracted her. He it was who had awakened in her the first realization of love that she had ever known. He was a scholar, and she was in love with learning. He called himself an atheist, and she, though a believer, was thrilled by his intellectual audacities. Finally, he was a sick man, and she had a passion for tending the sick. In 1827 he was living in Paris, where he had just joined the staff at the Museum in order to work with Cuvier. A Latinist, a Hellenist, and a student of Natural History, he was busy translating the scientific works of the great writers of Greece and Rome. He had written a Preface, full of erudition but with no spark of genius to illuminate it, for the *De Natura Rerum* of Lucretius. There were moments when Aurore believed that she had found in him the master she was seeking. It was not long before La Châtre society decided that she was compromising herself with him. When Stéphane was not in Berry, Hippolyte Châtiron who, with his young wife, Emilie de Villeneuve, had taken an apartment in Paris, entertained him and sent to Aurore such news as there was to tell.

Hippolyte Châtiron to Aurore Dudevant; I rather think that his troubles are, to a large extent, due to his undisciplined temperament. Money seems to burn a hole in his pocket: when he has any he thinks only of his friends, and his purse is at the service of all who make a call upon it. I am more intimate with him than with anyone else. Few realize the extent of his knowledge or the brilliance of his mind. His poor brain is all on fire. I have no doubt that, given time, he will make a name for himself, and a pretty good income as well. . . .

and again:

Our friend Stéphane, because he will *not* take care of himself, has fallen ill again. He insisted on working all night, with the result that he has succumbed to a fever. I tried preaching to him, but he merely asserted that, of the two of us, I was the madder. . . .[1]

Aurore to Hippolyte: What you say of Stéphane gives me much pain. He will take care neither of his health nor of

[1] Unpublished letters: Madame Aurore Lauth-Sand's Collection.

his affairs, and does not spare his strength or his purse.
Still more serious, he becomes annoyed when he is given
good advice, treats his true friends as though they were
his doctors, and receives them in such a manner as to
make it impossible for them to open their lips. I knew all
this even before you told me, and have, myself, more
than once been thoroughly snubbed . . . I wish I could
cease to be fond of him, because it causes me continual
anxiety to see his feet set upon the wrong road and to
realize that he refuses to see how mistaken he is. But one
has to be fond of one's friends to the bitter end, no matter
what they do, and once I have given my affection I
cannot withdraw it . . . People will always blame me for
being so much attached to him, and, though no one dares
to broach the subject to me, I can read condemnation in
the faces of those I meet, and that drives me on to defend
him . . . Stéphane will always be dear to me, in spite of
his misfortunes. He is so already, and the dearer he
becomes to me the less interest will others take in him.
Such is the rule of Society. I, at least, shall always do my
best to repair his misfortunes. Others may turn their
backs on him, but I shall remain within call . . . One does
not seriously suspect those one loves of being in the
wrong. . . .[1]

In the autumn of 1827 Stéphane paid a visit to the
country, at a time when Casimir was absent in Paris. He
brought a whiff of city air and a load of the very newest
ideas. Aurore saw a great deal of him, and spoke of their
meeting in her letters to her husband, all of them written
with that peculiarly feminine gift of telling the truth while,
at the same time, wrapping it up in a shimmering envelope
of apparent triviality.

Aurore to Casimir: Nohant, October 17th, 1827: Since
you left, my dear, I have had scarcely a moment to
myself. I have seen Stéphane, his brother, Jules Néraud,
Dutheil, Charles and Ursule, who, having learned from
Stéphane (he has left again for la Marche) that I was far
from well, have come to look after me. I have had a bad
attack of fever. . . .

[1] GEORGE SAND: *Correspondance.* Volume I, pp. 31-3.

October 19th, 1827: I am feeling much better. I have not yet recovered my appetite but I am sleeping well, and it seems highly unlikely that there will be any complications. I was afraid that I might be threatened with a serious illness. but realize now that this indisposition coincided with the bad time of the month for me . . . I am dropping with fatigue, and shall go to bed early. . . . I forgot to give you one of my gaiters as a pattern. If Stéphanie comes back in time, I will send it by him. But where he is now, and what he is doing, God alone knows. It would be the height of unfairness to ask him his plans. I saw him this week, as I told you, since when he has gone off with his brother to Guéret . . . They are planning to have some shooting . . . With you away I feel miserable and melancholy, and all at a loose end. Enjoy your freedom, be happy, and go on loving me. Write me when you plan to return if you want me to arrange to have you met at Châteauroux. . . .[1]

This letter was cordial enough, but no sooner had Casimir returned to Nohant than she set off for Paris with Jules de Grandsagne, and there saw Stéphane again.

Aurore to Casimir: December 8th, 1827: I breakfasted today with my mother. Hippolyte had told her that I got here the day before yesterday. She longed to fly into a rage, but when I proved to her that I had spent all the intervening time resting and unable to move, she grew calmer and was as charming as it is possible for her to be . . . Hippolyte had taken Stéphane to see her, introducing him by his real name. She received him well, in spite of all the things she had heard about him . . . I shall have to stay here all next week, but then, no matter what happens, shall start for home. Stéphane declares that he will return with us, but I do not really count on that, in view of his habit of blowing hot and cold. . . .[2]

The 'things she had heard' were to the effect that Aurore and Stéphane were conducting an 'affair'. Most of those who knew them regarded this as a certainty. She travelled in his company, was constantly with him in Berry, and trailed

1 Spoelberch de Lovenjoul Collection: Group E. 868, f. 46 and ff. 48-9.

2 Ibid., Group E. 868, ff. 53-4.

about with him in Paris. Stéphane's descendants have revealed the fact that the two lovers exchanged the most ardent letters.[1] Those that Aurore was writing to Casimir at this time were marked by the somewhat excessive expressions of affection in which women indulge who are suffering from a consciousness of wrongdoing. On December 13th, she begged him not to bother about meeting her, saying that Stéphane had undertaken to see her home. The reason she gave for her prolonged stay in Paris was her wish to consult a number of doctors. She had seen the most distinguished members of the Faculty, and they had given her a clean bill of health.

Her troubles were, in fact, only of the conscience. After her return to Nohant she relapsed into a condition of apathetic melancholy, and was as gloomy as though she were suffering from a sense of guilt. *To Zoé Leroy:* 'I don't ask you to go on loving me as once you did. I do not deserve the love of anybody. I am like a wounded animal that creeps into a corner to die. I cannot turn to my friends for peace of mind and succour.'[2] Why this sudden humility in so proud a nature? She was already with child again when she returned home, and it is at least possible that Stéphane was responsible, seeing that the child was born on September 13th, 1828, which would date its conception to the period of her stay in Paris. She herself always maintained that the birth was premature, and had been hastened as the result of a fright she had had when Hippolyte's daughter, little Léontine Châtiron, fell downstairs at Nohant. But it seems doubtful, to say the least, that Casimir entertained any illusions on the subject. One morning at the beginning of September, Aurélien de Sèze arrived unexpectedly at an early hour, to find Aurore in the drawing-room, laying out baby-clothes. 'What on earth are you doing?' said he. 'Surely it must be obvious. I am working against time in preparation for somebody who looks like arriving before he was expected.'[3]

He could not square this news of an unexpected child with those protestations of celestial love, and total—

---

[1] Cf. *Le Moniteur général* for January 6th, 1900, in which, under the heading 'Correspondence and Readers' Questions' there is a note by Paul-Emile Ajasson de Grandsagne, Stéphane's only son, who died in 1902.

[2] Spoelberch de Lovenjoul Collection: Group E. 902, f. 63.

[3] GEORGE SAND: *Histoire de ma Vie*. Volume IV, p. 48.

including conjugal—chastity of which her letters to him, and her talk, had never ceased to be full. When Zoé Leroy next saw Monsieur de Sèze, the wildness of his grief almost terrified her. He had become slightly unhinged, kept poking the fire, wandering to the piano, and playing with two fingers. *Zoé Leroy to Aurore Dudevant:* 'I could not help feeling, when I saw Aurélien again, that he had left behind him at Nohant a concourse of misery, agonizing dismay, and appalling loneliness. . . .'[1]

Aurore was brought to bed in circumstances that were painful in more ways than one. Hippolyte was so drunk that he fell down in his sister's room. From where she lay she could overhear a conversation between her husband and a servant-girl called Pepita, in the room next door, which left no doubt of the relationship in which they stood to one another. The child, a large, fine-looking girl, was given the name of Solange. 'Later on', wrote Louise Vincent, 'whenever Stéphane de Grandsagne went to Nohant, and his friends pulled his leg, he would say, "Why shouldn't I? I am going to see my daughter!" and Madame Dudevant herself frequently referred to the girl as "Mademoiselle Stéphane".[2] All the same, Monsieur Dudevant never breathed a word which might have led anyone to suppose that he intended to repudiate his wife. He clung to Nohant, to his son, and even to Aurore, who had established over him the sort of ascendancy which a strong personality exercises over a weak one. 'Lazy in mind, but preternaturally active on his legs,' he could do nothing, when the evening came, but snore. He had compromised their joint fortune by making a number of unfortunate investments, as a result of which he was now penitent and humble. Besides, if they did separate, where in the world could he go? Guillery belonged to his step-mother. Consequently, something in the nature of a truce was arranged between husband and wife. She tolerated his amorous escapades as well as his drunkenness, and he left her free to do as she liked, on condition that she did not ask him for money. Moreover, his continued mismanagement of their affairs put him to an even greater extent than formerly in her power. In 1828 he fell into the clutches of a crook called Desgranges, who had 'won his confidence

[1] Spoelberch de Lovenjoul Collection: Group E. 902, f. 113.
[2] LOUISE VINCENT: *George Sand et le Berry*, p. 122. The arguments for and against Grandsagne's paternity are given in the Appendix to this book.

by giving him a champagne dinner and the loan of his
mistress', after which he proceeded to sell him a fine
merchantman, of which he showed him a picture. The deal
cost Dudevant twenty-five thousand francs. The merchantman had no existence (except in the picture), and Monsieur
Desgranges turned out to be no more than a shipowner in
partibus. Aurore had mistrusted him from the start.

Aurore to Casimir: December 20th, 1829: It is as clear as
daylight that Monsieur Desgranges is having a good
laugh at your expense—and you can tell him so from me!
At least he did not pull the wool over *my* eyes! He has got
you to believe that there is somebody anxious to buy out
your interest in this affair. He arranges purely imaginary
interviews with this imaginary individual, puts you in a
good mood with amusing talk, and lulls you with
promises. You run all over the place, you are kept
dangling, you hope for the best. Meanwhile, Monsieur
Desgranges knows perfectly well that there is no buyer in
the offing at all. Each day you pin your faith to the next,
and the next brings nothing but increasing mystification
. . . See what consequences can flow from a moment's
stupidity! May what has happened be a lesson to you,
and teach you not to make business contracts after
dinner when, unfortunately, you are not as a rule sober.
It is no good you telling me that you did not conclude
this particular one with a glass in your hand. I am telling
you exactly what is in my mind at the moment. I won't
refer to the matter ever again, for the past is behind us. I
shall make it *my* business to keep a watchful eye on the
future. Up till now, I have avoided getting mixed up in
money matters, because I had complete confidence in
your judgment and good sense. But I have come to
realize that you are just as liable as anybody else to be
taken in. That that is so is due to an unfortunate
weakness which you contracted during your army days.
You got the 'better of it during the early years of our
marriage, but you have now fallen a victim to it again, in
spite of everything I could do. Don't be angry with me
for writing to you like this. We have a perfect right to tell
each other the truth . . . I am, above all things, a mother,
and I can be strong-minded enough when I needs must.
You will find me always ready to overlook your
shortcomings and to comfort you when you are in

trouble, but I do not intend to mince my words where the future of my children is at stake. . . .

What *must* be avoided is, as you put it, throwing good money after bad, and leaving in the hands of a shady customer, whom nobody trusts, twenty thousand, or even fifteen thousand francs, which represent a considerable bite out of a fortune such as ours. Your impatience and discouragement are *not* indicative of good sense. When one has made a blunder, one does not repair it by swearing and groaning and indulging in orgies of self-reproach until you make yourself, and everybody else, ill. Be a man! When you have to do with a hypocrite, browbeat him! *Don't* accept his invitations to dinner (two are more than enough). One does not accept hospitality from someone whom one suspects of dishonesty. . . .

How this affair of the mill is going, I don't know, but I have a strong feeling that it is going to be another case of a bad bargain . . . . Cannot you ever carry through a deal without getting yourself caught up in a tangle of trickery? You never have any luck with this sort of thing, so why go on trying? We should get much better results by combining our practical talents—all of us, I mean—than by each going off on his own and making decisions on our separate judgments. Dutheil understands business, and Hippolyte—though I know you think him a bit mad—has more sound horse-sense in matters of this kind than you and me put together. Why not let them regulate the household expenses? You can look after the cabbages and the roots . . . If you want to, and can, you may buy a few more parcels of ground every year, though I think I ought to warn you that you are a by-word in the neighbourhood for always paying higher prices than anybody else. . . .[1]

For some time now Aurore had given up sharing a bedroom with her husband. She had installed the two children in Madame Dupin de Francueil's yellow room on the ground-floor, and herself moved into the boudoir adjoining, where she felt perfectly safe since it communicated with no other room in the house except the children's. She slept in a cot, and did her writing on one of the wooden panels of the wall which let down to form a desk. The small room was filled with books, plant-specimens, mounted

[1] Spoelberch de Lovenjoul Collection: Group E. 868, ff. 97-8.

butterflies and fossils. There she wrote, there she dreamed, there she meditated. Out of love with life, she sought such compensation as she could find in sketching out the plans of novels. She was still, as in her Convent days, seeking to enter into some sort of direct contact with God. To formal worship, and the practices of institutional religion, she attached but little importance.

> What absorbed me, at Nohant, as, once, in my Convent, was the fervent, the melancholy, but unremitting effort to find the relationship which can, which should, exist between the individual soul and that Universal Spirit which we call God. Since neither in fact nor intention did I belong to the ordinary world, since my contemplative self lived withdrawn from its influences, since, in short, I neither could, nor wished to, act save in harmony with a law which is superior to the customs and opinions of the majority, it was desperately important for me to seek in God the answer to my life's enigma, the knowledge of my real duties, the justification for my most secret feelings . . . .[1]

Was this hypocrisy? Everything goes to show that it was not. There never had been any separation between her and her God. But, as every human being needs to come to terms with himself if he is to go on living, she obliterated from her mind the idea that adultery is a mortal sin. She had come to believe, as her mother had done before her, that 'these things don't really matter, provided that one is sincerely in love'. It was a pity that Aurélien had come into her life too early, and at a period when she was not yet ready to 'take the plunge'. Had circumstances been different, he might have been just the romantic lover she needed. She made several trips to Bordeaux and renewed acquaintance with her one-time friend, but only to find him 'older and less attractive'. But they never laid their cards on the table, and, for some time still, continued to correspond.

Maurice was growing into a big boy. Aurore, true disciple of Rousseau, began to pay attention to the education of her 'Emile'. From Duris-Dufresne, the Deputy for whom the Dudevants had waged so energetic campaign at La Châtre, she asked for information. On the occasion of a visit to the neighbourhood he had told Châtiron that one of the children of General Comte Bertrand had, thanks to a new method, learned to read in a few lessons. She wanted to hear all about this.

Aurore Dudevant to Duris-Dufresne, August 4th, 1829: I must apologize, my dear sir, for bothering you with details, and for taking up the time of one whose every moment is precious to us. I find comfort in the thought that you will not regard the advice I ask for as merely an important service rendered to the mother of a family, but as a partial means of giving a wider circulation to the improvements now being carried out in the field of primary education. Your career and your heart have ever been at the service of your fellow citizens, and the knowledge that this is so emboldens me to make this approach to you, and to seek your opinion in preference to that of anybody else. . . .[1]

The Deputy sent her the name of the man who had acted as tutor to the Bertrand children. He was a young fellow called Jules Boucoiran. With him Madame Dudevant now entered into a correspondence, and, in September 1829, engaged him to teach her son for a trial period of three months.

Aurore to Casimir, December 14th, 1829: Tell me what I ought to pay Monsieur Boucoiran, and I will give him notice. I suppose you will reply, as you always do, 'Please yourself'—which tells me nothing . . . I must know where I stand, and how I am to find the money, because I don't want to keep this young man indefinitely. I do not altogether like him, and think he will not much mind being sent away.[2]

Boucoiran returned to General Bertrand. It was not true that he had failed to please Madame Dudevant. He was a young Southerner, whom she found sympathetic and obliging. Naturally enough, he fell in love with her, but she kept him at arm's length. The most she did was to promise him a 'kiss' in return for certain commissions which he had carried out for her in Paris. He had proved himself to be a

---

[1] Unpublished letter in the possession of Monsieur Jacques Suffel.

[2] Spoelberch de Lovenjoul Collection: Group E. 868, f. 92.

good teacher, a 'superbly accurate grammarian'. At six
years old Maurice could read fluently, and was beginning to
study music, spelling and geography. *Aurore to Boucoiran:*
'Maurice's education is beginning, and yours is not yet
finished . . . Farewell, my dear son . . . The children and I
send you affectionate greetings . . . You can always rely on
your old friend . . . Did you get your waistcoat?'

Boucoiran's presence, even allowing for the fact that he
was 'somewhat lethargic', had helped Madame Dudevant,
for a few weeks, at least, to put up with a pattern of life
which no longer had anything married about it. Casimir
was fully occupied by two liaisons which he made no
attempt to conceal, one with the Castilian, Pepita—Solange's nurse—the other, with Claire—Madame Châtiron's
maid. Aurore was trying her hand at writing novels, *La
Marraine, Aimée.* Boucoiran was astonished by 'an elasti-
city and force of character which makes it possible for her,
on the morrow of the most violent domestic scenes, to
laugh as though nothing had occurred, and to refuse to
be overwhelmed by the weight of her unhappiness'.[1]
Sometimes , as she rode back from La Châtre in the
darkness, alone beneath the stars, along the road on which
her father had lost his life, she would reflect upon the
strange situation in which she found herself. She looked on
the people among whom she was living as, almost without
exception, thoroughly second-rate. But was she herself any
better? Certainly, she had had a wider education, was more
sensitive, and, so she thought, more genuinely pious. But
might she not, after all, be guilty of self-deception?

I sought God in the light of the stars, and remember how,
on dark Autumn nights, I sometimes watched the heavy
banks of cloud rolling above my head, and shutting out
the firmament from my eyes. Alas! I said to myself, it is
thus that Thou whom I pursue so diligently dost for ever
escape me! Dear God, whom I blindly serve, Great
Mystery which I have embraced as a real presence,
elusive, flickering, of which I have made the blazing
beacon of my life, where art thou? Dost thou see me?
dost thou hearken to my voice? . . . Am I an elected soul
whom thou hast charged with the duty of accomplishing
something on this earth, some sweet and saintly mission,

1 WLADIMIR KARENINE: *George Sand, sa vie et ses
oeuvres.* Volume I, p. 303.

or am I just the plaything of some romantic fantasy born of my own poor brain, a seed which the wind blows about the spaces of the air, and then lets fall at random? . . .

. . . Then, weighed down by despair, and feeling scarcely sane, I would spur my horse blindly into the encircling blackness . . . There was one spot upon that road which had a peculiarly sinister significance for my family, a point at which it made a sharp bend, just beyond the thirteenth poplar. There it was that my father, but little older than I was then, returning home on a more than usually dark night, had been thrown. Sometimes I would draw rein when I reached it, striving to evoke his memory, and, in the light of the moon, looking for the imagined traces of his blood upon the stones. But more often, when I drew near to it, I would dash forward at full speed, letting my horse have his head and spurring him on round the bend where the road dropped between steep banks and made my progress dangerous. . . .[1]

She felt convinced that somewhere, far from La Châtre and Nohant, there existed a gracious, elegant, and enlightened society, where men and women of parts could engage in the free exchange of their thoughts and feelings. She would have travelled 'ten leagues just to see Monsieur de Balzac pass by'.[2] She worshipped Hugo as a god, but so frightened did she feel at the prospect of such magnificence, that it never so much as occurred to her to take the first step in their direction. When she went with Maurice to Paris, staying there in the apartment lent by Hippolyte, she saw no one but her mother (always in the company of an old friend of hers named Pierret), Caron, the Duplessis family and, of course, Stéphane.

Aurore to Casimir, May 2nd, 1830: Stéphane is another of those I have seen, once yesterday morning, and again today. I have no idea how he knew that I was here. He found a letter for me left in charge of Hippolyte's concierge, and wrote his name on the cover—as a sort of makeshift for a card. Next day he appeared in person, scrubbed and brushed and gracious. Today, *ditto.* It re-

1 GEORGE SAND: *Journal intime,* pp. 162-7.
2 Ibid., p. 171.

mains to be seen how long this honeymoon will last.
. . .[1]

From Paris she made a sudden descent on Bordeaux.

I can get there in thirty hours. My idea is to make a stay
of two days and then return home at the end of next
week. I find the idea of this trip rather tiresome, and it
took me some time to make up my mind, because I shall
see scarcely anything of Aurélien, who is away in the
country . . . I will tell you what decided me. Something
happened which put me thoroughly out of temper, hurt
my feelings badly, and made me feel that I had got to
move. Up till that moment my mother had been
charming to me, and I am not aware that I had been
otherwise than charming to her . . . Then, suddenly, I got
a letter, eight pages long, filled to the brim with all the
ingenuities which fury and hatred could contrive. She
informed me, among other things, that I had come to
Paris with the deliberate purpose of 'going on the loose',
and that I had used *her* as an excuse with *you* for the
journey, etc. etc. . . .

As soon as I reach Bordeaux I will send you news of
myself. I won't ask you to promise to write to me there,
because my stay will be so short, and I might quite well
not get your letter . . . I am telling *nobody* here about
Bordeaux . . . I have merely put it about that I am going
to spend several days in the country, without giving any
details . . . so don't say anything about it to Madame
Dudevant, if you happen to be writing to her. . . .[2]

The husband was changing his role, and becoming a
confidant.

[1] Spoelberch de Lovenjoul Collection: Group E. 868, f. 102.
[2] Ibid., Group E. 868, ff. 109-10.

IV

LITTLE JULES

EIGHTEEN HUNDRED and thirty. Things were jogging along as usual at Nohant, with Casimir tramping the woods and fields, and in the evenings either snoring or playing about with Pepita.

Aurore to Jules Boucoiran: 'You know what life at Nohant is like: Wednesday is a replica of Tuesday, Thursday of Wednesday, and so ad infinitum. The change from winter to summer and back again provides the only movement in this state of permanent stagnation . . . I can be happy anywhere, thanks to my philosophic outlook, or, perhaps, to the fact that I am a complete nonentity. . . .'[1] Her one and only pleasure was to exercise her powers over the men of the neighbouring great houses. Almost every day she mounted her horse and, without bothering about her husband, rode over to La Châtre, or to one or other of her friends.

On July 30th she paid a visit to Charles Duvernet, at the Château du Coudrey. There she found Fleury (The Gaul), Gustave Papet and a young man of nineteen, whom she had never met before—Jules Sandeau. He was a charming youth, with a head of golden curls, who 'looked for all the world like a little Saint John the Baptist'. His father was Collector of Taxes at La Châtre, and Jules had grown attached to the small town 'where there is not a street corner but contributes to my happiness'. Since he had shown signs at an early age of possessing a sharp and nimble mind, his parents, in spite of their poverty, had made great sacrifices to give him a good education. He had done well at the Collège de Bourges, and, in November 1828, had gone to Paris with the intention of studying law. He spent his vacations at La Châtre, and it was sheer delight for him to rattle across the bridge in the stage-coach, to bump over the cobbles of the rue Royale, and to see once again the tiny Square, the empty, solitary streets, the disused stable which

---

[1] GEORGE SAND: *Correspondance.* Volume I, pp. 100-1.

served as a theatre, and the barn in which the local dances were held. The gilded youth of La Châtre had tried to rope the visitor into their round of pleasures, but little Jules had no taste either for shooting or for noise. Temperamentally lazy, and cursed with a weak constitution, he preferred to lie under a hedge with a book, to doze away the hours, and to dream of future happiness.

When Madame Dudevant turned up at the Duvernets, this attractive stranger tactfully withdrew from the assembled group, and wandered off with a book to a grassy bank under an old apple tree. This shyness acted as a stimulant on the young woman. She led the others in the direction of the tree, and the general talk went on around the seated Sandeau. It turned on the revolution which had recently broken out in Paris. Such news as had so far penetrated into the country was partial and confused. Apart from the fact that barricades had been set up in the streets, and that a certain amount of shooting had taken place, nothing was known. Had a Republic been proclaimed? Aurore, always enthusiastic and always active, said that she would ride into La Châtre to find out what had been happening. As she mounted her horse, she called back: 'Charles, you must bring all your friends over to dinner tomorrow . . . I shall be expecting you, gentlemen . . .' then with a touch of her crop, she galloped off on Colette, and disappeared.

Next day, the 31st, Sandeau, as one of a party, paid his first visit to Nohant. Aurore read aloud a letter she had received from Boucoiran. No doubt about it, there really had been a revolution. This little group of liberals received the news with every sign of enthusiasm. Casimir roused by politics from his usual lethargy, was appointed lieutenant in the National Guard, and soon had a hundred and twenty men under his orders. Aurore felt anxious about her mother, and, more particularly, about her aunt, Lucie Maréchal, whose husband held a position in the royal household. But, 'at such moments the blood is on fire, and the heart too full for sensibility'.[1] She was proud in the knowledge that La Châtre was more resolute than Châteauroux, and that, should the Gendarmes attack, or a regiment of infantry be sent from Bourges, the citizens would defend themselves. 'I feel in myself an energy which I did not know I had. The spirit grows with the movement of events.'[2]

[1] GEORGE SAND: Correspondance. Volume I, p. 103.
[2] Ibid.

The young Sandeau was fascinated by the wild beauty, the Quixotic, assertive character, the black and gleaming eyes, the lithe figure, of the mistress of Nohant. She was clearly interested in him, and it needed no more to set him falling desperately in love. He turned to Aurore Dudevant because he found her enchanting, because she liked talking of the same things as he did—but talked about them better; mainly, however, because she was strong and he was weak. Young men without much character choose as mistresses women of the maternal type, while women who lack the ability to humble themselves, find in the generous protection of others an excuse for becoming the slaves of love.

For some weeks she struggled—which considering the state of her heart, was nothing less than heroic. Everything about him tempted her—his extreme youth, his pink and white complexion, his golden hair, the cast of his mind, the aura of Paris which surrounded him, his weakness for romantic dreaming.

If only you knew how I love that poor young man, how, from the very first moment of our meeting, his expressive eyes, his frank, brusque manners, his awkward shyness where I was concerned, woke in me a longing to see more of him, to explore his nature. I find it difficult to describe the interest he aroused in me. All I know is that each day it grew stronger, and that it never so much as occurred to me to resist . . . The day I told him that I loved him, I had not even admitted it to myself. It was a feeling which, somehow, my heart did not wish to acknowledge, and Jules was made privy to it at the very same moment as myself. How it happened I really don't know. Fifteen minutes earlier I had been sitting alone on the front steps, with a book which I was reading only with my eyes. My mind was occupied by one single thought, a sweet, ravishing, lovely thought, but vague, uncertain and mysterious. . . .[1]

For a long time she was to think with peculiar tenderness of the little copse where they had declared their love.

[1] *Lettres de George Sand au Docteur Emile Regnault.* Bibliothèque nationale: department of manuscripts. Recent acquisition.

There is one place of which I am especially fond, a bench standing in a lovely grove of trees which forms part of my garden. It was there that, for the first time, our two hearts found words in which to express their feelings. It is there, too, that he often went and sat when he had arrived straight from La Châtre, tired, breathless, on a day of sunshine and storm. He would find my book and my scarf lying there, and when he heard me coming would hide in one of the nearby paths. I would see his grey hat and his cane lying on the bench. There is nothing silly in such trivialities when two persons are in love, and you won't laugh at me, will you, dear friend, when I talk to you about these nonsensical details? . . .

. . . Even the red cord he wore round his hat could set my heart fluttering with joy. All the other young men, Alphonse, Gustave, and the rest, had grey hats just like his and I would glance at them as I passed through the drawing-room. I knew by the red cord when Jules was among the visitors: the other cords were blue. And so it was that I kept that little length of cord as a relic. The mere sight of it awakens in me now a whole world of memories, heart-throbs, and happiness. . . .[1]

At length she took the final plunge. There was a summer-house at Nohant. One side gave on to the park, the other overlooked the road. Aurore had had it furnished in 1828, and it made an admirable meeting-place. He could reach it without going into the village at all, and without putting in an appearance at the front door of the château. There was little danger that the curiosity of the servants would be aroused. At other times, the lovers would meet in the woods, at a spot called the 'Clearing'—while their friends kept a sharp look-out and warned them of possible discovery. As was only to be expected there was a deal of ill-natured gossip in La Châtre on the subject of this intimacy between a married woman with a family, and 'young Jules'.

Aurore Dudevant to Jules Boucoiran, October 27th, 1830: The tittle-tattle of La Châtre pursues its way and gathers strength. Those who do not much care for me say that I *love* Sandot (you realize, of course, what they mean by the word): those who don't care for me at all, that I

[1] Ibid.

love Sandot and Fleury at one and the same time: those who detest me, that the idea of throwing in you and Duvernet as make-weights by no means alarms me. So, you see, I now have four lovers—which is not one too many for a woman with an appetite as keen as mine. The spiteful fools! How I pity them for being alive! Bless you, my child. Write to me. . . .[1]

How could the tittle-tattle of La Châtre affect her happiness? 'I concentrate my life upon the objects of my affection. I surround myself with them as with a battalion pledged to my service, which keeps at bay all black and gloomy thoughts. . . .'[2]

Those who would understand the Aurore Dudevant of 1830, and her need for adventures of the heart and head, must know something of the intellectual fermentation which at that time was going on in France. Passion was king, as Reason once had been, and the Irrational was worshipped as a God. The new poets, the new philosophical and social theories, had gone to the heads of the new Young. They found a species of exultation in claiming to be 'Hugolatrers', 'Saint-Simonians' or 'Fouriérists'. Everywhere in France Romanticism was a live issue. The individual was no longer, as he had been in the seventeenth century, a responsible member of a social and religious community. He had become an end in himself, an object of aesthetic contemplation. 'Tigers are more beautiful than sheep, but we prefer them behind bars. The typical romantic removes the bars and enjoys the magnificent leaps with which the tiger annihilates the sheep. He exhorts men to imagine themselves tigers, and when he succeeds the results are not wholly pleasant.'[3] Reality imitated fiction. In the days of *Astrée*, men had loved like Scudéry's heroes. In the time of Goethe, they loved like *Werther*, until such time as they should love like *Hernani*.

At La Châtre the young Baronne Dudevant, a potential tigress, figured as the local Muse. But she felt very lonely

---

[1] This letter, published *in extenso* in the *Revue des Mondes*, was mutilated by Maurice Sand when he prepared it for inclusion in his mother's *Correspondance*. The words italicized above are stressed in the original text, and Sandot, instead of Sandeau, is the spelling used by George Sand.

[2] GEORGE SAND: *Correspondance*. Volume I, p. 111.

[3] BERTRAND RUSSELL: *History of Western Philosophy*, p. 19.

when the holidays came to an end and her great men departed for Paris. She wrote them letters in which irony, and a vein of almost Shakespearian poetry, did their brave best to disguise a deep and underlying melancholy.

Aurore Dudevant to Charles Duvernet, December 1st, 1830: Happy, thrice happy, thou City of La Châtre, nurse of great men and classic haunt of genius! . . . Since thy departure, Oh Charles of the Golden Locks, young man of melancholy dreams, gloomy and brooding as a day of storm, hapless misanthrope who dost feel the gay frivolity of thoughtless youth, only to give thyself over to the dark meditations of an ascetic mind—the trees have yellowed and been stripped of their glittering crowns . . . And thou, gigantic Fleury, man of the huge hands and terrifying beard, and eyes that strike terror, denizen of a younger world . . . since thy vast bulk no longer, like the Gods in Homer, fills all the countryside, now that thy volcanic lungs no longer draw in all the air that mortals need for life—our climate has become less warm, our atmosphere is thinner . . . And thou, little Sandeau, charming and gay as the humming-bird that haunts the scented prairies, graceful and sharp-pointed as the nettle that sways before the driving winds upon the towers of Châteaubrun . . . now that thou dost no longer speed across our little Square, hand in pockets, swift as the chamois . . . the ladies of our city stir not, save, like the owls and bats, at setting of the sun, nor doff their nightcaps to lean from their windows, so that now the curl-papers are taking root for ever in the dense forest of their locks . . . As for your hapless friend, she, not knowing what to do to drive away the leaden-winged birds of boredom, aweary of the light of the sun which shines no more upon our erudite walks and grave discussions in the woods, has decided to be laid low with a fever and an attack of rheumatism, for the sole purpose of seeking distraction and passing the time. . . .[1]

But the time passed in a far from satisfying manner. For company she had no one but her sister-in-law, Emilie Châtiron, a kind, good creature who went to bed at nine, leaving Aurore with no alternative but to retreat to her boudoir where she could occupy herself with writing and

[1] GEORGE SAND: *Correspondance.* Volume I, pp. 116-19.

drawing. The two children lay snoring in the next room.
Solange was still chubby and fresh. Maurice was working
hard, and his mother was teaching him to spell. Casimir and
Hippolyte were almost always closeted together. Such a
state of stagnation could not last. Madame Dudevant
played with the idea of joining her little Jules in Paris. More
and more, her married life was coming to seem to her a
hollow mockery. Only by taking flight could she become
herself.

What was there to stop her? Religion? She still had one,
to be sure, but it was tolerant of love. Morality? Those were
the days when even the most solemn Saint-Simonians were
preaching the Right to Pleasure. The great artists, the
pioneers of reform, had laid it down that the 'sacred
phalanx', sworn to a life of experiment and daring, should
hold in contempt the conventions of the stodgy bourgeoisie.
She was young: she was a woman; she was intelligent, and
she wanted to follow in the footsteps of the leading spirits of
her time. Her husband? He had his mistresses, and she did
not see why freedom in that sense should be unilateral.

Aurore Dudevant to Jules Boucoiran, December 1830:
You have witnessed my life here: you know whether it is
tolerable. Many and many a time you have been amazed
to see me raise my head again twenty-four hours after I
had been crushed and beaten to the ground. There is a
limit to what one can stand . . . Searching the other day
in my husband's desk for something I had lost, I found an
envelope addressed to me. I was struck by its air of heavy
solemnity. On it was written *not to be opened until after
my death.* I did not feel sufficiently patient to wait until I
should have become a widow . . . The thing was
addressed to me, so I had a perfect right to open it
without feeling that I was being indiscreet, and, my
husband being in excellent health, could read his
testament with a calm and easy mind. Dear God! What a
testament! Nothing but curses! He had concentrated in
that document all the petulance and all the anger he had
felt at my expense, all his broodings on my *perversity,* all
his contemptuous comments on my character. And he
had left it to me as a pledge of tenderness! I thought I
must be dreaming. Till then I had kept my eyes tight shut
and refused to see that I was to him an object of scorn.
But this letter at last jerked me into wakefulness. I told
myself that to go on living with a man who feels for his

wife neither respect nor confidence is tantamount to
trying to bring the dead to life. I have made my decision,
and here and now I venture to assert that nothing shall
turn me from it. . . .[1]

Without letting a day elapse, she announced her
unalterable decision. 'I want you to make me an allowance.
I am going to Paris. My children will remain at Nohant.'
Casimir was staggered by his wife's firmness. She had the
iron will of Maurice de Saxe, and even the strategic
cunning, for her demands were in excess of her wishes. She
felt no desire to abandon her children, Nohant, or even her
husband, permanently. She was prepared to accept an
arrangement by which she should spend six months of every
year in Paris, six months at Nohant, and receive an
allowance of three thousand francs. If these conditions were
agreed to, she would maintain the fiction of a 'home'. They
were.

It remained to decide what should be done about the
children. Aurore fully intended to have her 'bouncing
daughter' with her so soon as she should be in a position to
keep her in food, and give her a roof over her head. Three
thousand francs was a mere pittance for somebody who, as
she did, loved to give, and hated the keeping of accounts.
Somehow or other she must find a way of making money.
She was sure that she could do so with her pen, with her
brush, and by decorating snuff-boxes. Maurice's father
proposed that the boy should be sent to a boarding-school
in Paris, but he was still too young for that, and too
delicate. He would have to have a tutor, and Aurore
expressed a wish that this should be no other than
Boucoiran. 'So long as you are at Nohant,' she wrote to
him, 'I can breathe freely. My son will be in good hands, his
education will progress, his health will be watched over, his
character will not be spoiled either by excessive laxity or
excessive discipline. . . .'[2]

Casimir Dudevant, to be sure, was not a very agreeable
person, but neither, if it came to that, was the Comtesse
Bertrand. If Boucoiran stayed on with the Bertrand family,
it would, of course, mean that he could live in Paris, for the
General had just been appointed Head of the Ecole
Polytechnique. But did a woman's gratitude, a mother's

love, mean nothing to him? 'My heart is *not* cold, as I think you know, and will not, I feel sure, fail to rise to the level of its obligations. . . .'[1] Jules Boucoiran, like all the other young men, was fascinated by Madame Dudevant. That concluding sentence of her letter opened up the most delicious possibilities. He accepted. But when he suggested that she should make a trip with him to Nîmes, where he was going to visit his family, she hung back. She must, she said, behave with the greatest circumspection, and not give her husband reason to be suspicious of their son's tutor-to-be. 'I will pursue you, till the day of your death, with my thanks and my ingratitude—and you must give to that word *what meaning you will* . . . as my old curé is so fond of saying.'[2]

> *Aurore Dedevant to Jules Boucoiran:* I think I ought to tell you of the idiotic inferences people are drawing from your attentiveness to me, and my familiarity with you. Do you know that that creature talks of me, half mockingly, half seriously, as though I were a female Don Juan formed in his own image? Never were more pointed sallies directed by a lost woman against an honest one. According to her, I have had lovers in Paris, Bordeaux and Havre—in fact, everywhere. The deflowering of you was, she hints, just the occupation of an idle hour. . . .[3]

Once the tutor was settled in, there was nothing further to keep her. Hippolyte Châtiron was the only person who tried to prevent Aurore from leaving. One night that nimble-witted drunkard, when he was obviously flown with wine, went in tears to his sister's room. 'You're not really proposing to live with a child in Paris on two hundred and fifty francs a month?' he said. 'The idea's fantastic! Why, you don't even know the price of a chicken! You'll be back here within a fortnight without a penny to bless yourself with!'—'That's as may be,' she replied, 'but I am going to try.' It was perfectly true that this great heiress, legally stripped by marriage of her fortune, no longer had a halfpenny she could call her own. But she hoped one day to regain possession of children, house and money. If she was

1 Ibid., Volume I, p. 135.
2 Ibid., Volume I, p. 139.
3 Spoelberch de Lovenjoul Collection: Group E. 920, ff. 12-13.

now choosing to live a bohemian existence, it was not
because she wanted to be free of household duties. 'I am not
one of those airy-fairy souls who cannot come down from
the clouds.' She loved making jam and planting cabbages.
She might be a romantic in her desire to break with the
conventions, but in her love of Nohant and domestic chores
she was a full-blooded bourgeoise. She would gladly have
applied to herself the saying that 'The man who is really
extraordinary is he who is truly ordinary'. She was not
afraid of sewing, cooking, and doing her own laundering,
but she would not serve a husband whom she did not love.

Casimir, faced by his wife's imminent departure, dissolved in lamentations. 'Today,' she said, 'he came to me
in tears! Well, that is his look out! I am going to prove that
my idea of married life is not that I should be endured as a
burden, but sought and claimed as a companion. . . .' She
was going to Paris, back to the graceful, fluttering Sandeau
to whom she dreamed of being mistress, housekeeper and
mother. As Casimir's wife she had been sunk in lethargy.
Now, at last, she was going to live. 'To live! how wonderful,
how lovely that will be, in spite of husbands, and troubles,
and embarrassments, and debts and relations and gossip,
in spite of deep anguish and wearisome vexations! To live is
to be in a state of constant intoxication! To live is happiness! To live is Heaven!' On January 4th, 1831, Madame
Dudevant left Nohant. She was full of joy at having won
her freedom, full of sadness at having to abandon her
children. Maurice cried, but the promise of a National
Guard uniform, complete with red-plumed shako, soon
comforted him.

PART THREE

GEORGE SAND

'Was what led her on a hunger of the senses? No, it was a craving for something very different—a furious desire to find that true love which ever beckons, ever flies.'

Marie Dorval

I

TWO DISTINGUISHED PROVINCIAL GENTLEMEN IN PARIS

SHE ARRIVED, tired and thoroughly chilled. The hood of
the post-chaise had given very insufficient protection from
the weather. Jules Sandeau was waiting—all eagerness, all
emotion—and saw her settled into Hippolyte Châtiron's
apartment, No. 31 rue de Seine. In next to no time they
became the centre of most of the Berrichons of the
capital—Félix Pyat, law-student, journalist and republican
who, in a public restaurant, just before the 'Three Glorious
Days', had substituted a bust of Lafayette for one of
Charles X, thereby achieving momentary fame: Emile
Regnault, a medical student who was Sandeau's intimate
friend and counsellor: the gigantic Fleury, moustachioed
like a Gaul: Gabriel de Planet, who had founded a
Berrichon Club in Paris, and Gustave Papet, the 'Mylord' of
the group, who stood refreshments whenever they went to
the theatre.

Among these young men, all more or less in love with
her, Aurore was happy. The Paris of 1831 went to her head.
'The Revolution, like the Chamber, is in permanent session.
Life is as gay among bayonets, rioting and rubble, as it
would be in the piping days of peace. I find it all enormous
fun.'[1] Literature was no less revolutionary than politics.
The first great Romantics were getting a hearing, and
demagogues were defying the bourgeoisie. In the February
of that year, *Notre Dame de Paris* made its appearance,
Michelet published his *Introduction à l' Histoire Univer-
selle,* and Buloz assumed the editorship of the *Revue des
Deux Mondes,* A little later, Marie Dorval, the adored
actress of all the young rebels, took the leading part in
Dumas's *Antony,* a play which glorified adultery and
bastardy. 'It is difficult now to realize the excitement, the

1 GEORGE SAND: *Correspondance.* Volume I, p. 168.

uproar the general emotional effervescence, with which it
was greeted.' Aurore and her friends were present in the pit
to give their support to the performance. In those days
women never sat anywhere except in the circle or the boxes.
So as to be free to go where she liked, and in order to spend
as little as possible on clothes, Madame Dudevant had taken
to dressing as a man. She had been accustomed in the old
days to go shooting with Deschartres in smock and leggings,
and this form of disguise caused her no embarrassment. The
prevailing fashions helped her. Men had taken to wearing
square-cut coats, known as 'redingotes à la propriétaire',
which fitted loosely and fell almost to the heels. Aurore's
was grey in colour and had a hood. A grey hat and woollen
muffler went with it. The impression she produced was that
of a young, first-year student. More than anything else, her
boots delighted her. What joy to be free of those pointed
shoes which slipped about on the mud like skates!

But, still more, what joy to have ceased to be a female
slave—to be able to go walking arm-in-arm with a young
man, and not have all La Châtre whispering!—to hear
people saying: 'how very typical of Madame Dudevant!' To
make her change of scene even more complete, she had
broken entirely with the world in which formerly she had
moved. She never thought of her husband now except when
she had need of him. *Aurore to Casimir:* 'Please let me have
some money for stockings, shoes, etc. . . . Write at once to
Monsieur Salmon telling him to send me three hundred
francs. Goodbye, my dear. I have seen my mother, my
sister, Charles Duvernet, and Jules de Grandsagne. I am
just off to hear Paganini . . . fond love.'[1] Such letters were a
matter of duty, and she kept them short.

She made one last visit to her beloved English Convent.
The gunfire of July had badly upset the community. Mother
Alicia, melancholy and preoccupied, could spare only a few
moments for the woman who once had been her 'dear
daughter'. Aurore realized that friendships in the outside
world meant nothing to the nuns. She went to see her two
friends of Cauterets days, Jane and Aimée Bazouin. Both
were now married: both were countesses: both were rich
and universally admired. She left with her mind made up
never to see them again. Charming they might be, but they
had chosen, as they had every right to do, a conventional
and orthodox existence. Aurore Dudevant preferred to

[1] Spoelberch de Lovenjoul Collection: Group E. 868, f. 146.

move freely, and with head held high, through a desert of
men, 'with feet set on the slippery ice, shoulders covered
with snow, hands in pockets, stomach sometimes empty,
but with the imagination, for that reason, more than ever
stuffed with dreams and songs, with colours and forms, with
sunlight and fancies. . . .'[1]

Meanwhile, she had got to live. She could not stay on
indefinitely in Hippolyte's apartment. He came often to
Paris and needed it for his own use. Even an attic would
cost three hundred francs a year. She could find a woman to
do her cleaning for fifteen francs a month. A cookshop man
would bring in her meals for two francs a day. It might
be just possible to keep alive on her allowance of three
thousand francs, but there would be nothing over for the
purchase of books and furniture. She tried to settle down to
some serious work in the Bibliothèque Mazarine, but
unfortunately she felt the cold, and the library was not well
heated. She was faced with the grim necessity of making
money—but how?—by decorating boxes? by painting
portraits at fifteen francs a head? There were plenty of poor
devils who would do them for five. She tried to paint one of
her 'daily woman', but made a mess of it, with the result
that her reputation in the neighbourhood sank. Write? Why
not? 'I knew that I could write, easily, quickly, and over
long periods without getting tired: I knew that the ideas
which lay sluggish in my mind had a way of coming to life,
of linking up, as soon as I put pen to paper. . .'[2] Though
slow to express herself in conversation, she could be lively
and witty in her letters, and knew it. She had always found
pleasure in noting down her impressions. She had brought
with her a novel, *Aimée*, which she had completed at
Nohant. But how was she to make a living from what, until
then, had been no more than an amusement? How was she
to break into the world of letters?

At that time the most powerful man of her acquaintance
in Paris was Duris-Dufresne, the Deputy for La Châtre. In
the course of a few days, he became: 'my dear old friend,
Duris-Dufresne'. He showed himself courteous and gallant
towards his charming compatriot. 'Your father', said the
ushers of the Chamber when she sought out *her* Deputy in
the lobbies. To him she spoke of her plan to become a
writer. The natural reaction of a man in an official position

1 GEORGE SAND: *Historie de ma Vie*. Volume IV, p. 102.
2 GEORGE SAND: *Histoire de ma Vie*. Volume IV, p. 60.

when asked for help is to refer the applicant to the leader of his party. He suggested that he should introduce her to Monsieur de La Fayette. 'We had better not set our sights so high,' she said: 'men who are too famous have no time to spare for matters of secondary importance.' He fell back on one of his colleagues in the Chamber, a certain Monsieur de Kératry, from Brittany, a novelist who had been a Liberal at the time of the Restoration but had become a Conservative after 1830. Aurore Dudevant had read a ridiculous story which he had written called *Le Dernier des Beaumanoir*, in which a priest violates a dead woman. 'Your illustrious colleague', she said to Duris-Dufresne, 'is completely mad. Nevertheless, a man may be a good critic though a bad practitioner.' She later described the interview. It had been both comic and disastrous. Monsieur de Kératry, an old gentleman with white hair, had received her, very ceremoniously, at eight o'clock in the morning, in a handsome room where his young wife was lying in bed under a pink silk coverlet. 'I am going to be frank with you,' he had said, 'a woman ought not to write . . . Believe me, you had far better produce children than books.' 'Really sir,' she had answered, choking with laughter, 'would you not do better to practise what you preach?'[1] But this account of the incident dates from twenty years later. There is documentary evidence that what happened was, in fact, very different.

Aurore Dudevant to Jules Boucoiran, February 12th, 1831: I went to see Kératry this morning, and we sat by the fire, talking. I told him how we had shed tears over *Le Dernier des Beaumanoir*. He said that a success of that kind meant more to him than all the applause of fashionable Paris. He is a man of great worth and dignity. I very much hope that he will take my little novel under his wing, and find a purchaser for it. . . .[2]

A friend at La Châtre, Madame Duvernet, had given her a letter of introduction to a Berrichon man of letters, Henri de Latouche. With him Aurore had much in common, for he was a cousin of the Duvernets, and his father had been one of Maurice Dupin's friends. But he had the reputation of being difficult. Born Hyacinthe Thabaud de Latouche, he

[1] Ibid., Volume IV, pp. 121-2.
[2] GEORGE SAND: *Correspondance*. Volume I, p. 159.

was an aristocrat who 'hated democracy but found it amusing to be a demagogue'. So exquisite was his language that most people took it to be an affectation, whereas it was merely his way of expressing himself. He had turned his hand to everything—the writing of plays and novels, journalism, scholarship—and in everything he had achieved success, of a second-rate kind. One of his books, *Fragoletta,* in which a woman dressed as a man leads a licentious life, had had some small *succès de scandale,* and had enchanted Théophile Gautier. He had acted as the posthumous editor of André Chénier, had introduced Goethe to French readers, but had never, in his own person, managed to conquer the 'dragon'—Fame. As a result of his failure to do so, he had become conceited, sensitive, and ever ready to take offence. Physically, he suffered from nerves and a bad digestion. But he was an excellent critic of others, and had nursed more geniuses than any man of his generation, though never himself attaining to genius. For instance, he had become the cross-grained mentor of the young Balzac, whose attention he had, very wisely, directed to Walter Scott and Fenimore Cooper. Nevertheless, Balzac did not much like him. One man, and one man only, had a burning belief in Latouche—Charles Nodier, whose daughter, irritated by her father's ardent championship, once said: 'How fortunate it is that God made the world, for, had He not, Monsieur de Latouche would most certainly have done so.'

In the eyes of the young Madame Dudevant, Latouche was a great personage. She went to see him at the Quai Malaquais, where he lived, and found a man of forty-five, with a stoutish figure, a face alive with intelligence, and beautiful manners. His voice, which had a muffled quality, was gentle, penetrating, caressing, and, at the same time, touched with mockery. The loss of one eye in childhood had left him by no means disfigured, and the only trace of this early accident was a sort of reddish gleam which showed in the dead pupil, and imparted to his physiognomy a kind of 'fantastic *glow*'. He had had much success with women, and had inspired Marceline Desbordes-Valmore with a tragic passion. By her he had had a son.

Aurore Dudevant to Casimir, January 15th, 1831: I have seen Monsieur de Latouche, who was most agreeable and is taking me on Sunday to see Madame Récamier at l'Abbaye-aux-Bois. Delphine Gay is to read some poetry, and I shall meet all the celebrities. This evening I am going to read my novel to him, and am very busy with an article which is going to appear in the *Revue de Paris*. He has also offered me some editorial work on the *Figaro*, but the idea does not appeal to me . . . All these promises are very fine, but will they amount to anything? I can't say. . . .[1]

Latouche listened patiently to the reading of *Aimée*, which Aurore had brought with her in manuscript. When it was finished: ' . . . "Have you any children, Madame?" he asked. "Unfortunately, yes, but I cannot have them with me, nor bring them back when I go home."—"And you mean to stay on in Paris and make a living by your pen?"— "I must."—"That is tiresome, for I can detect in your work none of the elements which make for success. Believe me, you would do much better to return to your husband". . . .' She listened respectfully to what he had to say, but stuck, with native obstinacy, to her point. When he said that her book lacked common sense, she replied 'True'; when he told her that she would have to re-write it from the beginning, she said, 'Maybe'. To Casimir she wrote: 'To you I can say, though you must not let it go any further, that I could never get on with a man like Latouche.' But she was to discover before very long that once he had got rid of 'a certain superfluity of intelligence' he showed himself the possessor of a heart capable of tenderness, devotion and generosity.

He had just become the proprietor of a little satirical periodical called the *Figaro*. Having had his baptism of fire with the Republicans on the barricades of 1830, he was now engaged in bombarding the régime of the Citizen-King with a brisk verbal fusilade of witticisms and epigrams—for he was the sort of man who, whatever the government, would always be in opposition. He offered to enrol the young woman in his team of sub-editors—'a brood of young eagles just feeling their wings'—as he proudly called them. The paper was made up in the unceremonious intimacy of the Quai Malaquais fireside, where each member of the editorial group had a small table to himself. Aurore ensconced herself close to the hearth, and did her best not to dirty the owner's fine, white carpet. It was his delight to instruct, criticize, and make suggestions. He would fling subjects for treatment at his 'eagles', together with scraps of paper

which he had cut to the required dimensions, into which
they were expected to fit articles or 'miscellaneous pars'
(which was what news items were called in the *Figaro*
office). It was an admirable training in concision for the
neophyte, but concision was precisely what Aurore could
not achieve. In vain did Latouche reserve for her such
sentimental anecdotes as came their way: 'I could neither
begin nor end within the strictly limited space at my
disposal, and by the time I had *begun to begin* it was time
to finish . . . I suffered agonies . . .' But there was plenty of
talk and laughter in the 'office'. Latouche was brilliantly
caustic, charmingly paternal. 'I did a lot of listening. I
enjoyed myself hugely. I produced nothing of the slightest
value, but at the end of the month I raked in twelve francs,
fifty centimes. . . .'

For all her self-criticism, she did manage to achieve a
minor triumph on March 5th, 1831, when, with the object
of poking fun at the precautions recently adopted by the
Government, she turned out the following 'Leader':

The Prefect of Police is about to publish a new decree.
Here are its main provisions. (1) All citizens capable of
bearing arms will parade every day from 7 a.m. until 11
p.m. for the purpose of guarding the Palais Royal, and
every night, from 11 p.m. until 7 a.m. for the purpose of
protecting the churches and other public buildings.
During these periods all women, children and old men
will do sentry duty at their own front-doors. Such
families as fail to fulfil these obligations will be ineligible
for protection by the armed forces, and will be exposed to
the violence of the mob. (2) So that the peace of the
population shall be no longer disturbed, twenty-five
rounds of cannon-fire shall be discharged every day, at
dawn, on the Public Places of the city. The tocsin will be
rung in all churches, and the call to arms sounded in the
streets throughout the night. A patrol of the National
Guard will make the rounds, calling on citizens to be on
the alert, as is the custom in fortified places. (3) It will be
the duty of every householder to see that a ditch, seven
and a half feet wide, is dug round his premises, that his
yard-entry is barricaded, that his windows are fitted with
bars, and that at least twenty muskets are available for
his tenants and domestics in case of need. Provided these
precautions are taken, the Government is prepared to
guarantee conditions of absolute and durable tranquillity.

It undertakes to discover no more than twelve conspiracies in any one month, and to put up with a maximum of three alarms per week. Each Monday, Wednesday and Friday shall be devoted to the forestalling of treasonable assemblies, and each Tuesday, Thursday and Saturday to the dispersing of the same. . . .[1]

The mockers in the cafés greeted this effusion with approving laughter, but the Citizen-King was thoroughly annoyed. The *Figaro* was seized. For a while, Madame Dudevant lived in hope that the law would attempt to discover the identity of the anonymous author of the offending article, and that proceedings would be instituted against her.

Aurore Dudevant to Charles Duvernet, March 6th, 1831: Heaven be praised! What scandal at La Châtre, what horror and despair in the bosom of my family! But my reputation is made. I have found a publisher to buy my platitudes, and fools to read them. I would gladly give nine francs, fifty centimes for the joy of being sentenced! . . .[2]

To her great sorrow, the Public Prosecutor stopped proceedings. 'Monsieur Vivien has instructed the Courts to take no further steps. What a shame! A political trial would have made my fortune. . . .'[3]

'Little Jules', too, had made his *début* upon the literary stage. Aurore had at first hesitated about introducing him to Latouche, whom she knew to be sparing of his patronage. But as soon as she had won her own enfranchisement, she plucked up courage to submit one of Jules's articles. The great man's verdict was favourable. It was now Sandeau's turn to be accorded a table with a handsome cloth in the editorial sanctum. Somewhat later, he offered to the *Revue de Paris* a quite 'incredible' piece of copy over which the two lovers had collaborated, though the signature was Jules's alone. Dr. Véron, the editor, had liked it very much. 'I am delighted, for Jules's sake: this proves that he has it in him to succeed. I have decided to take him as a collaborator

---

[1] This text, published in the *Figaro* for March 5th, 1831, is quoted by Frédéric Ségu in *Le Premier Figaro*, p. 50.

[2] GEORGE SAND: *Correspondance*. Volume I, p. 172.

[3] GEORGE SAND: *Correspondance*. Volume I, p. 152.

in my work, or to become a collaborator in his—whichever
way you like best. But I have made it a condition that he
shall give me the shelter of his name—having no wish to
sail under my own colours. In return, I will help him
whenever the need arises. . . .'[1] She insisted, however, that
this literary partnership should remain secret. 'I am in such
bad odour at La Châtre, that this, were it known, would
finish me off completely.'[2] There could be no question of
her writing under her own name. Her mother-in-law, the
dowager Baroness, after expressing considerable astonishment that she should remain in Paris for so long, without
Casimir, had asked whether it were true that she intended
to have her books printed: 'Yes, madame.' 'I have no objec-
tion to that, but I do sincerely hope that you will not set the
name I bear upon their title-pages.' 'Of course not, madame;
you need have no fear on that score.'[3]

Consequently, to begin with, the two collaborators signed
their joint productions 'J. Sandeau'. As lovers, they believed
that they had at last found happiness. To Emile Regnault,
her friend and confidant, Aurore wrote:

> I needed a heart of fire to love me as I understand love,
> and to console me for all the ingratitude which turned my
> youth into a waste land. Though I am already growing
> old, I have found such a heart—young as my own, and
> that lifelong affection which nothing can destroy and the
> passage of the years makes even stronger. Jules has given
> me a fresh hold on life. I was growing weary of it, and
> put up with it only out of a sense of duty to my children.
> He has made beautiful a future with which I had become
> disgusted in anticipation, but which now is filled with
> him—with his work, his success, his fine and modest
> behaviour . . . Oh, if only you could realize how I love
> him! The poor boy suffers so terribly from fits of
> melancholy, and he can do nothing to resist them . . .
> People blame him for them: but you, at least, never cause
> him to blush for his weakness. To forgive him for the
> seeming coldness which sometimes masters him, one
> must realize of what burning friendship, of what un-
> limited devotion, he is capable. . . .[4]

1 Ibid., Volume I, p. 106.
2 Ibid. Volume I, p. 153.
3 GEORGE SAND: *Histoire de ma Vie*. Volume IV, p. 175.
4 *Lettres de George Sand Emile Regnault*. Bibliothèque
nationale: department of manuscripts.

She felt it necessary to plead for Sandeau, because he was not much liked by the Paris Berrichons. 'He had a great deal of intelligence,' wrote Duvernet, at a later date, 'but he was a dry creature, eaten up by petty vanities and foolish ambitions.'¹ Sandeau, well aware of the hostility he aroused, was a mass of self-pity. 'The knowledge that he has a few friends would make him perfectly happy,' said Aurore, 'but when he finds reason to doubt them he suffers atrociously.' More a mother than a mistress, she consoled and tended him. His health was bad, and he often forgot to eat. It was she, at such times, who saw to it that he was properly fed. He was not, by nature, a worker, and she kept his nose to the grindstone, as a mother might have done a son's. To exercise so sweet a tyranny was joy for her. She regarded work not as slavery but as a natural function:

Aurore Dudevant to Jules Boucoiran, March 4th, 1831:
I am more than ever resolved to follow a literary career. In spite of occasional moods of disgust, in spite of periods of laziness and exhaustion which break in upon my work, in spite of the more than modest way in which I live, I know that I have found fulfilment. I have an object in life, a task, a—let me be frank, and say a *passion*. The trade of authorship is a violent, an indestructible, obsession. Once it gets hold of one, it never lets go. . . .'²

This laborious, bohemian existence would have been enchantment for her, if only she had not been deprived of her children. Her brother wrote to her, on that subject, letters from Nohant full of threats and thunder: 'The best thing you ever gave yourself to the making of is your son. He loves you better than anyone in the world, and you'd better be careful not to take the edge off that feeling of his.' The fierce Hippolyte was not far wrong. But Jules and Aurore were convinced that they could build, on the foundations of free love, a home where Maurice and Solange could come, in a short while, to live with them. They had the same tastes, the same likes. 'They would climb the narrow, twisting stair, in an access of joy, and it was never without a feeling of ecstatic delight that they shut the door of their tiny room behind them . . . It was a modest

¹ CHARLES DUVERNET: *Mémoires* (unpublished).
² GEORGE SAND: *Correspondance*. Volume I, pp. 165-6.

refuge, high-set near heaven, and the noises of the street could never reach it . . . They had neither carpets nor hangings, but flowers maintained within those walls eternal spring.'[1]

II

JULES SAND TO GEORGE SAND

IN APRIL 1831, true to the promise she had made to Casimir, she returned to Nohant. She was welcomed as though she had come back from the most ordinary of journeys. Her 'bouncing daughter' was lovely as a summer's day. Her son almost stifled her with kisses. Her husband guzzled and talked loud. She was delighted to renew acquaintance with her small world of Berry. But she had left her heart behind her in a room in the rue de Seine.

Aurore Dudevant to Emile Regnault: Dear Heaven! how gay our room must be looking in this lovely sunshine, with light reflected as in flaming mirrors from the windows opposite, covering with great plates of gold the ancient house-fronts which so much resemble Indian pagodas . . . The country here is very beautiful. Each evening my room is invaded by great gusts of lilac scent and lily-of-the-valley, by yellow, black-striped moths, and the song of nightingales from beneath my window, and cockchafers thrusting their faces into the beam that falls from my lamp. No doubt all this is most delicious, but Oh! how I dream of Paris—the misty evenings, the pink clouds above the roof-tops, and those charming little willows with their leaves of tender green, which stand about Old Henry's brazen statue, and the poor little slate-coloured pigeons that nest under the arches of the Pont-Neuf. How dear my Paris is to me, how sweet her liberty to live in love, and to be with my Jules who loves me so, and my Gaul, and my darling humming-bird . . . I think

1 JULES SANDEAU: *Marianna*, p. 131.

so often of that little room above the Quay where, in imagination, I can see you all, Jules in his dirty, tattered artist's coat, with his cravat twisted under one ear and his untidy left-off shirt sprawled over three chairs, stamping his foot and breaking the fire-tongs in the heat of argument. . . .[1]

She begged Regnault to keep a friendly eye on Sandeau. 'Good night, dear Emile: make much of little Jules, and see that he doesn't starve himself to death, as he might very well do . . .' She was all eagerness to get back to Paris. What was it she wanted?

To have enough to live on and to be together. That is all that matters: that is happiness . . . Two cutlets and some cheese; an attic with a view of Notre Dame and the river; work, so as to be able to pay the landlord and the cookshop man. Let others make a name and sacrifice their affections on the altar of precarious public praise. We will never imitate them, or only when we have lost our senses. The little 'un is well on the way to earning a living for himself and me. That Balzac is a charming fellow—if he becomes his friend, I'll grant that he is worth while, for I judge people nowadays by the degree of consideration which they have for Jules. . . .[2]

Honoré de Balzac, the man from Touraine who, like themselves, was one of Latouche's protégés, had struck up a friendship with the lovers. They moved him to a show of affectionate good-will. From time to time he would come to see them, and fill the attic with his boisterous vitality.[3] The date of Aurore's return to Paris was drawing close, and she was eager that Regnault should find them somewhere to live, since Hippolyte was now insisting that she must vacate his apartment. 'Jules is quite incapable of taking the necessary steps, but with you it is different . . .' Regnault's first suggestion was a room on the fifth floor of a house in the Ile Saint-Louis.

[1] Lettre II de George Sand à Emile Regnault. Bibliothèque nationale.

[2] Lettre II de George Sand à Emile Regnault. Bibliothèque nationale.

[3] GEORGE SAND: *Histoire de ma Vie*. Volume IV, pp. 126-32 and p. 183.

Aurore Dudevant to Emile Regnault: The fifth floor is a
bit high, and the Ile Saint-Louis is a bit far . . . One room
is not enough. I have a mother, an aunt, a sister and a
brother, all of whom are bound to get on my tracks . . .
With only one room I run the risk of being cornered, of
not being able to make my escape, of being caught red-
handed . . . I want something that would provide some
means by which Jules could slip away at any hour of the
day or night, for who knows but what my husband might
drop in on me, one of these fine days at four in the
morning, having nowhere to go and doing me the honour
of coming straight to my address! Just imagine what I
should feel like if I suddenly heard his ring, and knew
that his charming person was just on the other side of the
door! He could break it down if he felt so inclined, for I
certainly would not open it. All the same, the situation
would be the highest degree dramatic![1]

It appears from the above letter that there was a limit to
Monsieur Dudevant's willingness to keep his eyes shut,
though where precisely that limit lay it was not easy to
determine. The good Emile tried again, and this time offered
an apartment, consisting of three rooms, at 25 Quai Saint-
Michel.

May 30th: I am strongly in favour of the Quai Saint-
Michel. I adore the position. I shall see to it that nobody
knows anything about the back room. It shall be kept
barricaded and forbidden to strangers. Everyone will
think that I have got only two rooms. The third shall be
the mysterious room of doom and darkness, the haunted
chamber, the monster's lair, the place where I keep the
performing dog, the home of the hidden treasure, the
vampire's cavern . . . or anything else that comes into my
mind . . . Please make the necessary arrangements: I
leave everything in your hands. . . .[2]

She asked for a plan of the apartment, with all the dimensions clearly indicated, so that she might move some of

[1] Lettre X de George Sand à Emile Regnault. Bibliothèque
nationale.
[2] Ibid., Lettre XI.

her furniture from Nohant. For even when she was at
Nohant she thought only of her life with Jules. She would
wander away into the little copse where they had so often
met in the old days, and dream of the future. It was a
constant wonder to her that a 'boy of twenty, with pink and
white cheeks, should have lost his heart to a decrepit and
ailing old mummy'.

> *June 15th, 1831:* I felt, as it were, exasperated with the
> past. Why, when I was twenty, when I still possessed the
> beauty I have since lost, when my heart was calm,
> innocent and confident, when I still believed in that love
> of humanity which dies with experience—why, at the
> time when I was ripe for love, could I not have met Jules
> as he is today? I am old and battered and bruised,
> whereas he is still young, and capable of burning passion.
> . . .[1]

No woman in love but regrets that she cannot offer lost
virginity, an untouched body, and an innocent heart to the
man of her choice—not but what Aurore was fully aware
that plenty of young men found her still attractive. She was
insatiable in her demands, and delighted in the knowledge
that Regnault and Fleury were, both of them, her devoted
slaves. Her dearest dream was that the four of them should
set up house together. 'Our love, our friendship forms so
close a bond that especial fondness between two could never
mean alienation of the others. There is such identity
between us four that every thought we have is common
property . . . do not you agree? . . .'

She was certainly not 'old'. She was twenty-seven and,
apart from an occasional indisposition, as strong as a horse.
When she was at Nohant, she would work in the garden,
gallop over to La Châtre to applaud Duvernet in some
theatrical performance, nurse Maurice when he was ill, and
still find time to throw off a 'literary trifle, exquisitely romantic, and as black as fifty devils', complete with conspiracies and executioners, daggers, deaths, gurgles, blood,
oaths and curses. 'It is six in the morning. I have been
working since seven o'clock last night. I have written enough
in five nights to make a volume. During the day I teach my

[1] Lettre XIII de George Sand à Emile Regnault. Bibliothèque
nationale.

son Latin—of which I know nothing, and French, of which
I know very little . . .' There were no serious clashes with
Casimir.

*Aurore Dudevant to Madame Maurice Dupin, May 31st,
1831:* The truth is, my husband does exactly as he likes.
Whether he has mistresses, or does not have mistresses,
rests entirely with him. He can drink wine or water just
as the fancy takes him, and is free to save or to spend. He
can build, plant, sell, buy, run the house and the estate,
as he thinks fit. I have washed my hands of his concerns
. . . But it is only fair that he shall grant me the same liberty that he enjoys. If he does not, then I shall think
him odious and contemptible—and he would hate that to
happen. Consequently, I am completely independent. I
go to bed when he gets up: I visit La Châtre or Rome as I
please. I come home at midnight or at six a.m. All that is
my business, and no one else's. . . .[1]

Thus it came about that when in July she decided to
return to Paris and set up house there she consulted
nobody. Her mother, her sister, and her brother were all
loud in their condemnation of the plan. She did not hesitate
to put them in their places.

*Hippolyte Châtiron to Casimir Dudevant, Paris, July
6th, 1831:* I have just, this moment, had a letter from
Aurore . . . Your wife wants to be left perfectly free. She
longs for a life of dissipation and constant movement.
You have not been a bad husband, and people here, no
less than at home, realize that fact. Let her do as she
likes. If things turn out badly she will have no cause of
complaint against you, me, or her relations. Since she is
doing exactly as she wishes, without let or hindrance,
what line ought you to take?—Resign yourself to the
inevitable, don't worry, keep a watch on your tongue,
and look after your interests and your children. . . .[2]

Aurore liked her lodgings on the Quai Saint-Michel, on
the attic floor of the tall building which stood at the corner
of the Place. She had three rooms opening on to a balcony,
with a fine outlook, plenty of sky, water, air, swallows, and

1 GEORGE SAND: *Correspondance.* Volume I, pp. 182-3.
2 Spoelberch de Lovenjoul Collection: Group E. 868, f. 236.

a view of Notre-Dame in the distance. In order to buy furniture she had to borrow five hundred francs from Latouche, and as much again from Duris-Dufresne. How could she ever manage to pay back such enormous sums?— Why not run a Fair-Booth?

Aurore Dudevant to Emile Regnault: Planet can be an elephant and squirt water out of his trunk at the passersby: the Gaul will make a fine giraffe, and little Jules can be a South-American *chappard*.[1] We'll have a tub on which you can give a performance as a seal or a crocodile. The Gaul can sell hair-oil, Planet a tooth-ache cure, I embrocation for rheumatism, little Jules ointment for skin troubles, and you, rat-poison. If, with all that, we can't make our fortunes, we can always as a last resort jump from the balcony into the river *Sequana*.[2]

Aurore to Casimir: No one could well live more modestly than I do. I allow myself no luxuries. My furniture is of walnut and cherry-wood, my rooms are on the fifth floor. But there are certain necessaries I must have, It would ease my mind considerably if you would let me have a thousand francs over and above my monthly allowance . . . I should have thought you could borrow money at La Châtre . . . I am in a very different position. I have had to buy what I needed to set up house, and it never occurred to me that my brother and my husband would leave me in the embarrassing position of having to apply to strangers for the money I required to settle my more urgent debts . . . I should have known better what to expect! I have had to give my upholsterer a Bill for 250 francs, which falls due on August 15th. My mother lent me 200 francs. I have got to live, and I still owe for a number of articles—a hat, some shoes, and the cabinetmaker's account which comes to 300 francs . . . One thing is certain, that however economically I may live there is no middle way between begging and paying. The only alternative that I can see is the Morgue, which stands

[1] This word appears in no French-English dictionary. It may conceivably be a 'hyena' or possibly an 'ant-eater'.— TRANSLATOR.

[2] Letter quoted by A. GUET in an article entitled 'George Sand inconnue', which appeared in *La Vie Moderne*, June 10th, 1882.

opposite my windows. Every day I see the bodies of
persons being carried in there who have died for the lack
of twenty francs. I cannot live on nothing . . . I shall await
your answer before turning for help to strangers . . .
wish you a good appetite. . . .[1]

Her brother Hippolyte came to see her, and she treated
him to a scene straight out of Molière, accusing the family,
which *she* had ceased to see, of egotism and indifference.

*Hippolyte Châtiron to Casimir Dudevant, August 5th,
1831:* I have been several times to see Aurore. She has
treated me most unfairly. She has been doing all she can
to keep her family at a distance, and now accuses me of
selfishness and indifference. She told me that she had
gone hungry for three days, though my wife and I have
sent her at least twenty invitations, not one of which has
she accepted. What is to be done I simply do not know.
She seems to be surprised at the privations to which she
has had to submit, though she has incurred all of them
with her eyes open. She thought she could make a living
with her writing, but it is now, I gather, quite disillusioned
on that score . . . In the last letter she wrote to me she
said that if I go on conspiring with you to make her
miserable, to deprive her of her children, and to keep her
perpetually short of money, she will throw herself into
the river! She has asked me to tell you this, that you
may not have her death on your conscience. I have taken
it upon myself to advance her five hundred francs in
return for a Bill drawn on you, and dated October. I have
no doubt you will meet it, because, in spite of her
extravagances, we cannot leave her without anything,
and a prey to melancholy reflections which might result
in a desperate act for which we should never forgive ourselves. I told her that you would certainly not refuse to
pay for the furniture, and that you would continue your
allowance of a thousand *écus.* I said, too, that it was your
intention to send Maurice to a boarding-school in Paris
as soon as Boucoiran has finished with him. I added that
if, instead of setting a third person between you and
herself, she behaved to you in a spirit of trust and
friendship, she would get from her husband all she needs,

[1] Spoelberch de Lovenjoul Collection: Group E. 868, ff. 148-
50.

and more. The result of our talk was we were both of us
in tears, because, in spite of her pig-headedness, I cannot
help being fond of her. She has promised me that she will
return to Nohant in September. . . .[1]

She was as good as her word; but Jules settled down at La
Châtre, and the two lovers, to the great scandal of the 'three
societies', continued to live much as they had been doing in
Paris. They were working together at a long novel, *Rose et
Blanche,* for which a Paris publisher, Renault, had signed a
contract. He had undertaken to pay a sum of one hundred
and twenty-five francs on the delivery of each volume, and
a further five hundred three months later. Regnault was
given the task of working on Renault's feelings.

You must paint a moving picture of our poverty, describe
the condition of Jules's black frock-coat, and his lack of
waistcoats, indicate the appalling state of my shoes and
the grim condition of my neckerchiefs . . . Tell him that
Niort has started a subscription for the purpose of getting
Jules shaved, and that the people of La Châtre are
contributing to a fund for keeping me in food . . . I have
twice seen the Gaul. I flew at him, rolled him over and
over on the ground, and embraced him. He is as kindly as
a great cow, but talks about nothing but seducing,
abducting, attacking, robbing, and generally cleaning out
the men he meets in the streets, and, as Paul-Louis
Courier says, behaving in just the opposite way to the
ladies. . . .[2]

She made no attempt to conceal the fact that she and
Sandeau were lovers. She was excessively annoyed when she
was taken for the kind of woman who begs that 'her secret
may be respected' and that 'her reputation be handled with
kid gloves'.

I am sufficiently proud to feel humiliated when my
position is judged by the scale of their 'respectable'
females. How little they know me! They are quite
determined that I shall have a reputation. They blush,
and drop their eyes when they hear me referred to as a

[1] Ibid., Group E. 868, f. 238.
[2] Lettre XIX de George Sand à Emile Regnault. Bibliothèque
nationale.

woman who . . . Self pride in friendship is like the lees in a wine bottle. Our friends are ready to forgive us for being unhappy, boring, tiresome, decrepit: they will pardon us for anything except forfeiting public esteem. . . .[1]

It was not only in La Châtre that she met her lover. Intoxicated by her feeling of independence, she went so far as to receive him in her room at Nohant, although she was now occupying one on the first floor. The good Papet kept watch.

Not a grumble from Gustave. He is the most devoted of friends, and is up to the ears in our mad pranks. He stationed himself in a ditch in the garden, and stayed there all the time Jules was in my room—because, you see, he paid me a visit last night under the very nose of *Brave*, my husband and my brother, my children, my maid, etc. . . . I had planned everything and foreseen everything. The only risk Jules ran was of being peppered by a charge of shot as he was climbing up to my window—a bare six feet from the ground—a risk about as serious as being overturned in a coach, or of breaking a leg while dancing. He came—and oh, how happy we were! . . . There he was, in my tiny little room, and in my arms, happy, exhausted, hugged, bitten, shouting aloud, crying, laughing. Never, I think, have we experienced so violent an access of delight. You can't, can you, try to read a lecture to such a sensible and happy couple? I hope that he will come again tonight. Twice is not too often. More than that might be imprudent . . . My husband is bound to find out that he is distant only about three gunshots from Nohant, but so far he knows nothing. He is busy with his grape-harvest. At night he sleeps like a hog . . . I feel battered and bitten all over. I can scarcely stand on my feet . . . I am in a condition of ecstatic joy. . . .[2]

Aurore Dudevant to Gustave Papet: Dear Gustave: what a good fellow you are! How you love Jules, and how truly do I repay you in kind. You spent the night bivouacking in a ditch, for all the world like a wretched soldier, while

[1] Lettre XXI de George Sand à Emile Regnault.
[2] Lettre XX de George Sand à Emile Regnault. Bibliothèque nationale.

we, made egotists by happiness, could not tear ourselves from one another's arms. It was not for want of saying, thirty times at least: *We really must . . . Gustave is down there . . . poor Gustave!* I expect Jules has told you about it all. In the midst of our wildest transports, we called down blessings on your head. Your name was mingled with our kisses, our every thought was for you . . . I truly believe that your devotion, your presence so close to us, your anxious care in watching over our happiness, made it sweeter still. This holy, this fervent, friendship which surrounds and overwhelms us, is part and parcel of our lives, and makes our world a Paradise. How happy you, too, should be in the knowledge that you are loved so ardently. Do not weary of your well-doing. Put us to the test. But, meanwhile, my poor, dear friend, do not, please, get an attack of rheumatism. Oh dear, how egotistical love is, compared with friendship! . . .[1]

Little Jules, however, had never been physically strong, and this kind of life did not agree with him.

You will notice how thin and pale he looks. If he goes on like this he will kill himself. He gets no sleep. During the day he is as idle and lazy as a dog, and at night he cheats himself on rest in order to make up for lost time. I have many other bones, too, to pick with him, but it would be difficult to explain what they are. You and I must have a good talk about it all: we are both old troopers, and do not mince words when we are together. The long and the short of the matter is that I am in despair. So far as he is concerned there is only one opinion in La Châtre. Everyone is convinced that he is consumptive. I know it is not true, but I know, too, that his health is decidedly worse than it was . . . It has been so lovely to see him here, such ecstasy to hold him in my arms. But the knowledge that this passion which is eating us up is inflaming his blood and exhausting his vitality is quite frightful. . . .[2]

---

[1] This letter is quoted by Marcel Coulon in an article entitled 'L'Amoureuse George Sand', which appeared in the *Mercure de France* for August 15th, 1928.

[2] Lettre XVIII de George Sand à Emile Regnault. Bibliothèque nationale.

Meanwhile, at Nohant, work kept pace with love. The five volumes of *Rose et Blanche* were drawing to a close. The novel was about an actress and a nun. Latouche saw in it no more than a *pastiche* of the Romantics, and of Sterne. But this time the man of taste was wrong. For all its simple-minded crudities, it contains much that is charming: descriptions of the countryside of the Pyrenees and the Gironde: a deal of forceful characterization—old Sister Olympe, for instance, with her heart of gold and her barrack-room language: the arrival of a Bishop, and many scenes of back-stage life. Aurore's part in it was the best. She had drawn on her memories of the Convent, on her mother's intimate conversations, on her own impressions of travel. Sandeau had added a certain amount of rather coarse bawdiness—such as the recollections of a bogus castrato—and the cynical tone of these portions, when the book appeared, shocked Sophie-Victoire who, like many women of easy virtue, wanted her novels to be 'clean'.

Aurore Dudevant to Madame Maurice Dupin: I gladly bow to your criticisms. If, however, you find too much of the sergeant-major about Sister Olympe, the fault is hers rather than mine. I knew her well, and you can take my word for it that, in spite of her swearing, she was one of the best and noblest of women. Still, I am prepared to admit that I ought not, perhaps, to have taken her as my model for the character in question. The truth should not always be put into words, and, possibly, I was guilty of bad taste in making the choice I did. But I told you that the book is not my unaided effort. Of many of the comic parts I thoroughly disapprove, and put up with them only to satisfy my publisher, who wanted strong meat. . . .[1]

From the commercial point of view the publisher was right, as is shown by the fact that this 'realistic' novel sold well. Aurore had already started on a new work, this time alone. When Sandeau left for Paris she did not follow him at once. For some time now she had been finding her husband 'quite nice'. What, if it came to that, did she ask of him?—to have confidence in her, and to 'shut his ears to all the grubby gossip which is the standby of this particular world, and makes it peculiarly boring'.[2] That seemed to

present no great difficulty. There was, too, Maurice, who
was becoming more and more charming as he grew older.
She began to teach him history, trying as best she could to
clear his mind of political passion and religious prejudice.

But in November Regnault wrote that Jules was ill, and
she hastened to his side. The people of La Châtre had not
been wrong when they had said that he was consumptive.
He had a perpetual fever which gave rise to the worst
suspicions. She was filled with remorse. Had an over-
indulgence in the pleasure of the flesh been responsible for
his present condition?

Aurore Dudevant to Emile Regnault: Would it be better
if I sent him to sleep at your house? All these details are
hateful. Please forgive me, you cannot possibly know the
horrible anxiety, the terrible remorse, that I feel when I
see the one being for whom I would gladly give my life,
dying in my arms. It is frightful to see him growing
thinner and thinner and more exhausted, to realize that I
am bringing death ever closer to him, that my caresses
are poison to him, that my love is a fire which consumes
and does not warm, a fire that destroys and leaves
nothing but burnt-out ashes. That is a hideous thought.
Jules refuses to understand it. He merely laughs . . . and
says that death in such a shape is what he longs for, that
he wants to die like that . . . I have done him nothing but
harm. For three months I have let him sicken unto death
in my arms. Many and many's the time I have seen him
in a half fainting condition, and have resisted his desires.
But I have always yielded in the long run, for fear of
killing him. In the hope of curing him I have sacrificed
my own dearest wishes, and that is saying a good deal.
And now I tremble at the thought that I have done him
more harm by my devotion than by my resistance. I am
killing him, and the pleasure I give him is bought at the
cost of his life. I am his scrap of wild ass's skin. . . .[1]

Rose et Blanche was published in December. Its re-
ception by the public and the critics was fairly favourable.
Casimir came to Paris. The safety precautions at the Quai
Saint-Michel were put into operation, and Monsieur
Dudevant passed a few happy days in the capital.

[1] Lettre XXIV de George Sand à Emile Regnault. Bibliothèque nationale.

Aurore Dudevant to Casimir, December 1st, 1831: So used have I become to the simplest sort of existence, that your stay has been for me a time of feasting and self-indulgence. Thank you for it, and for the lovely dress which has just come home. On the evening of your departure I had a sort of rush of blood to the head . . . Goodbye, my dear. Keep me posted in your news, and kiss the tinies for me. I send you my fondest love . . . Please let me know the length of your foot. I am embroidering a pair of slippers for you, but don't know the measurements. . . .[1]

She did not wait long before following her husband to Nohant. The old house had need of her. There had been a number of domestic upheavals. Boucoiran was accused of having got Claire, Madame Hippolyte's maid, with child. Aurore did not take the matter very seriously. *To Jules Boucoiran:* 'Whether my husband and my brother are the guilty parties, and whether Dutheil, Jules or Charles have lent a hand, is a matter of complete indifference to me. They are all of them mean enough to jib at paying the piper. They had better open a subscription! I have no doubt you are involved, but you are poorer than they are and ought to be let off lightly. . . .'[2]

This time her stay in Paris had been short. She was complaining of feeling far from well, and Regnault had prescribed country air. What she really wanted was the chance to write in peace, and nothing could better suit her than the silent nights at Nohant. It was not long, however, before she thought that she was getting worse, that, maybe, she was dying, and a cry for help was dispatched to the admirable Regnault. 'The trouble is advancing with giant strides, my poor, dear Emile, and I can no longer refuse to recognize its progress. I am continually short of breath, and cannot walk round my room without almost collapsing. There is a burning sensation in my stomach. Oh, please, Emile dear, don't let me die . . .'[3] He offered to come to her, but she beat a retreat. 'I cannot ask you to come. My

1 Spoelberch de Lovenjoul Collection: Group E. 868, f. 156 and f. 160.

2 Spoelberch de Lovenjoul Collection: Group E. 920, f. 26.

3 Lettre XXV de George Sand à Emile Regnault. Bibliothèque nationale.

brother and my husband would look very much askance at you. They are quite certain that it is all imagination on my part. . . .'[1]

In this they were almost certainly right, but she was convinced that she had the cholera, which was the fashionable ailment of the moment. Finally, she reassured her friend. 'The *cholera morbus* has been arrested. I am once again sleeping soundly. I should hate Jules to see me return in my present state—pale, and with blue shadows round my eyes, great deep shadows that come half way down my cheeks, unable to walk three minutes on end, and looking like nothing on earth when I sit down to a meal. . . .'[2]

When she next put in an appearance at the Quai Saint-Michel, in the Spring of 1832, she brought with her her 'bouncing daughter', Solange, and a novel, *Indiana*.

III

THE BIRTH OF GEORGE SAND

THE ARRIVAL of Solange had surprised her young Berrichon friends. Was it decent to let a child of three and a half live in such ambiguous surroundings?

Aurore Dudevant to Emile Regnault: Yes, my friend, I am bringing Solange to see you. There is nothing that I know of in my bachelor life likely to do her the least harm. I shall adjust my manner of existence to suit her. That will be neither very difficult nor particularly meritorious. Jules, certainly, will not shed bitter tears. All it amounts to is that we shall have to adjust our rate of walking to the requirements of our small daughter's legs. We shall spend two or three hours every day in the Luxembourg, with our books and the child. We shall eat at home, as usual. She will sleep on our sofa, with the

[1] Ibid. Lettre XXIX.
[2] Ibid., Lettre XXVIII.

addition of a mattress, and, seeing that she is three and a
half years old, you can rest assured that she will make no
remarks or comments, that she will ask no questions, and
indulge in no gossip. It would be the same with Maurice,
so guileless is he. So you can set your moral qualms to
rest. I am no more anxious than the most virtuous of
mothers to be a cause of scandal to my daughter . . .
Besides, she has about as much brain as a goose. . . .[1]

It did mean, however, that Jules and she would have to
do without jaunts to the theatre. But what did that matter?
They were more than ready to sacrifice *Robert le Diable*,
and the Malibran, to one of Solange's tears. Everything, as
a matter of fact, went 'swimmingly'. Jules was mad about
'his daughter', took her to the Jardin des Plantes—filled,
just then, with the scent of acacias—showed her the giraffe,
which she pretended that she had seen already in one of the
Nohant meadows, and held her by the hand when she went
out on to the balcony at the Quai Saint-Michel to water the
dozen flower-pots which made up her mother's hanging
garden. She broke one or two stalks, and, fearing to be
scolded, mended them with letter wafers. The licentious
engraving was rapidly turning into a picture by Greuze.

As to *Indiana*—Sandeau read his mistress's manuscript
with feelings of admiration, astonishment, and, to some
extent, of embarrassment. It was too well done, and, for his
taste, rather too serious. Honesty forbade him to put his
name to a book on which he had done no work at all. What
nom de plume, then, should she take? 'J. Sand', their
collective appellation, had already, thanks to *Rose et
Blanche*, acquired some small degree of notoriety. *Dudevant* was impossible: her mother-in-law and her husband
would have been up in arms at once, while her own mother would, doubtless, raise objections to *Dupin*. A compromise was arrived at: she would keep *Sand*, and alter the
Christian name. In this way George Sand was born, because she insisted on passing for a man. Obsessed by the
idea that all women were slaves, she wished to escape from
her destiny by using a man's name and by wearing a man's

[1] Lettre XXXIV de George Sand à Emile Regnault. Bibliothèque nationale. This letter has been already published,
by Madame Aurore Lauth-Sand, in the *Revue de Paris*, for May
1st, 1937.

clothing. From then on, she gave a masculine termination to all adjectives which she applied to herself.

Towards the end of May, her publishers (J. P. Roret et Dupuy) sent round to the Quai Saint-Michel the first copy of the book to come off the press. It so happened that its arrival synchronized with Latouche's. He took the novel, and sniffed at it with an expression of uneasiness, curiosity and, as usual, of mocking scepticism. He turned the pages. 'Why, this is just *pastiche*—School of Balzac: pastiche— what d'you mean by it?—Balzac—what d'you mean by it?'[1] Aurore was on the balcony. He joined her there, holding the book in his hand, and proceeded to prove, point by point, just how she had copied Balzac's manner. She knew that the censure was undeserved, but said not a single word in self-defence. Latouche took away the volume, which she had, on the spot, inscribed to him. Next morning when she woke, she found the following note. 'George, this is just to take it all back and to say how sorry I am. I am at your feet. Forget how beastly I have been for the last six months. I spent the whole night reading your book. My child, I am proud of you!'

What rapture! Those sincere words of admiration, coming from so sharp-tongued and severe a critic, went to her head. They were soon being echoed in the papers. Balzac, in the columns of *Caricature,* wrote: 'Here is a book in which truth takes its stand against the fantastic, the modern world against the Middle Ages, intimate drama against the tyranny of the great Historical Manner . . . Nothing could be more simply written or more delightfully imagined. Incidents crowd upon one another in such a way as to give the impression not of art but of life—where all is confusion and mere chance produces more tragedies than Shakespeare ever succeeded in doing. In short the success of the novel is assured . . .'[2] In *La Revue des Deux Mondes,* Gustave Planche—that same 'Gustave the Cruel' who was the writer's terror, who treated even Hugo with contempt, and maintained with an air of disgust that Balzac's work stank of 'opium, rum and coffee'—praised the young woman novelist to the skies. He held her to be superior to Madame de Staël, extolling her 'eloquence of the heart' and

[1] GEORGE SAND: *Histoire de ma Vie.* Volume IV, p. 148.
[2] Quoted by Bernard Guyon in *La Pensée politique et sociale de Balzac,* p. 582.

her simplicity of expression. 'Doubtless, in the course of time, the author of *Indiana* will acquire a greater skill: but it is much to be wondered whether technical perfection will ever outweigh the boldness of conception which sheer ignorance has made possible. . . .'

She thanked him. He went to see her, with a request from Buloz, the new editor of the *Revue,* that she should become a contributor. George's first impression was of a strange creature, ill-tempered and morose. As a result of having had to struggle in youth against a father who was obstinately opposed to his adopting literature as a profession, he had grown into a rebel and a misanthrope. 'Aged, perhaps as a result of the embittered solitude in which he lived, and by a life of excessive cerebration, he spent his time examining the mental processes of others, unsystematically and aimlessly . . . He was the Turk of the intelligence . . . Criticism was his opium, and his harem of other men's books had disgusted him with the idea of ever producing any of his own. . . .'[1]

Planche's wide culture was housed in a dirty and uncared-for body. In vain did Buloz buy new clothes for him—he merely sold them, and returned happily to his greasy old suits. Convinced that there was nothing he did not understand, he lived 'in rapt contemplation of himself set against the immensities of his intellectual kingdom, and ignored the fleshly envelope with a scorn worthy of Diogenes'.[2] Sand liked men of his type, men who were independent, proud and poor. They struck up a friendship, and she made a bargain with Buloz. In return for four thousand francs a year, she undertook to supply a weekly quota of thirty-two pages of 'copy' to the *Revue*. Since, too, the publishers of *Indiana* had offered her an advance of fifteen hundred francs for a new novel, *Valentine,* about which she had already spoken to them, she found herself suddenly rich and famous.

What sort of a book, then, was *Indiana?* Sand has herself answered that question in the Preface:

To those who seek a full explanation of the book's intention, let me say that *Indiana* is a type. She stands for

[1] BALZAC: *Béatrix.* Volume I, pp. 280-2. The description is of Claude Vignon for whom, as Balzac admitted in a letter to Madame Hanska, Planche had served as a model.
[2] Ibid., Volume I, pp. 280-2.

woman, a weak creature charged by the author with representing those passions which have been compressed, or, if you will, *suppressed* by human laws. She is Choice at odds with Necessity; she is Love blindly butting its head against all the obstacles set in its path by civilization. . . .[1]

The novel, that is, was a medium through which its author had expressed what lay closest to her heart. But the artistic transposition is complete. We shall seek in vain among its characters for portraits either of Casimir or of Sandeau. Something, perhaps, of Aurore's Indian colouring—so much admired by her friends—is to be found in the heroine's Créole origins, and she shares certain features with her creator. 'She did not love her husband, for the very reason that love had been imposed upon her as a duty, and that to resist all forms of moral constraint had become, with her, a second nature, a principle of behaviour, a law of conscience . . .'[2] Indiana is disappointed in her lover, Raymon de Ramière (whose high principles are reminiscent of Aurélien de Sèze) no less than in her husband, the rough, coarse, but not ill-natured Colonel Delmare. The central theme is the contrast between Woman seeking the absolute in emotion, and Man, always more vain and sensual than passionate. Salvation comes, ultimately and artificially, in the person of a noble and calm English cousin, Sir Ralph Brown, who takes Indiana away to the idyllic valley of his childhood. (She had found some lovely descriptions of the Ile Bourbon in the notebooks of Jules Néraud, the 'Madagascan'.)

Valentine, the protagonist of her second novel, is also an unhappily married woman of noble family who, having been taken to wife by a mediocre individual of her own class, becomes aware that Benedict, a farmer's son, is in love with her. The book found favour with the public, in part because escape to the 'People' seemed no less romantic than escape to the Past, in part, because Aurore described in it the corner of Berry which she knew so well. It appears in the book under the name of 'La Vallée Noire'. Slowly its poetry had taken possession of her heart, and slowly her prose became suffused with a lyrical quality. For twenty-four years she had lived among its maimed trees, its

[1] GEORGE SAND: *Indiana*, p. 7.
[2] GEORGE SAND: *Indiana*, p. 60.

'bosky' dells and murmuring streams. She painted them with a sure and charming touch, and her readers adored the rural setting of the story. As to its social thesis—the intermingling of classes—some found in it matter for praise, others for blame, according to their political leanings.

'Saint-Simonism' had enjoyed some years of outstanding success, but had recently been undermined as a result of disagreements among its followers over the question of marriage. *Père* Enfantin, high-priest of the new 'church', taught that the enfranchisement of women could never be attained so long as they were bound by the law of marital fidelity. The ban on carnal love, pronounced by the authorities of Christendom, must be lifted. Those who held these views turned, after the publication of *Indiana* and *Valentine*, to George Sand. Might not this daring young woman, who had become suddenly famous, and was leading a direct attack on the institution of marriage, turn out to be the long awaited *Mother?* The Saint-Simonians hoped so, and tried to enlist her in their ranks. But she eluded their clutches. She had too much peasant caution, too much feminine wisdom, to let herself be caught. Nevertheless, the din of battle transformed her life. She no longer attended regularly at the Editorial Office, but many visitors, far too many, pursued her into the privacy of her home. When evening came, she shut herself away with her pens, her ink, her piano and her fire. Chilly and hard-working, she loved these nights of warmth and application. A number of long short-stories came to effortless birth beneath her fingers—*Metella, La Marquise* (which contains a portrait of her Dupin de Francueil grandmother) and others. Sandeau was a somewhat humiliated witness of all this flow of words. She urged him to imitate her, but in vain. 'You want me to work', he wrote to her: 'I, too, want it, but I cannot! I was not born, as you were, with a little steel spring in my brain. I am incapable of just pressing a button, like you, and setting my imagination functioning . . .' His mistress's inflexible industry filled him with a vague fear of losing her.

She defended her freedom against her lover, as, formerly she had defended it against her husband. 'I go where I like,' she told him, not without a certain severity; 'and I give an account of my movements to nobody.' In 1832 Latouche, in embittered mood, feeling himself to be generally destested,

left Paris and settled down at Aulnay, in Chateaubriand's
Vallée-aux-Loups.

> Il fuit, il se cache, il se couche
> Aù fond de la vallée aux loups,
> Sol où les lauriers sont des houx.
> Dormez bien, monsieur de Latouche[1]

He offered Sand his apartment on the Quai Malaquais
where she had paid him her first visit. Hers, now, was the
great white carpet, and the acacia clambering round the
window. What a 'move up'! On several occasions, during
the Summer of 1832, she went to see him at Aulnay,
travelling by diligence as far as Sceaux, and continuing on
foot along a path which brought her to the retreat of the
misanthropic literary recluse. These visits were happy and
delightful. They would spend the time until midnight deep
in talk. George would go and look for eggs in the chicken
run, gather fruit in the orchard, and cook dinner. 'People
have said that he was in love with me, that he was jealous,
though not admitting it even to himself, that he was hurt
because I never guessed. That is not true . . .' Balzac
believed that they were lovers, but Latouche's letters sound
a note rather of sentimental, regretful, wistful friendship.

Latouche to George Sand: That you are changeable, who
should know better than I?—but that, after all, is only to
say that you have the frailties of human nature as well as
its advantages. Your adorable letter brought me the only
moment of happiness I have known for a year past . . . I
don't, my dear, accuse you of ingratitude to Destiny . . .
I am prepared to maintain that you are right, and that all
the rest of the world is wrong—still, if ·you look around
I think you will agree that you have reason to be patient
with it. You have everything: children, pride, friends; you
have a just claim to all the good things of life. Do not talk
of such a wretched creature as myself! For a long time
now I have been more dead than alive, and now that I

---

[1] Alfred de Musset.
> He flees, and he goes to ground
> In the valley where, freed from his quarrels,
> He can substitute Holly for Laurels.
> Oh, Monsieur Latouche, sleep sound.

have grown used to the grave, now that I am acclimatized
to the other world, do not, I beg you, summon me back
to this one! Here, if one is not to feel forsaken, one must
be continuously happy. All the virtues are contained in
the single word *success*. Take my word for it, one is
better off when dead than plagued by ambitions . . . Had I
lived elsewhere, I should have loved you too fondly, and I
rejoice—as I did the other day when I re-read Rousseau's
four letters to Sara—to think that I have lived my life and
handed in my resignation. Goodbye, I remain, as ever,
your fond old host of the Vallée d'Aulnay, of the Vallée-
aux-Loups. Bring him a small pot of butter, and, above
all, another novel from the pen of the author of *Indiana*.
. . .[1]

An unexpected, and warmly welcomed, guest at the Quai
Malaquais, was Marie Dorval, the great romantic actress,
and interpreter of plays by Dumas and de Vigny. George,
moved by passionate admiration, had written asking her to
come. One morning, when she and Sandeau were talking,
the door opened, and a woman in a state of considerable
breathlessness exclaimed: 'Well, here I am!' Sand had never
seen her off the stage, but recognized her immediately.
Small, dark and fragile, with a fringe of curly hair,
brimming eyes, a trembling lip, and a face which expressed
poetic sensibility in every line, Dorval was more than
merely pretty—she was charming. Not that she *wasn't*
pretty, but so great was her charm that good looks seemed
to be an unnecessary addition. Hers was not so much a face
as a 'countenance', the outward and visible sign of an inward and spiritual grace. She was still slim. Her figure was
like a supple reed, swaying in obedience to some mysterious
breeze which she alone could feel. On this particular
occasion Jules Sandeau compared her to the 'drooping
feather that adorned her hat' . . . 'I am sure,' he said, 'that
one might search the whole world over without coming on a
feather so light, so soft, as the one that she has found. That
unique and wondrous feather has floated towards her in
obedience to the law of affinities, or has fallen upon her
from the wing of a flying fairy. . . .'[2]

[1] Letter quoted by Frédéric Ségu, in his *H. de Latouche*, p.
446.
[2] GEORGE SAND: *Histoire de ma Vie*. Volume IV, pp. 212-
13.

Dorval played a leading part in George Sand's life. In spite of appearances, in spite of the wild abandon of some of her letters, Sand had never found in the love of men that absolute passion, that ecstacy of happiness, that loosening of tension, which was her heart's desire. The sickly Sandeau lacked human warmth. Sand had done everything she could to convince herself that she loved him wildly. With him she had sought with frenzied determination a satisfaction of the senses which she had never found. Marie Dorval was all that George would have liked to be:

Only those who know how differently we were made can realize how utterly I was in thrall to her . . . She had been given by God the power to express what she felt . . . She was beautiful, and she was simple. She had never been taught anything, but there was nothing she did not know by instinct . . . I can find no words in which to describe how *cold* and incomplete my own nature is. I can express nothing. There must be a sort of paralysis in my brain which prevents what I feel from ever finding a form through which it can achieve communication . . . When she appeared upon the stage, with her drooping figure, her listless gait, her sad and penetrating glance . . . I can say only that it was *as though I were looking at an embodied spirit. . . .*[1]

Marie Dorval was the natural child of two strolling players. She had been brought up in a world of violent and sordid passions. When she lost control of herself she could bawl like a fishwife. In real life she had seen everything, said everything, done everything. On the stage she produced an impression of sublimity, vibrant, inspired, and brimming over with vitality. There was something in her of the devil, something of an unrepentant Magdalene. Allan Dorval, her actor husband, had died when she was twenty-two years old, and she was left a widow with three daughters. In 1829 she had married Jean-Toussaint Merle, the Director of the Porte-Saint-Martin Theatre, and the sort of man who, after marriage, was willing to keep his eyes conveniently closed. In 1831, Alfred de Vigny began to pay her assiduous attentions. They made a strange couple: the Comte de Vigny, a Knight of Malta, a haughty dreamer, and the

[1] GEORGE SAND: *Questions d'Art et de Littérature*, pp. 62-3.

cynical, passionate Marie Dorval. Sainte-Beuve reproached
Vigny with playing the part of a 'remote, unneighboured
obelisk'. Dorval was fond of mixing with her fellow
mortals. She was easy to get on with. But the mask of
austere stoicism concealed a sensualist. Vigny in love
thought of himself as one who was raising a fallen angel.
What more adorable in the whole world than an actress in
her dressing-room 'trying to spread the wings of her soul'?
Their relationship resolved itself into an exchange of
mystical thoughts and wild caresses. To Dumas she said
with a laugh: 'I am learning wisdom: I have put on a new
virginity . . . When, I wonder, will the Count's parents ask
my hand for their son?' At first, Vigny regretted nothing,
not even his remorse: 'We are two persons at the heart of a
single devouring flame.'

Almost immediately, Dorval invited the Sandeau-Sand
couple to dine at her house in the company of her husband
and Vigny. George appeared in close-fitting trousers and
tasselled high-boots. Vigny was shocked. 'She would seem
to be about twenty-five. Her appearance is that of the
famous *Judith* in the Gallery. Her black and curling hair
falls over her collar in the manner of one of Raphael's
angels. Her eyes are large and dark, their shape such as is to
be found in mystics and in the most magnificent Italian
faces. Her features are severe and impassive. The chin is
less pleasing, the mouth badly formed. There is an absence
of elegance in her bearing, and her speech is harsh. She
looks and talks like a man, and has the voice and
forthrightness of one . . .'[1] Sand's view of him was more
balanced. 'I don't at all like Monsieur de Vigny's *person*,
but I can assure you that when our minds meet, I feel quite
differently.' Intimacy grew rapidly between the two women.

George Sand to Marie Dorval: Do you really think you
can endure me? That is something you cannot know yet,
nor I, I am such a bear, so stupid, so slow to put my
thoughts into words, so awkward and so dumb just when
my heart is fullest. Do not judge me by externals. Wait a
little before deciding how much pity and affection you
can give me. I feel that I love you with a heart
rejuvenated and altogether renewed by you. If that is just
a dream, like everything I have ever wanted in life, do not

[1] ALFRED DE VIGNY: *Journal d'un Poète*, January 21st.
1832.

wake me from it too soon. It does me so much good.
Goodbye, you great and lovely person. Whatever happens, I shall see you this evening.[1]

To Madame Dudevant, still a little provincial bourgeoise,
in spite of her raid into Bohemia, the brilliant Marie
revealed a world of pleasures. Vigny was worried: Vigny
smelled danger. 'I cannot, as yet, altogether *place* this
woman. From time to time she goes into the country to see
her husband, though in Paris she lives with her lover . . .
Her relationship with Jules Sandeau and Latouche is one of
free and easy comradeship. . . .'[2]

The Paris of the literary côteries was a very small town.
As formerly at La Châtre, so now in the capital, the
accepted opinion among respectable folk was that Aurore
had three lovers—Sandeau, Latouche and Planche. Sandeau, who was aware of this, grew jealous. He knew, only
too well, that he had never overcome the essential coldness
of his mistress, and if, at times, he sought elsewhere a few
brief and short-lived consolations, he reflected bitterly that
she, too, was probably doing likewise. But he could not
break with her.

IV

LOOSENED BONDS

NOHANT, SUMMER 1832. After a few months of
independence back she went to the scenes of childhood,
with the nimbus of celebrity about her. The event had
outstripped her most ambitious dreams—yet life was as dust
and ashes in her mouth. In vain did she explore the ways
that she had loved so well. 'All has turned ugly. Where are
the days of youth and green fields and poetry, those days
that gave life to this river, this valley, and these pretty
fields? . . .' Only the little stream had still retained its old
delicious smell of mint and aromatic herbs. 'It is like a heart

[1] Unpublished letter. Spoelberch de Lovenjoul Collection:
Group E. 881, *bis*. f. 2.
[2] ALFRED DE VIGNY: *Journal d'un Poète*, February 1832.

untouched by storms and the ruination of time . . .' She
looked for the tree on which Sandeau had cut their names.
Casimir had had it pollarded. 'How happy I was, how
young we were, in those days!—and Oh, how empty now
this country seems! Nothing stays . . . happiness goes,
places change and the heart grows older.'

The sad truth was that she was growing tired of a lover
who gave her neither sensual satisfaction nor the joy that
comes with admiration. 'Separated from him, she was
conscious of a feeling of relief—and was appalled.' Sandeau
paid no visit to La Châtre that year . . . His father had been
appointed to Parthenay. Aurore sent him no summons. To
other men she was writing letters so tender that it is
impossible to be sure whether the feelings they expressed
were those of love or friendship: 'Good night, beloved . . .
soon, my dear, I shall be in your arms . . . All myself is in
the kiss I send you . . .' It was the typical Madame
Dudevant style, and, in itself, proved nothing. But Jules was
fearful, and sought to reassure himself:

Sandeau to Papet. Parthenay, August 4th, 1832: I sent
you a letter from Saumur, begging you to write to me
often. I implore you again, on my knees, to do so. I want
you to tell me about Aurore, about her daughter . . .
Dear friend, this year I shall not disturb your sleep, or
force you to unbolt your door so that I may carry you
off—you, who have never been the slave of passion, nor
the victim of love—to scour the roads and cross the
furrowed fields, and then lie hidden in a ditch at Nohant,
and hear the church-clock at La Châtre sound the hours
of darkness. Sleep sound . . . but sometimes give a thought
to those mad night escapades, as I would wish to do, and,
remembering them, love you the more. See Aurore; see
her often. You ask me to commend you to her
friendship—why, you must be mad! Do you not know
how fond she is of you? Are we not all your friends? If
you see her, speak of me. Tell her to live happy and at
peace: recommend to her sleep and a calm mind. Tell her
that I love her, and have no life that is not hers. . . .[1]

---

[1] This letter is now the property of Monsieur Joseph Pierre,
who quotes it in an article—'Jules Sandeau en Berry'—which
appeared in the July/August number of *La Revue du Berry et
du Centre*, 1933.

Aurore had lost her faith in this love of his. But what man was there who would not have disappointed her? For her, the ideal lover must be both God and tyrant, yet she had chosen one who was weak and human, because she must at all costs dominate him. She was a man in her insistence on freedom, but a woman, too, craving the shelter of a 'home' with her children about her. She had longed to leave Nohant and live a life of independence, and then, deprived of house and household cares, had found that passion reduced to the bare bones of her solitary ardours could never bring a lasting satisfaction. Sandeau, a young man without experience, loved badly because he loved too well. He did not know that 'a woman's pride has nothing but contempt for the lover who is foolish enough to sacrifice his own life upon the altar raised to the beloved'. All the same, Aurore had no wish to break their relationship. After so brilliant a beginning, her happiness had dwindled into a mere matter of self-love. Nevertheless, she could look on her own stubbornness with disillusioned eyes. When she made up her mind to go back to Paris, she wrote to Gustave Papet: 'I take the road with fever in my blood but despair in my heart—but you must not let yourself become involved in all that . . . I am going to see Jules. If we cannot find a way to come to terms unaided, we are beyond all help that others can give. . . .'

In the month of October 1832 she resumed her life with Sandeau. There was a reconciliation, clinched by an exchange of rings—but it did not last for long. Boredom came between them. Jules was dragging out an aimless existence—'squandering his unhappiness as he had once squandered his joy'. His idleness got on the nerves of his industrious mistress. 'This life of artists and bohemians which once had so much attracted her, these alternations of success and failure, of wealth and poverty, which at first she had found so poetic, seemed to her now to be no more than a rather stupidly vulgar eccentricity, or, at best, a form of childishness.' Among their best friends there were some who judged George harshly. For them, the young couple had been the very incarnation of romantic love, and, as such, they had adored them. They resented the fact that their heroine should have shown herself to be vulnerable. Stronger and stronger grew the rumour which linked her name with both Latouche and Planche. Balzac believed it to be true. Sainte-Beuve insisted that it was. Sand denied it, but Emile Regnault, an intimate friend, blamed her 'insatiable coquetry'. She, on her side, had reason to complain of Jules. Using her work as an excuse, she had insisted on their no longer living tobether under the same roof, and had taken for him a small apartment at 7 rue de l'Université. She accused him of entertaining women there. During the summer of 1832 she made the following entry in her *Journal intime*. 'Were it anybody else, I could slip into a lazy routine of habit, could be forgiving in a lukewarm way, but with *us,* if the wound strikes deep there can be no turning back into the past. . . .'[1]

Should it turn out that her lover was not the God she had hoped he would be, then he was nothing but an idol which must be toppled from its pedestal.

From day to day the air about them thickened. 'At first there were scenes which started no one knew how, and ended in crying and kissing, tiny storms which, when tears ensue, are for love what showers are for the earth in summer heats. But very soon their nature changed. Words streaked through the air and struck like lightning. . . .'[2]

Aurore, ordinarily so hard to rouse, was capable, in moments of crisis, of sudden angers and violent outbursts. Till now she had regarded it as a point of honour not to part from Sandeau. But once her decision was taken, as it was at the beginning of 1833, she made the break complete, as a man would have done.

It was she who disposed of Jules's apartment, who got him a passport, who reserved him a seat in the coach for Italy, who lent him money for the journey. Later, he recounted this strange rupture to Paul de Musset, who was guilty of a breach of confidence in using the story for his own purposes. Aurore, if we are to believe him, said to Jules: 'You must go away', and promised to visit him, dressed as a man, to say goodbye. She was as good as her word, and appeared in a long grey coat and pleated trousers, walking with a firm step. 'Now we are going to do your packing together.'[3] As a matter of strict fact, Sandeau did not leave at once. It was only on June 1st, 1833, that Balzac wrote to 'l'Etrangère'—'Sandeau has just started for Italy. He was in despair. I really thought him mad.'[4] Little Jules

1 GEORGE SAND: *Journal intime,* p. 129.

2 JULES SANDEAU: *Marianna,* pp. 185-7.

3 PAUL DE MUSSET: *Lui et Elle,* p. 12.

4 HONORE DE BALZAC: *Lettres à l'Etrangère.* Volume I, p. 26.

had, in fact, swallowed some acetate of morphine, but the
dose was too large and he was sick. It was he, really, who
had been the woman in the case, she the man. Their friends
were severe in their opinion of her behaviour, but nothing
in human relationships is ever simple. She had acted
ruthlessly in order to put an end to an attachment which
had become a burden too heavy to be borne. She could not,
however, help being sorry for her victim. While the breach
was widening, she had sent Regnault to see Sandeau:

Please look up Jules and do what you can so far as his
bodily health is concerned. His heart is broken and
beyond help. You can do nothing for it, so do not try. I
need no attention: in fact I would rather be left alone.
Life no longer holds anything for me. Do what you can
to bring Jules back to life. He will suffer terribly for a
long time to come, but he is very young. One day,
perhaps, he will cease to regret that he has lived . . . Do
not, I beg, abandon him. I certainly shall not. I am going
to see him today, and shall do so every day. Persuade him
not to give up working, not to add deliberate penury to
his other miseries. He will never have any right to keep
me from being a mother to him . . . Go and see him, my
friend, go and see him. . . .[1]

The chain once broken, she grew calmer, and once again
became the woman of action she had always been.

George Sand to Emile Regnault: June 15th, 1833: I have
just written to Monsieur Desgranges to give notice for
Jules's apartment. I am asking him to let me have a
receipt for the last two rent payments, which I intend to
settle. The lease will then stand in my name until January
1834 . . . I am taking possession of my few pieces of
furniture, and will make a bundle of such of Jules's
clothing as he has left in the cupboards. This I will have
sent to you, since I wish to have no meeting, no contact
of any kind, with him after his return which, from what
he says in the letter you showed me, may not be long
delayed. I have been too deeply hurt by what I have
discovered about his behaviour to feel anything for him
beyond compassionate affection. That, his pride will

[1] Lettre XLVIII de George Sand à Emile Regnault. Bibliothèque nationale.

prevent him—or so I hope—from accepting. Please make
it quite clear to him—if it should be necessary to do so—
that nothing can again bring us together. Should this
hard commission *not* be necessary, that is to say, should
Jules understand—without being told—that that is how
things are, then I should like him to be spared the
unhappiness of learning that he has lost everything—
including my esteem. I have no doubt that he has lost his
own. He has been punished enough. I do not like telling
you all this, and hope, dear friend, that you are a little
sorry I should have to. Oh, why was it not you I fell in
love with? If I had, I should have been spared the
shedding of many bitter tears. But never again shall I
make the same sort of mistake . . . In the future nothing
shall ever again come between me and sensible, uncomplicated friendship. . . .[1]

But something always does come between sensible
friendship and a pretty woman. The breach with Sandeau
was not the only one which darkened that year of 1833 for
Sand . . . Latouche, bitter, over-sensitive, and a jealous
master (like old Porpora in *Consuelo*) could not, when he
had 'watched over the growth and emergence of a talent'
bear to see the eagle feel its own wings. He had once been
Balzac's patron, but had recently broken with him. To
'l'Etrangère' Balzac wrote: 'Latouche is envious, full of
hatred and all uncharitableness; a storehouse of venom'—
and composed the only epitaph which, said he, that proud
spirit would have accepted: *'To Henri Latouche—From the
Nineteenth Century—in Gratitude.'* The two men were no
longer on speaking-terms, and Latouche had gone so far as
to upbraid Sand for continuing to see Balzac, who, in
return, said to George: 'Look out! you'll find that Latouche
has become your mortal enemy—and not know why!'

Latouche wrote an article on *Literary Friendships,* aimed
at the Romantic côterie. Planche replied with another,
entitled *Literary Hatreds.* This was the last straw. Latouche
was bitterly offended. 'I have just, as a writer, been exposed
to an attack from a number of disgruntled critics . . . The
man primarily responsible for these insults is, not to put too
fine a point upon the matter, the boon companion of
Madame Dudevant . . .' Officious friends did not scruple to
inform Aurore that Latouche spoke of her now only in

[1] Ibid., Lettre L

terms of execration: 'Success has gone to her head. She sacrifices her true friends and is impatient to all advice . . .'[1] The same kindly persons hurried back to Aulnay, eager to recount what George Sand had said. 'I recognize the true Madame Dudevant in that,' was his comment; 'she is eager to swell and make known the list of my evil-wishers, and so, the more safely, to become their leader. But I had rather suffer outrage at the hands of those to whom I have striven to be useful than ever myself to show ingratitude.' He sent word that she was never again to go to Aulnay. She realized that a breach had opened between her and the first of her masters. The knowledge made her very unhappy.

With Balzac she had, so far, been on the best of terms. She admired him, found him amusing and brilliant, and loved to listen to his enthusiastic description of the books he meant to write. But Balzac had taken a liking to Sandeau, and, when the rupture came, was not slow to make his choice.

Balzac to Madame Hanska, end of March 1833: Jules Sandeau is a young man, George Sand is a woman. I took an interest in both of them, because I found it magnificent that a woman should give up everything in order to go with a poor young fellow whom she loved. This woman, whose real name is Madame Dudevant, has uncommon gifts . . . I was fond of this pair of love-birds living proud and happy on the top floor of a house on the Quai Saint-Michel. *Madame Dudevant had her children with her*—that is a point to be noted. Then success came and left a load of trouble on the doorstep of the dovecote. Madame Dudevant made out that it was her duty to leave him on account of the children, but the real reason for their separation is, I truly believe, that George Sand, or Madame Dudevant, has formed a new attachment for the most malevolent of all our contemporaries —Henri de Latouche, a former friend of mine, one of the most attractive men you could hope to meet, but hatefully rancorous and spiteful. Even if I had no other proof of this than the way in which Madame Dudevant has taken to cold-shouldering me, though in the old days I was glad to entertain both her and Jules Sandeau in the friendliest fashion, it would be enough. She has spread a number of epigrams to the detriment of her former host, and

[1] CHARLES DUVERNET: unpublished *Mémoires*.

yesterday I met Sandeau in a condition of complete
despair. So much for the author of *Valentine* and *Indiana*.
. . .[1]

All this was pure fiction, and very far removed from the
truth. But what, after all, was to be expected of Balzac save
imagination and generosity? When, a few months later,
Sandeau returned from Italy, Balzac was deeply affected.
Little Jules paraded his bleeding heart, and Balzac, acting
upon a kindly impulse, offered to give him a home and to
keep him until such time as he should have made a success
in the theatre. 'The poor battered wreck, so full of warm
affection, must be salvaged, and then piloted upon the
ocean depths of literature . . .'[2] In point of fact, though the
abandoned lover had not yet forgotten the past, he was
already over the first bitter pangs.

Jules Sandeau to Emile Paultre: I have stripped my
sorrows of the ridiculous importance which I attached to
them at the moment of my departure. I have realized at
last that the Harmony of the Universe has not been
disturbed, that the world goes on its way no worse, that
the movement of the stars has not been halted for one
single movement. My misery by becoming less solemn has
become less powerful. I see it now as something trivial
and vulgar. I realize now the true value of a solitary and
ruffled heart . . . and I tell myself that in great
unhappiness even more than in great good fortune there
is more than a little pride, and a deal of vanity. There is
something fatuous in grief that makes one drunk. It
makes us think of ourselves as the centre of everything.
We like to think that no one has ever suffered as we do
what, in fact, all have suffered before us. We look upon
ourselves as the accurst of Destiny, as Fallen Angels
condemned to suffering—and I know not what else—
blood brothers of the *Giaour* and of *Lara* . . . when,
Heaven knows, we are just men deceived in love—of
whom the world is full. . . .[3]

[1] BALZAC: *Lettres à l'Etrangère.* Volume I, pp. 19-20.

[2] Ibid., Volume I, p. 194.

[3] Unpublished. Spoelberch de Lovenjoul Collection: Group
E. 1031 ,f. 179.

In two years he had changed amazingly. Premature baldness was beginning to take toll of his curly, golden locks. His eyes looked more deeply sunken and more expressive. He had suffered, and called down curses on Aurore's head, but from that suffering his own small talent was born. A day would come when Sandeau would turn his experience into material for a novel, *Marianna,* a work not without something of truth in it. There he set down an objective portrait of his first, his unforgettable mistress.

The silence of the countryside, a life spent in study, dreams, and reading, had developed in Marianna more of strength of mind than tenderness, more of imagination than of heart, more of curiosity than of genuine sensibility. Till then, she had lived only in a world of fantasies. In her lonely walks beside the Creuse, on the hillsides and by the leafy hedgerows, she had indulged in visions of an heroic future which was to be all compact of devotion, sublimity and sacrifice. She had fed her imagination on ardours and endurances, on ill-starred love and tormented ecstasies. Long before she had tasted any of these emotions in fact, she had, in fancy, sucked them dry.[1]

Not other was the judgment which George herself, sad and clear-headed, passed on her own case.

V

NEW FRIENDS — LELIA

THE PASSAGE of time and the accidents of life wash ceaselessly about our feet many strangers, some of whom, thus wrecked upon the coast of our own lives, remain there. New deposits of friendship take the place of those sucked backward by the ebb. George had lost her first adviser, Latouche, and now it was the turn of Sainte-Beuve to be, for a while, her confidant.

[1] JULES SANDEAU: *Marianna,* p. 64.

He was, at that time, a young critic (like Sand, he was twenty-nine in 1833), who had already made a reputation by the acuteness of his literary judgements. 'His full, shrewd, clean-shaven face' had no claim to good looks. The impression he made was that of a man who was concupiscent, affectionate and spiteful. 'His spirit seemed to have put forth the white and sickly foliage of a waterlogged poplar.' A prey to every wind that blew, he had sought an anchorage in Hugo's household, until, in love with Adèle, he had grown to entertain feelings of hatred for Victor. In the secrecy of his heart and his notebooks he had mocked at the puerile and titanic poet, deriding his 'crude and obvious' sallies and his plays: 'Puppet-shows for Cyclops' isle'—and described him as a 'Caliban posing as Shakespeare'. Sainte-Beuve, the commentator, regretted, quite wrongly, his failure to create—as though the highest form of criticism is not creative. 'A doorkeeper in the Temple of Cnidos', he loved to lay his finger on women's secret thoughts. He wormed his way into their homes, acted as their confessor, gave them advice, and raised indiscretion to the level of genius. In conversation he shone fitfully, like some iridescent fly. 'He seems to hide his intelligence behind the banality of his words, but at each flutter of the wing a flash betrays it. . . .'[1]

Ever since the publication of *Indiana,* Sainte-Beuve had been loud in his praises of its mysterious and brilliant author. She was aware of this, and, on the first night of *Lucrèce Borgia,* had written to him asking for two seats for herself and Sandeau. 'You are the friend of Victor Hugo, and we, my pseudonym and I, are his fervent admirers . . . If I seem importunate, tell me so, but come and tell it me in person . . .'[2] He sent the seats. But she was insistent that he visit her. 'You must come whenever it is convenient to you. I shall always be at home when you call . . . Whatever happens, you must not hate me, for I much desire your friendship. You may think it ridiculous that I should tell you so, but when one feels oneself to be right one should never be put off by the fear of being misunderstood. . . .'[3]

[1] Letter from Henri Lehmann (June 18th, 1839) to Marie d'Agoult published in *Une Correspondance Romantique*, p. 30.

[2] GEORGE SAND: *Lettres à Alfred de Musset et à Sainte-Beuve*, p. 99.

[3] GEORGE SAND: *Lettres à Alfred de Musset et à Sainte-Beuve*, p. 100.

She was a fine catch for this fancier of female confidences. For George, Sainte-Beuve soon became a valued counsellor in matters literary and sentimental. When the storm and tumult of the Sandeau separation arose and echoed, he sat back comfortably and watched the pleasing spectacle. More than once he dined as her guest at the Quai Malaquais, in the company of the charming and cynical Hortense Allart—at that time Chateaubriand's mistress —from whom he obtained many precious details about the old age of René. On one occasion Hortense brought with her a young, but silver-haired, Genevese—Charles Didier, who had once been her lover in Florence. Every woman is interested in the men who have been her friends' lovers, and George examined Didier with an eye that was at once curious and predisposed in his favour. He was good-looking, with somewhat chilly manners—which he owed to his Protestant upbringing—but virile, and much attracted to women. At this, his first, meeting with Madame Dudevant, he was not impressed. 'Rather dry and unforthcoming,' he wrote: 'She has a remarkable face, but is, I should say, incapable of passion.'

The sensual have a sure instinct. In spite of appearances the young man from Geneva was not wrong. The novel of which, at that time, George was in labour during a period of great unhappiness, and of which she had read a part to Sainte-Beuve, *Lélia*, is little more than a long avowal of physical impotence. As a book it is spoiled by exaggerated characterization, but as a frank confession it is of captial importance. It should be read, not in the standard edition which was expurgated by its author when she came to regret the extent to which she had given herself away, but in the original version of 1833. In this she had found a melancholy relief from unhappiness in describing her disappointments in love, and analysing their causes.

Lélia is a woman who denies love. She is beautiful, she is fine, but she is as cold as a statue. 'How shall I free myself from this marble envelope', she says, 'which grips me round the knees, and holds me as totally imprisoned as a corpse by its tomb?'[1] Stenio, the young poet, loves her passionately, but strives in vain to move her. 'Lélia', he says, 'is not a complete human being. What is she then?—a shadow, a

[1] GEORGE SAND: *Lélia* (original edition, 1833). Volume 1, p. 292.

dream, at best an idea. Where love is absent there can be no woman.'[1]

Lélia's romantic confidant, Trenmor, a man of the world and an ex-convict, begs her to let Stenio live, and not to blow with her icy breath upon one who is little more than a boy, and so destroy his happiness. But Lélia cannot summon up the courage to renounce him. 'I love to fondle you', she says to Stenio, 'and gaze at you as though you were my child . . .'[2] That is the disturbing and discordant theme—the theme of the maternal woman in love. It was to reappear more than once in the course of Sand's life. But it is not as a mother that Lélia longs to love, but as the courtesan, Pulchéria, her own sister, who stands in the novel for the type of sensual passion. She tries to do so, and suffers a terrible disappointment.

> My senses had been weakened by a long course of austere and mystical contemplation, my blood wearied by the immobility of study. I had forgotten how to be young, and Nature had forgotten to awaken me. My dreams had moved too much in the world of sublimity, and I could no longer descend to the grosser level of fleshly appetites. A complete divorce had come about, though I did not realize it, between body and spirit. . . .[3]

Then begins for Lélia a life of what she calls 'sacrifice and abnegation', because she consents to give the pleasure which she cannot not share. Here are the passages essential to an understanding of Sand.

> What led to my loving him for so long . . . was a feverish irritation which took possession of my faculties as a result of never achieving personal satisfaction. When I was with him I was seized with a strange, delirious hunger which no embrace could satisfy. I felt as though burned up by an unextinguishable flame, but his kisses brought me no relief. I crushed him in my arms with superhuman strength, only to collapse beside him, exhausted, hopeless. Desire, in my case, was an ardour of the spirit which paralysed the power of the senses even

[1] Ibid. Volume 1, pp. 104-5.
[2] GEORGE SAND: *Lélia* (original edition, 1833). Volume I, p. 207.
[3] Ibid., Volume II, pp. 9-10.

before they had been awakened, a savage ecstasy which took possession of my brain, and became exclusively concentrated there. My blood remained frozen, impotent, and poor, while my will took flight into remote immensities. . . .[1]

When he was fulfilled, satisfied and sated, I lay there motionless beside him, a victim of appalled dismay. I spent hours like that, watching him while he slept. He looked so beautiful . . . The agitated beating of my blood sent the colour to my face. An unendurable trembling took possession of my limbs. It seemed to me that I could feel the agitations of physical passion, the mounting imperative of bodily desire. I was violently tempted to awaken him, to hold him in my arms, to demand a renewal of those caresses from which I had as yet drawn no satisfaction . . . I fought against these lying urgencies of my suffering, knowing full well that it was not in his power to calm them. . . .[2]

Sometimes in sleep, a prey to the voluptuous ecstasies which feed upon ascetic minds, I felt as though swept towards him. Then I would swim on tides of inexpressible delight, clasping my nerveless arms about his neck, and fall upon his breast, murmuring vague words. He woke, and all my happiness was ended. I found myself again at grips with a brutal and voracious man, a man who had become like a wild beast, and I fled from him in horror. But he forced himself upon me, insisting that not in vain had he been roused from sleep, and took his bestial pleasure of a woman who had become well-nigh senseless and half dead.[3]

My senses, far from being impoverished, had been renewed. The splendours and the scents of Spring, the stimulus of warm sun and fresh air . . . threw me into fresh torments. I felt the prickings of a new restlessness, of vague and impotent desires. It seemed to me that I could love, and this time, and for ever, feel. A second youth, more vigorous, more feverish than the first, set my heart racing. In these recurrent and alternating moods of

---

[1] Ibid. Volume II, pp. 25-6.

[2] Ibid., Volume II, pp. 26-7.

[3] GEORGE SAND: *Lélia* (original edition, 1833). Volume II, p. 28.

desire and fear, no sooner was my strength renewed than I consumed it . . . I dreamed of the embraces of some unknown demon lover, was conscious of his hot breath upon my body, could dig my nails into his body, could feel the fierce sharpness of his teeth, I craved pleasure even at the cost of eternal damnation . . . But when daylight came it found me broken with fatigue and paler than the dawn . . . I tried to find relief in uttering cries of pain and anger. . . .[1]

Exhausted by a fall, the more headlong because her imagination has raised her hopes too high, Lélia ceases to have any feelings for her first lover. But how to share in a pleasure which she has never known, though it is so easily enjoyed by other women, the pleasure of physical passion, becomes the one subject of her thoughts, the sole controlling influence of her life, the one and only goal of her desires.

Having let my longings float away towards the land of dreams, I ended by following them in fancy, seizing them on the wing and imperiously demanding of them, if not happiness at least the ephemeral emotion of a few days . . . Since this unseen life of licence could not shock . . . I gave myself to it without remorse. In imagination I was unfaithful, not only to the man I loved but, each morning, to the one whom I had loved the day before. . . .[2]

Don Juan went from woman to woman because not one of the Thousand and Three could give him happiness. Lélia goes from man to man because none of them give her pleasure. The drama is, transformed into feminine terms, the drama of Don Juan Tenorio. The novel proves that a light had dawned in its author's mind, and that George, nearing her thirtieth year, could bring a lucid analysis to bear upon herself. On the day following the reading, Sainte-Beuve wrote to her:

Sainte-Beuve to George Sand: March 10th, 1833: Madame, I cannot wait longer to tell you how much yesterday evening, and what I then heard, has set me

[1] Ibid. Volume II, pp. 44-6.
[2] Ibid. Volume II, p. 83.

thinking, to what a degree Lélia has haunted my mind, and how greatly it has increased the very real feelings of admiration and friendship which I have for you . . . The general public which asks at the Library for 'any sort of a novel' will baulk at it, but it will raise you high in the estimation of those who see in fiction only a more vivid form of the eternal verities of the human mind . . . To be a woman, to be less than thirty, to have plumbed such depths and yet to show no outward sign of the adventure, to be able to endure the knowledge that you have— knowledge which would seam *our* brows, and turn *our* hair white—with ease and lightness, and to write of it in measured terms—*that* is what I most admire . . . Yours, Madame, is a rare and powerful temperament. . . .[1]

She replied next day. Her letter sounds a note of embarrassment, because she realized how monstrous and morbid she might appear to keen-sighted readers, who would identify her with Lélia.

George Sand to Sainte-Beuve: March 11th, 1833: After listening to *Lélia*, you said something which has caused me pain. You said that you felt afraid of me. Please do not confuse the author with the sufferings she has recorded. What you heard was the tale of those sufferings, and nothing more . . . You still cling to your faith, and often pray. Make my peace with God and do not attach too much importance to my Satanic posturings. I swear to you that they are no more than a literary attitude deliberately adopted . . . You are nearer in nature to the angels. Stretch out a friendly hand to me, and do not leave me with the Devil. . . .[2]

This letter proves two things: that she knew little of Sainte-Beuve, and that men are better hands than women at assuming the mask of virtue.

In every woman who is in love with love there is, unknown to herself, something of the bawd. Sainte-Beuve had a feminine side to his nature which led him to be 'accommodating' in matters of sex. Living alone in Paris,

---

[1] SAINTE-BEUVE: *Correspondance générale*. Volume I, p. 347.
[2] GEORGE SAND: *Lettres à Alfred de Musset et à Sainte-Beuve*, pp. 102-3.

and without ties, George Sand could not for long be a woman without a man. But it was no easy task to find a lover capable of satisfying a Lélia. Sainte-Beuve conceived the strange idea of posing the candidature of one of his friends, the philosopher, Théodore Jouffroy. This blue-eyed, slow, and serious-minded man from the Jura had a kindly but austere appearance. 'His tall figure, his simple, honest ways, combined with a certain roughness which he had never succeeded in shedding, marked him out as the very type of a mountain race. It was clear that in matters of love he was, as yet, entirely unawakened, and that he was proud of his backwardness. His friends had nicknamed him *'The Sicambrian . . .'*[1] Jouffroy had presented to the Sorbonne a thesis on 'The Beautiful and the Sublime' which had attracted a considerable amount of attention. He shared with Madame Dudevant a taste for lofty poetry of the pastoral and natural kind, but it was nothing short of madness to couple him with Lélia. She would have made a single mouthful of him. Nevertheless George, who regarded Sainte-Beuve as her Director of Conscience, replied with seeming humility to his offer of an introduction:

George Sand to Sainte-Beuve: April 1833: Dear friend: since it is you who send me Monsieur Jouffroy, I will receive him. Little disposed though I am to surround myself with new faces, I will overcome the immediate promptings of my boorishness, and have no doubt that I shall find in the individual whom you recommend so warmly to my notice every quality deserving of esteem. Please warn him against my dry, cold manner, my insurmountable laziness, and the shameful ignorance which keeps me for the most part silent, for I should not like him to interpret as impertinence what is in me a habit, a failing, but not deliberate ill-will. Monsieur Jouffroy's face tells me that he may be found to have an exquisite nature and a polished intelligence, but it may be that I shall note his possession of these qualities (all too rare, and worthy of the greatest respect) without any accompanying sense of admiration. There are men who come into this world fully formed, and who do not have to struggle with the shoals upon which others are cast up bruised and bleeding. They sail over them without so much as realizing that they are there, and feel astonished

[1] SAINTE-BEUVE: *Portraits littéraires.* Volume I, p. 306.

at the sight of so much wreckage floating around them. I am rather frightened of these men who are born virtuous. . . .[1]

At the last moment, in a sudden access of common sense, she countermanded the appointment.

But she remained in a condition of melancholy, the prisoner of a hard and mocking wretchedness. 'Go on with *Lélia*,' wrote Sainte-Beuve, 'but make of it a thing of prose, of real, practical life. Do not despise the half-cure, the half-happiness, which is no small comfort to the heart when certain storms have been weathered . . . You must once again acquire a more just, a more tolerant, view of mankind and of the world in general . . . In this miserable world of ours, even the true saints go through many bad times. . . .'[2] She thanked him, saying that among the 'writing people'—the *écriveurs*, as Solange called them, she had found but one true friend—himself. But her real confidante during these terrible months, was Marie Dorval, whose mingling of the cynical and the natural, of greatness of soul and ardent passion, suited the chaotic state of her own mind. It seems probable that the duologues between Lélia and Pulchéria, the wise courtesan, are reports, taken over bodily into the book, of the talk that went on between George and Marie.

They were much together, meeting often in one another's apartment. George, always devoted to the theatre, never missed a play in which Dorval was appearing. Offers of, or requests for, seats form the main subject of most of their letters. But George always managed to slip in a few fond words.

I can't see you today, darling—no such luck! But on Monday, either in the morning or the evening, at the theatre or in your bedroom before you are up, I must come and give you a kiss. If I don't, I cannot guarantee that I may not do something mad! I am working like a galley-slave, and seeing you is my only form of relaxation. Goodbye, you loveliest of women. . . .[3]

[1] GEORGE SAND: *Lettres à Alfred de Musset et à Sainte-Beuve,* pp. 104-5.

[2] SAINTE-BEUVE: *Correspondance générale.* Volume I, pp. 361-2.

[3] Spoelberch de Lovenjoul Collection: Group E. 881, *bis.* f. 8.

February 1833: Marie, my sweet, when you came I was at Aulnay. How miserable it makes me to lose even one day in which I might have been with you! Tell me when you would like to come in for a good gossip, after midnight. Send me word, and I shall be waiting. You, my dear, have so much in your life, and I nothing—*except you.* I send you a thousand kisses. . . .[1]

Dorval's replies were shorter. No doubt, from a wish not to displease Vigny, she was keeping her friend on 'short commons'. This became a matter of complaint with George.

March 1833: Marie, why has such a long time gone by without our seeing one another? One reason, of course, is that I have been ill. You, I know, have been much occupied and could not come, for you have a good heart, and would have done so had you not been prevented. But it is terrible, Marie, to love you so much, and yet to have to pass so many days away from you! That makes me sad, Marie, and gloomier than usual. Would you condemn me because I need pity? . . . You are a great and noble soul, and the thought that I so little deserve your friendship terrifies me! I am so much afraid of losing what I have gained—and cannot help wondering whether there is some flaw in me which keeps you away. Is there? You are so far superior to all other women, Marie, that, even were I guilty, you would be tolerant and compassionate. I do not feel that I have been guilty, but, even if I had, you are sweet enough to love me still in spite of everything . . . When can we have another of our evenings, here, or with you? Your friend is sad, be good happiness. . . .[2]

George would have dearly liked to accompany Marie on tour at least once, if necessary in the çapacity of dresser. She found a strange delight in listening to Marie Dorval's passionate upbraidings of God and of men. 'She concealed nothing of herself, was entirely without artificiality or affectation. In her moments of complete abandonment she could speak with a rare eloquence which, though it was sometimes violent, was never trivial. There was a chaste

[1] Unpublished letter. Ibid. E. 881, *ter.* f. 2.
[2] Ibid. E. 881, ff. 5-6.

quality in even her crudest outbursts, and every word she spoke told of an ideal beyond her ability to attain, of private dreams of pure happiness, of some Heaven here on earth . . .'[1] In this woman who had seen so much more of life than she had ever done, she detected that craving for the absolute which had ever been her own obsession. Vigny was jealous of their passionate friendship. The poor man, in his simple-mindedness, feared the influence upon his mistress of this apostle of free love. *Sancta simplicitas!* The lovely and sublime Dorval, so madly indulgent of her senses, had nothing to learn of such matters from any woman.

Now it so happened that while the tormented Lélia was seeking consolation and revelation, she met a cynic who promised her both. Prosper Mérimée, Sainte-Beuve's great friend, was, like Henri Beyle, one of those men who, from youth up, had suffered from a species of sentimental frustration. He was of the race from which the Devil picks his Don Juans. He took especial pleasure in talking of love as a technician, with all the coarseness of a medical student. The habit had gained him some successes in the Green-Room at the Opera, and in a few boudoirs. Meeting this charming oddity of womankind, unattached, intelligent and famous, he set himself to add one more scalp to his collection. Early in 1833 he began to lay siege to her, but in vain. She promised to let him visit her, but, at the last moment, always made some excuse: either she was suffering from neuralgia, or her husband had unexpectedly turned up. He became ironical, and faintly bitter. 'I should be much obliged if you would tell me whether you are now recovered, and whether your husband sometimes goes out alone; in short, whether there is any chance of my seeing you without making a nuisance of myself. . . .'[2]

He conquered her reluctance—'for forty-eight hours, by the sheer effrontery with which, in defiance of public opinion, he showed himself to the eyes of all fashionable Paris, standing at the top of the great staircase of the Opera, carrying in his arms the child Solange, who had fallen asleep during the last Act of *Robert le Diable*'.[3] She found in him a man 'both calm and strong', who fascinated her by

[1] GEORGE SAND: *Histoire le ma Vie*. Volume IV, p. 208.

[2] PROSPER MERIMEE: *Correspondance générale*. Volume I, p. 229.

[3] MAURICE PARTURIER: *Une Expérience de Lélia; ou le Fiasco du Comte Gazul*, p. 12.

the display of a 'powerful intellect'. She told over, for his benefit, the beads in Lélia's rosary of woes. It made him laugh. One evening in April 1833, as they were walking together along the Quai Malaquais, beside the Seine, she offered him a 'loving friendship'. To this he replied that he could love 'only in one way' and that anything else was just poetical nonsense. It was an utterly false conception of love, but she was in that mood of extreme misery which will lead a woman to snatch at any straw. 'I believed'—she wrote to Sainte-Beuve—'that he had the secret of happiness and would make me a party to it . . . that his attitude of careless contempt would cure me of my childish susceptibilities.'

He managed at last to convince her that there might be a form of love which would not exacerbate her senses but might inflame her heart. She was only too anxious to be persuaded, and let herself be dazzled by the prestige that always attaches to technical skill. 'All right, then,' she said at last, 'I will consent. Have your wish, since you will find in the experience such a deal of pleasure, though I, you may rest assured, shall have none!'[1] They went back to her apartment where they ate a light supper, after which, with the help of her maid, she assumed her *negligée*, a confection reminiscent partly of Turkey, partly of Spain. Mérimée later declared that during this part of the proceedings she had been guilty of a lack of modesty which had had the effect of killing all desire in him. No doubt she did, in his presence, behave more brazenly than she felt. However that may be, the evening ended in a wretched and ridiculous fiasco. Don Juan, like his friend Stendhal on a similar occasion, failed utterly to come up to scratch. Much to his surprise, he found that he was dealing with a prude who, whether from ignorance or a feeling of self-respect, would do nothing to help him in his embarrassment. Deeply vexed, he attempted to pass the whole matter off with a flourish of bitter and superficial mockery. When he had left, she succumbed to a fit of tears provoked by strained nerves, disgust and despondency.

She told the whole story to Marie Dorval. It was her view that she was to be rather pitied than blamed. Dorval, though pledged to a not very probable secrecy, passed on the news to Dumas—that prince of babblers. It made the round of Paris. Dumas put the following witticism into

[1] MAURICE PARTURIER: *Une Expérience de Lélia; ou le Fiasco du Comte Gazul*, pp. 16-17.

Sand's mouth: 'I had Mérimée last night:—but it didn't amount to much . . .' Several kind friends hastened to assure George that Marie Dorval had betrayed her confidence. They were not well received.

You say she has betrayed me. I am well aware of that, but which of you, my dear friends, have not done as much? She has betrayed me once only, but you do it every day. She passed on something that I told her, but you, every one of you, have put into my mouth words I never uttered . . . Leave me the freedom to love her still. I know her, and what she is worth. I am familiar with her faults and with her vices . . . Who are you to talk? You are afraid of vice, yet eaten up by it. Perhaps you do not know that, or perhaps you shrink from the knowledge. Vice, indeed! Where are your eyes? Don't you know that it is with you at every moment of your lives, round you, within you? . . . [1]

Fourteen years later, re-reading her *Journal,* she confirmed this judgment.

1847: She is ever the same, and I love her still. Hers is a lovely nature, generous and kind. In intelligence she ranks with the greatest. Her life had been filled with wretchedness and loose ends, and for that, dear Marie Dorval, I love and respect you the more! . . .[2]

To Sainte-Beuve, that trained specialist in human frailty, whom the rumour had reached, she made a full and fair confession:

George Sand to Sainte-Beuve, July 8th, 1833: You have not asked me to tell secrets, nor, in saying what I am about to say, am I doing so, since I ask for no discretion on your part. I would willingly relate—and print—everything that has ever happened to me, if I thought that the relation would be of the slightest use to anybody else. To you, because your esteem is helpful and necessary to me, I am entitled to show myself in my true colours, even though you refuse to accept my confession . . . One day recently, when I was feeling bored and desperate, I met a man whose nature it is to be completely self-

1 GEORGE SAND: *Journal intime,* pp. 134-5.
2 GEORGE SAND: *Journal intime,* p. 135.

confident. He failed utterly to understand me, and merely
laughed at my troubles . . . One thing I had never realized
about myself, and that is that I am utterly and completely Lélia. I wanted to convince myself that that was
not so, and hoped I might be able to abjure the cold and
hateful role . . . There is within the circle of my friends
one woman who lives free from all constraint, and her
I regard as sublime. I see myself, on the other hand, as
austere, well-nigh virgin, and a prey to hideous egotism
and appalling loneliness. I have tried to overcome my
nature, to forget the mistakes of the past . . . I am tormented by that romantic restlessness, that form of
nervous exhaustion which turns one giddy, and has the
effect, when one had denied everything, of putting
everything once more in doubt, so that one ends by
committing errors far worse than those one has forsworn.
And so it was that, having convinced myself that long
years of intimacy could not bind me to another's life, I
imagined that the fascination of a few days could settle all
my problems. I behaved, at thirty, as no girl of fifteen ever
would have done . . . Cheer up! . . . I hate having to tell
the rest of the story, though why should I feel ashamed of
cutting a ridiculous figure since no blame attaches to me?
. . . The experiment failed completely. I wept from sheer
nervous exhaustion, disgust and despondency. Instead of
having come upon an affection which might have pitied
me and so made up for disappointment, I found myself
confronted by bitter, superficial mockery. That is the sum
total of all that happened. The incident has been 'potted'
in a phrase which I did not utter, which Madame Dorval
neither betrayed nor invented, and which does small
credit to Monsieur Dumas's powers of invention.[1]

She felt no remorse. She stated the facts without lying,
and without making any plea in self-defence. She had
hunted happiness in dangerous coverts, and had failed to
bring down her bird. This final contretemps had confirmed
all her fears. To have been able to be, like Dorval, a woman
of unbridled passions, would have meant for her a triumph
absolute. It would have opened the way to redemption. She

[1] This letter, which was published in the *Revue de Paris* of
November 15th, 1896, was not included in the volume *Lettres de
George Sand à Alfred de Musset et à Sainte-Beuve* issued in the
following year by Calmann-Lévy.

harboured no resentment—not even against Mérimée. 'Had Prosper Mérimée understood me, he might have loved me. If he had loved, he would have dominated me, and if I had found a man capable of dominating me, I should have been saved, for liberty is eating my life away, and killing me . . .' But, had she been able to bring herself to accept a man's domination, she would not have been George Sand.

VI

WHAT CONFUSION of mind and heart! Ten years earlier she had been a young woman filled with hope and good intentions. She had believed herself to be capable of *forming* the men who might love her, of leading them to make her high and mystical ideal of love their own. She had been Stenio—credulous, inexperienced, fearful of the future yet aflame with expectation. She had failed with Aurélien de Sèze, she had failed with Casimir Dudevant. The reason for these disasters she found in a badly organized social system, in the imprisoning effects of marriage. She had believed that by liberating themselves from petty prejudices and outworn laws, lovers could live the free lives of their dreams. But free love had proved itself to be as disappointing as love within the bonds of marriage.

Confined to the limits of her country world, at odds with small-town conventions, she had fed on fantasies of a world of art, polite manners, and eloquence. She had imagined that in Paris she would find the 'life of her choice, an agreeable, elegant and enlightened society, where gifted individuals would be received with acclamation, and find it possible to indulge in a free exchange of ideas and sentiments'. She did not know then that genius is always solitary, that there is no such thing as a moral hierarchy to be accepted without cavil by the élite. She had thought of every poetaster as a poet. Two years of hard experience had taught her that great men are seldom giants, 'that the world is strewn with brutes, that one cannot take a step without

rousing them to snarl and snap'. She had searched for
masters, and found only cautious hypocrites. She had
learned the dangers of frankness.

> Men do not wish to be shown for what they are, nor to be
> made to laugh at the masks they have assumed. If you are
> no longer capable of love, then you must lie, or draw a
> veil so close about you that no eye can penetrate it. You
> must treat your heart as ageing libertines treat their
> bodies—hide it beneath a disguise of paint and subter-
> fuge. You must conceal behind a wall of boasting and
> bluster the decay that has killed your faith: you must
> shut yourself away from the society that has made you
> impotent. Above all, you must never confess that your
> intelligence has aged, nor tell to anyone how old your
> thoughts have grown. . . .[1]

Weary, tormented, bleeding from her recent wounds, her
mind 'hovering between the horror of suicide and the
eternal peace of the cloister', she was, in this Summer of
1833, Lélia in very fact, a woman thirsting for love and
worthy to be loved, yet incapable of that humility without
which no love is possible. 'Léila,' she told herself through
the mouth of Stenio, 'your heart is as cold as the marble of
the tomb!' . . . and yet, . . .

And yet, deep in her heart she knew that the young girl of
the English Convent, the Amazon of Nohant ever ready to
give her help to the unhappy, eager to learn, pure-minded
and serious, was not dead. In Lélia there were some of the
characteristics of Manfred and of Lara. But Byron, even in
his diabolic attitudinizing, was still an impenitent calvinist,
a sentimental lover. When she was dining gaily with
Hortense Allart, when she was listening greedily to Marie
Dorval, George Sand ceased to be George Sand. For the
space of an evening she lived again the youth of Aurore
Dudevant, and knew her hopes once more. At those
moments her thoughts turned to the garden paths of
Nohant, to the star-spangled sky, to that solemn, lovely
silence so suited to familiar converse, to those Berrichon
friends on whose arms she would one day lean and tell them

---

[1] GEORGE SAND: *Sketches and Hints.* This extract by
Wladimir Karénine, in *George Sand.* Volume I, pp. 420-1. The
manuscript book from which it is taken, is in the Bibliothèque
nationale.

of the storms she had survived. And then, her guests departed, alone with the sleeping Solange in the apartment of the Quai Malaquais, the stormed-tossed heart knew that once again, in spite of shipwreck, it must still believe in love; in a love, perhaps, that is more than human.

PART FOUR

LOVE AND GENIUS

Women believe that all they dare is innocent.

Joubert

I

BORN OF THEIR CENTURY

WE HAVE just left a young woman sitting in a tiny apartment on the Quai Malaquais, disenchanted and desperate. She has failed in adultery, she has failed in marriage. Through the medium of a novel she has tried to express her feeling of revolt. But we should do wrong to think of her as lost in tears. She has too much life in her, and too much strength, to weep for long. She tells herself that she made the wrong choice, that somewhere there must exist that ideal lover who can respect her delicacy yet overcome her repugnance, and that when she has found him passion, the messenger of conscience, and so of God, will guide her. She would go on looking for him, letting her eye range over all the men of talent who surrounded her, summing them up like a Sultan inspecting odalisques in the privacy of his harem.

Sainte-Beuve in spite of his baby-face, in spite of his look of 'a Cherub prematurely turned churchman', might have found favour in her sight, and she would have been glad, after her fiasco with the Cynic, to cast her Father Confessor for the part of the Young Lead. But Sainte-Beuve, though at first assiduous in his attentions, had withdrawn. She would not understand his silence, and would have preferred 'a flare of temper to this attitude of haughty immobility'[1]. Had she, because of some appalling blemish, frightened his 'august dignity'? Was he avoiding her because he found her presence disagreeable? Had the despairs of Lélia disturbed

1 GEORGE SAND: *Lettres à Alfred de Musset et à Sainte-Beuve*, p. 116.

his youthful confidence in life? Or was he caught in the enchanted web of some jealous mistress who forbade him to see more of so dangerous a woman? 'If that is so, cannot you reassure her, cannot you say that I am three hundred years old, that I ceased to be a woman before even her own grandmother was born, and that a man is now no more to me than Jean de Werth? . . .'[1]

That was precisely what neither Adèle Hugo nor Sainte-Beuve himself believed. He had leaned above the depths which George's charm concealed, and started back in terror. This he explained to her less bluntly. He praised in her 'the man's loyalty that dwells within a woman's grace', but had to admit that friendship with her was difficult. Friendship between the sexes is possible only when the age of change and adventure is over. Both parties in such a relationship must have reached years of discretion, must be at ease with life, and he able to sit sunning themselves on a bench in the afternoon glow . . .'[2] Put briefly, what he wanted was to remain her *serious* friend—at a safe distance. There must be no intimacy. This she found sad and foolish. 'After all, dear friend, if I have ceased to please you, you are free . . . I will trouble you no longer. If you are happy, so much the better. I thank Heaven for it, and find it well that you should avoid me. . .'[3] But she was careful not to break with him. He was an influential critic, and she a woman without rancour, save in love—and of that there was no question.

Her other familiar critic, Gustave Planche, had become, since the publication of *Indiana,* a frequent visitor to the Quai Malaquais. Was he her lover? Paris said so, as Paris always does say. Casimir was convinced that he was. George vehemently denied it. Truth to tell, there always hung about Planche a faint suggestion of sweat and toil, and it would be difficult to imagine him as a tempting morsel. But he was powerful. She had made of him her faithful slave, and he had proudly accepted the role. She often sought him out in the squalid furnished room in the rue des Cordeliers where he lived, and entrusted him with strange missions. When Casimir came to Paris, it was

[1] Ibid., p. 118.

[2] SAINTE-BEUVE: *Correspondance générale.* Volume I, pp. 374-5.

[3] GEORGE SAND: *Lettres à Alfred de Musset et à Sainte-Beuve,* pp. 118-21.

Planche who had to take him to the theatre. When Solange
was ill, it was Planche who had to go for the doctor. It was
Planche who accompanied Maurice to the Lycée Henri
Quatre at the beginning of term, and Sand to Madame
Dorval's first nights. Gustave the Cruel had been completely
domesticated by little Madame Dudevant.

Marie Dorval was still, of all her friends, the best
beloved. But she could not play a very constant part in her
life. Vigny was doing everything in his power to detach his
mistress from what he called 'that monstrous woman'. Marie, always in need of money for her three daughters, found
it necessary to go on tour after tour. On these occasions the
faithful Planche was hastily sent round to Vigny's apartment, and told to drag an address out of him.

George Sand to Marie Dorval: Where are you? What has
become of you? . . . Why did you go off like that, you
wicked creature, without so much as saying goodbye, and
without giving me a programme of your movements, that
I might follow hard on your heels? Your leaving without
a word hurt me. I was in a villainous mood. I imagined
that you cared nothing about me. I cried my eyes out . . .
I am a fool, and you must forgive me. My character is
full of flaws, but my heart is yours: that I know full well.
In vain do I explore a world of others—no one, not a
soul, comes up to you. Nowhere can I find a nature so
frank, true, strong, supple, good, generous, great, odd,
excellent and, in a word, so complete as yours. I want to
love you always: to cry with you, to laugh with you. I
long to join you somewhere, to spend a few days in some
place where you are staying. Where must I go? Shall I be
a nuisance to you?—not that I shall care if I am. Tell me
where you are. I will try to be less grumpy than usual. If
you are sad, I will be sad, too. If you are gay, then long
live gaiety! Is there anything I can do for you? I would
bring you the whole of Paris, had I the money to buy it.
Send me a line and I will start at once. Should occasions
arise when I might be in the way, you can always pack
me off to work in another room. No matter where I am, I
can always find something to occupy my mind. I have
been told more than once to beware of you, and, no
doubt, you have been similarly warned against me. Oh
well, let the prattlers prattle . . . you and I are the only
people concerned. . . .

Answer soon. You need send only the single word 'come', and I shall set off at once—even if I have got the cholera—or a lover. . . .[1]

Marie Dorval showed this letter to Vigny, pretending, so that he might be reassured, to make fun of it. In the margin he wrote: 'I have forbidden Marie to answer this Lesbian who is for ever plaguing her'; and Dorval: 'Madame Sand annoyed that I did not answer.'[2] But George was too full of admiration for Marie to remain annoyed for long.

Though her heart was dormant, George went on as usual with her work. But life seemed to her to have lost all meaning. Early in the Spring of 1833, the *Revue des Deux Mondes* gave a great dinner to its regular contributors at Lointier's, 104 rue Richelieu.[3] The whole of the permanent staff was invited. Gustave Planche, the magazine's leading critic, took George Sand, and chance, or Buloz's love of mischief, so arranged matters that she found herself sitting next to Alfred de Musset. Earlier, in the days when Sainte-Beuve was trying to 'find somebody for her', he had spoken of introducing the young poet with the tumbled locks, the slim, golden-haired youth who was beautiful as a God. Musset at this time was twenty-three, six years younger than Sand and Sainte-Beuve. The reason, perhaps, why the latter admired him so wholeheartedly was that Musset was the visible expression of everything the older man would have liked to be. 'He was all Spring, a dazzling Spring of poetry', was how he described him: 'no one at first sight ever produced so vivid an impression of youthful genius . . .'[4] From Byron Musset had learned to be a dandy. Dressed in a frocked coat with a velvet collar rolled to his waist, with

[1] Letter printed by Henri Guillemin, and quoted by Françoise Moser, in *Marie Dorval*, pp. 94-5.

[2] FRANCOISE MOSER: *Marie Dorval*, p. 96.

[3] Every one of Musset's biographers, with the single exception of his brother Paul, and all George Sand's, state that this dinner was held on June 20th, at the *Frères Provençaux*. Marie-Louise Pailleron, however, Buloz's grand-daughter and heir, owned a notebook in which appear the words *Diner-Lointier*. The date is given as the end of March or at some time in the first fortnight of April.

[4] Sainte-Beuve, quoted by Paul Mariéton in *Une Histoire d'Amour*, p. 250.

an extremely high hat tilted over one ear, and sky-blue,
close-fitting trousers, he produced an impression of rather
exotic elegance. When Sainte-Beuve had suggested taking
him to see George Sand she had refused the offer: 'He is very
much the dandy: I feel sure that we should not get on
together.'[1]

It is easy to understand why she should have felt
frightened, for the literary world spoke much evil of
Musset. In 1830 he had made a dazzling *début,* and Buloz,
the Cénacle and the Salon de l'Arsenal had at once adopted
him. The lovely Muses of the Romantic Movement were
fond of repeating, in tones of passionate admiration, some
of his highly-coloured and new-fangled verses: *'Un dragon
jaune et bleu qui dormait dans du foin . . .'*—but the
ungrateful youth mocked at his fame and ridiculed his
colleagues. He imitated them, he caricatured them, he gave
them irreverent nicknames. He called Sainte-Beuve—so
generous with his praise—sometimes *Madame Pernelle,*
sometimes *Sainte-Bévue.* He was the spoiled darling of the
women, a cherub who had read *Les Liaisons Dangereuses*
and *Manfred.* He had known pleasure before love, and
found no happiness in it. Then, with a sort of simple-minded enthusiasm, he had given himself over to champagne,
opium and prostitutes. Like Byron, he had been fascinated
by debauchery—in which woman resumes her ancient role
of witch, and man breaks free from the tyranny of society. Deceived by his venal mistresses, he had been left with
bitter memories. 'For the women of our day,' he said, 'loving means to play at lying as children play at hide-and-
seek . . . a mean and dreary game.' But in Musset, side by
side with the libertine who had become prematurely blasé.
there dwelt a sensitive and tender-hearted Squire. From
this contrast sprang his poetry. No artist turns from what
feeds his genius. Musset knew only too well the discords
sounding in his loveliest verse. He made a fetish of his
wildness. At first it had been little more than a game—part
sham, and part resentment. But 'debauchery is no laughing matter'— *on ne badine pas avec la débauche*—and,
from a very early age, his nerves had suffered. His inspiration had become intermittent, his purse was empty.

At the *Revue des Deux Mondes* dinner, Sand was

[1] Letter from George Sand to Saint-Beuve, dated March
11th, 1833. Spoelberch de Lovenjoul Collection: Group E. 899,
f. 11.

agreeably surprised to find that the dandy was a thoroughly nice young fellow. 'He was neither fatuous nor profligate, though he would have liked to be both.'[1] He shone. The beautiful and silent woman with the absent gaze laughed at his sallies. She stood in need of laughter. George, who had no wit of her own, could appreciate wit in others. 'Fantasio felt that he was being a success.' He had smiled at sight of the tiny dagger which his neighbour wore at her belt, but was fascinated by the eyes, so large and black, so heavy-lidded, so brilliant and so soft, which turned on him an interrogative look. They were enormous eyes, like an Indian's. Her face was olive-hued with bronze highlights. We know from his poems that he hymned an 'Andalusian girl with sun-browned breast', that he loved 'a virgin breast as golden as the swelling grape'. Something, it seems, in a rich, warm tint spoke to his deep-concealed desires.

When he got home he read *Indiana,* crossed through most of the adjectives—for he had a surer taste, a better style, than Sand—and wrote her a very sober letter, ending with: 'Believe me, Madame, yours most respectfully.' But with it was enclosed a set of verses: 'After reading *Indiana*':

> Sand, quand tu l'écrivais ou donc l'avais tu vue,
> Cette scène terrible ou Noun, à demi nue,
> Sur le lit d'Indiana s'enivre avec Raymon?
> Qui donc te la dictait, cette page brûlante
> Où l'amour cherche en vain, d'une main palpitante,
> Le fantôme adoré de son illusion?
> En as-tu dans le coeur la triste expérience?
> Ce qu'éprouve Raymon, te le rappelais—tu?
> Et tous ces sentiments d'une vague souffrance,
> Ces plaisirs sans bonheur, si pleins d'une vide immense,
> As-tu rêvé ca, George, ou t'en souveiens-tu?[2]

1 GEORGE SAND: *Elle et Lui,* p. 42.
  2 How came it, Sand, that you could so devise
     That terrible scene, where Noun half naked lies
     On Indiana's bed, and with Raymon
     Takes heady pleasure? Whence came that saraband
     Of words that paint a love striving with nerveless hand
     To seek and hold its fond illusion?
     Was it your own sad heart then speaking
     Raymon's long misery? Were you remembering it?
     And all those agonies of endless seeking,

The intimate tone, the urgency of his questions, served to create a poetic bond. A mild flirtation followed. Musset knew how to give charm to the airy nothings of such a relationship. George recovered her gaiety. She was soon calling him 'my urchin Alfred'. They made all sorts of romantic plans: they would climb together to the top of Notre-Dame, they would visit Italy. She received him in the most unconventional attire—a loose dressing-gown of yellow silk, Turkish slippers, and a Spanish mantilla. She gave him Egyptian tobacco to smoke, and sat on a cushion at his feet, puffing away at a long pipe of Bosnian cherry-wood. Alfred knelt beside her, stroking her slippers under pretence of following with his finger the oriental intricacy of their design.[1] But the tone of their conversation remained light and fanciful.

In July *Lélia* was finished, and Musset received a set of proofs. He was enthusiastic. 'There are, in *Lélia,* twenty or so direct and vigorous pages which strike straight to the heart. They are as beautiful as anything in *René* or in *Lara* . . .'[2] Then Cherubino returned to the subject of love.

You know me well enough now to be sure that my lips could never form the ridiculous question—*Will you, or won't you?* In this matter, there is a whole Baltic Sea between us. You have nothing to offer but a chaste love, and that is something I can give to no one (and who knows but what, if I had offered it, you might have sent me about my business?) But I can, if you think me worthy, be to you—not perhaps a friend, for even that sounds too chastely in my ears—but an inconsequent comrade, who makes no claims and will therefore be neither jealous nor quallelsome, but will smoke your tobacco, crumple your *negligées,* and catch a cold in the head as a result of philosophizing with you under all the chestnut trees of contemporary Europe. . . .[3]

Those aimless, grey, unhappy pleasures reeking
Of Hell and hopelessness? Was it a dream, or was it memory?

[1] PAUL DE MUSSET: *Lui et Elle,* p. 55.

[2] *Correspondance de George Sand et d'Alfred de Musset,* edited by Félix Decori, pp. 9-10.

[3] Ibid.

She needed some blasphemous verses for Stenio to sing in a husky voice when drunk. Who could better supply them than this young poet, only too familiar with drunkenness, who claimed to play the part of sentimental clown for her amusement? Musset duly composed the *Inno ebrioso*: or *Drunken Hymn*:

Si mon regard se lève au mileau de l'orgie,
Si ma lèvre tremblante et d'écume rougie
   Va cherchant un baiser,
Que mes désirs ardents, sur les épaules nues
De ces femmes d'amour, pour mes plaisirs venues,
   Ne puissent s'apaiser.

Q'en mon sang appauvri leurs caresses lascives
Rallument aujourdhui les ardeurs convulsives
   D'un prêtre de vingt ans,
Que les fleurs de leurs fronts soient pour mes mains
   semées,
Que j'enlace à mes doigts les tresses parfumées,
   De leurs cheveux flottants,

Que ma dent furieuse à leur chair palpitante
Arrache un cri d'effroi; que leur voix haletante
   Me demande merci.
Qu'en un dernier effort nos soupirs se confondent,
Par un dernier défi que nos cris se répondent,
   Et que je meurs ainsi! . . .

Ou, si Dieu me refuse une mort fortunée,
De gloire et de bonheur à la fois couronnee,
   Si je sens mes désirs,
D'une rage impuissante immortelle agonie,
Comme un pâle reflet d'une flamme ternie,
   Survivre à mes plaisirs,

De mon maître jaloux, imitant le caprice,
Que ce vin génereux abrège le supplice
   Du corps qui s'engourdit;
Dans us baiser d'adieu, que nos levres s'étreignent,

Qu'en un sommeil glacé tous mes désirs s'éteignent,
   Et que Dieu soit maudit.[1]

For some time longer he continued to write to Sand on a
note of Shakespearian comedy. Then, on July 29th, the post
brought her a definite 'declaration'.

My Dear George: I have something stupid and ridiculous
to say to you . . . You will laugh in my face, and hold
that, in all I have said to you so far, I was a mere maker
of phrases. You will show me the door, and you will
believe that I am lying. I am in love with you. I have been
in love with you ever since the day when I came to see
you for the first time. I thought I could cure myself by
continuing with you on the level of friendship. There is
much in your character that might bring about a cure,
and I have tried hard to persuade myself of this: but I pay
too high a price for the moments which I spend with you
. . . And now, George, you say—'Just another importunate bore!' (to use your own words) . . . I know precisely how you regard me, and, in speaking as I have
done, delude myself with no false hopes. The only result
will be that I shall lose a dear companion . . . But, in very
truth, I lack the strength of mind to keep silent. . . .[2]

She hesitated. It is important to make that clear, because
she has been too often represented as a *femme fatale,* as an
ogress in quest of fresh and tender food. Such, on this
occasion, was far from being the case. She had found much
pleasure in the company of a young man whom she thought
both brilliant and delightful, but what she knew of his
habitually wild life made her frightened. 'I love all women,
and despise the lot of 'em', he had told her. The love of

[1] GEORGE SAND: *Lélia.* Original version, 1833. Volume II,
pp. 209-10.
English lacks an accepted vocabulary of physical passion.
Swinburne might, just conceivably, have translated the above
verses, though even in his rendering they would, probably, have
sounded faintly ridiculous. But, Swinburne being dead, and the
age of romantic diabolism having (for the time being, at least)
fallen out of favour, I have chosen to leave them un-anglicized.
'They order this matter better in France.'—TRANSLATOR.

[2] *Correspondance de George Sand et d'Alfred de Musset,*
edited by Félix Decori, pp. 12-14.

which she dreamed must strike deep and last long. Unfaithful she might herself have been, but that, she thought, had been the consequence of disappointment and despair. Musset guessed the nature of her feelings, and came to grips with them in a further letter.

> Do you remember how you once said that someone had asked whether I was Octave or Coelio, and that you had answered—'Both, I think' . . . I was a fool to show you more than one side of myself, George . . . You should love only those who know how to love. I know only how to suffer . . . Goodbye, George, I love you like a child. . . .[1]

Like a child . . . Did he know, when he wrote those words, that he had found the one certain way to her heart? 'Like a child', she murmured, clutching the letter in fingers that trembled as the result of some obscure emotion. 'He loves me like a child! Oh, my God, what is he saying!—and does he know the pain that he is causing me?'[2]

She saw him again. He wept. She yielded. 'But for your youth, but for your tears which have made me weak, we should still have been to one another as brother and sister . . .' Very soon, Musset went to live at the Quai Malaquais. Once more she felt the need of a settled life and a shared routine. She must be for the man she loved not only a mistress, but housekeeper, sick-nurse, and, above all, mother.

The new favourite was not installed without the event starting angry repercussions in the circle of their friendships. The members of the Berrichon colony in Paris, and Gustave Planche, all of them faithful dogs, all of them accustomed to sit at George's feet, set up a noisy barking at sight of the intruder, and maintained that this open intrigue with a young fop, a man of the world, a conceited ass, would have a damaging effect upon her literary reputation. Planche, whose general grubbiness much offended the sensitive Musset, was got rid of. At precisely that moment, *Lélia* appeared. Sand had dedicated the book to 'Monsieur H. Delatouche', in the hope of making up her quarrel with the sage of Aulnay. He protested, however (no doubt ir-

[1] *Correspondance de George Sand et d'Alfred de Musset*, edited by Félix Decori, pp. 15-16.
[2] GEORGE SAND: *Elle et Lui*, p. 87.

ritated as much by her faulty spelling of his name as by her audacity in taking the step at all), and she removed the inscription from subsequent editions. On the fly-leaf of the copy of the first volume which she gave to Musset, she wrote: 'For my urchin Alfred—George', and on that of the second, 'For Monsieur le Vicomte Alfred de Musset, with the respectful homage of his devoted servant, George Sand'.

The book produced a sensation among the critics. The hypocrites had a field-day. One journalist, a certain Capo de Feuillide, called for a 'red-hot coal' with which to purify the lips that had uttered such shameless and disgusting thoughts . . . 'When you open *Lélia*', he went on, 'see to it that your library door is locked (lest others be contaminated). If you have a daughter, and wish her to retain her innocence, send her out to play in the fields with her young companions. . . .'[1]

Poor Planche, who was nothing if not chivalrous, sent a challenge to the writer of this insulting notice, and himself published a courageous appreciation of *Lélia,* and of its author, in the *Revue des Deux Mondes* for August 15th, 1833. 'There are', he wrote, 'certain characters marked by destiny to live for ever in a world of struggle. Of them it may be said that, whatever their faults, they pay for them with the torment and agony of sleepless nights. Only those who do not know them would dare to condemn . . .'[2] He added that *Lélia* would be understood by women.

They will underline those passages in which they have found, set down in words, the memories they harbour of their own past lives, the record of their own unpublished miseries. With tears in their eyes, and veneration in their hearts, they will acknowledge the impotence which here proclaims itself and reveals its torments. They will stand amazed at the courage of such an avowal. Some will blush to think that their secrets have been fathomed, but, in the privacy of their own minds, they will admit that *Lélia* is a speech not for the prosecution, but for the defence. . . .[3]

[1] Capo de Feuillide, quoted by Marie-Louise Pailleron in *La Vie littéraire sous Louis-Philippe*. Volume I, p. 386.

[2] GUSTAVE PLANCHE: *Portraits littéraires*. Volume I, pp. 356-7.

[3] Ibid., Volume I, pp. 359-60.

Then he sent his seconds to Capo de Feuillide. The Paris of Bixiou, Blondet and Nathan, went into ecstasies of laughter over this duel. By what right had Monsieur Gustave Planche set himself up as the hired bravo of Monsieur (or Madame) George Sand? Was this his manner of proclaiming his rights just when he had lost them? The wretched man pleaded in his own defence.

Gustave Planche to Sainte-Beuve: If I had for George Sand anything but feelings of true friendship, my conduct of yesterday would be of the grossest possible description. I should give the impression that I was asserting a right, and so appear as a man of the coarsest instincts, and entirely without breeding. I never had such a right, and am merely a man in a ridiculous position. But the world cannot be expected to know the truth, and is little concerned to know it. . . . [1]

Musset made a great display of anger: 'It was my intention to fight, and I have been forestalled.' From this moment, his feelings of disgust for Planche turned to hatred.

> Par propreté, laissons à l'aise
> Mordre cet animal rampant.
> En croyant frapper un serpent,
> N'écrasons pas une punaise. [2]

Sainte-Beuve, for his part, waited prudently until the storm should pass. Sand went on plaguing him to write an article about her in the *National:*

---

[1] Quoted by Marie-Louise Pailleron in *François Buloz et ses Amis.* Volume I, p. 388.

[2] Alfred de Musset; quoted by Marie-Louise Pailleron in *François et ses Amis.* Volume I, p. 389.

> Let's give the biting thing its head
> For health and cleanliness's sake,
> Lest, thinking we have scotched a snake,
> We find we've crushed a bug instead.

George Sand to Sainte-Beuve, August 25th, 1833: As you know, my friend, I have been much insulted, but all that leaves me cold. Still, I am not insensible to the zeal and enthusiasm with which my friends have rallied to my defence. . . .[1]

Then she made an official announcement to him of her new attachment:

I have fallen in love, and this time very seriously, with Alfred de Musset. This is not just one of my whims, but a feeling that goes deep. I will give you more of the details in a future letter. It is not in my nature to promise a permanence which would range this relationship with those sacred affections to which *you* are susceptible. I once loved for six years on end, and, in another case, for three. At the moment I do not know what my capabilities in that line may be. My *mind* has been the scene of many vagaries of fancy, but my heart has not been so much rubbed smooth with use as I feared it might have been. This I can say now, because I *feel* it. Instead of being hurt and misunderstood, I have found, this time, a combination of ingenuousness, loyalty and tenderness which has quite gone to my head. I have been blessed with the love of a young man, and the friendship of a true companion. That is something I have never known before, and did not dream that I should anywhere encounter, least of all in *him* . . . I set my face against this affection, and kept it at bay. At first I refused, but eventually surrendered, and am now rewarded for having done so, with happiness. It was friendship rather than love that urged me to give way, and now love, which I did not know I could feel, has been revealed to me, and without the accompaniment of those sufferings which I thought I should have to accept. I am happy, and would have you offer thanks to God on my behalf . . . And now that I have told you what is in my heart, I will explain my proposed behaviour.

Planche has been generally assumed to be my lover—not that I care: he never was. But it is important for me now that people should realize that, and realize, too, that I am more utterly indifferent to him than they will believe

[1] GEORGE SAND: *Lettres à Alfred de Musset et à Sainte-Beuve*, p. 124.

to have been the case. You will understand that I cannot live on terms of intimacy with two men who might be held to have been in a similar relationship to me. It would be uncomfortable to all three of us! I have, therefore, taken the painful, but inevitable, step, of parting altogether with Planche. We talked the whole thing out in a spirit of loyal comradeship, and separated with a handshake, each feeling for the other deep affection and lasting respect . . . Whether my action in thus cutting the Gordian knot will please you, I do not know. You may, perhaps, think that a woman should conceal her feelings: but I do beg you to realize that I am in a quite exceptional situation, and am compelled, from now on, to live my private life in the full light of day.[1]

Three weeks later, she made a further appeal to his somewhat sluggish devotion: 'You will write about *Lélia* in the *National*, won't you? I still live in hopes.[2]

He made excuses. He made promises: 'During the next two days, I shall live through *Lélia* again with you, but all the time I shall keep on telling myself that you are no longer the incredulous, despairing woman who wrote it . . .'[3] She reassured him: 'I am happy, my friend, very happy. Each day the bonds that link me to him grow stronger . . . Our intimacy is as precious to me as is the knowledge that he picked me out. . . .'[4]

She had grown ten years younger. In the company of this *child* (she made frequent use of the word, dwelling on it with incestuous delight), she had recovered the gaiety which had marked her early years with Sandeau. Once again the apartment on the Quai Malaquais echoed to the sound of singing and of laughter. Alfred filled his sketchbook with portraits and caricatures. There was wit in his drawings, and lightness in the occasional verses he threw off at this time:

---

[1] Ibid., pp. 125-8.

[2] GEORGE SAND: *Lettres à Alfred de Musset et à Sainte-Beuve*, p. 130.

[3] SAINTE-BEUVE: *Correspondance générale*. Volume I, p. 389.

[4] GEORGE SAND: *Lettres à Alfred de Musset et à Sainte-Beuve*, p. 131.

George est dans sa chambrette
Entre deux pots de fleurs,
Fumant sa cigarette,
     Les yeux baignés de pleurs.[1]

The 'pleurs' were there only for the rhyme, or perhaps
because she had been laughing till she cried. Alfred played
all sorts of mad pranks. One evening he dressed up as a
servant-girl, in a short skirt with a cross suspended round
his neck, and handed the dishes at dinner, in the course of
which he emptied the water-jug over the head of Lerminier,
the philosopher. George had always had a weakness for
practical jokes. Melancholy being habitual with her, she
needed the relief of crude fun. This student-life of theirs
enchanted her. 'All beginnings are delightful,' says Goethe;
'the threshold is the place to pause.' This is particularly true
in love. It is in the early days that two young people find
one another, that each displays treasures of mind and heart
for the other's delectation. The first weeks in their
apartment, with its windows opening on to the loveliest
spectacle in all the world, were filled with magic. 'A life of
freedom, delicious intimacy, tranquillity, and a sense of
hope expanding! Oh, God! what cause have human beings
to complain!—what can be sweeter than love?'

Strange bedfellows: George, serious-minded and punctual, was concerned to deliver her novel on time, and would
jump out of bed in the middle of the night to work, while
Alfred slept like a dormouse. When he woke, she would
read him a lesson, as formerly she had done with Sandeau,
for she was as much, or more, a schoolmistress than a
lover. Laughingly on these occasions he protested. 'I had
worked all day,' he said, 'and by the evening had produced ten lines and drunk a bottle of brandy. She, on the
other hand, had polished off a litre of milk and written half
a volume.' But in the early days he thanked her for having
saved him from the slow suicide which, up till then, his life
had been, and George revelled in the pleasure of 'bringing
back a choice and exquisite spirit to greatness'.[2]

There were, however, friends who uttered words of

---

[1] About her attic room she slips,
       With potted plants for company,
       A cigarette between her lips,
       And a tear-drop in her eye.

[2] GEORGE SAND: *Elle et Lui*, p. 101.

warning, and reminded Alfred of what had happened to Sandeau. 'Remember,' they said, 'that deadly sandbank at Quillebeuf on the Seine, where, above the surface of the stream, black flags flutter from the masts of sunken ships. There is a black flag visible in this woman's life, and it marks a hidden reef . . .'[1] But Musset belonged to that race of lovers who seek out danger and give their hearts, by preference, to those who, they know, will tear them to pieces.

In September he suggested to his mistress that they should go to Fontainebleau and spend a few days among the Franchard woods and rocks. She welcomed the idea, being fond of combining love with Nature. She feared neither fatigue nor darkness, but strode through the woods, dressed as a man, treading the sandy path 'with determination and a charming combination of feminine delicacy and childish bravado . . . She would walk ahead like a soldier, singing at the top of her voice . . .'[2] On the way home she would lean on her companion's arm, and they would murmur sweet nothings as they wandered. At first, most certainly, this holiday was happy, for later, when the time of fond regrets had come, Musset used always to recall the 'Lady of Franchard'. But one evening there was an occurrence which had the effect of ruining everything. They had visited a cemetery by moonlight, and there, suddenly, Alfred had fallen prey to hallucinations. He saw a pale ghost, with torn clothing and flying hair, leaping across the heath. 'I was overcome by fear, and flung myself face downwards on the ground, for the man I had seen was . . . myself!'[3] Next morning he made light of the incident and joked about it. Under a caricature of himself he wrote: *Lost in the forest and in the mind of his mistress;* and, under one of her, *Her heart as tattered as her dress.* The drawing annoyed her. She refused to see the comic side of a crisis which had genuinely frightened her.

It has been said that Sand exaggerated Musset's hallucinations. But, apart from the fact that he himself described them in *Nuit de Décembre,* we have irrefutable proof of their existence in a description from the pen of Louise Allan-Despréaux, the beautiful actress who, sixteen years

[1] PAUL DE MUSSET: *Lui et Elle,* p. 63.

[2] ALFRED DE MUSSET: *Confession d'un enfant du Siècle,* p. 227.

[3] GEORGE SAND: *Elle et Lui,* p. 112.

later, was his mistress. Her account coincides exactly with
the one given by George, and tells of a lovely, moonshiny,
Shakespearean figure transformed suddenly into a creature
of madness.

Madame Allan-Despréaux to Madame Samson-Tous-saint, July 17th, 1849: We spent the first few days in getting to know one another, and then a terrible storm
broke in which there was a lot of love, and other things as
well which I could not endure. On going home he was
suddenly seized by a fit of delirium. He is subject to these
attacks when his brain has been working at high pressure.
They are the result of his old disastrous habits. When
they are upon him he suffers from hallucinations, and
talks with spirits . . . Never have I seen a more striking
contrast than that between the two persons who seem to
co-exist in one and the same individual. On one side there
is the kind, tender, ardent man, overflowing with
intelligence and good-sense, simple (yes, surprising as it
may sound, as simple as a child), affable, uncomplicated,
unpretentious, modest, sensitive, excitable, prone to weep
over nothing at all, an artist in the fullest meaning of the
word . . . Then, turn the page and look at the contrasting
picture. You find yourself at grips with a man possessed
by some sort of a demon, weak, violent, arrogant, blindly
obstinate, self-centred and egotistical to the extreme,
blasphemous, and taking as wild a pleasure in the bad as
in the good, whipping himself into a frenzy of evil. Once
he is mounted on this devil's horse, the only thing to do is
to let him ride it till he breaks his neck. Excess is the
keynote of his temperament, excess in beauty, excess in
ugliness. In the latter case, the fit ends always in a bout of
sickness, which at least has the beneficent effect of
restoring him to his senses, and making him conscious
of his misdeeds.[1]

Such was the double-natured man by whom Sand found
herself confronted. What chiefly bound her to him was that
quality of weakness which she could never resist. He knew
it, and would play upon her sensibility by explaining that
his genius was a poor, frail thing—all this in an outburst of

[1] The letters of Madame Allan-Despréaux were published by
Léon Séché in the April number of the *Revue de Paris*, 1906, pp.
519-56.

sincerity and endless self-pity. Then, as soon as she had
succumbed to these proofs of weakness in himself, he would
recover sufficient strength to make her suffer, and himself
as well, for his masochism demanded suffering as a background to his work as well as to his pleasure. And all the
while Sand brooded over him like a mother-hen. She called
him 'My poor child', and he her, 'My great big George, my
Georgey'. Once more, it was she who was the man of the
family.

LOVERS IN VENICE

There are so many things between lovers of which only
they can judge.   *George Sand*

THEY BOTH longed to see Italy. Musset had sung of it,
but had never been there. Sand, attracted by the idea of
Venice, hoped that a change of scene might at last produce
in her a secret revelation. Taking her courage in both hands,
she went to see Alfred's mother. She promised that she
would watch over him with maternal affection and
solicitude, and, on those terms, obtained the old lady's
consent. Casimir, informed of her plans, urged her to travel
'for her instruction and her pleasure'. For so studious a
person Italy would not be lacking in instruction. Whether it
would be pleasurable was another matter.

They set off in December 1833. George, wearing pearl-
grey trousers, and a cap with a tassel, laughed a great deal.
Their departure, however, did not augur well. When they
reached the courtyard of the Hôtel des Postes, they found
that the Lyons coach was number '13'. As it was turning
into the street, it collided with a post and very nearly
crushed a water-carrier. But the lovers braved gods and
devils alike. From Lyons to Avignon they journeyed down
the Rhône Valley in the company of Stendhal. At
Marseilles they embarked for Genoa. Musset, wrapped in
his cloak, suffered from seasickness. George, her hands in

her pockets and a cigarette in her mouth, looked at her
companion with a superior air. He wrote a verse on the
subject.

> George est sur le tillac
> Fumant sa cigarette:
> Musset, comme une bête,
> A mal à l'estomac.[1]

He also made a drawing in which he stressed George's
solidity and his own woebegone appearance. Underneath it
he scribbled: *Homo sum; humani nihil a me alienum puto.*

Homo sum . . . Alfred was finding his mistress's virility
excessive. He complained of her priggishness, her reserve,
her coldness. No journey, however romantic, could change
by an iota Sand's laborious routine. She was busy finishing a
novel for Buloz. At Genoa, and later at Florence, she
insisted on putting in eight hours' work each night. If her
daily ration was unfinished, she locked her door. If her
lover protested, she urged him to work too, and suggested
Lorenzaccio as a subject. 'Man's true victory is woman's
willing recognition of him as her destiny.'[2] Sand's destiny
remained distinct from her love. Humiliated, and with his
patience exhausted, Musset became brutal. He called her
'boredom incarnate, dreamer, idiot, nun'. He reproached
her with 'never having known how to provide the pleasures
of love'. That was Lélia's Achilles heel. Deeply wounded in
heart and pride, she hit back. 'I am well content to know
that those pleasures have been more austere and less obvious
than those you find elsewhere. At least, when you are in
other women's arms no memories of me will spoil your
transports.' But such bravado brought solace to neither.

At Genoa she fell sick of a fever. Desire and sickness do
not go comfortably in harness. Musset, self-banished from
the sickroom, started to run after women, and to drink. He
was weary of what George called 'exalted love', and longed
with every fibre of his being for the 'deadly headiness of
days gone by'. He relapsed into sophistries. 'What is change
but renewal? The artist is not made to be a slave.' The

---

[1] George is above on the deck
   Puffing away like a good 'un,
   While Musset for his part just couldn'
   Feel more like an absolute wreck.

[2] Simone de Beauvoir.

woman who is too much mistress of herself worries and
exacerbates her lovers. She remains clear-headed and
collected just when the man is seeking to forget himself in
passion. He wants not only to overcome a shrinking
modesty, but to put liberty in chains, to transform a
thinking being into an object. Sand irritated men because
she always remained a subject.

Their arrival in Venice, of which she had hoped so much,
was mournful. Darkness had fallen. The black gondola
looked like a coffin. For one moment, as they entered the
city, she saw the dull red moon shining upon Saint-Mark's
with its domes looking like alabaster. The Doges' Palace,
with the Arab fretwork of its stones, and its Christian bell-
towers, raised on a thousand little columns, stood out
against the luminous horizon, and they felt as though they
were gazing at a Turner. But it is love that gives
enchantment to the scenes and cities over which it spreads
its radiance, not the beauty of a setting that brings love to
birth. The rose-red palaces and the golden domes of Saint-
Mark's were powerless to change their hearts. That evening,
in the Hotel Danieli where they had taken rooms, Musset
said to his mistress: 'George, I was wrong about my
feelings: I ask you to forgive me, but the fact is I do not love
you.' She felt utterly crushed, and would have left at once
but for the fact that she was far from well, and also felt a
scruple of conscience at the thought of leaving such a child
alone and without money in a foreign country. 'The
communicating door between our two rooms remained shut
from now on, and we tried to get back on to the old footing
of frank friendship . . . But that was impossible: you were
bored, and what you did with yourself in the evenings I do
not know. . . .'

It was not difficult to guess what he did with himself in
the evenings. Having kept away from her, at first from
tedium, because she insisted on treating him like an
'urchin', and was for ever preaching at him; later, from
disgust, because she was suffering badly from dysentery;
perhaps, too, as Maurras has suggested, 'from a tactful wish
to spare her the sight of his too obvious repulsion', he
abandoned himself to his fancy for romantic debauchery.
He took to haunting the Venetian slums with their stench of
stagnant water, and sampling strange new alcoholic drinks.
He 'sought the embraces of the dancing-girls of the Fenice'.
George, as a result of ill-health and a strong feeling of
resentment, was condemning him to a life of chastity;

consequently, he turned to other women. Never, in all her life, was she to forget those long hours of lonely waiting, when she lay listening to the mysterious plash of water round the steps, to the measured pacing of the 'sbiri' on the quay, to the shrill squeaking of field mice scuttling over the immense flagstones—a sound that was almost like that of children's voices; all those furtive, curious noises which faintly break the silence of Venetian nights.

One morning he came home covered with blood as the result of some casual brawl. Shortly afterwards he became a prey to one of his terrible crises. It may have been due to genuine mental derangement, to brain-fever, or to typhoid —whatever the cause, the spectacle of him in such a state was terrifying. She was frightened. He was quite capable of killing himself, or he might die of his infection, here, in Venice, far from home. What a responsibility for her! What a hideous end to the story she had hoped would be sublime! She called in a certain young Doctor Pagello, who had previously been attending her, and, in order to help him make a sound diagnosis, wrote a full account of what had happened at Franchard. This she sent him with a covering letter:

> On one occasion, three months ago, after a period of great anxiety, he behaved like a madman through the whole of one night. He saw spirits round him, and kept on screaming. He was in a mingled state of horror and fear . . . I love him more than I love anybody in the world, and it is agony for me to see him like this. . . .[1]

This letter is a document of no little importance, for it shows that, even after her many disappointments, Sand could still refer to Musset as the person she 'loved more than she loved anybody in the world'. Much heated discussion has raged round the question of what happened next. There has been charge and counter-charge: books pro-Musset, books pro-Sand. Volumes have been written to prove that Sand and Pagello had, on one occasion, drunk from the same cup, that they had made love at the very bedside of the stricken man. Much effort has been expended in attempts to prove just where the guilt lay. The answer to that question is simple: there was guilt, and there were

[1] Letter from George Sand to Pietro Pagello, quoted by Paul Mariéton, in *Une Histoire d'Amour*, pp. 84-5.

grievances, on both sides. 'By what right do you interrogate me about Venice?—asked Sand at a later date: 'Did I belong to you when we were there?' She put the question in perfect good faith. In her moral code (and everybody has a personal moral code) passion was something sacred, always with the reservation, however, that a woman should never 'belong' to more than one man at a time. Musset had ceased to treat her as a mistress, and, *therefore*, she held that she was free. He admitted himself that he 'deserved to lose her'. But Musset, with the traditional self-indulgence of the male, regarded his own shortcomings with a tolerant eye, but considered that the woman to whom he had been unfaithful should still remain faithful to him. What is beyond dispute is that for three weeks of delirium and madness Sand and Pagello nursed him devotedly.

Why did Sand encourage in herself a wakening desire for Pagello? The problem is extremely complex. In the first place, clinging, as she did, to the hope that she would somewhere find an *absolute* love, satisfying to both mind and body, she looked on every young man, provided he were young, strong, and reasonably personable, as capable of providing a possible solution to Lélia's difficulties. Furthermore, alone in Venice, in a foreign land, with only strangers round her, and with a half-mad 'child' upon her hands, she needed that form of moral support which women, in moments of distress and anxiety, sometimes confuse with love. Finally, since she was playing with the idea of using the Venetian scene as a setting for future novels, she wanted to acquire an intimate knowledge of Italy, and every artist knows that love alone can provide a key to a relationship of flesh and blood with a different nation and a different race.

Pagello and Sand were compelled to spend whole nights at the bedside of a sick man who was either sleeping or delirious. Shared anxiety and a common duty from a strong bond between the sexes. Physical exhaustion is a pander. Pagello was moved by admiration of a beautiful foreigner. He gazed at her with passion, but lacked the courage to woo her. She was a famous writer, he but a poor beginner in his profession. He had an Italian mistress: Sand was there, in Venice, with a lover. Besides, this lover was the doctor's patient, and his duty was obvious. The situation provided a difficult case of conscience for a decent young fellow of twenty-six, plump, fair-haired, and innocent of all emotional sophistication.

One night when Musset, wishing to get some sleep, had begged his mistress and his doctor to move away from the bed, they went and sat by a table near the fireplace, and Pagello put a harmless question:

'Are you planning a novel, Madame, which shall have to do with this beautiful Venice of ours?'

'Who knows,' was her reply.

She drew some paper to her, started to write at furious speed, put the pages in an envelope, and gave it to the doctor. He asked to whom he should deliver the packet. She took back the envelope, and wrote upon it the words: 'To the Stupid Pagello.' When he got home, he read the romantic effusion which was nothing less than a declaration of love couched in language far more beautiful than any she had put into the mouths of her own fictional heroes. It consisted of a series of breathless questions, in the true Sand style, for this deeply unsatisfied woman's attitude to life was one of never-ending interrogation. Curiously enough Musset was to reproduce this literary trick on more than one occasion in the future, both in his *Nuits* and in his plays.

Sand to Pagello: Are you to be my master or my stay? Will you console me for the sufferings that I endured before I met you? Do you know why I am sad? Have you the gifts of patience, compassion and friendship? Have you, perhaps, been brought up to believe that women have no souls? Do you realize that that is untrue? . . . Am I to be your comrade or your slave? What is it that you feel for me—desire or love? When your passion has been satisfied will you give me thanks? When I have made you happy, will you know how to tell me so? . . . Have you any conception of that desire of the heart which no human embrace can dull or weary? When your mistress lies asleep in your arms, do you stay awake, gazing at her, praying to God, and weeping? Do the pleasures of love leave you panting and besotted, or do they plunge you into a state of divine ecstasy? Does the movement of your heart outlive the prickings of your flesh when you have parted from her you love? . . .

I can interpret your broodings and find eloquence in your silence. To your actions I will give the meaning which I hope to find in them. When you look tenderly at me, I will believe that heart speaks to heart . . . Let us stay as we are . . . do not learn my language. I would rather not seek in yours the words which would tell you of my doubts and fears. I wish to remain ignorant of what you do with your life, of what part you play among your fellow men. I could wish even not to know your name. Hide your heart from me that I may continue to think it beautiful. . . .[1]

If Proust had read that letter, how he would have loved it! For what is Pagello's forced silence if not the sleep of Albertine? Exacting lovers always want the idol to be voiceless, and so, never disappointing. In this adventure, the beloved was not only voiceless but terrified. Sand's declaration broke into his tranquil existence like a clap of thunder. As has happened with many conquerors, Pagello felt that he had been defeated by his own success. What scandal there would have been in Venice had it been known that he was conducting an intrigue with 'The Sand'—as he called her! As a young doctor, he was just building a practice and must needs preserve appearances. But how resist the temptations offered by this fascinating foreigner? She became his mistress.

How much did Musset see? How much did Musset know? He was suffering from brain-fever. He had periods of delirium interspersed with moments of lucidity. He saw a woman seated on a man's knee, two mouths joined in a kiss. He believed that on the table close to which Sand and Pagello were sitting there stood a single cup, and that both had sipped their tea from it. He later laughed at the agitation into which the sight had plunged him. 'Has ever a farce been put upon the stage in which a jealous character is stupid enough to work himself into a state over a vanished cup? Why should they have drunk from the same cup? . . . What a fine thing to brood upon!' . . .[2] Paul de Musset tells us that on one occasion his brother found George writing a letter: that he accused her of corresponding with Pagello: that she denied the accusation, threatened to have him shut away in an asylum, tore the letter into scraps and threw them from the window, but at dawn ran out in her petticoat to collect them. Was all this hallucination or reality? Who can tell? Paul de Musset, as a witness, is prejudiced and suspect.

---

[1] Letter quoted by Paul Mariéton in *Une Histoire d'Amour*, pp. 95-7.

[2] ALFRED DE MUSSET: *Confession d'un enfant du Siècle*, p. 291.

The only thing that we can say for certain is that Pagello's entry on to the stage had the effect of creating a world from which Musset felt himself to be excluded, and that Sand triumphed in thus excluding him. Alfred had diminished her in her own eyes by saying that, as a mistress, she was heavy-handed. She found her revenge in working him up to that state of jealousy which is always the portion of the 'third person' when there is an understanding between two others, in which he has no share. Such jealousy could be dispersed only if an understanding between Sand and Musset might be re-established from which Pagello, in his turn, would be shut out. In that event, it would be Pagello who would suffer. But why, if it comes to that, *should* Musset have felt jealous, seeing that he had himself confessed that any love he might once have had for his mistress was over? The answer to that question is that jealousy re-awakens love, and endows with new and heightened value the very being whom the lover has come to spurn, and thought to understand.

Did Musset really believe that George was planning to regain her freedom by having him shut up? The state of delirium from which he suffered for so long makes it impossible to speak with any certainty. The prolonged devotion of his nurse would seem to give the lie to such a charge. If she used the word 'madness', the reason was that she was afraid of it, and that his recurrent crises had seemed to justify her fear. Why should she have wished to have him shut away? She was already free. She could leave him whenever she might wish to do so. She insisted that as soon as he was better she must tell him the truth. Pagello begged her to keep silent. The doctor held the view that Musset was not strong enough to bear such a blow. But all the Koenigsmark in Sand took hold of her. It was incumbent, she said, upon her self-respect that she should be sincere. Later, she noted in her *Journal*: 'Oh God, give me back that ferocious strength which was mine in Venice; restore to me that ruthless love of life which seized upon me like an access of rage in the midst of the most horrible despair!. . .[1]

Ferocious strength, *ruthless* love of life . . . strange language that, to use of dear, decent Pagello, with his smacking kisses, his simple airs, his girlish grin, his spread of waistcoat, and his sheep's eyes. But we must remember what it was she hoped to find in him—love perfected. 'Ah! I

[1] GEORGE SAND: *Journal intime*, p. 14.

have endured such suffering, have so endlessly sought
perfection without ever finding it! Is it in you, my Pietro, in
you at long last, that I shall see my dream fulfilled? . . .'[1]

Did she tell Musset, as she longed to do, that she was in
love with Pagello? Undoubtedly she did, for he speaks of
that 'melancholy evening in Venice when you told me that
you had a secret. You thought that you were speaking to a
stupid man obsessed by jealousy. But you were wrong,
George; you were speaking to a friend . . .'[2] It may even be
that he found a bitter pleasure in the whole incident: who
can say? In the *Confession d'un Enfant du Siècle* occurs
this passage: . . . 'Some intimate and secret pleasure held me
motionless, that evening, in my chair. As the moment
approached when Smith (Pagello) was due to arrive, I felt
restless until I heard the sound of the door-bell. How
explain the presence in ourselves of that something which is
love conjoined with misery?' . . .[3] The explanation is that
the certainty of misery is less painful than suspense. The
sufferings of jealousy are essentially the products of
disappointed pride and curiosity. The lover has wished to
dominate another human being. He has failed. His partner,
now his enemy, remains free. Her thoughts and feelings are
unknown to him. The sole way in which he can steal that
freedom from her is by *knowing*. With knowledge, the
emotion of jealousy grows less, and, sometimes, vanishes
altogether.

Musset was well aware that Sand was in love with
Pagello, but what he did not know was whether she had
been possessed by Pietro before his own departure from
Venice, and that splinter remained firmly embedded in his
flesh. She refused to answer him precisely on the point.
That, she said, was her secret, and, since she no longer
belonged to Musset, she saw no reason why she should be
answerable to him for her actions. At the end of March
George and Alfred had ceased to live under the same roof,
and sent notes to one another by the hands of gondoliers.

Musset left for Paris on March 29th accompanied by an
Italian servant. He took with him 'two strange companions,
sadness, and an inexhaustible joy': sadness, because he had

[1] Cf. PAUL MARIETON: *Une Histoire d'Amour*, p. 111.

[2] *Correspondance de George Sand et d'Alfred de Musset*,
edited by Félix Decori, p. 132.

[3] ALFRED DE MUSSET: *Confession d'un Enfant du Siècle*,
p. 284.

lost a mistress with whom he was again in love now that she had escaped from him; joy, in the knowledge that he had behaved well, and had made the great sacrifice of leaving her with a fine gesture. George went with him as far as Mestre, and there, after parting from him with a tender, motherly embrace, did as she always did in moments of moral crisis—went for a long walk in order to expend the excess of energy by which she was consumed. Then she returned to Venice with seven centimes in her pocket, and settled down with Pagello in a small apartment. *Sand to Boucoiran:* 'Address your letters to Monsieur Pagello, c/o Pharmacie Ancillio, near San Lucca, "to be forwarded to Madame Sand" . . . If Planche is busy correcting my proofs, ask him to tone down the style and correct my grammatical mistakes.'[1]

She spent five months in her Venetian retreat, finishing her novel, *Jacques*, which she sent to Musset with a dry little inscription, written in pencil—*George to Alfred*. She also wrote the first of her *Letters d'un Voyageur*, and made a number of notes for her Italian stories. *Jacques* displeased Balzac, who found the book 'false and empty'.

> *Balzac to Eve Hanska, October 19th, 1834:* Madame Dudevant's latest novel is a word of advice to husbands who are in their wives' way, to kill themselves, and so leave their partners free . . . A simple young girl, after six months of marriage, leaves a man of *superior* gifts for a young puppy, a solid, passionate and loving husband for a dandy. There is no reason at all for her action, either physiological or moral. There is, as in *Lélia*, a lot about how fond she is of mules—in other words, of sterile creatures, which is odd in a woman who is a mother, and also a very fair practitioner of love in the German, instinctive, manner. . . .[2]

It is true that many of Sand's novels are well below the level of her letters and her gifts.

In her moments of leisure, and with her customary zeal, the industrious novelist did a great deal of knitting and

---

[1] Unpublished. Spoelberch de Lovenjoul Collection: Group E. 920, ff. 56 and 66.

[2] HONORE DE BALZAC: *Lettres à l'Etrangère*. Volume I, p. 196.

embroidery. With her own hands she worked for her
handsome Italian a whole set of furnishings—curtains,
sofa-cover, chair-covers. With her, adultery was nothing if
not domestic. Pietro Pagello was deeply enamoured and
faintly embarrassed. His Venetian mistresses tried hard to
get him back, and one of them, in the course of a jealous
scene, sadly damaged his *bel vestito*. His brother, Roberto,
pulled his leg about the thin, yellow-complexioned foreign
lady: *'Quella sardella'*—he called her—'a regular sardine'.
But Pagello loved his Frenchwoman, and, since he was out
all day on his rounds, Sand could be sure of her eight
peaceful working hours—a sure guarantee that their love
would last. Since Pietro was too poor to buy flowers, he
used to get up at dawn and go to pick bouquets for her in
the outskirts of the city.

Did all this amount to happiness? If it did, it was a
happiness which already had gone slightly stale. No sooner
had Sand and Musset parted than they began to regret the
days of their misery. After leaving Alfred at Mestre, she had
written to him: 'Who will look after you, and whom shall I
have to look after? Who now is there that needs me, and
whom, henceforward, shall I tend? Goodbye, my little bird.
Think over with affection of your poor old George. I send
no message from Pagello, but this I can tell you, that he
sheds almost as many tears as I do . . .'[1] Ah! how difficult it
was for her to abandon that old ideal—the *ménage à trois*!
As to Musset, no sooner was he out of range of her scolding
tongue, than he regretted the friend whom he had lost. 'I
love you still,' he wrote, 'and I use that word in its full
meaning.' His emotions now crystallized about the absent
fair, and he set himself, in all sincerity, to play a
magnanimous part. He hoped she would be happy with
Pietro!—'A fine young fellow! tell him how fond I am of
him, and that when the thought of him comes into my
mind, the tears steal from my eyes . . .'[2] The good nurse
wept, too. 'On my knees I implore you—no more wine, and
no more women . . . It is too soon . . . Do not abandon
yourself to pleasure until such time as Nature calls on you
imperiously to do so. Do not seek it as a mere escape from

---

[1] *Correspondance de George Sand et d'Alfred de Musset*,
edited by Félix Decori, pp. 22-3.
[2] Ibid., p. 26.

tedium or unhappiness . . .[1] They concluded an agreement
that neither would lay the blame for what had happened on
the other. Their violent temperaments, their duty as artists,
made it impossible for them to live as normal lovers do.

They remained devoted to one another. 'Poor Mussaillon'
was charged by Sand with endless commissions for her in
Paris'. Would he please buy her a dozen pairs of kid gloves,
four pairs of shoes, and some patchouli? He could get the
money from Buloz. Would he go and see Maurice at the
Lycée Henri IV? Alfred continued to bewail his lot and
revel in his bleeding heart. He went to the Quai Malaquais
and burst into sobs at the sight of a cigarette which George
had left in a saucer. But the tears he shed were delicious
tears. 'You must not be angry with me; I do what I can . . .
Please realize that, for the present, there is not in my heart a
trace either of passion or of anger. It is not the lover that I
miss, but George, my comrade . . .'[2] On his return to Paris
he had found their little world much incensed against Sand.
Planche and Sandeau 'vomited' their disgust. Musset, drunk
with forgiveness, planned to issue a defence. 'I am going to
embark upon a novel. I feel a craving to write our story. To
do so would, I think, work a cure on me, and raise my
spirits. I long to build an altar to you, if need be, of my
bones . . . You should feel proud, my great, courageous
George, for you found me a child, and made me a man
. . .'—which was true. A little later: 'I have started the novel about which I spoke—and that reminds me, if you happen to have kept the letters I have written to you since my
return, would you be so very kind as to let me have them
back? . . .'[3]

Unhappy race of poets, for ever driven on to cut into the
very living flesh of grief! Musset had to have his letters
returned to him, as Rossetti had to exhume his poems. But
his own were not enough: he must have Sand's as well, and
from them he carefully extracted whole passages which he
afterwards used in *On ne badine pas avec l'Amour* . . .
'Perhaps the last of all your loves will be the youngest and
the most romantic. But never, I pray you, kill your good
heart—for good it is. May it be present, wholly or in part,

[1] Ibid., p. 42.

[2] Ibid., p. 39.

[3] *Correspondance de George Sand et d'Alfred de Musset*,
edited by Félix Decori, pp. 51, 56 and 122.

in all the loves of your life, there to play a noble role, so that one day you may be able to look back and say, as I do: "I have suffered often; sometimes I have deceived myself, but I have loved . . ."' In his play, however, this speech is transferred from Camille to Perdican.

At the same time, so complex are men's minds, so well can they secrete a store of sorrow when they want to, that Musset suffered with increasing intensity. 'What stage do you think I have reached now? I know men say that time cures every ill, but I was stronger a hundredfold that day when I returned to Paris than I am now . . . I am reading *Werther* and *La Nouvelle Héloïse*. I devour all the sublime lunacies at which I so often used to mock. I may, perhaps, go too far in this direction, as I once went too far in the other. But what do I care? . . . on I shall go.'[1] To these rallying cries of the passionate spirit of romance, George's heart, as may be imagined, duly responded. Pietro was a good lad, but he did not suffer. He had a way of seeing everything in simple terms. There was no need to sweat blood over his happiness. 'But I feel the need of suffering for somebody. I have to use up that superfluity of energy and sensibility which dwells in me. I needs must find nourishment for that maternal solicitude which has grown used to watching over some suffering and exhausted being. Oh, why, why, cannot I live with both of you, making each happy, but belonging to neither? I could have, indeed, I have, spent ten years in that way . . .'[2] *But belonging to neither*. In those words sounds the authentic cry of Lélia.

While in Venice, she heard by chance that Aurélien de Sèze had married Mademoiselle de Villeminot. She wrote, wishing him all happiness and asking him to send back her letters to him. He replied as follows:

My Dear George: I was on the point of acceding to your request, and sending back the papers you have asked of me. I realize that I have no right to keep them, but I feel that they belong no more to you than they do to me, and fear that if you read them through some echo from them might find its way into one of your future books. I have therefore burned them, sparing only the story which you

1 Ibid., p. 73.
2 Ibid., p. 83.

sent me once. That I beg you most earnestly to let me keep. Goodbye, George, goodbye. My heart will treasure the memory of you until I die. . . .[1]

Tombstones in the garden of love.

At last, in July 1834, she began to think about returning to France. She had finished her novel, and absorbed all that Venice could give her for her work. She had very little money. Buloz, Boucoiran and Casimir had neglected to keep her supplied. She had not seen her children for eight months. She wished to be present in Paris at Maurice's prize-giving. She longed to spend the autumn at Nohant, and thought with nostalgic craving of its elms, its acacia trees and shady lanes. The problem was—should she take Pagello back with her? She made the suggestion to him. 'I could not make up my mind,' we read in the doctor's Journal, 'and told her I would take the night to think it over. It was revealed to me in a flash that I should go to France, and return without her. But I loved her above all things, and would have put up with a thousand inconveniences sooner than let her make so long a journey alone . . .'[2] He accepted the proposal, knowing that the end of the story would not be long delayed. To his father, for whom he had a deep respect, the doctor wrote: 'I am entering upon the last stage of my madness. Tomorrow I leave for Paris, and there I shall part from Sand.'[3] The good Pagello had a clear head and a fund of common sense. He was sad to think that he must lose his mistress, but happy in the knowledge that by doing so he would bring happiness to his family, and would free himself from the load of a great sin.

[1] GEORGE SAND: *Le Roman d'Aurore Dudevant et d'Aurélien de Sèze*, p. 212.
[2] PAUL MARIETON: *Une Histoire d'Amour*, p. 138.
[3] Ibid., p. 183.

EXIT PAGELLO

THIS RETURN to Paris posed a number of difficult problems on three different levels.

On the Public Opinion Level Sand had been ready to laugh at the social verdict of La Châtre, but she attached great importance to her legend in the world of letters, the world of Buloz and Sainte-Beuve. When Musset's best friend, Alfred Tattet, came to Venice, she said to him: 'If anybody asks you what you think of the ferocious Lélia, you need say no more than that she does not live off sea-water and the blood of men . . .'[1] She found, when she got back, that the ferocious Lélia was in very bad odour. People turned from her. Pagello was a surprise to Paris, and a disappointment. What had been looked for was an Italian Count of quite irresistible beauty. It was agreed that he was a pleasant enough young man, but—the very idea of preferring him to Musset! . . . George could feel this general atmosphere of censure.

The Pagello Level. She wanted to treat him with tenderness and generosity. She gave him introductions to several doctors who would act as his guides through the hospitals of Paris, and also to Buloz, in the hope that the latter might commission from Pietro a series of articles on Italy. He had no money, and she wanted to provide him with some in such a way that his feelings should not be hurt. It had occurred to her that the best way of doing this would be to persuade Pagello to bring with him from Venice four pictures of no particular value, which she could then say that she had sold, and present him with the sum that they had 'fetched'. By this stratagem she managed to hand over to him fifteen hundred francs. Thus were generosity and honour both satisfied. But Pietro, whom she

[1] PAUL MARIETON: *Une Histoire d'Amour*, p. 126.

had always thought so trusting, suddenly took it into his head to grow jealous. 'From the moment he set foot in France, he ceased to understand anything.'[1] In the vocabulary of the comedy of love, that 'he ceased to understand *anything*' meant: 'he came to understand *everything.*'

And there was a good deal for him to understand, seeing that on the *Musset Level* drama was once again in the ascendant. Musset was unwilling to admit that there are cases of love going awry, in which a clean break is the only remedy. He wanted to see George again, but could not stand the shock. She told him that she was happy with Pietro. This was no longer true, but she was too proud to admit it. Musset decided that he must go away, but asked her for one last meeting, one last kiss. 'I send you my final farewell, beloved . . . I will not die until I have finished my book on me and you (on you, especially) . . . I swear by my youth and by my genius that on your grave shall grow only lilies without stain. With these hands I will inscribe your epitaph, cutting it deep in marble more pure than that which furnished forth the statues of our momentary glory. Posterity shall speak our names as it does those of the immortal lovers who are for ever linked—Romeo and Juliet, Héloïse and Abélard. Never shall one be spoken without the other.'[2] Then on August 25th he left for Baden, and she on the 29th for Nohant. Casimir, at his wife's request, had sent an invitation to Pagello. But the doctor had a deep respect for marriage, and refused it, content to stay on 'in this great capital, in order to visit the hospitals'. At Nohant, George renewed acquaintance with her old home, the pretty village 'Place', her trees, her friends, her children, and even her mother, who had made the journey from Paris. At once, the members of her old Berrichon circle flocked to see her—Néraud the 'Madagascan', Dutheil and Rollinat. They at least did not reproach her. 'A reprimand serves only to embitter the suffering heart; a friendly handshake is the most eloquent of consolations.' She felt herself broken and torn asunder between her two men, and thought of suicide. Only the love of her children, she said, bound her to life.

[1] *Correspondance de George Sand et d'Alfred de Musset*, edited by Félix Decori, p. 146.

[2] *Correspondance de George Sand et d'Alfred de Musset*, edited by Félix Decori, p. 136.

On the 'Madagascan' she poured a stream of questions:
'Are you calm? Can you bear the vexations of domestic life
without bitterness and without despair? Do you fall asleep
as soon as you get into bed? Is there not, hovering above
your pillow, a demon in an angel's shape, that cries to you:
"Love, love, happiness, life and youth"—while your
desolated heart replies, "It is too late: it might have been,
but was not"? Oh, my friend, do you spend whole nights in
tears and dreaming, do you say to yourself: "I have not
known happiness" . . .'[1] For Sand considered that she
had not been happy. She saw herself blamed, pursued
by calumny, and felt that she was innocent. Had she not
behaved with frankness? Had she not been disinterested,
eager to help? To François Rollinat, the closest of her
friends of the spirit, she addressed an eloquent defence.
'You, at least, know me for what I am. You can say
whether this torn, tormented heart has ever harboured vile
passions, cowardice, the least hint of treachery, the merest
trace of vice . . . You know that a great pride devours me,
but a pride that is neither petty nor stained with guilt, and
that it has never driven me to the commission of any
shameful fault, that it might have guided me to an heroic
destiny had I not been born a slave.'[2] With him she walked
at midnight through the Park at Nohant, exchanging sad
confidences at that hour when the stars look pale, when the
air is damp and mild, and the rides are wrapped in darkness.
'I wanted to play the part of a strong man,' she said, '. . .
and I have been bruised and broken like a child. . . .'[3]

During this month of September 1834, she read
'enormously': the Abbé Gerbet's *Eucharistie*, Madame de
Staël's *Reflexions sur la Suicide*, the *Vie de Vittorio Alfieri*
by Alfieri. A sermon, a dissertation, a confession. But,
above all, she read and re-read the letters she had once
received from Musset, passionate letters, wild letters, which
heralded his *Nuits*. 'Tell me that you give to me your lips,
your teeth, your hair, yes, all of them, and that head which
I have held between my hands. Say, oh say, that you
embrace me—you—me. Oh God! when I think of these
things a lump comes into my throat, my eyes grow dim, my
knees tremble. Ah! it is horrible to die, it is horrible to love
as I love! How thirsty, George, oh, how thirsty I am for

---

1 GEORGE SAND: *Lettres d'un Voyageur*, p. 104.
2 Ibid., p. 112.
3 GEORGE SAND: *Lettres d'un Voyageur*, p. 112.

you! Send me, I beg, I implore, a line. I am dying—
farewell! . . .'[1] Poetic exaggeration? Yes, most certainly.
People die less often of love than is generally supposed.
Musset, at Baden, had his hours of relaxation, and even one
stroke of good fortune which inspired a poem. But his
jealousy was real enough, and his passion for the woman
who, he thought, had escaped from him.

Sand, at Nohant, took refuge in the little wood, and
answered him in pencil. She did what she could to calm
him. "Ah! you still love me overmuch. We must not meet
again.' She spoke to him of poor Pietro, 'that good and pure
young man' who, after so often saying, '*Il nostro amore per
Alfredo*', was now caught, he, too, in the net of jealousy,
and, in his letters was overwhelming George with reproaches. But her heart no longer hesitated between the poet who
wrote those wonderful, those burning, letters from Baden,
and the weak, suspicious Pagello who 'struck at her' with
wounding, clumsy words.

> *Sand to Musset:* He may, by now, have gone, and I shall
> not try to keep him, because I have been wounded to the
> quick by what he has written. He has lost his faith in me,
> I know it: and that means that he has lost his love. . . .[2]

Jacqueline's delicious speech to Maître André, in the
first Act of *Le Chandelier,* sprang out of that. 'You no
longer love me . . . Even innocence in your eyes would now
seem guilty . . . You no longer love me, because you can
accuse me. . .'[3]

For, it must be confessed, the drama of this episode was
fast turning to comedy. George was perfectly sincere when
she put her slightly rhetorical questions to Musset: 'Is there,
really, anywhere, such a thing as a love that moves upon the
heights, and has absolute trust in the beloved? Am I fated to
die without ever meeting it? I am weary of finding that what
I clasp is only a ghost, that those I pursue are merely
shadows! And yet, I loved him, sincerely, seriously. For he
was generous, and his nature was romantic as my own. I
thought him stronger than myself.' . . . But the Comic Spirit

---

1 *Correspondance de George Sand et d'Alfred de Musset,*
edited by Félix Decori, pp. 143-4.

2 Ibid., p. 146.

3 ALFRED DE MUSSET: *Le Chandelier.* Act I, Scene 1.

was smiling when she added: 'I loved him as a father, and you were our child . . .'[1] She wanted everybody to be happy and to believe what she said. Her wish was that all her lovers should remain devoted, and that each should generously agree that she must be allowed to give happiness to his rivals. But human beings are not made like that. Love is not of a nature to take a tolerant view of the claims of others. It is mistrustful, exclusive, uneasy, jealous. What a disappointment!

On September 15th Musset wrote to her from Baden: 'You may be somewhat shocked, and he as well, at the news that I am about to return to Paris. I may as well confess that I am in no mood to treat the sensibilities of others with tender consideration. If this Venetian suffers, then suffer he must. He has taught *me* suffering. His handling of my education in this respect has been masterly, and I am merely paying him back in his own coin . . .'[2] George hastened to Paris in order to comfort Pagello prior to sacrificing him. The beauty of the situation was that Pagello stood in no need of comfort. When he had made the journey from Venice to Paris, he had known perfectly well that this was how it must all end. His time in France had been full of interest. Famous doctors had overwhelmed him with kindnesses. Life without his mistress had seemed to him to be deliciously tranquil. This is how he described the rupture:

Pagello's Journal: I have just had a letter from George Sand telling me that the pictures have been sold for fifteen hundred francs . . . In an ecstasy of delight I went off at once and bought a case of surgical instruments, as well as several new books all dealing with medicine . . . Our parting was conducted in silence. I shook her hand but could not look at her. She seemed perplexed. Whether she was suffering I do not know. She found my presence embarrassing. . . .[3]

Exit Pagello. The good doctor returned to Venice, married, had a number of children, and lived to the age of

[1] *Correspondance de George Sand et d'Alfred de Musset*, edited by Félix Decori, p. 146.

[2] Ibid., p. 154.

[3] PAUL MARIETON: *Une Histoire d'Amour*, p. 210.

ninety-one (1807-98). This adventure of his young manhood surrounded him with a sort of legendary glory similar
to that which crowned the Guiccioli. Happy are those
who, having been caught for a while in the white heat of a
brilliant destiny, have been able to escape from the danger
zone before they have suffered too much damage.

IV

THE QUEST OF THE ABSOLUTE

THERE WAS nobody now to bother about Pagello.

No sooner had they met again than Sand and Musset
resumed their relationship as lovers—he, mad with passion,
she, touched and softened.

He had promised to forget the past—but that could be no
more than a drunkard's word. Can those who revel in
suffering ever wholly renounce an opportunity for renewing
it? He gave George no respite from his probing and
incessant questions. When had she become the doctor's
mistress? In what circumstances? She refused to answer,
pleaded the claims of modesty. 'Had Pietro asked me about
the intimate secrets which you and I have shared, do you
think that I should have satisfied his curiosity?'[1] Musset
became once more a prisoner within a hellish treadmill. He
was the victim of a masochistic need to know the worst.
There was jealousy, there were upbraidings, terrible scenes,
followed by remorse, pleas for forgiveness, exquisite
tenderness, or, if he met with opposition, illness. And so the
vicious circle travelled round and round. Not for the first
time, she went to nurse him at his mother's house. She had
borrowed from her maid a bonnet and an apron, and
Madame de Musset, a willing conspirator, pretended not to
recognize her.

As soon as he was better, Alfred returned to the Quai
Malaquais and resumed his life with George. But they could
no longer be happy. Very soon everything was as it had

[1] *Correspondance de George Sand et d'Alfred de Musset*,
edited by Félix Decori, p. 162.

been before, furious scenes alternating with passionate notes. She realized that the situation was desperate. 'We are playing a game, you and I, but our lives and our hearts are the stakes, and it is not quite so amusing a pastime as it seems. Do not you think we had better go to Franchard and there blow out our brains?—it would be by far the quickest way of reaching a conclusion . . .'[1] Then, since neither of them really wanted to commit suicide, she thought it better to make a break, and left for Nohant.

There began one of those see-saw situations which are the stock-in-trade of the classic drama. Man is so made that he turns from what he can have, and pursues what he cannot. It must have been with no small a feeling of surprise that George Sand realized Musset's willingness to accept the breach, and, having done so, she at once ceased to want him to take her at her word. Wounded in the sensitive spot of her pride, she hurried back to Paris and tried to see him. Ridden on a tight rein by Alfred Tattet and his other friends, he maintained a strict silence. She knew that he spoke of her coldly and in anger. She was told that he did not wish to see her again. During the terrible days of November 1834 George Sand kept a very full *Journal intime*. It is one of the best things she ever wrote.

What if I run to him when the promptings of love are too strong, and tear at his door-bell until he opens to me? What if I fling myself across his threshold? . . . What if I say to him—You love me still. You may suffer from that knowledge, and blush to find it true, but you pity me too much not to love me. You know only too well that I love you, that I can love no other. Take me in your arms without a word. Let us not argue. Speak but a few soft sentences, and then make love with me, since even now you find me beautiful . . . And then, when you feel yourself grow tired and your irritability revive, send me away, maltreat me, but never, never pronounce that terrible phrase—*This is the last time!* So long as you want me to suffer, I will suffer, but let me sometimes, if only once each week, come to you in search of a tear, of a kiss that shall help me to live, and give me strength. But that you cannot do. You are weary of me, and, like so many others, have been quickly cured. . . .[2]

---

[1] Ibid., p. 170.
[2] GEORGE SAND: *Journal intime*, pp. 4-5.

She tried to see some of her friends. At Buloz's request, she sat to Delacroix, who poured oil upon the flames of her despair by talking about the great promise which Musset's sketches showed. She played with the idea of having herself portrayed looking like one of the Goya women whom Alfred so much admired.

She saw a good deal of the kind, but rather too sophisticated Hortense Allart, who explained that one must always use craft when handling men, that only by losing one's temper will one get them back. But such advice was mere lunacy. One can use craft only when one is not in love. Sainte-Beuve was the sole person who did not talk nonsense to her. 'What is love?' she asked him, and he replied: 'Tears . . . if you weep, you love.' She sought refuge in loneliness. 'I can no longer work', she wrote. That was something that had never happened to her before.

She knew that if Musset had been left to himself he would have returned to her. But there was his pride, his terrible masculine pride, to be taken into account, and there was Alfred Tattet, for ever saying, with that stupid look of his: 'How weak you are!' If only she could have won back Musset's friendship, that would have been something:

If only I had an occasional line from you, a word, permission to send you now and again some cheap print picked up on the Quais, cigarettes rolled by my own hand, a bird, a toy—so that I could cheat my grief and tedium, and see you in imagination thinking of me when you got such foolish nothings. . . .[1]

And then, this other passage, superb and heartrending:

Blue eyes that will never look at me more! Fair face that I shall never see again bending above me in a drooping languor. Dear body, so warm, so lissome, never more will you cover me as Elisha covered the dead child to give it life again. Never again will you touch my hand, as Jesus touched the hand of Jairus's daughter, saying—'Child, rise up!' To that fair head of yours I must now say goodbye, and to those white shoulders. Goodbye, then, to all that once was mine! Henceforward, in the night-time,

[1] GEORGE SAND: *Journal intime*, p. 25.

when I feel on fire I shall embrace the pine trees and the rocks deep in the forest, crying your name: and when, in dreams, I have enjoyed delight, shall fall back senseless on the cold, damp earth. . . .[1]

When December came she was at the end of her tether, and left for Nohant. She fancied that she was half resigned. Alfred wrote her a letter, not lacking in affection, in which he said that he repented of his violent fits. 'So now, then, all is over. I do not wish to see him again, it would be far too painful . . .'[2] It reached her ears that he had said to Tattet that the breach was final. The blow was too violent for her to bear. Like Mathilde de la Mole, she cut off her lovely hair, and sent it to him. Delacroix, in his portrait of her, now in the Carnavalet Museum, shows her with a cropped head—'the forehead seamed with care, a look of wildness in her eyes, the nostrils pinched, and the trembling lips made thin and pale by sleepless nights'.[3] When Musset received the heavy, raven locks, he burst into tears. Once again he was caught, and George, in triumph, could write to Tattet: 'Sir: there are certain surgical operations which, no matter how well performed, nor by how skillful a practitioner, cannot prevent the ailment from recurring. Such a recurrence, in the present case, was always a possibility. It is now a fact. Alfred has again become my lover.'[4]

But they were both afflicted by that worst of follies—a craving for the Absolute. From breach to breach, from reconciliation to reconciliation, their dying passion twitched and gibbered in the nervous spasm of approaching dissolution. They were like two men fighting to the death, both drenched with blood and sweat, clinging together, raining blows on one another, beyond the power of the onlookers to separate. On one occasion he threatened to kill her, then, in a short note written in Italian, begged for a final meeting:

'*Senza veder, e senza parlar, toccar la manò d'un pazzo che parte domani . . .*'—'Without a look, without word to

[1] Ibid., p. 29.

[2] GEORGE SAND: *Lettres à Alfred de Musset et à Sainte-Beuve*, p. 157.

[3] RAYMOND ESCHOLIER: *Delacroix*. Volume II, p. 125.

[4] Letter published by Maurice Clouard in the *Revue de Paris* for August 15th, 1896.

touch the hand of a madman who leaves tomorrow. . . .'[1]

Of this last fight Sainte-Beuve was referee, and now he intervened to stop it. She gave up the struggle.

> *Sand to Musset:* My pride is bruised and bleeding: my love is nothing now but pity. To you I say—'It is essential that a cure be found. Sainte-Beuve is right.' Your conduct is deplorable, impossible. But, Oh, my God, to what sort of a life shall I be leaving you?—drunkenness, wine and women, now and for evermore! But since I can do nothing to save you, there can be no point in prolonging what to me brings only shame, and to you, torment. . . .[2]

Since Alfred was obstinately determined to visit her, she fled to Nohant. The final scenes were once more presided over by the Comic Spirit. Tossed on a storm of passion, George made it clear that she could still retain her presence of mind, and exercise her gifts for organization. When things were at their emotional worst, the middle-class housewife of La Châtre and the hostess of Nohant had a way of taking control of the romantic heroine of drama.

> *George to Boucoiran, March 6th, 1835:* My friend, I need your help if I am to leave today. Please go, at noon, to the coach-office, and book me a seat in the Mail. Then come here, and I will tell you what to do.
>
> However, since, as is perfectly possible, I may not be able to give you my instructions orally—for I shall have my work cut out not to arouse Alfred's suspicions—I will explain everything to you now, in a few lines. You must call on me at five o'clock, and, with an air of urgency, say that my mother has just arrived, that she is very tired and seriously ill—adding that her servant is not to be found, that she needs my presence immediately. I will put on my hat, saying that I shall be back before long, and then you will see me into a dab.
>
> You must come round in the course of the day for the bag containing what I shall need for the night. You can easily take it without being seen, and you must leave it for me at the coach-office. Please have the holdall which

---

[1] *Correspondance de George Sand et d'Alfred de Musset,* edited by Félix Decori, p. 179.

[2] Ibid., p. 180.

I am sending, mended. I have mislaid the fastening . . .
Goodbye for the present. Come as soon as you can. But if
Alfred is here when you arrive, don't look as though you
had anything special to say to me. I will slip into the
kitchen and talk to you there. . . .[1]

Alfred de Musset to Boucoiran, March 9th, 1835: Sir:
I have just come from Madame Sand's, after being
informed that she is at Nohant. Please be good enough to
let me know whether that is so. You saw Madame Sand
this morning, and must be aware of her intentions. If she
is not to leave until tomorrow, you will be in a position to
tell me whether, in your opinion, she has any reason for
not wishing to see me before she goes. . . .[2]

George Sand to Boucoiran: Nohant, March 9th, 1835:
My friend, I arrived in good health, and not over-
fatigued, at Châteauroux, at three o'clock in the
afternoon. Yesterday I saw all our La Châtre friends.
Rollinat accompanied me from Châteauroux. I dined
With him at Dutheil's. I am settling down to do some
work for Buloz.

I am very calm. I have done what had to be done. The
only thing that causes me concern is Alfred's health.
Send me news of him, and tell me, without modifying
anything or trying to soften your words, whether he
showed indifference, anger or pain at the news of my
departure. The only thing that matters is that I should
know the truth. Nothing can weaken my resolution.

Give me, too, news of my children. Is Maurice still
troubled by his cough? Was he all right when he went
back to school on Sunday night? Is Solange also
coughing? . . .[3]

On the very first evening of her return to Nohant she
began work on a novel for Buloz, and produced the daily
quota of twenty sheets covered with her large, tranquil
writing.

[1] Spoelberch de Lovenjoul: *La Véritable Histoire de Elle et
Lui*, pp. 104-6.

[2] Letter published by Maurice Clouard in the *Revue de Paris*
of August 15th, 1896.

[3] Spoelberch de Lovenjoul: *La Véritable Histoire de Elle et
Lui*, pp. 106-7.

V

AFTER THE THUNDER, THE COUNTRY SONGS

THE TURMOIL subsided: the storm withdrew: from the last rumblings of the thunder rose the strains of rustic song. But the great adventure had ended in failure. Once again Lélia had thought to defy the world, impose her independence, live at once a life of passion and of freedom. Her most faithful friends, including her Spiritual Director, Sainte-Beuve, blamed her by implication and advised her to make fewer demands of love. The medicine *he* prescribed was, as he said himself, 'thin and saddening'. It took the form of a suggestion that she should resign herself to the imperfections of love.

She no longer hoped to find a love that would be tender and lasting, nor a love that would be violent and blind. She had reached a point where she understood that the sentiment of love was a beautiful and holy thing which she had wrongly used, which others had wrongly used, in their dealings with her. She decided that she was too old now ever to inspire it in anyone again. She was left without faith, without hope, without desire. It was not that she had denied the God of her childhood, but that she had loved Him imperfectly. He had loosed His lightnings upon her. Over for her were the long days of companionable riding. Never again would she set foot in stirrup.

George Sand to Sainte-Beuve: end of March 1835: I see now that at the root of all my wrong-doing and all my suffering lay the devouring pride which has been my undoing . . . Cursed be the men and the books that strengthened it with their sophistries. I should have stuck to Franklin, who was my delight until the age of twenty-five and whose picture above my bed always makes me want to cry, as would that of some friend I had betrayed.

But I shall not return to Franklin, nor to my Jesuit confessor, nor to my first Platonic love which lasted for six years, nor to my passion for collecting plants and insects, nor to the joy of suckling babies, nor to fox-hunting, nor to galloping my horse across the country-side. Nothing of what has been will ever be again: that I know only too well. . . .[1]

All human beings, when they are in the trough of the wave, are guilty of the error of forgetting that never-ceasing movement which, so long as they live and are capable of action, will sooner or later inevitably sweep them up again to the crest. It was doubtless true that what once had been could never be again. But there remained innumerable possibilities. Had it ever occurred to her, when she repented of the harm she had done to Musset, that he would make so rapid a recovery? Only eight or nine months later he was consoling his friend Tattet, a victim, in his turn, of a faithless mistress. 'Alas! alas! how quickly I have got over it all. New hair is sprouting on my head, new courage is in my guts, and a new indifference in my heart. . . .'[2]

Poetry is emotion recollected in tranquillity. Musset, because he had ceased to suffer, could, at will, re-open the old wounds in the interests of his art. The memory he retained of his season in Hell, the pictures he could conjure up of his days of passion, joy and violence, were to provide inspiration for the whole body of his work. Sometimes that past issued in a cry of hatred, but more often it was with feelings of regret that he recalled the woman, with her black locks and lovely eyes, who had been mad with pride.

The book which he had promised George that he would write about her appeared in 1835 with the title: *Confession d'un Enfant du Siècle.* In it he painted Sand's portrait— giving her as name, Brigitte Pierson—without bitterness, and even with something of respect. Octave, the hero, after a life of debauchery has contracted the habit of turning to derision all that is most sacred, most mysterious, in happy nights of love. He treats Brigitte now as a faithless mistress, now as a kept woman. She remains maternal. 'Yes,' she says, 'you make me suffer and I see you no longer as a lover. You are nothing but a sick child whom I must nurse back to

[1] GEORGE SAND: *Lettres à Alfred de Musset et à Sainte-Beuve,* p. 171.
[2] JOHN CHARPENTIER: *Alfred de Musset,* p. 165.

health before I can find again the man I love . . . May the
God of mothers and lovers permit me to fulfil that task . . .'
George, as we know her, had certainly used such words to
him. The novel ends with a rough indication of forgiveness.
'I do not believe, dear Brigitte, that we can ever wholly
forget each other. But I do believe that as yet it is too soon
for us to forgive, as forgive we must, no matter what the
cost, no matter if it means that we must never see one
another again . . .'[1] When Sand read this passage, she shed
many tears. 'Then I wrote a few lines to the author to say—
Oh, I don't know what—that I had loved him much, that I
had forgiven him everything, that I wished never to see him
again . . .'[2] On this last point they were in agreement.

One day towards the end of 1840, Musset, on his way
through Fontainebleau, remembered that 'Lady of Franchard' who had wrought his youth to fever-heat. Some time
later he met George at the theatre. She was still young, still
beautiful. There was laughter on her lips. She looked at him
as a stranger might have done. That same night when he got
home, he wrote *Souvenir*, the theme of which is: 'Love
passes, as all human emotions pass, as even human beings
pass.'

Oui, sans doute, tout meurt: ce monde est un grand rêve,
Et le peu de bonheur qui nous vient en chemin,
Nous n'avons pas plut tôt ce roseau dans la main
    Que le vent nous enlève. . . .

But what does it matter? Because love is fleeting, that does
not mean we have not loved.

Je ne veut rein savoir, ni si les champs fleurissent,
Ni ce qu'il adviendra du simulacre humain,
Ni si ces vastes cieux éclaireront domain
    Ce qu'ils ensevelissent

Je me dit seulement: 'A cette heure, en ce lieu,
Un jour je fus aimé, j'aimais, elle était belle.

[1] ALFRED DE MUSSET: *Confession d'un Enfant du Siècle*,
p. 350.
[2] Letter from George Sand to Marie d'Agoult, published in
her *Correspondance*. Volume I, pp. 365-72. Everything, however, that had to do with Musset was suppressed by Maurice
Sand.

    J'enfouis ce trésor dans mon âme immortelle
    Et je l'emporte à Dieu.'[1]

It is possible to conceive of a form of love more beautiful than romantic love. One may long for a passion that shall be transformed by the passage of time and by human endeavour into a sentiment of affection. Great natures may swear fidelity in perfect good faith, and keep their oath. But we cannot weigh in the same scales the acts of artists with those of other men. Every artist is a superb actor who must, and knows that he must, go beyond the tolerable in emotion, since only so can his thought be transformed into something rich and strange. A moralist has the right to conclude that Sand and Musset might have been able to conduct their lives more wisely. But the works of art which were born of their mistakes and sufferings would not, in that case, have been possible. Musset, before George Sand came into his life, had known desire, but not passion. In those days he was capable of writing *La Ballade de la Lune,* but not the dialogue between Camille and Perdican. And that is why we cannot regret that on a day of 1834, in a room peopled by phantoms, high above rose-coloured Venice, with the sound of stagnant water, and its heavy smell, coming up to them, two lovers of genius lived in agony, each tearing the other's heart to shreds. No doubt there was something turgid in their cries, and in their ecstasy some pretence:

    Mais qui sait comment Dieu travaille?
    Qui sait si l'onde qui tressaille,
    Si le cri des gouffres amers,
    Si les éclairs et les tonnerres,
    Seigneur, ne sont pas nécessaires
    A la perle que font les mers?

---

[1] The translator, while prepared to try his hand at translating doggerel or light verse, does not feel it incumbent upon him to mangle serious poetry.

PART FIVE

PROPHETS AND POETS

Do you know, the older I grow the more sure do I become that the only man one can really love is the man one does not respect.

Marie Dorval

I

MICHEL DE BOURGES

NOHANT. THE end of March 1835. How beautiful the garden was looking in those days of early Spring. Madame Dudevant, still in a somewhat depressed mood, would sit on a bench among the periwinkles and wild hyacinths, reading Sainte-Beuve's letters which were full of reproaches, encouragements, and warnings. His advice to his 'penitent' was that she should make her peace with God. Buloz, on the other hand, was badly scared because she had asked him to send her Plato and the Koran. He dreaded all the 'mystical stuff' which might descend upon his head—and on the *Revue*. 'Write to George,' he said to Sainte-Beuve, 'and tell her not to get too deeply involved in the mystical. I wish I'd had the courage not to send her those books, but she does so lose her temper!'

Buloz had good reason to be afraid. His lady novelist was doing a lot of 'dabbling in the mystic', though no longer in the mystical aspects of love. George declared that she would sooner blow her brains out than embark again on the sort of life she had been leading for the past three years. 'No, no . . . neither the gentle love that lasts, nor the love that is violent and blind. Do you think it likely that I could inspire the first, or that I am tempted to endure the second? Both are precious and beautiful emotions, but I am too old now for either. . . .'[1]

Panic-stricken at the thought of love after so many failures, she was anxious to find elsewhere a cure for her unsatisfied desires. But where? but how? In God, as in her Convent days? That was what Sainte-Beuve had recommended, and that was what she would have liked. She had never ceased to love that unknown God whose presence

[1] GEORGE SAND: *Lettres à Alfred de Musset et à Sainte-Beuve*, p. 169.

240

she could feel behind the heavenly constellations, on those dark nights shot with melancholy, when, under the pale stars, the Park at Nohant lay wrapped in silence and in mystery. She was feeling gloomy unto death. She thought: 'God does not love me, I am no concern of His, for He has left me here on earth in weakness, ignorance and wretchedness . . .'[1] First love, now Heaven, had abandoned her!

Of all that Sainte-Beuve had put into his letters, she remembered two words only: *surrender, sacrifice*. She longed to give herself to some great cause, to find some way of using up the superfluity of energy which was choking her, to tear herself free from pride and egotism. But these longings of hers eddied in the void. There was no object to which they could attach themselves. On whom should she expend the force of her devotion? Her children were far away, Maurice at the Lycée, Solange at boarding-school. The 'bouncing girl' had now become a 'handful', obeying nobody, but always being forgiven for her naughtiness because she was such a comic little creature, and so lovely to look at. Maurice had not outgrown his sentimental phase, and asked nothing better than to be tied to his mother's apron-strings. She would have liked to have him back at Nohant, but knew that the problem of his education would bring about a permanent breach with Casimir. Dutheil, who was her lawyer at La Châtre, and one of the few people in whom she could confide, counselled Aurore to 'make it up' with her husband by the simple expedient of 'becoming his mistress'. But such an idea was hateful to her. 'The very thought of coupling without love is loathsome. A wife who turns to her husband with the object of dominating his will is no better and no worse than a prostitute who plies her trade in order to live, or than a courtesan who sells herself in return for luxury.'[2]

Dutheil argued that the interests of her children demanded the sacrifice, but instinctive repugnance was too much for her. It was not that her husband caused her feelings of greater physical disgust or moral aversion than other men. What decided her was her strongly held view that no woman should allow herself to be used as a chattel. 'Human beings are compact of body and soul . . . The body, it may be, performs certain functions, such as eating and

[1] GEORGE SAND: *Histoire de ma Vie*. Volume IV, p. 305.
[2] GEORGE SAND: *Histoire de ma Vie*. Volume IV, p. 291.

digesting, with which the soul has nothing to do, but the act of love cannot be so regarded. The very idea is revolting.'[1]

Any 'seduction' of Casimir being, therefore, out of the question, there was nothing for it but to eliminate him entirely. She longed ardently for a 'separation of person and property' which should leave her mistress in her own house. Dudevant, for his part, was sick and tired of the country, and showed himself by no means averse to the idea of living in Paris as a gay young bachelor. They reached an agreement in accordance with the terms of which they could proceed to the business of getting 'unmarried'. Aurore would keep Nohant. Casimir should have the Hôtel de Narbonne, in the rue de la Harpe, which brought in six thousand seven hundred francs annually in rents. Out of that sum he would meet his son's school charges, all taxes and the concierge's wages. Aurore would be responsible for Solange. This agreement was to come into operation in November 1835. No sooner was it signed than Casimir began to have second thoughts. He regretted the loss of his little kingdom of Nohant, and felt that, in renouncing his rights, he was performing an act of sacrifice worthy of a Roman. His wife refused to take him seriously; still more, to regard him as a tragic figure. 'My creed is that of liberty, and I have no wish to be in anybody's debt, not even when I am made to be an object of charity on the proceeds of my own money . . .'[2] Above all, she did not wish the 'Baron' to pose as a victim in the eyes of the children, whose respect she valued. What was to be done? Dutheil advised her to go to Bourges and there consult a lawyer who already enjoyed a high reputation, Louis-Chrysostom Michel, known as 'Michel de Bourges', who was a close friend of Planet.

George Sand was filled with curiosity about this militant republican. He was the oracle of the Departments of the Cher and the Indre, and the uncrowned king of Aquitaine. 'Michel thinks . . . Michel wants . . . Michel says . . .' Dutheil, Planet and Rollinat were for ever repeating these words with an astonishing air of respect. Michel de Bourges appeared to be the unchallenged leader of all opposition to the existing régime, south of the Loire. He exercised over the Liberals of the district an almost despotic influence. Although he was only thirty-seven, he had the appearance of a bent old man. He was bald, and his head looked as

1 Ibid., Volume IV, p. 292.
2 GEORGE SAND: *Correspondance*. Volume I, p. 297.

though it were composed of two separate skulls welded together. He had a pale face and magnificent teeth. He was shortsighted, but his eyes were gentle and appealing. Lamartine described him thus: 'He is a man cut from a block of granite, all straight lines and sharp angles, like the statue of an ancient Gaul. There is something of the peasant, of the primitive, about him. His cheeks are pale and hollow, his head is sunk between high shoulders, his voice deep, solemn and sepulchral. . . .'[1]

Michel was the son of a poor woodcutter of the Var who had been assassinated by the forces of the counter-revolution. He had been brought up as a peasant, and still wore a shapeless reefer-coat and wooden clogs. Since he was in bad health, and suffered from the cold, he had taken to wearing, no matter what the weather, a sort of turban consisting of three knotted handkerchiefs, and this gave him a fantastic appearance. Under these aggressively rustic paraphernalia, he sported a white shirt of fine material which always looked as though it were freshly washed and laundered. The redoubtable Tribune of the People had a way with him, and was fond of women, whose favour he won by his eloquence. When he talked he became almost handsome.

On April 7th, 1835, walking the streets of Bourges from seven o'clock in the evening till four in the morning, he indulged in a display of verbal fireworks for the benefit of George Sand, Planet and Fleury, 'The Gaul'. George had come to ask his advice, but he would speak of nothing but *Lélia*, and his own theories. By the light of the moon, they spent the magnificent hours of the Spring darkness strolling about the austere and silent town of Bourges. Michel speechified till dawn.

It was as though a torrent of ideas were taking form in music. He could spread before his listeners vast spaces of measureless Heaven, and then, without effort or apparent contrast, but by a logical progression and the softest of soft modulations, bring them back to earth and the whisperings of nature. . . .[2]

[1] This passage appeared originally in one of the issues of the *Conseiller du Peuple*, and is quoted by Magon-Barbaroux in *Michel de Bourges*, pp. 58-9.

[2] GEORGE SAND: *Histoire de ma Vie*. Volume IV, p. 20.

To what end was he talking? To rally George to the cause
of militant revolution, to force her from her attitude of
'social atheism', to cure her of that intellectual pride which
had as object a condition of abstract perfection, and held all
action in contempt. She was fascinated. Her defence of her
own point of view was weak, and she felt a peculiar delight
in hearing herself out-argued. Michel's trump-card was his
admiration of *Lélia*. But he found the author even more
attractive than the book. 'I have never seen him like this
before,' Planet told her; 'I have been in his company
constantly for the past year, but never till tonight have I
really known him. He has surrendered to you uncondition-
ally, and has brought all the powers of his intelligence and
sensibility to work upon you.' George had her own view of
the meeting. *To Gustave Papat:* 'I have met Michel. He has
vowed to send me to the guillotine on the first opportunity
. . .' *To Hippolyte Châtiron:* 'I have met Michel. He strikes
me as a fellow with all the makings in him of a Tribune of
the People. We shall, I think, if trouble comes, hear a great
deal more of him.'[1]

She quite genuinely believed that, after her experiences
with Musset and Pagello, she had been cured of the passion
of love. What innocence! Who is there who has ever been
cured of passion while youth and hope remain? She was
like a mettlesome charger, happy when battle is done to
return to the quiet pasturage, but, at the first sound of the
trumpet, leaping the fence and galloping straight for the
sound of the guns. The gift of herself, provided it were
disinterested and accompanied by deep feeling, seemed to
her to be perfectly legitimate, no matter how sudden it
might be. She was introduced to Michel on April 7th. There
still exists an enamelled ring which she gave him as a
memento of their first love-making. It bears a date: April
9th, 1835. After all, she did not regard him as a new lover.
Far from it: he it was 'whom she had loved from the day of
her birth, and in spite of the unreal phantoms in whom, for
a brief moment, she had thought to find him and make him
her own.'[2]

All the same, she did manage, even while listening to
him, to retain her freedom of judgment and her Franklin-
inspired good-sense. Her own instinctive politics were all

[1] GEORGE SAND: *Correspondance*. Volume I, p. 292.

[2] Letter to Michel de Bourges, published in the *Revue
Illustree* of December 1st, 1890, p. 386.

love and justice. Michel's, on the other hand, saw power as
the goal, and the guillotine as the means. As soon as she got
back to Nohant, she began her *Sixième Lettre d'un
Voyageur* (in which she addresses him by the name of
Everard). It is at once eulogistic and rebellious. What, *he* a
philanthropist? she asks:

> Philanthropy produces Sisters of Charity. Love of fame is
> quite another emotion, and fathers quite other careers. I
> know you for a magnificent hypocrite. When you are
> with me you had better leave that subject alone! You
> deceive yourself if you take for duty what is merely the
> consequence in action of your instinct for power. I know
> perfectly well that you are not of those who live obedient
> to the voice of duty. Your part is to impose it on others.
> You have no love for your fellow-men, nor are you their
> brother, since you are not their equal. You out-top them
> all. You were born to sit upon a throne. . . .[1]

Her wish was to be a poet, and a poet only. She knew that
great men of action for the most part write their deeds in
sand, and that the selfsame wind that blew Sulla into history
swept away the memory of Marius.

He bullied her. To what use had she turned her
powers?—to the confection of novelettish love-affairs: just
that and nothing more. She was prepared to admit that her
life had been full of faults, but to them she attached no
doctrinal value whatever. 'All those who have known me
for some time are sufficiently fond of me to look with an
indulgent and forgiving eye on the harm I may have done
myself. My writings, since they set out to prove nothing,
have been the cause neither of good nor evil. . . .[2]

'When *will* you set out to prove something, then?' he
impatiently demanded: 'what if you die with nothing
proved?' She loved to feel his strength lashing at her. For
the first time in her life she had been brought up against a
man who was more strong-willed than herself. He called her
'Fool!'—and that was a new sensation. She stroked his great
bald forehead. She could wish that he were old and sick, so
that she might take care of him. But he *was* sick, sick of
unsatisfied ambition. Greatly daring, she said to him: 'You

[1] GEORGE SAND: *Lettres d'un Voyageur*. Volume VI, p.
152.
[2] Ibid., Volume VI, p. 159.

find that the accomplishment of a great destiny is long in
coming! The time drags, your hair recedes, your spirit burns
itself up, and the human race refuses to move forward.
. . .'[1]

At the end of April, Michel went to Paris to take part in
the great political trial of the year—the prosecution of the
Lyons insurgents. All the leaders of the republican party
were appearing for the defence—Marie, Garnier-Pagès,
Ledru-Rollin, Carrel, Carnot, Pierre Leroux and Barbès.
George wanted to go, too, so as to be with Michel and to
follow the proceedings. Sainte-Beuve, a stage behind in the
computation of her love-affairs, warned her against the
danger of a meeting with Musset. 'Don't imagine for a
moment, my dear, that you won't see him, that he won't be
fully informed, that he won't come . . . What will happen if
you are at the place of danger?—what if you let him cross
your threshold, with no third person there to act as a
buffer . . .'[2] She must have smiled at that! As though she
were bothering her head about Musset! Little by little she
was letting herself succumb to that passion for politics
which is no less intoxicating than the passion of love.
Michel brought with him into the Quai Malaquais apartment the great seething republican excitement. 'We must
get to grips with the social question,' Planet, the good-
hearted and simple-minded, would say each evening, and he
would be echoed by the young and handsome Liszt whom
Musset had introduced to George in the old days. It was for
the purpose of getting to grips with 'all the burning
questions of the hour' that Liszt invited her and the Abbé
Lamennais to dinner. Sainte-Beuve trembled to think what
these firebrand doctrinaires might have said!

Michael, who did not spare himself in his conduct of the
defence, would leave the Court at the end of each day in a
state of collapse. George, with her passion for nursing, took
him in charge, and developed 'a deep emotional attachment
for this man who was like no one I had ever known'.[3] As
soon as Michel was better he would start on a new bout of
oratory, this time with the object of persuading George. Not
that she was hostile. Like him she hated the 'Juste-Milieu',
the Middle of the Road régime. In a confused sort of a way,

[1] Ibid., Volume VI, p. 169.

[2] SAINTE-BEUVE: *Correspondance générale*, edited by Jean
Bonnerot. Volume I, p. 521.

[3] GEORGE SAND: *Histoire de ma Vie*. Volume IV, p. 336.

and in so far as Napoleon had been the incarnation of the
Revolution, she was a Bonapartist. In her girlhood she had
been a republican, from hatred of the 'old countesses', and,
as her mother's daughter, a friend of the People. Equality of
possessions she accepted in principle, though she understood
it rather as a 'general right to happiness' rather than as a
splitting up of property, 'which would make men happy only
at the cost of turning them into barbarians'.[1] The system
about which she heard Michel dilate one night on the
Pont des Saintes-Pères, with the lights of the Tuileries
shimmering on the trees below, was the pure milk of the
word as preached by Babeuf, the ending of inequality by
violence. The mistress of Nohant was jerked from her
dreamy enjoyment of the lovely night, the distant sounds of
an orchestra, and 'the soft radiance of the moon mingled
with the illumination of the royal festivities',[2] by the sound
of Michel's voice. 'I tell you' he was shouting, 'that this
corrupt society of yours will never be rejuvenated until this
fine river runs red with blood, until that cursed palace is
reduced to ashes, until the whole vast city at which we are
looking has become a bare waste on which the poor man
and his family can drive his plough and build his cottage!'

He made such a noise that night, striking his stick against
the old walls of the Louvre, that Sand and Planet, sick at
heart and dispirited, turned from him and walked towards
the Quai Malaquais. He followed on their heels, imploring
them to listen. On each of the following days, the argument
continued. She complained of the intellectual tyranny
which Michel was seeking to impose. She believed more in
wisdom and in love than in violence. She was grateful to
him for having revealed to her an ideal of perfect equality,
but feared that all this vehement eloquence could lead only
to headstrong action and to shooting in the streets.
Prompted by her importunate common sense, she asked
him what sort of society he aimed to build. What was his
programme? 'How can I know that?' he replied. Events
would decide. 'The truth is not revealed to thinkers who
withdraw into a mountain fastness. If they are to discover
what truths are applicable to a society in its birth-pangs,
men must unite and act.'

He reproached George with her impatience. 'Hurry!
hurry!' he said ironically: 'reveal God's secrets to Monsieur

---

[1] Ibid., Volume IV, p. 328.
[2] Ibid., Volume IV, p. 329.

George Sand, who does not want to wait!' She could, if she liked, of course, fold her arms and so preserve her precious liberty, but '. . . truth does not mount behind runaways and gallop along with them . . . The divine philosopher, of whom you are so fond, knew that well enough when he said to his disciples: *where two or three are gathered together in my name, there am I in the midst of them.* It is in the company of others that we must watch and pray . . .'[1] One morning when she was about to answer him, she noticed that he had left the room and locked her in. More than once he went off like that, and she was imprisoned for the whole day. 'I leave you in solitary confinement,' he would tell her, with a laugh, 'so that you may have time for reflection.'

At first, she derived a certain amount of pleasure from his bullying, but it did not in any way change her views. She had always been of the opinion that the last shall be first, that the oppressed are worth more than the oppressors, the slaves than the tyrants. 'I have always felt a hatred of the towering image with feet of clay.' But this hatred of hers remained passive. Except for an occasional outburst of warlike enthusiasm, she relapsed into an existence where poetry was the only thing that mattered. But at last, out of affection for Michel, she did adopt, if not his doctrine, at least his colours.

I warn you that I am, alas, fit for nothing but to carry out orders faithfully and courageously. I can act, but not think, because I know nothing, and have no certainties. I can obey only if I shut my eyes and stop my ears so that I may see nothing and hear nothing that might dissuade me. I can march with my friends, much as a dog that sees its master sailing away in a ship will plunge into the water and swim after him until it dies of exhaustion. The ocean is wide, and my friends I am weak. I am fit for no more than to be a soldier, and I am only five feet high . . . Let us go forward! No matter what the subtle colours of your banner so long as your companies march ever along the road that leads to the ultimate Republic. In the name of Jesus, who has upon this earth no single true apostle; in the names of Washington and Franklin, who failed to finish their work and have left us a task still to accomplish; in the name of Saint-Simon, whose sons bravely tackle the sublime and terrible problem (may

[1] GEORGE SAND: *Histoire de ma Vie.* Volume IV, p. 342.

God protect them!)—provided only that the good prevail, and that those who believe can give proof of their faith . . . I am but a poor drummer-boy, but take me with you. . . .[1]

It would have needed a prophet with more of religion than Michel had, a prophet who could have brought Socialism into harmony with Christianity, to turn the drummer-boy into a soldier of the Revolution, and to have satisfied not only Sand's heart, but her mind as well.

II

NEW FRIENDS

LAYERS OF friendships are renewed as slowly as, but no less inevitably than, layers of humus. One man dies, another slips out of our social world, a third finds his way into it bringing with him a whole new group. When Madame Dudevant first went to Paris she was surrounded by her Berrichon familiars—Regnault, Fleury and the rest. Then Latouche and Sainte-Beuve had become her intimates, the two persons of all others in whom she most confided. The break with Sandeau had alienated Balzac and Regnault, and passion had created about her an area of emptiness. When Musset took his departure he left behind him Franz Liszt, whom he had been instrumental in introducing to the Quai Malaquais. There were many reasons why Liszt, who was a musician of genius, should appeal to George Sand. She had been brought up by her grandmother to have an instinctive appreciation of all that was best in music. But it was not only music that drew them together. Liszt, since the days of his youth, had been mystically inclined. His piety was more fervent than hers. Like her, he felt a tender compassion for all unfortunates: like her, he combined aristocratic manners with democratic opinions: like her, he wanted to know everything. He read the poets and philosophers, and was for

[1] GEORGE SAND: *Lettres d'un Voyageur*, p. 183.

ever in search of noble emotions. He was her junior by seven years. He had flashing eyes, and when he played his long silken hair was never still. She could have fallen in love with him.

Paris gossip maintained that she had, and for a short while Musset was jealous of him. Aurore and Franz always denied the charge, and they lived, both of them, sufficiently in the world's eye, and sufficiently freely, to give an air of verisimilitude to that denial. Liszt admired Sand's novels, and thoroughly approved of her views on romantic love. The 'Corinne of the Quai Malaquais' awoke in him no carnal desires. As for her: 'If I could have loved Monsieur Liszt, I should have done so out of sheer spite,' she wrote, 'but I could not . . . It would annoy me intensely to love spinach, because if I loved it I should eat it, and spinach is a vegetable I cannot endure. . . .'[1] Besides, 'Liszt thought only of God and the Holy Virgin—in which he was very different from me. Good and fortunate young man'.[2] Was there, in all this, a touch of annoyance? Can it be that the spinach was a little too tart? The truth of the matter was, Liszt loved another woman, the Comtesse d'Agoult, granddaughter of Bethmann, the German banker, and daughter of the Comte de Flavigny. She was a golden-haired, blue-eyed creature, 'straight as a candle, white as a sanctified wafer', and ready to espouse all the extremes of romantic passion.

Musset had presented Liszt to Sand, and Liszt, in his turn, had brought about a meeting between her and the Abbé Félicité de Lamennais, for whom he felt an almost filial respect. He loved his burning eloquence, his readiness to sacrifice himself for his ideas, his gloomy, sterile melancholy, his alternating moods of tenderness and violence. This Breton priest, simple-minded, high-souled and obstinate, was eaten up by an imperative need to be loved. He was, emotionally, 'a skin short,' grumpy and irritable. His vocation had come to him late in life, and he took his First Communion at the age of twenty-two after passing through a prolonged crisis of unbelief. 'Life', he said, 'is a sort of gloomy mystery, the secret of which is Faith.' Though the phrase was fine, the doctrine which lay behind it was somewhat obscure. Lamennais had at first looked on the Church as the Spiritual Champion at odds

[1] GEORGE SAND: *Journal intime*, p. 21.
[2] Ibid., p. 23.

with arbitrary power. Everything is Caesar's, except men's souls. Then, after the revolution of 1830 had filled him with reforming zeal, he remembered that the role of the Church had always been to identify itself with, and confer its blessing upon, the great formative movements of history. Consequently it was the duty of nineteenth-century catholicism to be liberal, socially-minded and democratic. Lamennais, at once prophet and plebeian, believed that he had been marked out to achieve the regeneration of the Church. Disowned by his religious superiors, condemned by Rome, cast out from the company of the faithful, he had grown embittered and disenchanted. 'I should like', he said, 'to break with myself.' He lived in a small room in the rue de Rivoli, and dreamed of building a hermit's cell, over the door of which should be a coat-of-arms displaying an oak split by lightning, with, beneath it, the motto *I break but do not bend*. 'He was not' said Sainte-Beuve, 'of a stature to stand up against that most painful of all forms of persecution, which Pascal called the persecution of silence.'

All the same, Sainte-Beuve felt no little admiration for Lamennais, though he judged with his customary severity a man who was 'a Pope by temperament', who had to have as listeners young enthusiasts of the type of Liszt, and who described people as 'believing in nothing' when what he meant was that they did not believe in him. He noted in him that incontinence of thought, combined with credulity, which was reminiscent of Lafayette. Lamennais was physically short, slender and sickly. He had 'an enormous head which was out of all proportion to his body, shy and unforthcoming manners, an ugliness that was really monstrous, and eyes to which shortsightedness imparted a spurious air of gentleness'.[1] He was contemptuous of women, and used to say there was not one of them who could follow an argument for more than fifteen minutes. George Sand, however, found him enchanting. He provided just that mixture of religious faith and social enthusiasm which she needed if she was to come to terms with her new Socialist friends. She sang his praises: 'Never has there existed on this earth a tenderer heart, a more fatherly concern for his fellows, or patience more worthy of an angel . . .' To admire generously is the mark of a generous spirit.

[1] EUGENE FORGUES: Introduction to *Correspondance inédite entre Lamennais et le baron de Vitrolles*, p. 16.

Liszt paid a long visit to the Abbé at La Chesnaie, in Brittany. and described to George his threadbare coat, his blue woollen stockings such as peasants wear, and his shabby straw hat. He also gave her an account of how his own affair with the Comtesse d'Agoult was progressing. He was hoping that she would follow Aurore's example, leave her husband, and live openly with her lover. In June 1835 he gained his point. 'It is a final and severe ordeal', said the Countess, 'but love is my faith, and I am hungry for martyrdom.' She was with child by Liszt, and expected to be brought to bed in December. George could not but be touched by the spectacle of such a woman behaving like the heroines of her own novels.

> *George Sand to Marie d'Agoult:* Lovely Countess of the golden hair. I do not know you personally, but I have heard Franz speak of you, and have seen you. I feel, therefore, that I have the right to say, without presumption, that I love you, that I regard you as the one beautiful, estimable and truly noble product of the patrician world. You must indeed have a strong personality to make me forget your rank. Just now you are for me the very type of a fairy princess, loving, artistic, noble in speech and manner and appearance, like a King's daughter of legend. That is how I see you. I want to love you as you are and for what you are . . . I live in the hopes of paying you a visit. It is one of the most delightful projects on which I have ever set my heart. I have a feeling that you and I will really love one another when we are better acquainted. You are worth a thousand times more than I am. . . .[1]

It was a gracious letter, and yet—the two women were not made for mutual understanding. Madame d'Agoult, like Madame Dudevant, had broken free from her family and from the world in which she had been brought up. But George genuinely loved her freedom, whereas Marie was filled with regret for her lost rank. Sand, the cousin of kings, boasted of her grandfather, the bird-fancier. Marie was for ever reminding those who seemed to have forgotten it that she had been born a Flavigny. Sand loved to roam the countryside in a blue smock and trousers. Madame d'Agoult was never really at her ease, said Liszt, unless she

1 GEORGE SAND: *Correspondance.* Volume I, pp. 299-302.

had on a dress that had cost a thousand francs. George went
from man to man and hope to hope. Marie, having yielded
once to passion, did her best to make fidelity legitimize
adultery. 'I am not envious', wrote Sand, 'but I do admire
and respect you. I know that lasting love is a diamond
which calls for a casket of pure gold, and that your heart is
precisely such a tabernacle. . . .'[1]

Liszt took his Countess along to the 'attic' on the Quai
Malaquais. She turned out to have a long, thin face framed
in curls worn after the English fashion. Seen from the side,
it gave the impression that it 'had been squeezed in a door'.[2]
George praised, not without an almost imperceptible touch
of irony, the 'Péri in a blue dress' who had deigned to
descend from Paradise to visit a mere mortal. She never,
now, called her anything but 'la Princesse' or 'Arabella'.
Their first meeting was not a great success.

George Sand to Marie d'Agoult: The first time I saw you
I thought you charming; but you were cold. The second
time, I told you that I detested the aristocracy. I did not
then know that you belonged to it. Instead of slapping my
face, as I richly deserved, you spoke to me about your
soul, as though you had known me for ten years. It was
delightful, and I was straightway filled with a desire to
love you. But I do not love you yet. That is not because I
do not know you well enough. I know you as well now as
I shall do twenty years from now. It is *you* who do not
know *me* sufficiently. Since I cannot be sure that you love
me for what I really am, I do not wish to love you *yet* . . .
You may not realize it, dear friend, but I suffer from
shyness more than from anything else. That had not
occurred to you, had it? I am generally held to be a
person of audacious mind and character. But that is a
very mistaken idea. My mind is apathetic, my character
capricious . . . It is no use your hoping that you will be
able at once to cure me of my fits of abruptness which
find expression only in moods of reticence. . . .[3]

She added: 'You must quickly so arrange matters that I
can love you. That should not be difficult. To begin with, I
am fond of Franz, and he has told me to love you. He has

[1] GEORGE SAND: *Correspondance.* Volume I, p. 314.
[2] HONORE DE BALZAC: *Béatrix.* Volume I, p. 262.
[3] GEORGE SAND: *Correspondance.* Volume I, pp. 315-17.

answered for you as for himself.' The tone was not
noticeable for its warmth, but the two cats kept their claws
sheathed, and, when Liszt and Madame d'Agoult were in
Switzerland, whither, in spite of the Faubourg Saint-
Germain, they had gone as lovers, the correspondence
continued. It was not altogether without pleasure that
George read between the lines of Liszt's letters, in which he
announced his complete and utter happiness, and guessed
that he was thoroughly bored at Geneva. 'If you come', he
wrote, 'you will find me in a somewhat numbed condition.'
That was not true. He had never been more inspired, but
artists are just as coquettish as women. The lovers of
Geneva re-read *Lélia* and drew the most pungent conclu-
sions about its author's temperament. They adored their little daughter, Blandine, who was born on December 18th,
1835, and suffered from the disapproval with which a Puritan society treats an irregular union. Both of them, in every
letter they wrote, urged George to come to Switzerland. But
before she could make the journey, she had got to get her
affairs at home in order.

III

THE LAW AT WORK

THE AGREEMENT which Aurore Dudevant and her
husband had signed in February 1835 was due to come into
operation in November, but Casimir showed signs of in-
decision and irritability. His wife's new political friendships
were displeasing to him. Domestic squabbles became more
frequent. Aurore wanted to take the administration of her
property out of the hands of Casimir, who she said was
ruining her. She consented to maintain him even after the
separation should have taken place. 'My husband may be a
worthless creature.' she wrote to Hippolyte. 'but you don't
surely, think I should let him starve?—though he, for that
matter, would cheerfully let me go to the Morgue for a
matter of twenty francs.[1]

[1] Spoelberch de Lovenjoul Collection: Group E. 920, f. 80.

On November 19th, 1835, there was a scene. In itself it was nothing very serious, but it made a rupture inevitable. The family, with a few friends, was gathered after dinner in the drawing-room for coffee. Maurice asked for some more cream. 'There is no more', said his father; 'leave the room, and go to the kitchen.' The child took refuge with his mother. An altercation followed, in which Aurore remained calm but Casimir lost his temper. He told his wife, too, to leave the room. She replied that she was in her own house. 'We'll soon see about that,' he said, 'leave the room at once, or I'll box your ears!' The friends who were present, Dutheil, Papet, Fleury, Rozane and Alphonse Bourgoing, intervened. Casimir, beside himself with rage, went across to where he kept his guns, exclaiming as he did so, 'This sort of thing has got to stop!' Dutheil saw him take down a gun, snatched it from him, and read him a lecture. 'When I'm annoyed,' said Casimir, 'I lose control of myself. For two pins I'd have given you a punch on the nose!' Of such a nature was the quarrel as described by witnesses. It should be borne in mind that those present were friends of the wife rather than of the husband, that Dutheil had been in love with Aurore, and that public opinion in the neighbourhood was far from sure that the witnesses were impartial. Probably the scene was not so much frightening as unpleasant. George Sand herself gave an account of it to her friend Adolphe Duplomb, couched in comic dialect form.

Dear Hydrogène: You have got what happened at La Châtre all wrong. There was nothing in the nature of a brawl between Dutheil and the Baron de Nohant-Vic. Here is what really occurred. The Baron seemed to have got it into his head that he was going to give me a proper drubbing. But Dutheil wasn't going to have nothing like that, he wasn't, and Fleury and Papet felt about the same. So off goes the Baron and gets his gun for to pepper the lot of 'em. But they didn't feel like being peppered at all, they didn't. So the Baron ups and he says—'that's 'nuff', he says, and goes back to his boozing. That's how things was. No one didn't get across him. But I was just about through, seeing as I'm sick of working for my living and leaving my little bits and pieces in the hands of that old devil, and being turned out of house and home each year, and having all the loose madams in the place a-sleeping in my beds and filling the house with fleas, so I ups and I says—'I'm not going to stand for it,' I says, and off I goes to the Big Judge at La Châtre and tells him to get on with the business. . . .[1]

She hurried off to Châteauroux to consult the wise François Rollinat, and then to Bourges, where Michel was serving a not very rigorous prison sentence for his political misdemeanours. All the gentlemen of the Law were in agreement. No time must be lost, advantage must be taken of this providential incident, an immediate separation must be demanded, and Casimir must be persuaded to let the judgment go by default. This might be managed, because the *marito*, so long as the old baroness remained alive, was badly in need of money. In the event, he consented to leave for Paris, after first handing in his resignation as Mayor of Nohant. He took the children with him, and saw them safely settled, one at his Lycée, the other in her boarding-school. Aurore warned her mother to handle Casimir carefully, should he take it into his head to pay her a visit. At all costs they must avoid wounding his self-esteem, and so give him an excuse for 'quibbling'. She added:

Nothing is going to stop me from doing what I ought to do, and shall do. I am my father's daughter, and preconceived ideas don't matter a row of beans to me when my heart tells me that justice and courage are the order of the day. If my father had listened to a lot of fools and lunatics, I should never have been here at all to inherit his name. He left me a fine example of independence and paternal devotion. I shall be true to his memory even though the whole world seethes with the scandal. What do I care for the whole world! The only people I care about are Maurice and Solange. . . .[2]

November found her again at Nohant, awaiting the judgment of the Court. In the silence of the great house she wrote an excellent cloak-and-dagger novel, *Mauprat*. There were no servants. Casimir had dismissed the lot. The gardener and his wife looked after her. Since the judgment

---

[1] Letter quoted by René Doumic in *George Sand*, pp. 184-5. It was shown to him by Charles Duplomb.

[2] GEORGE SAND: *Correspondance*. Volume I, pp. 312-13.

would, to a great extent, depend upon her behaviour, she modelled herself upon 'Sixtus V.[1]

George Sand to Marie d'Agoult: At this very moment, a bare mile away, four thousand fools believe that I am on my knees in sackcloth and ashes, weeping for my sins, like the Magdalene. They will have a rude awakening. The very day after the victory is mine, I shall throw away my crutches, jump on my horse, and go careering all over the town. Don't be surprised if you hear it said that I have been made to see reason, that I have bowed my head to the edicts of public morality, that I am willing to throw myself on the mercy of the Court, that I have developed a fondness for Louis-Philippe, the Father, and Poulet-Rosolin, the Son, and for the whole blessed Catholic Chamber . . . I am quite capable of writing an Ode to the King, or a sonnet to Monsieur Jacqueminot.[2]

In January 1836, the 'Big Judge' in La Châtre heard the witnesses. The charges were matter of common knowledge —that Casimir had boxed her ears at Plessis in 1824: that he had used insulting language to her: that he had been intimate, in her house, with several of the servants, among them Pepita and Claire . . . that there had been nocturnal orgies.

Petition laid by Aurore Dudevant before the Court: So dissolute and so brazen did Monsieur Dudevant's conduct become, so vulgarly did he boast of his licentious behaviour in my presence, so frequently did the noise of his revelling disturb my rest, that it became impossible for me to remain in the same house with him, though that house happened to be mine . . . In the month of January 1831, I told Monsieur Dudevant that I wished for a separation, and an amicable agreement was reached between us, as a result of which I went to live in Paris . . . I made a trip to Italy, in the course of which Monsieur

[1] Sixtus V (1585-90) was elected Pope because the Cardinals believed him to be at death's door. No sooner, however, had he ascended the throne of St. Peter, then he threw away his crutches, and showed himself to be remarkably active. (TRANSLATOR—with the help of Larousse.)

[2] GEORGE SAND: *Correspondance*. Volume I, pp. 321-2.

Dudevant wrote me a number of perfectly polite letters, in which he expressed himself as being entirely indifferent to my absence, and not in the least anxious for my return. . . .[1]

Not a word was said about Sandeau or Musset. Hippolyte Châtiron, in spite of the fact that he was the plaintiff's brother, had sided with Casimir, and now urged him to enter a defence, assuring him that the whole neighbourhood was behind him. Casimir, however, had given his word that he would say nothing. He did not wish to lose the promised allowance. He let the case go by default. The Court at La Châtre gave Aurore the custody of the children.

But when she claimed a hundred thousand francs as her share after the property held by them jointly had been liquidated, he lost his temper and refused to accede to her demand. Hippolyte encourage him in this attitude. 'There are people close to you who could ensure your winning of the case. You have only to let them tell what they know . . .' George was surprised and irritated by her husband's sudden change of attitude. The period of friendly separation was at an end. She had to leave Nohant which, until the finding of the Court should be promulgated, belonged legally to Casimir, and went to live in Dutheil's house. It had become more than ever necessary for her to make her peace with public opinion. In a small country town it could bring much silent pressure to bear on the Judges. She was as charming as only she knew how to be; childlike with the children, innocently coquettish with the men, careful with the women. She roamed the countryside in search of insects, and managed stolen meetings with Michel, under Casimir's very nose, in the lonely summer-house at Nohant between the Park and the road. To her son she wrote affectionate letters, full of the praises of virtue. But over and above all she worked. Neither the case, nor her quarrels with Michel, nor her immense correspondence could reflect her from her ant-like labours. Both sides in the litigation were busy. Witnesses were summoned. Boucoiran came from Nimes to give evidence.

George Sand to Boucoiran, January 6th, 1835: I know you did not actually see either Claire or Pepita in Mr.

[1] Spoelberch de Lovenjoul Collection: Group E. 948, f. 23 and f. 28.

You-Know-Who's arms. All the same, you feel quite sure about what was going on. You have proof of it, insofar as such things can be proved, from what you saw happening all around you, and heard everybody in the house and in the village saying. . . .[1]

Casimir Dudevant to Caron, April 25th, 1836: There is one thing which I am told might make things difficult for Aurore when this case comes up again. She seems to think that I have in my possession certain letters which it amused her to write to Madame Dorval. Now these letters, from what I hear, and from what I discovered in Paris, are of a highly compromising nature. Could you not manage to get hold of a few of them by trickery, through the instrumentality of Dumont, or somebody else?[2]

Casimir, roused from his lethargy, drew up a tearful memorandum in which he enumerated his grievances. It began as follows:

August 1825: Trip to the Pyrenees. Meetings and correspondence with Aurélien de Sèze—*October*: Trip to Bordeaux. Aurore Dudevant and Aurélien de Sèze surprised in one another's company.

1827: Exchange of intimate letters between Aurore Dudevant and Stéphane Ajasson de Grandsagne— *November 1827*: Trip to Paris with Stéphane Ajasson de Grandsagne, on grounds of health!

1829: Letter written by Aurore Dudevant to Stéphane Ajasson de Gransagne, asking for poison, and saying that she was sick of life—*April 1829:* Departure of husband and wife to Bordeaux, where, it was agreed, they should spend three weeks or a month, at most. Daily visits of Madame Dudevant to Monsieur de Sèze. Excuse given, that she was going to the baths.

November 1830: Madame Dudevant arrived in Paris and stayed with her brother in the rue de Seine, where,

---

[1] Spoelberch de Lovenjoul Collection: Group E. 920, f. 120.
[2] Ibid. Group E. 948, f. 63.

according to the concierge, she shocked everybody by her behaviour . . . Monsieur Jules Sandeau.

1831: She returned to Nohant where she spent a few days, and then left again for Paris, taking with her, as maid, a country girl called Marie Moreau. This girl can give evidence of fierce disagreements with Jules Sandeau, accompanied by blows.

1832: Monsieur Gustave Plauche. . . .

1833: She left for Italy with Monsieur Alfred de Musset, and stayed there for eight months . . . Quarrels and reconciliations.

The last date in this Memorandum is 1835:

1835: Mutual antipathy between husband and wife. Madame Dudevant behaving like a young man—smoking swearing and showing herself habitually in man's clothes. Had quite abandoned the delicate manners of her sex—author of *Lélia*.[1]

In May 1836 the case came up once again before the La Châtre Court. The Bench took a serious and unsympathetic view of the husband's very displeasing accusations. Portions of the statement were true, others defamatory, but whether the charges were substantiated or dismissed their presentation in this form was ridiculous, in view of the fact that the man Dudevant was seeking 'not the dissolution of marital cohabitation, but its continuance'. The accusations being of such a nature that there could be no hope that husband and wife could be reconciled, the Court granted 'separation of bed and board' in favour of the woman Dudevant, forbade the husband to have anything more to do with her, and awarded her the custody of the children.

Urged by his advisers, Casimir lodged an appeal with the Court of Bourges. There Michel could appear on her behalf. George Sand, therefore, installed herself at Bourges so as to be near the man who combined the functions of lover and Counsel. She lived with a friend of hers, Eliza Tourangin, who, with her father, Félix Tourangin and her three small

[1] Unpublished. Spoelberch de Lovenjoul Collection: Group E. 948, ff. 40-1.

brothers, occupied a huge house in the rue Saint-Ambroise. On the evening before the hearing, George Sand scratched a prayer on the panelling of her room:

> Oh God! protect those who will the good, cast down those who intend evil . . . Destroy the blind rule of the scribes and pharisees, and open a way for the traveller who seeks Thy holy places. . . .[1]

From Paris, from La Châtre, from Bordeaux, came all her friends to rally round her. Only Madame Maurice Dupin refused to commit herself, since she did not know which side would keep her in funds. Michel pleaded with unashamed eloquence for his mistress. 'This woman's home,' he said, addressing the appellant, in his deep, solemn tones, 'has been profaned, and it is you who have profaned it. You introduced beneath her roof debauchery and superstition . . .' He read with emotion the letter-journal which Aurore had sent to Aurélien, maintaining that it proved the purity of his client at the time of her first love. He described the paradoxical situation of a young woman who, having brought as dowry to her husband a great house and a considerable fortune, was forced to live on a miserable pittance, while he used her house and property for the purpose of enjoying 'an existence of opulence and vice'. He alluded with horror to the slanderous imputations of Monsieur Dudevant, who had gone so far as to 'represent his wife as being no better than a prostitute.' He praised to the skies this irreproachable wife forced by a miserly and licentious husband to quit the conjugal roof. George listened, looking charming in a simple white dress, a white hood, and a falling collarette of white flowered lace. All those present in the courtroom were overcome by Michel's eloquence. The Bench, unable to agree, adjourned the case, but next day an amicable settlement was reached. Hippolyte, convinced that things were going badly, advised his brother-in-law to give way so far as Nohant and Solange were concerned.

Hippolyte Châtiron to Casimir Dudevant, June 18th, 1836: I am not suggesting that you should accept the La

---

[1] This prayer was published in 1878 in *Le Magasin pittoresque*, p. 190. It was partially reproduced in the *Souvenirs de 1848*, by George Sand.

Châtre ruling, but only that you should take the Hôtel de
Narbonne and your son, and let Aurore have Nohant,
where you know that, in any case, you could not go on
living. As to Solange, you had better resign yourself to
the inevitable . . . I can at least give you proof that this
wild, undisciplined creature has been a good deal stricter
with her daughter than any respectable woman would
have been . . . Don't worry your head about those who
are influencing her now. Before two years are out they
will all of them have been sent packing, Dutheil, Michel,
Duvernet and Fleury among the first. I won't say that her
character will have changed, but it seems probable that,
having her daughter to look after, she will become more
human. I think that self-esteem, if nothing more, will
lead her to save Solange from the abyss into which she
herself has fallen. . . .[1]

Casimir withdrew his appeal, and Aurore, in order to
have done with the whole business, agreed to his keeping
Maurice, and having a life-interest in the Hôtel de
Narbonne. She, for her part, kept Solange and Nohant
which brought in, at that time, nine thousand four hundred
francs a year in rents. And so, after all this washing of dirty
linen, and all this flow of eloquence, they were back where
they had started.

IV

THE HANDSOME DIDIER

MICHEL HAD spoken as a trained pleader rather than as a
lover. He and George had already drifted apart. It had not
taken him long to antagonize her. In their personal

<hr />

[1] Spoelberch de Lovenjoul Collection: Group E. 868, ff.
261-3.

relationship he was too insistent. He wore her out. She said little in reply to his entreaties, but he had a feeling that her mind was locked and bolted and would never yield to assault. He was bent on making her understand what he called 'political necessity'—a point of view which she decided was either criminal or puerile. She decided that he was more ambitious than sincere, and that made her afraid. His ideas were never the same for two days together. Montesquieu turned him into a moderate, *Obermann* into a hermit. Mental instability so abnormal left George unsatisfied. She had thought to find a master: she had found herself saddled with a tyrant. 'I sometimes think', she said to him, 'that you are the very spirit of Evil, so coldly cruel, so wickedly despotic you are to me.' Why, then, had she not already broken with him? Because, strangely enough, this worn-out, ugly man in whom there was no touch of benevolence, this 'faithless, jealous dictator', had succeeded, if not in bringing her fulfilment, at least in sometimes waking in her the woman whom her younger lovers, Sandeau, Musset, Pagello, had thought of as being 'wholly Lélia'.

George Sand to Michel de Bourges: March 25th, 1837: When destiny threw us together, we were neither of us looking for love. Passion overwhelmed us. We did not fight it, nor did we stop to think. Your desires outstripped mine: they led, I followed. I submitted to the onrush of your love, before ever I had realized the strength of my own, but I submitted with a sort of frenzied violence, because I had a presentiment that, though it had blazed a trail, had set the pace, it would be the first to grow weary and to cease. I knew how deep my own affections are, how concentrated, how calm, and how tenacious . . . When you first made love to me, I wept . . . For some days your passion was strong enough to make you dream that we might really, might wholly, link our fates. You went so far as to make me a promise that that should be so by a certain date which is now rapidly approaching. Cheer up! it is in my heart that the promise was written, and my heart belongs to you. It is a page of the book of life which you are free to tear up when you will. When all my supports were knocked away one by one, and my resistance overcome, when every nerve in my being, stripped of protection and wholly exposed, was quivering beneath your touch, my fondness grew so strong, and

struck so deep, that I could imagine no sweeter aim in life
than to be for ever at your side. . . .[1]

She wrote him burning letters full of mystifications and
code-references, because there was a Madame Michel, of
whom the 'Tribune' went in dread. Michel was regularly
referred to in them, as *Marcel;* Nohant became *Le Chesnay*;
Maurice Sand, *Marie;* April 7th (anniversary of their first
meeting) *Genril*. Eliza Tourangin, the young woman of
Bourges, their confidante and accomplice who arranged for
them to meet under her hospitable roof, figured as
Speranza. Sometimes, as a further precaution, George
pretended to be writing to a woman, and referred to *Marcel*
in the third person. These letters of hers are filled with a
sense of restlessness and sensuality. As with everything she
wrote, their style is breathless. The two lovers were for ever
accusing one another of infidelity, and both were justified.

It is natural enough that Michel should have been
jealous, since Sand, when her love grew weaker, was not the
woman to let any opportunity of happiness slip by untaken.
A young Swiss, Charles Didier by name, thirty years old
and very handsome, was on terms of intimate friendship
with her both in Paris and at Nohant, throughout the
'Michel' period. Hortense Allart had introduced him to the
Quai Malaquais some time before. Born at Geneva of a
Huguenot family, a botanist, a mountaineer, and a poet,
Didier had in him something of both Rousseau and
Benjamin Constant. Each evening he drew up in his Diary a
species of 'intellectual balance-sheet'. Being full of romantic
feelings and an ardent Puritan, he felt ill at ease in the
bourgeois-aristocratic society of his native country. He
therefore set off on his travels and at Florence became the

[1] *Revue illustrée*, November 1st, 1890, pp. 296-7. This letter
is one of those published without signature under the title of
Lettres de Femme. The series ran from the beginning of 1890
through 1891, and appeared in the following issues of the
periodical: 118, 119, 120, 121 and 122. Spoelberch de Lovenjoul
and Wladimir Karénine, both of them friends of Madame
Maurice Sand, have certified that they were written by George
Sand to Michel de Bourges in the course of the year 1837. The
Sand family was, however, very anxious that the writer's name
should not be divulged, and the date 1837 was systematically
altered to 1832. Publication of the letters was suddenly
discontinued in 1891.

lover of Hortense Allart. Round about 1830, he turned up
in Paris with fifty francs in his pocket. Victor Hugo, who
was his God, made him welcome, and he became a regular
member of the 'Cénacle'. He had written a novel—*Rome
souterraine*, which had enjoyed some small success, but,
having at about the same time read *Lélia*, had come to the
conclusion that 'in the light of such powers of passion and
composition, I feel myself to be a poor, weak writer and a
very minor artist'.[1]

When this handsome admirer was presented by Hortense
Allart to Sand, the latter sat for a while silently taking the
measure of the newcomer. Didier talked well (too well,
Sainte-Beuve said), and more or less continuously, in a
rather high voice, with lowered eyes and a vague smile
flickering about his lips. There was something pleasing
about his air of disdain and deep self-assurance. That
Hortense, an expert in men, should have fallen in love with
this eloquent Genevese, was a fact worth noticing. He was
invited to come again, quite quietly, was loud in his praise
of George's modesty, but disgusted by Planche's grubbiness
and the familiar manners of the young provincials who, at
that time, were more or less permanently encamped in the
Quai Malaquais apartment.

Though Didier had been very strictly brought up, he was
an extremely virile young man, who needed women and was
popular with them. Sand asked him to come and see her
alone. He responded eagerly to the suggestion. *Didier's
Diary*: 'Madame Dudevant, charming and wanton. She
breathes love. I am rather worried by her connection with
Planche—not at all the right man for her . . .' When Sainte-
Beuve told the young man about 'Madame Dudevant's
depravity', and, especially, about the Mérimée incident, his
warnings fell on incredulous ears. Then, Musset came on
the scene, and Didier was forgotten until one fine day when
Sand lent him a hundred francs 'to settle his bill for
firewood before starting for Italy'. The gentleman from
Geneva decided that these Frenchwomen were 'very odd
fish'. But by the time he returned from Spain at the end of
1835 looking handsomer than ever with his prematurely
white hair, Musset had disappeared. George offered him her

[1] Cf. JOHN SELLARDS: *Charles Didier, 1805-64*. (Paris,
Honoré Champion, 1904), and also, Sainte-Beuve's portrait of
Charles Didier, under the name of *Phanar*, in *Causeries de
Lundi*, Volume XI.

good offices with Buloz, the run of her purse, and, in fact, anything he might want.

Their intimacy was renewed. On March 26th, 1836, he accepted an invitation to supper in the company of Emmanuel Arago. 'A fantastic evening. We did not leave until 5 a.m. Arago was drunk . . . I was tired and lay on the divan, propped up with cushions. She was rather melancholy, not markedly imperious, and ruffled my hair, calling me her old philosopher . . .' By the time they left she had so managed things that both were head over heals in love with her. Next evening he hurried round to the Quai Malaquais with three bottles of champagne: 'George, gay and laughing. I don't like her rather vulgar side, but I forgive her. She was in a melting mood, and so was I. She gave me a kiss, and I returned it. When I left her at eight o'clock a terrible storm was raging. She gave me her cashmere shawl in exchange for my white silk muffler.' Serious young men cannot play sentimental games of this kind without getting their fingers burned. He wanted her. But what did she want? 'Fortoul is quite sure that George Sand has set her heart on having me . . . I don't want my feelings to become too deeply involved. With characters like hers and mine, things would be bound to go wrong.' Still he found her great fun. 'She talks a great deal to me about Michel de Bourges, and has explained that the bond between them is purely intellectual. She swears that she has had no lover since Alfred de Musset . . . she is beautiful and charming.'

On April 25th she moved into the house where he was living at 3 rue du Regard. He gave up his room to her.

Didier's Diary: 'Her settling into this house has provoked all sorts of gossip. We are more than ever intimate. This complicated creature is unintelligible to me in more ways than one, and I fear her impetuous restlessness. I study her too intensely: I don't understand her. Is she loyal? To questions like that there is no answer . . .' *May 2nd, 1835*: 'She went out this evening, and we did not see one another again until midnight. She finished her sixth *Lettre d'un Voyageur*, and then became tender and loving. She sat at my feet with her head on my knee, and her hands in mine . . . Siren, what is it you want of me?' Others were also wondering what she wanted of him, and whether the reign of Michel was already at an end. Liszt, writing from Geneva, asked bluntly how much truth there was in this 'new story'. She replied that there was none.

George Sand to Franz Liszt, May 5th, 1836: Charles Didier is an old and faithful friend. Which reminds me—you ask about a story that is going round, in which he plays a leading part. What precisely *are* people saying? I am sure I don't know. After all, people said things about you and me, and you know just how true *they* were. That ought to give you some idea. I have heard it said both in Paris and in the country that it is not Marie d'Agoult who is at Geneva with you, but I . . . Didier is very much in the same position as you, the lady in question certainly not being me—which does not alter the fact that I spent a week under his roof, in Paris. . . .[1]

It was true that she had been lodging in the same house as Didier, because she was afraid that her husband might distrain on her furniture at the Quai Malaquais. But another friend, David Richard, had made a third, and the days had passed in an atmosphere of 'patriarchal family life'. As for Musset, she had not thought of him for ages.

I have no idea whether he thinks of me. If he does, it is because he wants to write a bit of poetry and earn a few sous from the *Revue des Deux Mondes* . . . As a matter of fact, I am not now thinking of anybody in that way. I am a great deal happier as I am than I have ever been in my life. I am growing old. I have had my fill of emotions on the grand scale. I am one of those who like to sleep peacefully, and my temperament is naturally gay and carefree. Solid, lasting affection is what I need after thirty years of a life ravaged by violent emotions . . . That is all behind me now. Time does not stand still, and, thank. Heaven, one gets used to everything, and sick of everything. What I do not get sick of is kindness linked with intelligence. I think you have found a treasure in Marie. Don't let her go. You will be asked about her at the Day of Judgment, and, if you haven't used her well, will be deprived through all eternity of the sound of the celestial harps. I am quite certain that I shall hear nothing in the next world but the Devil's tattoo and the drums of Hell. I, too, had one great treasure—my own heart—and I have made bad use of it. . . .[2]

[1] Spoelberch de Lovenjoul Collection: Group E. 920, f. 140.
[2] Spoelberch de Lovenjoul Collection: Group E. 920, ff. 138-40.

In May she left for La Châtre where she was needed in connection with her lawsuit. Didier, mad with love and still unsatisfied, was more than ever inclined to say to himself, 'Siren, what is it you want of me?' There were times when he hoped that he would never see her again, and refused to play the painful role of confidant: others when he was devoured by desire and hope. The scarcity of her letters filled him with alarm, and he followed her into the country.

Charles Didier's Diary: Gloomy journey: struggles and perplexities. When I got to La Châtre she had gone to bed. I woke her and flung myself into her arms without a word. She held me tight and our reconciliation was accomplished in a long and silent embrace. No words of explanation were uttered between us until the evening, when she took me to Nohant. I spent five days with her, which are among the loveliest of my life . . . The world forgotten; country solitude; evenings under the trees at Nohant; moonlight. We were quite alone . . . Nights on the terrace beneath a starlit sky, my arm about her, and her head resting on my breast. . . .[1]

George, among her trees and flowers, and far from other men, could be an easy-tempered mistress. For several days, Didier was satisfied, charmed, intoxicated. 'At heart, she is a thoroughly good woman . . . Michel is very jealous of me —he says so in all his letters . . .' When he got back to Paris, he received from her several admirable pages on the happy days they had spent together, after which there was silence.

Truth to tell, she gave him scarcely a thought. She was moving hither and thither about the countryside, appearing in Court, plunging fully dressed into the Indre, then flinging herself on the grass in her soaking clothes, covering four leagues on foot, and, in the evenings, working at a revised edition of *Lélia*. The confession of impotence must be deleted. In the new version Pulchéria and Stenio are sacrificed to the wisdom of Trenmor. The novel becomes moral, and socially conscious. Lélia turns her back on love. *George Sand to Marie d'Agoult*: 'She is of the family of the Essenes, who dwell in solitude among the palm trees, that *gens solitaria* of whom Pliny speaks. His fine passage on the subject will figure as the epigraph of my third volume. Do

1 Cf. JOHN SELLARDS: *Charles Didier.*

you approve the plan of my book?—as to the plan of my life, you are not competent to judge. You are too happy and too young to pay a visit to the health-giving verges of the Dead Sea (again, Pliny the Younger), and to become one of that family in which nobody is born, and nobody dies.'[1]

This letter leads one to conclude that after all that had happened, even after Michel, George was Lélia still.

> I have had my bellyful of great men (forgive the expression). I quite like to read about them in the pages of Plutarch, where they don't outrage my humanity. Let us see them carved in marble or cast in bronze, and hear no more about them. In real life they are nasty creatures, persecutors, temperamental, despotic, bitter and suspicious. Their arrogant contempt includes both sheep and goats. They behave worse to their friends than to their enemies. God preserve us from them! Be good, and, if it comes to that, stupid. Franz will tell you that the people I love can never be foolish enough for my taste. Times out of number I have found fault with him for being too intelligent. Fortunately, that 'too' doesn't amount to much, so I can still go on being very fond of him. . . .[2]

She was rather fonder of him than Marie d'Agoult could stomach. 'What you say about Franz', George wrote to her, 'fills me with a wild, an almost morbid, longing to hear him. Did you know that whenever he plays I hide myself under the piano. I have very strong nerves, and no instrument is ever too loud for me.'[3]

It was true that she had 'very strong nerves', and the more ethereal Marie was deeply suspicious of her. Nevertheless, she kept on urging her to join them in Switzerland. Suddenly, in August 1836, when the lovers of Geneva had already left for Chamonix, George announced her impending arrival. Her case had been won. She turned up with her two children, a couple of old friends, and her maid, Ursule Josse, who, never having been further than La Châtre in her life, was convinced, when she reached Martigny, that she was in Martinique. Sand travelled, like Byron, with a whole menagerie at her heels. It is not difficult to imagine the effect produced in the small

---

[1] GEORGE SAND: *Correspondance*. Volume II, p. 3.

[2] GEORGE SAND: *Correspondance*. Volume II, p. 9.

[3] Ibid., Volume II, p. 4.

mountain inns by the sight of a page dressed in a blouse throwing her arms round the neck of a beautiful lady with long fair hair, by Liszt in a béret à la Raphael, and by his little pupil. 'Puzzi' Cohen, whom the inn-keepers called 'the young lady'. For Liszt and Marie also had their travelling circus, and trailed along with them not only Hermann Cohen, but an amusing Genevese major, called Adolphe Pictet, who wrote a brilliant account of the Chamonix episode, which he called *Conte fantastique*.

And it was a fantastic story! Liszt and Marie took the name of Fellows. Marie became Mirabelle, or Arabella, or the Princess. Sand called herself and the children Piffoëls, because of George's and Maurice's long noses. In the Hotel Register she wrote:

> *Travellers' Names*. The Piffoëls family
> *Home Address*. Nature
> *Coming from*. God
> *Travelling to*. Heaven
> *Place of Birth*. Europe
> *Occupation*. Loafers
> *Date of Passport*. Eternity
> *Issued by*. Public opinion[1]

They lived in a whirl of intellectual activity, discussing philosophy, music, the stars, the Creation, Schelling, Hegel and God . . . In the major's little book George figures as the genius, the creative force, at once poet and gutter-snipe. Liszt is the spirit of music, Arabella the analyst, the thinker. On the cover, George was depicted with a cigar in her mouth. All the illustrations were designed to contrast the two women: the gutter-snipe complete with smock, the countess with her hair beautifully done and a rather serious, remote, expression on her face. George herself produced a caricature of the party in true Musset style, with, underneath it, the words: 'The Absolute is Identical with Itself.' Liszt, with his hair on end, is asking 'What exactly does that mean?'—the major replies: 'It's a bit vague', and Arabella, her head buried in the sofa-cushions, 'I've been lost for ages!'[2]

Maurice, a young artist of thirteen, also produced

[1] WLADIMIR KARENINE: *George Sand, Sa Vie et ses Oeuvres*. Volume II, pp. 329-30.
[2] ADOLPHE PICTET: *Une Course à Chamonix*, p. 144.

numerous sketches and caricatures. The travelling circus took the road. At Fribourg, Franz played Mozart's *Dies Irae—Quantus tremor est futurus,* on the cathedral organ. . . .

'Suddenly,' wrote Sand in her tenth *Lettre d'un Voyageur,* which gives an excellent description of the trip, 'suddenly, this threat of an ultimate Judgment instead of depressing me seemed rich with promise, and a strange sense of happiness set my heart pounding. I felt completely confident, and something seemed to tell me that the Eternal Justice would not crush me . . .'[1] Her conscience was at peace. By *her own* moral standards she had incurred no blame. Didier? She had merely taken pity on his morbid self-love. How, without wounding him, could she have refused to him what she had given to others? Michel? She had been ready to devote her life to him, but he was married, inconstant, indifferent. She was certain that for her the 'Day of Anger would be the Day of Forgiveness'.

They returned to Geneva. Liszt composed a *Rondo fantastique* based on a Spanish song by Manuel Garcia, father of La Malibran, and dedicated it to *Monsieur George Sand,* who immediately wrote a 'story in verse', *Le Contrebandier,* as an amplification of Liszt's rondo. In October George had to return to France. It was agreed that Franz and Marie should join her in Paris, and that the Fellows and the Piffoëls should not be separated. They were happy in one another's company, for genius recognizes genius. All the same, George was not a little envious of this happy love-affair, and thought that the Princess showed insufficient gratitude to Liszt. Marie d'Agoult, somewhat embittered, felt at Geneva like a 'fish out of water', and complained of the insipid life she was leading. 'The unfortunate thing was that we were earning our daily bread there, which led to my making a change in the *Lord's Prayer,* and saying to the Good God, *Spare us this day our daily bread.*' Arabella disliked Franz's having dedicated his rondo to George, and the way in which he praised the musical appreciation of this very much too feminine 'boy', who slipped under the piano when he was playing. Still, George Sand had dedicated a novel, *Simon* (a rather nebulous portrait of Michel), to

Madame la Comtesse d'A . . .

---

[1] GEORGE SAND: *Lettres d'un Voyageur,* X, p. 309.

Mysterieuse amie, soyez la patronne de ce pauvre petit
conte
Patricienne, excusez les antipathies du conteur rustique.
Madame, de dites à personne que vous êtes sa soeur.
Coeur trois fois noble, descendez jusqu'a lui, et rendez-le
fier.

Comtess, soyez pardonnée.
Etoile cachée, reconnaisez vous à ces litanies[1]

They parted on a note of friendship: 'Goodbye, sweet and
charming Princess; goodbye dear idiot of the Valais . . . My
daughter is superb. As for me I am "baked to a turn", as
Henri Heine says.'[2] She returned from Switzerland with the
two children, and young Gustave de Géveudan, a casual
adorer. She had waited in vain for Michel to join her there,
and now hoped that he would meet her at Lyons.

George Sand to Michel de Bourges: After six weeks of
waiting, yearning, hope and frustration, you don't even
come to meet me because, according to your Pasha
views, it was for me to come humbly to you like an
odalisque. I was hoping to see you in Lyons, and dragged
my children all the way there, with that hope in view.
Five mortal days did I spend in an inn with my little
ones—both of them bored to · distraction—and my
travelling companion, who is a nice enough young man
and extremely obliging, but not sufficiently amusing to be
closeted with for so long. Still no sign of you! Finally,
time being short, and money shorter, I came on here,
worn-out, discontented and, I don't mind admitting, half
stifled with virtue, and with no outlet for the poetry and
the fire with which Switzerland had filled me. And what
do I find!—the sort of letter which an elderly banker
might write to his kept woman! It is heartbreaking that
you should treat *me* like that. . . .[3]

He accused her of fresh infidelities. She protested:

[1] GEORGE SAND: *Simon* (*Revue des Deux Mondes:*
January 15th, 1836).

[2] Spoelberch de Lovenjoul Collection.

[3] Unpublished. Spoelberch de Lovenjoul Collection: Group
E. 881, f. 31.

I have told you once and for all that, in the event of my being unfaithful to you, as a result of weariness, physical weakness, or morbid craving, I would confess it to you and leave you completely free to decide whether you would punish me by putting me out of your mind for ever . . . Resentment carried that far would have been a chastisement out of all proportion to a fault which, though vulgar in the extreme, should be easy enough to forgive—a fault, moreover, of which you have been guilty with your wife ever since we belonged to one another . . . Still, however that may be, I would endure, without servility, and without any show of weakness, the consequences of my misconduct. I should be sorry, but only to the extent warranted by my deviation from the strict line, and I certainly should not go out into the desert and do penance for a sin which you—and many respectable men, too—have committed I don't know how many times. . . .

I don't mind confessing that enforced chastity has been very troublesome to me. I have had dreams of the kind that leave one exhausted, and have suffered, over and over again, from a rush of blood to the head. At noon, in the exquisite depths of mountain valleys, with the song of birds in my ears, and sweet forest smells in my nostrils, I have more than once withdrawn from my companions to sit apart, my heart full of love and my knees trembling with desire. I am a young woman still. I may tell other men that age has brought me tranquillity, but there is fire in my blood, for all that . . . I can still walk ten leagues, and, when I fall into my bed at the inn, can still dream that the shoulder of the man I love is the only pillow which can bring rest to body and soul alike. Still, I have managed to assume an air of calmness convincing enough to take in even my dear friends Franz and Marie . . . The rest of the party believe that I am Lélia through and through, and that my pallor is the result of overmuch walking. There have been plenty of opportunities, as you may well believe, for me to relieve my urgencies. I have had about me a multitude of men, younger than you, at whom I only had to look . . . There was nothing to stop me. Many and many a time I could have deceived you with impunity, and enjoyed under the cover of darkness a moment's animal satisfaction which even Catherine II would scarcely have refused. What saved me from this blemish—in itself unimportant, but, for those who love, ineffaceable—was not what women call their 'virtue' (the word has lost all meaning for me) but the love in my heart which makes the idea of lying in the arms of any man but you, insurmountably disgusting to me. It is you of whom I have been dreaming when I wake in a cold sweat, your name that I cry aloud when nature breathes her passionate summons in my ear, and the mountain air assails my flesh with a thousand pricklings of desire. . . .[1]

No, she declared, never had she yielded to temptation, whereas he . . . On her way through Bourges there had been no lack of friends to tell her that Michel had 'fallen for' a woman of the most 'disgusting fatness'.

I had it for certain, from the lips of somebody who is as innocent of guile as a child, that you have been spending all your time with this woman. Why should I ever have doubted it, or how, not doubting, should I not have suffered? You have no feelings of friendship for her—if you had, you would have told me, and that, most certainly, you never did. I know from what you have said that you do not care two pins about her husband. What, then, takes you to her house? She can sing, but abominably out of tune, and with an intolerable air of affectation. That I know because I have heard her . . . Such imperfect talent can neither charm nor distract you. She is full of spite, and she hates me . . . She loses no opportunity of blackening my reputation and covering me with mud. I am convinced that what I say is true. I can almost hear her. How comes it that you can bear to be intimate with somebody who hates me? . . . I could not listen to my best friend, even my own son, speaking evil of you, without being filled with hatred of him, and parting from him for ever.

Tell me, Marcel, what is it you do when you are with her, and why you spend in her house the hours that you can spare from work? Is it just that she relieves your physical needs, as any pick-up might do? I, alas, am younger than you: I have hotter blood in my veins, stronger muscles, tougher nerves, than you, and a constitution of iron, as well as a superfluity of energy for which I can find no outlet—and yet there is not a man,

[1] Unpublished. Spoelberch de Lovenjoul Collection: Group E. 881, ff. 28-30.

no matter how young or how handsome, who could tempt me to be unfaithful to you in spite of your forgetfulness, your contempt, even your infidelity. When the fever takes me I get the doctor to relieve me of a pound of blood. He tells me that it is a crime, that it is tantamount to suicide, and that, in any case it won't help me much. What I need, he says, is a lover, failing whom my life will be in danger from the very excess of the demands it makes on me. Well, no matter how much I might wish to take his advice, I cannot. The mere thought is intolerable to me. . . .

It is hateful to me to think that your lovely body which I adore so fiercely, which has been so deeply impregnated by my kisses, drained so often by my passion, and revived by my lips, so often martyred by our frenzies, revived and cured by my endearments, by the touch of my hair and by my burning breath . . . Ah! whither are my memories wandering? Once when I revived your failing senses with my sighs, I thought I should have died, so hard did I try to impart to your failing powers something of the life that filled my breast. How sweet I should have found it then to die in the very act of injecting into you some of the rich sap of youth that was to me so heavy a burden! Oh, God! to think of your body sullied by the contact of unworthy flesh! . . . Is it true that your mouth has sucked in the breath of lips which have been prostituted by self-love and the worship of social trivialities? No, Oh no, that is impossible. . . .[1]

Seeing that he was avoiding her, she took refuge with *Speranza,* and begged him for a meeting of no more than fifteen minutes.

'I cannot believe that you are as frightened of me as you are of Madame Michel, that you recoil from granting me the opportunity to appeal to your honour. . . .'[2]

He came. Their wretched affair was patched up, and then she left for Paris. Didier, haunted by happy memories of Nohant, hoped that she would stay with him, but she had taken a room on the first floor of the Hôtel de France, 23 rue Laffitte. Franz and Marie were occupying a suite

[1] Unpublished. Spoelberch de Lovenjoul Collection: Group E. 881, ff. 16–18.
[2] Unpublished. Spoelberch de Lovenjoul Collection: Group E. 881, f. 4.

immediately above her. They shared a sitting-room which Madame d'Agoult, ambitious though ostracized, did her best to fill with writers and artists. She had been cast out from the Olympus of the Faubourg Saint-Germain, and wished to take her revenge by being acclaimed as Queen of a very different world. Her 'regulars' included Heine, Mickiewicz, Lamennais, Ballanche, Michel, Charles Didier and Eugène Sue. It was there that Sand heard, for the first time, a young Polish musician, Frédéric Chopin, the only pianist who, for genius and good looks, could hold a candle to Liszt. There, also, she made the acquaintance of Madame Manoël Marliani, wife of the Spanish Consul, an excitable Italian woman, a figure in society, kind-hearted, full of a wild passion, and a dangerous gossip.

Poor Didier was invited to the Hôtel de France, where he saw George, lovelier than ever, courted by all but treating him with cold aloofness. He burst into tears in the middle of the drawing-room. After much begging, she consented to his paying her a visit on November 25th, at midnight. But unlucky lovers are always clumsy. Instead of plucking the fruit of the passing moment, they weep over a past which can never come again. *Didier's Diary:* 'The night ended with a scene of horrible frankness, and a series of appalling confessions. What she said, so far from giving me new life, froze my blood, so that I was little better than a corpse in her presence . . . There are depths of ferocity in her. She loves to make others suffer, and takes pleasure in the pain she causes. She has no heart. Imagination is her predominant quality, and it rules her life . . .' He forgot that he had once thought her 'a good woman at heart'. But that had been in the days when she had preferred him to Michel.

After she had once more left Paris for Nohant, he decided that it might be a good thing to see Marie d'Agoult, and talk to her about his fickle mistress. He had a high opinion of this other woman, who was as serious-minded as himself, and knew, better than Sand, how to arouse a sense of pity. 'I like her better than I do Liszt', admitted the dear, good, young man with innocent frankness; 'she is a noble creature, and very unhappy . . . I find their present relationship puzzling, and rather think that they are deliberately acting, that their affair is at its last gasp'. This was not altogether true, though, since the return from Switzerland, a terrible state of tension had developed between two temperaments, both of them ardent and often noble in their way, but 'bitterly proud and fundamentally

insatiable'.[1] Didier opened his heart to Marie, who, judging
Sand as she did with the clear-sighted severity of an equal
and a rival, found it not unpleasant to listen to the lamentations of this handsome Swiss. She promised to plead his
cause at Nohant, where she was due to stay.

V

THE PROPHETS

DURING THE period of Sand's residence in Paris, the
Abbé de Lamennais had been one of the most welcome of
the visitors to the Hôtel de France. George was still ap-
preciative of his rough manners, his hot-headed obstinacy,
his heavy, seedy garments, and his blue woollen stockings.
'Those who came across him for the first time when he
was in one of his brooding fits, and saw no more than a
greenish, rather wild, eye, and a great nose edged like a
sword, were apt to take fright and say that his appearance
was positively devilish.'[2] George loved him for his
kindliness, his ingenuousness, his courage, and the sublime
simplicities of his talk. The Abbé was nervous, irascible,
and by no means an easy man to get on with, but Sand
accepted him for what he was, with his infatuations, his
suspicions, and his unpredictable changes of mind. Nothing
if not maternal, she found a real delight in protecting this
elderly child. When Sainte-Beuve, in the pages of the *Revue,* brought against the Abbé a charge of inconsequence,
she struck back at the risk of enraging both Buloz and the
influential critic. Indeed, the incident did lead to a marked
cooling off in the friendly relations till then existing between her and Sainte-Beuve. Through the instrumentality of
Buloz, she managed to get a box at the Théâtre Français for
the Abbé, who was anxious to see Rachel. *Sand to
Lamennais*: 'You will be alone in the box . . . I will be

---

[1] COMTESSE D'AGOULT (DANIEL STERN): *Memoires,*
1833-1854, p. 74.

[2] GEORGE SAND: *Histoire de ma Vie.* Volume IV, p. 358.

answerable for Buloz not starting any gossip . . . Yours, with
every expression of affectionate devotion . . .'[1] When the
Abbé took up his permanent residence in Paris, and
announced his intention of starting a paper, she said that she
would gladly work with him.

> *George Sand to Marie d'Agoult:* He needs to found a
> school: he needs disciples. In the spheres of morals and
> politics he will have neither unless he is prepared to make
> enormous concessions to the spirit of the times in which
> we live, and the stage of knowledge to which we have
> attained. From what his intimate friends tell me, I gather
> that there is still a great deal more of the *priest* in him
> than I had supposed. I had hoped to ensure him a
> position of considerably greater prominence than I have
> been able to do. He resists my efforts. We have fierce
> quarrels, and then we make them up: but so far we have
> reached no sort of a permanent understanding. I should
> dearly like us to be in agreement: only so can I see any
> future for virtue based on intelligence. Lamennais cannot
> march forward alone . . . If, abdicating from the position
> of prophet and apocalyptic poet, he flings himself into
> progressive action, he must have an army. The greatest
> general in the world can do nothing without soldiers. But
> they must be seasoned soldiers, and they must have faith
> in him. . . .[2]

She offered herself as a recruit, on condition that she
should be allowed a certain liberty of conscience, and
contributed a number of unpaid articles to *Le Monde*—the
Abbé's paper—at a time when the *Débats* was making her
the most tempting offers. The ill-natured tried to 'spread a
story to the effect that a sort of intimacy existed between the
Abbé Féli and George Sand.[3] One of the Nohant
neighbours claimed to have seen Lamennais on the terrace
'in an oriental wrap and smoking a *narghile,* in the
company of the author of *Lélia*.[4] Only those could have
talked like that who were ignorant of the Abbé's austerity
and innocence. No, she had enrolled under his orders for

[1] Ibid.

[2] GEORGE SAND: *Correspondance*. Volume I, pp. 369-70.

[3] MARIE-LOUISE PAILLERON: *George Sand*. Volume II,
p. 154.

[4] Ibid.

the simple reason that, like her, he was a Christian and a democrat, and also because he was a victim of persecution. 'He is so good, and I am so fond of him, that I am prepared to give as much of my blood and my ink as he may need.' This was generous, but Lamennais's friends were worried by his 'literary marriage' . . . 'The match which seems to have been brought off between Monsieur de Lamennais and George Sand is provoking a great deal of talk', wrote Madame de Girardin in *La Presse* for March 8th, 1837. 'She treats all her friends as "subjects", and each new relationship is a fresh novel. The history of her affections is to be found complete in the catalogue of her works. . . .'[1]

The Abbé, who was not an outstanding example of the virtue of making allowances, began very soon to find this friendship something of an embarrassment. Under Sand's roof he lived in a mingled atmosphere of comfort and charity, and this he found hard to bear. He regarded the Great Lady of Nohant much as, later, Leo Tolstoy's enemies regarded him—as a condescending aristocrat.

The Abbé de Lamennais to the Baron de Vitrolles, December 21st, 1841: The Lady of Nohant wears nothing now but shirts of Indian silk. Give her time and she'll come to cashmeres—all the while preaching the brotherhood of man, much to the edification of those who are dying of hunger, to whom she sets an example of how life *should* be lived. She has one room hung entirely with velvet—a remarkably useful guide to the poor fools who've not even got glass to their windows. . . .[2]

Hard words, and unjust; poverty, like physical courage, cannot be feigned.

George Sand to Eliza Tourangin, March 13th, 1837: I am a great deal of the Abbé de Lamennais, and have a perfect passion for him, which fact has given rise to talk which would seem odd to you if you had any idea how old he is and what he looks like! I have even heard it said that I am going to settle in Paris for the purpose of running his home for him. Not a bad idea! He would at

[1] VICOMTE DE LAUNAY (DELPHINE DE GIRARDIN): *Lettres Parisiennes*. Volume I, p. 82.
[2] *Correspondance inédite entre Lamennais et le baron de Vitrolles*, pp. 387-8.

least be well looked after . . . Let me know if you have
managed to get my two letters to Michel. If there is any
news of him, tell me. He is very lazy, and I am anxious.
. . .[1]

'The Abbé de Lamennais has been far from clever in his
handling of George', said Madame d'Agoult. 'He does not
seem to realize that she came to him in a mood of complete
surrender, full of a longing to devote herself blindly to the
furthering of his views, and to make herself in some sort the
handmaiden of his thought . . .' He did not feel how great a
source of strength she could be to him, and replied with
grumpy ill-humour to her emotional outpourings. When she
sent him her *Lettres à Marcie* for *Le Monde*, the
contumacious old priest found their romantic mysticism
displeasing. George, however, had behaved with great
circumspection. The *Letters* are presented as written by a
man friend to a bored young woman who has been
complaining of her loneliness and of the poverty which
makes it difficult for her to marry. 'Marcie, do not indulge
in overmuch complaining, and do not be ungrateful. You
are beautiful, you are well educated, you are pure-minded.
These things give you a great advantage, and form the
elements of true happiness. The rich unfortunates, who are
reduced to buying husbands, ought to inspire you with
feelings of deep pity . . .'[2] To support her argument she tells
Marcie two stories: one of a rich and ugly young woman
who thought that when she married she could keep her
husband true to her by virtuous behaviour, and died of
despair in a setting of detested luxury; the other of the three
nieces of a Lombard priest, so devoted to one another that
they decided to eschew marriage altogether rather than
break up their happy family, and found satisfaction in
celibacy: 'Truth is the love of perfection, and perfection is
the eternal effort of spirit to subdue matter.'[3]

The *Lettres à Marcie,* a fictional correspondence,
paraphrase in an abridged form the numerous letters which
Sand was addressing at this time to Eliza Tourangin

[1] Unpublished. Spoelberch de Lovenjoul Collection: Group
E. 917, ff. 91 et seq.

[2] GEORGE SAND: *Impressions littéraires, Lettres à Marcie,*
pp. 244-5.

[3] Ibid.. p. 252.

(*Speranza*). Félix Tourangin, the father of a large family (and a typical Micawber) had ruined himself. Creditors were threatening to seize his château of La Frée. Eliza, ever since coming of age, had had one overriding fear—that she might die an old maid, and Sand, to comfort her, had been instructing this Marcie-in-real-life in the contempt of riches and 'arranged' marriages.

> *George Sand to Eliza Tourangin:* My poor sister: if the expropriation which hangs over your head is not circumvented, if the assistance of which I live in hope fails to arrive in time, even so, nothing irreparable will have occurred. Why should the loss of your fortune seem to you so terrible an evil? If, as I believe, the human race is at the dawn of great changes, the kind of false shame, and the very real privations which are now the lot of rich people who have lost everything will cease to have any meaning or any effect . . . All is not lost. You will not fall into a condition of penury. Lands and Château you will no longer have, but you will have your own family, and peace of mind . . . And then, dear sister, if you are fated to be an old maid without a penny, you at least will not have to earn your bread in the house of strangers: you will come to me and share mine, and we will make jam to spread on it. . . .[1]

The sixth *Lettre à Marcie* is a plea for the equality of the sexes in love: equality, not likeness, and still less identity. Men in their egotism try to stifle women's intelligence, the better to rule them. There is in these pages 'an echo of the brutal scenes which had taken place between her and Michel de Bourges'.[2] Lamennais was shocked. Never having been a young man of the world, never having had anything to do with women, he went in mortal dread of the demon of lust. The subject which Sand suggested for her next letter—*The role of passion in a woman's life*—frightened him still more, and he suspended publication of the series.

[1] Unpublished. Spoelberch de Lovenjoul Collection: Group E. 917.

[2] ERNEST SEILLIERE: *George Sand, mystique de la passion*, p. 181.

Marie d'Agoult to Franz Liszt: She wrote to him very
properly very affectionately, very reasonably, to say that
she could not go on working blindly, that she intended to
talk of divorce and many other things, and wanted first to
know how much latitude he was prepared to allow her.
To this question he replied very coldly. He did not, he
said, want anything about divorce. All he asked for were
the flowers that fell from her hands, in other words,
stories and bits of nonsense of the Piffoëls variety. To
make matters worse, the Fourth Letter was not used. She
is thoroughly annoyed.[1]

It had given Arabella great pleasure to come on a 'very
beautiful passage in George's letter about exceptional cases
of love, about those noble, sacred and imperishable
passions, to the inspiring qualities of which we, I think, are
not strangers'. The reader judges a text, as a Jury the
accused, by the light of his own emotional reactions.
Lamennais would perhaps have come to a happier understanding with George if she had not been surrounded
by women whom he disliked—Marie d'Agoult, and the wife
of the Spanish Consul, Carlotta Marliani. He had an
especial detestation of Pierre Leroux, a man who, for some
time past, had been playing a prominent part in the spiritual
life of the group. 'It is not', said the rough-tongued
Lamennais, 'as though they understood one single word of
the doctrines which they so much enjoy. The truth is he
exudes a vague sort of brothel stench which they snuff up
with delight. . . .'[2]

It was Sainte-Beuve who was responsible for introducing
Leroux into George Sand's life. When she told him how
confused her ideas still were in matters of philosophy and
social theory, Sainte-Beuve, himself rather shaky in these
departments of thought, had recommended the writings of
Pierre Leroux. The whole affair is somewhat disconcerting.
How could Sainte-Beuve ever have admired such rubbish?
How could Sand dare to write, 'Can I ever harbour a
grievance against one whom I regard as a new Plato, a new
Christ?' and, much later, to a young woman who had asked
her for a philosphy of life: 'My child, read the works of

[1] *Correspondance de Liszt et de Madame d'Agoult.* Volume
I, pp. 199-200.

[2] *Correspondance inédite entre Lamennais et le baron de
Vitrolles,* p. 318.

Pierre Leroux. In them you will find peace of mind and an answer to all your doubts. It was Pierre Leroux who saved me. . . .'[1]

Who, precisely, was this Pierre Leroux?

He was the son of a man who ran a small Bar in the Place des Vosges. He had had a brilliant scholastic career, and had tried to enter the Ecole Polytechnique, but, having to start earning a living at once, had become first a stockbroker's clerk, and then, by his own choice, a working printer. He had invented an improved typesetting machine, a piano-type, which had no success, though it was the forerunner of the linotype. With his friend, Jean Reynaud, he joined the staff of the *Globe*. This Saint-Simonian periodical published a *New Encyclopaedia* by Leroux and Reynaud, which, like its prototype of the eighteenth century, was a manual in the service of an idea.

This idea, or, rather, this philosophy, contained nothing new. From Bonnet and Ballanche it had borrowed the idea of *palingenesis,* or, in other words, of the *metempsychosis* of the entire human race. Human beings die only to be born again (which is obvious), and each rebirth brings a movement upwards (which is less so). Thus, mankind climbs uninterruptedly, and the plan of Providence is wholly logical. The individual can live only in Society. This Society is capable of reaching perfection. By reason of our union with it, we ourselves are perfectible and immortal. Property and the family were necessary in past ages, but, so soon as they begin to hinder men's movement to perfection, became harmful. Man is neither all spirit nor all animal. He is animal transformed by reason and united with humanity as a whole. God is everywhere, in the material world no less than in the spiritual. We should not, therefore, fight against the life of the flesh, but uplift and sanctify it.

Without religion Society would be no more than a scattering of individuals. Either Christianity will turn out to be the religion of which the world stands in need, or a new religion will be born. Only religion can, to take a special case, make women able to accomplish their mission, which is one of sacrifice. In the absence of a religion, they must have a philosophy. Leroux believed himself to be the evangelist of the philosophy which his century needed. Actually, all that was best in his doctrine had been

[1] WLADIMIR KARENINE: *George Sand, sa Vie et ses Oeuvres.* Volume III, p. 2.

borrowed from Christianity. 'It is remarkable how many of its ideas Christianity stole from Leroux.'[1] All the same, Pierre Leroux did not, like the Christians, attribute immortality to the individual. Our bodies, he said, are our memories. When the body perishes, we cannot expect to achieve immortality with our load of memories. The River of Lethe is a wise symbol. But we shall participate in a collective immortality.

Leroux was at one with George Sand in refusing to admit any inequality of the sexes in love. Before ever the Man-Woman complex was formed, woman was a human being, a moral entity. Why, then, should marriage destroy her dignity? If the human *person* is not respected in love, the love becomes no more than license and prostitution. Woman will no longer claim freedom in love when she has obtained equality of status in the Man-Woman relationship. 'Only when marriage is perfect will the emancipation of women be truly achieved'—a dogma very sweet to Sand's ears.

All this is very far from being ridiculous, but far, too, from being a mark of genius. Contemporaries often commit the most astonishing mistakes. The highly intelligent Sainte-Beuve, who suffered from illusions where Leroux was concerned, wrote that the Lord sometimes raises up:

Quelques rares mortels, grands, plus grand que les rois,
Avec un sceaux brillant sur leurs têtes sublimes . . .
Ces mortels ont des nuits brillantes et sans voiles;
Ils comprennent les flots, entendent les étoiles,
Savent les noms des fleurs, et, pour eux, l'univers
N'est qu'une seule idée en symboles divers.[2]

Sand, too, believed that she had found in this 'rare mortal', in this 'idea incarnate', the solution of all the

[1] Emile Faguet.

[2] Rare mortals no less great, nay, greater than the kings,
    Who bear a seal that glows upon their godlike brows . . .
    Such mortals shine in the unclouded dark;
    They know the secrets of the tides, and hear the music of the spheres,
    Are privy to the names the flowers are called by, and for them
    The universe is one idea expressed in symbols manifold.

difficulties which had caused her so much anguish. It was her conviction that Leroux possessed the 'Open Sesame'. She caught in his pronouncements an echo of the great heresies which had always fascinated her—the heresy of the Hussites, the heresy of the Taborites, the rehabilitation of the flesh, and also the rehabilitation of Satan, that liberator of humanity who had 'too long been misrepresented, too long degraded, by the doctrine of Original Sin'. She wished passionately to meet Leroux. In 1836 she wrote asking him to dine with her and explain 'in two or three hours' talk the republican catechism'.

The man who entered the room in response to her invitation was scarcely older than she was, and very dirty. He had 'a big, knobby head, a lopsided face, and deep-set eyes under great tufted brows'.[1] She was enchanted. Here was the very type of the philosopher: here was Socrates: here was Leibnitz. She listened to him enraptured. Passionate rather than critical, she failed to see 'the gaps in his knowledge, the unsoundness of his thought'. From that day on, she asked all her friends in Paris and La Châtre: 'Have you read Leroux? I am convinced that a day is coming when people will read Leroux as they now read the *Contrat Social*.' She sat at the master's feet. She praised the unsullied purity of his childish mind and his ignorance of practical affairs, even though this simplicity took the form of incessant requests for money. She plagued Buloz to commission articles from Pierre Leroux for the *Revue*. But her bringing together of the two men was not a success. Buloz said to Leroux 'God is not news', and Leroux was justifiably indignant.

Sand trailed her philosopher round with her to a number of literary salons. 'I think you should know', wrote Béranger to a friend, 'that our metaphysician has surrounded himself with women, chief among them Mesdames Sand and Marliani. He now declaims his theories, and displays his muddy boots, in gilded drawing-rooms. This press of adorers has gone to his head, and, to my mind, his system is beginning to feel the effects . . .' In short, Leroux was Godwin to a female Shelley. 'She has persuaded him'—the comment is again Béranger's—'to lay a small religious egg that she may have the pleasure of hatching it.'

[1] MARIE-LOUISE PAILLERON: *George Sand*. Volume II, p. 46.

Unfortunately that was not the only egg Leroux had laid. He was a widower with a large family of children, and he had to be provided for. What with unpaid articles for Lemennais, subsidies to Leroux, and passionate appeals to Michel, Sand's prophets were costing her dear.

VI

A SUMMER IN THE COUNTRY

SHE RETURNED to Nohant at the beginning of January 1837 with her two children. There was a lot to be seen to in connection with the estate over which she now ruled as undisputed sovereign. She needed peace and quiet in order to finish *Mauprat,* and she wished to be near Michel whom she was set on recapturing for no better reason than that he was in the process of escaping from her clutches. It had been agreed that Liszt and Marie d'Agoult should join her in Berry, but when Arabella came at the end of the month she came alone. The relationship between the two women was drawn tighter. They went for long rides together. George, very manly in her blue blouse and trousers, kept a hand on the bridle of the golden-haired 'Princess's' mount whenever a grassy slope became too steep or a ford too deep. Arabella brought a none too friendly eye to bear upon the household. Solange, she thought, was beautiful and admirably proportioned, but in character 'passionate and unmanageable':

When the wind plays in her long fair hair, and the sun catches her vivid little face, I feel that I am looking at a young hamadryad who has escaped from the woods . . . Her character is as forceful as her body . . . Solange is destined to live always in extremes, whether of good or evil. Her life will be a series of struggles and fights. Hers is not a temperament to yield to the common rules of existence. There will be something heroic in her faults, something sublime in her virtues. Maurice seems to me to be the exact antithesis of his sister. He will grow into the kind of man who is commonsense incarnate, with a scrupulous regard for regulations, and an equipment of easy-going virtues . . . His taste will be for quiet pleasures and the life of a country gentleman, unless his talents, which are really remarkable, pitchfork him into the world of art. . . .[1]

A new tutor, Eugène Pelletan, had arrived on the scene to look after the boy. He was a Protestant, the son of a Royan lawyer, infuriatingly slow of speech, as ardent a republican as Michel but too serious-minded to fit easily into the mental climate of Nohant. As to George herself, it was the Princess's view that she was burning herself up in the fires of a ridiculous and hopeless passion. In vain did she cling to Michel in an effort to fan the flames of a dead desire. The 'Tribune', self-centered and worn out, was anxious only to free himself from an exhausting mistress. George was loud in lamentation.

Sand to Michel, January 21st, 1837: You must not concern yourself with my melancholy. It is deep and incurable, but I have the strength to bear it whereas you have none to bring it alleviation. I will speak of it no more to you. It is doubtful whether you would even understand it, for the world has set a great gulf between us. The concerns of our earthly existence have made of you one sort of person; disgust and horror of them have made of me another. And yet, there *is* an invisible and unknown world in which you and I once lived and were as one! . . . It was not because of your love for me that I loved you. Others have had love far greater, but so little was I moved by it that I could not be bothered so much as to look at them. Nor yet was it because of those fine sentiments which you know so well how to express to women. I have known other glib talkers to whose words I have barely listened. It was not because I expected happiness, fame, or even affection. I am contemptuous of the pinchbeck, and was well aware, when I gave myself to you, that the world's torrent would always separate us. I realized that the ambitious can spare for love no more than an hour a day . . . I loved you because you delighted me, and because no one else can do just that . . . You have vices which I have not, for you have never known how to

[1] COMTESSE D'AGOULT (DANIEL STERN): *Mémoires,* p. 82.

discipline your passions. I know every scrap of you, for
we are *one* person, and you the half of me. . . .[1]

To these long, these interminable, letters he had ceased to
reply. It is doubtful whether he even read them. *January
28th, 1837:* Why do you not write? What does this new
mood mean? Are you ill? Oh God!—are you sulking still?
Are you in love with somebody else? I believe you are—
that certainty has been with me continuously ever since I
came back and saw you again. Your face is not as it used to
be, and, despite your brief fits of tenderness, you do not
succeed very well in concealing your boredom and the
eagerness you feel to get away from me . . . Do precisely as
you wish. I am quite capable of preserving a proper air of
dignity. I am even capable of saying nothing if you find my
affection tedious. . . .'[2]

She realized that she had been unfair, bitter, temperamental. But was it her fault that she could not do
without him? Was it her fault that she was jealous of all
other women, and, in particular, of 'the Person' (Madame
Michel). 'How could you be so devilish as to take me into
your house and show me your marriage bed? It is
extraordinary to me that love can stand up against such
trials—yet, mine does.'[3]

What was it that he still could give her? From time to
time she would gallop through the darkness to La Châtre or
Châteauroux, just in order to spend a few hours in
Michel's arms. But those brief times of love-making were
followed by 'a drenching flood of icy water on my poor
heart'. It was she who had to beg for every one of such
meetings. 'I was looking for a miracle when I hoped that
you would let nothing stand in the way, that you would find
some means of escaping for *one whole night* from work and
your marital duties . . .' With abject and surprising humility,
however, she told herself that she was prepared for
anything. Would he like her to take a house in Bourges?
She would live there shut away as in a hermit's cell, ready
for him whenever he might want her. Was he afraid of the
physical exhaustion of love? Well, then, she would willingly
consent to a sentence of chastity.

[1] Letter published in *La Revue illustrée*, November 1st, 1890,
pp. 291-2.
[2] Ibid., p. 293.
[3] Ibid., p. 297.

George Sand, 1830 Portrait by Eugene Delacroix *(Musée Carnavalet)*

Alfred de Musset by Charles Laudelle *(Louvre)*

Michel de Bourges *(Bibliotèque Nationale)*

Chopin at Marseilles. Sketch by Maurice Sand

Baron Dudevant. Sketch by Maurice Sand

George Sand. Painted by Eugene Delacroix

Page from a letter of George Sand to Charles Marchal
(Simone André-Maurois Collection)

Marie Dorval *(Musée Victor Hugo)*

Solange, daughter of George Sand. Bust
by Jean-August Clésinger
(Barnard Barbary Collection)

George Sand aged sixty *(Photograph by Nada)*

George Sand's house *(Photograph by Match)*

Puppets *(Photograph by Match)*

George Sand's pavilion at Nohant
(Photograph by Combier, Macon)

Printed in U.S.A.

Ah, if only we lived close to one another!—then, at least, you could sleep upon my breast when sickness held you in its paralysing grip. My love, which is ever wakeful, would store yours up as in a treasure-house, to be returned when you awoke. I would not torment you, not I, with reminders that you *ought* to love me. I would let you forget love altogether, because it would be sweet just to have you sleeping there beside me, and I would be skilled at holding nothingness at bay should it come to claim you . . . My love for ever leans above you like a willow-tree above the waters which gladden its heart, and my sweetest dream, when I yield to the cheating hope of one day living with you, is thinking of the care with which I would look after you when age and weakness come upon you. The delights of love are to be found not only in those fleeting hours of feverish passion which send the soul careering madly to the stars, but also in the innocent and persevering tenderness of intimacy . . . To be with you all day and every day, to anticipate your smallest wish, to hold you in my arms and lull you to sleep, letting you gently, quietly, withdraw into yourself, to guard your senses from the storm of passion, so that it shall not beat upon and break you, and then, when we are too old to feel the sap rising in our veins, to make of my love so soft a pillow and so sure a refuge, so silent, so warm, so calm a world of darkness, that the thought of the grave soon to gather us is no longer a haunting horror, no longer a threatening dread. That is the hope I hug to myself, dear compensation for all the weariness of a useless life, for all the cares untouched by enthusiasm, beneath whose weight I have lived so long. . . .[1]

Arabella, basking in the warmth of long and peaceful days, watched these raging storms. 'All evening', she noted, 'George has been as though numbed in a state of brooding not-being. Poor great woman! The sacred flame which God has kindled in her can find nothing outside her to lay hold upon, and now consumes what faith and hope and youth still live in her. Charity, love, desire, those three aspirations of soul and heart and senses, all of them too ardent, too extreme, in a nature marked out for too high a destiny, have

[1] Letter published in *La Revue illustrée*, November 15th, 1890, pp. 343-4.

been thrust headlong on doubt, disappointment and satiety, and driven down deep within herself to make her life a martyrdom . . . Dear God, grant to George Goethe's gift of serenity! . . .'[1]

By thus coming to a fuller knowledge of her illustrious friend, Marie d'Agoult believed that she had attained to a deeper awareness of her own worth. Not that she failed to admire the enormous vitality of her horse and gallop to a lovers' tryst. She recognized in George a deep sense of natural poetry, a curious charm, a genius for friendship. But, in the last analysis, she judged her sternly. Why, when she was talking of dying of love for Michel, did she fill her house with young men from La Châtre and Paris—Scipion du Roure, Gévaudan, and others, all madly enamoured of her? Why this absurd, this high-falutin' expression of maternal passion? The fruitful Marie had no liking for a 'love of young things which is not a feeling governed by intelligence, but a blind instinct in their response to which the lowest members of the animal kingdom are superior to the human female . . .'[2] Of her own two daughters born in wedlock, Louise and Claire, she had lost one and abandoned the other to the Comte d'Agoult. She had put her natural child, Blandine, out to nurse near Geneva, and was now, without any feeling of pleasure, awaiting the birth of a second, also Liszt's.

Arabella's earlier diagnosis had been the fairer. What George suffered from was an excess of vitality. She frequently had herself bled. 'In your place I should prefer Chopin', said the Princess, ironically—for she had not failed to notice that the handsome, sickly musician had made a deep impression on Sand, and knew that she would like nothing better than to lure him to Nohant. In May, Liszt arrived from Paris, pale, ardent, inspired, and it was George's turn now to observe the other couple. Here was a similar case of two persons violently at odds: Franz, young and untamed, Marie, proud and brooding. This love of theirs, thought George, would not go on for ever. Nevertheless, beneath the trees at Nohant, the summer of 1837 was a season to be remembered. Sometimes it flickered with the lightning play of genius, sometimes was darkened

[1] COMTESSE D'AGOULT (DANIEL STERN): *Mémoires*, p. 75.

[2] COMTESSE D'AGOULT (DANIEL STERN): *Mémoires*, p. 81.

by the storms of passion. Lime trees motionless and all a-
glitter, golden light beneath the leaves. Each evening,
George entered up Dr. Piffoël's Diary:

Arabella's room is on the ground floor, immediately
under mine. There stands Franz's wonderful piano, just
under the window with its screen of lime-leaves which I
can see from here. From that window float sounds which
the whole world would give its soul to hear; and there are
none to be jealous of them but the nightingales. What an
artist!—sublime when great matters are toward, and ever
superior even in the trivial. But, for all that, he is
melancholy, and bleeds from a secret wound. Fortunate
man, beloved of a beautiful woman who is as generous,
intelligent and chaste as she is lovely. Ungrateful wretch!
what is it, then, you crave? Ah, if only I were loved! . . .
When Franz plays the piano, the burden is lifted from
my heart. All my agonies are turned to poetry, all my
instincts mount into the empyrean. Above all, he sets the
cord of generosity vibrating. He touches, too, the note of
anger, so that it sounds almost in unison with the beat of
fever in my blood, but never the note of hatred. Hatred
feeds on me: hatred of what? Oh God, shall I ever find
anybody worth the expenditure of hatred? Grant me that
grace, and never more will I ask to be allowed to find one
who deserves to be loved. . . .
I adore the broken phrases which he strikes from his
piano so that they seem to stay suspended, one foot in the
air, dancing in space like limping will-o'-the-wisps. The
leaves upon the lime trees take on themselves the duty of
completing the melody in a hushed, mysterious whisper,
as though they are murmuring nature's secrets to one
another. . . .[1]

In a hand which she wished to be firm and steady she
weighed all those 'miserable baubles' which so delight a
man—fame, love . . . Dear God! what should she do with
all the power she felt within her? Work?—it was nothing
now to her but a task. 'I hate my trade.' Only cigars and
coffee could keep going 'that wretched industry of mine at
two hundred francs the page'. Then, suddenly, the world
grew bright, because Michel had agreed to a meeting. On
April 7th, anniversary of their first experience of love, he

[1] GEORGE SAND: *Journal intime*, pp. 45-7.

had written rather more tenderly than usual, and she had felt crushed under a weight of happiness. For she had lost the habit of delight. 'Tell me that it is really true, that you love me, that you will come, that I shall see you on our shadowed path when the moon rises, that I shall press you to my heart under the acacia trees! . . . April 7th!—will you bring me happiness?' In May she rode to him on horseback and, for one night, knew joy.

May 7th, 1837: Dear angel of my life! If you love me, I am happy. That is all that I can say tonight. I am dropping with weariness. I rode seven leagues in two hours. I found the children well. Liszt and Madame d'Agoult have arrived. I am weighed down by exhaustion, but not mainly as a result of my galloping. What a delicious feeling it is, and how calm a sleep lies heavy on my eyes! Good night: be mine for ever, as I am yours. Remember now and then those hours of madness and delight . . . Write to me, it is your turn. I shall wait for you upon the sun-drenched lawns sprinkled with violets. Till then I shall live in the memory of the days just past, those wonderful days which fled so swiftly by. Tell me that they did not overmuch disturb your habits, did not too much harm your work, nor wake a sickness in your heart? . . . Love me, and, please, please, tell me so . . . That is all I have to live upon. . . .[1]

What power a màn can wield who will not give himself! It is well we should remind ourselves once more how strange a lover it was to whom a beautiful young woman galloped her horse through all a livelong night—a man prematurely aged, with a bald and knobbly head tied in a handkerchief! Yet what love he woke in her! She was worn out with fatigue.

May 8th, 1837: My eyes are heavy; I can scarcely bear the brilliance of the early sun. The world is all on fire, but I am cold. I am hungry but I cannot eat, for appetite comes with health, hunger with weariness. Hurry to me, dear love. When you stand before me, then, revived like the earth when the sun of May returns, I will cast aside my icy winding-sheet, and tremble with love . . . In your

[1] Letter published in *La Revue illustrée,* December 1st, 1890, p. 392.

eyes I shall be young and beautiful, because, in an ecstasy of joy, I shall fling myself into your arms of iron. Come, come . . . strength will be mine, and health, and youth, and hope . . . I shall come to meet you like the spouse her lover in the *Song of Songs*. Love or death . . . for me there is no middle way. . . .[1]

When all the elements of a situation, and of the two persons concerned, make happiness impossible, how can it last? She would arrive at Bourges, exhausted, ardent, panting, to hear trotted out at her, the 'Person', the Republic, the electors. 'Damn the lot of 'em!' she would exclaim: 'it remains to be seen whether the love of the moon will give you such warmth as you can find in my heart and in my arms!' Michel's reply was to complain of being loved:

Michel de Bourges to George Sand: Hell! . . . because of you, and for your sake, I live in a constant state of warfare, which never ceases night or day, within the bosom of my family. Well, that's as should be. Nothing in this world is ever won without fighting and struggling. If only I could, at least, find in your arms a refuge from all this wretchedness . . . But I don't: you are for ever wanting, for ever demanding, so that I have to fight against you, too. Enemies to the right of me, enemies to the left. Things can't go on like this . . . I must be able to live in peace and quiet. There is something unspeakably beastly in sex warfare. It has not been granted me to fight with adversaries of my own stature, with tyrants. Well, then, for Heaven's sake, let me know absolute tranquillity. I am going to settle down in a hut on a hillside . . . within sight of the Mediterranean. . . .[2]

This time, George hit back:

George Sand to Michel de Bourges, May 31st, 1837: You class me with the Person, who causes you so much suffering . . . and you roar and you rant at being made uncomfortable because of me, as though a determined and disinterested devotion could ever be comparable to domestic squabbles! . . . You threaten to go and live in a

[1] Letter published in *La Revue illustrée*, December 15th, 1890, p. 1.
[2] Ibid., January 1st, p. 1.

hut . . . I should feel nothing but gratitude to God if He forced you to be as good as your word. In no time at all I should be with you. In me you would find the faithful negro slave, ready at all times to tend your poor, bruised body . . . and you would understand then that a woman's love is not something 'unspeakably beastly', and that the men of clay with whom you long to measure swords are not, and never will be, your equals. . . .[1]

In the secrecy of his *Journal intime,* Dr. Piffoël took himself to task:

It is your belief, Piffoël, that one can say to the object of one's passion—'You are being in all ways like myself. I chose you out from among my fellows, because I thought you the best and greatest of them all. Today, I no longer feel at all certain *what* you are . . . It seems to me that you have blemishes like other men, for you often make me suffer, and no man is perfect. But I love your blemishes, I love my sufferings . . .' No, no, Piffoël!—you may be a Doctor of Psychology, but you are no better than a fool. *That* is not the sort of talk a man wants to hear. He sets no value on devotion, because he holds devotion to be his by natural right, merely by virtue of his being his mother's son . . . A man knows when he is necessary to a woman . . . The woman knows but one way of lightening her burden, and of keeping her tyrant, when that tyrant has become essential to her—and that is, to flatter him abysmally. Her submission, her loyalty, her devotion, her care, are things of no worth in the man's eyes. Without them, so he thinks, he would not bother to put up with her at all. She must humble herself in the dust, and say—'You are great, you are sublime, you are incomparable! You are more perfect than God: your countenance sheds brightness, your feet distil sweet perfume, you are without a single vice, all the virtues are yours. . . .'

My dear Piffoël, the sooner you learn the truth about life, the better. When next you set about writing a novel, try to know the human heart a little better. Do not take as your ideal of womanhood someone who is strong of mind, disinterested, brave, and artless. The public will

[1] Letter published in *La Revue illustrée,* January 1st., pp. 101-2.

merely boo her from the stage, and call her by the hateful
name of *Lélia the impotent.* Impotent, indeed! Yes,
impotent where servility is concerned, impotent in
adulation, impotent in baseness, impotent in fear of you,
man the stupid, who lacks the courage to kill without the
support of laws which punish murder with murder, who
can take your vengeance only by employing calumny and
defamation! But when you find a female who can do
without you, then your power is vain: it turns to fury,
and your fury is punished by a smile, by a farewell, by
eternal forgetfulness. . . .[1]

This is a key passage, because it shows, at one and the
same time, why it was that Sand hated the men whom she
thought she loved when she could not dominate them, and
why she found it impossible to keep them. She was too
clear-headed to satisfy a tyrant whose dream of love was to
see at his feet an adoring woman willing to accept all his
ideas as Gospel truth, giving everything, and asking
nothing. She was too proud to feign submission. At last, on
June 7th, 1837, for the first time, she was brave enough to
cancel a meeting that had been arranged.

George Sand to Michel de Bourges, June 7th, 1837: I am
ill. I cannot go trapesing tomorrow through this heat. I
do not feel strong enough to start off this evening. I
should arrive in an exhausted condition, and I do not
suppose it would be much fun for you to hold me in your
arms at the Inn when I was like that! . . . I shall sleep
until you can find time to come and see *me.* Goodbye.
. . .[2]

Resentment and pride had driven out passion. The
pleasing Dr. Piffoël made melancholy obeisance to this
triumph of wisdom:

Dawn. My room. June 11th: Friendly walls give me a
kindly shelter. How freshly gay is this sheet of blue and
white paper! How full the garden is of birds! There is a
sprig of honeysuckle in my glass: how sweet it smells!
Piffoël, Oh, Piffoël, how frightening is the calm within

[1] GEORGE SAND: *Journal intime,* pp. 56-60.
[2] Letter published in *La Revue illustrée,* January 1st, 1891, p.
104.

your breast! Has the flame really been extinguished?

Hail Piffoël full of Grace. Wisdom is Thine. Thou hast been chosen from among all dupes. The fruit of Thy suffering has ripened. Blessed weariness, mother of rest, descend upon us, poor dreamers, now and in the hour of death: Amen. . . .[1]

Exit Michel.

The evenings at Nohant were superb. The family and the friends were gathered on the terrace. The old house was bathed in the soft light of the moon. Each of those present was occupied with private dreams. Arabella was wondering why all lovers regret the first hour of awakened passion, and weep over its ruin . . . George was whispering to himself some lines from Shakespeare: *Je ne suis pas de ces âmes patientes qui acceuillent l'injustice avec un visage serein.*[2]

Franz got up, went into the house, and sat down at the piano.

Piffoël's Diary, June 12th, 1837: That evening, while Franz was playing one of Schubert's most fairylike airs, the Princess wandered about the terrace in the darkness. She was wearing a light-coloured dress. A long white veil was draped about her head, and covered almost all her slender figure. The moon went down behind the tall limes. The motionless pines looked black and ghostly against the night-blue of the sky. A deep calm lay upon the flowering shrubs. The breeze had dropped, dying of weariness in the long grasses at the first notes of that superb instrument. The nightingale was still struggling to compete, but his voice was shy and swooning. He had drawn close in the darkness, and sounded his little organ note of ecstasy, keeping true time and tune, like the excellent musician that he is.

We were all seated on the steps, our ears attentive to the sometimes charming, sometimes mournful phrases of the *Erlkönig,* tranced like all nature in a bleak beatitude. We could not take our eyes from the magic circle which the silent sybil in her ghostly veil was tracing all about us

---

[1] GEORGE SAND: *Journal intime,* p. 55.

[2] The combined efforts of many friends have failed to trace this quotation. The words, therefore, have had to be left in French.—TRANSLATOR.

. . . At the far end of the terrace she was barely visible. Suddenly she would be lost to view among the pines, and then appear again, when least expected, in the lamp-beam from the window, as though she were some creature born of the flame. Then she vanished once more and seemed to float, vaguely blue and indistinct against a clearing in the trees. Finally, she came and sat upon a bending branch, weighing it down no more than would a ghost. At the same moment, the music stopped as though some mysterious bond linked the living notes to that lovely pallid form which seemed poised for flight to regions of unending harmony. . . .[1]

On June 8th, the actor Bocage had arrived. The object of his visit was to try to persuade George to write a play. He was the perfect type of a romantic 'star', tall, slim and endowed with Byronic good looks. He had been superb in *Antony,* dressed in a black frock coat buttoned over a white waistcoat, his deep blue eyes and pale face showing to advantage. In 1837 he was thirty-eight years old, but was still slender, still ardent, and given to expressing Republican sentiments with fiery passion. The conversation turned to plays, players and authors. There were mocking references to Victor Hugo's vanity and Marie Dorval's depravity. George defended both. Arabella thought Bocage stupid, and, indeed, he could scarcely be called a cultured man. Marie Dorval, in a letter to Vigny, refers to his 'conceited, silly, talkativeness', but adds, 'all the women are mad about him, and follow him in the streets'. Marie d'Agoult tried to talk to him about Mickiewicz. 'Miss qui?' he asked. But what chiefly annoyed Arabella was to see him paying court to Sand, and to take note that the latter seemed far from displeased by his advances. On June 15th the handsome, sinister Charles Didier put in a sudden appearance. 'Our hostess would rather it had been *Zopin*,' said Liszt. This was the way in which he facetiously pronounced his friend's name.

Marie d'Agoult, true to her promise, pleaded Didier's cause, but no sooner was he at Nohant than he regretted having come. He had ceased to be a favourite, and there was an air of embarrassment about the welcome which was extended to him. 'She talks to me in that nasty, teasing way she has . . . my coming here was the worst of blunders . . .

[1] GEORGE SAND: *Journal intime,* pp. 60-2.

where I am concerned, she is solid ice . . . she is bent on making fun of what she calls my "stateliness" . . . Oh, these artistic women!—their hearts are cold and unstable!'[1] He found not only Bocage of the party, but François Rollinat, and a young playwright, Félicien Mallefille, who was a friend of the *Fellows*. At night, on the terrace, seated round the lamp, they discussed God, Dorval, and a song-bird recently acquired by Sand, who busied herself with making punch. The blue flames lit up her scarlet dress. Arabella noted, with somewhat mocking sympathy, how touchy Charles Didier had become.

> At the slightest word his forehead would flush. He sat withdrawn behind his gold-rimmed spectacles, watching with deep attention the expression of our faces, and often a smile would be checked from his lips, frozen by mistrust or doubt. He is an unhappy creature, with the feverish ambition of a consumptive and the heart of a lion beneath a hedgehog's prickles. All the same, I am fond of him. . . .[2]

Unfortunately for Didier's peace of mind, his desires were still set on George, though he had a strong feeling of respect for Marie. Walking under the limes with the diaphanous Princess, he spoke of his disappointment and his pain. Sand seemed to be wrapped up in Bocage, and that was too much for the poor young man. Marie d'Agoult, in an outburst of exasperation and brutality, told him that their hostess seemed determined to embark on a career of casual intrigues. 'She maintains that George is now incapable of either love or friendship.' He could not sleep, and played with the idea of killing Sand. It was no more than an idle fancy, but he felt that his feet were set upon a dangerous slope, and took refuge in flight. He very nearly left Nohant without saying goodbye to his hostess. She came upon him suddenly, just as he was strapping his bags. 'I do hope you are not leaving us?' she said. 'I am, and at once!' She held up her face to him. He kissed the great eyes so fathomless and dry. 'Experience of the world and of life bears bitter fruit,' he noted in his Diary.

Exit Didier.

[1] Cf. JOHN SELLARDS: *Charles Didier*.
[2] COMTESSE D'AGOULT (DANIEL STERN): *Mémoires*, p. 88.

The *Fellows* departed on July 24th. Sand and Mallefille accompanied them on horseback as far as La Châtre. Mallefille, suddenly promoted to the role of favourite, was staying on at Nohant, and there was a plan afoot for him to act as Maurice's tutor. Warmth sounded in the farewells, but it was a warmth of the lips rather than of the heart. Still, the visit had been a success. Each one of the party had shone in his or her way. Arabella left firmly convinced of her own superiority.

It has been of use to me to see George and the great 'poet' together: George the undisciplined child, George the weak woman, even in her audacities, with feelings and opinions that are never the same for more than a moment, illogical in her life, for ever influenced by chance occurrences, rarely governed by reason or experience. I see now how childish it was of me to think (and the idea has more than once saddened me) that perhaps only she could have given Franz's life its full development, that I had been but an impediment, keeping asunder two destinies made to merge and to bring completion each to each. . . .[1]

George had recovered the equilibrium which, for a moment, had been set rocking by Michel, and, in the space of two months, had completed one of the best of her novels, *Les Maîtres Mosaïstes*. She had written it for Maurice, finding pleasure in evoking the Venetian scene and the old mosaic masters of St. Mark's, whilst Liszt sat playing the piano, and the nightingales, intoxicated by the music and the moonlight, sang with furious intensity among the lilacs. She was herself amazed at her recovered calm. Since that day, so rich in hope, when she had gone from Nohant to give herself to a great love, she had seen three passions come to birth and die. Now she could sleep as soundly in her bed, 'as Buloz in his'.

[1] COMTESSE D'AGOULT (DANIEL STERN): *Mémoires,* p. 81.

VII

BEATRIX

FELICIEN MALLEFILLE, left like a piece of driftwood high and dry with George and the children on the foreshore at Nohant after the ebb of the great summer tide, was a young Créole with a 'beard seven foot long'. He had been born in the Ile de France in 1813, and had come, at the age of nine, to France, where he had done brilliantly at school. At twenty-one he had had a play, *Glenarvon,* performed at the Ambigu, and in the following year another at the Porte-Saint-Martin. He was 'a thin man with a magnificent profile, and an eye that struck terror, and he affected a pair of bristling moustaches which made him look as though he had stepped straight out of a picture by Velasquez'.[1] Being poor and friendless, he was looking for some employment that would provide him with a living. In the Hôtel de France, Marie d'Agoult, who had constituted herself his protector, had introduced him to George Sand who had found him 'outrageously ugly, vain and stupid'. Marie, on the other hand, considered him as 'loyal, good and even witty', and had taken up the cudgels on his behalf. George was driven to exasperation by her friend, because 'how could anyone have the bad taste to find such a creature endurable? She was even more annoyed when Liszt revealed the fact that Mallefille was in love with her. She 'riddled' the unhappy youth with a 'great deal of unkindly sarcasm', and went so far as to say that he inspired her with feelings of 'physical repulsion' which she found it 'impossible to overcome'.

Nevertheless, when she broke more or less completely with the austere Pelletan she was in the position of having to find a new tutor for Maurice. Marie d'Agoult suggested Mallefille's brother, Léon (because she dared not mention Félicien), but it was on the latter that Sand decided to

1 Jules Claretie.

confer the succession. Somewhat later, she settled down with him at the Hôtel Britannique, at Fontainebleau, while Maurice was sent to board with Gustave Papet at Château d'Ars near La Châtre. Mallefille had become 'a sublime character' whose devotion left nothing to be desired, and it was with him that she resolved to make a pilgrimage to those Franchard 'gorges' where she had once spent an unforgettable night with Musset. Her stay at Fontainebleau was cut short by the receipt of bad news. Sophie-Victoire-Dupin had been taken seriously ill, and her daughter hurried to Paris to nurse her.

George Sand to Gustave Papet, August 24th, 1837: Dear old friend: I have lost my poor mother. I could not have wished for her an easier or a quieter end. There was no struggle, nor had she any idea that death was approaching, but just dropped off to sleep, fully expecting to wake up again as usual. You know how neat she was, how careful of her appearance. Her last words were, 'please tidy my hair'. Poor dear, so sensitive, generous, intelligent, and artistic, inclined to fly into rages over small matters, but splendid in big ones. She caused me much suffering, and the worst things that have happened to me were all due to her. But, latterly, she more than made up for them, and I had the satisfaction of knowing that she had, at last, come to a complete understanding of my character, and that her attitude to me was one of justice. It is a consolation for me to know that I did for her everything that duty demanded. . . .[1]

George Sand to Marie d'Agoult, August 25th, 1837: I wrote to you at Geneva, and hope that the letter reached you . . . I told you in it that I was in deep distress, that my mother was approaching her end. I spent several days in Paris in order to be with her during her last moments. While I was there, some disturbing news reached me which turned out to be a false alarm. I was told that my son had been carried off, and I sent Mallefille post-haste to Nohant to look for him. While I was awaiting his return at Fontainebleau, my mother breathed her last, quite quietly, and without suffering at all. Next morning I found her stiff and cold in her bed. As I kissed her dead face, I realized that what people say about blood-ties and

[1] GEORGE SAND: *Correspondance*. Volume II, p. 84.

natural affections is not the dream I had so often thought it in my moods of dissatisfaction . . . My poor mother is no more! She lies at rest under the sun, and in the lovely flowers above her grave the butterflies are fluttering without a thought of death. I was so struck by the gaiety of the Montmartre cemetery in this lovely summer weather that I wondered why my tears should flow so copiously. . . .[1]

Thus ended the greatest drama of her life and the most unhappy of her passions.

She thought it was by Casimir that Maurice had been carried off. One of her friends in La Châtre had written saying that her husband was in the neighbourhood. Such, however, was not the case. Papet delivered Maurice to Mallefille, and agreed to take charge of Solange.

Félicien Mallefille to George Sand, August 16th, 1837: I have got Maurice. Everything has been carried out according to your wishes, and with the most scrupulous care . . . Forgive this disjointed letter. I have so many details to attend to that I don't know where to begin nor where to end. Maurice is being very good and very nice. He is much looking forward to seeing you again. He is in excellent health. Nobody at Nohant, nor at Ars, has seen any sign of Monsieur Dudevant . . . Before you return to Fontainebleau, ask my brother for your *Dzyady* and your straw hat, so that you may have the wherewithal to fill your head and cover it: There now! Pray for me, *Santo Giorgio!* I am longing for sleep. *Veni, vidi, dormi.* *Vostrissimo*

FELICIEN MALLEVILLE[2]

Strange to tell, Casimir, who in August, had *not* been tempted to carry off Maurice, had in September the ridiculous idea of kidnapping Solange, and taking her to Guillery. George, beside herself with anger, obtained a Court Order, went as swiftly as post-chaise could carry her to Nérac, taking with her Mallefille and a lawyer, warned the Sous-Prefet, and had a police cordon thrown round Guillery.

---

[1] Ibid., Volume II, p. 86.
[2] Spoelberch de Lovenjoul Collection: Group E. 920, f. 212.

George Sand to Alexis Dutheil, September 30th, 1837:
Dudevant, turned suddenly polite and gracious, led
Solange by the hand as far as the entrance to the Royal
Residence, having first invited me to enter, a request
which I most ceremoniously refused. Solange was handed
over to me, like a Princess on the frontier between two
States. The baron and I then exchanged a few polite
words. He threatened to take his son back by order of the
Court, and we parted, mutually charmed. . . .[1]

This incident ended, she entertained the idea of a second
sentimental pilgrimage as she was not far from the
Pyrenees. Mallefille had already been made the legatee of
the emotional disturbance occasioned by Franchard. This
time he was to be associated with the recollections evoked
by the arena at Marboré . . . As soon as the journey had
been made, the family, once more reunited and now in good
heart, returned to Berry. There each spent the winter
absorbed in work.

George Sand to Marie d'Agoult, March 1838: My home
life has nothing much of interest to offer you. It is quiet
and hardworking. I pile novels on short stories, Buloz on
Bonnaire. Mallefille piles dramas on novels, Pelion on
Ossa . . . Maurice, caricatures on caricatures, and
Solange, legs of chickens on false notes. Such is the
strange, heroic life we lead at Nohant. . . .[2]

To himself, Dr. Piffoël addressed admonishment:

Recapitulate all that has happened during these three
months of self-forgetfulness. Do you really remember,
have you not already forgotten, the facts? Your mother
has died, your son been saved, your daughter carried off
and recovered—what of the rest? You have seen
Franchard again—and with whom? You have seen
Marboré again, and with whom? You have come back
here. What are you going to do? what fate awaits you?
Whom are you going to love? what sufferings are you
going to endure? Whom will you be hating a month from
now?—a year from now—tomorrow— . . . What a fine
fellow you are, dear Piffoël! You would drink the blood

---

[1] GEORGE SAND: *Correspondance*. Volume II, p. 91.
[2] Ibid., Volume II, p. 103.

of your children from the skull of your best friend, and
feel not so much as a stomach-ache. . . .[1]

The *Fellows* were travelling in Italy, but no longer happy.
'Storm is in the air', notes Liszt: 'my nerves are on edge . . .
Visions of desolation, of profound disenchantment, lower
over my destiny . . . I have but one thought, one sole
remorse—I ought to have made her happy. I could have
done so once, but can I still?' Suffering breeds injustice in
the heart. A note from Mallefille, enclosed in a letter from
Sand, exasperated Marie, who thought it cavalier and
lacking in politeness. The truth was, she resented the fact
that her former protégé had crossed into her friend's camp.
She complained to George, who reacted unsympathetically:

George Sand to Franz Liszt: And now about Mallefille. I
should really like to know why Mirabella seems to hold
me responsible for all the idiocies he writes to her. As
though I were in duty bound to read Mallefille's letters, to
understand them, to comment upon them, to correct
them, or even to approve them! Thank Heaven, I am not
compelled to give intelligence to those who lack it! . . .
Mallefille writes a letter to the Princess. It is a stupid letter, which does not in the least surprise me. Believing
the Princess to be well used to Malefille's letters, and not
holding it to be my duty to take responsibility for them, I
enclose the said letter in one of my own to the Princess.
Bless you! I know nothing of its contents. I have enough
stupid letters to read every day as it is. If Mallefille's is
rather stupider this time than usual, I should, I think, be
thanked for having found room for it in mine, and so
saved the Princess from having to pay thirty sous for a
stupid letter. When one lets Mallefille write to one, one
cannot complain of what one gets. Knowing Mallefille
and his manner, one should be prepared for anything.
That I should set myself to form Mallefille's epistolary
style would be the worst of mistakes! I know, for my
part, that I shall always find his letters utterly delightful,
for I hope that I shall never read a single one of them. I
love him with all my heart. He could ask me for one half
of my blood and I would give it gladly—on condition
that I should not have to read his letters. . . .[2]

1 GEORGE SAND: *Journal intime*, pp. 85-6.
2 GEORGE SAND: *Correspondance*. Volume II, pp. 96-8.

Marie d'Agoult to George Sand, November 9th, 1837: I
am amused by what you say about Mallefille. What odd
creatures you writers are . . . Do you remember the
quarrels we used to have about him?—how ugly and
stupid he was, how dunderheaded, vain and intolerable?
You seemed to judge him with the sort of angry feelings
which Homer attributes to Juno and to Venus, and I was
reduced to say, *mezza voce*, that if one did not school
oneself to live in peace with other people's vanities, one
would, in all probability, live alone . . . How your
enthusiasms do fade: how many of the stars in your
firmament are shooting stars . . . Perhaps, one day, it may
be even Mirabella's turn! . . .[1]

It was, and that soon. She had never been *persona
gratissima* at Nohant. George and Mallefille were at one in
criticizing her severely.

George Sand to Dutheil, Paris, October 1837: Thou hast
forgot to seek a dwelling worthy of the Lady d'Agoult (I
need not point out that this is my normal manner of
speech). Strive, my sublime and radiant friend, to procure
for the Princess Mirabella, of whose most humble slaves I
count myself as one, a curule chair on which her
ravishing and revered posterior may be borne through the
vistas of those Elysian Fields which go by the name of la
Vallée Noâre. . . .[2]

The velvet paw was still in evidence, but the claws were
already being sharpened. The instrument of vengeance was
Honoré de Balzac, who 'was set down at the Château of
Nohant on the last Saturday in Lent', February 24th, 1838.
There had been a coolness between Balzac and Sand since
the Sandeau affair. Not only had he sided with 'little Jules',
but, after the latter's return from Italy had, as has already
been recounted, taken him in and provided him with
a livelihood in exchange for certain vaguely specified
services which Sandeau had undertaken to perform,
but, because of laziness, had failed to do. Balzac, like Sand,
was a perfect devil for work, who could turn out a novel in

1 Cf. SAMUEL ROCHEBLAVE: 'Une Amitié romanesque',
in the *Revue de Paris*, December 15th, 1894.
2 Spoelberch de Lovenjoul Collection: Group E. 883, f. 50.

two months, and if need be in seventeen days. The flabby
indolence of little Jules exasperated these 'tough-fibred
monsters'. Sandeau, for his part, soon grew weary of living
in a perpetual condition of spate. Balzac said of him: 'He is
a man adrift. He spends his life making plans which he
never carries out.'

> *Balzac to Eveline Hanska, March 8th, 1836:* Jules
> compelled to give intelligence to those who lack it! ...
> Sandeau has turned out to be one of my mistakes. You
> could never imagine such slothfulness and unconcern. He
> is completely lacking in energy and will-power. He will
> talk fine sentiments, but nothing ever comes of them. He
> cannot discipline mind or body to anything. When I had
> spent more on him than a great lord would spend on a
> fancy, when I had nursed his talent and said—'Here's the
> subject for a play, Jules; get on with it, and when that's
> done, start on another, and then try your hand at a
> Variety Show for the Gymnase ...' his only comment was
> that it was *impossible* for him to work straight on end like
> that. Not wishing to seem to be trading on his sense of
> gratitude, I did not insist. He would not even sign his
> name to work we had done in collaboration. 'All right,
> then, make a living out of books ...' In three years he has
> not turned out enough to fill half a volume! Criticism?—
> he finds that too difficult. He is a carriage-horse, that's
> what he is ... He makes friendship impossible, as he has
> made love. I am finished with him.[1]

The two men separated. At the beginning of 1837,
Sandeau was in Brittany, working on a novel about Sand,
Marianna, when information reached him that Balzac was
himself engaged on a book based upon the Sandeau—Sand
episode (*Un Grand Homme de province à Paris*).

> *Jules Sandeau to Balzac, January 21st, 1837:* What ex-
> actly *is* this *Illusions perdues*? I hear from Paris that it
> is the story of me and a certain person known to you.
> That story is one with which everyone is now familiar,
> and the people who have written to me in this strain may
> well be wrong. All the same, I am assured that every page
> of your book is a day from my own youth. Two things

[1] HONORE DE BALZAC: *Lettres à l'Etrangère.* Volume I,
pp. 303-4.

worry me in all this. The first is that, out of friendship for
me, you may have shown the other person in too harsh a
light: the second, that, since I, too, am at present busy on
the task of telling the whole sad business, I may be too
late. You cannot but realize that if Ulysses had come out
with his Memoirs *after* the Odyssey had appeared, he
would have been regarded as a fool and a figure of fun.
Do, please, write and tell me about the book, I shall be on
tenterhooks until I hear from you. . . .[1]

Balzac reassured him. Lucien de Rubempré had nothing
in common with Jules Sandeau. The only character who in
the least resembled him was Lousteau (which did not much
improve matters).

Having now come to share George's feelings about
Sandeau, Balzac need no longer deprive himself of a
powerful and charming friend. Besides, Madame Hanska, a
great collector of such items, very much wanted the lady-
novelist's autograph. In February 1838, when he was staying with the Carrauds at Frapesle. Balzac wrote to Sand asking her permission to 'make a pilgrimage to Nohant . . . I
don't want to go home without having seen either the
lioness of Berry in her lair or the nightingale in its nest . . .'[2]
George, no more than he, liked to be on bad terms with
writers of genius, and sent him a cordial invitation. He
arrived on February 24th and it is impossible to improve on
his own account of this visit to Lélia.

I fetched up at the Château of Nohant on the last
Saturday in Lent, at about half-past seven in the evening,
and found friend George in a dressing-gown, smoking her
after-dinner cigar by the fire in an enormous, desolate
room. She was wearing a handsome pair of fringed
yellow slippers, coquettish stockings, and red trousers. So
much for the general setting: now for her appearance.
She has developed a double chin, which gives her the
look of a Church dignitary. There is not a single white
hair to be seen in spite of all the appalling experiences she
has been through. She is as swarthy as ever, and her fine
eyes are as brilliant. She has that way I remember of
assuming an almost stupid expression when plunged in

[1] Spoelberch de Lovenjoul Collection: Group A. 316, f. 110.
[2] Letter published by Madame Aurore Lauth-Sand in *Les
Nouvelles littéraires* for July 26th, 1930.

thought, the reason being, as I told her after prolonged consideration, that it is her eyes only that are expressive. She has been at Nohant for the past year, very low in spirits, and putting in an enormous amount of work. . . .

So there she is, hidden away in the depths of the country, inveighing against marriage and love alike because in both she has had nothing but disappointments. All it means is that the right male for her is a rare bird, and will continue to be rare because she is not the type that invites love, and she will find it difficult to find anyone to give it to her. She is masculine, she is an artist, she is great-hearted, generous, devoted and temperamentally chaste. She has all the finer characteristics of a man; *ergo* she is not a woman. During the three days I was there we talked together with the utmost frankness, and not once did I feel, any more than in the old days, that physical thrill which one ought to feel in the company of a woman, whether in France or in Poland. It was just as though I were with a friend of my own sex. She has outstanding virtues, virtues of the kind that society misunderstands. With the utmost seriousness, with perfect sincerity, absolute candour, and a conscientiousness worthy of noble shepherds entrusted with the care of the human herd, we discussed the all-important problems of marriage and freedom. . . .

It was one up to me when I compelled Madame Dudevant to admit the necessity of marriage, but I have no doubt that she will see that I am right, and will feel that I have done her a good turn by providing my point. She is an excellent mother, and adored by her children: but she dresses her daughter Solange like a little boy, and that is not a good thing. In the matter of morals, she is like a young man of twenty, fundamentally chaste and prudish. She is the artist only in externals. . . .

She has done many foolish things, but in the eyes of the fine-spirited and high-souled they redound to her credit. She has been taken in by Dorval, by Bocage, by Lamennais, etc. etc. . . . The same feeling to which they appealed has led to her being taken in *now* by Liszt and Madame d'Agoult, but she has come to realize it in her case, as she did in Dorval's, because she has the type of mind which can see clearly enough when it is alone with itself, but is easily set on the wrong track when brought up against realities. It was while we were talking about

Liszt and Madame d'Agoult that she gave me the subject for *Les Galériens ou les Amours forcés*, which I am going to write because, her position being what it is, she cannot very well write it herself. But all that is a dead secret. What it all comes to is that she is a man: all the more so since she wants to be one. She has given up playing the woman, and is *not* a woman. Women attract; she repels. If she produces that effect on me, who am very much of a man, it is very certain that she will produce it on all men who resemble me. She will always be unhappy. At this very moment she is in love with someone who is decidedly her inferior, and that sort of relationship is bound to end in disenchantment and disillusion for a high-spirited woman. A woman should always love a man who is her superior, or be so blinded by passion as to think him so. . . .[1]

No doubt in order to reassure the jealous Madame Hanska, Balzac somewhat exaggerated Sand's inability to attract him physically, and stressed her masculine character. Fundamentally, however, what he said was true. He never did feel desire where she was concerned, and that meant that there could be perfect frankness between them. They could talk together as two persons of high intellectual distinction. Their conversation must have been lively and good. They agreed about nothing. Sand, the faithful disciple of Rosseau, believed in original freedom and in progress. Balzac, a penitent Rousseau-ist, believed in original sin, and was convinced that men's natures could not be changed. George Sand was feeling her way back to the variety of Christianity preached by the *Vicaire savoyard*, which she called the Gospel according to Saint-John. Balzac, whose faith was of much the same kind, nevertheless upheld the Roman form of catholicism, partly, like Bonald, for political reasons, partly because he admired some of the saints. George Sand was a republican, Balzac a monarchist. George preached the emancipation of women, and marriage for love: Balzac upheld the marriage of common sense, and feared the effect of too much freedom on married women. George Sand had created fictional heroes of a stainless idealism, and had then tried to find their equivalents in real

---

[1] HONORE DE BALZAC: *Lettres à l'Etrangère*. Volume I, pp. 462-6.

life, without success. Balzac, who had been loved since early youth by a woman of ideals, *la Dilecta,* described adultery and debauchery with pitiless realism.

Balzac believed that he had converted Sand in the matter of marriage. His efforts to that end had been undertaken not in her interests so much as in those of other women, and it is possible that that great and wise man did exercise upon her thought a beneficent influence. When he came to work out the subject for a novel which Sand had suggested, he turned *Les Galériens de l'Amour* into *Béatrix, ou les Armours forcés,* and as such it was a masterpiece. The title contains a cruel allusion to Marie's one-time determination to make of Liszt and herself the new Dante and the new Beatrice. 'Dante! Beatrice!'—said Liszt bitterly: 'it is the Dantes who make the Beatrices, and the real ones die at eighteen.' Madame d'Agoult, Liszt's senior by six years, was thirty-three.

George herself was portrayed by Balzac as Félicité des Touches, who wrote books under the name of 'Camille Maupin'. The choice of the name Maupin could be taken as a veiled reference to Théophile Gauthier's equivocal heroine. The picture of her was, however, flattering: 'She had even more heart than talent . . . She was gifted with genius, and led one of those exceptional existences which cannot be judged by ordinary standards . . .' Béatrix de Rochefide, on the other hand, was a severe satire on Marie d'Agoult: 'There was something of affectation about her: she had rather too much the air of being able to understand difficult matters . . .' Claude Vignon was made, in certain respects and with the model's full consent, to resemble Gustave Planche. Balzac always swore that Gennaro had not been suggested by Liszt, and the musician, with his habitual dignity, refused to see himself in the character, or to take offence. Actually, and as always with Balzac, the transposition was at a very deep level. But Marie never forgave Balzac for this novel which, she said, had been written after 'a week's hobnobbing at Nohant'.

In September 1839, *Béatrix* appeared serially in *Le Siècle.*

Balzac to George Sand: I hope you will be pleased, and that should there be anything not to your taste you will tell me. I count on that sincerity which has always marked our friendship . . . My dear, I have read *Marianna,* and thought sorrowfully of our talks at your fireside. There will soon be a whole tribe of authors ready to have their entrails pulped into paper so that they can print the secrets of their lives on it . . . The horrors of a literary Coliseum are threatening . . . I thought *Les Amours forcés* a pleasanter title than *Les Galériens.*[1]

For *l'Etrangère* he provided a 'key' to the novel.

Balzac to Eveline Hanska, February 1840: Yes, Sarah is Madame de Visconti; yes, Mademoiselle des Touches is George Sand; yes, Béatrix is almost too much Madame d'Agoult. George Sand is in the seventh heaven. The book gives her a nice little revenge on her friend. The story, a few changes of detail apart, is true. . . .[2]

Nevertheless, when the book was put on sale, and George, uneasy about the *Fellows'* possible reaction, asked him to 'cover' her by writing a letter which she could show if the necessity arose, he played up nobly:

Balzac to George Sand, January 18th, 1840: I knew that something of this sort would happen about Béatrix. Thousands of people who are intent on putting us on bad terms—but they won't succeed—must have tried to make you believe that Camille Maupin was but one among many strokes of malice, and that the name Claude Vignon cloaked a dig at you. Since, in spite of our friendship, we have never really had eight days together over a period of eight years, and it is difficult to see how I could possibly have known much about you or your home life . . . I have been told, too, that Béatrix is a portrait, and that the whole novel bears a remarkable resemblance to something which occurred in your circle . . . Alas! something similar has happened with all my books! . . . As a result of *Le Lys dans La Vallée* I was credited with knowing the secrets of at least four or five families about which, in fact, I knew absolutely nothing. But when it comes to the assumed original of Béatrix (on whom I have never set eyes) it really is a bit too much! My reasons for writing *Béatrix* are set forth in the Preface, and I have nothing to add to

[1] Letter published by Madame Aurore Lauth-Sand in *Les Nouvelles littéraires* for July 26th, 1930.

[2] HONORE DE BALZAC: *Lettres à l'Etrangère.* Volume I, p. 527.

what I have said there. I love Liszt both as a man and an artist, and to assert that Gennaro has any points of resemblance with him is a double insult, for it strikes both at him and at me. . . .[1]

George Sand to Balzac: Good evening, dear Dom Mad. Please don't worry yourself over my susceptibilities. Whether or no I feel flattered about the 'cousin german' about whom you speak, I am too used to writing novels not to know that the novelist never indulges in *portraiture,* that, even if one would, one cannot, copy a living model. Heavens! where would art be if one did not invent, for good or bad, three quarters of the characters in whom the stupid, inquisitive, public likes to think that it can see originals who are known to it? I am told that you have, in this book, terribly blackened a very spotless person of my acquaintance, and her companion in what you are pleased to call the 'galleys'. She is too intelligent to see herself in your story, and I rely on you to exonerate me should it ever occur to her to accuse me of malicious tale-bearing. . . .[2]

And so it was that this dramatic summer in the country became a masterpiece. It was no bad harvest.

---

[1] Letter published by Madame Aurore Lauth-Sand in *Les Nouvelles littéraires* for July 26th 1930.

[2] Spoelberch de Lovenjoul Collection: Group A. 311, f. 46.

PART SIX

FREDERIC CHOPIN

'No doubt about it,' said old Buloz one day, when he was talking of me, 'she is very proud in love, and very good-hearted in friendship.'
George Sand

PRELUDES

ALL SAND'S friends had noticed that, in the course of that
wonderful, sublime and absurd summer of 1837, one of the
persons to whom, in the chaos of her emotions, her
thoughts had turned, was the young Polish pianist whom
she was trying in vain to attract to Nohant. It seemed, as
though Chopin, as she might have said, had been marked
out for her by Providence. He was a sensitive and unhappy
exile. His constant feeling was one of regretful longing for
Poland, for his family, and, above all, for a mother's tender
love. 'If I thought', he said, 'that anybody wanted to put me
into leading-strings, I should be very happy.' Now, what
somebody very precisely wanted was to find in him a
combination of son and lover. Chopin was seven years
younger than Sand, and this difference in age led her to
hope that he would adopt towards her that filial, that almost
childlike, attitude which the tyranny of a man like Michel
had made her long for. She saw in the young musician
somebody who was weak, ailing and feverish—three
characteristics which this nurse-mother found irresistible.
In physical beauty he was Liszt's equal: 'of middle height,
slim, with long, tapering fingers, very small feet, ash-blond
hair with a suspicion of auburn in it, brown eyes more
marked by liveliness than melancholy, an equiline nose, a
very sweet smile, a rather husky voice, and something about
his general air so noble, so indefinably aristocratic',[1] that
those who did not know him took him to be some great
Lord in exile. Many and many a time while she sat gazing
musingly at the golden limes of Nohant, that handsome face
had danced upon the paper beneath her pen, and kept her
from writing—a rare and dangerous sign.

Mallefille was a thoroughly nice fellow—'one of Heav-
en's best gifts to friendship', but his talents were mediocre,

[1] WLADIMIR KARENINE: *George Sand, sa Vie et ses
Oeuvres.* Volume III, p. 29.

whereas Chopin had genius. Sand, so truly musical, both by heredity and upbringing, Sand who, as a small girl, had sat beneath her grandmother's harpsichord revelling in that romantic hiding-place, and, later, had crept under Liszt's piano and crouched there, delighting in the thrilling power of his playing, understood more than most people the language of sound. On top of all this, if Marie d'Agoult, having captured Liszt, were to be allowed to annex Chopin as well, she would have felt it to be a bad mark against herself. Everything combined to waken in her a passionate wish to harness the frail and brilliant pianist to her chariot.

But the task of winning him was far from easy. Chopin, so delicate that he seemed almost a wraith, and looking as though he were out of his element among earthly scenes and flesh and blood people, had a horror of noisy argument, untidy clothes, and, above all, of scandal. The spiritual climate best suited to him was a drawing-room full of fine furniture and beautiful women, high-born, too, as well as beautiful, musically inclined and prepared to sit in half-darkness listening to a *Nocturne* which was also a confession. He loved to plunge an aristocratic audience into a mood of rapt contemplation, and then lift it suddenly to heroic heights by making his piano body forth in sound and martyrdom of Poland. In politics he was a Conservative. In love, he was shy and gentle. A somewhat hazy Platonism was well suited to his not very strong character. Taken for all in all, he was a rather unhappy mortal whose life was but 'an immense discord'.

When they first met he passed severe judgment on this woman novelist who wore a man's clothes and smoked cigars, who addressed her odd friends in the second person singular, who had broken with all society save that of artists, and paraded her socialistic and democratic theories. How different she was from those fair-haired, those angelic, Polish ladies for whom, till then, he had entertained so chaste a passion! It is easy enough to understand why he should have set his face against going to her house, and that after visiting the Hôtel de France he should have said: 'How antipathetic this Sand woman is! Is she really a woman at all? I am inclined to doubt it.'

When, however, she returned to Paris in October 1837, he agreed to meet her again. He was the victim of profound unhappiness. 'I am of those', he said, 'who have come from the workshop of some celebrated master, some incomparable Stradivarius, who is no longer here to turn to account. Unskilled hands were powerless to draw new music from us, and we bury it deep within ourselves, because we lack a player to make it audible . . .' The young Polish woman whom he had hoped to marry, Marie Wodzinska, had gradually come to see less and less of him, obedient to the orders of her parents who were alarmed by his weak physique. He never spoke of his melancholy, but felt an urgent need to be consoled. Sand was prepared to give him all the consolation he required. In one of Chopin's notebooks a piece of George's letter-paper was found, folded in two. On one side she had written the words—*I adore you!* with her name. Below her signature, Marie Dorval had added—*I, too! I, too! I, too!*[1]

Chopin's Journal, October 1837: I have had three further meetings with her. She gazed deep into my eyes while I played. I had chosen some rather sad music, Legends of the Danube. My heart was dancing with her in a country scene. What were her eyes saying, those dark, those curious eyes, so intently fixed on mine? She leaned on the piano, and her gaze was like a fiery flood . . . Flowers all about us. My heart was captured! Since then I have seen her twice again . . . She loves me . . . Aurore, what a lovely name! . . .[2]

He found in George a strength by which, in spite of himself, he was attracted, because of the support with which it furnished him. Here was a woman knowledgeable in music, a woman capable of appreciating him, of inspiring him, even of advising him; a woman free with her person, who asked nothing better than to give herself. Despite his naturally chaste, and almost chilly, temperament, he was tempted.

Heinrich Heine, who admired both of them, has given us some idea of this strange pair. '*She*—beautiful auburn hair falling to her shoulders; eyes rather lustreless and sleepy, but calm and gentle; a smile of great good nature; a somewhat dead, somewhat husky voice, difficult to hear, for George is far from talkative, and takes in a great deal more than she gives out. *He*—endowed with abnormal sensitive-

[1] MARIE-LOUISE PAILLERON: *George Sand*. Volume II, p. 131.
[2] Printed by G. Knosp in *Le Guide Musical* for September 15th, 1907. Quoted by Louise Vincent.

ness which the least contact can wound, on which the tiniest sound will strike like thunder: a man made for intimacies, withdrawn into a mysterious world of his own, from from which he sometimes emerges in a sudden spate of violent, charming and fantastic speech.'

During the Spring of 1838 she made several visits to Paris. They saw one another in the evenings, often alone. Chopin would play, and then the two of them would respond to the 'breeze of the moment' and be fanned to 'a celestial glow'. Poor Mallefille was quite forgotten. But Chopin was not a man with whom it was easy to take things for granted. His friends, Albert Grzymala, the Pole, and Madame Marliani, the Consul's wife, were the recipients of confidences every whit as moonstruck as his *Nocturnes*. With Chopin, 'the weather of love's season is changeable. One keeps on saying *yes—no—if*—but, and often, in the morning, one says, *really this is quite intolerable*, only to declare, when evening comes, *this is the very crown of happiness!'*[1] Shyness and sexual modesty awake desire more surely than does coquetry, which merely apes them, with less of nature. George was infatuated by this remote young man, who kept himself withdrawn.

It was in this changeable, uncertain climate of the heart that, in the early Summer of 1838, she wrote to Chopin's best friend, the Count Albert Grzymala—'a gigantic Pole, of extremely smart appearance, frock-coated in the latest fashion in a monstrous, a pyramidal garment, all braid and trimmings', whom Sand called her husband, because Chopin was their 'small child'. The letter was thirty-two pages in length. It has been severely criticized. Indignation —and sometimes amusement—has been expressed, because, in the course of it, Sand spoke frankly of matters which most people, then as now, might think but not put into words. To hypocrites all sincerity has the appearance of cynicism.

Let us face the question frankly, once and for all—wrote Sand to Grzymala—because on your considered answer all my future conduct will depend. Your gospel is the same as mine in laying down that one should think of oneself last of all, and not at all when the happiness of those one loves calls for the exercise of all one's strength

[1] Letter from George Sand to Grzymala, printed in full by Wladimir Karénine, in *George Sand*. Volume III, pp. 44-63.

of mind. Listen carefully, and send me a clear,
categorical, and definite reply. . . .

What was all this about? In the first place, she wanted to
know whether the young Polish woman, Marie Wodzinska,
whom Chopin felt bound, or thought he felt bound, to love,
could still make him happy. Sand had no wish to play the
part of evil genius. She did not want to be the *femme-fatale*
fighting against a childhood's sweetheart, if the latter was
beautiful and pure. On the other hand, she admitted that
she was 'as good as married' to the best of men, against
whose honesty of heart and personal honour no charge
could be brought (Mallefille), who had given himself to her
utterly, and whom she did not want to abandon. If 'our
poor little chap' (in other words, Chopin), should decide to
put his life into George's hands, she would feel definitely
afraid. Such love 'could not exist save in accordance with
the dictates of his temperament—that is to say, by fits and
starts. When a kindly wind blows us into one another's
arms, we shall pay a fleeting visit to the stars. . . .'
There were two possible solutions. If the 'person in
question' was capable of giving Chopin a pure and genuine
happiness, and if he in his 'excessive scrupulosity' found it
impossible to love two different women in two different
ways, then she, Sand, would make herself scarce, and do
her utmost to forget him. If, on the contrary, marriage with
the 'person in question' was likely to become the 'grave of
his artistic soul', or, if Chopin's domestic happiness and
religious scruples could come to terms with 'occasional
interludes of chaste passion and sweet poetry', then she
would continue to see him. She would be a stranger to his
ordinary day-to-day existence, and would not in any way
seek to influence his religious, political or social attitudes.
He, for his part, must refrain from asking her to give an
account of her actions. 'We should not see one another
every day, for not every day would the sacred fire have hold
of us, but we should know moments of great beauty, and
heaven-sent ardour. . . .'
There was another problem—though of secondary
importance—which must be faced: the problem of total
surrender—possession or non-possession? It is in this
matter that George's attitude of detachment has surprised
and shocked so many people. She had never, she confessed,
where physical relations were concerned, been able to bring

wisdom and feeling into harmony. 'I have made no secret of
my attitude: I have no theories, fixed views, nor prejudices
. . .' She had always trusted to her instincts. She had much
that was foolish to reproach herself with, but nothing that
was squalid or wicked.

With me, feeling has always been stronger than reason,
and such constraints as I have wished to place upon myself have never been of the slightest use. I have changed
my mind twenty times over. The one thing I have placed
above all else is faithfulness. That I have preached, that I
have practised, upon that I have insisted. Others have
shown a want of it, and so, for that matter, have I. But I
have never suffered from remorse, because, whenever I
have been untrue to faithfulness, it has always been
because I seemed driven on by a sort of faith, an instinct
for the ideal which has compelled me to leave the imperfect for what I thought was closer to the perfect. . . .

She was not—that was what it came to—inconstant by
nature. She had always been faithful to what she loved, in
the sense that she had never *deceived* anybody, and had
'never ceased to be faithful except for very good reasons
which, because of others' faults', had had the effect of
'killing love'. In the present case she felt morally uneasy,
because, in fact, she had no sort of a grievance against
Mallefille. She was appalled by the effect which the 'little
chap' (Chopin) had had upon her. She knew that if she had
had time to fight against her passion, to bring her powers of
reason to bear on it, she would have been guilty of
wrongdoing. But, as things had turned out, she had been
swept off her feet, and it was not in her nature to let reason
decide her course of action when she was in the grip of love.
On this point she was influenced by Rousseau and his view
of the moral standards of the heart. In any case, insofar as
there was a fault at all, the mere fact of physical possession
did not make it worse. A simple kiss was a consummation
of infidelity. 'When the heart is lost, all is lost' . . . If a man
and a woman want to live together, they ought not to
outrage nature by recoiling from complete union. With
Chopin she would, if driven to it, accept the necessity of
sacrifice and remain chaste, but only if he insisted on
abstention out of feelings of respect for her, or even from a
sense of loyalty to another, but *not* if he was influenced by

that contempt of 'human grossness' felt by the excessively pious. *Contempt of the flesh* was an expression which Sand held in abhorrence.

> He has said, I believe, that *certain facts* might spoil the memory. Don't you think such a view sheer stupidity, and that he does not really believe it? Or is it that some wretched woman has left him with this view of physical love? Has he had a mistress who was unworthy of him? Poor angel! I should like to see all women hanged who have *dirtied* in men's eyes the thing in life most worthy of respect, the most sacred fact in all creation, the divine mystery, the most serious of all human actions, and the most sublime in the whole universal range of life.

That is the gist of the famous letter which is outstandingly remarkable for its good sense. It has been said: 'She wanted to have Chopin without having to give up Mallefille, and was trying to find virtuous reasons for persuading herself that she was acting only in the best interests of both ...' That may be so. But who is there, among those endowed by nature with strong passions, who has not sometimes had recourse to casuistry when it was a question of reconciling sense and sensibility? 'What sort of life do *you* lead, my fine men and women in the street?'—asks Sand. 'What has become of your eyes, your ears, your memories? You call me a cynic because I see and remember, and because I would blush to owe to blindness that sham kindliness which makes you at once fools and knaves . . .'[1] Who shall say that she was wrong? The woman who sins, and confesses her faults, is accepted and absolved by the moralists, because, so far from weakening moral principles, she has, by accusing herself, strengthened them. Byron and Baudelaire, both dissipated, both tormented, still stand as witnesses for virtue. It is the serenity, the clear conscience, of the rebel, that exasperates society. What the hypocritical reader, 'mon semblable, mon frère', will never find it possible to put up patiently with in this letter of Sand's, is its note of unperturbed frankness, and, above all, the fact that it was written *by a woman*. Change the sex, and it will be generally agreed that it expresses the feelings not of one man only, but of *all men*. Now, Sand lived as a man. In that lay her originality, her weakness, and, as she thought, her honour.

1 GEORGE SAND: *Journal intime*, p. 135.

PRELUDES 321

The problem, as it happened, was quite different from what Chopin's extreme reserve had led George to imagine. His engagement to Marie Wodzinska had been broken off a year before, and it was because he was suffering, because he stood in need of generous-hearted tenderness, that he had let himself seek consolation in George Sand's arms. What form Grzymala's answer took we do not know, but it must have been reassuring, because George lost no time in leaving Nohant and returning to Paris.

The Summer of 1838 was a time of happiness. Little by little the image of Marie Wodzinska faded from Chopin's mind, until it was little more than a romantic memory. He worked hard and published a collection of *Etudes,* dedicated to the Comtesse d'Agoult. His excessive sense of modesty had not allowed him to dedicate it to George. It was the man of this paradoxical couple who insisted on secrecy. Besides, this time, George felt obliged to take certain precautions because of Mallefille. She had believed that she could get rid of him without much difficulty. 'He is so good, and so wise that, given time, I shall be able to let him know what has happened, and to bring him to a mood of understanding. He is yielding wax on which I have set the imprint of my seal, and when I want to change the superscription, I shall, if I go carefully and have patience, succeed.'[1]

When it came to the point, however, the wax proved to be less soft than she had expected. Mallefille, finding himself forsaken, because jealous and wished to put up a fight. He had the hot passions of a créole. During the Summer of 1838 he had already sent a challenge to a friend of his who, in the course of a visit to Nohant, had paid court to George. She, obedient to the dictates of loyalty, now warned the young tutor that a chapter in his life had been closed, and that he must consent, from now on, to relinquish love for friendship. But violent trouble might, at any moment, break out again with somebody else, and, at all costs, that somebody must not be Chopin. The very idea of a Velasquez *caballero* attacking the sickly musician with his rapier was terrifying. Pierre Leroux, whom Mallefille intended to visit in company with Rollinat in order to clear up certain philosophical problems, was asked to use all his influence in an attempt to appease the angry lover. 'When

[1] Letter from George Sand to Grzymala: quoted by Karénine. Volume III, p. 45.

the question of women crops up between you, tell him
straight out that they do not belong to men by virtue of
brute force. and that the cutting of throats settles nothing.
. . .'¹

The whole adventure delighted Marie d'Agoult. 'Poor
Mallefille!—there he is, confined to his bed, suffering from
ingrowing vanity, for ever *dis*abused, *dis*illusioned, *dis*enchanted—and all the other *dis's* in the world. And do you
know why? It really is a perfectly priceless story . . .'—
whereupon she describes the return to Paris of Mallefille
(who had been sent to Le Havre in charge of Maurice). The
wretched man was quite ignorant of the new love affair, and
had actually published in the *Gazette musicale à Ballade* in
Chopin's honour.

Finally, prompted by what devilish inspiration I do not
know, he began to get suspicious, and hung about,
watching the door of Chopin's apartment where George
was in the habit of going every night. The dramatic
author became a character of drama. He shouted, he
yelled, he was terribly fierce and all out for blood. Friend
Grzymala flung himself between the illustrious rivals.
Mallefille was calmed down, and now, off George has
gone to bask in the sunshine of a perfect love under the
myrtle trees of Palma! Confess now, that is a far better
story than any novelist could invent. . . .²

¹ Letter from George Sand to Pierre Leroux: quoted by
Karénine. Volume II, p. 444.
² Letter from Marie d'Agoult to Major Pictet (Florence,
January 10th, 1839), quoted by Marie-Louise Pailleron, in
George Sand. Volume II, p. 141.

II

A WINTER IN MAJORCA

SAND HAD a number of excellent reasons for 'basking in
the sunshine of a perfect love' elsewhere than in Paris. She
ran the risk, if she did not go away, of having to face fresh
outbursts of jealousy. Maurice's health would be benefited
by a warm climate. Chopin's cough was causing considerable anxiety, and he feared the scandal of a public 'liaison' which would have horrified his pious family. As to
George, she could work no matter where she was, and felt,
as always, the need to live in conditions of 'married'
domesticity with her new lover. For five years now she had
been suffering from a series of troubles and worries, and
longed for peace and quiet. Her Spanish friends, the
politician, Mendizabal—half genius, half adventurer—and
Marliani, the Consul, painted, for her benefit, a glowing
picture of Majorca. It was agreed that she should travel by
short stages, with her two children, going by way of Lyons,
Perpignan and Barcelona. Chopin was to join her somewhere on the way, and they would take ship together for the
Balearic Isles. At Perpignan, as arranged, he appeared 'fresh
as a rose and rosy as a turnip'.

They reached the Majorcan town of Palma in November
1838. They had left Paris in cold weather. Sunshine
welcomed them to Spain, and the first impression was one
of beauty.

Chopin to Jules Fontana, November 15th, 1838: Here I
am at Palma in the shade of palm trees, cedars, aloes,
oranges, lemons, fig-trees and pomegranates . . . The sky
is of turquoise blue, the sea of lapis, the mountains
emerald. The air?—the air is as it must be in Heaven.
The days are sunny: everybody goes about in summer
clothes, and it is hot. At night there is singing and guitar-
playing for hours on end. The houses have huge
balconies from which depend great vines which cover
walls dating from the time of the Arabs . . . The town,

like everything else here, reminds one of Africa . . . In short, a delicious existence! . . .[1]

But the sense of enchantment did not last long. They had two badly furnished, or, rather, unfurnished rooms: trestle beds with slabs of slate in place of mattresses, and one straw covered chair. Their food consisted of fish and garlic. The sickly stench of rancid oil was everywhere. Houses, people, even the fields, seemed impregnated with it. There was more than enough in all this to upset a delicate constitution. Sand, ever active, found a house and proposed to put it into habitable state, only to discover that the Majorcans were disinclined to do much work, and that what they did was bad. They lived at the mercy of every wind that blew, without glass to their windows or locks to their doors. At last the lovers found a certain Señor Gomez who leased them a cottage at the foot of the mountains, for which he charged a hundred francs a month.

At first, with love to help, their existence was delightful. They spent delicious days in idling, and lovely evenings on the terrace, though by now it was December. Sand remembered the nights in Venice, filled with the sound of water plashing against marble steps, and other nights at Nohant, loud with the songs of nightingales. In Majorca the silence was profound, broken only by the tinkle of donkey-bells and the distant, vague, scarcely audible murmur of the sea. But neither here did the enchantment last. The rainy season started, and life became a perpetual deluge. The *Maison du Vent* which Señor Gomez had leased them, lived up to its name. Damp, and innocent of chimneys, it had not been built as a shelter against storms. So thin were the walls that the plaster absorbed moisture like a sponge. It was as though an icy cloak had descended upon their shoulders. The asphyxiating atmosphere of braziers was the worst possible thing for Chopin. He had terrible fits of coughing.

From that moment, the local population regarded him with fear and horror. The aggressive Gomez wrote a letter in which (said Sand) he asserted that 'we were *harbouring* an individual who was *harbouring* a contagious ailment. He trusted that we would move out of his "palace" . . .' . . . The three doctors of the town assembled in consultation. *Chopin to Fontana:* 'One of them sniffed at my sputum, the second tapped the part of my anatomy from which the said sputum

[1] Letter quoted by Edouard Ganche: *Frédéric Chopin*, p. 155.

had come, the third listened to my chest while I was producing the sputum . . .' He had the greatest difficulty in staving off their bleedings and blisters. The Spanish doctors having declared, not unreasonably, that consumption is contagious, Señor Gomez showed his tenants the door. They were compelled to settle in a ruined monastery from which the monks had been expelled—the Charterhouse of Valdemosa. A political refugee who was in a hurry to get out of the country bequeathed them his cell and his furniture. In the middle of December they moved to this mountainous retreat, travelling to it across heaths and fields of asphodel.

The Charterhouse of Valdemosa, built to accommodate twelve monks and a Superior, overlooked the sea on two sides. The Order having been dissolved by a decree of 1836, the building had been put up for lease by the State, but superstitious fear had so far kept anyone from occupying it. Sand and her 'family' found themselves living almost completely alone except for an apothecary, a sacristan and a neighbour called Maria-Antonina, who offered her services, for the love of God, *por l'assistencia*, though, in fact, she helped herself pretty extensively to their clothes and their food. The work of the establishment was done by Catalina, a powerful local witch, and Nina, a small, shaggy monstrosity. The Oratories and the Cloisters were adorned with mosaics in the Arab taste. At night, when the moon was shining, the old buildings took on a fantastic appearance. Solange and Maurice clambered about the roofs, which they reached by a spiral staircase.

Green-draped mountains, wild rocks, palm-trees silhouetted against the pink sky—on sunny days the scenery was superb. Nevertheless their stay at Valdemosa was a failure. Since Chopin could not stand the local cooking, Sand had to prepare the meals with her own hands. There was no end to her work—she did the cleaning and the cooking, explored the Palma shops, went walking with the children in the rain, crossed swollen rivers in a ramshackle carriage, and, at the same time, was busy revising *Lélia* and writing *Spiridion*, since, somehow or other, money had got to be earned, and Buloz, who had provided the travellers with funds, was clamouring for copy. But, hard though the life was, it suited her energetic nature. Eagles hovered above their beds. The mountains were often enveloped in fog, and the small lamp by the aid of which they found their way about the cloisters, glimmered like a will-o'-the-wisp. No dwelling could have been more romantic. Chopin worked away in his 'cell, the doors of which are taller than those of Paris carriage-entries'. His hair was no longer curled, he had discarded his white gloves, but he was as pale as ever . . . He had at last recovered his *pianino* which had been for a long time in the clutches of the Customs officials at Palma. On it stood the works of Bach together with his own scribbled sheets of music-paper. But he suffered from the break in his usual habits and the absence of all the familiar objects which he liked to have about him.

The small French group was not popular with the neighbours, who were deeply shocked by the failure of its members to go to church. The *alcade* (or local Magistrate) and the curé spread it about that they were heathens, Mahommedans or Jews. The peasants were in a plot to refuse to supply them with fish, eggs and vegetables except at exorbitant prices. Solange's smock and trousers were a cause of scandal. A young girl of ten years old ought not to dress like a boy. The climate, however, suited the children. Solange flourished and Maurice's health improved miraculously. Their mother, with her usual diligence, kept them hard at work. 'I am deep with Maurice in Thucydides and Co. and, with Solange in the rules of indirect speech, and the agreement of the participle . . .' But Chopin was wasting away in the most terrifying fashion. His 'catarrh' (for Sand refused to admit that his cough was anything worse), made him appallingly weak and listless. It was a matter of extreme distress to Sand that she could not give him better food, and she would fly into towering rages when she caught the servants stealing his broth, or when the bread failed to arrive freshly baked. As the winter deepened, so did melancholy. It lay like a paralysis upon her every effort to be gay and serene.

> The condition of our invalid grew ever worse. The wind sighed in the valley, the rain beat against the windows, the voice of the thunder penetrated the thickness of the walls and mingled its mournful sound with the laughter of the children at their play. The eagles and the vultures, emboldened by the fog, ventured quite close and ravened on the poor sparrows in the pomegranate tree which filled the window of my room. The raging sea kept the boats in harbour. We felt ourselves to be prisoners, far from all enlightened assistance and practical sympathy. Death seemed to be hovering above our heads, intent on seizing

one of our number, and there was nobody to help us keep it from its prey. . . .[1]

The local doctor diagnosed laryngeal consumption, and prescribed diet and bleedings. It was her view that bleeding would have been fatal, and she refused to believe that he was suffering from consumption. 'I had nursed many cases of sickness,' she wrote, 'and my instinct in such matters was reliable.'

In spite of his intense sufferings, Chopin worked hard. During his stay on Majorca he composed a number of *Ballades* and *Preludes,* many of which, it is said (though this is doubtful), were inspired by his feeling of anxiety when George, having gone walking at night with the children, was late in returning.

We hurried [wrote Sand] because we knew he would be anxious. And so he had been, very anxious, but the feeling had, as it were, become frozen into a sort of despairing calmness, so that he played a wonderful *Prelude* for us with the tears streaming down his cheeks. When he saw us enter the room he jumped up with a great cry, and, in a strange tone, and with a wild look in his eyes, said—'Ah! I was so sure that you were dead! . . .' When he had recovered his spirits, and saw how we were, he made himself quite ill by imagining all the dangers we had faced. He later confessed to me that, while he had sat there waiting for us, he had seen everything happening as in a dream, and then, finding it impossible to distinguish dream from reality, had grown quiet, and as though numbed, while he played the piano, to sure was he that he, too, was dead. He had a vision of himself drowned in a lake. Heavy, icy, drops of water, he said, were falling rhythmically upon his breast, and when I made him listen to the raindrops which were, in fact, dripping with measured regularity upon the roof, he denied that they were what he had heard. He even grew angry when I used the phrase *imitative harmony*. He protested as strongly as he knew how—and he was right—against the childishness of such aural imitations. His genius was rich in the mysterious harmonies

[1] GEORGE SAND: *Un Hiver au Midi de l'Europe, Majorque et les Majorcains (Revue des Deux Mondes,* March, 15th, 1841, p. 822).

suggested by natural happenings, but they were always transposed into the sublime equivalents of his musical thought, and were never a mere slavish repetition of sounds that had struck upon his ear from the outside world. What he had composed that evening was full of the sound of raindrops on the monastery roof, but they had been transformed in his imagination and in his music into tears falling from Heaven upon his heart. . . .[1]

And so it was that Chopin in that romantic setting gave birth to masterpieces. But he soon developed a horror of Majorca. The stay at Valdemosa became for him an ordeal, and for Sand a torment.

Though Chopin was tender, vivacious and charming in society, in the intimacy of the sickroom he could drive one to despair . . . It was as though his spirit had been flayed. A crumpled rose-leaf, the mere shadow of a fly, would make it bleed. With the exception of me and the children, everything beneath the Spanish sun was, for him, antipathetic and repellent. He was dying with impatience to be gone. The longing to leave irked him far more than the discomforts of our life there.[2]

At last it was decided that they should go. The journey from Palma to Barcelona was frightful. On board the *El-Mallorquin* the air was thick with the stench of a cargo of live pigs. The captain, having noticed Chopin's cough, had given him the worst bunk so that a better one should not be contaminated. The pigs, whom the sailors regularly beat in order to cure them of seasickness, made the most appalling noise. Chopin spat a great deal of blood, and, by the time they reached Barcelona, was within measurable distance of dying. They made the trip from Barcelona to Marseilles in a French ship, *Le Phénicien*. The medical officer did everything he could for the sick man, but there could be no question of a return to Paris in February. Sand installed the whole 'family', for every member of which she had now become responsible, at the Hôtel de Beauvau in Marseilles.

---

[1] GEORGE SAND: *Histoire de ma Vie.* Volume IV, pp. 439-40.

[2] Ibid., Volume IV, p. 443.

George Sand to Carlotta Marliani, February 16th, 1839:
I must send you news of my patient, for I know, dear
sister, that you take as much interest in him as I do. He is
much, much better. He came very well through thirty-six
hours of rolling and pitching in the Gulf of Lions,
though, as a matter of fact, except for a few squalls of
wind, the crossing was comfortable enough. He has
stopped spitting blood, sleeps well, coughs but little, and,
what chiefly matters to him, is back again in France! He
can sleep in a bed with the comforting assurance that it
will not be burned because he has used it. When he
stretches a hand in welcome people do not recoil from it.
He will be well looked after, and have every possible
medical attention. . . .[1]

She found little to attract her in Marseilles. 'I have only
to stick my nose out of the window, venture into the street,
or visit the harbour, to feel that I have been turned into a
sugar-loaf, a box of soap, or a packet of candles.
Fortunately, Chopin with his piano, keeps boredom at bay,
and brings poetry into our lodging.'[2] The time-wasters, 'the
lazy, the curious, the literary hangers-on', besieged her
door.

George Sand to Carlotta Marliani, March 15th, 1839:
There is a crowd outside my door. All the riff-raff of
literature persecute me, and all the riff-raff of music is at
Chopin's heels. For the moment, I am giving it out that
he is dead, and, if this sort of thing goes on, we shall send
out an intimation to all and sundry announcing that we
are both dead, and so be mourned and left in peace. We
are planning to lie concealed in various Inns during this
month of March, sheltered from the mistral which, now
and again, blows with extreme violence. In April we shall
take a furnished house somewhere in the country, and in
May we shall go to Nohant. . . .[3]

Although the children made a great deal of noise, she
managed, while staying at the Hotel, to get through her

[1] Letter printed by Wladimir Karénine in *George Sand*.
Volume III, p. 94.

[2] GEORGE SAND: *Correspondance*. Volume II, p. 138.

[3] Letter printed by Wladimir Karénine in *George Sand*.
Volume III, p. 96.

fifteen or twenty pages a day. She had brought back with her from Majorca the refurbished *Lélia,* and a metaphysical-mystical novel, *Spiridion.* Intoxicated by Leroux and his philosophizing, she wanted to have no more to do with 'mediocre' sentimental subjects. *Spiridion* had been hatched from the 'little religious egg laid by Leroux', and had even, in part, been written by him. The monasteries of Barcelona and Majorca had supplied the setting. The book is the story of a Benedictine monk, Alexis, who narrates to a novice the story of his life, and that of the founder of the monastery, the Abbé Spiridion, who is a symbol of humanity's journeyings through various religious faiths. It is also the story of Sand's own spiritual evolution, from the agnosticism of her childhood, through the emotional catholicism of her time in the Convent, to the beliefs of Lamennais and Leroux. Spiridion, born a Jew, has been successively a Catholic, a Protestant and, finally, a Christian Deist. In his grave are buried a copy of the Gospel according to Saint-John, and a manuscript containing an exposition of his own doctrine. This is a synthesis of all the religions. Alexis, reveals the document to the young monk, Angel, who is the hero of the book. A party of French Republican troops comes to the monastery, and the old man, Alexis, is killed. But he dies without hatred in his heart, because he knows that his murderers, who are fighting in the cause of liberty and equality, will help to advance his ideas.

It does not need much imagination to realize how exasperating these mystico-revolutionary dissertations must have been to the regular readers of the *Revue des Deux Mondes.* Even the author's friends raised their eyebrows. *Sainte-Beuve to Madame Juste Olivier*: 'Can you make head or tail of *Spiridion*? I am told that Father Alexis is Monsieur de Lamennais, and that the famous book of the *Spirit* is Leroux's *Encyclopédie*. But I speak only from hearsay, not having read the novel, nor wishing to read it . . . '[1] Madame d'Agoult who had, confessed 'I do not understand a word', though it is true that she did not want to. Buloz begged Sand to come down to earth. What the public wanted was another *Indiana,* another *Lélia.* But she was convinced that these metaphysical bypaths would lead her to a nobler form of art. In *Les Sept Cordes de la Lyre,* a

[1] SAINTE-BEUVE: *Correspondance générale.* Volume II, p. 486.

detestable pastiche of Goethe's *Faust,* she repeated the offence.

George Sand to Carlotta Marliani, March 17th, 1839: I think I ought to tell you that anything which seems to show even the least little profundity of purpose terrifies our good Bonnaire and our good Buloz, because their regular subscribers prefer nice little stories of the *André* type, which circulate just as readily below stairs as above. These two gentlemen are counting on me to give them, in the near future, something in the Balzac line. I would not, for the world, condemn myself to turn out that sort of stuff eternally, and I hope that I have now escaped for good. Do not breathe a word of this to our old rogue-elephant, but, between you and me, unless a subject presents itself which will enable me to wrap up some elevated idea in these trivial fictions, I have finished with them for ever. . . .[1]

She continued to look after Chopin with truly maternal devotion. 'I cannot go out, because my poor Chopin must not be left alone. He gets bored when the children are not playing, and I am not reading, or sitting, near him . . .'[2] *To Bocage*: 'Dear brother: I am answering your letter from this city of the Phocaeans, which is no more Phocaean than you or I. However, I find it quite sufficiently charming as it is, after Spain. Chopin is becoming comparatively plump again, and is as gay as a finch when the mistral is not blowing . . .'[3] When he was better she took him on a Musset pilgrimage to Genoa, as once she had taken Mallefille to Franchard. The *Fellows,* now living at Lucca, sent them an invitation. But George was suspicious—not without reason. Marie d'Agoult, a confirmed letter-writer, had for some months been sending Carlotta Marliani spiteful descriptions of how George, in her 'Chopin mania', was making a fool of herself.

[1] Letter printed by Wladimir Karénine in *George Sand.* Volume III, p. 234.

[2] Spoelberch de Lovenjoul Collection: March 20th, 1839. Group E. 920, f. 309.

[3] Ibid., Group E. 879, f. 5.

*Marie d'Agoult to Carlotta Marliani, November 9th,
1838*: This trip to the Balearic Islands gives me a good
deal of amusement. What a pity it did not take place
earlier. When George was having herself bled, I always
told her—'in your place, I should much prefer Chopin!'
What a number of digs with the lancet that would have
saved her! There would have been no *Lettres à Marcie*,
no Bocage business, and everyone would have been the
better all round. Do you really think the experiment will
last long? Knowing them both as I do, I think they're
pretty sure to be at daggers drawn after a month of living
together. Their two temperaments are quite *antipodean*.
Never mind, it is all blissfully delicious, and I can't tell
you how pleased I am about it, both for her and for him.
What about Mallefille? How is he taking all this? Is he
going to re-invigorate his Castilian pride, as he said he
would, by plunging into the waters of the Manzanares?
May George, perhaps, have been right when she used to
tell me, *ad nauseam*, that he was outrageously stupid and
absurd? I have never felt seriously alarmed over the 'state
of Maurice's health', and, in any case, the Spanish sun
would seem to be an odd sort of cure for palpitations of
the heart. You do well to love Chopin's talent; it is the
beautiful expression of an exquisite nature. He is the only
pianist I can listen to not only without being bored, but
with a really deep sense of composure. Tell me what you
think about everything. Are you binding up Bocage's
wounds, or have you, too, sent him to the right-about?
How I wish we could have a good gossip . . . it really is
the oddest situation. . . .[1]

Lamennais, to whom this letter had been shown, and who
took a devilish delight in 'setting these females at odds',
advised Carlotta to communicate its contents to George—
which she did. George, very properly annoyed, scribbled
across the first page—*This is how one is judged and put
through the mangle by some of one's women friends!* Carlotta having made her swear that she would never reveal
how she had come by her knowledge of this effusion, she
thought it simpler not to answer Madame d'Agoult's letters
at all: *I don't like making a pretence of friendship.* Her

[1] Unpublished. Spoelberch de Lovenjoul Collection: Group
E. 872, f. 5.

silence surprised the *Fellows,* who wrote, complaining of it, to Major Pictet.

> *Liszt to Major Picet: Rome, August 1839:* George
> Dudevant Kamaroupi has left us without news of any
> sort since the beginning of the Chopin period (about nine
> months) . . . Dr. Piffoël's latest productions (*Les Aldini,
> Spiridion,* and *les Sept Cordes de la Lyre*) have made a
> painful impression on me. *Lélia* and *Les Lettres d'un
> Voyageur* are I must say quite a different pair of shoes.
> She has, since then, shown definite signs of weariness,
> exhaustion, and a general falling-off. Still, we must wait
> and see . . . and, since we have been her friends, let us
> keep all this to ourselves. . . .[1]

As though spitefulness can ever be kept confidential! . . .
Meanwhile, Chopin and Sand left Marseilles for Nohant at
the end of May 1839. They made the journey by short
stages 'sleeping at Inns like a good middle-class couple'.

III

'MY THREE CHILDREN'

BERRY IN June. Brilliant sunshine—the joy of being able
to work at home and reign as mistress in her own house. On
the left-hand panel in the window embrasure of her
bedroom she wrote in pencil a date which is still visible—
June 19th, 1839. Was it put there to mark the beginning of
a new life? One may, perhaps, be allowed to think so. She
realized that her 'wandering days' were over. She was the
head of a family, and felt herself to be responsible for three
children—Chopin, Maurice and Solange. She would try
now, with praiseworthy steadfastness, to live only for them
and for her art. All her real friends hoped that her life was
about to take a new direction, that it would become 'filled

[1] Quoted by Robert Bory in *Une Retraite romantique en
Suisse; Liszt et la comtesse d'Agoult,* p. 156.

with quiet, with almost patriarchal, domesticity,' Without
irony, and without reproaches, they were prepared to
include Chopin in the family circle. From 1839 onwards,
their letters to Sand ended with the formula: *Love to
Chopin, Maurice and Solange*. The situation was made
easier by Chopin's extreme delicacy. He invariably referred
to Sand as *my hostess* or as the *mistress of the house*.

This first Summer at Nohant was a time of happiness.
Chopin did not really much like the country. 'He was
always yearning for Nohant, but actually could never
endure Nohant . . . His thirst for rusticity was soon
assuaged. He would go for occasional walks, settle down
under a tree, or pick a few flowers. Then he would go back
to the house and shut himself in his room . . .' He could not
take part in that open-air existence which George and the
children found so enchanting. But he was feeling better, and
his piano was never silent from morning till night. 'Since he
has been here, he has composed some entrancing things,'
wrote George, and indeed it was during that Summer that
he produced the Sonata in B. Flat Minor, the second
Nocturne, and three *Mazurkas.* Her musical taste was very
precious to him. She was a 'sensitive listener'. Knowing him
so well, she was able to understand him as he understood
himself, and, as she listened to him playing, could follow
the movement of that inner life which never emerged from
its secret world except in the music which was its
mysterious and vague expression.

Chopin's Journal, October 12th, 1839: They tell me I am
better. The coughing has stopped, and so have the pains.
But I feel that deep down in myself something is wrong.
Aurore's eyes are misted: they shine only when I play,
and then the world is full of light and beauty. My fingers
glide gently over the keyboard: her pen flies across the
paper. She can write and listen to music at the same time.
Music above her, music all round her; Chopin's music,
soft, but limpid as the words of love. For you, Aurore, I
will creep and crawl. Nothing shall be too much for me: I
will give you everything! All I ask is a kiss, a smile, when
I am tired. I do not want to live except for you. For you I
wish to play sweet melodies. You won't be too cruel, my
dearest, will you, with your eyes all misted. . . .[1]

[1] Quoted by Louise Vincent in *George Sand et le Berry,* pp.
309-10.

You won't be too cruel, will you? Was she, then, being cruel to him?—Surely not: but there was a trace of condescension in her love. Not that her admiration of the musician and the poet in him had grown less. It was only that the Majorca experiment, and the extremely serious relapse which followed it, had proved to George that Chopin was not made for the ecstasies of passion. Always ailing, he could not endure their violence. Although he begged and implored, 'Aurore' very soon compelled him to observe a moderation which became, at last, complete abstention. Much later (May 12th, 1847), Sand was to write to their mutual friend, Albert Grzymala:

> For seven years now I have lived the life of a virgin, both with him and with others. I have grown old before my time, and it has cost me neither effort nor sacrifice, so weary had I become of passions, so disillusioned and beyond all remedy. If any woman in the world could inspire him with absolute confidence it was I, and yet he has never understood . . . I know that many people blame me, some of having exhausted him as a result of my sensual exigencies, some of having driven him to despair by my indiscretions. But you, I do believe, have understanding. He complains that I have killed something in him by deprivation: but I know that I should have killed him altogether had I acted differently. . . .[1]

Chopin would not have been human if he had not suffered from this attitude of hers, and suspected its cause to lie in other loves. But it was only later that his jealousy—probably unjust—became intolerable.

That Autumn, much to George's regret, they had to leave Nohant. In Paris, her heart was 'heavy all the time' when she thought of the ploughlands, of the nut trees round the fallow, of the ploughmen's voices urging on the oxen. 'It's no good; when one has been born in the country one can never really adapt oneself to the hurly-burly of the town. I have a feeling that the mud at home is lovely mud, whereas here it disgusts me.'[2] But Chopin had to get back to his pupils, and Sand herself wanted to live in Paris for the sake

[1] Letter quoted by Wladimir Karénine in *George Sand*. Volume III, p. 571.

[2] GEORGE SAND: *Correspondance*. Volume II, p. 243.

of economy. At Nohant, the house constituted a heavy
drain. Its mistress, robbed on all sides, did not want to play
the careful housewife and be accused of 'meanness'. Every
day self-invited guests had a way of descending on her, and
a dozen of them would appear even before she was up. In
the country she spent fifteen hundred francs a month, but in
Paris only half that sum. It was decided, therefore, that the
'family' should settle in Paris. At first George Sand and her
children occupied two 'follies'—'separated from the street
by a largish, attractive garden belonging to 16 rue Pigalle'—
and Chopin, an apartment at 5 rue Tronchet. But he needed
constant moral support and watchful care: consequently,
after a while, he moved to the rue Pigalle. Thus, for three
years, they all lived together in the same house (October
1839 to November 1842). Balzac visited the establishment,
and, with that usual accuracy of his which made him part
valuer, part novelist, described it to his 'Eve'.

Balzac to Eveline Hanska, March 15th, 1841: She is
living at the bottom of a garden, at No. 16 rue Pigalle,
over the coach-house and stables belonging to a mánsion
facing the street. She has a dining-room furnished in
carved oak. Her boudoir is done in café-au-lait, and the
drawing-room, in which she receives, is filled with flowers
in superb Chinese vases. There is a flower-stand which is
kept always full. The upholstery is green. There is a side-
table covered with odds and ends of bric-à-brac, and
there are pictures by Delacroix as well as a portrait of
herself by Calamatta . . . The piano is a magnificent
square upright in rosewood. Chopin is always there. She
smokes only cigarettes—nothing else. She doesn't get up
till four. At that hour Chopin is finished with his lessons.
One climbs to her establishment by way of a steep, rigid,
set of steps of the kind known as a 'miller's staircase'. Her
bedroom is brown. She sleeps on two mattresses laid on
the floor, Turkish fashion. *Ecco, contessa!* . . .[1]

In 1842 the obliging and formidable Madame Marliani
found for Chopin and Sand two apartments in the square
d'Orléans, a sort of self-contained block with plenty of light,
sanded paths and trees. It had the noble air of an Italian
Palazzo, and she lived there herself. It is situated at 80 rue

[1] HONORE DE BALZAC: *Lettres à l'Etrangère.* Volume I,
pp. 552-3.

Taitbout and it looks today just as it did then. In the same block lived not only the Marliani couple, but the sculptor, Dantan, Taglioni, the dancer, and a young husband and wife called Viardot. Louis Viardot, writer and left-wing politician, had been a close friend of Sand since 1838. He had been introduced to her by Pierre Leroux. Pauline Garcia, Marie Malibran's sister, a girl with a miraculous voice, had been brought into George's life, somewhat earlier, by Musset, at a time when he was paying simultaneous court to Malibran, the singer, and Rachel, the tragic actress. Sand was very fond of Pauline Garcia, and brought her and Viardot together. She thought him a fine fellow, and altogether worthy of the charming young woman. The Viardots had a great many children, and referred to George as their 'good angel'.

In this way, the square d'Orléans became a sort of 'Phalanstery'. 'We have even arranged to do only one lot of cooking, and to have our meals in common, which is much cheaper and more amusing than each of us living separately . . .'[1] They all met in the evenings for music and reading aloud. Sand and Chopin had pooled their friends. Sand's were Pierre Leroux, Delacroix, Balzac, Heinrich Heine, Emmanuel Arago—known as *le Bignat*—Bocage, Marie Dorval, Hortense Allart and all the Berry crowd. Chopin's were various musicians, ladies of fashion, and Poles: the Princess Sapieha, the Princess Marceline Czartoriska, Mickiewicz (a poet in exile, now a Professor at the Collège de France), the Countess Delphine Potocka, whose voice he admired, and James and Betty de Rothschild. The result of these gatherings was that Sand became violently pro-Slav, and sang the praises of Mickiewicz, while Chopin struck up an intimacy with Eugène Delacroix who, like himself, was much addicted to dandy-ism. Both were sensitive and impressionable; both were aristocrats in mind and manners, and much closer to one another than to their democratic patroness.

Heinrich Heine, another regular of the square d'Orléans, appealed to George because of his humour. Like every other man, he had been in love with her, but his 'mad passion' had gone unrewarded, and did not last. He called her 'my dear cousin', ended his letters with 'my heart embraces yours', and wrote—'I am sending back your novel, which resembles you closely, in being beautiful . . .'

Sand was amused by his calling Alfred de Musset 'a young man with a great past'. What she did not know was that he called her *l'Emancimatrice*. He could never resist the pleasure of coining a phrase, but admired her both as woman and as writer. Nobody has better described her serenity and her air of greatness. 'George Sand is beautiful: but she is not very dangerous even for the wicked cats who stroke her with one paw and scratch with the other; not even for the dogs who bark most fiercely at her. Like the Moon, she is a gentle queen, and looks down on everyone from a great height. . . .'[1]

Of Chopin she still spoke with affection: 'He is always an angel of goodness. Were it not for his perfect, his discerning friendship, I should often be tempted to lose courage.' . . . 'Chopin goes his modest way, still coughing. He is always the sweetest, the most retiring, and the least vain of geniuses . . .' For reasons of economy she did not take him to Nohant, and did not go there herself in 1840. But each of the next six summers (1841-46) saw her busily at work rebuilding the nest for her three chicks. From morning till night, great gusts of music from Chopin's piano would rise to where George was working overhead, mingled with the scent of roses and the song of birds. When Pauline Viardot was of the party, she would sing, accompanied by Chopin, the old, almost unknown scores of Porpora, Marcello and Martini. In the eyes of all three friends, Mozart's *Don Juan* was the height of perfection. Mozart and Bach were never absent from the music-stand. Quite often Delacroix, for whom a studio had been improvised at Nohant, Chopin and Maurice—now over twenty—would discuss their respective arts, while Sand listened with her mind far away. At that time she was writing *Consuelo,* the best of all her novels, and Pauline Viardot was being used as the model for a singer of genius. George has described these evenings at Nohant:

Chopin is at the piano, quite oblivious of the fact that anyone is listening. He embarks on a sort of casual improvisation, then stops.
'Go on, go on,' exclaims Delacroix, 'that's not the end!'
'It's not even a beginning. Nothing will come . . .

[1] HEINRICH HEINE: *de l'Allemagne.*

nothing bur reflections, shadows, shapes that won't stay fixed. I'm trying to find the right colour, but I can't even get the form. . . .'

'You won't find the one without the other,' says Delacroix, 'and both will come together.'

'What if I find nothing but moonlight?'

'Then you will have found the reflection of a reflection.'

The idea seems to please the divine artist. He begins again, without seeming to, so uncertain is the shape. Gradually quiet colours begin to show, corresponding to the suave modulations sounding in our ears. Suddenly the note of blue sings out, and the night is all around us, azure and transparent. Light clouds take on fantastic shapes and fill the sky. They gather about the moon which casts upon them great opalescent discs, and wakes the sleeping colours. We dream of a summer night, and sit there waiting for the song of the nightingale. . . .[1]

It was Chopin who devised the theatre at Nohant. At first he sat improvising at the piano, while the young people enacted scenes from various plays, or danced comic ballets. 'He led them on, precisely as he wished, making them pass, as the fancy took him, from the charming to the severe, from the burlesque to the solemn, from the elegant to the passionate.'[2] Chopin himself had a positive genius for miming, and would get up, now and again, and appear from behind the piano with an extraordinary imitation of the Emperor of Austria or an old Polish Jew. Then, too, there were expeditions into the forest, Chopin on his donkey, the others on foot; and dances on the green to the music of bagpipes, which suggested to Sand the subject of her *Maîtres Sonneurs*. All these things gave an idea of the brilliance, the happiness, the charm of this romantic paradise.

Nothing would be less true than to think of Chopin, during those years from 1840 to 1845, as always ill, as the prey of an unsatisfied bacchante. Sand's influence on his work and on his life was, at that time, entirely beneficial,

[1] GEORGE SAND: *Impressions et Souvenirs*. Chapter V, p. 86.

[2] GEORGE SAND: *Dernières Pages*.

whether it took the form of good advice or constant care. Throughout those Nohant summers, Chopin was as happy as he had it in him to be. Unfortunately, neither his temperament nor his ailment allowed him to be happy for long. Many of George's friends pitied her. Mickiewicz, though he was Chopin's compatriot, declared that—'he was George Sand's evil genius, her moral vampire, her cross', and that 'he will probably end by killing her'. Madame Juste Olivier, after dining with them, thought it unlikely that Chopin would ever bring happiness to Sand. 'He is', she wrote in her Journal, 'a man of soul, a man of talent, a charming creature, but I doubt whether he has much heart.'[1]

That was too harsh a verdict. Chopin had plenty of heart, but, like all neurotics, he was so obsessed by what he found repugnant that he could not put himself in the shoes of other people, and the ability to do that is the supreme secret of friendship. In politics he could never agree with Sand. He could not bear certain men whom she admired, nor the vehement nature of their judgments. He got on the wrong side of people (for instance, of his own pupil, Marie de Rozières, whom he blamed for carrying on a too obvious love affair with the Comte Wodzinski), and attacked them the more violently when George was active in their defence. Familiar by this time with his morbid 'crazes' and 'non-crazes', she would change the subject, as one might do with a child. Had she not done so 'there would have been whole days of silence, melancholy, suffering and extravagance . . .'[2] So long as he remained at Nohant she dared not invite to the house the proletarian poets in whom she took an interest. Hippolyte Châtiron got on Chopin's nerves with his boisterousness and boorish manners. In Paris, he was shocked by the appearance and behaviour of Madame Sand's visitors. Elizabeth Barrett Browning has described them:

Crowds of ill-bred men who adore her *à genoux bas* betwixt a puff of smoke and ejection of saliva . . . I did not mind much the Greek in Greek costume who tutoyéd her, and kissed her, I believe, so Robert said: or the other

[1] Cf. LEON SECHE: *Sainte-Beuve.* Volume II, chap. 111, pp. 109-11.
[2] Letter to Marie de Rozières (June 20th, 1841), quoted by Wladimir Karénine in *George Sand.* Volume III, p. 431.

vulgar man of the theatre who went down on his knees and called her 'sublime'. 'Caprice d'amitié,' said she, with her quiet, gentle scorn. . . .[1]

This society, which amused Sand, exasperated Chopin. Still, for a long time, political differences, a clash of tastes and jealousy were powerless to disturb a deep friendship which, on Chopin's side, was born of love, and on Sand's, of admiration and maternal feeling. She continued to watch over her 'patient' with a brooding care that nothing could diminish. If he went to Paris alone, she would warn Madame Marliani of his impending arrival, so that he might have hot water to wash in, and be sure of finding his room aired.

My little Chopin is on his way: I entrust him to you. Look after him, even though he may not want you to. He is so careless of himself when I am not there, and his servant, though a good creature, is stupid. I am not worrying about his main meals, because I know he will be asked everywhere, but I am so terribly afraid that, in the mornings, in his haste to go off to his teaching appointments he may forget to drink the cup of chocolate or broth which I insist on him taking before he goes out, in spite of all his protests . . . He is in good health now: all he needs is to eat and sleep in a normal fashion. . . .[2]

She had not, with all her devoted care, been able to cure him, but she had brought about an improvement in his condition, and was ready, at all times, to fly to his assistance. He, for his part, her 'little Chopin, her *Chip*, her *Chipette*, her *Chopinsky*' remained utterly devoted to her. When she kept her bed (which was frequently, because she suffered all her life long from liver and stomach troubles) it was wonderful to see him playing the sick-nurse, always zealous, always ingenious at getting round difficulties, always the faithful adorer. Their love of beauty was a constant bond between them. One evening, at Nohant, she talked to him, as only she knew how to talk, of the peace of the countryside and the wonders of nature. 'What you have

[1] ELIZABETH BARRETT BROWNING: *Letters,* edited by Frederick G. Kenyon.
[2] Quoted by Wladimir Karénine: *George Sand.* Volume III, p. 483.

been saying', he told her, 'is beautiful.' 'Do you really think
so?' she replied: 'then put it into music.' Immediately,
Chopin sat down and improvised a genuine pastoral
symphony. George Sand, standing beside him, with her
hand laid lightly on his shoulder, murmured: 'Pluck up
courage, velvet-fingers!'

Who can say whether, without that hand upon his
shoulder, without the magic influences of Nohant, Chopin,
in the course of his short life, would have composed so
many masterpieces? Who can even say whether he would
have gone on living?

IV

DEATH OF A FRIENDSHIP

IT WILL, no doubt, have been noticed that among the
visitors to Nohant, and to the rue Pigalle, the earliest
friends of the Chopin-Sand household, Liszt and his
Princess, no longer figured. Carlotta Marliani's communication to George of Marie d'Agoult's sarcastic comments
had created a situation for which there was no remedy. Sand
having given her word that she would not say from whom
the information had come, could not voice a protest. Marie,
ignorant of Carlotta's betrayal, quite failed to understand
why a cloud of silence had descended upon Nohant, and
found it as little explicable as the 'snub-nose of her son',
Daniel Liszt. In her letters to Madame Marliani, she
continued to speak of Sand without any sort of reserve.

Marie d'Agoult to Carlotta Marliani, January 23rd,
1839: What grounds, my fair, female Consul, have you
for saying, in your wisdom, that I am *a priori* incapable
of loving or understanding my friends?—and that, too, in
connection with the easiest person in all the world *to*
understand—our poor Piffoël! Why should you expect
me to take seriously what she does not take seriously
herself, unless it be in those brief moments when artistic
genius has hold of her, and she mistakes pebbles for

diamonds and frogs for swans? I don't expect you to talk
to me about her, beyond telling me whether she is alive or
dead. When I was living under her roof, I did all I could
not to know about certain details of her life which in no
way affected my feelings for her. Since that time, such
information as I have comes in public rumour—which,
you know, is habitually well informed on matters that do
not concern it. Well, I suppose that is how George wants
it to be. The only thing that worries me—and this I
would say to her face—is the falling-off in her talent . . .
Since the *Lettres à Marcie* (which don't count, because
she has not gone on with them, or made any attempt to
develop the many questions she has raised in them), she
has produced only a number of quite valueless novels. It
is clear that her emotional period (a period so mag-
nificently expressed in *Lélia* and *Lettres d'un Voyageur*)
is now over. Her greatest need at present is for study, reflection and mental concentration. But none of the three
men now round her, Bocage, Mallefille, Chopin, will
be of the slightest use in guiding her energies into a
new channel. My own view is (and this between ourselves) that Madame Allart is far more likely to
understand this phase of her existence. Led on by
passion, she has done many foolish things, and has now
reached a point at which she sees love as no more than a
purely physiological problem. When chastity becomes
intolerable to her, she takes a lover. I certainly won't say
that she deceives him, but he exercises no influence over
her, and counts for nothing in her life. What she is doing,
in fact, is what men do regularly when they find it
necessary to satisfy a physical need. The doing of it goes
against the grain with her, and she deplores the demands
of the body which force it upon her. Still, she remains
superior to the whole business by reason of her complete
self-knowledge, and of her absolute loyalty. . . .[1]

In August 1839, surprised, and not a little worried, by the
absence of any sort of a reply from George, she begged
Carlotta to forward a final appeal.

Marie d'Agoult to George Sand: c/o Madame Marliani:
Villa Maximiliana, near Lucca, August 20th, 1839

[1] Unpublished. Spoelberch de Lovenjoul Collection: Group
E. 872.

My Dear George: this persistence of mine in writing letters may, perhaps, astonish you, because your unbroken silence over the past eighteen months, the silence which you appear to have imposed on Carlotta about all that concerns you, and, above all, your *failure to reply* to my last communication, in which I begged you to come and spend the summer with us, make it clear that you no longer want to have anything to do with me. But, since our friendship was something that I took very seriously, and because certain words which once passed between us still retain for me the meaning which I took them to have, I cannot bring myself, if only from motives of self-respect, to allow a bond to be loosened, for no apparent reason, which I had always hoped would last our lifetime.

I cannot really believe that you have anything to complain of in my behaviour, for, if you had, you would have let me know at once, in order that a frank and open explanation should put an end to any passing misunderstanding. That, after all, is the simple duty which is binding on all friends in their mutual dealings. I have searched my conscience, and can find no shadow of guilt on my side. Franz, too, is wondering how it is that your close connection with a man whom he feels that he has the right to call his friend, should have had the immediate result of breaking off all communication between us . . . To be perfectly frank, there *was* one earlier occasion when your intimacy with another of our friends produced a very similar situation. At that time you announced your intention of 'writing less often', but what Franz then said to you had the effect of making you put off and defer what may have already been firm determination to bring about a gradual weakening and ultimate cessation of our mutual friendship. But I still refuse to accept such explanations as I might have found for this strange behavious. Frequent warnings, and the depressing experience of so many broken relations in your past life, seem to me, in this case, insufficient ground for such melancholy assumptions—as that you are incapable of lasting feelings; that a momentary caprice weighs more with you than old and proved affection; that words mean nothing to you; that you let any chance breeze take possession of your heart, and that there is no nook or cranny in your feelings where those who have been dear to you can shelter from the insulting competition of the latest comer.

I still hope for—I will go further, and say that I sincerely long for—some sort of an explanation, worthy both of you and of me, which will put an end to a state of affairs which I find wounding and intolerable. If, however, you persist in maintaining this silence, I shall *know* that you are deliberately bringing about a rupture. The same fickleness which can lead you to betray a solemn friendship will, in all probability, help you to forget it. But no matter what happens, I shall keep alive a memory which has for me the strength of *faith,* and shall bury deep in my heart all that might smirch or injure it.

Franz wanted to write to you, but a letter from him could have done little more than repeat the gist of mine. I have spared you what might have been pain and annoyance in taking the pen from his fingers; for, let me repeat, I still find it impossible to believe that you would light-heartedly turn your back on two such faithful friends.

MARIE[1]

Marie d'Agoult to George Sand (enclosed with the above)
Pisa, September 18th, 1839

You will see from the date at the head of the accompanying letter that it has been much delayed. I sent it to Carlotta, not knowing where you were. Carlotta sent it back, saying that *its effect on you would be very different from the one intended.*

The whole business seems to me to make less and less sense. In any case, since the effect I intended was that it should urge you to a frank and definite explanation, I am sending it to you now without changing a word. It is not like you, nor is it like me, to rest content with the unexplained and the unexplainable. I live in hopes of an immediate answer. Address it to Pisa: Hôtel delle Tre Donzelle.[2]

George Sand sent both these effusions to Carlotta Marliani, asking her how best she thought the relationship could be ended. She intended to answer, if only to exonerate Chopin, for whom Arabella was quite capable of making

---

[1] Unpublished. Spoelberch de Lovenjoul Collection: Group E. 872, ff. 25-6.
[2] Ibid., Group E. 872, f. 27.

difficulties in the musical world, difficulties which he, always so nervous, so circumspect, so exquisite, would take very hardly. 'I will make it very short, but very firm. There shall be no anger in it, no bitterness . . . Female malice has never worried me. It is something I observe with a cold and detached eye . . .' She would quite understand that Carlotta should continue to see the person in question, 'who is extremely intelligent, gracious and companionable'. In that case, it was inevitable that they should sometimes meet.

> But I would point out that such peaceful meetings, which I see may be necessary, will be possible only if there has been an explanation between the three of us. Otherwise she will make a scandal, and treat me to a rousing scene on the first possible occasion. I know her! Displays of injured dignity are her strong point. It will be highly amusing for the world at large, but not for you, the hostess, nor for me. . . .[1]

George pressed her demand for a three-cornered explanation—and for firmness. Carlotta Marliani must have been considerably put out. It was essential that she should confess to Marie the indiscretion of which she had been guilty. This she did, and, on the whole, not too badly.

> *Carlotta Marliani to Marie d'Agoult: October 1st, 1839:*
> My dear Marie, I owe you an explanation. I owe it also to myself, and it was my intention to give it you by word of mouth, on your return to Paris. The arrival here of Madame Sand, whom I expect at any moment, your persistent request to her that she should give an explanation of her silence, and, finally, the letter which you say you sent to her in the exact form in which I saw it, have made me decide to confide in you without further delay, and with the utmost frankness. I expect you remember those two letters which you wrote to me, on November 9th and January 23rd? In them you spoke of my friend with a dryness, a coldness, and a sour levity, which hurt me deeply, as my reply must have made clear, and, later, my complete silence on this painful topic. I had, until that moment, believed that you were fondly

---

[1] Letter printed by Samuel Rocheblave in *La Revue de Paris*, December 15th, 1894.

attached to Madame Sand, through whose good offices I had had the pleasure of first meeting you.

Convinced that you were most certainly *not* her friend, I did what I felt my own feelings of deep affection demanded. George having spoken to me of you, and of the time she had allowed to elapse without answering your letter, I wrote to her saying that I did not think she ought to count on your friendship, that I regarded it as my duty to warn her, but adding that she must not ask me to say more, because, if she did, I should not answer. George, in fact, never has asked me, nor have I spoken to her of your letters, and shall certainly never show them to her.

That my giving her the warning at all was an imprudence: that I mistook the duty which I owed to one who is so dear to me, I am prepared to admit. All that I can assure you is, that my approach to her in the matter—of which *you* may think that you have cause to complain, but which I, holding the views I do about what is owing between friends, cannot regret—had no other motive than the one I have just given you. . . .[1]

And so it came about that direct correspondence between George and Arabella was re-established. George did not deal gently with her former friend, in whom she had always suspected the presence of a concealed enemy. Her letter deserves to be read in its entirety. It is no less remarkable for the firmness of its style than for the acuteness of its analysis.

George Sand to Marie d'Agoult, I do not know, exactly, Marie, what Madame Marliani has recently told you . . . I have complained of you to nobody but her . . . You, on the other hand, complain of me to a great many people who hate me and blacken my character. If I live in a world of gossip, it is not I who produce it, and I shall do my best to follow in your footsteps as little as possible.

All this invocation of *our* past puzzles me. I do not understand what it is all about. You were generous with your offers of friendship, and you must realize that I flung myself into your proffered arms without the faintest

[1] Unpublished. Spoelberch de Lovenjoul Collection: Group E. 872, f. 11.

feeling of constraint. I will go so far as to say that I did so
with enthusiasm. *Infatuation* is one of the things in me
that you laugh at, and it is scarcely charitable in you to
do so at the very moment when you are busy destroying
what I had of it for you. Your view of friendship is very
different from mine. I can tell you that, because you used
to talk so much about it. You enter upon it with no trace
of illusion or indulgence. You should, therefore, exhibit a
degree of loyalty beyond reproach, and take the same
uncompromising line with those who criticize you, as you
do when discussing them behind their backs. That way of
behaving may not be particularly pleasant, but one can at
least get used to it: one will at least learn how to profit
from it. Priggishness always has its uses: spitefulness has
none. You are generous with soft words, tender endearments, and even tears of sympathetic gush, for those who
are fond of you, but when you talk, and, still more, when
you write of them, you are cutting and contemptuous . . .
You mock at them, you blacken their characters, you
humiliate them, you even slander them, and all with so
charming a grace, so delicate a touch! Those whom you
treat in this manner get a sharp awakening and a not very
pleasant surprise, and it is scarcely to be wondered at that
they should, for a while, be thoughtful, silent, and a prey
to consternation. *Your* behaviour when you are faced
with that very natural reaction is quite outrageous and not
easily to be explained away. You load them with
reproaches of a kind to which one is proud and even
pleased to submit when they come from those one
believes to be fond of one, but which are productive only
of pain and pity when one feels that one is an object of
hatred to those who give them utterance. You heap upon
them the sort of abuse which, when friends have
momentarily fallen out is no more than an expression of
unhappiness and regret, but, in other cases, is evidence of
a vindictive hatred. Yes, *hatred,* my poor Marie! It is no
use your trying to delude yourself: what you feel for me is
mortal hatred: and, since that feeling cannot have come
to birth in the course of a single year, and without sufficient motive, it follows that you must have
entertained it *always.* But why? I do not know, and
cannot even guess. But I do know that there are certain
instinctive antipathies against which one struggles in vain.

You have often told me that you felt just such an antipathy for me long before we met. It is in the light of that admission that I explain your later conduct. I always like to take the most favourable view—it is a small failing of mine which affords me some little pride. You were devoted to Liszt and, seeing that he was hurt in his feelings of friendship for me by your sarcasms, you were bent on giving him a noble proof of your affection. You made an immense effort to get the better of your instinctive dislike. You persuaded him that you were fond of me—you may even have persuaded yourself. That is why you have loved me by fits and starts. You may even, at times, have been defeated by my attitude of friendship for you. But you have always relapsed into your old mood of aversion the moment my back was turned, and as soon as an opportunity was presented of finding relief for bitterness long repressed. I believe that if you look into your heart you will find that I can excuse and pity you. I might, perhaps, have admired you had I not been the victim of this wretched attack. But I must be allowed to regret the error into which I so imprudently, so completely, fell and, above all, that you did not honestly adopt one of the only two possible alternatives—either to show your hatred frankly—since I did not know you then, it would not have much mattered—or honestly to express affection. Such behaviour on your part would have proved that not only could you indulge in dreams of magnanimity, but could act in accordance with them. I, too, was building up a dream—which is something, as you say, that I am only too prone to do. It is rather cruel to laugh at this tendency of mine to think that the moon is made of green cheese, at the amount that you are stripping me of one of my dearest illusions.

Now you are angry with me—as is only to be expected. La Bruyère has something to say about that! But be calm, Marie, be calm! I bear you no grudge, and I reproach you with nothing. Where I am concerned you have done what you could to substitute heart for intelligence, but intelligence has got the better of you. Beware of having too much, my poor friend! If an excess of benevolence leads—as I have often learned to my cost—to one's finding oneself ill-equipped in the matter of friends, an excess of clear-sightedness is apt to end in isolation and loneliness. And, since we are condemned to live on this earth in the company of our fellow mortals, better a perpetual round of quarrels and reconciliations than a complete severance of all relations with one's neighbours, with no hope of filling the consequent void.

Don't be upset, my poor Marie. Forget me as you would forget a nightmare which you have at last succeeded in throwing off. Try—not to love me, for that is impossible, but to cure yourself of a hatred which will do you nothing but harm. You must have suffered greatly, if the compassion I feel for you is any guide. Give up plaguing yourself in an effort to construct strange stories which shall account to your intimates for the mutual coldness which now exists between us. When Liszt comes into this part of the world, I won't ask him here. I don't want to give any colour to the version of our estrangement (put about, I think, by you) according to which we are fighting over his body. You know better than anyone that I have never thought of him in that way. It was only Balzac who seized on the idea, and I can assure you that even if it were possible for it to be true—which I don't *yet* think to be the case—no amount of resentment would ever put such a thought into my head. It would, therefore, be unworthy of you to believe it, to say it, and still more to let others say it. I accept—not, I must confess, without some slight feeling of pride—your aspersions on my *morals,* but where are certain insinuations against which I shall continue to react violently. Pull yourself together, Marie. Your part in this wretched affair has been wholly unworthy of you. I know you well, and that there is in your intelligence a craving for greatness against which petty feminine uneasiness wages perpetual war. You would like to act in a spirit of noble chivalry, but cannot abandon your role of a beautiful and witty woman who is for ever crushing and immolating others. That is why you find no difficulty in praising me as a 'good fellow', though you can find nothing bad enough to say of me as a woman. You have two forms of pride, one petty, the other great. Try to let the latter win the day. You can, you know, for God has richly endowed you, and it is to Him that you will have to give an account of the use you have made of His gifts of beauty, intelligence and charm . . . This is my first, and last, sermon to you. Please forgive it, as I forgive you the lectures you have read on me—without letting me hear them.[1]

Liszt, who was on tour, was kept informed by his mistress of the stormy course of these negotiations. Carlotta was blamed by everybody, including her own husband. She deserved to be. To convey an offensive utterance to somebody who may be deeply hurt by it, is more blameworthy than to indulge in the nasty, irresponsible gossip in which most human beings find pleasure. In order to exonerate herself, Madame Marliani asserted that it was Lamennais who had advised her to forward the letters—which, alas! is only too likely. When the three women saw one another again (in Paris, in November 1839), Marie d'Agoult's attitude towards Carlotta was icy: to Sand she had resolved to show herself sweet and kind. The part Sand played was one more of sorrow than of anger. She had never ceased, she said, to admire Marie's intelligence, and her loyalty in love, but she knew that she had never loved *her*. As to the letters . . . at this point Marie broke in to say that she would not let false shame stand in the way of her begging for forgiveness. At this, George held out her hand, and it was agreed that they would go on seeing one another, but that they would never again discuss either their love-affairs or their friendships.

'I accept the terms,' said Marie, 'because I feel convinced that time will modify them. Time is a great healer. In a few months, or a few years, you will confess that you have been wrong.'

'Perhaps,' replied George: 'I am extremely susceptible to charm, and you, Marie, are very charming.'[2]

Liszt thoroughly approved his mistress's attitude. 'Your behaviour to George has pleased me much . . . You must be patient and reasonable. You can be, because you are strong. It does not seem to me that the time has come to break with George . . . Make up your mind that you will ignore, if possible, a number of things, and forgive others . . . When you *do* break, it must be with an obvious, a definite

[1] Unpublished. Spoelberch de Lovenjoul Collection: Group E. 872, ff. 56-61.

[2] *Correspondance de Liszt et de Madame d' Agoult.* Volume I, p. 320.

advantage on your side . . .'[1] But the apparent reconciliation changed nothing, and the tittle-tattle went on.

Marie d'Agoult to Franze Liszt, January 21st, 1840:
Potocki has admitted that when I went off by myself to Nohant (in 1837) he was quite convinced that there was a sort of 'Dorval friendship' between George and me. . . .

Thursday, February 6th: Dinner, yesterday—George, Carlotta, du Roure, Grzymala, Potocki, the Seghers. George a bit glum. At dinner she made Grzymala (quite literally) feel her knee. He was pretty well 'lit', as a result of drinking champagne. There had been some talk about the beauty of the human knee. 'Tell me what *my* knee's like, Grzymala!'—she said. *Grzymala:* 'It's made of pink skin.' *George:* 'Oh, do stop! you're tickling! . . . I'll scratch if you're not careful!' . . . The conversation, rather constrained and half-hearted, continued until midnight. I really can't see *those people*[2] any more. . . .[3]

February 10th, 1840: Vigny came. He was very sweet and talked to me a lot about Dorval. He says it was George who debauched her! He had heard, he said, from Sainte-Beuve that I am seeing less of George, and uttered a heartfelt 'So much the better'. . . .[4]

March 10th, 1840: My relations with the Marliani are again excellent. I think it won't be long before the Chopin household breaks up. Some of our mutual friends say that he is morbidly jealous, that passion is killing him, that he tortures himself and others. She is at the end of her patience, and fears only that he might die at once if she left him. . . .[5]

Marie d'Agoult to Henri Lehmann, the painter, February 6th, 1814: The Abbé (Lamennais) is putting up pretty well with prison life. He won't have any women go to see

1 *Correspondance de Liszt et de Madame d'Agoult.* Volume I, p. 349.
2 In English in the original.
3 Ibid., Volume I, p. 376.
4 Ibid., Volume I, p. 379.
5 Ibid., Volume I, pp. 412-13.

him. The reason is, I think, that he doesn't want to have Madame Sand turning up. . . .[1]

April 21st, 1841: Madame Sand hates me. We no longer see one another.[2]

May 18th, 1841: Franz's Beethoven Concert at the Conservatoire was an occasion worthy of both (I may say *Beethoven and Liszt,* like that, to you, mayn't I?) Madame Sand, irritated by all these triumphs, persuaded Chopin to give a recital at Pleyel's—quite private—just a few friends. Liszt wrote a magnificent article on the said recital (I think it must have annoyed both of them!) . . . Do you know, she is so furious with me that she even went so far as to tell Franz that *you had been my lover*! Franz knows what to say to that sort of remark, and said it—which will serve only to intensify her hatred . . . I have withdrawn completely from the Marliani set.[3]

It was the moment to bring out that quotation of which the Abbé de Lamennais was so fond: 'We made it up: we embraced: since which time we have been mortal enemies.'

V

GREY HAIR

George Sand to Bocage, 1843: Nohant has changed a great deal since you reigned there as king of games and laughter. My forty years, which are now almost upon me, have brought with them a serious mood . . . and, then, our friend's sad state of health has set upon our minds the habit of melancholy, or, at least, of sober thought . . .

[1] *Une Correspondance romantique: Madame d'Agoult, Liszt, Henri Lehmann*, p. 149.

[2] Ibid., p. 165.

[3] *Une Correspondance romantique: Madame d'Agoult, Liszt, Henri Lehmann*, p. 170.

Forgive this scrawl—my lamp is on the point of going out. The breaking dawn is as grey as the head of her who writes this soon will be. . . .[1]

1845: Life is a long ache which rarely sleeps and can never be cured. I am very sad, and very gloomy, but, for that reason, love those who deserve my love even more than before.[2]

THE RIVER of Time was carrying not only her to the falls of death, but all whom she had loved and hated. In 1837 Casimir had inherited the Guillery estate from his stepmother, the Baronne Dudevant, but there were numerous legacies to be paid, with the result that his condition was that of a large landed proprietor in embarrassed circumstances. He settled down in the Château, and spent most of his time in Gascony, from which he rarely moved. He loved his pine-woods, his cork-oaks, his bracken, his gorse and his vines. In the eyes of his neighbours, he was the 'father and good genius' of the countryside. As a result of living with Aurore he had acquired a greater degree of culture and intelligence than his friends could boast. He liked to quote from Pascal and Seneca, and was temperate in talking of his own misfortunes. The people of Guillery found it difficult to believe that his wife had left him because he was coarse and brutal. The general view was that he was gentle and peace-loving, well-made and personable. A certain Dame de Boismartin, by no means young, was in love with him, and did her best to make him reciprocate her feelings. But she hoped in vain. He knew only too well the danger of passionate women. One day, he wrote to his son, Maurice: 'I have a piece of good news for you; Madame de Boismartin is dead . . .'[3] It was a harsh comment, but life had treated Casimir harshly. His children went each year to spend some part of their holidays at Guillery. From 1844 he lived in intimacy with Jeanny Dalias, who had entered his employment as housekeeper. By her he had a daughter, Rose. He would gladly have married her mother, to whom he was unflinchingly faithful, but because Aurore was still

[1] Unpublished. Spoelberch de Lovenjoul Collection: Group E. 879, ff. 14-16.

[2] Ibid., Group E. 879, f. 28.

[3] Quoted by Louise Vincent in *George Sand et le Berry*, p. 621.

living, could not regularize the relatioṅship. As a result
of his concubinage, he was debarred from taking the
Sacraments. As he grew older he had turned back to the
Faith, and suffered much from this deprivation. Nevertheless, he attended Mass every Sunday, sitting, as
befitted a great landowner, in the Choir, and bore with
dignity the burden of a past which made him look
ridiculous.

Sandeau, 'little Jules', was making his way in the world.
His first, unhappy love had marked him for life. For a long
while he could neither forget nor forgive. One day when
Marie Buloz, as a child, was turning over the pages of a
portrait album, he showed her Sand's. 'Look well at that
woman, my dear: she is a walking graveyard. Do you
understand what that means?—a walking graveyard!'[1] All
the same, he owed her everything. When she had first met
him he was completely without talent. In 1839, when he
published *Marianna,* readers acclaimed it as a work of true
passion. The success of the book was as marked as the
failure of the adventure had been. Publishers and editors of
Reviews clamoured for novels from his pen. Women threw
themselves at his head. He became the lover of Marie
Dorval, who, tired of Vigny, had embarked on other
adventures and remained George Sand's friend. Thus, by
the strange play of circumstance, little Jules and his first
mistress had now but a single bond, their shared admiration
for this mad, adorable, woman of the stage.

When first the liaison started, Dorval had thoughts only
for Vigny. 'It is impossible that we should ever come
together again, but I weep for the love that is gone . . . I
have nothing to put in its place. I do not love Sandeau,
though I will try to do so. I have a feeling that I shall not
succeed. I talk to him of nothing but Alfred . . .'[2] Later,
when she felt old age approaching, she clung passionately to
Jules. *Dorval to Sandeau:* 'Oh, how I love you! You are the
joy of my eyes, the delight of my being, the madness in my
blood, the sweet magic of my heart! . . .'[3] Did he, one
wonders, read again those so similar letters written from
Nohant in 1831? In 1840, he accompanied his mistress on

[1] MARIE-LOUISE PAILLERON: *George Sand.* Volume I,
p. 187.

[2] Letter to Pauline Duchambge, quoted by Charles Gaudier
in *Marie Dorval: Lettres à Alfred de Vigny,* p. 203.

[3] Quoted by Françoise Moser: *Marie Dorval,* p. 198.

one of her tours. 'Our dear Marie is having an immense success . . .' But little Jules wanted more than anything else to make a rich marriage, and was casting longing eyes at the dowry of Pauline Portier, the daughter of a paymaster in the Navy. Félicie Sandeau, Jules's sister, to whom Marie Dorval poured out her troubles, was made the recipient of many tearful letters. 'I am overwhelmed by a wretchedness for which, I think, there can be no cure . . . It is now two months since he left me on the road, and returned to finish his book . . . I am on my way home. I have discovered that Madame and Mademoiselle Portier are in Paris. I am miserable, and have discussed the matter with your brother. He tells me it is true . . . I have returned with death in my heart. For three days I waited for Jules in a state of the most horrible anxiety. At last he visited me, but only to say that we must separate. I was appalled. It was impossible, I cried, to tear myself from the man I loved! He replied that he had made up his mind, once and for all. My misery, Félicie, can be understood only if it be thought of in terms of my feelings for him. That, my dear sister, I *must* say . . .'[1] The marriage took place at Nantes, in 1842. Marie Dorval, who was on tour at the time, received, while at Luxeuil, an official announcement sent by Sandeau in person. She hurried to Sand and poured out her misery to her friend. The two women exchanged sad memories of their 'sentimental braggart'. The young man of the fair, curly hair, was growing prematurely bald and turning out novels with a moral. Already he was being spoken of as a likely Academician.

Henri de Latouche was still living, a misanthropic hermit, at Aulnay. He had followed from a distance, with feelings of bitterness, the brilliant and scandalous career of the woman whom once he had launched on the seas of the literary world. In the letters which he wrote to his cousin Duvernet, he deplored the novels in which a woman made public display of her most intimate sorrows. But he still hoped for a reconciliation. In 1840, he published a novel of his own, *Léo*, the hero of which, Arnold, travels through La Vallée Noire, and visits Nohant. The door is opened to him by a maid dressed from head to foot in a blue stuff gown, and wearing a cap of unbleached linen. In the drawing-room, with its floor of small waxed bricks, he gives his hostess (George Sand) a letter of introduction.

[1] Unpublished. Simone André-Maurois Collection.

'I thought,' she said, 'that I had quarrelled for ever with the old bear who wrote this.'

'He said as much himself,' replied Arnold . . . 'But so great is the enthusiasm which he has retained for the authoress, so sincere the affection, that he feels he could never be wholly a stranger to her.'

'The absent have but one crime upon their consciences—and that is, absence', replied the young woman . . . What has that madman gained by courting nothing but solitude, by seeking approval other than that of his own conscience? He is a peasant, lacking a peasant's health, an anchorite, lacking an anchorite's virtue. He who would never have kicked his heels in the ante-rooms of kings, will die, for lack of companionship, in the anteroom of fame . . . A soldier in the service of the victorious press of 1830, he has lacked the courage to become a Prefect. He was a man of letters who enjoyed the unheard-of good fortune of bringing barbarism to flower in the language of Voltaire, but he will never achieve membership of the Institut. . . .'[1]

George Sand herself never read the novel of her first master, but she got others to read it, and learned that she had been gently treated in its pages. And so it was that, somewhat later, when she founded *La Revue Indépendante*, she sought contributions from 'Monsieur Delatouche' (she persistently refused him the particle to which he had a perfect right).

George Sand to Duvernet: I have seen Delatouche. He was charming, admirable, and we are friends again until further notice . . . If only he were less crotchety, what a wonderful editor he would make for a serious, intelligent Berry periodical . . . But how can one be sure that he won't fly into a temper over nothing? . . . What can we do to persuade him that we are not plotting his overthrow? . . .[2]

After a deal of hesitation, mistrust and intellectual flirtation, he felt himself again almost at ease in her

[1] HENRI DE LATOUCHE: *Leo* (Michel Lévy, Paris, 1840).

[2] Unpublished. Spoelberch de Lovenjoul Collection: Group E. 921, f. 85.

friendship. But she saw in him an embittered man, a prey to concealed grievances, irritated by the politics, the manners and the style of his day. He was the very type of Alceste. This condition of spiritual agony lasted for fifteen years. There are men whom life torments, and others who torment themselves. Of these latter was the unhappy Latouche.

Aurore Dudevant's second mentor, Sainte-Beuve, had become an all-powerful critic. From the very beginning, his authority had been recognized—as it had every right to be—but now it had grown greater. He had emerged from his mystic-social stage, and was a welcome figure in the aristocratic circles which moved about such figures as Madame d'Arbouville, Madame de Boigne, the Duc de Broglie and the Comte Molé. There he gave much satisfaction by keeping the ladies informed of the latest news from the literary underworld. Very imprudently, George Sand had constituted him the guardian of her correspondence with Musset. The letters made the round of the boudoirs—'in a large envelope on the back of which Sainte-Beuve was at great pains to tick off the names of the great ladies to whom it was successively sent'. Though not made to shine in the lists of love, he had a number of adventures. The charming Hortense Allart granted him her favours, in exchange for which he lent her a copy of Marcus Aurelius.

> Voici donc le stoïque et sa mâle sagesse,
> En retour d'un présent plus doux.
> Il faut être Aspasie ou vous
> Pour songer à tels noms le soir d'une caresse
> Ou le matin d'un rendezvous.[1]

He showed himself a better poet in these lines in the manner of Lafontaine than in those earlier Elegies which he had addressed to Adèle Hugo. With Sand he was now polite, prudent and remote. To a friend who said to him, 'How exquisite those letters to Musset are: Madame Sand

[1] Quoted by Léon Séché in *Hortense Allart de Méritens*, p. 184.

> Your gift was a sweet one; here's mine in return,
> The old Stoic's rigour: there are no more than two
> Who would dream of such matters, Aspasia and You,
> When the furnace of passion had just ceased to burn
> Or the love-birds of Venus were starting to coo.

must have a beautiful soul!'—he replied, 'Yes, indeed, a beautiful soul and a big bottom!' He quoted with delight something that Félix Pyat had once said: 'She is like the Tour de Nesle: she imprisons her lovers, but instead of dropping them into the river, she beds them down in her novels.' All of this, however, belonged to his more intimate conversations. The articles which he wrote about her were still courteous, and even enthusiastic.

Of Pierre Leroux, who had once been his own personal gift to Sand, he now said: 'That fellow Leroux flounders about in philosophy like a buffalo in a bog', and Victor Hugo: 'If Pierre Leroux were only good, he would be the best of men.' Such were far from being George's own sentiments. In spite of the fact that Leroux was gradually falling into discredit, she continued to support him. Needless to say, the philosopher had fallen deeply in love with his disciple. George herself asserts that she had resisted his advances. 'There are some who maintain that only love can produce such miracles. If, by that, they mean spiritual love I am prepared to agree with them, for I have never so much as touched a hair of the philosopher's head, nor had closer dealings with his thick mane than I have had with the beard of the Great Turk . . . This I say in order to assure you that my attitude to him is the outcome of a serious act of faith—the most serious in all my life—and is not inspired by the sort of equivocal infatuation which frivolous women feel for their doctors or spiritual directors . . .'[1] Leroux-the-philosopher owed too much to George not to forgive her for repulsing Leroux-the-man.

Pierre Leroux to George Sand: How good you are, and what a blessing is your friendship! Not a word of yours but has struck deep into my soul, not a phrase but I have dwelt upon a hundred times in memory, and made the subject of my daily, nightly, meditations! How grateful I am for your belief in me! No, oh no! the dogs must not follow the scent of your blood. Your sorrows are sacred. You must live and triumph. Queen, queen, queen! I, poor wretch, detest only the *goodbyes* in your letters, though even so I kiss them, I am ravished by them, for they are better than nothing to me, and so command my adoration. *Yours in heart and mind,* say you. I would rather it were just *Yours* however vaguely. Such common stamps, as I have told you, are all false, are all

1 GEORGE SAND: *Correspondance.* Volume II, pp. 293-4.

appearances, stamps of *sentiment, intelligence* and *act.*
Nothing is real but *being,* and *being* under these three
aspects is present always in friendship as in love. What,
then, do your goodbyes mean? Alas! I know only too
well! I should find more to treasure in an infinite *Yours*—
Yours perhaps, Yours vaguely, Yours in this life or the
next . . . With all the strength of my being, I say to you—
'Yours'. . . .[1]

If she was not *his,* she did all in her power *for him.* She
abandoned the generous Buloz in order to found, in
collaboration with the penniless Leroux, *La Revue Indépendante.* Lamennais commented ironically upon this close
association.

*Lamennais to the Baron de Vitrolles, October 19th,
1841:* A new Periodical, I am told, is about to appear
under the joint editorship of Leroux and Madame Sand.
They want to create a rival to the *Revue des Deux
Mondes,* perhaps because one world is all that they will
recognize. Not that it amounts to much just now, but no
doubt they will refashion it with the help of Carlotta . . .
and when the work is duly finished, there we shall be, the
lot of us, swimming round like so many fish in a tank. I
was about to add—'Praise be to God'—but, alas! He is
one of the things they have suppressed. Their God is Life
Universal. And what to goodness may Life Universal be?
and how, I ask you, can one address words like 'Praise
be—' to Life Universal? I should be happier in my mind
of this Periodical of theirs were likely to be amusing. In
this matter of launching a new religion, the ability to
make people laugh in a bored century like this of ours
would offer some chance of success. Unfortunately, I feel
far from reassured by what I hear. . . .[2]

November 25th, 1841: I have just been given some details
about Leroux and his *Revue Indépendante.* He, it seems,
is more than ever committed to the idea of founding a
new religion, and appears to be quite certain of his
success. Within ten years, he says, all forms of property

[1] Letter quoted by Wladimir Karénine in *George Sand.*
Volume III, p. 16.

[2] *Correspondance inédite de Lamennais avec le Baron de
Vitrolles,* pp. 370-1.

in France will have been abolished. Since his *Revue* is to be conducted along those lines, since he has made a beginning by stuffing it with old odds and ends of his own reprinted, at least some of them, for the third time, and since he has added to his already well-known views another one to the effect that Jesus Christ formally sanctioned adultery—a number of those who had promised to contribute, are now thinking better of it. It seems, from all I hear, as though it will not be long before he finds himself alone with Madame Sand. She, faithful to her prophet, is busy preaching communism in a new novel, the first instalment of which appeared in the initial issue. I fear that it won't contain much evidence of her earlier talent. How can people who have been blessed with such rare natural gifts so light-heartedly throw them away? . . .[1]

There was, in fact, no 'throwing away of natural gifts'. In *Consuelo* Madame Sand revealed herself as a far greater novelist than she had been in the days of *Indiana*. But Lamennais was perfectly right when he spoke of the political influence which Leroux was exercising over her. George's mistake, ever since she had grown up, had been to believe that the world can be explained by a formula. Leroux, who claimed to hold the key to the only true formula, had laid a spell on her. In him, far more than in Michel de Bourges, she had found an intellectual master. 'His is the only philosophy which is as clear as daylight and speaks to the heart as directly as the Gospel. I have steeped myself in it, and it has made a different person of me. It has restored to me tranquillity, strength, faith, hope and a patient, persevering love of humanity.'[2]

Through Pierre Leroux she had come to learn something about the system of Workers' Trade Guilds. This system had started in the Middle Ages, and now, in 1840, was showing new signs of life under the influence of a few proletarians, like Agricol Perdiguier, who had recently become intensely class-conscious. The medieval Journeymen had wandered about France, and, in each village, had been welcomed by a *mother* who conducted a species of co-operative Inn. Perdiguier restored this custom to a place of honour, revived the code of *obligations*—part cor-

[1] Ibid., p. 380.
[2] GEORGE SAND: *Correspondance*. Volume II, p. 259.

porative, part Masonic—and preached to working-class audiences a form of Christian-Socialism which bore a close resemblence to Leroux's own creed. George Sand, who became his friend and patroness, made him the central figure of a novel, *Le Compagnon du Tour de France*. which was something new in fiction in that it dealt with working-class life. It was also very simple-minded in the pictures it drew of Journeymen in love with the ladies of great houses. It was George's way of absolving herself from the sin of having been born the lady of a great house—and enabling her to continue as such.

Buloz, with whom she had a general agreement to publish all she wrote, raised numerous objections. The readers of his *Revue* would be shocked. The new word *communism* was coming into general use to describe the doctrine of equality of goods. The middle classes were already taking fright. Sand went for advice to her philosopher, Leroux. He answered her questions by telling her that there was communism *and* communism; that certain forms of it were sheer lunacy, and that he himself preferred the type of communism which implied fraternity. There was no reason, he said, why Sand should identify herself with a *word* which seemed so alarming to Buloz, but that, at the same time, she must not reject the underlying idea. Above all she must be firm in her refusal to allow Buloz to tamper in any way with the text of her story. Her group of proletarian friends now contained a number of poets—Charles Poncy, a builder from Toulon; Savinien Lapointe, a cobbler; Magu, a weaver; Galland, a locksmith; Jasmin, a barber, and Reboul, a baker. They all of them sent her their verses, and she instructed them in the principles of Leroux's philosophy.

From these friendships sprang a new novel, *Horace*, in which she contrasted Paul Arsène, a great-hearted, heroic working-jeweller, and a selfish, lazy bourgeois intellectual. There is something in Horace of the young Jules Sandeau, something, too, of Emmanuel Arago, with an occasional touch of Mallefille. He is an intelligent and gifted youth, who talks about work instead of working, and lives a life of amusement in Paris on his parents' hard-earned savings. He leaves his mistress—a woman of the people—when she is with child, for a 'Vicomtesse de Chailly'—who is a cruel portrait of Marie d'Agoult.

Her thinness was terrifying, and her teeth doubtful, but she had magnificent hair which was always exquisitely dressed. Her hands were long-fingered, and dry to the touch, white as alabaster and loaded with rings from every country in the world. There was a certain grace about her which deceived a great many people. In short, she possessed what might be called an artificial beauty . . . She prided herself on being educated, erudite and eccentric. She had read a little of everything, even of politics and philosophy, and it was curious to hear her bringing out as her own, for the delectation of the ignorant, things that she had read that same morning in a book, or had heard the night before from the lips of some serious-minded man of her acquaintance.

The Vicomtesse de Chailly came of a family of financiers who had purchased titles under the Regency. She wanted it to be thought, however, that she was an aristocrat of the bluest blood, and was lavish in her display of coronets and armorial bearings which she went so far as to have painted on the handles of her fans. In her intercourse with young women she was intolerably arrogant, and she never forgave those of her men friends who married for money. She was passably hospitable to budding writers and painters, affecting for their benefit alone to care only for merit. In short, her nobility was as artificial as everything else about her—teeth, bosom, and heart. . . .[1]

Marie d'Agoult was stamping mad with fury, but Liszt, as on a previous occasion, advised her to be patient and to say nothing. *He,* after all, had put up with *Béatrix,* surely *she* could pretend not to recognize herself in *Horace*? He added, rather cruelly: 'No doubt about it, Madame Sand *did* mean to paint your portrait in her description of Madame de Chailly's artificial mind, artificial beauty, and artificial aristocracy . . .'[2] All of which proves that Sand and Balzac were right in their contention that Liszt's love for *Béatrix* had, for some time now, ceased to exist.

Horace appeared in the *Revue Indépendante*. George was determined to break loose from Buloz, who had ventured to blue-pencil her 'copy', and to make Leroux's fortune. She

1 GEORGE SAND: *Horace.*

2 *Correspondance de Liszt et de Madame d'Agoult*. Volume II, p. 186.

contributed to the first number of the new periodical not
only the opening instalment of *Horace*, but an essay on the
proletarian poets. The second contained the balance of
Horace, and an article on *Lamartine, utopiste*. She then
made an offer of *Consuelo*. She was, indeed, 'showering her
riches with a lavish hand', and the cream of the joke was
that she really believed the appeal of *La Revue Indépendante* to lie in Leroux's preaching.

The general theme which the new periodical tried to
elaborate was the creation of a new world, and, consequently, of a new literature, by 'the People'. *La Revue
Indépendante* gave pleasure to a few friends, like Liszt and
Duvernet, but it had no regular body of subscribers, and
was never successful. For three weeks Leroux could not be
found, and the proofs went uncorrected. In George's eyes,
however, his prestige remained undiminished.

> *George Sand to Carlotta Marliani, November 14th, 1843:*
> I received a long and terribly sad letter from him the
> other day. I know only too well what causes all his fears
> and anxieties—the state of poverty which makes it
> impossible for him to carry on his great enterprise, and
> also, I doubt not, to satisfy the needs of his family. Today
> I sent him five hundred francs . . . I know that this year
> has not been too kind to you, but could not you find a
> little something tucked away somewhere? . . . We, you
> and I, cannot let him founder . . . The bright glow of his
> mind must not be allowed to be extinguished in the
> struggle . . . We must not allow him to be terrified and
> discouraged for the sake of a few banknotes. Make
> yourself his confessor: get out of him the true secret of
> his distress. No doubt he is shyer than ever in your
> presence because of the numerous kindnesses for which
> he is already in your debt. You must break down that
> shyness . . . Send me news of him. I cannot bear the
> thought that the torch may be extinguished, and we be
> left in darkness. . . .[1]

At La Châtre, too, George Sand would dearly have liked
to 'dissipate the shadows'. There was great need of an
Opposition paper. She rallied her friends, Planet, Dutheil,
Fleury and Duvernet, and with them founded the *Eclaireur
de l'Indre*. Each of the *patriots* was asked to subscribe 'in

[1] GEORGE SAND: *Correspondance*. Volume II, pp. 281-2.

proportion to his dose of enthusiasm', and even Monsieur de Chopin, who at heart was a disinherited aristocrat, was prevailed upon, willy-nilly, to give fifty francs. The first idea had been to produce the paper in Paris, but Leroux had bought a printing-house in Boussac with the idea of installing his family there. George entrusted the *Eclaireur* to him. Chopin observed these generous activities of his 'hostess' with a sceptical eye, and did not keep his ironical attitude to himself.

VI

LUCREZIA FLORIANI

BETWEEN GEORGE and Chopin there had never been any insurmountable obstacles. Their mutual tenderness was built on firm foundations. Chopin was in love with George, and for him she had a gentle and maternal affection. She admired in him the musician of genius, and he respected in her the great writer. Nevertheless, 'there is no longer any question of passion', wrote Marie de Rozières, the ageing spinster who was the intimate friend of both and had been Chopin's pupil: 'there is no longer any question of passion, at least not on one side (*Sand's*), but much tenderness and devotion, mingled, according to her changing moods, with regret, melancholy and boredom . . .'[1] That was true enough, but tenderness and devotion might have sufficed, might have lasted, had it not been for 'the others'. George had always felt herself to be strongly bound to friends and children, but Chopin's extreme sensibility could not endure the idea of sharing. Maurice was now a man. He adored his mother. He regarded the constant presence of Chopin as a matter of scandal, and suffered much because of it.

Solange was sixteen in 1844. She had been brought up in a world of indiscipline, and respected nothing and nobody. Turn and turn about she laughed at Chopin and flirted with

[1] Letter quoted by le Comte Antoine Wodzinski, in *Les Trois Romans de Frédéric Chopin*.

him—not without success. She fascinated him for the simple reason that she was the only person among the whole lot of them who did not treat him as a spoiled child. In face and colouring she closely resembled her great-grandmother, Aurore de Saxe. Her beauty was of a virile type. She was by nature cold and odd. Whatever she did was apt to be inspired by a spirit of contradiction. Slightly unbalanced, she had her mother's daring without her mother's genius. 'You have a good heart, but too violent a character', Sand had written to her while she was still a child. The bad streak in her nature had remained, the goodness of heart, when she grew older, was less apparent. The relationship between parents and children is no less difficult, no less fraught with drama, than that between lovers. The growing child, developing into an independent individual, surprises and annoys its parents. What once was a charming plaything becomes an adversary. A mother like George Sand expected obedience and devotion in exchange for unquestioning affection. These Maurice could give, but Solange was a rebel. Her mother could not tolerate in a child the independence which once she had claimed as her own by right. When the mutual love of mother and daughter encounters disappointment, it may well turn to hatred.

For a time George, who could no longer put up with Solange, sent her to live in the charge of Mademoiselle de Rozières, hoping that separation might produce a change. The choice was unfortunate. Marie de Rozières, though she came of a good family, was without money. She had been seduced and later abandoned by Antoine Wodzinski (the brother of Chopin's inconstant betrothed). Thus jilted, she had become a victim to obsessions, and a romantic introvert. She loved tittle-tattle and scandal. It was necessary to call her to order.

George Sand to Marie de Rozières: There comes a moment when little girls are little girls no longer, when it is necessary to keep a watchful eye on what the effect of the things they hear may be. *Not a word,* however casual and harmless, about the masculine sex—that is the sole caution I would have you observe. . . .[1]

---

[1] Unpublished. Spoelberch de Lovenjoul Collection: Group E. 921, f. 159.

She did not mince her words. She forbade Mademoiselle de Rozières to speak to Solange about 'Monsieur So-and-So's figure, or Monsieur the-other's moustache'. Disappointment in love, said Sand, had changed Mademoiselle de Rozières for the worse. 'You had better know exactly what I think. In the old days you were *not* a coquette, but now, my love, your eyes have become terribly voluptuous . . . All the men have noticed it, though of course if *you* do not mind, why should I? . . . All the same, I have decided that Solange had better not see quite so much of you—until this little nervous trouble of yours is over, and you have taken either a lover or a husband *ad libitum* . . .'[1] This letter wounded the poor creature to the quick, and she never forgave Sand for writing it.

Now, it was only too easy for Mademoiselle de Rozières to rouse Chopin's feelings against his 'hostess'. Pierre Leroux had brought to La Châtre, from Tulle, a young man called Victor Borie, who shared his political ideas, and frequently stayed at Nohant. The idea was that he should act as editor of the *Eclaireur de l'Indre*. Chopin was jealous of him in a vague sort of way. There was also the fact that quarrels were constantly breaking out between Jean, his Polish valet, and the Berrichon servants. 'Monsieur de Chopin' was generous with his money, and paid his valet as much as the *Eclaireur de l'Indre* paid its editor. Everything seemed to be combining to produce a state of friction.

In 1844, Chopin's sister, Louise Jedrzeïewicz, paid a visit with her husband, to Nohant, where they exercised a calming influence. The two women struck up a warm friendship. But the beneficial effects of this happy intrusion did not last for long. The state of Chopin's health was deteriorating. He became more and more touchy, susceptible and jealous. 'More irritable', said Sand, 'and more than usually inclined to pick quarrels. I laugh at it all, but Mademoiselle de Rozières cries, and Solange answers scratches with bites. . . .'[2]

George Sand, for her part, found relief for her feelings in true writer's fashion—by making a book of them. Her enemy, Marie d'Agoult, now separated from Liszt, had just torn his to pieces in a novel called *Nélida*. George, in *Lucrezia Floriani*, with due regard for the distortions and

transpositions demanded by the art of fiction, set about
painting a picture of her own strange relationship with
Chopin.

She later denied that Lucrezia was a portrait of herself.
Nevertheless, the great Italian actress who, while still
young, retires into the country to bring up her children,
bears a remarkable resemblance to her creator. Lucrezia has
written successful plays. She has had numerous adventures
which she explains away much as Sand had done. She is not
a *courtesan* because she has always *given herself* to her
lovers, and has never *received* anything, even from her
friends. She has loved much, but always with the sincere
wish to share her life with those who have awakened her
passion, and has never entertained the illusion of an eternal
fidelity. She has had affairs which sometimes lasted a week,
sometimes only an hour, but, on each and every occasion,
her intention has been to dedicate her life on the altar of
love. We know only too well that this firm resolution was all
that mattered in Sand's eyes.

Lucrezia, believing that the life of the senses is over for
her, meets an adorable youth, gentle, sensitive, in every way
exquisite, an angel—'with the beauty of a fine and
melancholy woman'. He has a slim and unspoiled body; the
expression of his face is eloquent at once of chastity and
passion. His name, in the novel, is Karol, and it is quite
clear that he is intended for Chopin. This Prince Karol is in
love with an imaginary woman whom he has created in his
own image. He is less a lover than a nice young man—but
how should she have guessed that? His enchanting beauty
pleads in his favour, and his frail health makes him
interesting to women—or, more precisely, to women like
George Sand and the Floriani, women who combine
passion with maternal yearnings. He has one terrible
fault—intellectual intolerance. He believes that the virtue of
all virtues is abstention from sin, and forgets that love of the
repentant sinner which is the great glory of the Gospel. He
has been trained to help the poor, if need be, to pity them,
but never to treat them as his equals. The necessity of
charity he will admit, but not of social reforms. He will not
agree with the view that Humanity can find salvation on
this earth. In fact, he sums up in his character all that Sand
had found politically estranging in Chopin.

Naturally, Karol falls in love with Lucrezia. She tends
him as though he were one of her own children. He loves
with a mixture of timidity and ardour, and this gives him an

irresistible charm. Lucrezia believes (as she has believed before) in the eternity of this sublime passion. She gives herself to the prince, and for some weeks they are blissfully happy. But gradually the egotistical side of the enchanting Karol comes uppermost. He is jealous, intolerant and intolerable.

One day Karol would be jealous of the curé who had come asking for money: on another, of a beggar whom he took for a lover in disguise. He was jealous of a servant who, spoiled and petted as were all the members of the domestic staff, had answered his mistress with an insolence which he regarded as unnatural. Turn and turn about, everybody caused him jealousy, a pedlar, the family doctor, a great oafish cousin . . . Karol was jealous even of the children. But why should I say *even*, when the word should be *especially*? . . . They were, in truth, his sole rivals, the only living creatures to whom Floriani gave as much thought as she did to him. . . .

But the more Karol's irritability increased, the more polite and reserved did he appear: his icy courtesy was the measure of his fury.

It was at these moments that he was truly insupportable, because it was then that he tried to argue, to force real life—which he had never begun to understand—into the mould of principles which he was incapable of defining. The mood bred in him a false and brilliant wit, and with this he tormented those who loved him. He assumed the airs of a mocker and a prig. He became mannered. He affected to view everything and everybody with disgust. It was as though he were indulging in a game of mild biting for his own amusement, but the wounds he made went very deep. When he lacked the courage to contradict and jeer, he took refuge in disdainful silences and fits of heartbreaking sulkiness. . . .[1]

This constant atmosphere of bickering is finally too much for Lucrezia. She loses her beauty. Her complexion fades to an unhealthy pallor. She suffers because she is condemned to a premature old age by the ill-treatment of a lover who does not respect her. She ceases to love Karol. She feels that

[1] GEORGE SAND: *Lucrezia Floriani*, pp. 246-9.

she is breaking under the strain, and one morning, suddenly, she dies.

In this abrupt, and not very convincing, way the novel, like life itself, comes to an end. It was meant to be a lesson and a warning to Chopin. The strange thing is that he never recognized himself in Karol. Delacroix describes how, one evening, Sand read *Lucrezia Floriani* aloud to Chopin and himself as audience. 'I was in agonies all the time the reading was going on'—Delacroix said to Madame Jaubert: 'but I don't know which surprised me most, the executioner or the victim. Madame Sand appeared to be completely at her ease, while Chopin expressed the warmest admiration of the story. At midnight, we left together. Chopin wanted to walk home with me, and I took the opportunity to find out, if I could, what he really felt. Was he playing a part for my benefit? No, the truth was that he just had not understood. The musician never for a single moment ceased to express his admiration for the novel . . .'[1] It may be, too, that Chopin's exacting code of good manners led to his assuming a mask of unconcern.

> *Hortense Allart to Sainte-Beuve, May 16th, 1847:* I have not told you how indignant *Lucrezia* has made me . . . Madame Sand, in the general holocaust of pianists, has drawn a picture of Chopin enriched with every kind of unsavoury domestic detail, and with a cold relentlessness which nothing can justify. It is as though some second self had taken control of her. Women can never be too much on their guard against these betrayals of the bedchamber. They can have the effect only of keeping lovers at arms' length. Nélida's outburst of fury was excusable. For Lucrezia's cold exacerbation there can be no excuse. Why does so fine a genius allow herself to be so ill inspired?[2]

Hortense was by nature frank and impulsive. She wrote to Sand, repeating what she had said to Sainte-Beuve. Sand, quite naturally, denied that she had had Chopin in mind when she was creating Prince Karol.

---

[1] CAROLINE JAUBERT: *Souvenirs, Lettres et Correspondance*, pp. 43-4.

[2] Letter quoted by Léon Séché in *Hortense Allart de Méritens*, p. 207.

George Sand to Hortense Allart, June 22nd, 1847: I am more susceptible to your blame than to your praise, because, when praise comes my way, I always suspect that it is due to some extent to the politeness and enthusiasm of friendship, whereas in blame I find something of the sadness and frankness of true concern. That is why I hasten to tell you that your letter made me feel very melancholy, and that I had to read it twice, and to stop each time at the word Prince, before I could fully understand it. Who on earth put that idea into your head? Was it Marie d'Agoult? . . . If she knew Chopin really well, she must have realized that there was nothing of him in it: if not well, then how can she be so sure?

But how can *you* know him so well as to recognize him in the character of a novel? Some spiteful tongue, inspired by malicious intention, must have given you some very inaccurate and ridiculous information. Do you really take *me* for the Floriani? Have *I* had *four* children, and all those adventures? I never thought of myself as so richly endowed, nor believed that I had anything like her vitality. I am neither so great-hearted, not so mad, nor so good. Had *I* been so closely linked to Prince Karol, I give you my word that I should not have let myself be killed off, but should have stood my ground. My health is excellent, and I should not so much as dream of allowing myself to be estranged from a friend whom eight years of mutual devotion had made invaluable to me. How is it possible that I should have written this novel under his very eyes, reading it to him, chapter by chapter, accepting or rejecting his comments as I always do when we are working in close harmony, without his even beginning to recognize *us* in these lovers of the Lake of Iseo?

Apparently we know one another less well than the public knows us. The whole business is so odd that I should have laughed it out of court had it come to me from any other source than you. Still, your blame is serious, and my reply to it is no less so. I know nothing of Prince Karol, or, rather, I know him as a combination of fifteen different persons, as is always the case in creative fiction, where no existing man or woman can give the novelist who is really absorbed in his art the material for a fully rounded person.

I think I have told you all this before, and I am surprised that you, who are also an artist, should share

this simplicity of the vulgar, who always want to see in a
novel a *true* story, and the portraits of people they have
known. . . .[1]

All of which is both true and false, as is every gen-
eralization.

VII

SOLANGE AND AUGUSTINE

LOVE BEGINS with fine feelings, and ends in trivial
quarrels. When a number of human beings live in close
contact, there are bound to be misunderstandings. When
marriage and family affection make it possible to get the
better of them, all goes well. In the freedom of a loose
intrigue, everything falls to pieces, and that is why
'marriage is the only bond that time draws tighter'. The
atmosphere at Nohant *seemed* to be one of gaiety, poetry
and genius. The various members of the party spent their
time in reading, composing, wandering about the countryside, and bathing in the river. There were *tableaux vivants,*
charades and ballets, for which Chopin provided improvisa-
tions on the piano, but peace of mind was absent.

In 1845, George Sand invited to Nohant, and later
'adopted', a young girl named Augustine Brault, who was a
distant cousin of hers on the bird-fancier's side, and a
relation of Sophie-Victoire's. She was the daughter of a
working tailor and a kept woman. This latter, Adèle Brault,
middle-aged and thoroughly depraved, had conceived the
idea of turning to account the fact that her daughter was
young, and gave promise of great beauty. Sand, the self-
appointed protectress of the afflicted, intervened. She
offered money in exchange for Augustine, whom she
proceeded to take into the family as companion to the
children. Maurice, as was only natural, warmly welcomed
the advent of such a pretty young woman. Solange played

1 Spoelberch de Lovenjoul Collection.

the great lady, and adopted a patronizing attitude to her cousin. The company soon divided into two camps, Sand and Maurice taking the side of Augustine, Solange and Chopin attacking her. Sand much preferred the sweet and docile Augustine—whom she called her 'real daughter', to the hard-baked Solange. She spoke of her to Maurice in all her letters.

> Titine is still beauty and goodness incarnate. She has taken it into her head to become a true countrywoman. She is already one at heart, and is well on the way to becoming one in appearance, though she still confuses gooseberries with green peas . . . She is tanned by the sun, and tormented by her cousins, but that does not matter. She is daily becoming more and more like a peasant girl in health and strength. She is invariably sweet and charming, and Solange, for all her grand airs, can scarcely do without her. . . .[1]

The summer of 1846 was swelteringly hot.

> *George Sand to Marie de Rozières, June 18th, 1846:* Chopin is amazed to find himself sweating so much. He finds it a great hardship. He says that no matter how much he washes, he stinks! We laugh ourselves sick to see that ethereal being refusing to perspire like everybody else . . . I have dismissed the gardener who has been consistently robbing me. Chopin was thoroughly shocked by my firmness in the matter. He cannot understand how one should not put up all one's life with what one has endured for twenty years. . . .

> *August 8th, 1846:* Ever since he came back this year, he has been very sweet. I did well to lose my temper with him. It gave me the necessary courage to tell him a few home truths, and to threaten him with the possibility that my patience might not last. Ever since then, he has been in a more reasonable state of mind, and you know how good, admirable, and excellent he can be when he is not mad. . . .[2]

---

[1] Unpublished. Spoelberch de Lovenjoul Collection: Group E. 921, f. 207 and f. 212.

[2] Unpublished. Spoelberch de Lovenjoul Collection: Group E. 921, ff. 220-1.

That Autumn, Solange broke the news that she was
engaged to be married. She had achieved the conquest of a
young local landowner, Fernand de Préaulx, a man of good
family and Olympian dignity. Maurice depicts him in one of
his drawings as an antique bust, looking very haughty and
slightly ridiculous. George Sand, though she did not oppose
the plan, was in no haste to bring it to fruition. Solange was
only eighteen, and not yet (according to her mother)
physically awakened. 'She only wanted to marry so as to be
called Madame.' Sand would have preferred some show of
passion, however little, to such futility. 'The young man is
very good looking and kindness itself. His intelligence is not
very apparent, especially when it comes to talking . . .
Personally speaking, I am quite devoted to him, but he
certainly will not set the Seine on fire. He knows nothing of
our modern civilization. He has spent his life in the
backwoods with horses, wild boars and wolves, whose heads
he cracks with his whip-handle . . . The Princess loves him
and he is her slave. . . .'

George Sand to Hetzel (P-J. Stahl): My daughter, as
proud as Mauprat's Edmée, has let her affections become
involved with a sort of Bernard Mauprat, though the
young man in question lacks Bernard's harsh and brutal
education, and is, in fact, gentle, obliging and as good as
gold. He is a country gentleman, a man of the woods,
who is as simple as nature, dresses like a gamekeeper, is
as beautiful as an antique statue, as hairy as a savage, and
as generous as our friend le Petit-Loup . . . For the time
being he has not a penny to bless himself with, and in
politics is a legitimist. The bourgeoisie say we are mad,
and I am quite sure that my republican friends will stone
me. I confess it had never occurred to me that my son-in-
law would be an aristocrat, a royalist and a hunter of
wild boars. But life is full of surprises, and it turns out
that the young man in question is more of an egalitarian
than any of us, and gentler than a lamb for all his lion's
mane. Anyhow, there it is, we love him and he loves us.
. . .[1]

[1] Unpublished letter supplied by Madame Bonnier de la
Chapelle.

Another match was in the offing, between Maurice and Augustine, and this was much closer to her heart. But Maurice was a creature of conflicting impulses, and could not make up his mind. Sand swore that there had never been anything between the young people but a feeling of brother for sister. A letter, however, exists (written at a later date) from her to Maurice in which, while on the subject of another of her son's infatuations, she makes mention of Augustine.

The first time you fell in love, you were clear sighted—and so much the better for you, since the girl could never have been yours.[1] The second time[2] you were capricious, often unjust, and, finally, anything but heroic—and not a little cruel. So much the worse for you . . . You were racked by uncertainty, and oscillated between alternating fits of attraction and disgust which can cause such acute suffering to the human heart . . . But you *must not* make the same sort of serious mistake again, involve yourself in a hasty engagement, and then write from Guillery—*My father does not much care for the idea, and perhaps he is right* . . . You are grown up now, and cannot go on behaving like a child. . . .[3]

One can only conclude that Maurice had led Augustine to entertain great hopes, and had then taken shelter behind Casimir (a very transparent excuse) in order to make his escape. Meanwhile Solange, jealous of the dark-haired Augustine, told Chopin, without producing any proof at all, that the girl was Maurice's mistress. The puritanical Chopin was shocked. Once again the air of Nohant was heavy with quarrels. 'The only thing to do', said Sand, 'is to wrap oneself up in oiled silk, and let the external world run off one's back like water to its heart's content.'

The end of that Autumn was painful in the extreme. The two girls went about with their arms round one another's waist, apparently on terms of the closest affection, but really filled with hatred and suspicion. Chopin was at his worst. Solange alone, to whom he was infinitely indulgent,

[1] Pauline Viardot.

[2] Augustine Brault.

[3] Unpublished letter from George Sand to her son, Maurice (December 17th, 1850): Spoelberch de Lovenjoul Collection: Group E. 922, ff. 95 and 98.

because 'la baronne', like himself, was a mass of class prejudices, escaped the cold impact of his anger. To Augustine he behaved with quite terrifying bitterness. Maurice, attacked by Chopin, on the ground that he was misbehaving with his Brault cousin, talked of clearing out altogether. 'I could not, and ought not, to allow that', wrote Sand. 'Chopin could not bear my interference, natural and necessary though it was. He hung his head, and muttered that I no longer loved him. What blasphemy after eight years of maternal devotion! But I really believe the poor man was so worried and upset that he did not know what he was saying.'[1]

In November 1846, Chopin left Nohant, not thinking for a moment that he would never return. He continued to send friendly, and even gay, letters to Sand, but, when writing to others, indulged in mocking criticism of the family whose guest he had been. Solange's marriage was a new subject of irritation. Chopin had thoroughly approved of the engagement. Fernand de Préaulx, her aristocratic suitor, fitted in well with his own prejudiced outlook. But when, early in 1847, Solange and her mother went to Paris to order the trousseau, their peaceful existence was suddenly shattered by the irruption of a 'noisy, disorderly creature, a former cavalry soldier turned sculptor, who carried with him wherever he went, the manners of the canteen and the studio'.[2] The name of this apparition was Auguste Clésinger. In March 1846, he had sent Sand a turgid letter, full of emphatic statements and bad spelling, in which he asked her permission to 'carve in eternal marble the affecting title of *Consuelo*'. She had replied, giving the required authorization.

Auguste Clésinger to George Sand, March 19th, 1846:
May happiness be yours, madame, and pride, for the bliss you have brought to a poor young man. He will cry it aloud from the house-tops, for he hopes that in his works he will perpetuate the name of George Sand to whom he owes what now he is. . . .[3]

[1] GEORGE SAND: *Histoire de ma Vie*. Volume IV, p. 473.
[2] ARSENE HOUSSAYE: *Confessions*. Volume III, p. 241.
[3] Letter quoted by Samuel Rocheblave in *George Sand et sa fille*, p. 93.

No sooner had the two women arrived in Paris in February 1847, than the cavalryman, all beard and enthusiasm, flung himself upon them, craving the honour of perpetuating their busts in 'eternal marble'. He represented Solange as a huntress, with distended nostrils, bare shoulders and flying hair. The sittings seem to have had a strangely disturbing effect upon the girl, because she broke off her engagement to the Vicomte de Préaulx on the very day before the contract was to be signed. 'He is too much the plaster saint . . .' she declared. Her own preference was for marble. 'I deplore the whole business', wrote Chopin, 'and am sorry for the young man, who is deeply in love and worthy of better treatment . . .'[1] Even Sand agreed with him. 'The poor young fellow who has been left in the lurch is a noble-minded youth, who has behaved like a true flower of French chivalry . . .'[2] Nevertheless. she had a weakness for the cavalryman, or, as she called him, 'the monumental mason'. Such information, however, as she could collect about Clésinger was deeply disturbing. He was said to be stupid, brutal, heavily in debt and a drunkard. In a vain attempt to separate Solange from him, she hurried her back to Nohant. But the bearded lover appeared at La Châtre, and, by the sheer violence of his exuberance, extracted Sand's consent to his marriage with her daughter.

George Sand to Maurice: He will get his way because his mind is set on it. He gets everything he wants on the spot by dint of sheer persistence. He seems to be able to go without sleep or food. He was here for three days, and, during all that time, slept no more than two hours in all, and appears to be none the worse. I am amazed, I am even rather pleased, by the spectacle of such strength of will, which never weakens nor grows tired . . . I think he will be the saving of your restless sister. With him at her side, she will steer a straight course. . . .[3]

Some time later—'Solange is ill', she wrote, 'because, for the first time in her life, she is violently in love, and Clésinger, you know, is all fire and flame. . . .'
Truth to tell, George was dangerously taken by this

[1] *Lettres de Chopin*, p. 447.

[2] GEORGE SAND: *Correspondance*. Volume II, p. 363.

[3] Unpublished. Spoelberch de Lovenjoul Collection: Group E. 921, ff. 255-6.

bandit of a man. To her friends she explained the suddenness of her decision by saying that the wild ex-trooper had been plotting to elope with Solange. 'This marriage must be rushed through as though on the spur of the moment . . .'[1] *George Sand to Maurice, April 16th, 1847:* 'Not a word of all this to Chopin. It is none of his business, and when once the Rubicon has been passed, *ifs* and *buts* will do nothing but harm. . . .'[2]

She, herself, made the best of a bad job, generously financed the bride, and was loud in her praises of the groom. 'Clésinger will bring glory to his wife and to me. He will inscribe his name in marble and in bronze.'[3]

George Sand to Grzymala, May 12th, 1847: I do not yet know whether my daughter will be married here in a week's time, or in Paris in a fortnight's. In any case, I shall be in Paris for a few days at the end of the month, and, if Chopin can be moved, shall bring him back here with me . . . I think he has suffered a good deal in his solitude from knowing nothing and being unable to give any advice. But it is no good paying attention to anything he says when the problem to be solved has to do with real life. He has never been able to face facts, nor can he even begin to understand human nature. His being is all poetry and music, and he cannot bear what is different from himself. Any influence he might exert in the concerns of my family would mean for me the loss of all dignity and all love in my relations with my children . . . Do, please, have a word with him, and try to make him see, in a general way, that he must really stop worrying about them . . . It is all very difficult and very delicate. I can think of no way of calming and restoring a sick mind, when every effort to effect a cure merely irritates the invalid. The evil which is eating away the poor creature, both morally and physically, has been for me, over a long period of time, a form of slow death. I see him slipping

[1] Cf. SAMUEL ROCHEBLAVE: *George Sand et sa fille,* p. 99.

[2] Letter quoted by Wladimir Karénine in *George Sand.* Volume III, p. 560.

[3] George Sand to the Princess Galitzin, *née* La Roche-Aymon, quoted by George d'Heylli (Edmond Poinsot) in *La Fille de George Sand,* p. 54.

away without being able to do a thing to help him, because it is the very uneasiness, jealousy and moodiness of his affection for me that is the chief cause of his melancholy. . . .[1]

Since Solange was still a minor, it was necessary to obtain Casimir Dudevant's consent. Clésinger rushed off to Guillery. There could not be a moment's doubt of what the upshot would be of a discussion between this walking thunderstorm and Casimir the Easygoing. All that now remained to be done was to inform Chopin—who had been very ill—at the last possible moment, of what had been decided. Everything about Clésinger, including his wild and melodramatic nudes, shocked him. 'Next year', he said sadly, 'we shall be treated to a view of Solange's little behind in the Salon!' *Chopin to his family, June 8th, 1847:* 'Her mamma is adorable, but has not an ounce of common sense in her whole make-up . . . Maurice was on his side (*Clésinger's*) for no better reason than that he detests de Préaulx, who is a man of elegant upbringing and good family . . .'[2] The marriage took place on May 20th, at Nohant. Casimir travelled from Guillery to be present. He was very gracious to the 'stone-hewer' and to George.

Sand to Charles Poncy, May 21st, 1847: Never was a marriage carried through with such determination and promptitude. Monsieur Dudevant spent three days under my roof . . . We caught the Mayor and the Curé when they were least expecting us, and prevailed upon them to attend. We made it seem as though the actual wedding were entirely unpremeditated, and had been decided upon only at the last moment. Now it is all over and done with, and we can breathe freely. . . .[3]

But it was *not* over and done with. Solange and her husband returned, after a short wedding-trip, to Nohant. Maurice had invited a friend of his to stay, Théodore Rousseau, a famous painter of foliage, forests and grassy

---

[1] Letter quoted by Wladimir Karénine in *George Sand*. Volume III, pp. 570-1.

[2] *Lettres de Chopin.*

[3] Letter quoted by Samuel Rocheblave in *George Sand et sa fille*, p. 100.

meadows. Rousseau fell in love with the lovely Augustine, and Sand, feeling that she owed the girl a debt, did her best to promote his suit.

> *George Sand to Théodore Rousseau, May 15th, 1847:* If you could have seen how the colour rushed into her cheeks, and the tears into her eyes, when I showed her that beautiful letter, you would be feeling as calm and as radiant as she has been for the past two hours . . . She flung herself into my arms, saying: 'Then there really is a man who will love me as you love me!'[1]

Sand went so far as to tell Rousseau that, if his mind were made up, she would give Augustine a dowry of a hundred thousand francs, to be paid out of her author's royalties—which was more than generous. At this point, the redoubtable Solange came on the scene. She hated Augustine, and had no intention of letting any part of Sand's money go to her. Besides, by putting a spoke in this particular wheel, she would be serving the interests of her husband's family, because his younger brother was also in love with Augustine. She got somebody to tell Rousseau that her 'cousin's' heart was elsewhere engaged, and that if she consented to marry him it would be because her hopes had been disappointed. This news filled Rousseau with alarm. It was quite true, he told Sand, that he was very much taken with Augustine, but, as to marrying her . . .

> *George Sand to Théodore Rousseau:* Vile tongues are putting it about that I have behaved shamefully in giving shelter to an angelic creature, and that this noble girl, who refused my son's hand because she did not believe that he could give her the love which her pride demanded, is an intriguing miss who is capable of plotting with me to deceive an honest man. Why, she could become Maurice's wife tomorrow if she could put into words all that she is suffering. . . .[2]

It was a most deplorable situation. Sand had to play a wary game with Maurice who, now that he saw Augustine

---

[1] Unpublished. Spoelberch de Lovenjoul Collection: Group E. 921, ff. 314-15.

[2] Unpublished. Spoelberch de Lovenjoul Collection: Group E. 921, f. 328.

in a mood to marry, felt his own irresolute feelings for her revive. She tried to bring Rousseau up to the scratch, while he, for his part, felt nothing but amazement at the sight of one who was popularly supposed to have rooted objections to the state of matrimony, playing the 'match-maker'. What was really going on in his mind? Did he genuinely suppose that she would have been willing to see her 'adopted daughter' become her friend's mistress? 'If you think that I am an enemy to the idea of marriage, then all I can say is that you cannot have read a single one of my books . . .' Had he been lending a willing ear to abominable slanders? 'I am beginning to wonder whether you are not just such another as Lamennais, with whom nobody finds it possible to live because he is afflicted with emotional hallucinations . . .' Worried by an anonymous letter, and discouraged by Solange, Rousseau took himself off. Augustine remained as calm as 'roses after rain', but between Clésinger and Sand there were high words.

It was Solange, 'that strong-minded, tenacious, cold, cynical, remorseless and pitiless woman' whom Sand especially blamed.

George Sand to Charles Poncy, August 27th, 1847: No sooner married than she has trampled everything under foot, and dropped the mask. She has turned her hot-blooded but weak-minded husband against me, against Maurice, and against Augustine, for whom she entertains a mortal hatred, and whose only fault lies in being far too good and far too devoted. It is entirely owing to her that the poor child's marriage has broken down, and that Rousseau has gone temporarily insane. She repeated to him the most atrocious lies about Maurice and Augustine . . . she is doing her best to embroil me with my friends . . . she poses as the victim of my unjust preference for her brother and his cousin! She has fouled the nest in which she was reared by thinking—and saying—that it has been the scene of the most disgraceful conduct. Nor does she spare me—me, who for her sake, have condemned myself to the life of a nun. . . .[1]

The scenes that followed 'are scarcely to be believed . . . We have been within an ace of cutting one another's throat'.

[1] Partially unpublished. Spoelberch de Lovenjoul Collection: Group E. 921, ff. 281-2.

The sculptor threatened Maurice with a mallet. Sand resorted to physical violence in an attempt to save her son from her son-in-law. Solange spurred on the combatants. 'That is the way of things. One fine day Satan enters into a beautiful woman.' To herself Solange argued, 'Better be the executioner than the victim.'

> *Sand to Marie de Rozières:* The devilish couple took themselves off yesterday evening, crippled with debts, glorying in their impudence, and leaving behind them a scandal the effects of which they will never be able to shake off. Here I was, for three days, in my own house, at the mercy of a murderer. I never want to see them again. They shall never cross my threshold. This is the last straw! Dear God, what have I done to deserve such a daughter . . .[1]

VIII

SEPARATION

SOLANGE WAS well aware of the extent of her influence over Chopin. With the assistance of Marie de Rozières—who had grievances of her own—she planned to 'set him against' Sand. She explained the recent family quarrel as having arisen, not from the violent behaviour of her sculptor husband, but because, as she insinuated, George was the mistress of young Victor Borie, and perhaps also of Eugène Lambert, the painter—a studio friend of Maurice's—and did not want to have too many prying eyes about the house. Solange accused Maurice of putting up with Borie's presence at Nohant because he needed a shield behind which he could carry on his own affair with Augustine. Chopin was only too ready to believe all this. He gave a ready ear to the various charges—though Solange did not produce a single shred of proof—and left unanswered a letter in which

[1] Letter quoted by Wladimir Karénine in *George Sand.* Volume III, p. 578.

Sand, prompted by anxiety on his behalf, had asked him to return to Nohant.

George Sand to Marie de Rozières, July 25th, 1847: I am frightened and uneasy. There has been no news of Chopin for several days . . . It was all arranged that he should leave Paris—then, suddenly, he did not arrive here, and has not written. I should have set out myself before now had it not been that I feared we might miss each other on the road, and also that I dread returning to Paris and being exposed to the hatred of a woman whom you still persist in thinking so 'good' . . . Now and again, just to reassure myself, I think that he is very much fonder of her than I am, that he is taking her side, and sulking.

. . . At long last I received a letter by this morning's post from Chopin! I see now that, as usual, I have been the victim of my silly heart, and that, all this time, while I have been spending sleepless nights in worrying over the state of his health, he has been thinking ill of me and condoling with the Clésinger couple. A fine state of affairs, I must say! The solemnity with which he writes makes me laugh! He preaches at me for all the world like a good father and family man. His sermons, if it comes to that, have taught me a good deal . . . There is a lot behind this at which I can only guess, but I do know of just how much credulity and prejudice my daughter is capable . . . My eyes have been opened at last, and, from now on, I shall act accordingly. No longer shall my body and blood serve as food for ingratitude and perversity. . . .[1]

George Sand to Frédéric Chopin: Yesterday I ordered horses, and fully intended, in spite of my own ill-health and this appalling weather, to set out by chaise. I planned to spend a day in Paris in order to get news of you—to such a condition of anxiety had I been reduced by your silence. Meanwhile, *you* had been taking time to think things over, and your reply could scarcely have been cooler. So be it, my friend. Do as your heart tells you, and take its instinctive promptings for the language of your conscience. I quite understand.

As to my daughter . . . she has the bad taste to say that

[1] Letter quoted by Wladimir Karénine in *George Sand*. Volume III, pp, 578-9.

she needs the love of a mother whom, in fact, she hates and slanders, whose most sacred actions she sullies, whose house she fills with her own atrocious talk! You have undertaken to lend a willing ear to her, and perhaps you really do believe what she tells you. I will not be a party to this kind of squabble. It fills me with horror. I would rather see you go over to the enemy than myself take arms against that same enemy who was born of my body and fed on my milk.

Take good care of her, since you seem to have decided that it is your duty to devote yourself to her. I will not hold it against you, but you will, I hope, understand me if I say that I shall stick to my role of outraged mother ... To have been a dupe and a victim is quite enough. I forgive you, and will not, from this day forward, address so much as a single word of reproach to you, since you have confessed frankly what is in your mind. I cannot pretend that it does not somewhat surprise me, but if you feel freer and more at ease this way, I will not let myself be hurt by so strange a change of face.

Goodbye, my friend. May you soon be cured of all your ills, as I hope that now you may be (I have my own reasons for thinking so). If you are, I will offer thanks to God for this fantastic ending of a friendship which has, for nine years, absorbed both of us. Send me news of yourself from time to time. It is useless to think that things can ever again be the same between us. . . .[1]

It is a sad and silly business when two people who have loved each other dearly become estranged. As a rule the misunderstanding is not serious. Words never uttered, or uttered carelessly and irresponsibly in a moment of bad temper, are repeated by officious or malicious gossips. The victim of such slanders is either too deeply resentful, or too proud, to explain. Long, unbroken silence kills, in the long run, all tenderness. The stronger an attachment has been, the more surely will disappointment turn it to a kind of hatred. Only too many friends, when the breach occurs, burn the idol they once adored, and carry condemnation, as once they carried praise, to excess. George Sand was too generous-minded to let herself be swept down the slope to hatred, but she felt nervously exhausted. From now on she

[1] Bibliothèque nationale: Department of Manuscripts.

wanted to hear nothing about Chopin, except how he was.

George Sand to Carlotta Marliani, November 2nd, 1847:
Chopin has openly sided with her *(Solange)* against me,
and that without knowing the truth, which smacks of
ingratitude to me and of crazy infatuation for her—
Please behave as though you knew nothing—He has
changed so much that I can only assume that she has
worked upon his jealous and suspicious nature, and that
it is by her and her husband that this absurd slander has
been put about touching a *love affair* on my part, or an
exclusive friendship, in connection with the young man
you mention *(Victor Borie)*. It is the only explanation I
can find for so ridiculous a story, and one which nobody
could possibly credit. I have no wish to get to the bottom
of this particular piece of trivial nastiness.

I don't mind admitting that I am far from feeling
annoyed that he *(Chopin)* should have decided to take the
management of his life out of my hands. Both he and his
friends were beginning to put a great deal too much
responsibility on my shoulders. He was becoming more
and more soured as time went on, and things had come to
such a pass that he was indulging in scenes of temper and
jealousy in front of my children and my friends. Solange,
with the low cunning which is natural to her, made use of
them for her own purposes, and Maurice was beginning
to lose patience with him. He knew, from the evidence of
his own eyes, how chaste our relationship was, but could
not help seeing, too, how the poor sickly creature,
without wishing to, and perhaps because he could not
help it, behaved as though he were my lover, my
husband, and the master of my every thought and action.
He was on the point of bursting out and telling him to his
face that he was making me—a woman of forty-three—
look ridiculous, and that he was taking advantage of my
goodness of heart . . . I realized that a storm might burst
at any moment, and took advantage of Chopin's obvious
preference for Solange to let him sulk, and not to make
any effort to get him back.

For the last three months we have not exchanged a
line. How this cooling off will end I do not know. I shall
do nothing that might have the effect either of worsening
the situation or of terminating it altogether. I have been
guiltless, and I feel no resentment against those who are

to blame. But I cannot, and ought not to, let myself become once again the victim of that sort of secret tyranny which, as a result of a constant campaign of pin-pricks—some of which struck pretty deep—was beginning to make life impossible . . . The poor child could no longer maintain even that decent behaviour in company of which, by habit and conviction, he had become the slave . . . He had a horror, and a furious, insensate jealousy of everyone—men and women alike, and no matter what their age . . . The fit would come on him in the presence of my children, of my servants, and of men who, seeing how he behaved, might well have forgotten that respect to which my age, and my conduct over the last ten years, entitle me. I could stand it no longer. His own particular circle will, I know, take a very different view. He will be looked upon as a victim, and the general opinion will find it pleasanter to believe that I, in spite of my age, have got rid of him in order to take another lover. . . .[1]

George Sand to Marie de Rozières, November 22nd, 1847: Please tell Chopin to inform Monsieur Pleyel that the grand piano was despatched from here four days ago. Solange has sent me a message from Chopin to the effect that Monsieur Pleyel had not 'hired' it to him, that it is an exceptionally fine instrument, but that I could keep it, and that he, Chopin, would make himself responsible for the financial arrangements. I have no wish that Chopin should make me a present of a piano. I do not like being under an obligation to those who hate me. What Chopin has said to his friends in confidence—and like all confidences, it has been passed on—make it quite clear how he and I stand from now on . . . My dear child, I am perfectly well aware *why* his attitude and his behaviour has changed. It took some time for my eyes to be opened, but they are open now, and I forgive him with all my heart. I realize that he is no longer responsible for his actions. What would be a crime in anybody else is, with him, merely a form of wildness. I always knew that, in the long run, his friendship for me would turn to aversion, because he is a man who never does things by halves. I feel perfectly calm now, and all the past is

[1] Letter quoted by Wladimir Karénine in *George Sand*. Volume III, pp. 586-7.

explained. I want no more than that he *should not do me a service. . . .*[1]

Thereafter—silence. George made no further attempt to end the coldness. Their last meeting, tragic in its simplicity, has been described in a letter from Chopin to Solange, dated March 5th, 1848. 'Yesterday, I went to see Madame Marliani,[2] and, on my way out, found myself in the doorway of the ante-room, face to face with your mother, who was just coming in with Lambert in tow. I asked her how she did, and whether she had had any recent news of you. "I heard from her a week ago," she replied. "Not yesterday, or the day before?"—"No"—"Then, let me inform you that you are a grandmother. Solange has had a little girl, and I am delighted to think that I am the first to inform you of the fact." I bowed, and went on my way downstairs. Combes, the Abyssinian, was with me, and, since I had forgotten to say that your health was good—an important piece of information for a mother (as you will readily understand now that you are a mother yourself) I asked him to run back, not feeling up to facing the climb, and to tell her that both you and the child were doing well. I waited for him below. Your mother came down with him, and asked with every show of interest about your condition. I said that you had sent me a few pencilled words, *in your own hand* on the day following your daughter's birth; that you had suffered a good deal, but that the sight of the child had made you forget all your troubles. She asked me how I was, and I answered that I was well. I then told the porter to open the door, bowed, and returned to the square d'Orléans with the Abyssinian. . . .'[3]

Sand, too, has given an account of this meeting. 'I thought that a few months spent away from him would heal the wound, make possible a tranquil friendship, and pour balm on memory . . . I saw him for a moment in March 1848. I took his hand. It was icy cold and trembling. I should have liked to talk with him, but he took to his heels.

[1] Unpublished. Spoelberch de Lovenjoul Collection: Group E. 921, ff. 299-300.

[2] In 1848, Carlotta Marliani, like George Sand, left the square d'Orléans (where Chopin was still living at No. 5) and moved to 18 rue de la Ville-l'Evêque.

[3] Letter quoted by Wladimir Karénine in *George Sand*. Volume III, p. 592.

It was my turn to say that he no longer loved me, but I spared him that pain, and left everything in the lap of the Gods and the future. I never saw him again. There were black-hearted people between him and me—good-hearted, too, but they did not know how to help. There were also a number of trivial folk who preferred not to get mixed up in such delicate matters.'[1]

That is the way of the world. Two people may be all in all to one another, but habit plays a large part in their daily intimacy. Transplant them, separate them, and very soon they will strike new roots in strange soil. To the friend whom once we made the confidant of our every thought, we cannot bring ourselves to say a word. Silence covers all. The heart bleeds for Sand and Chopin meeting for a moment on the staircase of that house in the rue de la Ville-l'Evêque, going their ways, and never, for a moment, looking back.

[1] GEORGE SAND: *Histoire de ma Vie.* Volume IV.

PART SEVEN

THE REVOLT OF THE ANGELS

Humanity has shod the giant child, Progress.

Arthur Rimbaud

That women differ from men, that heart and intellect are subject to the laws of sex, I do not doubt . . . But ought this difference, so essential to the general harmony of things, to constitute a moral inferiority?

George Sand

I

THE PERSONAL POLITICS OF
GEORGE SAND

'WOMEN HAVE no moral sense,' said La Bruyère; 'they depend for their behaviour upon the men they love.' More than one biographer has been tempted to apply this saying to George Sand's political life. 'She held by no doctrine', they say; 'she took her ideas from any man she happened to be in love with at the moment.' That is not true. She had political views long before she was in love with anybody. Chopin was an aristocrat, Musset a sceptic: she, however, was neither, even though she was in love with each of them. True, she took over the ideas of Michel de Bourges, of Lamennais, of Pierre Leroux, 'but they were ideas with which she was already familiar'. It would be more accurate to say that she carried her passionate temperament into the field of politics. She was ever a woman of extremes— imprudent, ardent, violent, with lucid intervals of simple human charity and a basically simple common sense. She shares with Madame de Staël the glory of being one of those rare women who played a part in French nineteenth century history.

That statement needs to be explained and analysed.

I have said that she had already taken sides long before she came under the influence of any man. The road had been marked out for her in childhood. Because, in one sense, she belonged to 'the People', and liked to recall the fact ('I am of the People as much by blood as feeling . . . I am no intruder into their world'); because she had lived for a long time on terms of intimacy and friendship with the children of peasants; because her first strong emotion had been one of aggressive affection for a mother who, so she thought, had been unjustly treated; because she had learned from that same mother to distrust the rich—she had a spontaneous sympathy for all rebels. Because she had suffered from the corruption of the ruling class of her time, and had her own share in that corruption, her hopes had come to be centred on the virtues of the 'masses'.

Consequently, *first:* George Sand was by instinct a democrat, or thought she was. Later on it will become apparent that she had no very clear ideas about democracy. 'I am by nature a poet, and not a legislator. I could, if necessity arose, be a fighter, but never a parliamentarian.' That is a fairly serious admission, and explains her many disappointments. With her friends at La Châtre, she had always championed the republicans and the Bonapartists against the monarchists. In her eyes, every king, whether or no he called himself a citizen-king, was a tyrant. When Maurice was at school with the Duc de Montpensier, she always forbade him to accept the young prince's invitations. But even this was more, with her, a matter of instinct than of theory. She was a republican, but, like Jérôme Paturot, for ever in search of the best of all possible Republics.

Second: She was by nature, education and conviction an Evangelical Christian. She held that Christianity must be something that the 'People' could understand—a generous, socially-conscious religion, or nothing. Its morality must derive neither from an Epicurean philosophy, nor from the drawing-rooms of the great world. This explains Lamennais.

Third: In her fortieth year she still remained a mystic and a follower of Rousseau. Her faith tended to move away from a vague emotionalism, because her experiences of life had shown her that the heart is an unreliable counsellor. All the same, and in spite of her many disillusionments, she still held that direct communication with God was the best way to achieve knowledge. She was strong in her conviction that such communication can and does exist, not perhaps between God and the individual, but certainly between God and the soul of a people . . . She believed, with Rousseau, in the natural goodness of Man. She would have nothing to do with the dogma of Original Sin. In this she differed entirely from Balzac, who wanted to see a strong government because he was sceptical of the natural man. Even as late as 1848, Sand believed in the masses, *provided* they were instructed in the 'true' philosophy of religion and society.

Fourth and finally: She held these ideas sincerely, and not as a matter of self-interest. She had no personal ambition. Is it true that she was a feminist? Not if that word is given the meaning it acquired towards the end of the nineteenth century. George Sand never demanded, nor wanted, political equality for women. She thought that public life was incompatible with the duties of motherhood. 'Education', she said, 'will in time be the same for men and women, but it will be in the female heart par excellence, as it always has been, that love and devotion, patience and pity, will find their true home. On woman falls the duty, in a world of brute passions, of preserving the virtues of charity and the Christian spirit . . . When women cease to play the role, life will be the loser.'[1]

What she sought for women was not the right to vote nor to sit in Parliament, but the enjoyment of equality with men in Law and in Love. She believed that where the husband holds the wife in subjection, married happiness is impossible, that it can exist only in an atmosphere of freedom. Women would make no demands if they were loved as they wished to be. 'As things are, they are ill-used. They are forced to live a life of imbecility, and are blamed for doing so. If they are ignorant, they are despised, if learned, mocked. In love they are reduced to the status of courtesans. As wives they are treated more as servants than as companions. Men do not love them: they make use of them, they exploit them, and expect, in that way, to make them subject to the law of fidelity.[2]

That was her main grievance: that was the cry which, first uttered in her girlhood, echoed through every one of her books. In the name of what Justice, human or divine, could a woman be bound by a code of loyalty which a man refused, in his own case, to regard as other than empty and ridiculous? Why should a woman remain chaste while a man was free to wander at will, and indulge the coarse tastes of a libertine? 'In society as it exists today a man has only to multiply the number of his conquests to be greeted on all sides with tolerant smiles. This is especially true in the country, where he who keeps a rich table, and rides successfully in the lists of love, is regarded as a jolly fellow of whom no more need be asked . . . Very different is the fate of the woman taken in adultery. "Honour" in a woman is held to mean only one thing. If she is unfaithful to her husband, she is branded in the eyes of her neighbours, looked on as the lowest of the low, and exposed to the obloquy of her children. Nay more, she risks incurring the

---

[1] GEORGE SAND: *Impressions littéraires*, p. 282.

[2] GEORGE SAND: *La Fauvette du Docteur (Almanach du Mois*, November 1844).

infamous punishment of imprisonment.'[1] What Sand wanted was to see restored to women those civil rights of which they were deprived by marriage, and to have repealed a law which exposed the adulterous wife to degrading penalties—'a savage law, the only effect of which is to make adultery a permanent feature of our society, and to increase the number of cases in which it is committed'.

She could see but one remedy for the injustices which were rampant in all matters connected with the union of the sexes—freedom (in her day non-existent) to divorce and re-marry. 'Once a human creature, whether man or woman, has reached that high vantage-point from which true love can be seen for what it is, it is no longer possible for him—I would go further and say that it is no longer permissible for him—to turn back the clock and regard it as a mere animal function.'[2] For her the act of physical union, unaccompanied by strong emotion, was a crime of sacrilege, even *within* the bonds of matrimony, a crime which every woman had the right to avoid. 'I regard as mortal sin not only the lying evidence of the senses in matters of love, but also the illusion which the senses seek to create where love is not whole or complete. One must love, say I, with all of oneself—or live a life of utter chastity.'[3]

In her view, the fault, the sin, lies not in changing the object of one's passion, not in leaving one man and going to another in response to the call of love, but in giving oneself to somebody whom one does not love, even if it happens to be one's husband.

Those were the limits of her feminism. It should be clear that it did not imply, for women, any programme of militant action in the political field.

---

[1] GEORGE SAND: *Histoire de ma Vie*. Volume IV, pp. 392-3.

[2] Ibid., Volume IV, p. 294.

[3] Ibid., Volume IV, p. 295.

II

LADY OF THE MANOR —
AND SOCIALIST

BUT THE outlook of every individual is inevitably formed
or distorted by the intellectual climate of the society in
which he lives, whether he floats with the tide or struggles
against it. What chiefly characterizes the period in France
from 1830-48 is the fact that it attempted to achieve a social
revolution which should complete the political revolution of
1789. In 1830 the middle classes had finally reached a
position of power. The régime of the 'Juste-Milieu' had
meant the triumph of the Toms, Dicks and Harrys. But it
seemed obvious to the far-sighted that the religious
revolution of the eighteenth century ought to find its natural
term in a revolution of the proletariat. Why should the
working classes, now that they had lost their faith in a life
to come, be content to put up with poverty in the life they
were compelled to live here below? This line of reasoning it
was that produced in a man like Balzac the view that only
the re-establishment of the spiritual authority of Catholicism could save society from anarchy, and led Saint-Simon
to make an effort to establish on the ruins of Catholicism a
spiritual power which should direct the progress of industry,
science and art to the attainment of a goal which might be
described as 'the quickest possible improvement in the
conditions of the poorest and most numerous class of
the community'.

Though their doctrines were to have a future which, at
that time, nobody could foresee, Saint-Simon and his
disciples had suffered a temporary setback. The nineteenth
century, so rich in 'miscarriages', was treating its reformers
with mockery, and bowing down in the Temple of
Mammon. Saint-Simon and Fourier, flouted and laughed at,
had died in the wilderness. Their influence over Sand had

not been great. Michel de Bourges had tried to turn her into
a militant, but without success. He had, however, familiar-
ized her with the more daring views then current about
property, and had introduced her into 'advanced' circles.
Lamennais, though his own views were somewhat confused, had enlisted her under the banner of Christian-
Socialism. But the man to whom she really owed her
initiation was Leroux.

He had given her a new religion. He regarded himself as a
prophet, and wished to substitute human solidarity for Christian charity. Sand, as Sainte-Beuve said, 'took at their face-
value people who, in many respects, were her inferiors'.
She had made much of Leroux's doctrine her own. She had
accepted the ideas of human perfectibility (the Golden Age
is still to come), of the immortality, not of the individual,
but of the species, and of collective property. Society alone
could distribute the rewards of labour, and, though
Property was not theft (this statement did something to
soften the scruples of the Great Lady of Nohant), neither
was it a right, and the community as a whole had a right to
re-adjust it. Leroux confirmed Sand in a Socialism which
was less brutal than the brand favoured by Michel, more
sincere, and less vacillating. In 1843, Sainte-Beuve was
calling Béranger, Lamennais, Sand and Sue, 'the four great
corner-stones of Socialism and Philanthropy in the modern
world'.[1]

In what way did this Socialism of hers find expression?
Sentimentally, by the support she gave to the proletarian
poets—Magu, the weaver; Reboul, the baker; Jasmin, the
barber; and, above all, Charles Poncy, the mason of
Toulon, to whom she wrote: 'My child, you are a great poet,
the most truly inspired, the most highly gifted, of all the fine
poets who have sprung from the People . . . You have it in
you to be the greatest poet in France. . . .'

And, again:

June 23rd, 1842: It is not *we* of the literary world who
are poor, suffering humanity; not *I*, who (and maybe the
loss is mine) have never known either hunger or poverty;
not even you, dear poet, who will find in fame, and in the
recognition of your fellows, a noble recompense for all
your personal sorrows. No, it is the People, the ignorant,

[1] SAINTE-BEUVE: *Correspondance générale.* Volume V,
p. 323.

abandoned People, full of stormy passions which men rouse for their own evil ends, or suppress without a thought for that power which God has not given them for nothing. . . .[1]

She added: 'There have been times when Hugo has felt that, but he lacks the moral outlook which might have enabled him to follow his thought to the end, and give it significance. It is because his heart lacks fire that his Muse lacks taste.' Poncy's lacked genius, and even talent, but Sand made of him a faithful friend, a temporary confidant, and, in the long run, a prosperous bourgeois, since it was thanks to the notoriety which she obtained for him that he became Secretary to the Chamber of Commerce at Toulon.

Sand's Socialism expressed itself also in her works, for she took 'as the subject of her later novels the proletariat of the cities and the countryside, its labour and its poverty, setting its virtues in opposition to the selfishness of the rich and the great'.[2] It is the People, according to her, who are the trustees of divine inspiration: it is the People who manifest that natural goodness which Rousseau had attributed to the individual. In *Le Compagnon du Tour de France*, the good woodworker, Pierre Huguenin, is of the 'same divine stuff' as the carpenter, Jesus. When the old and sceptical Comte de Villepreux, in whose house he is working, says, with kindly benevolence, speaking of the City of the Future: 'Make your fine resolutions, build your systems, but do not too soon commit yourself to them!'— Huguenin feels nothing but contempt for this living corpse of a man and for the moribund society which he represents. In *Le Meunier d'Angibault* Sand paints the miller as a robust and attractive saint. She shows the aristocratic Marcelle de Blanchement rejoicing in the loss of her fortune and saying to her son, 'I would have you realize that you have been set *(as the result of the family's ruin)* among the sheep who stand at Christ's right hand, and separated from the goats upon His left!' To God she prays: 'Grant me, Oh Lord, the strength and the wisdom to make this child a man. I could have made him a patrician merely by standing aside with folded arms!' About this time Sand was prepared to admit that she was as much a Communist as a Socialist:

[1] GEORGE SAND: *Correspondance*. Volume II, pp. 218-20.
[2] ERNEST SEILLIERE: *George Sand, mystique de la passion*, pp. 200-12.

but, truth to tell, she was not an obscurantist and was eager to understand more precisely what the two words really meant.

Sainte-Beuve to Madame Juste Olivier, August 3rd, 1840: Madame Sand is going over to Communism, and is undertaking to preach to the workers. Her next novel will, I fear, reflect this tendency. She is not behaving any too well, and in order to keep in with her I am being very careful to stay out of her way.[1]

Pierre Leroux had once told her that he preferred the title *Communionism* to *Communism*, because what was at stake was not only a sharing of goods, but a 'brotherly communion of souls'. By 1848, however, she had left Leroux far behind. She was eager that Socialism should turn to action, while her 'philosopher' was interested only in the devising of systems.

George Sand to Bocage: I am a Communist now much as I might have been a Christian in A.D. 50. For me, Communism is the ideal which all progressive societies must set as their goal. It is a religion which will be a living reality centuries from now. I cannot swear allegiance to any of the formulae of Communism at present in vogue, because all of them are to some extent dictatorial and believe that they can establish themselves without any assistance from habits, manners and convictions. But no religion can be built up on force. . . .[2]

This Communism of hers has all the appearance of being idyllic rather than aggressive, and it has been pointed out before how the novels in which she found an opportunity of expressing it were, all of them, published in Conservative sheets, such as *Le Constitutionnel* and *l'Epoque*. Her own position as a rich woman did not cause her the slightest embarrassment. 'I have a positive hatred of landed property. At most, all I care about is the house and the garden. The meadowland, the plain, the heath, everything that is flat, I find boring, especially when the flatness belongs to me,

[1] SAINTE-BEUVE: *Correspondance générale*. Volume III, p. 332.

[2] Unpublished. Spoelberch de Lovenjoul Collection: Group E. 879, f. 271.

when I tell myself that it is mine, that I am compelled to have it and keep it, to surround it with prickly hedges, to keep the poor from grazing their animals on it, at the risk, if I don't, of becoming poor myself—and that, in certain circumstances, would inevitably mean the upsetting of honour and of duty'[1]—all of which is just an ingenious rationalization of her wish to keep Nohant, and to live there in brotherly simplicity.

In Berry, where her property was situated, Madame Sand had, since 1840, thrown in her lot with the advanced elements of the local opposition to Louis-Philippe. In 1843 she had contributed generously, as we have seen, towards the founding of the *Eclaireur de l'Indre*. The politics of *l'Eclaireur* approximated to those of the Parisian journal, *La Réforme*, which was controlled by Ledru-Rollin, a breezy lawyer with an imposing presence and a charming smile. At heart he was a lazy opportunist who had made a rich marriage and ran after every woman he met. Very much closer to Sand was Louis Blanc, a Socialist with Communist sympathies, who had changed his earlier slogan: 'To each according to his work' into 'To each according to his needs.' They corresponded, and she, like the honest Berry woman that she was, put a number of very direct questions to him before she would agree to espouse his cause. She loved at first sight the little man with the face of a child, who was for ever laughing and gesticulating, and had a gift of brilliant intellectual daring. She even played with the idea of arranging a marriage between him and 'the beauty'—which was Pauline Viardot's name for Solange. There is a portrait of him in her novel *Le Piccinino*: 'Great ambition lodged in a small body; a soft, insinuating voice, and a will of iron.'

It would, however, be a mistake to picture her, throughout the 'forties, as being entirely taken up with laying the foundations of revolution. She was, in fact, living quietly at Nohant.

George Sand to Charles Poncy: I shall be at Nohant until the Winter, as usual, my life being as straightly ruled henceforward, as a sheet of music-paper. I have written two or three novels, one of which is just about to appear . . . My son is still very thin and very delicate, though

[1] Quoted by Ernest Seilliere in *George Sand, mystique de la passion*, p. 205.

in other respects well. He is the best, the gentlest, the most even-tempered, the hardest-working, and the most upright person you could hope to meet anywhere. Our temperaments, to say nothing of our hearts, are so mutually attuned that we can scarcely endure to be separated even for a day. He has just entered on his twenty-third year, and I am in my forty-second . . . We both have a natural gaiety, not of the noisy but the constant sort, which obliterates the difference in age between us, and makes us contemporaries. After a week of hard work, we find our greatest pleasure in going some little distance and eating a picnic in a small wood, or among ruins. Uusally my brother comes with us, a great, sturdy country-fellow, brimming over with intelligence and good nature. He lives quite close, and takes his dinner with us every day. These little expeditions are our greatest treat. Maurice sketches; my brother lies on the grass doing his accounts; the horses graze peacefully . . . the dogs frolic, and the old hack which, on these occasions, conveys the whole family in a species of large, two-wheeled cart, nuzzles round and eats off our plates.[1]

Not all the novels she was writing at this time were concerned with social themes. 'So you thought, did you, that I was busy drinking blood from the skulls of aristocrats! Far from it, my friend; I spend my time reading Virgil and learning Latin . . .' The study of Virgil inspired her to undertake the *Georgics* of her own countryside. As a child she had been fascinated by the stories told in the dark by spinners at the fireside. Her dearest dream was to capture something of that rustic simplicity, to write a story which should have the strength and directness of a popular tale, while at the same time transposing its dialect medium into language which should be easily comprehensible to a Paris reader. This experiment resulted in two charming idylls: *La Mare au Diable* and *Francois le Champi*. The stories balance one another. In the first, a rich farmer marries a poor girl: in the second, the 'Waif' (a bastard child abandoned in a field) wins the affection of the comfortably-off woman who finds him. These touching, healthy-minded little Pastorals breathe the grace of the antique world. We are reminded, as we read, not only of Virgil but of Theocritus, and sometimes of the *Odyssey*. Saved by the

[1] GEORGE SAND: *Correspondance.* Volume II, pp. 339-40.

lyric qualities of her countryside from her obsession with ideologies, she succeeded in producing two masterpieces. In 1843, a bookseller said to Balzac: 'There's no longer any demand for George Sand. *Le Compagnon du Tour de France* killed her stone-dead, which is odd, seeing that popular writers are usually forgiven at least twenty shocking bad books.'[1] But, in the following year, Balzac, speaking of *Jeanne* to Madame Hanska said, 'You must read it: it is superb . . . The country background is touched in by the hand of a master. . . .'[2]

In 1847 Sand was more deeply disturbed by her personal troubles—the breach with Chopin, the Clésinger-Solange drama—than by politics. 'My heart and body have been bruised and broken by grief. The pain is, I think, incurable. For an hour or two I can banish it from my mind, but it always returns to tear at my feelings and darken my sky . . .'[3] She did, however, manage to work, to seem gay, and even, occasionally, to be so.

She had at last found a husband for her dear Titine. Karol de Bertholdi, a Polish exile of thirty-six, had been appointed to the post of drawing-master at Tulle with a salary of three thousand francs a year. Victor Borie had made his acquaintance there, and Sand had invited him to Nohant. Augustine had won his heart. All that now remained was to ensure the penniless young couple some security for the future. Sand gave the bride a dowry of thirty thousand francs, and managed to get the husband (sponsored at her request by Duvernet) made Collector of Taxes at Ribérac. Her own financial resources were seriously imperilled by this act of largesse, and by the ridiculous antics of the Clésingers. Consequently, she was compelled to make some more money, and, with that object in view, started to work on the ten volumes of the *Histoire de ma Vie*.

George Sand to Charles Poncy, December 14th, 1847: The whole thing will be a sequence of memories, professions of faith, and meditations, set in a frame the details of which will have something of poetry and much of simplicity. I shall not, however, reveal all my life. I

[1] HONORE DE BALZAC: *Lettres à l'Etrangère*. Volume II, p. 125.

[2] Ibid., Volume II, p. 456.

[3] GEORGE SAND: *Correspondance*. Volume II, pp. 374-5.

dislike intensely the arrogance and cynicism which go into most 'Confessions'. I do not think that one ought to expose all the mysteries of one's heart to the eyes of readers who may be worse than oneself and, consequently, inclined to draw from such a display bad lessons rather than good. Besides, our lives are closely knit with the lives of others, and we can never justify our actions without being compelled to accuse somebody, often our best friend. I do not wish to accuse, nor to bring sadness to, anybody. I should think it hateful to do so, and should harm myself more than my victims. So, you see, what I am planning is a *useful* book, free from danger and scandal, without vanity and without baseness. I enjoy working at it. . . .[1]

In the course of the year 1847 she saw scarcely anything of Pierre Leroux, and her former indulgent attitude towards him was now beginning to be shot through with criticism. 'I know nothing of Leroux's affairs. I am gradually getting used to the idea that he will always manage somehow to keep his balance on the invisible tight-rope which stretches between himself and actuality. How he will achieve the feat I have no idea, but achieve it he will. There is one part of him that is wildly undisciplined in face of facts, but another that is shrewd, tenacious, and always succeeds in getting what he wants from the world which he condemns. . . . I do not understand how he has managed to put on such a show of indigence, and yet never to want for anything, and that in spite of the fact that he has many mouths to fill. The problem is a difficult one, but it has existed now for so long that the edge of my anxiety has become blunted. If Boussac crumbles beneath him he will find somewhere else in which to build his nest. He is extraordinarily clever at tapping the most unexpected resources, and positively inspired when it comes to getting others to accept his code of behaviour . . . I confess that I cannot any longer accept the species of Jesuitry with which, on occasion, his fanaticism will come to terms . . .'[2] Hypocrisy is the tribute paid by the rebel to society.

1 GEORGE SAND: *Correspondance.* Volume II, p. 378.
2 Unpublished letter from George Sand to Carlotta Marliani Spoelberch de Lovenjoul Collection: Group E. 921, ff. 297-8.

THE MUSE OF THE REPUBLIC

EARLY IN 1848 Victor Borie, at that time a constant visitor to Nohant, was on tenterhooks at the idea that a revolution was brewing in Paris. George did not believe that there was anything in the wind, and the outbreak of February took her, as it took the whole of France, by surprise. She hated Louis-Philippe with a peculiarly feminine virulence, but the campaign of banquets which preceded and brought about the collapse of the régime appeared to her to be harmless though pointless. 'It is no more', she wrote to her son, 'than a matter of intriguing between Ministers on the way out and Ministers who would like to be on the way in, and I cannot believe that the People will rally to the cause of Monsieur Thiers against Monsieur Guizot . . . So don't have anything to do with it. You won't help the good cause by getting yourself knocked on the head in that sort of squabble. It would really be too stupid to be laid out for the sake of Odilon Barrot and Co. . . .'[1] When the rioting started, she advised Maurice to return to Nohant, and was surprised when he did not turn up. Delacroix wrote to her in a mood of high excitement: 'Maurice is absolutely radiant. He has just left me in such a state that he might, for all the world, have been drinking. I never believed him to be capable of such a degree of exaltation.' Feeling extremely uneasy, she set off immediately in search of her son.

When she got to Paris her first, and sudden, impression was that the 'great day' had indeed dawned, and that not only the Republic, but the *Socialist* Republic, was an accomplished fact. She went to see little Louis Blanc in *his* Palace of the Luxembourg. The marble galleries were

[1] GEORGE SAND: *Correspondance*. Volume III, pp. 2-3.
[2] EUGENE DELACROIX: *Correspondance générale*. Volume II, p. 343.

streaked with long files of proletarian visitors. Louis Blanc was aglow with enthusiasm. 'The strength of the people', he said, 'must show itself under a surface of apparent calm: calm is the majesty of strength.' Standing in talk with Lamartine in one of the windows of Guizot's house, she watched a procession passing below.

> *George Sand to Augustine Brault:* It was a beautiful sight, very simple and very moving—four hundred thousand people crowded shoulder to shoulder all the way from the Madeleine to the Column of July. There was not a gendarme, not a police officer, to be seen, and yet the whole affair passed off in so orderly, so decent, so serious a manner, with so much politeness on all sides, that not a toe was trodden on, nor a hat stove in. It was quite admirable. The people of Paris are the greatest people in the world! . . .[1]

The establishment of a Republic was assured. The opportunity was not going to be missed. If necessary, men would fight on the barricades to defend it. The Government, composed of decent, well-intentioned people, was not perhaps quite up to a task which demanded 'the genius of Napoleon and the heart of Jesus'. Nevertheless, most of them gave of their best.

Sand had never been on really intimate terms with Lamartine. After a speech of his in 1843, in which he had come out as a declared opponent of the régime, she had sent him her congratulations. The letter had pleased him greatly, and he had asked to be allowed to meet her. Though she was still in bed at five o'clock in the afternoon, she had got up to do the honours for her guest, and had appeared before him in 'a sort of a smock, partially unbuttoned. Cigars were brought, and they sat together discussing politics and humanity. It was the first time that these two great geniuses had met face to face. Until that moment George Sand had given the impression that she was faintly contemptuous of him . . .'[2] When she saw him again in Paris in February 1848, the impression she received was that the role he had been called upon to play had decidedly gone to his head. 'I

---

[1] Letter quoted by Wladimir Karénine in *George Sand*. Volume IV, p. 20.

[2] SAINTE-BEUVE: *Correspondance générale*. Volume V, p. 55.

have just made a speech', he told her, 'and embraced a
hundred thousand men.' She judged him to be more of a
Vergniaud than a Mirabeau, more of a poet than a man of
action. But the Republic still had need of him. He was its
'bewitching radiance'. His soft but powerful voice could
take the ugly edge off the word *Revolution*.

Sand watched the leaders of the Provisional Government
being pulled this way and that by the contending forces of
workers and bourgeoisie. Smock *versus* frock-coat; cap
versus hat. socialist republic *versus* bourgeois republic—
that was what 1848 amounted to. Flown with the heady
wine of victory, George did not want this conflict.
Bourgeois and Worker had together brought about the
overthrow of the 'abject system'. They ought to have shaken
hands.

> 'The People', wrote Sand, 'is in the mood to place full
> confidence in the bourgeoisie. The bourgeoisie will not
> abuse that confidence. It will not let itself be led away by
> false counsels, by empty scares, by baseless rumours, by
> slanders uttered against the People. The People will be
> just, calm, wise and good. The middle class will set them
> an example. . . .'[1]

In those early days she felt herself suddenly strong, and
therefore optimistic. She arranged that her friends should be
made Commissaries of the Republic at Châteauroux and La
Châtre. At Bourges, she brought about the dismissal of her
former lover, Michel, who, said she, was betraying the
democracy from dread of demagogy. She succeeded, thanks
to the good graces of Ledru-Rollin, in having Maurice
appointed Mayor of Nohant. Through her influence Pauline
Viardot was accorded the honour of being asked to
compose a 'new *Marseillaise* to words by Dupont. It is I
who have brought all that about', she added proudly.[2] She
herself was given a permit which entitled her to see all the
members of the Provisional Government whenever she
wanted to do so. Ledru-Rollin, 'in his usual impulsive and
slapdash way', put her in charge of the *Bulletin de la
République*. She became the muse of the Revolution.

[1] GEORGE SAND: *Lettre à la Classe moyenne*.
[2] Letter from George Sand to Maurice (March 25th, 1848)
quoted by Wladimir Karénine in *George Sand*. Volume IV, p.
48.

Action is apt to intoxicate artists. They lack experience of its dangers. It goes to their heads. They think it as easy to manipulate the real world as that of the imagination. Their awakening is sudden and painful.

This beautiful dream of hers did not last. That is the way of dreams. The rich took fright, and so did the poor. The People, still clinging to their bitter memory of 1830, when the Citizen-King had done them out of their republic, refused to lay aside their arms. 'I have seen', Sand was already writing in March 1848, 'distrust and scepticism creeping into the hearts of the rich. I have seen ambition and dishonesty assuming the mask of loyalty to the cause.'¹ She was suspicious of last-minute workers and overnight republicans, who were already taking part in popular manifestations with the object of bringing them to nothing.

She hurried back to Nohant in order to be present at Maurice's installation, and also to take the local temperature. There was a great celebration in the village square. The men of Berry came in on horseback with rifles slung. This cavalcade had all the appearance of a peaceful peasant rising. But in La Châtre the middle class was showing signs of hostility. 'I came back here to help my friends, as best I could, to establish the revolution in Berry, which has not yet awakened from its sluggish slumbers . . . Never mind! the Republic is not lost just because La Châtre will have none of it . . .'² All the same, this disappointment had a hardening effect upon her, and her aggressiveness increased. Back in Paris, she proudly believed herself to be the brain and pen of the régime.

> *George Sand to Maurice, March 24th, 1848:* Here I am, already doing a statesman's work. I have drawn up two government circulars today, one for the Ministry of Public Instruction, the other for the Ministry of the Interior. It amuses me to think that they will go out addressed to '*All Mayors*', and that you will be receiving through official channels your *mother's* instructions! Ho, ho, Mr. Mayor, you had better step carefully, and begin by reading out each Sunday one of the Bulletins of the Republic to your assembled National Guard . . . I do not know whether I am standing on my head or my heels.

¹ GEORGE SAND: *Seconde Lettre au Peuple.*
² GEORGE SAND: *Correspondance.* Volume III, pp. 11 and 13.

There is somebody at me all the time. But this kind of life
suits me. . . .'[1]

She was uplifted by a strong, sincere, gust of faith.
Lamartine she thought too lukewarm and too bourgeois.

George Sand to Lamartine, April 1848: Why do you
doubt? You, surely, who have been inspired as poet and
artist by revelations from on high, can judge of the
miracles which the Almighty holds in reserve for the
intelligence of the weak and oppressed? . . . Do you
believe that God will rest content to wait for centuries before making a reality of that magic picture which He
has designed to reveal to you in glimpses? . . . You may be
a great poet and a great man, but you have mistaken the
time of day! . . . Why do you range yourself with those
whom God does not will to enlighten, and not with those
on whom His light has shone? . . . If fear alone can shake
and conquer our adversaries, put yourself at the head of
these proletarians and make yourself the mouthpiece of
their threats, ready, the next moment, to fling yourself
across their path to prevent those threats from being
turned to action. . . .'[2]

Balzac, whose place was never among the political
enthusiasts, summed up the chances of the new régime with
a disillusioned eye. 'Since the Republic won't last more than
three years at the longest, one should snatch time by the
forelock . . .'[3] If he had had money available he would have
followed the example of the speculators in his own novels,
and taken advantage of the prevailing panic to buy up land
and State Bonds on a falling market. 'Before the Republic
can be solidly established', he wrote to Madame Hanska,
'everything will have to be demolished, everything rebuilt.
We have not got the men for such a task. So I think we shall
return pretty quickly to practical politics . . .' About what
form those practical politics should take he would not have
been in agreement with his old friend and comrade, George.
The General Elections were approaching. Sand exerted

1 GEORGE SAND: *Correspondance.* Volume III, pp. 15-16.
2 Ibid., Volume III, pp. 20-2.
3 HONORE DE BALZAC: *Lettres à l'Etrangère.* This letter
was printed by Marcel Bouteron in the *Revue de Paris* for
August 1950.

herself to the utmost in an endeavour to ensure that the People should vote on 'the right side', that is to say, for those candidates who would support the government and the revolution. But the whole of Berry, apart from a few industrial towns, seemed to be as Conservative as La Châtre. George, however, would not even consider the possibility of defeat. She went so far as to establish a dangerous distinction between *majority* and *unanimity*:

> The ideal expression of the sovereignty of all is not majority but unanimity. A day is going to come when reason will have been so completely freed from its blinkers, and men's consciences so wholly released from hesitation, that not a single voice in the Councils of Mankind will be raised against the Truth . . . Every period of History has known these moments of great decision, when Providence sets the stage and gives her sanction to the genuine aspirations and electrical assent of the Masses. There are times when unanimity is arrived at in the face of Heaven, and then, in comparison, mere majority counts as nothing. . . .[1]

In *Bulletin No. 16,* which was to achieve an unpleasant notoriety, she resorted to threats.

> If these elections do not assure the triumph of social truth, if they express only the interests of a caste, and if the trusting loyalty of the People is by violence deceived, then, beyond all doubt, instead of being, as they ought to be, the salvation of the Republic, they will sound its death-knell. Should that happen there can be but one road to safety for those who have already built the barricades, and that will be for them to manifest a second time their will that the decisions of a false National representation shall be adjourned. Does France wish to force Paris into having recourse to this extreme, this deplorable, remedy? . . . I pray God that the answer will be—NO. . . .[2]

This was tantamount to calling the People into the streets. But Madame Sand had no fear. In her eyes,

[1] GEORGE SAND: *Socialisme IV,* in 'La Cause du Peuple', April 23rd, 1848.
[2] GEORGE SAND: *Bulletin de la République,* No. 16.

Government, Press and the Nation were divided into two
camps. In the first stood the purely Political Republicans,
with their adherents, the Monarchists: in the second, the
Socialist Republicans, in whose ranks she had ranged
herself. Ordeal by Battle alone, she thought, could decide
the issue between these two groups. She felt no confidence
in the outcome of the elections, because they were to be
called upon to declare against the 'Communists'—fanciful
and wholly unreal Communists who were said to stand for
the Agrarian Law, for Pillage and for Theft.

> If by Communism you mean a plot to seize dictatorship
> by force, as was said on April 16th, then, assuredly, we
> are not Communists . . . But if by Communism you mean
> the wish and the determination to use every legitimate
> means which the public conscience has seen fit to place at
> our disposal in order to destroy here and now the
> revolting inequality of extreme wealth and extreme
> poverty, and to establish the beginnings of a true
> equality, then we are Communists indeed, and dare to
> admit as much to you who put the question loyally,
> because we believe that you are no less Communists than
> we ourselves. . . .[1]

Meanwhile, the members of the extreme Left (Blanqui,
Cabet, Raspail and, perhaps, Louis Blanc—'great ambitions
in a small body') were preparing a 'coup' for Sunday, April
16th. They suffered a severe setback. The whole of the
National Guard and of the bourgeoisie, as well as a large
proportion of the industrial suburbs, raised the cry of 'Long
Live the Republic!'—'Death to the Communists!'

George Sand to Maurice, April 17th, 1848: I must tell
you exactly what happened, for you will have got no
clear idea from the newspapers. Please keep to yourself
such parts of what I say as are not generally known. Well
then, for the last week three plots, or, rather, four, had
been actually going forward. To begin with, Ledru-
Rollin, Louis Blanc, Flocon, Caussidière and Albert
wanted to force Marrast, Garnier-Pagès, Carnot, Bethmont and all the supporters of a middle-of-the-road re-

[1] GEORGE SAND: 'Revue politique de la Semaine', in *La
Vraie République,* May 7th, 1848.

public out of the Provisional Government. They would
have retained Lamartine and Arago, who, being half-
and-halfers, and preferring power to opinions (of which
they have none) would have thrown in their lot with them
and the People. This plot was firmly based . . . It might
have saved the Republic by proclaiming an immediate
reduction in the poor man's taxes, taking measures
which, without bringing ruin to fortunes honestly
acquired, would have extricated the country from its
financial crisis, and changing the form of the electoral
law, which, as it stands, is bad and can produce only
parish-pump elections—in short, by doing everything
immediately possible to rally the People to the Republic
with which, as the result of bourgeois machinations, they
are already disgusted throughout the length and breadth
of the country, and giving us a National Assembly which
would not have found it necessary to employ force.[1]

And so it was that, from this moment, because they
anticipated a bad outcome to the elections, the more
advanced elements in the government began to conspire
against their own régime. The success of the countermani-
festation strengthened the moderates. Many readers of
Bulletin No. 16 held George Sand's 'incendiary' words to be
responsible for the ensuing disorders. Who, it was asked,
had permitted her to print them in an official Journal?
Naturally enough, neither Ledru-Rollin nor Jules Favre (the
Secretary-General of the *Bulletin*) was prepared to admit
that he had 'ordered' the article in question, and certainly it
was a fact that in conformity with the most solid of
administrative traditions, neither had read it before it went
into type.

George Sand attempted to explain through the medium
of other periodicals that she disapproved of manifestation
and counter-manifestation alike, both what she called the
'Caste' and the 'Sect'. By the 'Caste' she meant the so-called
ruling class, by the 'Sect' that small group of fanatics which
was busy preaching violence. But the fact remained that she
had encouraged the 'Sect', and there was a marked public
outcry against her. On April 20th, the Feast of Fraternity
gave her an opportunity of taking her revenge.

[1] GEORGE SAND: *Correspondance.* Volume III, p. 31.

George Sand to Maurice, April 21st, 1848: A million persons . . . This Feast was History's greatest hour . . . It means more than all the intrigues of the 16th. It proves that the People care nothing about our differences or our subtleties, but are deeply aware of the great issues at stake and are behind them to a man. . . .[1]

The elections were held on April 23rd, and resulted in the return of an aggressively moderate Assembly. The masses, now consulted for the first time, showed themselves to be even more Conservative than the voters on the old property-qualification register. Paris, by establishing universal suffrage, lost its influence over the country constituencies. A street rising in the Capital might contest the legitimacy of a government chosen by limited suffrage, but not one with the majority of the country districts behind it. The Palais-Bourbon had won a victory over the Hôtel-de-Ville. The French had shown themselves willing to accept a political—but not a social—revolution. 'We had foreseen that the results of the elections would be bad', said *La Réforme*, 'but the event, we must admit, has far exceeded our expectations.'

Sand still had freedom of access to the Ministers. On May 10th, while the Assembly was busily engaged with the election of its officials, 'Ledru-Rollin was lying stretched on the lawn of the Chamber of Deputies in the company of Madame Sand. A sentry had been posted to see that they should not be disturbed . . . Lamartine joined them somewhat later . . .'[2] The stout Ledru, who was nothing if not an opportunist, had taken the lesson of the elections to heart, and was now drifting towards Lamartine and the moderates. Louis Blanc was ousted from the government. On May 15th, the workers of Paris did what Madame Sand had advised them to do in *Bulletin No. 16*. Led by two veterans of street-fighting, Barbès and Blanqui, they stormed the Palais-Bourbon, declared the Assembly dissolved, and proclaimed a Socialist government. But the authorities had the alarm sounded, and the National Guard from the richer districts released the imprisoned members. Barbès, and the workman, Albert, were arrested. 'The democrats were victorious over reactionaries and demogogues

---

[1] GEORGE SAND: *Correspondance*. Volume III, pp. 46-7.
[2] MARECHAL DE CASTELLANE: *Journal*. Volume IV, p. 66.

alike.' That was the feeling of Lamartine's friends. The offensive epithet could scarcely be expected to please the friends of Louis Blanc or of George Sand.

She refused to admit that test of strength had been conclusive, and still held that the People would impose their will. Monckton Milnes, a British Member of Parliament (and the future Lord Houghton), happened to be passing through Paris and gave a luncheon party early in May. Among the guests were Sand, Auguste Mignet, Alexis de Tocqueville, Carlotta Marliani and Prosper Mérimée. 'One of the ladies', wrote the latter, 'had remarkably fine eyes which she kept fixed on her plate. She was sitting opposite me, and I had a feeling that her face was vaguely familiar. Finally, I asked my neighbour who she was. It was Madame Sand. I found her much improved in appearance since the old days. We did not, as you may imagine, exchange any words, but we did indulge in a good deal of mutual staring.[1] After luncheon I gave Colonel D—— a cigar, which he went across and offered to her as from himself. She accepted it very graciously. I was careful to keep her at a good cable's length, as sailors say. *Who sups with the devil needs a long spoon.*' Tocqueville, who was unaffected by personal memories, was more especially interested in Sand the 'politician'. Though strongly prejudiced, he fell a victim to the charm of her natural simplicity of speech and behaviour.

> I was much struck by what she said. This was the first time that I had been able to speak directly, and on familiar terms, with someone who could, and would, tell me what was happening in the enemy's camp. Political parties never really know one another. They get to close quarters, they indulge in elbowing, and they come to grips, but they don't *see*. Madame Sand painted for me, in great detail and with unusual vividness, a picture of the conditions in which the Paris workers lived, and explained the nature of their organization, their numbers, their weapons, their plans, their thoughts, their passions, and their terrible determination. I thought the picture exaggerated, but in this, as the future was to show, I was wrong. She seemed to be not a little frightened on her own account at the prospect of a popular victory, and to

[1] PROSPER MERIMEE: *Correspondance générale.* Volume V, pp. 303, 304, 306.

feel pity for *us* and for the fate to which we might have to look forward. 'Do try', she said to me, 'to work on your friends not to drive the People into the streets by a policy of pin-pricks and threats. I, on my side, will do all I can and will preach patience to those with whom I have decided to throw in my lot, because, believe me, if it comes to fighting the whole lot of you will soon be finished and done with.'[1]

This astonishing belief in the triumph of her ideas, at the very moment when they seemed to be in such danger, was a product of her amazing vitality. Feeling herself to be strong, she was convinced that the Socialist Republic was strong, too. In her articles she expressed her sympathy with the Republican Socialists, and her hostility to an immediate Communism 'which would be the very negation of true Communism, since it wishes to proceed by violent means and the destruction of that spirit of fraternity which is the keystone both of Communism and the Gospel'.[2] She thought the moment so fraught with grave issues, that she would not even return to the country to attend the wedding of her dear Titine, which took place on May 6th, 1848.

Of what did that young girl think as she stood with Bertholdi, the victim of a marriage of convenience, in front of the Mayor of Nohant who was none other than that cousin Maurice with whom for so long she had been in love? It is not hard to imagine her grief at the idea of leaving a house within whose walls she had formed such splendid hopes, and, when theatricals were toward, had known the happiness of real success. There had, of course, been moments when she had suffered, but, on the whole, she had had a deal of wonderful fun. To marry this 'brittle old creature' at her side was, she thought, to face the certainty of a life of boredom in a setting of mediocrity.

On May 15th, the storm foretold by George in her talk with de Tocqueville broke. Its occasion was a manifestation on behalf of oppressed Poland, the 'Christ of nations'. Lamartine, ever a prudent Minister, had refused to commit France to a hopeless war, and the world of the Polish émigrés was roused to a white heat of anger against him. Such was the ostensible cause of the outbreak. Actually, it

[1] ALEXIS DE TOCQUEVILLE: *Souvenirs*, 204.
[2] GEORGE SAND: 'Revue politique de la Semaine', *La Vraie République*, May 7th, 1848.

was designed to parade the power of the People, and to impose new elections upon the government. Many of the demonstrators were simple-minded enough to believe the official slogans, and loudly shouted 'Long Live Poland! Long Live the Republic!' Gradually, cries of a different kind made themselves heard: 'Long Live Louis Blanc!' Blanqui led the crowd in an attack on the National Assembly. Lamartine, Ledru-Rollin, and even Barbès, found it impossible to make themselves heard. Blanqui and Louis Blanc worked upon their following to cheer for the Democratic and Socialist Republic. They demanded that an army should be immediately dispatched to Poland. Suddenly the roll of drums was heard beating to arms. The National Guard was moving in to defend the Assembly. The day was lost. Panic seized the crowd. There were cries of 'Down with Barbès!' He was arrested. It was all over.

Where was George on that May 15th? She was one of the crowd in the rue de Bourgogne. She saw an unknown woman leaning from a first-floor window, haranguing the mob, and rousing cheers on her behalf. She asked the name of this heroine, and was told that it was George Sand! According to Maurice, the whole incident was a joke staged by a few idlers. He himself went off to the Ecole Militaire, with Adolphe Duplomb, of Berry, to search for cannon. All he found was beer-bottles. 'What a memorable and mirth-provoking day', he wrote. It is certain that Sand took no active part in the events which marked it. All the same, the newspapers held her responsible, on the ground of her having said in *Bulletin No. 16* that the People had a right to defend the Republic, even if it meant marching against the National Assembly. To this she replied that the *Bulletin* had appeared long before May 15th, and could not have been the immediate cause of the disturbances—which was true.

On the evening of that momentous day, she decided that the cause of the Socialist Republic was lost. She felt only one desire, to get back to Nohant. She waited, however, for two more days, because it was said that she was about to be arrested. She did not wish it to be thought that she was running away. Fully expecting that her house would be searched, she burned all her papers, including her *Journal intime*. But no one thought of interfering with her, and she left Paris, without incident, on the evening of the 17th.

I wanted to give the Law time enough to lay hands on me should it take the view that there were matters between us needing to be cleared up. It seemed unlikely that my friends' fears were well founded, and I could have drawn attention to myself, and gained a reputation for prominence at a cheap rate, had I gone through the motions of taking to my heels. In the event, nobody honoured me with so much as a thought, except, perhaps, a few gentlemen of the National Guard who were indignant at the idea that so dangerous a conspirator had been overlooked.

IV

NOHANT: 1848-1850

There are no principles; there are only events.

Balzac

WHEN ON the evening of May 15th in the rue de Bourgogne she had conjured up a picture of Nohant, it had seemed to her a refuge. The time had come for her to sing small. She would, she decided, run more risks in her country home, where she would be a target for the reactionaries, than in the confusion of the Paris streets where she was now forgotten. Her neighbours were accusing her of every kind of error, every kind of crime.

Here, in this gentle, good, tranquil and romantic Berry, in this countryside which I love so dearly, where I have given proof to the poor and simple that I am well aware of my duty to them, I am looked upon as an enemy to the human race. If the Republic has failed to implement its promises, that is, obviously, because of me.[1]

The story was going round that she had wheedled out of 'Monsieur le duc Rollin' all the vineyards, all the ploughland, and all the pastures of the parish, and that she had had the best of the Deputies imprisoned at Vincennes.

[1] GEORGE SAND: *Souvenirs de 1848*, p. 120.

George Sand to Carlotta Marliani: The effect of my presence here is to hold in check a considerable number of half-wits from La Châtre, whose daily talk is of burning my house to the ground. They lack both physical and moral courage. Whenever they show their faces in these parts, I go among them and they raise their hats. But when they have got to a safe distance, they summon up just enough spunk to raise a cry of 'Down with the Communists!'[1]

Old Aulard, the new Mayor of Nohant, a political adversary but a personal friend, advised her to leave the district until all the rumours and angers should have died down. She left for Tours, and the newspapers broke into a cackle of laughter. 'Where has George Sand got to? . . . We hear from Paris that George Sand has had her male or female nose put out of joint by the events of June, has packed up her furniture, her cigar-cabinet, and the rest of her belongings, and deprived the Capital of her presence, preferring to set up at Tours. All quite simple: just a matter of getting a man round with a pantechnicon.'[2]

Delacroix wrote her a letter thoroughly approving her decision to leave Nohant. 'You might have been accused of building barricades. How right you are when you say that in times like these party spirit is quite incapable of taking a rational line, and that guns and bayonets are the sole argument to which people will listen . . . Your friend Rousseau, who, by the way, never faced fire except when tending the kitchen range, once quoted in an access of bellicosity the remark of some Polish paladin who said, in reference to his turbulent republic: *Malo periculosam libertatem quam quietum servitium*—which being interpreted means: "I prefer a dangerous liberty to a peaceful slavery". I, alas, hold the contrary view, believing that liberty purchased at the cost of pitched battles is not liberty at all, seeing that true liberty consists in the freedom to come and go in peace, to think as one will and eat as one likes, and enjoy a great many other advantages to which political upsets pay no attention. Forgive these reactionary

1 GEORGE SAND: *Correspondance*, Volume III, p. 80.
2 Article by Th. Muret, published in *La Mode*, July 23rd, 1848.

reflections, my dear, and please go on being fond of me in spite of my incorrigible misanthropy. . . .'[1]

As a result of the crushing of the insurrection and the bloody massacres of June, thousands of persons were deported. The Socialist Republic, and, perhaps, Republicanism altogether, of no matter what colour, had been put down. A blood-filled trench had been dug out between workers and bourgeoisie. Sand was in despair, and gave up writing in the newspapers.

> *George Sand to Edmond Plauchut, September 24th, 1848:* You ask which of the papers I am writing for. I have given up writing altogether, for the time being, at least. I cannot speak my mind under siege conditions. It would mean making concessions to the so-called needs of the times, and of that I am incapable. For some time past I have felt bruised, beaten and discouraged. My mind is still sick, and I must wait until it has been cured. . . .[2]

Chopin was in London, talking with increasing spitefulness about the misfortunes of his former mistress. 'She has, recently, been plunging deeper and deeper into mud of every description, and dragging down others with her. She is held to be responsible for the abominable proclamations which were instrumental in stirring up civil strife'. . . .[3]

To her public misfortunes were added painful private troubles. Brault, the tailor, Augustine's father, had recently published a pamphlet, entitled: *One of Our Contemporaries. The Life Story and Intrigues of George Sand.* In this he accused her of having enticed Augustine to Nohant with the object of making her Maurice's mistress, and then, when the girl was hopelessly compromised, of having married her off to the first available man. It was a piece of blackmail, since Brault (who announced the forthcoming appearance of other pamphlets on the same subject) could have had no interest in throwing mud at his own daughter's reputation unless he had hoped to feather his own nest by doing so. George went for advice to the great lawyer, Chaix d'Est-Ange. She asserted that there had never been between her

1 EUGENE DELACROIX: *Correspondance générale.* Volume II, pp. 349-50.

2 GEORGE SAND: *Correspondance.* Volume III, p. 92.

3 *Souvenirs inédits de Frédéric Chopin,* edited by Karlowicz (*Journal:* entry for August 19th, 1848).

son and her adopted daughter anything but an innocent brother-and-sister relationship. 'They were never out of my sight. We lived together in a close family circle.'[1] Chaix d'Est-Ange brought pressure to bear on the tailor, and the second pamphlet never saw the light. But once again Chopin sided with the enemy. "It is a filthy business', he wrote, 'and all Paris is agog. The father has behaved disgracefully, but what he says is no more than the simple truth. So much for the "act of charity" against which I protested as hard as I knew how from the very moment that the young woman entered the house!'[2]

Prince Karol had reached a point at which he felt nothing but hatred for Lucrezia Floriani. To Solange, who was still Chopin's favourite, and constantly received from him gifts of carnations and roses, Sand wrote: 'I cannot bring myself to pay him back in his own coin for all this hatred and rage. I think of him often, and always as of a sick child who has become bitter and unbalanced. . . .'[3]

From the attacks of a hostile world she once again took refuge in work. She resumed her *Histoire de ma Vie,* and, also, on the advice of Rollinat, began to exploit the vein which she had opened up with her novels of the countryside. She started on *La Petite Fadette,* for which she wrote a charming Preface: *Why the Cobbler has returned to his Last.* In this she recorded a conversation with François Rollinat from which the story had emerged.

Still talking together of the Republic of our dreams, and of the Republic with which we had been fobbed off, we reached a spot on the shady road where a bed of wild thyme invites the wanderer to rest.

'Do you remember', said he, 'how we came this way a year ago, and spent a whole evening here? It is in this very place that you told me the story of the *Waif,* and I told you to write it in the easy, conversational style you had used in talking of it?'

'Which was my way of trying to capture the manner of

[1] Unpublished letter from Sand to Chaix d'Est-Ange (July 25th, 1848). Spoelberch de Lovenjoul Collection: Group E. 921, f. 414.

[2] *Souvenirs inédits de Frédéric Chopin,* edited by Karlowicz (August 19th, 1848).

[3] Item No. 6013 in the catalogue of the Auguste Blaizot Library, 51st annual issue (1942).

the spinner from whom I had heard it? Indeed I do, and it seems to me that, since that day, we have both of us grown ten years older.'

'And yet', replied my friend, 'nature has not changed. The night is still unsullied, the stars still twinkle, and the wild thyme smells as sweetly now as it did then . . . We may be afflicted and unhappy, but no one can take from us the sweet delight which is nature's gift to those who love her and her poetry. Since, then, that is the only offering that we can make to the unhappy, let us use art again as once we understood it. Let us sweetly celebrate this sweetest of all poetry, and pour it out, like the sap of some health-giving plant, upon the wounds of humanity.'

'So be it,' I replied; 'let the cobbler return to his last, or the novelist to the sheep-fold. . . .'[1]

This new rustic tale won back the affection of her public. Neither in the Preface nor in any of her articles, had she made the least gesture of recantation so far as her theories were concerned. But she had renounced active politics. From now on, she said, she was prepared to recognize two forms of property—individual ownership which only the mutual understanding of the classes could make tolerable, and collective ownership which she would like to see on as extensive a scale as possible.

George Sand to Joseph Mazzini: Only if all work together—reactionary bourgeoisie, democratic bourgeoisie, and socialists, will the People achieve self-government. The only way to their enlightenment is for these diverse elements to engage continuously in a legal and pacific struggle.[2]

On Christmas Day (December 25th, 1848) Hippolyte Châtiron died at Montgivray. 'He had been a sick man for close on two years, seeking in wine an artificial stimulus. He ate scarcely anything, and was drinking more and more every day . . . Death took him before he realized its approach. . . .'[3]

---

[1] GEORGE SAND: Preface to *La Petite Fadette,* published separately in *Le Spectateur républicain* (September 1848). The novel appeared, on December 1st, 1848, in *Le Crédit.*

[2] GEORGE SAND: *Correspondance.* Volume III, p. 73.

[3] Unpublished letter to Charles Poncy (January 9th, 1849), Spoelberch de Lovenjoul Collection: Group E. 22, f. 3.

In 1849, Augustine presented Bertholdi with a son. Like Marie Dorval's grandson, it was given the name of Georges. Marie, now an old woman, had broken with all her lovers, and devoted herself entirely to her grandchildren. Her daughter, Caroline (the fruit of an affair with Piccini during her young widowhood) had married the actor René Luguet. Their joint endeavours in the theatre met with only small success, and they were soon in the position of having to feed and clothe three children. Merle, who was paralytic, lived in a home. Dorval had to shoulder crushing financial responsibilities. With great courage she embarked on tour after tour, her penniless family being entirely dependent upon such money as she could make 'on the road'. Little Georges was a sickly child, and in order that his grandmother should have him with her when she was working in the South (at Nîmes, Avignon and Marseilles), Sand guaranteed the necessary travelling expenses. He died, however, of brain-fever, and Dorval outlived him for only a year.

René Luguet to George Sand, May 23rd, 1849: Dear Madame Sand—she is dead. That poor, wonderful woman is dead. We are inconsolable. Pity us.

Dear Madame Sand: you loved her dearly, and she admired you much. Let me tell you some part of what she suffered . . . It would be no more than the truth to say that she died of *grief* and *disappointment*. It was neglect that killed her . . . yes . . . neglect . . . A crowd of women nonentities who had remained obscure and unsuccessful for twenty years past, took advantage of the boom period to band themselves together. Money, passions, and the requirements of the majority of Directors, made them powerful. These creatures invaded the theatre: the gutter spilled over on to the stage . . . The poor dear went from theatre to theatre with nothing but her talent for sale, and the so-called 'Directors' merely stared when they heard the name Dorval . . . What did *they* care about her talent! She had lost one or two teeth . . . she was forty years old . . . she dressed in black . . . she could not force her features to express a gaiety she did not feel . . . it was too much to hope that she would prove an attraction to that mingled crowd of dandies and doorkeepers which throngs our theatres at the mere news that *Amanda, Frisette* or *Rose Pompon* is to appear . . . It was just when matters were in this desperate state that our first great tragedy occurred . . . little Georges died.

Poor Marie's life was drained away through two deep wounds—the death of an adored being, and neglect. She was forgotten in the world of the theatre: she was reduced to poverty. That was how things stood on April 10th last. I was at Caen. She was to join me there, but first wanted to make one last effort to make a *little niche* for herself at the Français, and earn five hundred francs a month!—*just enough to buy bread*. Monsieur Seveste, the Director, told her in my presence that it was absurd for her to dream of such a sum, but that he hoped very soon to be able to save three hundred on his lighting expenses, that he would do what he could to overcome the *reluctance* of his Committee, but could promise nothing. So there was our poor Marie, already suffering from two deep knife-thrusts, struck on the head by a brute like that! . . . More than once it was only her angelic sweetness that kept my indignation within bounds. But that interview was the last straw. She started for Caen, but, no sooner was she there, than sickness laid her low. Two hours later her condition had got so much worse that I called in a doctor. His verdict was that she was very seriously ill—a pernicious fever, and an ulcerated liver to boot! . . . It was as though I had heard *myself* condemned to death. I could not believe my eyes. When I looked at that angel of sorrow and patience who lay there never uttering a word of complaint, but smiling sadly at me, as though to say '. . . *You* are with me, Luguet, *you* won't let me die'—it was then, Madame Sand, then, that a lump came into my throat, a great roaring in my ears, and that I cursed God!

Although the doctors had refused to answer for her life if she were moved, I was terrified of her dying so far from Paris, and though, night and day, she called on death in accents that still, in recollection, freeze my blood, I reserved seats in the diligence . . . Next day she was in her own room, and we were standing round her bed. She had been drowsy during the journey, but now the disease reasserted itself, and at one o'clock on May 20th she said— 'I am dying, but I am resigned . . . my daughter, goodbye, my dear, good daughter . . . splendid Luguet.' Those Madame, were her final words; that, Madame, was her final act. She breathed her last with a smile on her lips . . .

Oh! that smile—it has burned itself into my eyes . . .
Dear Madame Sand, my heart has been struck down.
Your letter has given new life to my misery. Adorable
Marie—you were her last and latest poet. I read *Fadette*
aloud at her bedside, and we had a long talk about all the
wonderful books you have written. We wept as we
recalled the many moving scenes that they contain. Then
she spoke to me of you, of your heart . . . Ah! dear
Madame Sand, how deeply you loved Marie, how truly
you understood her spirit, and how sincerely I love you,
and how miserable I am! . . .

I see that I have written a very long letter. I must close
it now, and await the happy day when you and I can talk
together of our unhappy Marie . . . When next I know
that you are in Paris, I hope that you will spare me just
an hour so that I may tell you all the *amazing* things our
angel said to me in those days of pain and melancholy.
. . .[1]

Dorval had sent word to the elder Dumas and to Sandeau
that she would like to see them both again. Dumas hurried
round at once, reassured Marie, who dreaded that she might
be buried in a pauper's grave, and promised to raise the five
or six hundred francs needed to buy her a few feet of earth.
But little Jules came too late to this last meeting. A black
wooden cross was set above her, and on it the words:
MARIE DORVAL: SHE DIED OF GRIEF, were inscribed. All her life long she had been vilified, betrayed
and smirched, a 'victim of art and destiny'. She left behind
her a loved and honoured memory. George Sand generously
provided for her grandchildren, Jacques and Marie Luguet,
who, for many years, spent their holidays at Nohant.

Chopin died on October 17th, without seeing George
again. It was said that he murmured: 'She said that I should
die in no arms but hers', but the stories told about his last
days are so numerous and so contradictory that it is
impossible to be certain. Solange was one of those who
heard the Comtesse Delphine Potocka sing, in a voice
broken by sobs, at the bedside of the dying Chopin. When
the fatal news reached George, she enclosed a lock of his
hair which he had given her in an envelope, on which she

[1] Simone André-Maurois Collection.

wrote the words *'Poor Chopin! October 17th, 1849.'* The words, *Moia bieda'* inevitably come to mind.[1]

Two years later, Alexandre Dumas, the younger, came upon Sand's letters to Chopin somewhere on the Russo-Polish frontier. Chopin's sister had taken them from Paris to Myslowitz, where, fearing the indiscretion of the Customs authorities, she had left them with friends. It was they who, thinking to amuse the young Alexandre, had shown him these passionate epistles written by a French woman about whom they knew nothing.

> *George Sand to Dumas fils, October 7th, 1851:* Since you have had the patience to go through this collection, so much of which consists of unimportant repetitions and it seems to me can be of interest to nobody but myself, you will have realized how much maternal fondness filled nine years of my life. There is nothing secret about it, and there is for me more of pride than embarrassment in having tended and consoled that noble heart which nothing could cure, as though it had belonged to my own child. . . .[2]

Which was true.

Marie d'Agoult, since her breach with Liszt, had been living in Paris. She had made her peace with all her relations (excepting her husband), and was now conducting a political Salon in her 'rose-pink house' in the Champs-Elysées. She was also, under the name of Daniel Stern, publishing a number of solid works: *Essai sur la Liberté: Lettres Républicaines: Esquisses morales.* Having embarked on *l'Histoire de la Revolution de 1848,* she thought it might be a good thing to renew acquaintanceship with George Sand, who as an actress in the drama, could give her much valuable help by telling what she could remember of the happenings of that period. The two women had not been on speaking terms for eleven years.

> *Marie d'Agoult to George Sand, October 11th, 1850:* A mutual friend[3] recently gave me a message purporting to come from you (but did it really?) which touched my heart. Even now I scarcely dare surrender to the

---

[1] Two Polish words, meaning *my grief,* or *my sorrow.* This envelope is now the property of Madame Aurore Lauth-Sand.

[2] Spoelberch de Lovenjoul Collection: Group E. 882, f. 11.

[3] Emile de Girardin.

happiness it brought me. If you were alone I would set off at once in order to hear from your own lips whether, in fact, our dear and broken friendship has left you with some feelings of regret . . . to learn whether you feel, as I do, that it had a quality of lastingness which nothing can destroy. The world at large maintains that there were wrongs on both sides. If you think that I was in any way guilty, I am prepared to admit it, though my own view is that we both of us had but one thing with which to reproach ourselves—our youth. We were young in those days, that is to say, credulous, exigent and hot-headed. In our simple-minded way we believed a great deal of false, or irresponsible, gossip. Our lively affection seemed to us to have run on to the rocks, and that disaster found expression in violent words. But I have long retained a conviction which nobody can take from me. It is this— that if for an hour, if for a minute, at any time during those melancholy years, we could have looked into one another's heart, we should have found beneath the din of mutual anger a true and shared affection, a deep and indestructible love. Nevertheless, I hesitated when I took up my pen to start this letter. Would that old feeling of affection which I have for you still have any value in your eyes? Alas! time may have made me a better woman, though, I fear, a very much less attractive one! The golden-haired Péri has left her wings I know not where: the fairy Princess had lost her sky-blue draperies: the divine light has faded from Arabella's brow. All that now remains of those many visions conjured up by your genius is just a woman, with more courage than strength, who walks with slow steps along a dreary road, with, as her only, and only too familiar, companion—regret for dead hopes . . . Still, whatever the risk I run in writing to you like this, I have resolved to do so. You will, I am sure, realize that I speak seriously and with sincerity. You have occupied too great a place in my life for me to do less. As I write that dear name 'George', I seem to feel my youth revive. My doubts vanish. I hear a voice saying that our friendship will be reborn, that it will be more tender and more strong than it ever was in the past. I have never so longed for anything. And you, George, how say you?[1]

[1] Unpublished. Spoelberch de Lovenjoul Collection: Group E. 872.

Arabella was of the opinion that she had been magnanimous, and Dr. Piffoël's reply came as a sad disappointment.
It went back again over all the old ground.

Marie d'Agoult to George Sand, October 23rd, 1850:
Why, my dear George, do you compel me to talk again of
all my old resentments, to recall bitter memories, to go
into hateful details, when all I want is to shake hands,
and so wipe away the last trace of the injuries we did one
another? Why do you insist on what you call the *enigma*
of my behaviour? Cannot you realize, *a priori,* that a
woman as proud as I am, and accustomed to controlling
the movements of her heart, would never have taken the
initiative in a matter of this kind, unless she felt that she
had as much to forgive as you have? I am conscious of
an almost invincible repugnance at the idea of facing
once again all the charges you have brought against me,
because I know that to do so will, so far from bringing us
together, still further estrange us. Still, *since you have
never really understood the causes either of my anger or
of my silence,* I feel constrained to explain my motive in
acting as I did. The individual who, at that time, had the
greatest influence over me[1] had made me swear that I
would never speak to you of him. He seemed to be afraid
of the moment when you and I might discuss openly
together a *very delicate question.* I felt bound to make the
generous gesture of so promising, and I kept my word, at
very great cost to myself.

Certain serious and clearly defined charges—to which
public opinion and the attitude of *my* friends, as well as
of some of yours, gave considerable weight—were the
cause of those first outbursts of temper in Italy. There
was in them a note of irony *which was not mine.* It was
in strong contrast to my true feelings, and, as soon as I
got back to Paris, I saw how unjust it had been. At the
very moment when we two were trying to come together
in friendship, Liszt showed me a letter that you had
written to him. I have kept it. Its references to me were
cruel and severe. Also, if you will forgive me for saying
so, they were somewhat *treacherous,* seeing that the letter
was addressed to a man with whom I was passionately in
love, and had the effect of diminishing such affection and

[1] Franz Liszt.

esteem as he might have for me . . . But why must we bring up this unhappy past again? . . . The way you now write is sufficient proof that we are neither of us now in the same mood as once we were. You have forgotten me, you say, but I have never forgotten you . . . It seems that you are taking a rather high-and-mighty attitude towards me, I might almost say (if you will excuse the word) a *priestly* attitude. You want to be in a position to say *Absolvo te*. But mark this: I was brought up in, and still feel the effect of, the mental climate of the eighteenth century. I have become a believer in equality to an extent of which you can have no idea, and I am not prepared to admit that anybody has the right of granting absolution, or the privilege of exercising charity. Since the days of June I cannot see how there can be any relationship between us other than one of mutual amnesty, for the simple reason that you refuse to confess that you were ever in the wrong, and because you feel no emotional promptings where I am concerned . . . What, then, am I to do?

You may, perhaps, be right, and I regret now that I was too willing to believe friends who were animated by certain well-meaning illusions. They told me that you looked back on our old friendship with feelings of regret, and I was simple-minded enough to think that that explained everything. They reminded me of the cordial and kindly way in which formerly the artist George had extended the hand of affection to a 'fugitive Princess'. I concluded, therefore, that it was for me to take the first step . . . I knew that your suffering had been different from, but no less profound than, my own. That is why I have, inopportunely as I now see, broken in upon your peaceful retreat, first with a gush of ill-timed emotion, and now with a series of disgruntled recriminations. . . .[1]

George was not averse to the idea of a partial reconciliation. But before that could be brought about she was determined to empty the abscess, to throw light on all the points that were still obscure.

Marie d'Agoult to George Sand, October 28th, 1850: You really are a very much better woman than I am, not

[1] Unpublished. Spoelberch de Lovenjoul Collection: Group E. 872.

THE REVOLT OF THE ANGELS

426

to have taken offence at a letter which I, in your place, should probably have found supremely irritating. You have expressed yourself with that simplicity and frankness which there should always be between us, and have made it possible for me to look forward to seeing you again in a mood of joy and trust.

It would not be quite accurate to say that I believe you to have played a *double part* between Liszt and me, though I am not sure that any other woman would share my hesitation (you will agree about that when, some day, in intimate and easy converse at your fireside or at mine, I tell you the whole story). I alternately believed and doubted. I behaved in friendship in precisely the way I had so long behaved in love, admitting and rejecting, almost simultaneously, opposed and hopelessly irreconcilable certainties. Those two letters of mine were written at a time when your situation as between Bocage, Mallefille and Chopin, which had been painted to me in the most odious colours, had the effect of tilting my thoughts to the side of *treachery*. This does not excuse, it merely explains them. I was being neither wayward nor outlandish in my attitude. I did not even want to hurt you. I knew perfectly well that the person to whom I was writing had a deep fondness for you (not for the world would I have spoken in that way to your enemies!). I had been hurt, and I sought relief from pain without troubling to think how my conduct might affect others. Those two letters deserved no better fate than to be pitched in to the fire.

Things have completely changed since the days when Liszt 'forbade' me to speak. He has now unbosomed himself utterly to the person with whom he had always said he would do no such thing. The breach between him and the poor woman to whom he once set himself to give advice is final. I now no longer feel myself bound by the promise I gave so long ago. I am very much of the opinion that if I could put into your hands the clue which, from the date of our first meeting in 1835, leads through such a veritable labyrinth of intrigues, misunderstandings and doubts, you would feel and judge all that has happened as I myself do. If our friendship is destined never to revive, the fault will lie not in the past but in the present and the future. I lately mentioned the whole matter to our 'reconciler', and confess that I am not entirely unapprehensive. In many ways—and those the most important ones—you and I are much alike. I believe that our *ideals* are, to all intents and purposes, the same. But in practical affairs, in the day to day routine of our two lives, in our tastes, in our habits, in our minor views and interests, and in the nature of our respective circles, there are many contrasts which leap to the eye, and to which you, I think, attach much greater importance than I do. If you happen to meet in my house someone whose looks you do not like, or notice on some of my silver spoons an armorial crest which from indifference, a wish to save money, or dislike of seeming to behave like a coward, I have not had removed; if I do not approve the methods of some of your political friends etc. etc. . . . you will be shocked. If somebody, in the course of a visit to me, happens to say something stupid, you will hold me responsible. Finally, if, from having long lived a lonely existence and being driven in upon myself, I may seem sometimes to be less forthcoming than I mean to be, you will assume that I am mistrustful and deliberately cautious in my behaviour. It is all this, dear George, that makes me somewhat nervous, though not so much so as to prevent me from wishing to attempt the conquest of the Promised Land. . . .[1]

The truth of the matter was that a renewal of friendship was now impossible. Too many words, too many letters had been spoken and written. Each knew what her rival and her enemy was thinking. Excessive frankness is never forgiven. Its recipient is disturbed by the evidence of a too-piercing eye, by a comment which was cruel when it was spoken and may be cruel again. There can be no friendship without confidence, and esteem, even when feigned, does more to ensure it than an edged sincerity which, only too often, is no more than the expression of ill-humour or of spite.

Sand's children changed scarcely at all. Solange and her monumental mason continued to oscillate between passionate devotion and desperate quarrels. The Hôtel de Narbonne had been sold at a very low price by Order of the Court, 'at the suit, action and representation' of certain creditors in respect of unpaid interest on the mortgage. Since the daughter had lost her dowry through her own

[1] Unpublished. Spoelberch de Lovenjoul Collection: Group E. 872.

foolishness, her mother generously undertook to provide the couple with an annual income of three thousand francs, which was a heavy burden for her to shoulder. On May 10th, 1849, a little girl, Jeanne Clésinger, was born under Casimir's roof at Guillery. The stonehewer had been awarded a medal of the First Class at the Salon of 1848, and, a year later, received a decoration. Solange 'allowed herself to be caught up in the turbulent eddies of Paris life'. She entertained writers and actors to dinner. She had horses, a carriage, and an English coachman. God only knew how the bills were paid!

Maurice, still vacillating, always blowing hot and cold, was talking of making a home of his own, but his plans seemed never to get beyond the dream stage. 'But *of course,* I didn't look on this idea of yours of getting married in a tragic light'—his mother wrote to him on December 21st, 1850 . . . 'What nonsense to say that I reproach you for the past! I reproach you for nothing. All I did was to talk to you *about* the past . . .' She advised him, if he were really looking for a wife, to enlarge the circle of his Paris acquaintances, and to get to know people of different types. 'How about being introduced to Madame d'Agoult who entertains the fine flower of the intellectual world—that would be something quite new for you? There have been overtures of peace between us, and although I do not wish to see much of her myself, that is no reason why you should not meet her. She would receive you with open arms, for she is longing to be repatriated . . . She has daughters, and almost certainly fills her house with young people. One new acquaintance leads to others . . .'[1] All she asked of Maurice was that he should not make up his mind until he had seriously considered all the possibilities. Marriage was a step of the utmost importance, for her as well as for him, because if she did not get on with her daughter-in-law, she would have to leave Nohant. Made wise by experience, she warned her son that the only way to have a happy home life was to bend the whole of his will to that end, and not rest contented with mere vague good intentions. She preached fidelity—which may seem strange, coming from her, but the fidelity she had in mind was that based on true love, the fidelity on which her doctrine of the sexual relationship had always been based.

[1] Unpublished. Spoelberch de Lovenjoul Collection: Group E. 922, f. 104.

To marry without love is to serve a life-sentence in the galleys. I heard you say not so long ago that you thought yourself to be incapable of loving anybody *always,* and could give no guarantee that you would be faithful to your marriage vows. If you really mean that, then do not get married at all, because, if you do you will, in the long run, become a cuckold, and deservedly so. If you married in that state of mind you would merely be sharing your life with a brutalized victim, a jealous fury, or a dupe for whom you could feel nothing but contempt. When one truly loves one is quite certain that one will be faithful. One may be wrong, but one *believes* it; the vows one makes are made in good faith, and one is happy for as long as one remains true to them. If an exclusive love cannot last a lifetime (and I have never found any satisfactory proof that it can), it does at least give many happy years so long as the belief that such a thing is possible persists . . . On the day when I see you sure of yourself, I shall cease to worry. . . .[1]

Maurice brought to Nohant many young men of his own age, fellow-students and political friends. Several of them— Eugène Lambert, who painted cats, Alexandre Manceau, the engraver, Victor Borie, the journalist, Emile Aucante, the lawyer, settled down there for long periods. Sand gave them a permanent place in her life, and ended her letters to Eugénie Duvernet with the words: 'Maurice, Lambert and Borie send love and greetings to you both.' Relays of these young men used to turn up at Nohant. *Sand to Maurice:* 'Lambert left this morning, and should be with you tonight. He has been charming, devoted, and full of attention to me in our lonely existence. Now it is the turn of Manceau, who is also a dear. . . .'[2]

And so it was that four young men rivalled one another in their eagerness to give satisfaction to their illustrious hostess, and became her slaves. Aucante, shrewd and subtle-minded, was her man of affairs, and acted for her in all her negotiations with publishers. He was later employed on a salary basis. Lambert, for long her favourite, forfeited some of her affection when he decided that his career as a painter necessitated long stays in Paris. She insisted that

1 Spoelberch de Lovenjoul Collection: Group E. 932, f. 97.
2 Ibid., Group E. 932, f. 115.

Nohant should be regarded as the hub of the universe. He felt that he had been harshly treated, and put his grievance into words.

Eugène Lambert to Emile Aucante, May 30th, 1852: Madame Sand ends her letter with a *cruel* sentence . . . I she'd many tears, my friend, when I received a reproach which I had done nothing to deserve. If I leave Madame Sand for two or three months, the reason is that my future demands my presence elsewhere. That is what I told her in my reply: 'I have *got* to work from time to time in Paris, otherwise it will be all up with me.' I put the whole of my heart into that letter, and she could find nothing to say in answer to it. So all is over: ten years thrown to the winds just because stayed away a little too long. I may be wrong, but it does seem to me that she ought to love others a little more for their sakes, and a little less for her own. *Nobody knows better how to love, but nobody more quickly reduces those whom she does love to a state of utter prostration.*

June 4th, 1852: I shall spend all my summers at Nohant, and as soon as she wants me to occupy one of the rooms, I am at her orders. She has only to let me know . . . But I must, above all things, keep my liberty . . . A tiny cloud has passed across our sky, but large enough to cast a chill on her feelings. Mine remain unchanged. Never in my life shall I forget what she has done for me. . . .[1]

In 1850 Manceau had been promoted to the position of favourite, and continued to occupy it. He had just the qualities needed to satisfy in Madame Sand her political prejudices and her slightly dubious maternal instincts. He was thirteen years her junior. He had weak lungs, a quick intelligence, a handsome face and a proletarian back-ground—his father being one of the caretakers at the Luxembourg. He was an engraver on steel, and very much of an artist by temperament. He was first employed by George Sand as Secretary, but very soon became her confidential adviser. She managed to keep the peace between him and Lambert, but it was for ever trembling in the balance. *Manceau's Diary for 1852:* 'Manceau and

1 Unpublished letters. Spoelberch de Lovenjoul Collection: Group E. 953, ff. 139 and 142.

Lambert wanted to fight but Madame made them shake hands . . .' When Sand went to Paris, she planned to put up at Manceau's lodging, in spite of protests from Maurice, who was afraid that such behaviour might provoke gossip, in spite of his mother's mature years.

> *George Sand to Maurice, December 24th, 1850:* I will put up wherever you like, though Manceau's place would suit me better than yours . . . There could not be any 'talk' if you were with me. You could sleep in his studio. There would not be any even if you did not . . . Why, no one but the porter would know that I was there . . . For a young man to lend his apartment to a lady from the country is an everyday occurrence, especially when she is forty-six years of age! You could lend yours tomorrow to Titine, even if you were *not* away. So long as you slept under a different roof, nobody would so much as raise a whisper. . . .[1]

The Bertholdis were living at Ribérac, where 'the Pole' had been appointed Collector of Taxes. The fair Titine, however, who was bored in Périgord, and had high ambitions, paid frequent visits to Paris, where she stayed at the Hôtel du Helder. Her absence from Nohant was the more regretted, since private theatricals were a popular pastime there, and candidates for the star female parts (in which youth was required) were lacking.

> *George Sand to Augustine Bertholdi, January 15th, 1850:* You are very much missed, too, for the acting. Lambert and Maurice realize that they have lost their pearl among *ingénues*. Madame Fleury is elegant, and can make up young, but she is too fearful and mannered. Manceau—you know whom I mean, Maurice's and Lambert's friend—is now our leading man. He is equally good for serious parts and comedies, and is really tip-top when it comes to making dresses, designing scenery, and seeing to the make-up. You have no idea how excellent their pantomimes are now. If only you were here to play Columbine they would be perfect. But none of the women can make anything of her, and we have been

[1] Unpublished fragments from a letter only partially published by Maurice: Cf. *Correspondance*, part III, pp. 224-8, and the Lovenjoul Collection: Group E. 922, f. 105.

reduced to using a man made up as a girl, and
burlesquing the part. . . .[1]

And so it came about that Harlequin and Columbine
were now taking the place in George's life of the parts once
played by Ledru-Rollin and Louis Blanc. As always, when
storms threatened, she had made Nohant her homeport,
and, once the hostile feelings of her neighbours were
appeased, had found there a peaceful existence, the beauty
of heathland and irises, the quarrels and gaiety of young
men. With Manceau's health to watch over, her son to love,
her house to run, and twenty pages of a novel to complete
each night, she was once again leading a normal existence.

V

OUR LADY OF SUCCOUR

IN THE meantime, Louis-Napoleon Bonaparte had been
elected President of the Republic. The name had worked its
old magic. The new Head of the State was no stranger to
George Sand. In his youth he had been a Liberal, and even
a Carbonaro. Round about 1838 she had met him in a Paris
drawing-room, and a shared hatred of Louis-Philippe had
drawn them together. When the young Prince's plotting had
landed him in the prison of Ham, he had spent his time in
devising a rather muddled 'system' in which Order and
Revolution, Socialism and Prosperity, Liberalism and
Authority, had all played a part. In 1844 he had written a
pamphlet on the extinction of pauperism. Louis Blanc had
visited him in prison, and had made him the subject of an
article which Sand had published in *l'Eclaireur de l'Indre*.
The Prince knew that Madame Sand was interested in
him, and had sent her word to the effect that if she could
make the journey to Ham it would be a 'red-letter day for
one who is living in a condition of excommunication'. She
did not go, but wrote a letter in which, very politely, she

1 Unpublished. Simone André-Maurois Collection.

affirmed her staunch adherence to republican principles.
'You must not take it ill that we are careful to protect
ourselves against the charm which your character, your
intelligence, and the situation in which you find yourself,
exercise upon us . . .'[1] She could, she said, recognize no
Sovereign but the People—'no miracle, no incarnation of
the popular genius in a single individual . . .' Louis-
Napoleon answered with equal frankness.

> *Fortress of Ham, January 24th, 1845:* Madame, I trust
> you to believe me when I say that you could give me no
> finer title than that of Friend, because it implies an
> intimacy which I should be proud to know existed
> between us. You, Madame, who have a man's qualities
> without a man's faults, cannot be guilty of injustice
> towards me. . . .[2]

She was, at that time, tempted to believe in the sincerity
of the young Bonaparte. Her friends warned her against
him, but, when he was elected President, she published in
La Réforme an article which was far from hostile. 'In
rejecting the favourite of the Assembly,[3] the People were
voicing a protest, not against the Republic, which they
need, but against the form of Republic with which the
Assembly has saddled them. Let there be no doubt about it,
the greatest merit of Louis Bonaparte is that he has played
no part under the bourgeois Republic. . . .'[4] She found a
certain pleasure in the defeat of those 'moderates' on whom
she had lavished her warnings. To her publisher, Jules
Hetzel, she wrote:

> I have recovered my calmness of mind . . . This change
> has been brought about in me by the spectacle of the
> People registering their votes for Louis Bonaparte. I felt
> in some sort resigned when I found myself in the
> presence of this, their expressed will. It is as though they
> had said: 'This is as fast as we will go, and we will choose
> our own road.' So I have resumed my own particular

---

[1] GEORGE SAND: *Correspondance.* Volume II, p. 328.

[2] Letter of Louis-Napoleon Bonaparte to George Sand,
published in the *Figaro* in 1897.

[3] General Cavaignac.

[4] GEORGE SAND: 'Sur le général Cavaignac', an article
quoted by Wladimir Karénine. Volume IV, p. 166.

task, like a workman returning to his job, and have made good progress with my *mémoires*. It is an undertaking which brings me much pleasure and no fatigue. . . .[1]

In November 1851 she paid a visit to Paris in order to attend the rehearsals of her play, *Le Mariage de Victorine*, which was produced at the Gymnase on the 26th of that month. Solange attended the opening performance accompanied by her husband, and her 'protector', the Comte d'Orsay. The Clésinger household kept moving backwards and forwards from separation to reconciliation, from reconciliation to separation. In the following year, a Court Judgment finally put an end to the stormy domestic career of these married enemies. Lady Blessington had died in 1849, and Alfred d'Orsay, who was one of the most powerful influences behind the new régime, attached himself to the young Solange, and extended his protection, indirectly, to the mother of his 'friend'.

Everybody was talking about the probability of a coup d'Etat. Who was there to oppose it? The middle classes?— they were monarchists: the workers?—why should they defend an Assembly which had ordered the troops to fire on them? On December 1st, Emmanuel Arago said to Sand: 'If the President delays much longer before staging a coup d'Etat, it will be because he does not know when luck is with him. Nothing, at the moment, would be easier.'[2] That evening she went to the circus with Solange and Manceau. As they passed the Elysée Palace on their way home at one o'clock in the morning, they noticed that the gate of the courtyard was shut. A single sentry was on duty. The silence was unbroken. The street lamps shone on the greasy, slippery roadway. 'Well, anyway, it is not for tomorrow,' said Sand with a laugh. She slept soundly all that night.

Next morning, December 2nd, Manceau told her: 'Lamoricière and Cavaignac are confined at Vincennes. The Assembly has been dissolved.' The news left her unmoved. The Republic which was now on its deathbed had long ceased to be hers. The streets were quiet, but that evening at the Gymnase *Le Mariage de Victorine* was played to empty benches. 'So complete is my self-control at the moment,'

[1] Unpublished letter in the possession of Madame Bonnier de la Chapelle.

[2] GEORGE SAND: *Journal*, published in *Souvenirs et Idées*, p. 80.

said George to a friend, 'that nothing can any longer arouse my indignation. I regard the spirit of reaction as a blind fatality which only time and patience will conquer.' She spent the evening sitting beside her fire and listening for some sign of noise in the streets. 'Nothing—a silence as of the tomb: a silence bred of imbecility and terror'.[1] For some days she hoped that the new master would make some attempt to bring reconciliation to the French nation.

> *George Sand to Jules Hetzel, December 24th, 1851:*
> Some there are who thought that between the too recent and too-little-likely-to-last victory of socialism, and what has occurred in the course of the present month, there might be a middle term—a Constitutional Republic. You can see for yourself that such was not the wish of the People, and the explanation of their attitude is very simple. Extreme suffering demands extreme measures, even though those measures may be the product of quackery. The People prefer the unknown to the known, magic to palliatives . . . If the Man of the Moment has not been bereft of his senses, surely he will see that his strength lies in them? Today, he is the only man in a position to be strong, because he alone can unite the six, seven, or eight million votes, whether extorted or not, which he will receive. . . .[2]

But the first months of the new régime were bloody and tyrannical. As in the days of the White Terror, the *Ultras* demanded that the Prince should veil the statues of Mercy and Pity, that 'he should show himself to be a man of bronze, inflexible and just', that 'he should sweep through the century wielding a sword of harsh severity'. All that remained faithful to the Republic was brutally eliminated. Official repression was made worse by local acts of vengeance. 'One half of France is busy denouncing the other', wrote George Sand. As a result of decisions against which there could be no appeal, decisions which had been inspired by anonymous slanders, many poor wretches were imprisoned, transported to Africa, or sent to Cayenne. In the Province of Berry panic reigned. Several of the old Nohant circle were already in captivity, other were marked down for transportation. Pierre Leroux, Louis Blanc,

1 GEORGE SAND: *Journal*, p. 86.
2 Unpublished letter. Bonnier de la Chapelle Collection.

Ledru-Rollin, Victor Borie, went into voluntary exile. It was said that Sand was to be arrested. She refused to flee. On the contrary, she sought an interview with Louis-Napoleon.

Actually, she was in no danger. The prince-president respected her. All the same, she insisted on having an audience. She wanted to plead the cause of her friends. Maupas, the Prefect of Police, sent her a safe-conduct. On January 25th, she went to Paris and wrote to the Prince.

> I have always looked upon you as a man inspired by the genius of socialism . . . Deeply imbued with a sense of almost religious trust, I should regard it as a crime to strike a discordant note in all this vast acclamation by uttering a cry of reproach against Heaven, against the Nation, and against the man whom God has raised up, and the People have accepted. . . .[1]

He replied in his own hand on official Elysée notepaper: 'Madame, I shall be charmed to receive you on any day next week that you may like to name, about three o'clock . . .'[2] She prepared a long letter in which she set down what she feared she would not have the time to tell him by word of mouth. It was an appeal for mercy.

> Prince, I am no Madame de Staël. I have neither her genius nor that pride with which she set herself to fight against the twin faces of genius and power . . . Nevertheless, I approach you, greatly daring. Prince, the friends of my childhood and of my old age, those who have been my brothers and my adopted children, are in confinement or exile. The weight of your hand lies heavy on all who have assumed, who have accepted, who have been loaded with, the title of republican socialists . . . Prince, I cannot permit myself to discuss politics with you. To do so would be ridiculous on my part. But, from the depths of my ignorance and my powerlessness, I cry to you, with tears in my eyes—'Conqueror, enough, enough! Spare the strong as well as the weak . . . Be gentle, be human, as you wish to be. So many innocent, so many unhappy people have need of gentleness and humanity! Ah, Prince! this word *deportation*, this

---

[1] GEORGE SAND: *Correspondance*. Volume III, p. 264.
[2] Printed by Wladimir Karénine in *George Sand*. Volume IV, p. 179.

mysterious penalty, this eternal exile under foreign skies, is not of *your* invention. If only you knew what consternation it brings to the coolest heads, to the least politically involved of men . . . and preventive detention, which means that the sick, the dying, and those in prison, are herded together on straw, in foul air and a freezing temperature! Think of the anxiety felt by mothers and daughters who know nothing of reasons of State. Think of the dazed amazement of peaceable workmen who say: 'Are people to be thrown into prison who have neither killed nor stolen? Shall we all find ourselves there—we who were so glad to give him our votes? Ah, Prince!— my dear Prince of long ago, hearken to the man within, to the man you truly are, the man who can never, for the sake of governing, consent to be reduced to an abstract entity. Politics can achieve great things I do not doubt, but the heart alone can work miracles. Listen to your heart!

An amnesty, my Prince, an amnesty!—and may it be soon! If you will not listen to my words, what matters it to me that I have made one supreme effort before my death? But I feel that such an effort as I can make will not be unpleasing to God, will not sully in me the spirit of human liberty, that, above all, it will not have made me wholly undeserving of your esteem, which I value far more than length of days and a quiet end. . . .[1]

Louis-Napoleon took both her hands in his. He was deeply moved by her plea for an amnesty, by her denunciation of those acts of personal vengeance which were using politics as a pretext. He told her that he had the greatest respect for her character, that he would grant anything she might ask for her friends. He sent her, with his personal recommendation, to Persigny, the Minister of the Interior, and from him she obtained an order of release for many of her Berry intimates. He told her that the Prefect of the Indre had behaved like a brute. It is always easy for Authority to disavow the actions of its subordinates, and the task of the executive agent is never productive of a bed of roses.

A long period followed which does honour to the name of George Sand, who struggled with courage and tenacity to

[1] GEORGE SAND: *Correspondance*. Volume III, pp. 262-70.

win mercy for the unfortunate. It was a doubly thankless task. By pressing her demands she ran the risk of exasperating the Central Power, and the mere fact that she was engaged in parleying with Authority drew down upon her the blame of her republican friends. Not that she had been in any way false to her convictions. To the Minister, Persigny, she said: 'I am a Republican: but that does not alter the fact that in 1848 I spent many hours in this very office where you sit now, preaching mercy to those whom you have overturned.' To the Republicans she maintained that she was unshakably loyal to their—and her—principles, and that she would continue to compromise herself on behalf of those who now heaped calumnies upon her. 'I feel no disgust at the thought of my duty, which, as I see it, consists above all in pleading with the strong in the interests of the weak, with the conquerors in the interests of the conquered—no matter who conquerors and conquered may be, and irrespective of my own convictions . . .' The essence of her attitude was—'You may proceed against men for what they do, but not for what they think. There should be complete freedom of opinion.' In this contention she found an ally in the President's cousin, Prince Napoleon-Jérôme ('Plonplon'), to whom the Comte d'Orsay had introduced her, and who became her very true friend. This Jacobin, this *enfant-terrible* of the Bonaparte family, this 'Prince of the Mountain', came into the open as champion of the 'vile mob' against Thiers, thereby winning the esteem of advanced opinion. He was on intimate terms with his cousin, Louis-Napoleon, with whom he could take unheard-of liberties. His support, therefore, was very valuable to George, and she saw a great deal of him. *Diary, February 8th, 1852* (unpublished): 'Luncheon with Napoleon Bonaparte. Manceau kept the stub of his cigar and the dregs of his glass of brandy, saying—"who knows a day may come . . . How like his uncle he looks". . . .'[1]

For many months Sand spent most of her time in running from Minister to Minister, from Prince to Prefect, saving the lives of sick prisoners, securing assistance for their families, stopping deportations, sending books and money to the exiled, drawing up petitions in such a way as to safeguard the self-respect of their signatories, snatching four young soldiers who had been condemned to death from the very clutches of the firing-squad. The Communists

[1] Bibliothèque nationale: Department of Manuscripts.

called her 'The Saint of Berry'. To the proscribed Marc Dufraisse she was 'Our Lady of Succour'. Alfred d'Orsay wrote to her—'You are a much-loved woman, in addition to being the one outstanding man of our times.' When she found too many obstacles in her way, she thought nothing of making a further approach to the President in person:

> I trust that you will make it clear to all that you were speaking the truth when you said to me—*I do not persecute beliefs, nor punish men because of what they think* . . . But until such time as the amnesty promised by your true friends is granted, you should see to it that your generosity is known throughout the country. It is important that you should realize what the People, by whose will you occupy your present position, are saying: 'He *wants* to do the right thing, but is served by cruel men. He is not master in his own house. Our will has been thwarted. We wanted him to be all-powerful but he is not.' . . .[1]

She continued to believe in the good faith of the former prisoner of Ham, now the sleep-walker of the Elysée.

> *George Sand to Jules Hetzel, February 20th, 1852:* I am convinced, and shall remain convinced, that the President is a most unfortunate man, the victim of error and of the overriding necessities laid upon him by the end he envisages. Circumstances, in other words the ambitions of a party, have forced him into a position at the very heart of the storm. He flatters himself that he has it under control, but he is already half submerged, and I very much doubt whether, at the moment, he is fully aware of what he is doing. . . .[2]

After he had been made Emperor by the all-but unanimous decision of the country, she saw no more of him. Thenceforward, whenever she needed support in high places, she made her approach through the Empress, Prince Napoleon, or the Princesse Mathilde. Her behaviour throughout this difficult period was unfailingly fine, dignified and generous-minded. For a few weeks between the months of March and May 1848, she had let her

---

[1] GEORGE SAND: *Correspondance*. Volume III, pp. 290-1.
[2] Ibid., Volume III, p. 298.

passions run away with her. After the coup-d'Etat, she
controlled them in the interests of charity.

> *Diary, entered up by Manceau, December 5th, 1852:*
> Proclamation of the Empire at Nohant . . . Napoleon III,
> Emperor of the French . . . The whole household
> attended the ceremony, dressed in their best. After it was
> over, we went home. Work. Madame retired at half-past-
> eleven. *Pressoir.*'[1] Lambert leaves tomorrow.[2]

VI

PUPPETS

IN THIS way did George Sand fall on her feet like a
fortunate and nimble cat. Authority was handling her with
kid gloves. Her credit with the régime was high. She had
emerged from the rough-and-tumble if not untouched, at
least from this time forth untouchable. But she had suffered
a violent shock. Once again the Quest of the Absolute had
resulted for her in a painful disappointment.

Defeat is the time for play-acting. In the spiritual
confusion of the years which followed the disaster of 1848,
George Sand owed her salvation to the theatre. She had
always loved it: it was in her blood. At Nohant, ever since
the Chopin era, there had been a succession of pantomimes
and plays, all more or less improvised on the spur of the
moment. Then, in 1848, Maurice had set up a puppet
theatre. He himself carved the dolls from lime roots, and
his mother dressed them with no less wit than taste.

> *George Sand to Augustine Bertholdi, December 1848:*
> Maurice and Lambert have built a puppet theatre which

---

[1] *Le Pressoir* is a drama of country life on which George
Sand was then working. It was produced at the Gymnase on
September 13th, 1853.

[2] Unpublished. Bibliothèque nationale: Department of Manuscripts.

is really a marvel of ingenuity. There are arrangements for changing the scenes, and for displaying vistas, forests, moonlight and sunset effects, transparencies—it is all really most charming and cleverly contrived. They have constructed about twenty characters, and make this little group of puppets talk and gesticulate in the most amusing fashion. They write the plays themselves, and some of them are really quite good. They have even tried their hands at melodramas of the deepest dye . . . There are heaps of costumes for all the members of our wooden company.[1]

All the characters of the Italian Commedia dell'Arte were represented, as well as a hundred others invented at Nohant: Balandard, the Manager of the Company, an attractive person, though somewhat formal in his frock-coat and white waistcoat; Bassinet, the country policeman; Bamboula, the Negress; Colonel Vertébral, and the Comtesse de Bombrecoulant, with her generous display of bosom. The costumes were perfect: starched ruffs, embroideries, feathered hats. The upper parts of the bodies were covered in kid, and this allowed the ladies of the party to appear in low-necked gowns and the men to wrestle stripped to the waist.

In 1851, George Sand had a real theatre constructed in the former billiard-room of the Château. It was to be a surprise for Maurice. The great vaulted apartment on the ground floor was thrown into Solange's old bedroom, and given over entirely to the requirements of the drama. There was a stage at the far end on which actors of flesh and blood could strut. The whole of the central floor-space was turned into an auditorium, and an alcove provided accommodation for the puppet theatre, which was now better equipped than any similar construction in the whole world. By means of a rotating drum, moon and sun could be made to move in their nightly and diurnal round. Rain could fall, and lightning zig-zag across the backcloth. The scenes, painted by Maurice, produced an impression of depth. Each one of the characters was made in several different sizes, so that when he made his entry at the back of the stage, he could be made to increase in size as he approached the footlights. All were mounted on springs so sensitive that a puff of breath would produce a response. When one of them started on a set speech, the others could be made to express themselves

---

[1] Unpublished. Simone André-Maurois Collection.

in action at the appropriate moments. Maurice, who was an admirable improvisator, liked the audience to shout questions at his puppets, who answered in the most brilliant fashion.

George Sand to Augustine de Bertholdi, February 24th, 1851: Yes, Maurice was really staggered by the theatre. It was shut when he turned up one morning about three weeks ago. That evening, I blindfolded his eyes and led him into the billiard-room. Then the curtain rose to reveal the stage set for *Claudia,* everything beautifully fresh, and the whole well lit. You can imagine his surprise! We have had only two performances since he came back. I have made a rule that the stage shall be used no oftener than once a fortnight, because a great deal of work is involved in the preparation of the plays. Yesterday was splendid, a piece of the same general type as *Pillules du Diable,* half spoken, half mimed, with surprises, and devils, and bangings in every scene. We had an audience of sixty. Opinions differed: but there was a great deal of applause and stamping, and the actors gave an inspired performance.

April 28th, 1851: We had a performance of my latest play,[1] Oh! how we missed you! I am now condemned to take the young female leads. I can manage my face with a bit of make-up, but what I cannot do is to convince myself that I am young, which means that I never feel myself into the character I am playing, and so play badly.[2]

'No one knows how much I owe to my son's puppets', wrote George Sand. It was true. This particular form of game had, all through her bad times, taken her out of herself—which is the function of all games. After half a century of experiments, many of which had been violent and painful, George was beginning to get a pretty clear idea of what strings control the movements of life's human puppets. At Nohant, while she sat in the evening at the big table, busy with costumes for Harlequin and Columbine,

---

[1] *Nello, ou le Joueur de Violon.* This play, which was several times re-written, was produced at the Odéon on September 15th, 1855, under the title of *Maître Favilla.*

[2] Simone André-Maurois Collection.

for Balandard and Bamboula, she thought about the not very much more complicated mechanism of the heart's passions. She had known innumerable persons, and could group them under a few simple categories. There had been the 'old countesses' of her childhood; there had been a violent, noble-hearted woman of the people; there had been the garrulous reformer of the Michel type, eager for position, an opportunist with a touch of poetry; there had been the ardent and consumptive 'leading-man', and the 'leading woman' in search of love. She had reached a stage in her life at which she knew precisely how they would behave as soon as they had made their entries. It is a great temptation for the disenchanted heart, when it comes within sight of fifty, to look with an amused eye at the human mechanism and then withdraw, leaving the bewildered actors to their posturings. The theatre can provide a purge for the passions. It can also be their death.

But the finer spirits in the audience can see beneath the paint and powder. They can learn from watching a play how to 'kill the puppet in themselves'. They can make the discovery that when the technique which controls the human jerkings has been mastered, the last word has not been said. George Sand had set out in pursuit of an ideal love. She had not found it, but she did not regret having wanted it. She still felt convinced that in love a woman must stake all or nothing. She had hoped for an ideal Republic, and had seen that dream brought to nothing, but she did not regret having dreamed it. She still believed that there are in men, in spite of moments of baseness, vast possibilities for good, and that it is better to speak to them 'of liberty than of slavery'. She had seen the evil, but still clung to her belief in the fine. Mother Alicia and the Abbé de Frémond had been right to put their faith in her, ignoring all her faults. Now, with the approach of old age, she was moving into calm waters, and that, for all of us, is something that can be achieved only after much strenuous fighting.

PART EIGHT

MATURITY

THE DANGEROUS AGE

'THE DANGEROUS age' afflicts those women who have been cheated of a woman's life. It is they who, when signs show that the body is ageing, are obsessed by regrets which turn to manias. George Sand, who had known love and treasured its glories, was spared the sad task of asking herself, as so many others do, what love would have been like. She remembered what it had been. Doubtless, round about 1852, she went through that 'inevitable period of weakness which comes with the change of life'. But what mattered it that her beauty was fading? Her fame was guarantee enough that she would never be abandoned. For one who, like her, had always refused to be just a piece of 'luxury goods', it was now not only a matter of indifference (every woman looks at her mirror), but an easy necessity, to admit, when the moment came, that she was *no longer quite suited to play the leads*. She knew that, no matter what her age, she was more than ever a centre of attraction. She ruled at Nohant as a powerful matriarch. Maurice's friends, Borie, Manceau, Lambert, Aucante, paid her the tribute of devoted homage. Eugène Delacroix was amazed to find so many young men living under her roof. *Delacroix's Journal, February 21st, 1852:* 'The sight of all those young men circling round that poor woman, produces the oddest impression . . .'[1] for Delacroix, a traditionalist by temperament, and now the spoiled child of the régime, turned on Sand a gaze in which there was something of pity, and not a little of severity. But the way to keep young, she thought, is to live in the company of youth. 'My visitors enjoy themselves, and there is always gaiety at Nohant. . . .'[2]

In his four volumes of caricatures, Maurice has left us a

rather coarse record of this gaiety. We are shown the ludicrous side of Lambert, with his nose in the air, the heavy-footed *gaucherie* of Borie. Manceau is more delicately depicted, with his small, neatly clipped moustache and his thin body, shivering on the banks of the Indre after an icy bathe. He remained Madame Sand's favourite. He was a deferential prince consort, always ready to make himself useful, and with a heart of gold. 'If you knew him, you would realize that he is one of those who should be cherished and appreciated more than most.[1] Maurice and Lambert worked during the winter in Paris. Borie, after his return from Belgium, was hoping to make his fortune in a Bank. Manceau and 'Madame' (that was how he always referred to her) remained together in unbroken intimacy. Because of his strong character and unshakeable loyalty, Manceau acquired a greater influence over Sand than any man had ever had. She could not do without him, and always took him with her when she went to Paris. She dedicated five of her books to him. He stood between her and all material worries. He made it his business every evening to see that the necessary stacks of paper, together with a glass of sugared water, were standing ready on her writing table. 'All the same', said Théophile Gautier, 'Manceau did turn Nohant into a sort of writing factory! No sooner did she sit down in a room than he would materialize with a load of pens, blue ink, cigarette papers, Turkish tobacco, and foolscap!'[2]

Manceau's Diary, June 23rd, 1852: Lambert arrived this morning. He is growing fat. He has got some commissions for pictures, and curls his moustache round like a corkscrew . . . It is raining, and we can't go out. Conversation. Work. Dinner. Music. Embroidery. Maurice is writing a play. Lambert has gone to bed, so has Madame Solange. Went to my room at midnight. Madame settled down to write some letters.

George Sand's Diary, January 13th, 1853: Periwinkles, laurustinus, moss, primulas, gillyflowers, violets—some of them white. The japonica has been in flower for a fortnight past. Masses of violets everywhere, in the woods

[1] GEORGE SAND: *Lettres à Alfred de Musset et à Sainte-Beuve*, p. 212.
[2] *Journal des Goncourts*. Volume II, p. 119.

and garden. The red peony covered with great fat buds.
So far not a single hard frost . . . We have gone on with
our readings of Balzac. Wrote and sent off a very
restrained advance notice for *Leone Leoni* . . . Reread
Lucrezia preparatory to writing a notice tomorrow . . .
January 14th, 1853: Rather cold. Maurice leaves tomorrow. We read some Balzac, and laughed a good deal in
the evening so as to put as good a face as possible on
things . . . *January 28th, 1853:* At last, a letter from
Maurice. Lovely weather: roses, periwinkles, gillyflowers
of three colours, primroses, single, double, and parti-
coloured: the hyacinths just on the point of flowering:
almond trees in full bloom. Did fifteen pages of my
novel yesterday evening. This evening, wool-work. We
read *Ivanhoe* aloud. Borie fell asleep and snored. Solange
tied a kite-tail to his hair . . . He was furious, swore, and
tore a lock of hair away with the ribbon. He stormed and
roared, and ran after Solange shouting a few home truths
at her, which delighted Manceau. . . .

Manceau's Diary, February 1st, 1853: Madame Solange
quite early this morning—up at nine! She set the servants
at sixes and sevens, woke all of them who were still
sleeping, and even Madame! This was thought to be great
fun, but not by me! Madame working at her embroidery
all day to get the Iris chair finished. She is quite lost to
everything else, and looks very pretty when she is
working away at irises. In the evening Manceau read
aloud *The Fair Maid of Perth*. Borie and Emile went to
bed, but the rest of us not till midnight. *February 14th,
1853:* A fine day. Madame woke with a headache which
grew steadily worse all day until eight o'clock in the
evening . . . Madame dined off tea, bread and butter. I did
all I could to distract her. I took her into the garden to
plant some flowers on the island. I tried being amusing,
stupid, gay, but nothing was any good. . . .

George Sand's Diary, February 18th, 1853: Another
letter from Napoleon with a safe-conduct for Patureau
from Monsieur de Maupas. . . .

Manceau's Diary, February 27th, 1853: Weather cold,
grey and dreary. Madame going on well. Preface to *Les
Maîtres Sonneurs,* and corrections to the novel. Madame
has dedicated it to Lambert. I rather wonder whether that

hard-hearted scamp really deserves such good fortune?
. . .[1]

When the house at Nohant was full, or when friends
came over from La Châtre, nothing was allowed to break
the monastic regularity of the day: breakfast, walking,
work, dinner, a hundred up at dominoes, then reading aloud
'round the table'. This large, oval table had been made by
the village carpenter, Pierre Bonnin, now an old man, who
had known Aurore Dupin when she was four years old, and
who still said to George Sand when she went to see him in
his workshop—'Just you hop it, now! You're a-stopping of
me from getting on with my work!' The evening sessions
round the table played an essential part in the life of the
household. Its broad surface had been used for so many
purposes.

So much lunatic and ingenious scribbling—charming
drawings or mad caricatures, painting in water-colour or
tempera, the making of models of all kinds, flower studies
from nature by lamplight, sketches dashed off from
imagination or impressions of the morning walk, the
preparation of entomological specimens, building of
cardboard models, copying of music, somebody writing
letters, somebody else writing comic verses, piles of wool
or silk for embroidery, construction of scenes for the
puppets, costume making for the same, games of chess or
piquet—a hundred and one things. Everything that
people do in a family party in the country, with talking
going on all round, during the long autumn and winter
evenings. . . .[2]

'Not till the table has been bundled into the lumber-room,
and I into my grave,' said George Sand, 'will anything here
be changed.' It was round this table that the communal
readings took place. When Hugo sent Sand a copy of *Les
Contemplations*, Duvernet read them to the assembled
company. They argued about the rhymes, and praised the
poet's lyrical quality. More often than not Madame Sand
occupied herself with puzzles or did her embroidery,
without speaking a word until midnight, or sewed away at

[1] All these extracts are unpublished. Bibliothèque nationale:
Department of manuscripts.
[2] GEORGE SAND: *Author de la Table,* p. 8.

costumes for the puppets, and at trimming clothes. At midnight she broke up the party. Manceau prepared her oil-lamp and accompanied her to her writing-room, where she would work until six the next morning, smoking cigarettes and dropping the stubs into a glass of water.

In the afternoons she busied herself about house and garden. There was a great deal to be done. The staff was large—eight or nine regular domestic servants, to say nothing of 'dailies' when the house was filled with guests, or when Madame was busy making her current jams, for that was work she always did herself, and took great pride in her recipes. Bonnin, the carpenter, and a house-painter, were engaged by the year. Everyone got good wages. Sand made it a rule always to pay rather more than her neighbours. She did not like to hear people talk of *masters* and *servants*. One is not the master of free individuals. There are just so many house-workers, each with his or her especial job. She liked things to be well done, and insisted on a high standard. But she never expected anybody to do work which might humiliate them. She allowed neither liveries nor the form of address in the third person. When she gave an order she always used the local formula: 'Would you mind doing this?'—and was always delighted by the reply—'Indeed I would not.' The quality by which she set most store in those who served her was *discretion*. It was an unwritten law that there should be no gossip about what went on at Nohant. A left-over, this, of her adventurous and secret youth.

Though she was a revolutionary by conviction, she ran her house with bourgeois thoroughness. Similarly, though she was a romantic at heart, she attached much importance to the 'scientific approach'. This strange conjunction of words may help us to understand her. 'The whole secret of the study of nature', she said, 'lies in learning how to use one's eyes', but she added that it was impossible to 'use one's eyes properly' even though the object to be examined might be no larger than a square-yard of garden, if one did not bring to its contemplation some idea of classification. 'Classification is Ariadne's clue through the labyrinth of nature'.[1] Ever since the days of Deschartres, she had been busy enlarging her collection of plants. Deschartres had long been dead, and the poor 'Madagascan', another companion in her natural studies, was dying. She continued

[1] GEORGE SAND: *Nouvelles Lettres d'un Voyageur: Le Pays des Anémones*, p. 51.

to seek with absorbed attention the four species of heath which would provide food for her caterpillars—'the common fibrous type, the light-coloured heather, broom, and the four-leafed species which, in my opinion, is the prettiest. The loveliest of all, the "vagrant" variety, we have not yet found. . . .'[1] Intoxicated by nature, she had neither the taste for, nor the need of, Paris. She went there only to superintend her theatrical enterprises. 'I have shaken the accursed dust of that city from my feet.'

The study of nature makes the changes in the human body easier to bear. The reddened leaves of autumn are the forerunners of winter but do not curse its coming. And so did George now accept with equanimity the old age that was creeping on apace.

The old woman I shall become [says one of her characters] will be quite different from the woman I am now. Another *I* is beginning, and so far I have not had to complain of her. She knows nothing of my past errors. She knows nothing because she would not understand them, and feels herself incapable of renewing them. She is as gentle, patient and just as the other was irritable, exigent and tough . . . She mends all the evil that her predecessor committed, and, in addition, forgives that other the actions for which, a prey to remorse, she could never have forgiven herself. . . .[2]

Such, on her best days, was Sand's attitude on the threshold of fifty. She wanted to substitute kindliness for passion as the mainspring of her actions. It was a virtue that had always been hers, though sometimes it had been overlaid by her violent temperament. In the old days she had been kindly by fits and starts, but from now on she would be kindly in a settled and continuing way. Her quest, she thought, was ended at last. It was not that she had become resigned, but rather that the effects of violence had given her a disgust for violence. For the future, she would fight only for the happiness of others, without hate and without resentment.

This state of mind was to have its set-backs. Old age is much like any other period of life, and has its ups and

---

[1] GEORGE SAND: *Impressions et Souvenirs: Entre deux Images*, p. 352.

[2] GEORGE SAND: *Isidora*. Volume II, p. 258.

downs. In the years ahead she was to know moods of
relapse and irritation, appetites and regrets, weaknesses and
moments of injustice. From all this arose her occasional
periods of excessive gaiety. 'Frivolity is violent', and the
noise of it sometimes drowns the quiet voice of the spirit.
All the same, because she longed to be consistent, she not
only forgave herself for the past, but transformed it, quite
sincerely, in her own mind, so that she might make it
worthy of her deliberate choice of charitableness. Musset?
—for him she had been nothing but an angel of devotion. The woman of passion, hanging like a leech to her
prey, was now for her no longer even a remembered puppet.
The mysticism of love? the hatred of marriage?—well, they
had been, at worst, a form of romanticism. The period, not
the writer, deserved the blame. As to her early novels, those
witnesses to a tumultuous past, she had had them re-issued
with new Prefaces designed to adapt them to her later
philosophical beliefs—a procedure which had had the effect
of exasperating a few of her more churlish critics; Barbey
d'Aurévilly, for instance, who parodied her on a note of
sarcasm:

> You believed me to be the enemy of marriage . . . you
> thought that I held more liberal views on the ordinary,
> decent relationship of man to woman? Well, after thirty
> years of illusions which I myself encouraged, I tell you
> now that such was not the case. You overrate my
> intelligence. I have never had, nor ever wished to have, so
> penetrating an eye. I am just a simple-minded woman of
> genius who produces novels as a peach-tree produces
> pink blossom, and has never sought to do more than
> please. . . .[1]

In the books she was now writing, marriage played an
increasingly respectable part. Love, which is God's will, is
dictated by the heart. That, of course, is true, but it differs
from mere animal instinct in that reason plays a part in the
choice, which is a total surrender of heart and body and
ought to be lasting. 'But what if love dies?' asks one of her
characters in *Constance Verrier*, the actress Sofia Mozzelli,
who was drawn from Marie Dorval—'should one not in
that case seek elsewhere?' 'Why elsewhere?' replies the

[1] BARBEY D'AUREVILLY: *Les Oeuvres et les Hommes du
XIXe Siècle*, V. *Les Bas Bleus*.

heroine: 'you should rather use that power which you attribute to the heart to cure it of its guilty lassitude.' A woman can know the happiness of marriage only if she kills the savage demon of desire within herself, and, instead of seeking out another lover, tries to acquire a deeper knowledge of the man to whom she is united. Balzac had congratulated himself in the old days on having made George realize that truth, but in such matters time is a better teacher than the advice of friends.

> *George Sand to Sainte-Beuve, December 15th, 1850:* I am a slope which leads up or down without my having any say in the matter. Life takes me whither it will, and for many years now I have felt my own intentions to be so little involved that I no longer have to put up any sort of a struggle. I move through regions of calm, and thank God that He has seen fit to let me enter them. But how all that has come about, I do not know. Perhaps I had a good intention. *Pax hominbus bonae voluntatis. . . .*[1]

II

THE FAMILY CIRCLE

THIS NEW philosophy of marriage had come to George too late to save poor Casimir's domestic happiness, though it is doubtful whether their union could ever have been steered clear of the rocks. There are cases in which the more a woman tries to acquire a deeper knowledge of her husband the less she finds in him to like. When that happens it is useless to preach the blessedness of reconciliation. Sand must have known that better than most. But age does not see these dramas with the eyes of youth. Old women no longer cherish marital peace for their own sakes, but for the sakes of their daughters, their daughters-in-law, or their granddaughters. We are all of us strong enough to put up a

---

[1] GEORGE SAND: *Lettres à Alfred de Musset et à Sainte-Beuve*, pp. 225-9.

successful fight against the passions of others. The mother of Solange Clésinger found it impossible to judge or to feel as the wife of Casimir Dudevant had done.

Solange and her mother showed no mercy to one another. Sand and Maurice had presented a united front against the nasty little girl who had tangled her denunciations with such a mingling of treachery and plausibility that all who came within her orbit ended by hating each other without ever really knowing why. 'While Solange was in the house even the cocks were more pugnacious, the dogs more ill-tempered.' From childhood she had witnessed all her mother's love affairs. She had at first condemned, but, later, come to envy them. 'When I spoke to her of God', said Sand, 'she laughed in my face . . .' Admittedly, Solange had learned about easy love in a first-rate school, but of that Sand was not aware. She could not see herself as Solange saw her. 'She flatters herself', wrote Sainte-Beuve in harsh comment, 'that no one ever believes things to be as they are, and that fine words will always, in the long run, carry the day.' But her attitude was more sincere than he supposed. Her daughter's crude outlook and hardened cynicism genuinely shocked the bourgeoise and the romantic sides of her nature. For all their calling one another 'sweet, darling, dearest', there was no love lost between them. During the Chopin episode they had been secret rivals. Solange's behaviour at that time had been most blameworthy. Sand had wished to be, quite honestly believed that she had been, forgiving. On two separate occasions she had financed her daughter, once when she had given her the Hôtel de Narbonne, and then, after the creditors had distrained on that, when she had provided her with a yearly allowance. Her only wish had been that the Clésinger marriage should hold together.

But that was an empty hope. Clésinger was a crazy creature who, in a single year, ran so far into debt that he was compelled to sell the house, mortgaged though it was. He ruined his wife and considerably embarrassed his mother-in-law's finances. Sand struggled in vain to save him. Meanwhile Solange, true to her system of spreading slanders among her intimates, told her friends, the Bascans, that her mother's creditors were hard on her heels! Ever a lover of mystification, she concealed from George the reality of her domestic situation. 'I can get nothing out of her but what she is willing to tell, and she tells no more than

what she thinks may further her interests . . .' The birth of
the little Jeanne Clésinger, 'Nini', had led to a truce, if not a
reconciliation, between mother and daughter. 'Clésinger
may be the crazier of the two', said Sand, 'but he is certainly
not the more malicious.' In February 1851, Solange and
Nini turned up at Nohant.

*George Sand to Augustine Bertholdi, February 24th,
1851:* To turn for a moment to serious matters, let me tell
you that Solange put in an appearance here shortly
before Maurice was due, and spent four days under my
roof with her child, who is pretty enough but a regular
handful. Sol had come with the intention of being
agreeable, and agreeable she was in an artificial sort of
way, like a great lady without a heart. That is all I can tell
you: for what the purpose of her visit was, or what she
hoped to get out of it, is beyond the ingenuity of mortal
man to discover. She talks of spending the summer
months in this part of the world, and is looking about for
some house to lease, but she won't find one for the very
simple reason that such do not exist. It may have been
her way of getting herself invited here. I told her to her
face that I would *not* give shelter to her husband, his
servants and his friends, his horses or his dogs; that I was
prepared to receive only herself and her child, and that
even so I should be pretty wary, and keep a weathereye
open for storms. To this she replied that she had no
intention of staying with me, seeing that there was no
room here for all her 'people'. According to her, her
husband is making a lot of money. He may be, for all I
know, but I have yet to learn that he is paying his debts.
She is for ever standing up for him, saying that he has a
good heart but a bad character. If she can find
satisfaction in *that,* so much the better. From what I can
see, the only thing she thinks about is being a woman of
the world, but such of the world as she sees she does
nothing but run down continuously, mocking at it in the
unkindest way. What is bad is that her health seems to be
far from good, but that, in my opinion, is entirely her
own fault. She recently had a miscarriage, but went out
riding the very next day, and does not seem able to make
a proper recovery. She writes me letters full of the most
pretentious expressions of affection. I have decided on
the best line to take in all this, and am sticking to it. I am

no longer angry, miserable, or deluded. I am quite calmly
facing the facts of the situation, and they are not likely to
change. . . .[1]

So great was Sand's horror of the pair, that she believed
them to be quite capable of carrying on criminal activities.
She begged Maurice not to dine at his sister's.

George Sand to Maurice, January 2nd, 1851: I do not
like the idea of your eating with them . . . Clésinger is
completely mad. Solange is without any bowels of
affection. Both of them are so utterly amoral in their
principles of behaviour that there is no knowing what
they might not do in certain circumstances . . . Your
ceasing to exist would be very much to their interest and
with them interest is everything. Solange has always been
eaten up with jealousy. They are hard on your tracks, and
Clésinger is sticking to you like a leech . . . You must act
with extreme caution. Once again I say, *do not eat or
drink at their table* . . . Burn this letter, but memorize its
contents. Crime does not always take the form one thinks
it will. When one is dealing with monsters, it is well to
remember that it is not the slow germination of deliberate intention, or the rounding out of a foreordained tendency, with which one has to deal, but, rather the result
of some sudden brainstorm, an act of blind rage. . . .[2]

She was driven to admit to herself that she felt no
affection whatever for her daughter: 'So far as I am
concerned, she is just a bar of cold iron, somebody I never
have known, and cannot know.' To Solange herself she
wrote: 'The way you are going on, my child, is qu'te
fantastic. The older you grow, the more incomprehensible
do I find you.'[3] Fantastic?—the word was no exaggeration.
Solange was behaving in the oddest possible manner. She
settled down for some considerable time with her father at
Guillery. Though the wretched Casimir was by no means
certain that he could, in her case, claim to be adjudged the
honours of paternity, he shouldered full financial responsi-

[1] Unpublished. Simone André-Maurois Collection.

[2] Letter quoted by Wladimir Karénine, in *George Sand*.
Volume III, pp. 607-9.

[3] Letter quoted by Samuel Rocheblave, in *George Sand et sa
Fille*, p. 148.

bility. But this did not save him from being the target of her bitter complaints. Clésinger having been guilty of infidelity, his wife determined to follow in his footsteps. She had a fine figure, remarkable beauty, and a keen wit. Consequently, she found no difficulty in equipping herself with a bevy of adorers. In 1852 she left Clésinger, who, she said, 'treated her like a model', and, from the shelter of a Convent, continued her lamentations.

Solange Clésinger to George Sand, April 23rd, 1852: Is it thus that I am to pass the best years of my life—without parents, without friends, without my child, without even a dog to break the monotony of existence? . . . To live in isolation, with sound and movement going on all about me—people enjoying themselves, horses galloping, children playing in the sunshine, happy lovers—is not so much boredom as despair! People wonder how it is that poor girls without minds of their own, or any sort of education, allow themselves to slip into a life of pleasure and vice! Can even women of judgment and warm affections be sure of keeping themselves unspotted? . . .[1]

George Sand to Solange Clésinger, April 25th, 1852: I spent many of the best years of my own youth living in what you call 'isolation', and working hard between four dirty walls, and let me tell you that though I regret much, I do not regret them . . . The sort of isolation of which you complain is another matter . . . It is the result of your own deliberate choice. It may be that your husband does not wholly deserve to be so bitterly disliked or so impulsively set aside. If separation there had to be, I cannot help thinking that it might have been achieved rather differently, with greater dignity, more patience, and more prudence. But you wanted it this way, and this is the way you have got it . . . In my view it is not very pretty of you to complain of the immediate consequences of a resolution which you took entirely of your own accord, and in spite of the *parents, the friends and the child,* of whose absence you are now so painfully conscious. The thought of your child should have persuaded you to possess yourself in patience for a while longer. As to parents—and it is to me that you refer—I

[1] Letter quoted by Wladimir Karénine in *George Sand*. Volume III, p. 610.

was for ever urging you to wait until a better opportunity
should occur, and a sounder motive be provided . . . I fail
to see why the friends whom you made for yourself when
you deliberately chose to live away from me in the great
world, should be likely to show themselves more loyal
than those whom I could have provided . . . There is
not one of my old acquaintances who would not readily
have forgiven your extraordinary behaviour to me, and
welcomed you as of old . . . There are not many of them,
it is true, and such as there are are neither important nor
fashionable. But that is not my fault. I was not, as you
were, born in the purple. and, when it came to making
friends I followed the promptings of my own simple
tastes . . . All your misfortunes have flowed from the fact
of your being my daughter, but about that I can do
nothing. . . .

The only thing that will console you is money—and a
great deal of it. In luxury, laziness and the whirl of
fashion, you might succeed in forgetting the emptiness of
your heart. But I could give you what you need only by
working twice as hard as I do now, which means that I
should be dead in six months, since even my present
programme is beyond my strength. You would not be
rich for long, so that my sacrifice would go for nothing,
since what I shall have to leave will by no means provide
wealth for you or your brother. Besides, even if I could
work twice as hard, and keep going for a few more years,
what proof have I that it is my duty to turn myself into a
galley-slave or an old horse merely to supply you with
luxuries and a life of pleasure? What I can give you, you
shall have. You can treat this house as your home, on
condition that you do not upset everybody by your idiotic
behaviour, or drive them to despair with your ill-natured
ways. I will keep your daughter and see to her bringing-
up for as long as you wish, but what I will *not* do is to
pretend to sympathize with the difficulties and privations
which you will have to endure in Paris. That remark in
your letter about *women of judgment and warm
affections* who let themselves slip, like poor girls without
minds of their own, into *a life of pleasure and vice,*
makes me think that your husband may not always have
been lying when he claimed that you had uttered certain
threats. He may be mad, but so are you—diabolically
mad . . . There are moments when you seem not to know
what you are thinking or what you are saying. You were

in that state when you put that odd paradox into your letter to me . . . If you often say such stupid things, I don't wonder at your sending Clésinger out of his mind . . . So you find it difficult, do you, to be lonely and poor and not to *slip into a life of vice*? It is all you can do, is it, to endure being cooped up between four walls, while women are laughing and horses are galloping outside? 'What a terrible fate!' as Maurice would say. The real tragedy is to have the sort of mind that thinks, as yours does, that you *must have a life either of happiness or vice*. All right then, just try a little vice: just try being a prostitute! I do not think you would make much of a success of it. Why, you could not so much as *begin* to hunt out luxury at the cost of self-love! It is not so easy as you seem to think to accept dishonour. A woman has got to be a great deal more beautiful, and more intelligent, than you are before she can hope to be pursued, or even sought out by men who are eager and anxious to pay for her favours—or else she must be a great deal more experienced in the art of making herself desirable, more skilled in *feigning* passion, and wantonness, and those allurements of the dubious delicious kind of which, thank God, I do not even know the names! Men with money to spend want women who know how to earn it, and that kind of knowledge would make you feel so physically sick that the preliminary haggling would very soon be broken off. . . .

I have known young women who have fought down the passions of heart and body, and been terrified out of their wits lest domestic unhappiness might lead them into giving way to the mad impulse of a moment: but I have never known a single one brought up as you have been, in an atmosphere of personal dignity and moral freedom, who has dreaded unhappiness and isolation because of such dangers as *you* talk of. A woman of heart and judgment may, no matter how strong her character, feel frightened of being swept off her feet by love but never by cupidity. If I were the Judge appointed to deal with your case, and had read the precious reflections to which you have just treated me, I should certainly *not* give you the custody of your child. . . .[1]

---

[1] Letter quoted by Wladimir Karénine in *George Sand*. Volume III, pp. 611 and 616.

Solange must have given vent to bitter laughter when she read those words: *brought up as you have been, in an atmosphere of personal dignity and moral freedom* . . . Nevertheless, her mother had written them in perfect good faith. A genuine passion into which no thought of wealth or poverty entered, she could have understood. But with the sale of self she would permit no compromise. To all of which Solange might have replied: 'It is easy for you to talk like that. You have always been rich. *I* have got nothing but the miserable allowance you make me. I have got to live somehow.' The breach with Clésinger was followed by a writ (chimerical, as matters stood) for the restitution of her dowry, and by quarrels on the subject of Nini who, fortunately, had been bundled off to Nohant.

> *Solange Clésinger to George Sand, April 29th, 1852:* If ever there was a fool in this world, it's my husband . . . I'm only too glad that the child's being sent to you. You or me, it's all the same, but nothing would induce me to let *him* have her for two months in each year . . . She is still far too young to be handed over to the tender mercies of a man like that, who would keep her short of everything. Later, when she has grown into a young lady, the danger will be just as great—that of leaving her in the hands of so coarse-grained and cynical a creature. . . .[1]

George Sand had had some experience of kidnappings, and now, to make sure that Nini should not fall into the monumental mason's hands, put Nohant into a state of defence. If the worst came to the worst she would mobilize Manceau's Fire Brigade. With the child to look after, she could taste again the pleasure she had once known of living in the constant proximity of the very young. She adored being a grandmother. The instinct to love and protect meant more to her than anything else. Nini and she became inseparable. Together they tended the 'dolls' garden' which Madame Dupin had had made for Aurore, who had called it her 'Petit Trianon'. It contained miniature mountains, tiny chalets, paths carpeted with moss, and waterfalls fed from a zinc tank concealed among the trees.

---

[1] Letter quoted by Samuel Rocheblave in *George Sand et sa Fille*, pp. 173-4.

George Sand to Augustine de Bertholdi, October 28th, 1853: I work every day at the Petit Trianon, carting stones in a wheelbarrow, weeding and planting ivy. I tire myself out in a doll's garden, with the result that I sleep and eat better than I have ever done before. . . .[1]

George Sand to Solange Clésinger: I have bought her a straw hat for the garden, four morning frocks, shoes, etc. . . . She will need only one ordinary hat—and that can be as simple and as cheap as possible, so long as it is not in the appalling taste of La Châtre . . . I have also bought her some stockings. The tuckers and drawers are ready. Our little girl is charming, a perfect picture of health, and getting along quite well with her reading. From noon until nine o'clock at night we are inseparable. The mornings she spends with Manceau, who adores her. . . .[2]

The 'Queen of Ninis' ruled at Nohant. 'When she has to have her little enema, she will submit only if the syringe is decorated with flowers and ribbons. Manceau has to whistle a little tune all the time the application is going on.' In the calm following on one temporary reconciliation, Solange resumed her charge of the child, 'after whom she was hungering and thirsting', but grandmamma protested. 'I will keep Nini as long as possible. The poor mite will never know peace or happiness so long as this struggle continues.' Sand was particularly opposed to constant comings and goings. 'It is my misfortune that I become attached to those for whom I assume responsibility. I dislike bolts from the blue . . . If this reconciliation comes to nothing, Nini will be ailing, unsettled, irritable, and difficult to handle when you bring her back to me . . .'[3] And that, as it turned out, was precisely what happened. But once again Nohant magic had its effect.

George Sand to Solange Clésinger, September 21st, 1852: Nini is getting along marvellously, and you would scarcely recognize her as the same person . . . With me,

[1] Simone André-Maurois Collection.

[2] Letter published by R. de Bury in the *Mercure de France* for June 1900, p. 590.

[3] Letter quoted by Samuel Rocheblave in *George Sand et sa Fille*, pp. 175-6.

Ninette is quite enchanting . . . She is much less nervous
than she was, and is filling out. She is prettier than ever.
She talks a great deal about you, but does- not fret,
because she is quite sure you may turn up at any moment
. . . Her intelligence is making astonishing progress, and
she has taken to describing the garden—the flowers, the
sun ('wearing its grey dress'), the stars ('which have little
golden feet'), the night-stocks which open in the evening
when the mallows have gone to sleep, the glow-worms,
etc. . . . No little girl could be sweeter. . . .[1]

George Sand's unpublished diaries, more often than not
entered up by Manceau, though sometimes by her, have
preserved an account of the games played by the grandmother and the little girl, of the works carried out at the
Berry Trianon, of the fantastic Paris evenings, when George
would take Solange, Nini, Maurice and Manceau to dine at
Magny's, and later drag the four-year-old girl along to the
Odéon or the Ambigu, because neither her mother nor her
grandmother, both of them devoted theatre-goers, knew
what to do with her when they went to the play.

George Sand's Diary, April 19th, 1853: Gave the
finishing touches to my Petit Trianon. Manceau arranged
a waterfall. I constructed the Grove of Bacchus. Emile
was struck all of a heap—so were the nightingales . . .
Read, by myself, the last volume of my memoirs. . . .

April 20th, 1853: Heavenly weather, slightly overcast,
but mild. The trees are bursting into leaf almost as one
watches. I made a mountain next to the Trianon, but two
hours later Manceau knocked it down and put in its place
a dolmen containing an invisible reservoir which supplies
a fountain in the Grotto of Trianon. What a surprise for
Nini, and still more for me, who am much more of a
child than she is . . . The fountain played for two hours
. . . Did absolutely nothing today beyond embroidering
a narcissus. I am being thoroughly lazy . . . If only that
condition could continue! . . . Sent off the first volume of
Maîtres Sonneurs to Dutacq . . . *April 21st, 1853:* The
garden clean as a new pin. It really is superb. No tulips
yet, but narcissi. The small copse is positively carpeted

[1] Ibid., p. 180.

with violets. The pansies very lovely. Daisies, daffodils, blackthorn . . . Made a second hillock at Trianon to disguise the tanks . . . Started the chair with the birds'-nest pattern . . . .

At this point Manceau takes up the tale: She has resumed work on the remaining portions of *Ma Vie*, the fourth part of Volume VII . . . *April 13th, 1853:* Nini is becoming a really sweet little girl, but she is fond of eating with her fingers, and grandmamma does not approve . . . Nini will be as nice as nice when her mummy comes and builds grottoes—with her fingernails all painted red . . . *June 16th, 1853:* Madame Solange did not turn up—as was only to be expected! *June 18th, 1853:* Madame Solange arrived this morning . . . In the evening she made Nini eat her dinner without a stitch on, and, in the morning complained of the cold and the country—Oh Lord! . . .

George Sand's Diary, August 29th, 1853: Rain and cold. Corrected my *memoirs*. Did not stick my nose out until after dinner. Fine night—the sky cloudless. Got a good view of the comet in the west—sky very red. Manceau as a hermit. Maurice as Bertram, Lambert as Lélia, etc., performed an improvised play in the forest 'set'. Their costumes made me almost die of laughing. All great fun: much ranting and absurdity. Gave me a lot of amusement, all the more since I wasn't expecting anything of the kind . . . *Pas de deux* by Lambert (as a female devil) and Manceau (as a monk)—Temptation of Saint-Antony —first rate! . . . The play was called *La Croyance et le Doute*. . . .

Manceau's Diary, November 71th, 1853: Left Nohant at 3 a.m. Maurice insisted on going to bed for an hour, and could not eat any of the woodcock which Manceau had cut up so beautifully. Arrived at Châteauroux before six, couldn't hold the horses in! Left for Paris at half-past nine . . . Took a *coupé*—all there was! The train reached Paris at six in the evening. Jean[1] looked after the luggage. Dined at *Magny's*. Went home. Madame put away the linen, and retired to rest at half-past ten.

[1] George Sand's servant.

November 19, 1853: Madame pretty well . . . Rehearsal
of the first six scenes.[1] Cuts. Baez[2] lost his temper with
the actors. Dined at *Magny's,* then on to see *Champi* at
the Odéon, with Maurice, Madame Solange and Nini. . . .

George Sand's Diary, Nohant, December 19th, 1853:
Weather magnificent. Drove to the Bois du Magnier with
Nini and her doll. Took Jean on the box, with plenty of
spades and baskets. We skidded about in the mud, but
brought back a splendid collection of things for the
Trianons . . . Nini very sweet: asked me a lot of questions
on the way, about 'what happens to people when they are
dead' . . . *December 27th, 1853:* Snowed all day. The fish
are imprisoned under the ice. We worked hard at trying
to cut a way out for them. The birds don't know what to
say. My Trianon looks quite Swiss . . . Wrote some
letters, and worked a bit on the fair-copy of *Teverino* . . .
Old Aulard[3] and Pierre le Noir came to dinner. The
peasant didn't make much of a meal (because peasants
will never touch dishes they don't know). Emile managed
to get him to try a brandied orange. Played cards with
Manceau, then worked with Emile at collating *Daniel.*
Went upstairs at ten. Scribbled some verses for old
Aulard and Emile, then back to *Teverino.*

Manceau's Diary, December 28th, 1853: Much snow.
Madame well. She pushed snow about with a rake to get
some exercise, and worked so hard that she was as hot as
though it had been August! The carp are still dying.
Manceau will never kill a blackbird as long as he lives . . .
December 29th, 1853: Nini came back from Madame
Perigois[4] with a whole heap of toys. She is quite

---

[1] i.e. of *Mauprat,* a dramatization by George Sand of a novel
which she had published in 1837. It was, at this time, in
rehearsal at the Odéon, where it was produced on November
28th, 1853.

[2] Gustave Vaez was co-director (with Alphonse Royer) of the
Odéon. George Sand stood godmother to a child he had by the
actress Bérengère.

[3] Mayor of Nohant.

[4] Angèle Néraud, daughter of the 'Madagascan', who had
married Ernest Perigois.

overjoyed with the clothes her mummy has sent. They arrived this morning.[1]

For a few days the child brought mother and grandmother together, as once another child had done in the case of the two Dupin ladies. They were enchanted by the odd things she said.

George Sand to Solange Clésinger, February 9th, 1854: No one here can hold a candle to Nini for fun. She is the life and soul of the house, or, rather, I should say, she and Manceau are, for he puts himself on her level so successfully that she keeps on asking me: 'Grandmamma, am I really sillier than him?' She is a perfect little darling. . . .[2]

George Sand to Augustine de Bertholdi, March 12th, 1854: Everything goes on as usual at Nohant. Just now Solange is here, but she is not what I should call enjoying herself wildly, and so won't be with us for long. The most sensible thing she does is to leave Nini with me. The child is charming, and I can't do without her. Manceau is as efficient as an old woman in the way he looks after me. He is a good fellow, and sticks to me faithfully, no matter how black my mood. Maurice is having some success in Paris. . . .[3]

But no arrangement between Solange and her 'trooper' was destined to last. In May 1854, a new catastrophe occurred. Clésinger, having been informed that his wife was carrying on an affair with Comte Carlo Alfieri, Deputy for Alba in the Piedmontese Parliament, burst one day into her room. After a terrible scene, he seized all her lover's letters and sent them to Bethmont, his lawyer, with these words: 'What's to be done? I was sufficiently courageous not to kill her. . . '[4] He shook the dust of the domestic hearth from his feet, went to Nohant, accompanied by a man 'who could

[1] Unpublished extracts. Bibliothèque nationale: Department of Manuscripts.

[2] Letter quoted by Samuel Rocheblave in *George Sand et sa Fille*, p. 185.

[3] Unpublished. Simone André-Maurois Collection.

[4] Cf. GEORGES D'HEYLLI: *La Fille de George Sand*, p. 78.

boast a decoration', to fetch Nini, and applied for a legal separation, this time as the innocent and injured party. Once again the poor child was passed from hand to hand. Sometimes she was left with her godmother, Madame Bascans, sometimes she lived with her father, who finally settled her in a boarding-school. George Sand's letters to Madame Bascans are proof that for a whole month she was left in complete ignorance of the whereabouts of her granddaughter.

The first consequence of this adventure was unexpected. Solange—exhausted and broken by so much emotional strain—began to hanker after conversion. Her cousin, Gaston de Villeneuve, a man of deep piety, 'pushed her into the arms of Father de Ravignan', and the next thing she knew was that she was taking a Retreat at the Sacré Coeur. 'If I do not achieve faith,' she said, 'it will not be for want of trying. In any event, I shall plagiarize Henri IV, and say: "My daughter is well worth a Mass" . . .'[1] In her hope of heavenly succour, she displayed, for the first time in her life, a noticeable degree of humility. 'Only by a miracle can my child be restored to me. God can work miracles, but what have I done that He should work one for me? . . . No . . .' George Sand, never lacking in shrewdness, took the ball on the rebound: 'If your piety is genuine, now is the moment to exchange the kiss of peace with Augustine.' Solange, truly transformed, consented to this idea of a reconciliation.

The hoped-for miracle took place on December 16th, 1854, when the Courts granted a separation, and gave the custody of the child to her grandmother.

George Sand to Solange Clésinger, December 17th, 1854: What joy!—my dear daughter. This, surely, will strengthen your faith! God has come to our aid, and no matter what the religion one adheres to, that aid is always granted if one only seeks and implores it. You must come here at once, but *with* Jeanne.[2]

New Year's Day was close at hand. What a festival they would make of it at Nohant, if Nini got back in time! But, alas! it was necessary to wait until the ruling of the Court

[1] Ibid., p. 188.
[2] SAMUEL ROCHEBLAVE: *George Sand et sa Fille*, p. 190.

should have been officially promulgated. Clésinger might still lodge an appeal, and the lawyer, Bethmont, knew no pity. When January 1st 1855 came, the most Solange would be able to do would be to take a present of toys to the Deslignières Boarding-School in the rue Chateaubriand. She had found four lines of doggerel from George pushed under her door, as she had so often done when she was a little girl. They expressed the anxious affection of a harassed mother:

> Pour ma Solange, en ce beau jour,
> J'ai trouvé tout mon amour
> Puisqu'elle veut être sage;
> Pourvu qu'elle en ait le courage![1]

An interim Order of the Court was issued to the effect that the child must remain at school for the time being. 'Her father took her out with him in mid-January', wrote Sand, 'without so much as noticing that she was wearing a summer frock.' That same evening he returned her to the establishment in an ailing condition, and went off to shoot at some distance from Paris, no one knew exactly where. Sand felt profoundly worried. *December 29th, 1854:* '*Gloomy*[2] day. Thought of nothing but Nini. Wrote some letters. Brooded.' Alas! her dark forebodings were to be justified only too soon. Scarlet fever set in, and the poor child died.

> *George Sand to Charles-Edmond:* The worst has happened! They have killed my poor child . . . I was about to see her again. The Court had put her in my charge. Her father resisted from sheer wounded vanity. He appealed, and there was a Stay of Judgment . . . I wrote in vain to his hard, cold-hearted lawyer, telling him that my poor mite was being insufficiently looked after at the school where he, yes, he, had placed her! . . . Her

---

[1] For dear Solange on this sweet morn
   I find my love has been reborn:
    At last she has heard wisdom's voice,
    May courage give support to choice!
These lines are quoted by Samuel Rocheblave in *George Sand et sa Fille*, p. 191.

[2] This word was written by Sand in English.—TRANSLATOR.

mother was sent for and allowed to tend the child when it
was clear that there could be no hope. She died in her
arms, smiling and talking to the last. Her whole body was
terribly swollen. Her last words were: 'You must go to
Nohant, mummy, for I can't. I shall never leave this
place!'[1]

Manceau's Diary, January 14th, 1855: About ten, an
express messenger came from Châteauroux with a
telegram which contained the news that poor Nini ceased
to suffer last night. Madame is in despair, and so is
everybody else . . . *January 16th, 1855:* Arrival of
Solange, Lambert, Emile . . . and Nini. They placed her at
once in the Church. Ursule,[2] Perigois, Vergne,[3] Madame
Decerfz, and Madame Perigois, came to the funeral.
The little body was laid in the earth at half-past one,
by Bonnin, Jean, Sylvain[4] and the Gardener.

George Sand's Diary, January 17th, 1855: I slept, after
weeping away all my repressed and accumulated misery.
I thought a great deal about her, and had the feeling that
she was responding. Sol is quite crushed, and, consequently, much calmer. I wrote some letters . . . Solange got up for dinner. We re-read *Laurence,* and she
did her best to listen. I went up stairs at one. I still feel
completely heartbroken . . . *January 18th, 1855:* Nothing
new today. Did no work. Idled. Spent the day talking
very sadly. Solange has caught cold and is far from well.
Read some Cooper. Wool-work. Maurice and Lambert
did some distempering. *Laurence:* patching.

Manceau's Diary, January 23rd, 1855: Madame fairly
well. Thaw . . . Madame and Madame Solange made
notes about poor little Nini's life (material for *Après la
mort de Jeanne Clésinger,* still to be written). Dinner.
Discussion about future worlds. Wool-work. Cooper.
Madame Solange has got a cold: she's a mass of

[1] GEORGE SAND: *Correspondance.* Volume IV, pp. 34-6.
[2] Ursule Josse, one of the Nohant peasant women, and a
contemporary of George Sand, with whom she had played as a
child.
[3] Vergne de Beauregard, the local doctor.
[4] Sylvain Brunet, George Sand's coachman.

compresses. Madame is going to go on with her story of Nini, making use of our day-to-day diary. . . .[1]

It would be wrong to judge too severely this need felt by Sand to write something about her granddaughter's death.[2] An author's deepest feelings find their natural expression in words and phrases. Quite often he feels only what can find a literary outlet. George Sand tried to work, but her attention kept wandering to Nini's toys, her wheelbarrow and watering-can, all her little odds and ends, and the garden which they had made together. 'Providence is hard on men', she wrote, 'but especially hard on women.'

> *George Sand to Augustine de Bertholdi:* Thank you, my dear, for your letter. I am broken and miserable, though not ill, so do not be anxious. I can summon up the necessary courage. Solange has been much overwrought, and has therefore shown such strength as is within her compass. Yesterday we buried the little victim next to my grandmother and my father. Today we are all feeling utterly crushed. How long my sorrow will retain its present intensity I do not know. Rest assured that I will do my best not to let it kill me. I want to go on living for the sake of those who remain to me. I love you, and send my fondest affection, my darling daughter. Solange is genuinely touched by the sweetness you have shown her. She feels it deeply, and understands.[3]

The kindly can never have too much of the sorrows of others. They want the sufferings of the unhappy always to be just a little greater. George Sand has been blamed because, in spite of her grief, she could still take an interest in watching the newts leaping in the tiny lake: because she asked Maurice, on February 23rd, whether, at a dinner-party given by Prince Napoleon, Solange was 'really looking her best, and was well made-up': because, in July, theatricals began again at Nohant. But George Sand, like

[1] Unpublished extracts. Bibliothèque nationale: Department of Manuscripts.

[2] Which she did, in an article, 'Après la mort de Jeanne Clésinger'. This was later included in a volume of Essays, *Souvenirs et Idées*, p. 187.

[3] Unpublished. Simone André-Maurois Collection.

Goethe, saw no merit in cultivating a sorrow. 'Others may die, but we must go forward'—would have been a motto entirely to her taste.

After Nini's death, her 'young men', Maurice, Aucante and Manceau, proposed a trip to Italy in order to take her mind off what had happened. The journey was delightful. They went by sea from Marseilles to Genoa—'where we lunched in the open air under orange trees smothered in fruit', and thence by land, across the Roman Campagna, 'piled into a species of diligence', and then to Florence by way of Foligno—'that Trasimene where Hannibal gave the Romans a drubbing'—the phrase is Maurice Sand's in a whimsical letter to Titine, describing the trip. 'We crossed the Possessions of the Duke of Modena, where everything is of white marble, from the walls enclosing the peasants' holdings to the ducal coronet. These Possessions are twelve leagues in circumference. The Duke has an army of thirteen men, including the band, and all his subjects are marble-workers. . . .'[1]

Reading between the lines of all this light-hearted nonsense, it is easy to see that the expedition was a gay one, with enough spending of money on a large scale to satisfy even Sand. Manceau clipped his moustache, and kissed St. Peter's toe. Sand recovered her strength, and clambered up mountains with unceasing energy and subsequent exhaustion. They found many strange plants and insects, and caught butterflies among the ruins of Tusculum. In short, the tone of this 'campaign of Italy' was vastly different from that of the *Lettre à Fontanes*. Sand was happy, but determined to see the bad side of everything, and to regret her native France at every step. Whence her many surprising judgments. 'Don't believe those who tell you that there is grandeur and sublimity in the spectacle of Rome and its environs. Compared with other sights it is all very trivial, though I admit that there is about it a sort of delicious daintiness . . . In many respects, Rome is a lot of *humbug* . . . One would have to be very much a lover of Ingres to admire all of it . . . It is strange and beautiful, it is interesting and amazing, but it is too dead . . . The City is a disgusting medley of ugliness and filth! It is La Châtre writ large . . .'[2] Oh, true daughter of Berry!

The truth is that she saw Rome with the eyes of

1 Unpublished. Simone André-Maurois Collection.
2 GEORGE SAND: *Correspondance*. Volume IV, pp. 47-51.

prejudice. To her friend Luigi Calamatta, who reproached her for not saying that Rome contained, as well as beggars and sharpers, many decent folk and not a few martyrs in the cause of Freedom, she replied that the Imperial censorship did not permit her to speak of the Italian Liberals, or of Mazzini and Garibaldi, whom she loved. 'Since, therefore, one cannot talk of what in Rome is gagged, paralysed, and invisible, one must tear Rome to pieces, all that one sees there, all that it produces—filth, laziness and infamy . . . Men should know what happens when a people becomes enslaved by the priesthood, and I have done well, at whatever cost, to tell them. . . .'[1]

This outburst of anti-clericalism is surprising, coming, as it does, so soon after her suggestion that Nini should be sent to a Convent, and at a time when she herself had many good friends among the curés of the Nohant neighbour-hood. In part it must be attributed to that deep, underlying love of Voltaire, which was always liable to come to the surface when anything occurred to shock her mind into awareness: in part, also, to a feeling of resentment against those who had led her to hope that a miracle might save her granddaughter. Chiefly, however, it was due to the horror inspired in her not so much by the religious, as by the clerical, policies of the Second Empire. She saw that freedom of thought was in dire risk of being threatened, that a number of young University Professors were being persecuted, and she judged it necessary to react to these stimuli. The book which she wrote about her Italian tour, *Daniella,* a pamphlet rather than a novel, was the cause to her of much embarrassment. The periodical which pub-lished it in serial form, *La Presse,* came within an ace of being suspended. George Sand was induced, out of pity for the innocent compositors and printing-hands, to ask the Empress to use her influence. This the Empress did—a courageous act on the part of a deeply religious Spaniard—but got little enough in the way of gratitude for her pains from Madame Sand.

III

TIME'S SCYTHE

DURING HER absence in Italy George learned of the
death of the poor 'Madagascan' to whom she had been
planning, so delightedly, to bring back a gift of strange
plants. In old age the human heart becomes a cemetery.
Those whom one has loved dearly, those whom one has
loved too little, wander at night among the tombs.
Handsome Ajasson de Grandsagne had died in 1847;
Hippolyte Châtiron in 1848; Chopin and Marie Dorval in
1849; Balzac and Carlotta Marliani in 1850; Latouche and
Aunt Lucie Maréchal in 1851; Planet in 1853; Nini
Clésinger and Néraud in 1855.

Nevertheless Nohant was crowded with guests. Manceau
never for a moment left his post, and the other young men
turned up as often as they could. Maurice's versatility was a
cause of anxiety to his mother. He did so many things well,
but nothing to perfection. His caricatures were amusing, his
illustrations clever and full of poetic feeling. The melodramas which he wrote for his puppet theatre were highly
comic, and he even produced a novel. He never, however,
emerged from obscurity. The burden of his mother's fame
lay heavy on his shoulders. Though Sand loved him
wholeheartedly, she could not help adopting a faintly
patronizing tone when she talked to him about his many
activities. 'Show me your novel to Buloz: he will accept it to
please me.' That is not the sort of encouragement an artist
wants. Maurice was approaching his forties. It irks a man at
that age to be nothing but his mother's son. She was eager to
see him married, but about that, as about everything else, he
could not make up his mind.

She still regretted his failure to make a wife of her dear
'Titine' with whom she corresponded regularly. There was
no end to the Bertholdis's requests. Neither Augustine nor
her husband was ever satisfied with what they had. When
they were appointed to Lunéville, they would rather have
been closer to Paris. When Sand got them moved to St.

Omer they would, for reasons of climate, have been better satisfied with Antibes. Augustine, who was still a handsome woman, would have liked George Sand to present her to that powerful patron, Prince Napoleon.

George Sand to Augustine de Bertholdi: I *do not want* to introduce you to the Prince. It would not suit me at all to put in his way a pretty woman with favours to ask. Get rid of the idea to which you so obstinately cling that I can ask kindnesses and assistance from the great, under the present régime . . . It is not for a white-haired old lady like me to kick her heels in the ante-room of a man young enough to be her son, and to grovel in gratitude for what he may deign to do for her . . . And don't expect me, either, to give you a letter to him. It is scarcely fitting that I should send a young and pretty woman to have an audience of a man who is only too fond of the sex. I have no wish to play the bawd . . . Maurice is still with us, but for a short time only. He sends you his love, as does Manceau, though the latter is not yet grey-headed. I am afraid he never may be. Poor, poor boy. . . .[1]

Manceau was coughing and spitting in a suspicious manner with which Sand was only too familiar. As to Solange, she was gadding about as unattached women 'of great beauty and little virtue' who run after men usually do. She was off, in turn, for Belgium, London, Turin.

George Sand to Solange Clésinger, July 25th, 1855: I should like to laugh at the fantastic travel adventures which you relate with such comic gusto. But I am always afraid that behind all the gaiety there may lurk sorrow and foolishness. On you go, constantly worried about where to make for next, while all the time Nohant would be much better for your morale and for your physical health . . . But the Devil's for ever at your back, pushing you whither I have no idea . . . Do, at least, keep me informed of your movements, and when you are tired of looking for, though never finding, amusement, come here and be bored. It will at least give you a chance of having a rest. . . .[2]

[1] Unpublished. Simone André-Maurois Collection.
[2] Letter quoted by Samuel Rocheblave in *George Sand et sa Fille,* p. 220.

To which Solange replied that Nohant without her dogs and her horses would be intolerable.

> I frankly confess that Berry—explored on foot—has lost much of its charm for me. Unfortunately, I am only twenty-seven, and, though I am often ailing, my blood still runs too swiftly, and my nerves are still too young, to make it possible for me to spend a whole winter doing wool-work, playing the piano, or giving all my attention to my vast correspondence. I need to be active in some way or other, whether in the frequenting of salons, stage-plays or race-meetings, etc. . . . or riding on horseback, which is the most restful of all varieties of activity.'[1]

George had no wish to find food for horses. Besides, for the first time in her life, she wanted to get away from Nohant. She had now to work harder than ever in order to keep her family, help political refugees, and provide for the grandchildren of Marie Dorval—and many others. Worn out, at Nohant, by a daily stream of visitors, many of whom came to ask her to use her influence on their behalf with Prince Napoleon, she longed for somewhere more remote, where she could settle down to her labours. In the course of an expedition which she had made with Manceau in the valley of the Creuse, which forms the hilly part of Berry, or, to use her own words, 'its little Switzerland', she happened upon a small village called Gargilesse standing on a river of the same name. The place had enchanted her. It must be admitted that this part of the country is extremely pretty. Cliffs clothed in brushwood make a frame for a river-bed studded with black boulders, at the bottom of which flows the Creuse, its blue surface streaked with white rocks and turned to foam by swirling eddies. The friendly air of the inhabitants, and their ready hospitality, had pleased her. A man called Moreau, whose trade was catching trout, had acted as their guide from Pin to Gargilesse, a village built in a hollow of the hills, where twenty or so streams nourished a vegetation of almost African density, so warm and

---

[1] Samuel Rocheblave: op. cit., p. 221. Solange's letter, dated October 6th, 1855, was in reply to one written by Sand on the 4th, inviting her to spend the winter at Nohant, but, 'on one condition—no horses'.

protected was the site. The place contained some seven
hundred souls, a romano-byzantine church, a romantic
château, and swarms of Algerian butterflies. 'It became an
obsession with us,' she said, 'since there was no need for us
to live in Paris, to establish a temporary residence in the
village . . . Every artist who loves the countryside has, at
some time or another, dreamed of ending his days in a place
where life may be reduced to the simplicities of a pastoral
existence. . .'[1]

She was suddenly seized by the desire to buy a small
house at Gargilesse. The price would have to be in the
neighbourhood of five hundred to a thousand francs.
Manceau asked permission to make her a present of the
kind of place she was looking for, found exactly the right
property, standing on the bank of the river, bought it, and
could soon talk of nothing but *his* terrace, *his* meadows and
his kitchen. For a sum of three hundred francs, the 'faithful
companion' had the house repainted and furnished. He
fitted it out like a ship, with a series of small but
comfortable cabins. Madame Sand took a great liking to it.
Whenever she felt the need to work in peace, she would
leave Nohant with Manceau and take refuge at Gargilesse,
where the two of them lived a life of idyllic happiness.
Maurice paid it a visit, as did the actress Bérengère. But
Gargilesse was to Nohant what Marly had been to
Versailles, a retreat reserved for a few chosen souls. Sand
rarely used it as an address. Later, Victor Hugo immortal-
ized the tiny stream:

> George Sand a la Gargilesse
> Come Horace avait l'Anio. . . .

In 1857 both Alfred de Musset and Gustave Planche
died, the latter after a long and terrible struggle, with the
faithful Buloz in constant attendance at his bedside.
Planche in his articles had figured to the end as the loyal
champion of George Sand, who held him to be 'the only
sound critic now writing'—which should be interpreted as
meaning the only one who wrote about her. Sandeau
mourned him: 'Poor Planche, poor Trenmor, as we here
used to call him, nobody will ever know how much I loved
him.' It may be doubted whether he himself knew, so long
as the other was alive. As to Musset, his heart, his 'poor

---

[1] GEORGE SAND: *Promenades autour d'un Village.*

heart', had been prematurely worn out by a lifetime of wild indulgence and excess. He had tried to find a substitute for George, but had never forgotten her. In 1851 he had revisited Italy, and found the memory of her there still living:

> Aveugle, inconstante, ô fortune!
> Supplice enivrant des amours!
> Ote-moi, mémoire importune,
> Ote-moi ces yeux que je vois toujours. . . .

These lines he repeated to himself whenever, in spite of himself, he saw again in brooding fancy the 'velvet-soft, the dark, unfathomable eyes' of that lover in Venice whom, no matter how much she might have disappointed him, he could never forget.

In 1834, when he was busily engaged on his *Confession d'un Enfant du Siècle,* George had written to him: 'I find it impossible, in my present state of mind, to write about you in a book. You, however, must do as you will: novels, sonnets, poems—you must speak of me as you would wish to speak. I deliver myself blindfold into your hands.'[1]

In 1858, after Musset's death, when she had made her peace with *La Revue des Deux Mondes,* she offered Buloz for publication an autobiographical novel dealing with the Venetian tragedy—*Elle et Lui.* Although she sincerely believed her treatment of the subject to be impartial, she cast herself in a role of sublime nobility. Her heroine, Thérèse Jacques, gives herself to her lover only from a feeling of compassion. When Buloz read the manuscript, he advised her to represent Thérèse as having been rather less perfect, and to put not quite so many *saintly* utterances into her mouth. Now that age had worked a transformation in George's philosophy of love, she had set herself, once again, to retouch the past, so that the story of her life might appear more consistent. It was but human to do so, and maybe it was wise. But her novel infuriated Paul de Musset, who retaliated with a cruel and unjust book, *Lui et Elle.* Then came the last straw. Louise Colet, a woman writer as lacking in talent as she was richly endowed with tempera-

[1] This letter, dated May 12th, 1834, was printed by Spoelberch de Lovenjoul in *La Véritable Histoire de Elle et Lui,* p. 136.

ment, produced a pamphlet entitled *Lui*, which fairly dripped hatred.

George Sand had in her possession Musset's love-letters to her, as well as her own to him. In 1860 she decided to publish them, hoping thereby to re-establish the truth on a basis of irrefutable documentation. There can be no doubt that this correspondence quite definitely proved the existence of a mutual passion—but was this the moment to make it public? She thought it best to consult Sainte-Beuve, who, in the old days, had been a witness of the emotional stress and strain which had led the lovers to separate. She had never actually quarrelled with him, though they had long since ceased to see anything of one another. In the intimacy of his 'poison-cupboard' he had been far from gentle towards her: 'a pot-house Christina of Sweden' had been one of the descriptions that went into his secret collection of literary notes. But in 1859, when Jules Sandeau was elected to the Academy, Solange had met him at the installation ceremony. He had spoken in a very kindly fashion to the young woman about George, and had asked her to come and see him. Solange was making great play at that time with her announced intention of writing the life of the Maréchal de Saxe, her great-great-grandfather. Sainte-Beuve gave her a certain amount of advice—in a strictly paternal spirit. 'His fatherly attitude to me is quite charming.'

Sainte-Beuve to Solange: What lovely weather. I expect you have already been to Versailles. Whether or no, Monsieur Soulié (the Curator of the Museum—he has quarters in the Palace) has been told of the piece of luck that is coming his way. You would do well to talk to him about the Maréchal de Saxe project. I am quite sure that he has information which might prove useful. *Mille respectueux et tendres hommages.*[1]

Sainte-Beuve received Solange at the rue du Montparnasse, in a Louis XV room panelled in white and gold, with windows opening on to a plum tree and a climbing clematis. The rather too good-looking serving maid had about her an air of Madame de Pompadour. A cat was suckling its kittens

[1] Unpublished letter, dated September 26th, 1859. Simone André-Maurois Collection.

behind the door. Sainte-Beuve lavished on his fair visitor all
his wealth of intelligence and erudition. The talk, and those
that followed, produced no *Life of the Maréchal de Saxe,*
but they did give birth to a friendship.

To Jeanne de Tourbey, the 'Lady of the Violets', whose
lover was Ernest Barache,[1] son of the all-powerful Minister
of Justice, Sainte-Beuve wrote:

> Here is something by which I set great store. The
> immediate necessity is to interest our good friend,
> Monsieur Bar[oche] on behalf of the charming daughter
> of Madame Sand, Solange, who has a case pending which
> is to come up for hearing on Tuesday. At the moment, in
> view of the age of the presiding Justices, she may appear
> to be slightly compromised. But the son of the Keeper of
> the Seals, can no doubt do a great deal towards
> influencing their decisions. And then, too, the Advocate
> General! Well, anyway, you have been told now what it is
> all about, and I shall be assured that Monsieur
> Bar[oche] will have been kept informed. . . .[2]

Solange's letters reminded Sand of the time when Sainte-
Beuve had produced a calming and comforting effect upon
herself. 'No one has a happier gift for saying the right
things. He expresses them in a form at once pleasing and
serious.' So she sent Emile Aucante to the rue du
Montparnasse with copies of the whole Musset correspondence. 'You see, dear friend, that all I ask is two hours of
your precious time in which to read the various documents,
to be followed by one hour of talk with my messenger who
will clarify anything that still remains obscure in this letter
of mine: finally, a further hour in which to chew the cud of
what you will have read, whenever you can fit it in, and a
considered verdict by which I will abide to the last iota.
. . .'[3]

The verdict, when it came, left her in no doubt: the
correspondence must not be published.

[1] Ernest Baroche was on the point of regularizing his liaison
with the Lady of the Violets, when he was killed at Le Bourget
in 1870. As residuary legatee of a hero, she inherited the whole
of his large fortune, and, in 1872, married the Comte de Loynes.

[2] Unpublished letter. Simone André-Maurois Collection.

[3] Letter printed by Spoelberch de Lovenjoul in *La Véritable
Histoire de Elle et Lui,* p. 223.

George Sand to Sainte-Beuve, February 6th, 1851: Dear friend: Emile has told me about his final interview with you, and the nature of your advice. It is good, and I shall follow it. The letters shall not be published until after my death. When they are, I think they will prove that three specific and hateful charges never for a moment weighed upon the conscience of this, your friend: that a dying man was allowed to witness the beginnings of a new affair while he was in extremis: that there was ever any threat, or any idea, of shutting him away in an asylum: that there was ever any intention on my part of getting him back, or of exercising my powers of attraction on him after he had become morally cured . . . Those are the three filthy charges which my accusers level at me. If the letters prove anything it is that there is, underlying the two novels, *Confession d'un Enfant du Siècle,* and *Elle et Lui,* a substratum of actuality. Anyone is at liberty to assume from such evidence as they provide, that there was folly on one side and affection on the other, or, perhaps, that there was folly on both, but most certainly that there was never anything either hateful or cowardly in the two hearts involved, nor anything that can leave a blot upon their sincerity. . . .[1]

Touched by Sand's confidence in him, and having learned through Solange that the Nohant establishment was in financial low water (George, by her own account, had not been able during the previous winter to afford a new coat or a new dress—which is hard to believe), Sainte-Beuve conceived the idea of getting the Académie Française to award the Gobert Prize of twenty thousand francs to the great woman novelist. Vigny gave his unstinted support to the scheme. He was big enough to let literary distinction take precedence of personal spite. Guizot, though lavish both of praise and regret, opposed the claims of the author of *Elle et Lui,* quoting in his justification a number of 'scandalous' comments on marriage and property which she had made. Mérimée and Sainte-Beuve protested. A vote was taken. Eighteen of the judges were against her, and only six chivalrous gentlemen for,—Sainte-Beuve, Ponsard, Vigny, Mérimée, Nisard and Silvestre de Sarcy. Jules Sandeau did not put in an appearance! Since a second vote had to be

[1] Ibid., pp. 224-5.

taken of the Institut as a whole, Mérimée, an active
campaigner on Sand's behalf, in spite of certain ludicrous
memories, canvassed 'little Jules' by letter. But Sandeau
could not forgive the woman who had caused the
'shipwreck' of his youth, and the prize went to Thiers.

The Court, which in spite of Sand's own wishes
continued to extend its protection to her, was annoyed by
this failure. The Empress suggested that perhaps the
Académie might, in default of awarding her the prize, elect
her a member. Somewhat later a pamphlet appeared from
the pen of an anonymous writer, entitled *Les Femmes
à l'Academie,* which described the installation of a woman
who could be none other than George Sand. She replied in a
pamphlet of her own: *Pourquoi les Femmes à l'Academie?*
In this she explained that, though she felt considerable
respect for the company, and had no doubts of the ability of
its members, she had no wish to be herself connected with a
body of men whom she regarded as being old-fashioned,
and out of touch with contemporary conditions. 'Sour
grapes', was the general comment. 'No', replied Sand, 'not
sour, merely over-ripe.'

IV

MAURICE'S MARRIAGE

IN 1861 Maurice Sand celebrated his thirty-eighth birthday. His mother was now fifty-seven. Feeling that she was
growing old, she put pressure upon her son to get married. She longed for a fresh supply of grandchildren.
The kind of life which the handsome Solange was leading
was not favourable to motherhood. Maurice was the last
hope. In 1854 he had sought the hand of Berthe Duvernet,
who had disappointed him by marrying Cyprien Girerd.
More recently, two other possible matches, with Aucante as
go-between, had come to nothing.

George Sand to Jules Boucoiran, July 31st, 1860: I
despair of your ever marrying him off if you seek a bride

for him among legitimists and Church folk. I, personally, should much prefer a Protestant family. Still, take your soundings and report results to me. I am terribly anxious that he should make up his mind, and set about starting a family. If you can discover some charming young person with serious tastes, a pretty face, intelligence, and a decent family behind her which won't try to impose its own ideas or its own ways of life upon the young couple, save by exerting such influence as comes of affection— then I shall certainly not let money considerations stand in the way. . . .[1]

I, personally, should much prefer a Protestant family . . . George Sand's links with Catholicism were growing progressively weaker. In the days when she had been an inmate of the English Convent, she had loved the ceremonies of the Church. Later, she had ceased to be a practising Catholic, and had given her allegiance to a Christianity which, as she herself put it, was limited to the Gospel according to St. John—the Christianity of the 'Vicaire Savoyard', to which Pierre Leroux and Jean Reynaud had given a new form. Her God was the God of all good men and true, of Béranger, of Victor Hugo. *George Sand to Flaubert:* 'My Christianity [of 1848] was only a passing *craze*, though I admit that at all times the Faith can exercise an irresisitible attraction on those who regard only its gentler aspects . . . I am not surprised that a generous-hearted man like Louis Blanc should have dreamed of seeing it purified anew, and brought into line with his ideals. I, too, once entertained that illusion, but one has only to take a few steps into the past of the Primitive Church to see that it can never be revived . . .'[2] However, she retained, from her fond memories of Father de Prémord, a predilection for the Jesuits, seeing them (and this was high praise, coming from her) as heretics who were within measurable distance of her own philosophy of life. 'The doctrine of Loyola remains the only practicable religion.'

As matters turned out, the woman whom Maurice did eventually marry was not a Protestant but an Italian girl without any religion at all, whom he had seen grow up from childhood, the daughter of Luigi Calamatta, the engraver. 'Either love or don't get married', had been his mother's

1 GEORGE SAND: *Correspondance.* Volume IV, p. 214.
2 Ibid., Volume IV, pp. 271-2.

advice. Lina Calamatta was a charming young woman. She
had been partially educated in Paris, was very pretty,
intelligent, and, what Sand regarded as being of the utmost
importance, 'an ardent Roman patriot'. There would
certainly be no political squabbles between son's mother
and son's wife.

> *George Sand to Lina Calamatta, March 31st, 1862:* Lina,
> darling, put your trust in us, put your trust in him, and
> believe in happiness. There is only one happiness in life,
> to love and to be loved . . . I feel certain that I shall be a
> true mother to you, for I need a daughter, and in whom
> could I find a better one than in the child of one of my
> dearest friends? Love your dear Italy, my child, for to do
> so is the mark of a generous heart. We love it, too,
> especially now that it has re-awakened in these critical
> and heroic days. . . .[1]

The two women got on well together at Nohant. Lina
had a delicious voice, fresh and rich, which was the delight
of her mother-in-law. 'She is a perfect child of nature, and a
regular character: she sings enchantingly; she can be both
tender and angry, and she makes sweets and goodies with
which to surprise us. Each day when work is laid aside, our
time of recreation becomes, as a result of her skilful
ministrations, a genuine interlude of celebration . . .'[2] The
girl was exquisitely sensitive, equally prepared to dissolve in
laughter at the antics of a fly, or to cry her eyes out over the
puppets, when there was the slightest excuse of sentiment.
Like everybody else at Nohant, she soon became madly
addicted to the study of geology and the collecting of
fossils, though these occupations did not stop her from
sewing away at baby-clothes and hemming nappies, for
there were soon signs that a child was on the way, and the
whole household was agog. The religious problem had not
been resolved. Sand would have been perfectly ready to
accept a Catholic marriage, as is proved by a letter of hers
to Lina, dated April 10th, 1862, during the period of the
engagement: 'God will give all three of us credit for faith,
because marriage is an act of faith in *Him* as well as in
ourselves. The words of the priest add nothing to it . . . It is
a matter for ourselves alone, and in church, while the priest

---

[1] GEORGE SAND: *Correspondance.* Volume IV, pp. 324-5.
[2] Ibid., Volume IV, pp. 238-9.

is busy with his mutterings, we shall be praying to the true God, the God who sends His blessings to the sincere of heart, and helps them to keep their vows. . . .'[1]

In this matter Maurice was even more intransigent than George, while Lina Calamatta, who had long suffered under the tyranny of a bigoted mother (after her husband's death, she took the veil, and the name in religion of Sister Marie-Josèphe de la Miséricorde), shared to the full the views of her betrothed. Consequently, the marriage had been a civil one only. The problem, however, about the bringing up of the children, remained. There is matter for a whole book on *George Sand in Search of the Best of all possible Protestantisms*. She corresponded with various Ministers of Religion, weighed their doctrines, and sought out Dissenters who did not carry Dissent to extremes—all for the purpose of so arranging matters that her grandchildren should, later on, be assured of the shelter and support provided by an organized church. She was concerned not for herself (her own attitude was fixed and final) but for Maurice and his children. Ultimately both he and his wife turned Protestant, went through a second ceremony in church, and got Pastor Muston to baptize their son, Marc-Antoine Dudevant-Sand, nicknamed 'Cocoton', who was born on July 14th, 1863— the anniversary of the Taking of the Bastille. 'We have shot off the little cannon' (it had been installed in 1848) 'and a piper from Auvergne came and played for us the most primitive of the Gallic chants. . . .'[2]

Cocoton's birth, like everything else connected with Nohant, took place in a picturesque and slightly lunatic atmosphere. It was a house in which 'theatre' played a more important part than life. Rehearsals and performances, whether of puppets or of full-sized stage dramas, were of daily occurrence. Manceau as an actor was 'perfection made perfect'. One of the young girls from the village, Marie Caillaud, at first known as 'chicken Marie' because her work lay in the poultry yard, but later promoted by Sand, who found her to be very gifted, to the position of forewoman, had been enrolled by Manceau in the company, of which she had become the star performer. Every evening there was a play, followed by supper. Then, 'Madame', as Manceau called her, would go upstairs to sleep for an hour,

[1] Letter printed by Wladimir Karénine in *George Sand*. Volume V, p. 415.

[2] GEORGE SAND: *Correspondance*. Volume IV, p. 353.

after which Manceau woke her, and she settled down to work. He, meanwhile, would sit by, 'coughing quietly', while Lina knitted baby-clothes.

Throughout the spring and summer of 1863, Sand was a constant visitor to the theatre at La Châtre, whither she brought many touring companies. On July 2nd, the pious Calamatta dowager arrived in order to be present at her daughter's lying-in. She was appalled to find the house filled with actors all busily rehearsing *Le Château de Pictordu*. Manceau, in spite of the fact that he was running a high temperature, Marie Caillaud, George, and even Lina, pregnant though she was, bathed regularly in the river, though not Maurice, whose rheumatism forbade such an indulgence. When Lina was near her time a midwife was installed at Nohant, and she, too, was taken to La Châtre to see *Le Fils du Giboyer*, and *Trente Ans, ou la Vie d'un Joueur*. When Lina's pains came on, the whole party was at the theatre, and the patient had to wait for a good part of the night before her nurse returned. Nevertheless, Cocoton was a magnificent baby, whom George Sand welcomed into the world, wrapped in 'her apron'.

The first friend to whom George Sand sent news of Marc-Antoine's arrival, was Alexandre Dumas, the younger. She had long felt a deep and strong affection for this 'dear son' of hers, who called her 'mamma', was twenty years her junior, and had much the same temperament as herself, the same liking for a 'responsible social' attitude in literature, the same ardent desire to stand as the protector of women and children. She had done her best to get him to Nohant, but had never succeeded in doing so until 1851, for Dumas was entirely taken up by his liaison with a Russian patrician 'with green eyes and long, amber-coloured hair', the Princess Nedefa Narishkine. At last, however, he promised to come.

Alexandre Dumas the younger to George Sand, September 20th, 1861: I thank you, as Monsieur Prudhomme would say, for your esteemed favour of the 15th, and take pen in hand to express my lively feelings of gratitude . . . I understand that my hostess has already written to you . . . I won't conceal the fact that she is looking forward immensely to being received at Nohant, and meeting you face to face . . . There remains the question of her daughter whom she does not want to

leave alone in the forty-four rooms of her vast barrack of
a house, and whom she would like to be allowed to
present to you. She can sleep on a settee in her mother's
room. That, as a young travelling Muscovite, is what she
loves—so you need not worry about her. But . . . and
here is the real difficulty . . . there is a friend of mine, a
very great friend, who is rather like one of your
Newfoundland dogs, is called Marchal, weighs 182
pounds, and has enough intelligence for four. He can
sleep anywhere, in the farmyard, under a tree, or under
the sink. May I bring him? . . .[1]

Dumas was full of admiration for the puppets, or said he
was, and read Musset's poems aloud to the company
assembled round the big table in the evenings. The choice
was an odd one. The 'giant', Marchal, was a great success
. . . 'Marchal is collaborating with Maurice in a puppet-play
. . . Marchal is well on the way to becoming my great big baby . . .' He stayed on for a long time after Dumas had
departed, painted portraits of Maurice, Sand, Manceau and
Marie Caillaud, but annoyed Madame Sand by failing to
write a 'bread-and-butter' letter after a prolonged visit, in the
course of which he had made the acquaintance of Prince
Napoleon, from whom he got a number of commissions.

Dumas the younger to Sand, February 21st, 1862: I shall
always feel a certain reluctance about introducing no
matter whom into your house at Nohant, where
everything runs so smoothly among friends that the
tiniest grain of sand threatens to bring the whole machine
to a standstill . . . So our friend Marchal has already
shown himself to be ungrateful, has he? It is early days
for that to happen. Still, he *ought* to have thanked you
for that six thousand francs commission which he got
from the Prince, entirely owing to you. Oh dear! oh dear!
I am very much afraid that human nature is not God's
masterpiece. . . .

February 26th, 1862: I am feeling quite furious, and the
silence of our mastodon is not a little to blame for that. I
have no more idea than you have where he is. A lack of
education, prolonged into maturity, can look remarkably

[1] Unpublished. Bibliothèque nationale: Department of
Manuscripts.

like a lack of feeling. Poor boy, he doesn't yet know that
when one has received from somebody like you such
extended, cordial, and useful hospitality, one ought at
least to answer the letters one receives, to say nothing of
writing one's thanks. . . .[1]

The fact of the matter was that charming though the
mastodon might be, he was an egotist. Sand forgave him,
and even retained a good deal of affection for him. It was
Dumas, too, who introduced George to Edouard Rodrigues,
the stockbroker.

Dumas the younger to George Sand, March 8th, 1862:
No one could be more of an artist than this chap
Rodrigues. He is devoted to music, and a great friend to
the arts (in the best sense of the word). He has just settled
forty thousand francs on young Emma Fleury, of the
Théâtre Français, and married her off to a sculptor of
promise.[2] This he did, not for the *obvious* reason, but
from sheer goodness of heart . . . He is a man for whose
admiration of you it would be difficult to find words,
were it not that he has already found them himself.
Summing up his debt to you, he said: 'Madame Sand has
made a better man of me . . .' I found that so touching,
and so worthy of you, that I promised myself to send him
along. And here I am, keeping that promise. . . .[3]

When his 'darling mamma' paid a visit to Paris that
winter, she agreed to go with him to dine with Rodrigues in
his 'gilded home'. Her host on that occasion promised to
give material assistance to several of her 'young men' who
were badly in need of money.

Sand's favourite themes became those of Dumas. They
both of them had a weakness for 'plays with a purpose'.
Dumas turned *Francois le Champi* into a piece for the
theatre, which was called *Le Fils naturel*. The subject was
one that, naturally enough, was close to his heart. *Claudie*,
the unmarried mother who, for no other reason than that
she has been betrayed, deserves, more than most women,

[1] Unpublished. Bibliothèque nationale: Department of
Manuscripts.
[2] Jules Francaschi (1825-93).
[3] Unpublished. Bibliothèque nationale: Department of
Manuscripts.

the respect of the masculine sex, suggested to him, first *Les Idées de Madame Aubray*, and, later, *Denise*. *Le Mariage de Victorine*, which is the glorification of a 'misalliance', seemed to them both so magnificent a theme that Sand wrote it up as a novel, *Le Marquis de Villemer*, from which Dumas helped her to construct a second play. He was a master of stage technique, and a past master at scenario-writing, at which Sand was always a poor hand. This did not stand in the way of his admiring her to excess. 'She thinks like Montaigne,' he said, 'dreams like Ossian, and writes like Jean-Jacques. Leonardo has put her phrasing into visual form, and Mozart into music. Madame de Sevigné kisses her hands, and Madame de Staël kneels when she passes.'

Le Marquis de Villemer is a commonplace story about a lady-companion who marries the son of the house, and the wit in which Dumas dressed this moral tale is not, all told, very scintillating. The play, however, was an enormous success, the reason being that George Sand, outraged by the religious intolerance of the Imperial Government, and provoked by the threat to freedom of speech and conscience, was becoming increasingly anti-clerical.

> *George Sand to Prince Napoleon, February 26th, 1862:*
> The Emperor is frightened of Socialism. I agree that, from his point of view, that fear is well founded. But by striking at the movement too hard and too soon, he has raised on the ruins of the old Party a new one which is clever in quite a different sort of way, and no less dangerous, a Party bound together by class-feeling and clannishness, a Party of nobles and priests. Unfortunately, I can see no counterpoise in the bourgeoisie. For all its faults the old bourgeoisie had its uses as a make-weight. It may have been sceptical, it may have owed a declared allegiance to Voltaire, but it had its own form of clannishness, its own *nouveau-riche* vanity. It resisted the priests, it flouted the nobles—of whom it was jealous. But all that is a thing of the past. Today it flatters them. Their titles have been restored, and today we see the middle class showing the utmost deference to the legitimists by whom it is surrounded, and who are raising their heads again with vengeance! The middle class is only too anxious to be on good terms with the nobles, whose influence is growing greater. The priests are acting as go-betweens. People now become church-goers in order that

they may be received in legitimist drawing-rooms. Civil
servants are leading the way, and it is no unusual thing to
see them at Mass, all smiles and bows. As for the wives
of the *Third Estate,* they have plunged head foremost into
legitimacy—for women never do things by halves. . . .[1]

Anti-clerical she might be, but she was not, nor had she
ever wished to be, anti-religious.

George Sand to Alexandre Dumas the younger: My
beliefs about death are all sunny, and far from harsh. My
own view is that I have deserved quite a pleasant fate in
the next world. I don't insist on being given a place in the
seventh heaven, with the Seraphim, nor on spending my
time in continual contemplation of the Face of the Most
High. For one thing, I don't think that there will be any
face, or profile, to contemplate, and, in the second, well,
though it is very nice to be in the front seats, it is not, for
me, a necessity . . . I remain an optimist in spite of all the
searing experiences I have gone through. I am not sure
that optimism is not my only really good quality. You
will come to it—just see if you don't! At your age I was
just as tormented, and, both morally and physically, far
worse off than you are. Then, one fine day, sick of
wearing myself and other people to shadows, I said to
myself: 'What *does* it all matter! The universe is great and
lovely. The things we think of tremendous importance
are so ephemeral that they are really not worth bothering
about. There are, in life, only two or three truly
important things, and it is precisely those things, for all
their obviousness, for all their ease, that I have failed to
see, or, having seen, have despised: *mea culpa.* But I have
been punished for my foolishness, and have suffered as
much as it is possible to suffer. Surely, I shall be forgiv-
en! It is time I made my peace with the Good God. . . .'[2]

With God, then, she had made her peace, but she could
believe neither in the Devil nor in Hell. The idea that a good
God could condemn anybody to eternal torment revolted
her. But she was far from imagining the extent to which she
herself shocked those whose temperament was naturally

[1] GEORGE SAND: *Correspondance.* Volume IV, p. 315.
[2] Letter quoted by Wladimir Karénine in *George Sand.*
Volume IV, pp. 407-9.

sombre and embittered. Nothing is so exasperating to the wounded heart as quiet optimism. Baudelaire detested her.

The woman Sand is the Prudhomme of immorality. She has always been a moralist, though there was a time when her morality took an anti-moral form. Besides, she is no artist. She has that famous, easy style so dear to the bourgeois heart. She is stupid, she is heavy, she is garrulous. There is in her moral ideas about as much depth of thought, as much sensibility, as you would find in a concierge or a kept woman. The things she said of her mother . . . the things she has said about poetry . . . her love of the working class! . . . That some people can become infatuated with such a *latrine* is sufficient proof of the abyss into which humanity in this century has sunk.

Take, for instance, her Preface to *Mademoiselle La Quintinie*, in which she maintains that good Christians do not believe in Hell. This Sand is all for the *God of decent, kindly folk*, the God of the concierge and the thieving servant-girl. She has good reasons for wishing to suppress Hell.

The Devil and George Sand. There is no reason to hold that the Devil tempts only men of genius. No doubt He despises fools, but He does not disdain their help. Quite the contrary, He has great hopes of them. Of this, George Sand is a good example. She is above all, and outstandingly, a great fool: but she is possessed. It is the Devil who has persuaded her to put her trust in her *good heart* and her *good sense*, in order that she may persuade all the other great fools to put their trust in *their* good hearts and *their* good sense. I cannot think of the stupid creature without a shudder of horror. If ever I met her I don't think I could keep myself from throwing a holy-water stoup at her head.

George Sand is one of those ageing *ingénues* who will never leave the stage.[1]

Such a reaction may have been natural, but it is unjust. How should anguish of spirit not hate serenity? Those who live in the shadows and those who live in the sun have never been able to get along together. Ever since her visit to

[1] CHARLES BAUDELAIRE: *Mon Coeur mis à nu*, pp. 53-4.

Rome, George had been 'haunted by the black spectre'. The church bells which, in her girlhood, and even as late as 1834, had brought her peace and consolation, now sounded in her ears like 'mournful thunder, like a sinister tom-tom'. It so happened that in 1862, Octave Feuillet, a novelist seventeen years her junior, published in Buloz's *Revue* a novel entitled *Sybille* which was imbued with a spirit of sentimental and mediocre religiosity. It is the story of a young girl who, after a childhood spent in unquestioning belief, begins to entertain grave doubts at the period of her first communion. One stormy night she sees the village priest put out, unaccompanied, in a boat to save some sailors who are in imminent danger. Moved by this spectacle of religion in action, she returns to God. Somewhat later, having fallen in love with a young sceptic, she strives to convert him, and dies after returning from a moonlight walk which has been full of 'theology and sentiment'.[1]

This book exasperated George Sand, and she determined to give tit for tat. A year later, in the pages of that same *Revue des Deux Mondes*, she delivered a counter-blow, also in the form of a novel—*Mademoiselle La Quintinie*. She had lost none of her ability to plan and execute a work of fiction at high speed. In this story she turned the situation imagined by Feuillet inside out. The heroine, Lucie, pious daughter of a General, is courted by a young free-thinker whom she loves. The man in question has four main grievances against the Catholic Church—the doctrine of Hell; the denial of progress; fleshly asceticism, and, above all, the practice of Confession. A woman, he says, cannot at one and the same time confess to her husband and to her director of conscience. He, Emile, cannot bear the thought of having to share his wife's thoughts with a priest who, for the purposes of the story, is made to be a man well on the way to being, if not actually unfrocked, a dangerous and suspect individual. Ultimately he succeeds in freeing his wife's understanding, and in leading her back into the path of true religion—in other words, the author's.

The literary world was thrilled by these goings-on, and Sainte-Beuve summed up.

The author of *Sybille* raised many profound issues in his novel, issues, perhaps, rather more profound than he at

---

[1] RENE DOUMIC: *George Sand*, p. 351.

first realized—theological problems, social problems, problems of the present and the future. George Sand, as is known, took the book much to heart. The strong-winged eagle waxed as angry as in the days of her highest flights. She pounced on the white dove; she swept it up into the high heavens, she flew with it across the mountains and the torrents of Savoy, and, at this very moment, is holding the prey suspended in her claws. Thesis and anti-thesis, theology and counter-theology . . . and all this in works professedly of fiction: is it not all a little uncivilized. . . .[1]

Sand sent him her thanks. 'I have read an excellent article of yours on Feuillet, which ends with a reference to me which is far more brilliant and flattering than I deserve. I am too old an eagle to carry off young hopefuls and gobble them up . . .'[2] At a time when clericalism was the official attitude of the régime, the position taken up by George Sand established her in the eyes of the young as the 'Great Woman' of the Opposition. She became a personage; she became a banner. When the Odéon announced the forthcoming porduction of a dramatized version of *Le Marquis de Villemer*, and there was talk of an organized demonstration against it, students and workmen went to the first performance, prepared to support Sand against all comers. She herself on this occasion, was perfectly calm: only Manceau felt sick. As matters turned out, there was no demonstration. The Emperor and Empress were both present, and their applause was of the eager, artlessly ostentatious kind which betrays an uneasy conscience.

George Sand's Diary, February 26th, 1864: First night of *Villemer*. Weather quite appalling—rain. Paris a river of mud. I drove with Maillard[3] to buy flowers, and gloves at Jouvins'. Paid a visit to the Prince . . . Spent the rest of the

[1] SAINTE-BEUVE: *Nouveaux Lundis*. Volume V, p. 40.

[2] GEORGE SAND: *Lettres à Alfred de Musset et à Sainte-Beuve*, p. 249.

[3] Louis Maillard, Manceau's cousin, an engineer and a naturalist who had lived much in the Colonies. In 1863, Sand had contributed to the *Revue des Deux Mondes* two articles about him, under the general title of 'M. Maillard et ses Travaux sur l'Ile de Réunion'. These were later reprinted in *Questions d'Art et de Littérature*.

day 'at home' to students, who arrived in groups of four
with their identity cards stuck in their hat bands, to ask
for seats! From ten o'clock in the morning there was a
crowd of them on the Place de l'Odéon, shouting and
singing . . . The Emperor and the Empress were in the
audience, also Princesse Mathilde, the Prince, and
Princesse Clotilde, in whose box I sat[1] . . . Incredible,
extravagant success; shouts, singing, bravoes, curtain-
calls. There was something very like a riot when six
hundred students who had failed to get into the theatre
went off and sang choruses under the windows of the
Catholic Club and the Jesuit 'House'. They were
dispersed and taken to the lock-up. I left through a
double line of demonstrators, all chanting '*Vive George
Sand!*'—'*Vive La Quintinie!*' They followed me into the
Café Voltaire, still chanting and shouting. We had to take
to our heels . . . More than two hundred people came to
congratulate me in the green-room—among others,
Déjazet, Ulbach, Camille Doucet, Alexandre, Montigny,
Lesueur, etc. etc. . . .[2]

Le Marquis de Villemer—a workmanlike melodrama—
benefited from this popularity. Takings soared: 4300 francs,
4500, 5000, 5310—compared with the normal receipts of
the Odéon which were usually in the neighbourhood of, at
most, fifteen hundred. 'You would think', wrote Sand, 'from
the way the Odéon people treat me . . . that I was God
Almighty. . . .'

Among the friends who stood by Sand on the steps of the
Odéon during this ovation, was Gustave Flaubert, 'crying
like a woman'. An impenitent romantic, and a penitent
realist, he had always admired George's talents. He saw her
sometimes at the *Magny* dinners, with Renan, Sainte-Beuve,
Théophile Gautier and the Goncourt brothers. She would
sit beside him, glance nervously about her at the company,
and whisper in his ear: 'You are the only person here who
does not make me feel uncomfortable!' All the same, the
Goncourts were full of admiration for 'that handsome,
charming face', which was daily coming to look like that of

---

[1] In 1859 Prince Napoleon had married Clotilde of Savoy,
daughter of King Victor-Emmanuel II.

[2] Unpublished. Bibliothèque nationale: Department of
Manuscripts.

a mulatto, and for the 'marvellous delicacy of those small hands half hidden in the lace of her sleeves'.[1]

George Sand's Diary, February 12th, 1866: Dinner at *Magny's* with my 'pals'. Their welcome could not have been warmer. They were all very brilliant, except Berthelot,[2] the great scientist . . . Gautier, dazzling as ever, and full of paradoxes. Saint-Victor, charming and distinguished.[3] Flaubert, with his ardent temperament, appeals to me really much more than the others. Why?— I don't know, yet. The Goncourts too sure of themselves, especially the younger. The best talker, and the most intelligent man of the lot, is still *Uncle Beuve,* as we call him . . . We pay ten francs a head: dinner only so-so. There is a great deal of smoking. Everyone talks at the top of his voice, and leaves when he feels so inclined . . . I have forgotten to mention Louis Bouilhet, who looks very like Flaubert:[4] he was very self-effacing. Met Madame Borie . . . Had a visit at home from the dressmaker, followed by Camille[5] and Lucien Arman.[6] Have been invited to dine at Sainte-Beuve's . . . *April 9th, 1866:* Our *Magny* dinner, with all the pals: Taine, Renan, Sainte-Beuve, Gautier, Saint-Victor, Charles-Edmond, the Goncourts . . . and Berthelot, who did not open his lips. He and I exchanged not a single word. Gavarnie's [*sic*] son, a nice-looking boy, and somebody else whom I could not identify. Conversation spirited, brilliant and awash with Gautier's paradoxes. Taine, level-headed, much *too* level-headed. The evening, as a whole, had nothing of the gaiety and good-natured charm one finds among theatre folk. . . .[7]

[1] EDMOND ET JULES DE GONCOURT: *Journal*. Volume III, p. 18.

[2] Marcelin Berthelot (1827-1907).

[3] Paul de Saint-Victor, the literary critic (1825-81).

[4] Louis Bouilhet (1822-69), poet and Flaubert's friend.

[5] Dr. Camille Leclerc, who was George Sand's doctor. He was a perfect tower of strength during Manceau's last days.

[6] Lucien Arman (1811-73); Deputy for the Gironde.

[7] Unpublished. Bibliothèque nationale: Department of Manuscripts.

. It was at one of these *Magny* dinners, when Sand was absent in Berry (September 14th, 1863), that Théophile Gautier, just back from Nohant, was asked to give a description of his visit.

Was it amusing?

About as amusing as a Monastery of Morvian Brothers. I got there in the evening. It's a long way from the railroad. My trunk was unloaded into a bush. I went through the farmyard—masses of dogs—positively terrifying . . . I had dinner. The food is good, though rather too much game and chicken for my taste . . . doesn't agree with me . . . Marchal, the painter, was there, Madame Calmatta, young Dumas. . . .

How does one spend one's time at Nohant?

Breakfast at ten. Everyone sits down on the stroke. Then in comes Madame Sand, looking like a sleepwalker, and remains apparently asleep all through the meal. After breakfast we adjourn to the garden, where we play at bowls—which seems to revive her. Then she sits down and starts to talk. The subject of these morning dissertations is usually linguistic—how, for instance, *d'ailleurs*, and *meilleur* should be pronounced, with much jollity and a great many lavatory jokes.

Ugh!

But not a word, mark you, about sex. I got the idea that if one so much as mentioned the horrid thing, out one would go! . . . At three o'clock, Madame Sand retires upstairs, and remains closeted with literature until six. Dinner is rather a hurried affair—rushed through, so as to let Marie Caillot [*sic*] have hers. She is the maid of all work, a 'Petite Fadette' whom Madame Sand picked up in the country to take part in their plays, and who joins the company of an evening in the drawing-room . . . After dinner, the hostess settles down to her puzzles until midnight, and doesn't utter . . .[1]

Such massive bulk, such forceful weight of age, foursquare in a world of fads and silences, is a sign of strength. Gautier observed Sand as Hegel observed the mountains: 'that's how they *are*'.

[1] EDMOND ET JULES DE GONCOURT: *Journal.* Volume II, pp. 116-17.

V

LET'S ALL MIGRATE TO PALAISEAU

George Sand to Augustine de Bertholdi, March 31st, 1864: The success of *Villemer* has made it possible for me to enjoy more freedom than of late. For the last few years I have had our good Berry folk on my shoulders, and that has kept me at Nohant. Everyone, from rural constables for miles around to the friends of friends, has looked to my influence to find them jobs. My life has been entirely taken up in writing useless letters, and being obliging, out of sheer lazy good-nature. Add to all this my visitors, who never seem able to understand that the evening is my brief interval of freedom, the day my long routine of work. I got to such a point that I had to do work all night, and it very nearly led to a complete breakdown. The expense of living at Nohant was far, far too much for me to carry unless I was prepared to shoulder a crushing load of work. But now I am making a change. I am delighted at the prospect, and it seems odd that others should pity me. It will be far better, too, for the children, because the presence of our visitors from Paris meant that they were cramped for room, whereas our new arrangement will mean that in the city we shall be within easy reach of one another, and can all come back here together whenever we feel that we should like a little time in the country. But the whole business has given rise to all sorts of tittle-tattle, and I cannot help laughing when people say to me: 'Are you really going away? How *will* you manage to live without us?' Oh, these good Berry folk!—they have been living *off* me for quite long enough. . . .[1]

BUT THERE was more to it than that, and the reasons which George gave to Augustine for wishing to leave

---

[1] Simone André-Maurois Collection.

Nohant were not the only ones. For some time past, Manceau had been getting on Maurice's nerves. It was hard for the son of the house to see somebody of his own age, somebody of whom he had always thought as occupying a subordinate position, now promoted to the rank of favourite. It was humiliating that 'Marcel le Vieil' should be officially recognized as Secretary, Accountant, and, to all intents and purposes, Agent, with real, if delegated, authority in the running of Nohant. There was a quite remarkable resemblance between Manceau and the heroes of George Sand's novels. Unselfishness had become with him almost a passion. Such little money as he had, he sought to give away. For Sand, his 'Lady', he had a doglike devotion. To the others his attitude was one of touchy pride. But in addition to all this he was a man of talent. Not only did art critics regard him as an excellent engraver. He showed also a considerable feeling for the theatre. Helped to a very considerable degree by George, he wrote a short play in verse, which was put on at the Odéon. He superintended Sand's rehearsals, and undertook the task of reading new plays to the actors. The 'friends of the family'—Dumas, Flaubert, Comte d'Orsay—treated him with affection. Princesse Mathilde invited him to dinner. Prince Napoleon was present at his First Night.

To the Goncourts, who had been surprised at Madame Sand's sober and tranquil bearing, at her appearance of being never more than half awake, at the monotonous, almost mechanical sound of her voice, Manceau explained rather like a lecturer demonstrating his exhibits, that 'she does not in the least mind being interrupted . . . Let me put it this way. Suppose you have got a tap running in your room. Somebody comes in, you turn it off . . . It is like that with Madame Sand's concentration. She can turn it on or off'.[1] His feeling for her was reciprocated. To Dumas the younger, George was loud in her praises of Manceau. 'He is a man of whom one can have the highest opinion without any risk that he may turn out disappointing. He is all heart, all devotion! I think it is the twelve years during which I have lived with him continuously, from morning till night, that have definitely reconciled me to the human race. . . .'[2]

In 1863, the tense atmosphere at Nohant became

[1] EDMOND ET JULES DE GONCOURT: *Journal*. Volume II, p. 23.
[2] Letter printed by Wladimir Karénine in *George Sand*.

intolerable. A quarrel broke out between Maurice and
Manceau on the subject of Marie Caillaud. Her success,
both as actress and as woman[1] had gone to her head, and
she had become insolently familiar. Just as formerly, in the
days of Chopin, Maurice now issued an ultimatum to his
mother: 'You must choose between him and me. One of us
must leave Nohant.' For a moment she played with the idea
of sacrificing Manceau.

> *Manceau's Diary, November 23rd, 1863:* There has been
> a long confabulation about which I know nothing. All I
> do know is, that, as a result of what was said, I have been
> told that I shall be free to leave at next Midsummer.
> Oceans of tears shed on my account!—but what do they
> amount to? So much for fifteen years of devotion! I put
> all this down in black and white now, so as never to
> return to the subject. I don't want to cry over it, and only
> hope the day will come when I shall be able to laugh at
> what has happened. Anyhow, what does it matter? . . .
> Human nature, on the whole, is pretty squalid . . . So now
> I am to be given my liberty, and, should I wish, in time to
> come, to place my love and devotion elsewhere—and
> devoting myself to others is the mainspring of my life—I
> shall be perfectly free to do so . . . I must say that, in the
> circumstances, that word 'free' is a bit much! . . . *There is
> a note added in Maurice's handwriting at a later date:* 're-
> read *Tartuffe!* Maurice'.[2]

But Sand, after thinking the matter over for a whole
night, decided that the situation differed from that of 1847.
Maurice, now happily married, and the father of a son,
could, henceforward, do without the constant presence of a
mother. Manceau, by this time seriously ill, could not be
left in the lurch. On the 24th, George chose Manceau and
departure.

[1] The dramatist, Edouard Cadol (1831-98), who spent a week
at Nohant (cf. *Juliette Lamber,* Volume II, p. 203), fell in love
with Marie Caillaud, though, in spite of what Karénine says
(Volume IV, p. 387) he did not marry her. In 1868, she gave
birth to a daughter, Lucie. It was never discovered who the
father was.

[2] Unpublished. Bibliothèque nationale: Department of
Manuscripts.

George Sand's Diary, November 24th, 1863: I feel no
sadness. Why? We knew how things were, and they have
turned out badly. I, too, am recovering *my* liberty . . .
After all, *we* are not parting. Are we not contented that
there should be a change? Wasn't I longing for some
change in this bitter and unjust existence? Let us go, my
friend. Let us go without rancour and without ill-feeling.
Let you and me not part . . . Let us give them everything;
let us give everything *for* them, always excepting our
dignity, always excepting the sacrifice of ourselves . . .
That we will *never* make.[1]

Note added in Maurice's handwriting: Re-read the
father in *Tartuffe*. My mother always was a dupe!
Maurice.

The days that followed were difficult in the extreme.
Madame Sand, overwhelmed by the gravity of her decision,
was ill, and slept 'fully dressed' upon her bed. Manceau, 'all
on edge', spent the time in continually running backwards
and forwards between Nohant and Paris in an attempt to
find somewhere in the country in which they might find a
temporary lodging. Meanwhile the puppet-plays went on.

Manceau's Diary, December 26th, 1863: Madame is
certainly far from well today. She is being a little
impatient. This afternoon she slept for a while. In the
evening she got very much excited over the dresses for
the puppets. There is more of frenzy than of silliness in
her behaviour! . . . What will happen when there are no
more puppets? . . .

Though Manceau had gained the victory, he was not a
little worried at the idea of tearing 'Madame' from her
familiar domestic existence. The year ended with the
customary ceremonies.

George Sand's Diary, December 31st, 1863: Cold: have
not stirred out. Talked with Maurice about *l'Homme de
Neige.* Dinner worthy of Lucullus: truffled partridges,
peas, meringues. After dinner, cigarettes, dominoes. Lina
sang. Midnight sounded. We looked at one another.

---

[1] George Sand underlined the word 'never' three times.

Cocoton was brought in, fully awake and as gay as a bird. We exchanged presents and munched sweets.[1]

In Paris there were changes in the habitual circle of friends. Sand settled down with Manceau at 97 rue des Feuillantines.[2] She saw a great deal of the Maillards— Manceau's cousins—of Rodrigues, the stockbroker and ex-follower of Saint-Simon, who continued to contribute generously to her charities, and of the Lamberts—those regular attendants at the *Magny* gatherings.[3] She had a set of false teeth fitted, went to the theatre four times a week, and combed the suburbs for a 'little house'. Maillard, who lived at Palaiseau, on the Versailles-Limours line, put her on the track of one. Delacroix had recently died. Sand owned more than twenty of his pictures ('I am pretty sure', she wrote, 'that they are worth anything between 70,000 and 80,000 francs). She decided to sell all but two—'La Confession du Giaour', which had been his first gift to her, and 'Le Centaur', his last. This deal enabled her to make Maurice a very welcome allowance of three thousand francs, 'which is better than unproductive capital', and to buy a small property. Rodrigues looked after the financial arrangements. The 'Villa George Sand' was bought in the name of Manceau, who undertook to leave it to Maurice. There was one last farewell visit to Nohant. 'Old Aulard', the peasant-Mayor, wept. Maurice and Lina preached wisdom to the mother whose heart had stayed too young.

George Sand's Diary, April 25th, 1864: Abstinence! abstinence from what, you fools! It would be well if you observed a lifelong abstinence from evil! Has God made what is good so that we may deprive ourselves of it? You had better abstain from enjoying the heat of the sun, from looking at the lilacs in flower. I, for my part, work, without abstaining from a regret that I do not work more.

---

[1] Unpublished. Bibliothèque nationale: Department of Manuscripts.

[2] The part of the rue des Feuillantines where George Sand went to live on June 12th, 1864, goes today by the name of the rue Claude-Bernard. In May 1866, Manceau having died in the meantime, Maurice Sand leased an apartment on the first floor of the same building.

[3] In 1862, Eugène Lambert had made a brilliant marriage.

But I am bored, and have little heart for working . . . This evening, Maurice's novel. During the day I have learned how to make *gnocchi*—a piece of knowledge that will come in useful at Palaiseau! . . .

Manceau's Diary, June 11th, 1864: Last evening at Nohant. We shall all, I think, long remember it, so there is no need to record it in writing. Still, in spite of myself, I cannot help thinking that in the course of my fourteen years of living here I have laughed oftener than cried, and *lived* more fully than at any time in the preceding thirty-three . . . From now on I shall be alone with Her. What a responsibility! but, also, what an honour, and what happiness!

    Note added in the handwriting of Maurice Sand. What a conceited ass![1]

There was no open quarrel, and everything went off in a friendly fashion. Nohant was put into dust-sheets, 'during owner's absence', since Maurice and Lina were unwilling to shoulder the weight of so large a house . . . 'The dear children do not want to look after Nohant. I cannot help feeling that, in their own interest, this decision is a mistake . . . but they have been influenced by certain scruples which, though I do not altogether understand them, are undoubtedly honourable and inspired by their tender feelings . . .'[2] They decided to go to Guillery and stay with Casimir, who remained his children's last refuge, and for whom both Maurice and Lina had a warm affection. George Sand 'winged her way to Palaiseau', accompanied by the lamentations of her Berry friends, who sent sorrowful addresses and affectionate petitions after her. There was talk at La Châtre of a family quarrel. Sand protested: 'We remain on the best of terms, God be thanked. But if the people of La Châtre had not, as usual, found *some* unworthy motive for my step, I should have suspected them of being ill . . .'[3] She loved her new Paris installation, 'so tiny, but so delightful, convenient, clean, and all in the most charming taste'. Palaiseau she found enchanting.

---

[1] Neither of these passages has hitherto been published. Bibliothèque nationale: Department of Manuscripts.

[2] GEORGE SAND: *Correspondance.* Volume V, p. 30.

[3] Ibid., Volume V, p. 33.

George Sand's Diary, June 12th, 1864: I am delighted
with *everything:* the countryside, the little garden, the
view, the house, the food, the maid, the silence. It is quite
fascinating. The good Manceau has thought of everything. *All is perfection . . . June 13th, 1864:* Slept like
a log. They tell me there was a gale of wind, and
thunder, but I heard nothing . . . Spent the day unpacking
and setting things to rights. It is fun arranging one's
belongings in a new house, especially when it is as clean
as this is. Lucy[1] prepared a most succulent meal, which
was served up with appetizing neatness. We had
strawberries *from our own garden,* fish, eggs, and coffee.
Manceau is not the only gainer . . . Scrumptious! . . .[2]

George Sand to Maurice, June 14th, 1864: This place is a
little patch of greenery, with a tiny diamond of water set
in the middle, and lovely country all round—a real
Ruysdael . . . I sleep well here. Not a sound, night or day,
it is just like being at Gargilesse. The trees are superb, the
meadows and cornfields splendid. Every scrap of land is
cultivated, but, for all that, there is a wealth of wild
plants all along the footpaths, and beside the streams. I
made a little tour of exploration this morning, and have
already found pink, blue and lilac larkspur of a kind we
do not get at home. What I should like to send you is a
species of pink meadow-sweet from my garden—an
enchanting thing. . . .[3]

Scarcely had she settled into the house at Palaiseau, than
George Sand received terrible news. The little Marc-
Antoine—'Cocoton'—had been taken ill at Guillery.

Manceau's Diary, July 19th, 1864: We received the
appalling news that Marc is dying: 'MUCH WORSE
LITTLE HOPE.' We sent the young men off at once to
tell Maillard to meet us at the Sceaux station. Packed our
bags, and started. We meant to catch the night express to

---

[1] Lucie (not Lucy) was the cook whom Manceau had
engaged.
[2] Unpublished. Bibliothèque nationale: Department of
Manuscripts.
[3] This letter is quoted by Wladimir Karénine in *George Sand.*
Volume IV, p. 478.

Bordeaux, but the local train was late, and we got to the Orléans Terminus five minutes after time. We can't set off until tomorrow . . . We sleep at the rue de Feuillantines . . . Did well to bring Lucie with us . . . *July 20th, 1864:* Another telegram IF YOU WANT SEE HIM COME AT ONCE. Visit from Maillard . . . and Camille. Persuaded them to come with us. Dined alone at home, rue des Feuillantines, and started from the station at seven-forty-five. Got a Coupé . . . *July 21st, 1864:* Breakfasted between Périgueux and Agen in our Coupé. Reached Agen at half-past ten. Found letters waiting for us, and hurried on to Guillery, where we arrived at two. We had learned half an hour earlier from the local postman that we were too late. The child died this morning. The first person we saw was Maurice—then M. Dudevant and Mme Dalias[1] . . . lastly, Madame Maurice. . . .[2]

This was the last occasion on which Sand saw her husband. Casimir, annoyed at the idea of receiving her under his roof, had said: 'I cannot stop her from coming to see her grandchild.' When 'Madame la Baronne's carriage' was announced, he went out on to the steps with his friends. Aurore had brought Doctor Camille and Manceau with her. 'Casimir . . .' she murmured in a very low voice. 'Madame,' he said, 'you know your room: it has been empty since you left.' The concubine politely took charge of the wife, who said to her, 'I entrust my old husband to you.'

George Sand was wearing a strange sort of a dress, looped up to reveal a red underskirt. She smoked enormous cigarettes. During the meal she did not speak a word. All those present at Guillery noticed 'her air of extreme depression, her fleshiness, her pendent cheeks'. She left again next morning. 'What was the impression made on you by this last meeting with your wife?' Dr. Selsis asked Casimir. 'Oh,' was the reply: 'I felt no wish to call her Aurore: she had more the appearance of a *setting* sun. . . .'[3]

Maurice and Lina returned to Nohant, Sand to Palaiseau.

---

[1] Jeanny Dalias, the Baron Dudevant's housekeeper-cum-mistress, and mother of his daughter Rose. She later became Madame Bergé.

[2] Unpublished. Bibliothèque nationale: Department of Manuscripts.

[3] Cf. LOUISE VINCENT: *George Sand et le Berry*, pp. 622-3.

Plunged in grief though she was, she once again surprised her friends by her quick powers of recuperation. 'What a tragedy! But I remand—I *command*—another child, for we must love, we must suffer, we must weep, hope, and create . . .' *Magny* dinners, music-halls, Gymnase, Odéon—life once again returned to its old, closed circle. Manceau, always coughing, looked after the house at Palaiseau, and, in the evenings, played at bézique with his 'Lady'.

VI

MANCEAU'S SUFFERINGS AND DEATH

EIGHTEEN HUNDRED and sixty-five was a year of wretchedness. Manceau, with his constant cough and a permanent high temperature, was clearly going downhill at a terrifying rate. George, too, complained of endless small ailments. She did not, however, let them interfere with her activities, and thought nothing of tramping about in the muddy garden, planting the onions sent her from Nohant, and then, in the evenings, going in to Paris for the theatre. Manceau and Maillard were worn out by a succession of errands and shopping expeditions. On January 23rd, Maillard developed peritonitis, and died suddenly. 'Madame was good and kind to everybody.' Nevertheless a few days later she dragged Manceau off in the pouring rain to visit the Fair at Palaiseau, where there was to be a performance of *Les Mémoires du Diable*. She could not resist the lure of a puppet-show.

There were times, indeed, when she seemed incapable of resisting a lure of any description. In 1864 she had once again, in Paris, come across the painter, Marchal—the 'Mastodon'—who, thanks to her, was now numbered among the friends of the Princesse Mathilde. As once before, it was the younger Dumas who brought them together, and now he begged her to get the Prince to have a ribbon bestowed upon this 'monstrous Apelles who is so fond of red'. In this she succeeded, and the monstrous Apelles went to Palaiseau to express his thanks. Manceau, already at death's door, became very easily a victim to despair. It was difficult to look after him properly, and Sand, by this time at the end of her tether, suddenly decided to spend a few days at Garbilesse with Marchal. *Manceau's Diary, September 29th:* 'Marchal is as insolent as an executioner's assistant.'

But this was the last flare-up of the old fire. In 1865, seeing that there was no hope for Manceau, she swore not to leave him again, and kept her word. He was panting for breath—'like a dog'—and spitting blood. George had the idea that if they set to work to collaborate in a novel, it might help to relieve his gloom, and draw the bond between them still tighter. The book was *Le Bonheur.* 'Madame is working at *our* novel.' All the same, she sent him into Paris for 'a pump and some other things.' He got back in a state of complete exhaustion. 'My dear Lady was waiting for me at the station, as though she were I, and I she! It was very sweet of her . . .' *May 30th, 1865:* 'Seeing me like this makes my Lady sad. I do what I can to get her to laugh whenever the fever leaves me for a while. . . .'

She nursed him with the devotion of a Sister of Mercy, washing him with her own hands, rubbing his chest, applying his damp compresses. Only she, now, kept the running record of their life, and, because Manceau read it each day, had to maintain a difficult balance between an only too obviously unfounded optimism and a feeling of despair which would have terrified the dying man.

George Sand's Diary, June 18th, 1865: He said to me this morning: 'I am sweating less and certainly improving.' He falls fast alseep after breakfast, which is all to the good, because his nights are broken. He is doing a little work, and can read a few pages aloud without coughing. He would like to have a drive if only the weather would get warmer, but at the moment the cold is terrible . . . Life is over for me! It is awful to see him suffering like this. After I had given him his rub this evening, he took two pills . . . He felt cold, even after the rubbing . . . *June 25th, 1865:* Miserable day. He is discouraged, irritable, despairing. I can do nothing but cry, and that does not make things better. He makes it a grievance against me that he is not getting well, and that the doctors are no good. He had a temperature all day long and coughed for two whole hours before dinner, grumbling at Doctor Morin, at his friends, at everybody

... *July 6th, 1865:* A day of storms, with a tropical heat which has completely exhausted him. There was a short while, round one o'clock, when he felt calmer. He called down to me that he did, poor dear, but it did not last. The fever is burning him up, and he is very, very weak. All the same, he eats. But in his present state how can he possibly fight against the heat which is too much even for the hale and hearty? He is being very brave, while I, instead of helping him, can do nothing but cry! He was my strength and my life—and now that he is the weaker physically, I am the weaker morally ... *July 8th, 1865:* Weaker and more irritable than ever. This has been a quite appalling day. Doctor Fuster arrived in the evening, with his secretary and Camille.[1] Doctor Morin came too. Fuster made a careful examination, and submitted the patient to an auscultation. He found nothing new. One lung is perfectly sound, but there is a small patch on the other. That, in itself, is not very serious. The real trouble is fever, nerves and general irritability ... Dr. Fuster says it is important that he should be cured *as a result of his own will to get well*, but that he must undergo the full rigour of the treatment. He is to have applications of cold water immediately, and there must be no flinching about giving them to him. He told me that he has cured much worse cases, but that I must not yield to entreaties, and should be prepared if need be, to see him develop a real hatred of me ... Poor boy!—he cried when I gave him his cold wash. It really is heartrending. I feel like killing myself. But no! I have got to nurse him and pull him through ... in spite of himself.

August 18th, 1865: He has been coughing uninterruptedly all night and all day. Forty-eight hours! It tears one to pieces to hear him, though he is far calmer than he has been for several days. It seems that he does get a little sleep, in spite of everything, because he looks sur-

---

[1] Dr. Fuster, a Professor of the Faculty of Medicine at Montpellier, believed that he had discovered a way of curing tuberculosis. There had been much talk in the newspapers about his 'wonderful treatment'. Sand corresponded with him, and persuaded Manceau to follow the system of treatment he laid down. It is clear from the above entry that she thought nothing of bringing Fuster all the way from Montpellier to Palaiseau for a consultation.

prised when I tell him what time it is, and has no idea
how many hours have elapsed . . . *August 19th, 1865:*
Unfortunately, *he has read all the above.* Sometimes I am
afraid of irritating him by making light of his troubles,
and sometimes I am afraid lest he may realize how
hopeless his condition is. I have known the worst, now,
for mor● than a month, and fought hard to keep it from
him. He is about as bad as he could be. At this moment,
he is sleeping, worn out by fever, and scarcely breathing.
He has even stopped coughing. Is this his last sleep?

Monday, August 21st: Died this morning at six o'clock,
after a night during which he appeared to be perfectly
calm. When he woke up, he spoke a little. His voice was
that of a dying man, his words wandering, as though he
were emerging from a dream. He struggled for breath,
then went deadly pale, and then—*nothing!* He wasn't—I
hope he wasn't—conscious. As late as midnight he had
been talking to me quite lucidly, and in a strong voice. He
spoke about going to Nohant! . . . I laid him out, and
arranged the bed. I closed his eyes. I put flowers on his
body. He looks very handsome and very young. Oh God!
to think that I shall never watch by him any more! . . .
August 22nd, 1865: I sat all night, alone, beside that
body wrapped in everlasting sleep. He is stretched out on
the bed. He has found peace at last. There is nothing
frightening nor ugly about him. No bad smell. I have
covered him with fresh roses . . . I am sitting here, quite
alone, with him beside me, in this little room. No longer
do I have to listen to him fighting for breath. Tomorrow
night there will be nothing, and I shall be *lonelier than
ever*—lonely now *for* ever! . . .[1]

There are few more moving incidents in the whole of
George Sand's life than that long watching beside a dying
man, than those brave lies, than that display of practical
affection. For five months she had not left him for as much
as a day. As soon as he was dead, she wrote to Maurice.

George Sand to Maurice, August 21st, 1865: Our poor
friend's sufferings are ended. He fell asleep at midnight,
with his mind perfectly clear . . . I am completely broken,

[1] Unpublished.   Bibliothèque   nationale: Department   of
Manuscripts.

but, after dressing him, and laying him out with my own hands on his death-bed, I am still possessed by that nervous energy which will not find relief in tears. Do not worry: I shall not be ill. I refuse to be ill, I want to come to you as soon as I have made arrangements for his poor remains, and put in order his affairs and mine, which are also yours. . . .[1]

Although Manceau's parents were still living, and a married sister, Laura, as well, he had left everything he possessed to Maurice Sand.

George Sand to Maurice, August 22nd, 1865: For two nights now I have been alone beside the poor sleeper who will never wake again. How deep the silence of this little room, which I enter, whether by day or night, no tiptoe. I seem all the time to be hearing that heartrending cough. Now, at last he is sleeping soundly. His face is peaceful. He is covered with flowers. He looks as though he were carved in marble, and yet, in life, how full of life he was, and how impetuous! No bad smell. He is as though petrified. His idiot of a sister arrived this morning, but would not see him. She said it would make too painful an impression on her! . . .[2]

After the funeral, 'a day of tears and emotion', Maurice took her back to Nohant. *George Sand's Journal, August 23rd, 1865:* 'My son is my very soul. I will live for him, and love these two brave hearts—yes, yes—but *you* . . . you who loved me so well! Be not troubled, your part in me remains imperishable . . .' She found Lina four months gone, 'fresh as a daisy and very stout, the house beautifully clean and well-ordered . . . Walked round the garden, visited the animals, went everywhere. Everything well kept and very pretty'. Maurice and Lina seemed to be growing more and more attached to Nohant. Her daughter-in-law was active, sweet-natured, biddable. Sand spent several weeks there, and then, when the autumn season began, returned to Paris, to the Théâtre-Français, to the Odéon. She endured sorrow, but she did not cultivate it. Of another woman, she said:

---

[1] This letter is quoted by Wladimir Karénine in *George Sand*. Volume IV, p. 490.

[2] Letter quoted by Wladimir Karénine in *George Sand*. Volume IV, p. 491.

'She draws sustenance from all these puerilities of suffering, which merely make things worse and fail to awaken the sense of duty. She spends many hours a day on her son's grave, not to pray, not to meditate on human immortality, but simply to stare at a patch of earth where there is nothing left of him but the temporary clothing of his imperishable essence . . . Time heals all scars, if she who has endured the wound does not deliberately pour poison into them.'

In a letter to Flaubert who, all through this terrible time, had been a faithful and friendly visitor, she described, with complete sincerity, the state of her mind.

George Sand to Gustave Flaubert, November 22nd, 1865: Here I am, living quite alone in my tiny house . . . All the same, this place makes me sad. That absolute solitude which, for me, has ever been rest and recreation, is shared now by one who ended here like a lamp blown out, but is still a presence. I do not believe that he is unhappy in the world where he is living now; but the pale reflection of himself which he has left behind seems always to be complaining that he cannot speak to me. Never mind! There is nothing morbid about sadness, and it keeps us from becoming desiccated . . . And you, my friend, what are you doing?—grinding away, I fancy, you, in solitude too, since your mother is probably in Rouen. The nights there must be very lovely, too. I wonder, do you sometimes spare a thought for 'the old troubadour of the ale-house clock, who sings, and will always sing, of perfect love?' Well, and so do I. You, my lord, are not enamoured of chastity, but that is your concern. Personally, I think it has its merits. And with that, I take my leave, with fondest messages of love. I am off to breathe speech, if I can, into the mouths of those who love in the old way. No need for you to write me letters when you are not in the mood. There can be no true friendship without absolute freedom. I shall be in Paris next week, and then again at Palaiseau, and then, at Nohant. . . .[1]

What, during these lonely times at Palaiseau, on the threshold of old age, was she thinking? So far as religion went, she confessed her ignorance. Man has not sufficient

[1] GEORGE SAND: *Correspondance*. Volume V, pp. 99-101.

power of understanding to form a definition of God, and
what he cannot define, he cannot assert. Still, she wanted to
believe.

George Sand to Desplanches, May 25th, 1866: This age
can make no firm assertion, but I hope that the future
may be able to. Let us believe in progress: let us, from
now on, believe in God. Feeling prompts us to. Faith is
an excitement and an enthusiasm: it is a condition of
intellectual magnificence to which we must cling as to a
treasure, and not squander on our way through life in the
small coin of empty words, or inexact and priggish
argument . . . Let time and knowledge work their
changes. Centuries must pass before men can hope to
understand the ways of God in His universe. Man as yet
knows nothing of the ultimate. He cannot prove that God
does not exist: he cannot prove that He does. It is already
so much ground gained that he cannot deny without
being challenged. Let us who are artists,—in other words,
men and women of feeling, rest content with that . . . Let
us, whatever happens, still have faith, and say—'*I
believe*', which is a very different thing from saying '*I
assert*'. Let us say '*I hope*', which is a very different thing
from saying '*I know*'. Let us shake hands on this notion,
this determination, this dream—which is the dream of all
good men. We *feel* that if we are to have loving-kindness
we must have hope and faith, just as, if we are to have
liberty and equality, we must first have fraternity. . . .[1]

And so she 'loved God', as Mother Alicia had said she
would. But, if she found her own solution in the life of the
spirit, she steadily refused to excommunicate the material-
ists. 'Make way for the atheists! Are not their eyes, like ours,
turned to the future? Are they not, like us, in arms to fight
the dark powers of superstition?'
In matters of politics, though more sceptical than she had
been about the action to be taken, she continued to hope.
The Empire left her cold, in spite of the friendship shown
her by the ruling House, and she had very little belief in the
liberalism which Napoleon III was beginning to announce
as his declared policy . . . In a novel which she wrote at this
time, *Monsieur Sylvestre*, two men engage in a dialogue
which, in fact, represents Sand talking to Sand. Monsieur

[1] Ibid., Volume V, pp. 114-15.

Sylvestre, an old anchorite, and formerly one of the men of
'48, has ceased to believe in any form of society, because he
has learned from experience that justice never triumphs . . .
His interlocutor, Pierre Sorède, is a young man who denies
the right of anyone to become a sceptic merely because the
earthly paradise has remained unrealized. Why seek to
impose perfect laws upon a people! 'That is the doctrine of
terrorism: Fraternity or death. It is also that of the
Inquisition: *no salvation save in the bosom of the Church.*
Virtue and Faith by decree are no longer faith and virtue.
They become hateful. Individuals must be left free to
understand the advantages of "community", and the right
to establish it themselves when the time is ripe.'

And so it was that the mystical and romantic revolutionary gradually acquired something of the critical spirit.
That she had done so she attributed to the practice of the
sciences. In another novel dating from this period, *Val-
èvdre,* she portrays with affection and respect a man of
science. 'Never tell me that the study of natural laws, and
the search for ultimate causes, chills the heart or checks the
full flight of human thought.' Like Renan and Berthelot, at
about the same time, Madame Sand was progressing from
popular to scientific romanticism. She was evolving with her
period, and remained, 'like a sounding board', at the centre
of the new thinking.

The books she wrote at this time were not very good, and
she knew it. They were novels 'with a purpose', in which she
opposed not human beings but incarnate theories. True art
must be more concrete. Sand's real genius had always been
bound up with her love of the earth, and it flashes out for
the last time in some scraps of the letters she was still
writing.

George Sand to Maurice, February 1st, 1866: My trip
was wonderful: a fantastic, superb, sunrise over the
Vallée Noire—golden tints, cold colours and warm alike,
reds, greens, yellows, purples, violets and blues, all from
the palette of the great master who has made the light.
The sky from zenith to horizon was aflame with colour,
the country lovely, with flowering gorse standing about
patches of water touched with pink. . . .[1]

1 GEORGE SAND: *Correspondance.* Volume V, p. 106.

Valvèdre is nothing but a creature of reason, the hero of a 'socially conscious' novel from which the irrationality of life is wholly absent. But Sand drove forward, head down, like one of her own Berrichon oxen, completing her daily furrow. Was she happy? Yes, because it was her *will* to be so.

George Sand to Charles Poncy, November 16th, 1866: One is happy as a result of one's own efforts, once one knows the necessary ingredients of happiness—simple tastes, a certain degree of courage, self-denial to a point, love of work, and, above all, a clear conscience. Happiness is no vague dream, of that I now feel certain. By the proper use of experience and thought one can draw much from oneself, by determination and patience one can even restore one's health . . . So, let us live life as it is, and not be ungrateful. . . .[1]

It was the philosophy which Sainte-Beuve had preached, years before, at the time of the great storms. Remembering this, she sent him a copy of *Monsieur Sylvestre*, inscribed as follows: 'To Sainte-Beuve—the soft and precious radiance of my days.' The fashion, in 1866, was to mock at the 'mal de siècle' which had caused her and her romantic friends so much suffering. Once more she raised the old and tattered flag. 'Maybe our sickness was more valuable than the reaction that has followed it; than this craving for money, than this search for pleasures untouched by the ideal, than all this unchecked ambition. They do not seem to me to prove that the century has recovered *its* health.'

[1] GEORGE SAND: *Correspondance.* Volume V, p. 106.

PART NINE

THE ART OF BEING A GRANDMOTHER

In spite of all I have been through, I am led, by the weight of my years and the greatness of my soul, to believe that all is well.   *Sophocles*

I

MY TROUBADOUR

MANCEAU'S DEATH strengthened the bond between
George Sand and Nohant. Her strange taste for a
multiplicity of dwellings resulted in her keeping on both the
small house at Palaiseau and the apartment in Paris. A love
of the theatre, of the *Magny* gatherings, of rehearsals, took
her often to the capital. She went to the Français to see a
Comedy by Musset—*On ne badine pas avec l'amour.*
'Nothing new,' she noted, 'but charming, all the same.'
Nothing new, indeed, for she found in it echoes of what she
herself had said, and the memory of long-dead passions.
Sometimes she would take Marchal the 'mastodon' to the
Circus or the Gymnase.

> *George Sand to Charles Marshal:* Have you heard *Don
> Juan* at the Lyrique? I am asking for two seats for
> Tuesday. Would you like one of them? If so, let us dine
> together, at any place you choose. If not, tell me where
> we can meet so that I may give you a hug and my
> blessing before starting for Nohant. I shall leave Paris on
> Thursday, and Palaiseau the preceding Monday. Drop
> me a line to the rue des Feuillantines, to await my arrival,
> so that I may dispose of the seat for *Don Juan* to
> somebody else if you cannot use it. How are you, my
> pet? I am fine. The only thing that worries me is this east
> wind. Much love. . . .[1]

But her friend was elusive, 'deeply involved' with lovely
models, and difficult to tempt away, even with the bait of a
ten-franc dinner at *Magny's* or *Brébant's*.

The Palaiseau house was kept spick and span by Jacques
and Caroline, a resident couple, pious-minded and prolific';
'everything seen to, the clock punctual to the minute, the

[1] Unpublished. Simone André-Maurois Collection.

Almanack to the day', as in the time of Manceau, so that
George, whenever she wished, could spend quiet and not
too melancholy evenings there, alone in silence and self-
communing. But at heart she remained a countrywoman of
Berry, and preferred her dear Nohant to every other place.

As child, as young girl, and as woman, she had allowed
scarcely a year to pass without paying it a visit, there to
saunter beneath the pollarded elms, and to make renewed
contact with her land and her remembered dead. The grass-
grown cemetery, the tall old trees, the little tile-hung belfry,
the rough wooden porch of the church, 'all those things
become dear to the heart when one has lived for a long time
in so quiet and silent a place'. Within the cottages which
huddled about the great house, were the playmates of her
youth, their children and their grandchildren. The sacristan-
cum-grave-digger was an old friend. There had, maybe,
been times when the lady of Nohant had shocked the
villagers. There were some who believed that they had seen
devils in the Park, and heard strange music and the sound
of masques and revelry, polonaises and mazurkas. But all
that was over now. Madame Sand had become the Good
Presence of the neighbourhood, a legendary figure, a
guardian angel who had 'brought fame to the quietness of
the Berry countryside'.

With her there lived not only Maurice and Lina, but a
granddaughter, Aurore, for the 'command' which she had
issued after the death of Cocoton had been duly carried out.
Aurore, nicknamed 'Lolo', was pretty, fresh and gay. She
had her grandmother's black velvety eyes, 'the most darling
feet and hands imaginable, and a serious expression even
when she laughs'. Aurore IV 'is determined to talk, and
produces an extraordinary series of consonants in a nasal
and throaty voice'. In 1868 she celebrated her second
birthday, and her grandmother to mark the occasion gave
her the Trianon garden, and a great bunch of white
primulas.

The house was always open to its mistress's friends, a
centre of hospitality. But the friends had changed. Borie
was now the all-powerful Director of a Discount-Bank,
earning twenty-five thousand francs a year,[1] much to the
scandal of George Sand. Lambert, now a successful painter,
with a ribbon in his buttonhole, and blessed in a happy
marriage, was living in high style—'much richer than I am,

---

[1] The equivalent of about five million in 1951.

better housed, better dressed, better fed', she said: 'but what does it matter? He is stepping on to the stage of life just as I am leaving it'.[1] A new generation of 'sons' was slowly growing up around her. There was Edmond Plauchut,'[2] with whom she had corresponded for years; because that great traveller had told her how once, when shipwrecked on Bôa-Vista, one of the Cape Verde Islands, he had been saved as a result of his admiration for her. He had made a point of always carrying with him, wherever he went, an album containing the autographs of Eugène Sue, Cavaignac and George Sand. On this occasion, ill-treated by the Negroes, and shown the door by the so-called French Consul, he had found a kinder welcome in the house of an educated Portuguese to whom he had exhibited his album-talisman. The universal fame of the Lady of Nohant had protected him. In 1861 he had put in an appearance at Tamaris, with the beak of a pirate and the beard of a conquistador, and been at once adopted. Then, too, there were Charles-Edmond, Managing-Director of *Le Temps*,[3] Henry Harrisse, an American who regularly attended the *Magny* dinners—a great authority in his own country on Christopher Columbus and George Sand—and a group of second-generation Berrichons, such as Maxime Planet and Angèle Néraud, as well as a few of a still younger vintage, as, for example, Hippolyte Châtiron's grandson, and René, Edmé and 'Bébert' Simonnet. But the great friend of Sand's old age was Gustave Flaubert. He had won her heart by going to Palaiseau, after Manceau's death, to keep her company. She, in her turn, had visited him at Croisset, and this new 'combination' had been an immense success.

George Sand's Journal, August 28th, 1866: I reached Rouen at one o'clock. Flaubert was at the station with a carriage. He drove me round the city, showing me its fine monuments—the Cathedral, the Hôtel-de-Ville, Saint-Maclou, Sainte-Patrice. It really is a marvellous place, a centuries-old charnel-house, full of ancient streets—all

[1] George Sand's Diary: February 7th, 1866. Bibliothèque nationale: Department of Manuscripts.

[2] 1814-1909. Buried in the Family cemetery at Nohant.

[3] Charles-Edmond Chojecki (1822-99), Librarian of the Senate, who had abandoned the use of his Polish surname, and was known only by his two Christian names.

very curious. Then we went on to Croisset . . . Flaubert's
mother is an old lady of great charm. The situation is
quite delicious, the house comfortable, pretty and well
arranged: attentive servants, cleanliness, water, and one's
every want *anticipated* . . . I live like a fighting-cock! . . .
In the evening Flaubert read me his magnificent
Tentation de Saint Antoine. We chatted away in his study
till two in the morning . . . *Wednesday, August 29th:* We
started off at eleven by river-steamer, with Madame
Flaubert, her niece,[1] her friend, Madame Vaas, and the
latter's daughter, Madame de la Chaussée. We went to La
Bouille. Weather terrible: rain and wind, but I stayed on
deck looking at the water . . . We spent ten minutes at La
Bouille, and then returned on the *flood*, or *surge*, or
bore—a sort of a tide-race. We got back at one. A fire
was lit: we dried ourselves, and drank tea . . . Then I
started out again with Flaubert, and made the round of
the estate; garden, terraces, orchard, kitchen-garden,
farm, and the 'citadel', a very curious old wooden house
which he uses as a store-room. *Moses' Path.* View across
the Seine . . . a beautifully sheltered spot on rising
ground. Soil dry, with a whitish surface: very charming
and poetic . . . Dressed. Excellent dinner. I played cards
with the two old ladies. Later, I had some talk with
Flaubert, and went to bed at two. Bed very comfortable. I
slept well but started to cough again. My cold troublesome: must have disturbed him a lot . . . *Paris Thursday, August 30th:* Left Croisset at noon, with Flaubert
and his niece. Dropped her at Rouen. Had another
look at the city—the bridge, huge and magnificent. Fine
Baptistery belonging to a Jesuit church . . . Flaubert
bundled me off.[2]

Sand to Flaubert: I was deeply touched by the way you
welcomed me into your orderly existence, where a
wandering creature of my sort must be a bit of an
anomaly, and might so easily become tiresome. You
received me as though I were one of the family. It is clear
that your good manners are born of the heart. Remember
me to my charming friends . . . You are a good, kind

---

[1] Caroline Commanville, later Madame Franklin-Grout.
[2] Unpublished. Bibliothèque nationale: Department of
Manuscripts.

person, even if you *are* a great man, and I am very much attached to you.[1]

She returned to Croisset in November 1866.

George Sand's Journal, November 3rd, 1866: Left Paris at one o'clock with Flaubert. The express travelled very fast. Lovely weather, charming country, good conversation . . . At Rouen station we found Madame Flaubert, and her other son, the doctor. At Croisset went round the garden, talked, dined, and then, more talk, and reading, until half-past one. Comfortable bed: slept like a log . . . *November 4th, 1866:* Wonderful day. Walked round the garden as far as the orchard. Worked. I am deliciously snug in my little attic room, which is very warm. The niece, her husband, and the old Crépet lady, came to dinner . . . She leaves tomorrow. Puzzles. Gustave read me his fairy-tale. It is full of admirable and charming things, but is too long, too richly orchestrated, too full. We had another talk which lasted until half-past two. I felt hungry. We went down to the kitchen in search of cold chicken. We poked our noses into the yard just long enough to get some water from the pump. It was as mild as a spring night. We ate. Retired upstairs again. We smoked. Went on with our talk. We separated at four in the morning . . . *November 5th, 1866:* Weather still lovely. After breakfast we went for a walk. I dragged Gustave along; he was positively heroic. He got dressed and took me to Canteleu, which is quite close, on top of the hill. What lovely country!—what a soft, extensive, wonderful view! I brought back a bundle of stone-crop. Nothing else grows there. We got home at three. Worked. After dinner had another talk with Gustave. I read him

---

[1] In Volume V of her published *Correspondance* (p. 126), this letter is dated *August 10th, 1866.* This must be a mistake, because the visit to Croisset took place later. The *Journal* which George Sand regularly kept for twenty-five years (1852-76), in a large desk Diary with a printed heading for each day, proves beyond a doubt that the two expeditions to Croisset took place between August 28th and 30th, and between November 3rd and 10th, 1866. Sand rarely dated her letters. When Maurice published the six volumes of her *Correspondance* (Calmann-Levy, 1882-84) he added a specific, but often erroneous, date to each letter.

Cadio. We went on talking, and supped off a bunch of grapes and some bread and jam . . . *November 6th, 1866:* Rain. We started off at one o'clock by steam-boat to Rouen, with his mother. I paid a visit with Gustave to the natural-history museum. We were received by M. Pouchet, who is as deaf as a post and generally ailing. He made a most tremendous effort to be nice to us. Impossible to exchange a word with him, but he occasionally explained something to us and was interesting . . . The nest measuring eighty-four metres in circumference, with its abandoned eggs . . . The little birds are born with feathers on them . . . Collection of magnificent shells . . . M. Pouchet's private room: his live spider which eats birds: his crocodile. Visited the museum in the Jardin des Plantes . . . Fragments of Corneille's door . . . Dined at the house of Mme Caroline Comenville [*sic*] . . . From there to the Schmith menagerie. Superb animals as tame as dogs. The foetuses. The bearded woman. A pantomime. St-Romain's Fair. Got back to Croisset at half after midnight, with his mother, who was very courageous and had walked a long way. Had another talk which lasted until two o'clock. . . .[1]

A regular correspondence began. He called her 'Dear Master' or 'Dearly Beloved Master': she, him—'My Monk' or 'My Troubadour', because she was fond of saying that they sat 'cooking our legs by the fire' like two old troubadour figures on a clock carved in the romantic manner. Looked at superficially this mutual affection of theirs seems strange, for never were two persons more unlike; she, a bohemian who loved walking and travel, he, inseparable from his house at Croisset, his manuscripts and his comforts.

Gustave Flaubert to George Sand, November 12th, 1866: Everybody here is devoted to you. Under what star were you born thus to combine in your person so many rare and diverse qualities? I do not know how to describe my feelings for you. All I do know is that you have awoken in me an affection of a very special kind, such as I have never, till now, felt for anyone. We get on well,

[1] Unpublished. Bibliothèque nationale: Department of Manuscripts.

don't we? It was so nice seeing you . . . I too, wonder
why I am so fond of you. Is it because you are a great
man or a charming creature, I really cannot say . . .
November 27th, 1866: How pleasant those nightly talks
were. There were times when I had to keep myself from
giving you a kiss, just like a great overgrown child. . . .[1]

George Sand to Gustave Flaubert, October 12th, 1867:
You have not, like me, an itching foot ever eager to be
off. You live in your dressing-gown—the great enemy of
freedom and the active life. . . .[2]

Flaubert was interested in nothing in the world but
literature. Sand wrote in order to make a living, but other
trades might have tempted her. 'I love classifying things:
there is a good deal of the schoolmaster in me. Then, again,
I have a weakness for sewing, and keeping children clean:
there is a good deal of the servant-girl in me. I love
amusements, and there is certainly a good deal of the fool in
me. . . .'[3]

And again:

'Literature the sacro-sanct, as you call it, occupies only a
secondary place in my life. I have always loved somebody
more than *it*, and my family more than the somebody . . .'[4]
Flaubert refused to write 'novels with a purpose' or
autobiographical novels. 'The novelist has no right to
express his opinion upon anything. When have you ever
found the good God expressing an opinion. . . . The man in
the street is a more interesting person than M. Gustave
Flaubert, because he is more generalized and, consequently,
more typical . . .'[5] To this Sand replied: 'I think that an
artist should, so far as is possible, live true to his nature
. . .'[6] Flaubert would lie awake all night sweating over a
single word. Sand would knock off thirty pages in the same
period, and start on a new novel a minute after finishing
the one she had just been working at.

---

[1] GUSTAVE FLAUBERT: *Correspondance.* Volume V, pp.
247 and 250.

[2] GEORGE SAND: *Correspondance.* Volume V, p. 229.

[3] Ibid., Volume V, p. 157 (November 30th, 1866).

[4] Ibid., Volume V, p. 371 (March 30th, 1870).

[5] GUSTAVE FLAUBERT: *Correspondance.* Volume V, p.
253.

[6] GEORGE SAND: *Correspondance.* Volume V, p. 253.

George Sand to Gustave Flaubert, November 29th, 1866:
I have never ceased to wonder at the way you torment
yourself over your writing. Is it just fastidiousness on
your part? There is so little to show for it . . . As to style,
I certainly do not worry myself, as you do, over that. The
wind bloweth as it listeth through my old harp. *My* style
has its ups and downs, its sounding harmonies, and
its failures. I do not, fundamentally, much mind, so long
as the *emotion* comes through. But it is no use my trying
to screw it out of myself. It is the *other* who sings
through me, well or badly, as the case may be. When I
begin to think of all that, I get frightened, and tell myself
that I count for nothing, for nothing at all . . . Let the
wind blow a little through *your* strings. I think you fret
about it all much more than you should, and that you
ought to let the *other* have his say more often. Everything
would work out all right, and it would be a great deal less
exhausting for you. . . .'[1]

There were times when she was less sure of herself.
'Seeing the agonies through which my old friend goes in
order to produce a novel, I feel depressed at the thought of
my own facility. I tell myself that the stuff I turn out is just
slipshod . . .' To this Flaubert replied very modestly: 'In
your case, the *idea* in a book is a broad river flowing
without check. In mine, it is a tiny trickle, and only the
most elaborate ingenuity of art will produce a waterfall. . . .'
One of their most constant subjects of discussion was
sensuality and the artist. Sand remained passionately
interested in this aspect of human nature.

George Sand to Gustave Flaubert, September 21st, 1866:
And how about you, dear monk? You are still, I imagine,
alone in your exquisite hermitage, hard at work and
never going out? . . . You are a man apart, very
mysterious, but, at the same time, as gentle as a lamb. I
have often longed to question you, but a feeling of
excessive respect has always kept me from doing so. I can
speculate only on my own disasters. Those which a great
spirit must endure in order to be in a fit state to produce
work of importance, I regard as sacred and not to be
touched with a rough or thoughtless hand. Sainte-Beuve,

[1] Ibid., Volume V, p. 154.

who, all the same, is very fond of you, maintains that you
are quite appallingly vicious. But, maybe, he sees you
with rather muddy eyes . . . I assume that the highly
intelligent man must be tormented by much curiosity. I,
personally, am not, probably because I lack the gift of
courage. . . .[1]

The statement seems an odd one in view of her youthful
experiments. But multiplicity is not the same thing as
variety. George knew better than most people that the artist
puts the best of himself into his work, and is often incapable
of enjoying the pleasures he describes.

Sand to Flaubert, November 30th, 1866: I have no great
belief in the Don Juan-cum-Byron type. Don Juan did
not write poetry, and Byron was, from all accounts, an
inept lover. There must have been times—such emotional
crises can be counted on the fingers of one hand—when
he knew complete fulfilment of heart, and soul, and
senses: certainly he had sufficient experience of such
moments to become one of the poets of love. But we
must not expect to thrill often to those mighty vibrations.
The constant winds of petty appetite dissipate the power
of response. . . .[2]

Flaubert referred her to one of 'old Montaigne's'
Essays—*Sur quelques vers de Virgile:*

Flaubert to Sand, November 27th, 1866: What he says
about chastity precisely expresses my own view. It is the
effort to achieve abstinence, not abstinence in itself, that
matters. If that were not so, then we should have to
anathematize the flesh, as Catholics do. God knows
where that leads! Great natures, which are the only good
natures, are, above all things, prodigal of themselves, and
do not too closely count the cost when it comes to giving.
We must laugh and cry, love and work, enjoy and
suffer—in short, vibrate to the limits of our capability,
and in the widest possible fashion. That, I believe, is what
makes man truly human.[3]

[1] Ibid., Volume V, p. 135.
[2] GEORGE SAND: *Correspondance*. Volume IV, p. 156.
[3] GUSTAVE FLAUBERT: *Correspondance*. Volume V, pp.
250-1.

They discussed the case of Sainte-Beueve, who had remained lecherous into old age, and seemed to be 'plunged in gloom at the thought that he can no longer haunt the Cyprian groves'. Sand was relentless in her judgment: 'He regrets what is least to be regretted, as he, that is, understands it.' Flaubert was more indulgent: 'How hard you are on old Beuve. After all, he is neither a Jesuit nor a green girl . . . Men will always be of the opinion that the one serious thing in life is sexual enjoyment. Woman, for all the members of my sex, is a groined archway opening on the infinite. That may not be a very elevated attitude, but it is fundamental to the male . . .'[1] That, however, was precisely what she refused to admit.

Sand to Flaubert, February 16th, 1867: I am *not* a Catholic, but I do draw the line at monstrosities! I maintain that the old and the ugly who buy young bodies for cash are not indulging in 'love', and that what they do has nothing in common with the Cyprian Venus, with groined arches or infinities or male or female! It is something wholly against nature, since it is not desire that pushes the young girl into the arms of the ugly dotard, and an act in which there is neither liberty nor reciprocity is an offence against the sanctity of nature. . . .[2]

Flaubert was working just then on *l'Education Sentimentale,* and asked her endless questions about her experiences in '48. In his judgment on the men who had been concerned to provoke the outbreak, he was severe. Sand, their faithful comrade, waxed hot in their defence. 'We have been floundering since '89. Is it not because we had been floundering that we were landed with '48? We may, in that year, have floundered still more, but it was in order to reach a necessary goal.'[3] She feared that Flaubert might be unjust. 'You cause me grave anxiety when you say that your book will lay upon the patriots the blame for all that was bad. Is that true? Besides, true or not, they were the ones who were defeated, and it is enough to be defeated by one's own fault without having one's stupidities flung in

1 Ibid., Volume V, p. 274.
2 GEORGE SAND: *Correspondance.* Volume V, pp. 180-1.
3 GEORGE SAND: *Correspondance.* Volume V, p. 145.

one's teeth. Be merciful! There were fine men among them, when all is said! . . .'[1]

What a difference, nay, what a contrast there was between them. Yet, for all that, they were just 'two old troubadours, who believe in love and art and the ideal, and can still sing while all around us hoot and jabber. It is we who are the young lunatics of this generation. Those who are to follow us have made it their business to be old and blasé and disillusioned in our stead . . .'[2] To which Flaubert replied: 'Ah, yes! I am only too ready to go with you into another world. The question of money will, before very long, have made it impossible to live in this one. Even the very rich will not be able to do so without giving constant thought to their possessions. Everyone, without exception, will have to spend several hours a day monkeying with capital. A delightful prospect!'[3]

They shared, too, many hatreds: 'Dear Master, dear friend of the Good God, let us roar and rant in unison against M. Thiers. No words can express the nausea I feel at the spectacle of that old addle-pated and intriguing fool nourishing his idiocy on the stinking compost of the bourgeoisie . . .'[4]

It is always easier to reach agreement *against* some*one* than *for* some*thing*. She would have dearly liked to get Flaubert to Nohant. It was there that her friends became more truly her 'sons'. But Flaubert had his book to finish, and would not take time off. 'That is why I cannot come to Nohant. It is the old, old story of the Amazons who cut off one of their breasts that they might the more efficiently draw the bow. I sometimes wonder whether, all things considered, it is really a very sensible proceeding.'[5] Sand thought it far from sensible. In spite of her masculine coats and her masculine trousers she had never been an amazon. She had always striven to be an artist and a woman, an artist *because* she was a woman. Round about 1868 she was explaining this attitude of hers to a young and beautiful woman friend, far better than she had ever done to Flaubert.

[1] Ibid., Volume V, p. 164.

[2] Ibid., Volume V, p. 271.

[3] GUSTAVE FLAUBERT: *Correspondance*. Volume V, p. 267.

[4] Ibid., Volume V, pp. 346-7.

[5] Ibid., Volume V, p. 348.

II

'DEAR CHILD . . .'

AT SOME time round about 1860, Juliette Lamber, a charming neophyte married to an intolerable husband, had made her bow upon the literary stage. Her father, Doctor Jean-Louis Lamber, had brought her up in an atmosphere of progressive idealism *à la* Sand. Her husband, a lawyer called La Messine, was a positivist, a conservative, and a bad lover. It was not long before he got on her nerves. Arrived in Paris, she soon made friends by reason of her vivacity and charm. She was welcomed not only in the republican circles of her choice, but also by men like Mérimée, who had given their allegiance to the Empire. She began her life of authorship with a small book in which she set out to defend women against the attacks levelled at them by Proudhon, and, in particular, indulged in passionate praise of George Sand and Daniel Stern (Marie d'Agoult), both of whom had dared to claim the right to live their lives as they chose. She at once received an invitation from the Comtesse d'Agoult, who was just then conducting a political Salon, and 'bureau of general intelligence'. George Sand wrote a letter of thanks to the young essayist, but refused to meet her when she learned that Juliette was in the habit of going to see her enemy. That old experience with Carlotta Marliani had taught her to be careful of divided friendships and conversational scandal. Better a clean break, she thought, than tittle-tattle. 'The day on which you fall out with Mme d'Agoult, you may rest assured that George Sand is your friend, and that you may visit her whenever you wish to do so. . . .'[1]

To the young Juliette, Madame d'Agoult seemed both elegant and virile. 'I have reached the age of manhood,' said Daniel Stern, but the statement was untrue, for her nervous

---

[1] MADAME ADAM (JULIETTE LAMBER): *Mes Premières Armes littéraires et politiques*, pp. 98-9.

system was still that of a woman. When she declared her democratic sympathies, and entertained Grévy, Pelletan and Carnot, people smiled, for, with her crown of white hair and black veil of Chantilly lace, she looked every inch an aristocrat. She could not resist the temptation to demolish the picture of George Sand which this young beginner had built up in her own mind. 'Dear child; let me give you a piece of advice. Never get to know Madame Sand. If you do, all your illusions about her will vanish. As a woman—I beg your pardon, as a *man*—she is quite insignificant. No powers of conversation. Her nature is of the brooding kind, as she herself very well knows. You can tell it from her eyes which, in other ways, are handsome enough.' Did Marie, then, refuse to allow George any virtues?—kindness, for instance? 'She has a sort of contempt for those to whom she has been generous . . . She treats her lovers much as though they were pieces of white chalk with which she has been writing on a blackboard. As soon as she has finished, she treads the chalk underfoot, and very soon it is no more than a cloud of fine dust which quickly dissipates.' The young woman ventured to express a regret: 'How sad an example for us *small* folk when two people as *great* as George Sand and Daniel Stern cannot be friends!' The 'great' person to whom these words were addressed, expressed impatience: 'Never!' she said.[1]

When Juliette La Messine left her husband, Madame d'Agoult approved the decision and gave her full support. But, in their walks together, her talk constantly reverted to Sand. 'What I cannot forgive in a woman of her ancestry and upbringing is her neglect of appearances, the way she dresses, her coarse country jokes, and her art-student behaviour. At her age, she ought to know better . . . She is well born. Now that she is growing old she no longer has any excuse for conducting herself like a gutter-snipe,'[2]—which, as Sophie-Victoire Dupin would have said was a typical 'old countess' remark.

In 1867 La Messine died. Juliette was delighted and made up her mind to marry, after the briefest possible delay, the man she loved, Edmond Adam, journalist and man of politics. All her friends congratulated her, with the exception of Madame d'Agoult: 'The misfortune of becom-

[1] MADAME ADAM (JULIETTE LAMBER): *Mes Premières Armes littéraires et politiques*, pp. 202-3.
[2] Ibid., p. 152.

ing a widow is that one is usually stupid enough to want to marry again. Surely, you will not be guilty of such a piece of idiocy? Any woman with a brain to bless herself with, should remain free.'[1] When news of the engagement reached her she flew into a violent rage, accused Juliette of being a little provincial ninny, and prophesied that before two years were out she would have stopped writing, and would be devoting all her energies to the keeping of the household accounts. Her behaviour on this occasion was scarcely sane, and it is not surprising to know that in the following year Madame d'Agoult had to retire for a while to Dr. Blanche's mental clinique.

The breach with Madame d'Agoult left Juliette free, at last, to make the acquaintance of George Sand. She asked for an audience, and was summoned to present herself at 97 rue des Feuillantines. She entered the drawing-room in a highly emotional state of mind, to see before her a somewhat small woman engaged in rolling a cigarette, who motioned her to a chair beside her own. George lit her cigarette. She appeared to be making an effort to say something, but without success. The visitor burst into tears. Sand opened her arms in a maternal gesture. The young woman flung herself into them. This wordless scene was the beginning of a long friendship.

In the eyes of Juliette Lamber, George Sand was infinitely superior to Daniel Stern in delicacy of feeling, nobility of heart, understanding of life, and the possession of a serenity of mind gained at the cost of much cruel experience. George Sand at once adopted her as a spiritual daughter. She decided to take her to one of the *Magny* dinners and there introduce her to the company. The presence of the pretty young woman had a tonic effect upon those present, several of whom embarked on stories of a not very delicate description. Sand lost her temper: 'You know that I detest talk of that kind, and how much it disgusts me!' Dumas was full of praise for Juliette's beauty: 'I do most sincerely trust that she has no talent!—fancy, with a figure and a phiz like that wanting to become a blue-stocking'— 'Young Alexandre,' said Madame Sand, 'I beg you to keep a check upon your contempt for blue-stockings! . . . I am prepared to wager that you are about to preach love to this little Juliette of mine—am I right?'—'Of course! When a

[1] JULIETTE ADAM: *Mes sentiments et nos Idées avant 1870*, p. 136.

woman's got all *that*, she's not going to bother about being a writer!'—'My child,' said Madame Sand; 'pay no attention to what they say. You have only to read what they do with their women in love, their Madame Bovary, their Madame Aubray, their Germinie Lacerteux. No good advice is to be hoped for from *them*.'—'You', said Dumas, 'have never loved anyone but the heroes in embryo of your future novels, puppets togged out in literary finery, incapable of doing anything except repeat what you put into their months. D'you call that love?'[1]

Sometimes, while she sat smoking cigarettes, which she threw into a bowl of water after taking a few puffs, George would try, for Juliette's benefit, to formulate the lessons she had learned in the course of her stormy life. 'When we know one another better I will tell you what roads I have followed on my journey through life, and how, when I expected them to be smooth, they turned out to be rough . . . Kindliness, which should be a clear-sighted and considered virtue, was, in my case, something torrential and tumultuous. It was concerned merely to spread itself. People had only to inspire me with compassion to possess me utterly. Sometimes I flung myself into the doing of good with a blind enthusiasm which, more often than not, had precisely the opposite effect to the one I intended. *When I take stock of myself, I realize that the only two genuine passions of my life have been motherhood and friendship.* Love, when it came my way, I accepted, but I never went out of my way to seek it. Consequently, what I contributed, what I demanded, was something very different from what it gave. In those who got love from me, I might have found friends and sons. After my first two choices, I no longer had the right to impose friendship. To do that, one must have moral authority. It is only reluctantly that men in love will play the role of friendship. So far as pleasure goes, one woman to them is as good as another. What they really like is to supplement sensuality with a warm flood of delicious emotion. . . .'[2]

This assured self-diagnosis would have caused no little surprise to those enemies of George Sand who saw in her a woman enslaved by her body. It was, however, quite

[1] JULIETTE ADAM: *Mes sentiments et nos Idées avant 1870*, p. 162.

[2] JULIETTE ADAM: *Mes Sentiments et nos Idées avant 1870*, pp. 169-70.

accurate . . . She had given herself, first from a sense of compassion, later, as she said, because she no longer had 'sufficient moral authority to impose friendship', and ultimately, because she had got into the habit of love, and needed a man in her life. The period had dictated an attitude. Aurore Dudevant had grown up at a time when a whole generation of artists was swept by a desire for love, by the urgent necessity to feel themselves to be in some way different from the bourgeoisie. 'We despised paddling in the shallows. What we wanted was to swim far out above unsounded depths, and the further we went the more hopelessly lost did we become. To get away from the ruck of our fellows, to put an ever greater distance between ourselves and the safety of dry land, to strike out onward and ever onward—that was what we longer for! Many of us lost everything. Those of us who suffered, who refused to drown, who struggled back to the shore, were cast up high and dry, scrambled to our feet, and, as a result of renewed contact with good, solid earth, and, in particular, with sensible and humble folk, became once more like other people. Often and often I have found health in peasant simplicities. Often and often, Nohant cured me and saved me from Paris . . .' She concluded with these words: Our great fault was to confuse the gratification of the senses with our sentimental ardours.'[1]

It was about this time that Alexandre Dumas, bathing one day with Sand in the Cher, asked her, in mocking mood: 'By the bye, what do you think of *Lélia*?' Still swimming, George replied: '*Lélia*?—don't talk about it! I tried to re-read it a short while ago, and could not get even to the end of the first volume!' Then she added: 'All the same, when I wrote that book, I was sincere.'[2] But who would have thought that Lélia was to end her life in her grandmother's Château, writing stories for her own grandchildren?

On another occasion, after explaining to Juliette for the hundredth time, that Musset had been 'the best action of her life', and that she had never had any other thought than to 'save him from himself', she begged her chosen 'daughter', should she ever hear George Sand accused of disloyalty, to make the following answer: 'George Sand may have lost the right to be judged as a woman, but she can still

[1] Ibid., pp. 170-2.

[2] JULES CLARETIE: *La Vie à Paris, 1904* (E. Fasquelle, 1905), p. 168.

claim to be judged as a man, and in love she has been more loyal than any of you. She has never deceived anybody, has never indulged in two adventures simultaneously. All that can be held against her is that, in the course of a lifetime during which art bulked more largely in her eyes than anything else, she sought the society of artists, and preferred the moral standards of the male to those of the female.'—'Let me admit, without further ado, my dear Juliette, that for a woman to cease to be a woman is productive only of inferiority. It is well that you, living, as I once lived, surrounded by men, and doubtless adored by many of them, should remember this: that any exceptional woman who has for friend a superior man is to be envied. As a lover, a man is the same for all women, and often the better lover where the woman is vile and stupid. I have known utter and complete love—not once, alas! but many times—but, *if I had to start my life over again, I should choose to remain chaste. . . .*'[1]

Juliette and her daughter Alice, nicknamed 'Topaze', had become Madame Sand's most constant companions. With them she made expeditions to Fécamp, Dieppe, Jumièges. It was in the company of Juliette and, her *fiancé*, Edmond Adam, the republican, who looked like a friendly dog, that she visited the Exhibition of 1867.

George Sand's Journal, September 22nd, 1867: Yesterday I made a lucky find—a perfectly delightful cab-driver. He fetched me again today, and I call for Juliette. She lives up a great number of stairs, but has a charming little eyrie with a beautiful view. We went to the Exhibition with Adam and Toto. The Chinese giant is superb, a real Tartar Apollo. There is also a horrible Chinese dwarf, and a far from good-looking Chinese woman, who appears to be bored to death by all the idiotic things people say to her. How stupid and crude the great public is! . . . The decapitated *Casque-de-Fer* looks a decent sort of a man. Salviati. Rumanian costumes. I ate some bananas and we had ices. I went back with Juliette, and we dined very pleasantly together. Home by ten, and sat down to correct *Cadio*. . . .[2]

[1] JULIETTE ADAM: *Mes Sentiments et nos Idées avant 1870*, p. 220.
[2] Unpublished. Bibliothèque nationale: Department of Manuscripts.

Juliette left Paris to spend the winter on the shores of the Gulf of Juan. The *Villa Bruyères*, which her parents had given her, was close to the *Grand Pin*, a property belonging to the 'friendly dog'. An invitation was sent to Madame Sand, who accepted. The visit was a great success. The weather was perfect, the villa comfortable and gay. Edmond Adam, whom Sand called 'my good oua-oua', showed himself no less devoted than his future wife to their old and illustrious friend. Sand had brought all her 'following' with her—Maxime Planet, Edmond Plauchut—who spent the evenings in describing his shipwreck, and how he had been saved by his album of autographs—and Maurice, 'delightfully paternal in his attitude to his mother, whom he looked after, amused and protected'. Lina, now in her third pregnancy, had stayed behind, alone, at Nohant. 'She is on the point of being brought to bed', said Sand, 'and, so that Solange should not spoil my stay here—for Maurice is the only person of whom she is afraid—Lina, quite unprompted, insisted that her husband must accompany me.' Solange, just then, was 'in luck's way at Cannes' with a foreign prince, and Madame Sand was careful not to meet them. Maurice was very popular with his hosts, who found him highly talented and vivacious. They called him the 'Sergeant', because he had inherited from the Maréchal de Saxe a passion for all things military. There were picnics, there was an excursion to Vallauris—'a large and interesting village where the manufacture of pottery is carried on'—there were boat-trips, botanical expeditions—with much poring over the seed-sacks of myrtle, mastic, arbutus-berry and anemone—and some insect-catching: there were games of croquet and 'boules' in the garden, and, at night-time, paper games, and the telling of fantastic stories. Each day brought its simple pleasures.

The band of happy friends made short trips to Nice, Cannes, Mentone and Monaco. In the Casino at Monte-Carlo Maurice liked playing the country bumpkin, and went up to perfect strangers, explaining that he had come there to 'play' and did not know how to go about it. Some just called him a fool to his face; others gave him advice, while his companions stood by, doubled up with laughter. The end of it all was that the police requested them to leave the Rooms. Madame Sand found it all great fun—'she still loved youth in others, and adored the sense of old age in herself, that happy period of life when one is a friend, a

mother, a grandmother, and nothing more.' So delightful
did they all find it to be together, that they made many
plans for the future—such as founding an Abbey of
Thelema, or touring France in a caravan . . . The group
became an army. George Sand was the Colonel, Maurice
the 'Sergeant', Plauchut and Planet the 'other ranks', Adam
the 'civvy' hanger on, and Juliette the camp-follower. By the
end of the holiday, Maurice had promoted the camp-
follower to the rank of Lieutenant-Colonel, an advance-
ment of which Madame Lamber was very proud. Then they
broke up, their hearts full of gay and happy memories,
pledging one another to meet again at Nohant whither
George was in a hurry to return in order to greet the brand-
new granddaughter who had been born there in her
absence—Gabrielle Sand.

III

NOHANT ON THE EVE OF WAR

ADAM AND Juliette were married in July 1868, and went
straight to Nohant. They had as travelling companion the
American, Henry Harrisse, who got on their nerves,
because he insisted on playing the part of guide with
portentous gravity, and, like a sort of Christopher Columbus in reverse, behaved as though he had discovered Le
Berry. But, once arrived, they fell in love with the poetic
atmosphere of the house. In the evenings, with the windows
open to the stars and the sweet scents drifting in from the
garden, they listened to Sand's accomplished playing of
Mozart and Glück by heart. They looked at the portraits of
the Maréchal de Saxe, with his shining breast-plate and
powdered hair, and of the lovely Aurore de Koenigsmarck,
whom Maurice so closely resembled. 'So you find the
ancestors impressive, do you?' he said to Juliette with a
smile. She admitted that she did. Royal blood combined
with such simplicity filled her republican heart with
astonishment.

Next day was the 'Bonne Mère's' name-day. Maurice let

off a salvo of artillery. All the members of the company offered bouquets of flowers gathered in the fields. In the evening there was a puppet performance. Juliette had long wanted to see these actors, and there exists no better description of them than the one she wrote.

We knew them by name before ever we saw them, Balandard, Coque-en-Bois, Captain della Spada, Isabelle, Rose, Céleste, Ida—all of them, both men and women . . . We were in full first-night fig, with low-necked dresses. Copies of the programme were hung up all over the place. The puppets had elected to play *Alonzi Alonzo le Bâtard ou Les Brigands de las Sierras*. Maurice had been working away for twenty nights in order to give his adored mother a single hour's amusement . . . At last the solemn moment arrived. We filed punctiliously in. Madame Sand had arranged the order of precedence. We entered the theatre which, till then, we had not seen. It was brilliantly lit. On the left was the stage on which full-sized plays are performed, and straight ahead the puppet-booth with an amazing curtain painted, of course, by Maurice. The curtain rose. The back cloth displayed a wonderful arrangement of perspectives. We were straightway transported to Spain, to *las Sierras*. It was announced that we were at liberty to speak to the performers, that the action of the piece, and its dénouement, might be radically influenced by the spectators—that being the only form of universal suffrage to which Maurice would bow.

Balandard, as Manager of the Company, entered and explained all this.Though somewhat stiff in appearance, he at once enlisted our affections. When he had made his announcement, he added: 'You will enjoy yourselves.' Dear Balandard, with his impeccable dress-coat and white waistcoat, grasping his enormous hat with so dignified an air! George Sand had been his tailor, and he missed no opportunity of boasting of the fact . . . The regular patrons of the theatre, who, so to speak, knew the actors apart from their roles, or rather, in all the roles which each was accustomed to play, care being always taken to fit the player to the part, since Maurice always showed the greatest deference to the individual, to the temperament of this one or that, to the position occupied in the company by each, so that none was called upon to play a part which did not accord with his or her talents, with his or her virtues and vices—the regular patrons, I say, were to a large extent responsible for giving life to the characters from the moment they made their appearance on the scene. All had their preferences, their weaknesses, for this one or that. For example, Plauchut could never see Mademoiselle Olympe Nantouillet without showing delight in every line of his face. Lina was devoted to Balandard. Madame Sand had a marked liking for the Doge of Venice, and for Gaspardo, the best fisherman on all the Adriatic. Planet paid court to Mademoiselle Ida. My own choice was, as it were, forced upon me. Coq-en-Bois had never loved anybody. He scorned the female sex as a whole, and had been known, quite often, to show lack of respect for its individual members. With us, it was a case of love at first sight. I declared my passion for him publicly, and he at once responded.

'What you, Coq-en-Bois, till now so faithful to your name, have you, too, unhappy man, been caught at last!' cried Lina.

'Hold your tongue! 'tis Juliette who speaks to me.'

Adam protested:

'That's a bit *too* much!' he exclaimed.

We all burst out laughing. Madame Sand, delighted, declared that Adam had been properly taken in and that Maurice had never had a greater triumph. . . .[1]

Juliette and Edmond made the discovery that only at Nohant was Sand truly herself. 'Nothing but my itch for wandering keeps me from the place', she would say with a laugh, and it was an increasing pleasure for her to believe that her 'expeditions' had never been more than casual absences from the one form of life which she had ever really loved. The visitors to Nohant at this time were the younger Dumas (who, in 1864, had married his green-eyed princess); Gautier, dear good Théo, who, on the occasion of his first appearance there had thought that Sand was hostile because she had looked at him without uttering a word; Flaubert, who had only with difficulty been prevailed upon to make the journey, and who teased Madame Adam, telling her that the Republic of the future would be the product of envy and stupidity; Turgénieff, brought by Pauline Viardot. Sand had

[1] JULIETTE ADAM: *Mes Sentiments et nos Idées avant 1870*, pp. 269-73.

a great admiration for his novels ('He was quite surprised when I told him that he was a great artist and a great poet'). Once, even, the whole of the Odéon Company, a *comic novel* on tour, turned up, on which occasion there was singing and laughter and iced champagne until three in the morning.

The daily programme never varied. *Sand to Flaubert:* 'I am, every day, immersed to my chin in the river. This cold, tree-shadowed stream, which I adore, has the immediate effect of restoring all my strength, and I have spent many hours of my life in its waters recovering from over-long closetings with the ink-pot . . .'[1] In summer, the day regularly began with a bathe in the river, which was always kept cool by the trees that overshadowed it. At noon there was luncheon together, followed by a long walk in the Park, a visit to the flower-garden, work, or giving lessons to Aurore. Sand even found time to instruct the trumpeter of the fire-brigade in how to blow a flourish.

> *George Sand to Juliette Adam, January 10th, 1869:* I have got my hands full and no mistake! But what I don't know now about bulging is not worth knowing!— Reveillé, Alarm, Parade, Action, Dismiss, Assembly, Doubletime, Quick-time, etc. I am taking this opportunity to give the good fellow an elementary grounding in music. He is a miller's boy, and quite illiterate. Still, he is naturally intelligent, and will learn. . . .[2]

Dinner was at six. Then, after another stroll round the garden, the company would assemble in the blue drawing-room and listen while Sand played the classics, or Spanish airs, or old country songs of the district, on the piano. After the children had gone to bed, their elders would gather round the table. Sand would play with puzzles, or cut out dresses for her grandchildren, while Maurice drew caricatures, and the others engaged in games of beggar-my-neighbour or dominoes. Sometimes there was reading aloud. Flaubert, Turgénieff, and Sand herself, tried out their as yet unpublished works on this audience. But, for the most part, the evening passed in jokes and rather puerile laughter. George Sand, though remaining silent, liked to

[1] GEORGE SAND: *Correspondance.* Volume V, p. 219: letter dated September 10th, 1867.

[2] Ibid., Volume V, p. 298.

hear plenty of noise about her. 'Gaiety', she said, 'is the best medicine for body and mind.' She believed in gaiety as she believed in good health and kindliness. She liked it to be of the rather obvious kind, what her friend Flaubert was fond of calling 'Henormous'. Even at sixty she still had a weakness for practical jokes. On one occasion she and Maurice hid a cock in the log-chest in the Adams' bedroom, and the wretched Edmond could not close an eye. Juliette took her revenge by bribing the sarcristan-gravedigger to ring the Angelus so loudly that it woke the whole household. Flaubert grumbled. He was, as might be supposed, 'quite intolerable at the puppet-shows, because he criticized everything and could not see what a fool he was making of himself'. By way of friendly reprisal, Sand dedicated to him *Pierre qui roule,* a story in which the Nohant puppets appear as characters.

For she was still writing novels, though without having much faith in them. 'One gets used to treating all that sort of thing much as a soldier treats the orders of his superiors, going into action without too much bothering about whether he is going to get killed or wounded . . . I just drive straight ahead, stupid as an owl and patient as a Berrichon peasant . . .'[1] Every evening, when her guests had gone to bed, she covered twenty sides of paper with her strong handwriting. She never re-wrote, and rarely corrected. 'I write much as another person might garden,' she said—not a very admirable method, but 'the old retired troubadour sings his little song to the moon without much caring whether he sings well or ill, so long as he can get rid of the tune running in his head . . .'[2] She remained the very incarnation of modesty. What she really admired was not her own work, but *l'Education sentimentale,* and was horribly depressed when hostile reviews made Flaubert gloomy. No one, she said, could have any idea of the lengths to which Flaubert carried artistic integrity, nor how sensitive was his professional conscience. She did, however, permit herself to make one very subtle comment on him. 'He does not know,' she said, 'whether he is a poet or a realist, and, since he is both, he feels cramped.'[3]

This acute critical gift makes its appearance also in the

[1] GEORGE SAND: *Correspondance.* Volume V, p. 277.

[2] Ibid., Volume V, p. 300.

[3] JULIETTE ADAM: *Mes Sentiments et nos Idées avant 1870,* p. 416.

letters which she was writing at this time to a young author called Hippolyte Taine, whom she had met at the *Magny* gatherings. 'You have placed Balzac where he truly belongs. Several great men refused it to him, and he suffered because of them. Many is the time I have said to him—"Don't bother: you will remain at the very top." '[1] When Taine sent her his *Thomas Graindorge*, she praised the intelligence of the book and the talent of its author, but made certain reservations.

> *George Sand to Taine, October 17th, 1867:* I have no great feeling for a work of fiction which serves merely as a convenient frame for Monsieur Graindorge's reflections. I don't like his name, I don't like his chiropodist, I don't like his pickled pork, I don't like his torffs, and least of all do I like his little dancer. There seems to me to be a lack of warmth about all those details: they have been too carefully thought out. The comedy, I feel, is too English, by which I mean that it is fantastic rather than gay. The French mind loves plausibility. Molière, the logician, is its true image. *Tristram Shandy* pricks us to astonishment, but it does not much amuse us. The only thing we really like about that book is its elegance and its sentimentality. I don't see why M. Graindorge, who is a painter of the first rank, a subtle-minded critic, and an entrancing artist, should be shown in so ridiculous and odd a light, still less do I understand why he is vicious. Obviously, there is an idea at the back of the author's mind, but the reader never really grasps it, and this element of puzzlement produces in him a feeling of melancholy impatience. . : .[2]

This is a typically French reaction, admirably expressed. The Lady of Nohant took her subjects from the life about her. *Mademoiselle Merquem* was suggested by her own daughter, Solange, whom she introduced under the name of Erneste de Blossay—'a woman whose character was haughty, capricious, and marked by a spirit of contradiction, part whimsical, part practical, and capable of exploiting all the advantages of her position.' Just as Solange had

---

[1] Letter from George Sand to Taine, published in the *Revue de Deux Mondes*, January 15th, 1933, p. 340.

[2] Letter from George Sand to Taine, published in the *Revue des Deux Mondes*, January 15th, 1933, p. 340.

broken off her engagement to Fernand de Préaulx, a
gentleman of Berry, in order to marry Clésinger, so, too,
does Erneste break off hers with M. de la Thoronay, a
country squire, in order to marry Montroger. It seems that
after an interval of twenty-one years, George Sand had
turned back to old letters which either she had kept, or
which had been given her by their recipients. Solange had
not ceased to be a problem. Still beautiful at forty, she had a
number of rich and well-born lovers from whom she
accepted sums of money which were far from negligible,
though that did not prevent her from taking an allowance
both from her father and her mother.

All things considered, and all passion spent, George was
happy. 'Why should I weep over the ruins of Palmyra? All
that, as Lambert says, will pass. The tragedy for my
contemporaries is *that they would like to return to the past,*
and returning to the past is something we can never do. One
is like a flowing, babbling stream, and, surely, when the
water has reflected beautiful things which one has loved and
sung, it has flowed and babbled for long enough. To go on
would be tedious: to begin again, terrifying. One grows old
in loneliness, sad or resigned as may be, but tranquil, and,
as the years pass, 'more tranquil still . . .'[1] She stood
foursquare to the world, as firm and as solid as the Pont
Neuf. She was burned by the sun like a brick. She was still
capable of walking all day long, and then, when she got
back, of bathing in the ice-cold Indre.

George Sand to Joseph Dessauer, July 5th, 1868: Today I
have completed sixty-four Springtimes. I have not yet felt
the weight of the years. I walk as much as I ever did; I do
the same amount of work. I sleep as well. My eyes are
tired but I have worn spectacles now for so long that one
year, in that respect, is much like another. When the time
comes for me to be no longer active, I hope that I shall
have lost the wish to be so. After all, this fearing of old
age is based on the assumption that one is going to reach
it. One never thinks of the tile that might fall upon one's
head. The best thing is to be always ready for whatever
may happen, and to enjoy one's latter years more than
one enjoyed those of one's youth. One wastes so much
time, one is so prodigal of life, at twenty! Our days of

[1] Unpublished Diary, entry under November 27th, 1866.
Bibliothèque nationale: Department of Manuscripts.

winter count for double. That is the compensation of the old. . . .[1]

As we march through life, the ranks ahead grow thinner. In 1869 her first 'Confessor', Sainte-Beuve, died. Towards the end of his life he had disgusted Flaubert by singing the praises of Napoleon III: 'To me of all people!—praise of Badinguet, indeed!—and we were quite alone, with nobody to overhear us!'

Gustave Flaubert to George Sand, October 14th, 1869: We shall meet on Saturday at poor Sainte-Beuve's funeral. How our little group dwindles! How rapidly the few shipwrecked mariners on the *Medusa's* raft now disappear! . . . *June 29th, 1870:* When the *Magny* dinners first started, there were seven of us, now only three remain—myself, Théo and Edmond de Goncourt! In the course of the last eighteen months, the others have all gone, one after another—Gavarni, Bouilhet, Sainte-Beuve, Jules de Goncourt—and that is not the full count. . . .[2]

But Casimir still lived. His wife continued to watch him from afar. She warned Solange and Maurice that he might leave everything to his natural daughter, and so cheat them of Guillery. Urged by her, they filed a suit against him, on the ground that he had falsely interpreted the Will of the Baronne Dudevant. George Sand conducted the whole business with 'the passion of a mother, the subtlety of a woman, and the shrewdness of a lawyer.' The proceedings plunged Casimir into gloom. He lost much sleep because of them, and his health deteriorated. He had never been strong enough to stand up to Aurore. Notice was served upon him to the effect that Guillery must be sold. He kept for himself one hundred and forty-nine thousand francs of the sum realized by the sale (the balance of one hundred and thirty thousand being divided between Maurice and Solange). He retired to the village of Barbaste, six kilometres from Guillery, and there, on March 8th, 1871, he died. His troubles had, no doubt, confused his judgment and brought on softening of the brain, for in May 1869 he addressed to

[1] GEORGE SAND: *Correspondance.* Volume V, p. 267.
[2] GUSTAVE FLAUBERT: *Correspondance.* Volume VI, pp. 7, 79 and 123.

the Emperor an astonishing letter in which 'the Baron
Dudevant, sometime officer in the Armies of the First
Empire', demanded the Legion of Honour.

> I feel that the time has come for me to address myself to
> Your Majesty's good heart, that I may obtain an honour
> to which it is my sincere belief that I have a right. Now,
> in the evening of my days, there is but one ambition left
> to me, namely, to obtain the Cross of the Legion of
> Honour. This is the supreme favour which I solicit from
> Your Imperial Highness. In asking for such an award I
> base my claim not only on the services which, since 1815,
> I have rendered to my Country and to its Government by
> law established—services in themselves, perhaps, of no
> great brilliance, and maybe, even insignificant—but on
> those, to, of my father during the period dating from
> 1792 until the return from Elba. Still more do I venture
> to invoke those private misfortunes which are now matter
> of History. Having married Lucile Dupin, famous in the
> literary world under the name of George Sand, I have
> suffered cruelly in my feelings both as a husband and a
> father. I am sure that I have deserved the sympathetic
> interest of all who have followed the miserable occur-
> rences of that period of my life . . .[1]

Napoleon III did not consider that these domestic
misfortunes, matters of History though they might be,
deserved the Cross. But that he found this letter to be
possessed of a certain piquancy, and that he showed it to
others, is proved by the fact that it was found upon his desk
after the abdication of 1870.

George saw little reason to pity Casimir. After a lifetime
marked by many trials and difficulties, she was now
enjoying a hale, honoured and triumphant old age. The
spectacle of her as she now was could not but remind her
friends of the picture she had herself painted of the old age
of one of the high-spirited heroines of her earlier fictions,
Metella: 'Even when she had reached the age at which love
is no longer in season, she was widely admired, and those
who saw the respect with which she was generally treated,
and the way in which Sarah's charming children flocked

---

[1] A copy of this letter is in the Spoelberch de Lovenjoul
Collection: Group E. 868, f. 291. The original reposes in the files
of the Chancellery of the Legion of Honour.

about her, felt something of the same emotion as touches
the heart at sight of a cloudless, fair and tranquil sky when
the sun has just disappeared from view . . .'[1] One day she
re-opened the romantically bound album—*Sketches and
Hints*—in which, in the time of Musset, and, later, of
Michel, she had recorded her more lively feelings and
impressions. This renewal of acquaintance with the woman
she once had been, surprised and displeased her.

September 1868: It is by the merest chance that I have
read all that again. How devoted I was to that album!
How many and beautiful were the thoughts I meant to
embalm within its pages! Actually, what it contains is the
most unadulterated idiocy. Today it all seems to me to be
terribly over-emphatic, though at the time I was
convinced of my sincerity. Can one ever really sum
oneself up? Does one ever truly know oneself? Is one
ever *a person*? I can no longer feel any certainty in these
matters. I have the feeling now that one changes from
day to day, and that after a few years have passed one has
completely altered. Examine myself as I may, I can no
longer find the slightest trace of the anxious, agitated
individual of those years, so discontented with herself, so
out of patience with others. I suffered no doubt from
illusions of *greatness*. It was the fashion of the times.
Everyone wanted to be great, and, since they were not,
relapsed into a mood of despair. I had my work cut out to
remain good and sincere. And now, here I am, a very old
woman, embarked on my sixty-fifth year. By one of those
strange oddities in my destiny, I am now in much better
health, much stronger, much more active, than I ever was
in my youth, I can go for longer walks, sit up later, and
wake without effort after sleeping soundly . . . I enjoy
complete tranquillity, and my old age is as chaste in
imagination as it is in fact. I am troubled by no hankering
after the days of my youth: I am no longer ambitious for
fame: I desire no money except insofar as I should like to
be able to leave something to my children and grandchildren. I am not at loggerheads with my friends. The

---

[1] The original version of *Metalla*, issued in 1834, in a volume
bearing the general tide of *Le Secrétaire intime,* does not contain
the final section depicting the heroine in old age. This 'extremely
virtuous conclusion' first appeared in Volume II of the *Complete
Works* (Hetzel-Lecou, 1852), p. 427.

only thing that worries me is the way in which mankind seems to be moving, the way in which human societies seem to have turned their backs on progress. But who knows what this apparent sluggishness conceals, or what eventual awakening may not be hidden under the banked ashes of apathy? . . .

Will my life continue for a long while to come? This astonishing old age which has brought me neither infirmity nor lowered vitality, may be the sign of a long life. I wonder. Am I destined to be struck down suddenly? What would it profit me to know the answer to that question since, at every moment of every day some accident may carry any of us off. Can I still make myself useful? That one may legitimately ask, and I think that I can answer 'Yes'. I feel that I may be useful in a more personal, a more direct, way than ever before. I have, though how I do not know, acquired much wisdom. I am better equipped to bring up children. I shall have faith, complete faith, in God. I believe in life eternal, and that evil will one day be conquered by science, a science made bright by love. But I have outgrown the symbols, the figures, the cults, and the gods whom mankind has made in its own image . . . It is quite wrong to think of old age as a downward slope. On the contrary, one climbs higher and higher with the advancing years, and that, too, with surprising strides. Brainwork comes as easily to the old as physical exertion to the child. One is moving, it is true, towards the end of life, but that end is now a goal, and not a reef on which the vessel may be dashed. . . .[1]

---

[1] GEORGE SAND: *Journal intime*, pp. 229-32.

THE WAR AND THE COMMUNE

ON JULY 1st, 1870, George Sand celebrated her sixty-sixth birthday. 'No decrepitude, excellent health, very active, no weight on my shoulders,' she noted. The heat at Nohant was tropical. The shade temperature rose to 113 degrees. There was not a blade of grass to be seen, and the yellowing trees were losing their leaves. This heat, of an African intensity, made everything look as though the end of the world was approaching, and to add to all this came scourges of another kind—forest fires, frightened wolves prowling round the houses, epidemics. 'Never have I known so miserable a summer, and now, as the last straw, war has been declared. . . .'

The last straw! This extra scourge still seemed to her more ridiculous than dreadful. She had accepted the necessity of force when it was a question of liberating Italy, but war between France and Prussia! . . . 'It is just a question of national pride, a matter of determining which country has got the better rifle.' Plauchut, in chauvinistic mood, wrote from Paris that the people were 'roaring mad with enthusiasm'. Sadly she replied—'things are very different in the country. The general feeling here is one of consternation. The whole business is looked on as a game played by our rulers . . .'[1] *To Flaubert:* 'I regard this war as dastardly . . . *Malbrough s'en va-t-en guerre* . . . what a lesson for the peoples who have chosen to place their destinies in the hands of absolute masters!'[2]

Early August was sheer agony. No news from the front. The gloom of waiting became a torment. The Press was gagged, and the papers told nothing. George Sand was a

[1] GEORGE SAND: *Correspondance*. Volume VI, p. 3.
[2] Ibid., Volume VI, pp. 4-5.

witness of the fury felt by the country-people against the
Emperor. 'There's not one of them you won't hear say—
"our first bloody bullet'll be for him" . . . It won't, of course,
they are too good soldiers for that . . . but everywhere is
distrust, disaffection, and a determination to get their own
back through the ballot-box . . .'[1] *To Juliette Adam:* 'We
have got to get rid of Prussians and Empires at one fell
swoop.'[1] Maurice wanted to enlist, but everywhere confusion reigned. *To Arms!*—but what arms? There was a
shortage of rifles, of foodstuffs, of everything. 'Three
Prussians could take La Châtre. No plans have been made
to meet invasion.'

Towards the end of August, news of disaster began to
spread. *George Sand's Journal, September 4th, 1870:* 'An
official communiqué at last! Gloomy! . . . The one
consolation is that the Emperor has been taken prisoner.
But our poor soldiers! How many of them have lost their
lives so that forty thousand might surrender! . . . This is the
end of the Empire, but how horrible the circumstances . . .'
September 5th, 1870: 'Maurice woke me with the news that
a Republic has been proclaimed in Paris without a shot
being fired—a terrific achievement, unique in the history of
any people . . . God save France! . . . she has become once
more worthy of His attention . . .'[2] *To Edmond Plauchut:*
'Long Live the Republic!—no matter what happens. . . .'

In September an outbreak of smallpox took dreadful toll
of Nohant. The little girls must be got away as soon as
possible. The whole family left for La Creuse. Lolo and
Titite played at Prussians with guns made from reeds. On
the public squares of the villages they passed through, boys
were drilling with sticks. George suffered in her feelings
both as a French woman and as a pacifist. The Germans
made a painful impression on her. 'They arrive cold and
harsh as a snowstorm, implacable in their determination,
quite capable of acting with extreme ferocity, though
normally, and in ordinary life, they are the gentlest of men.
They do not think at all. This, they hold, is no time for
thought. Only when they get home will they be capable of
reflection, of pity, of remorse. On the march they are mere
engines of war, oblivious of all other considerations, terrible

[1] Ibid., Volume VI, p. 11.
[2] Ibid., Volume VI, p. 13.
[3] Unpublished. Bibliothèque nationale: Department of
Manuscripts.

. . .'¹ Like Jules Favre, George Sand longed for peace, but not for a shameful peace.

When she got back to Nohant, she learned that two balloons, named respectively *Armand-Barbès* and *George Sand,* had taken off from the besieged capital. *Barbès* carried to Tours a young Deputy who had already made a name for himself as an orator, Léon Gambetta. This man had already declared it as his view that France might still be armed, and the war won. George did not share in this belief: 'Our dictators of Tours are the victims of a terrifying optimism . . .'² Gambetta's improvised armies inspired no feeling of confidence in the mind of Madame Sand, the shrewd countrywoman. A genuine Republic, legitimately established by elections according to law, was her dream: the thought of a prolonged dictatorship, lacking the justification of successes in the field, filled her with horror. *George Sand's Journal, December 7th, 1870:* 'No one understands a thing: the general atmosphere is one of lunacy. Alone in our solitude, we are like passengers in a ship blown by contrary winds, and incapable of movement . . .' *December 11th, 1870:* 'The Government has left Tours for Bordeaux. Gambetta is off to join the Army of the Loire. Does he mean to command it in person? Either he is the Consul Bonaparte, or a gambler who will lose all. He has reached his fifth act. The only alternatives for him are to succeed or to get himself killed . . . The closer the danger comes, the more work do I do. I have even got a sort of enthusiasm for work. It is as though I had undertaken a task which has got to be finished, so that I may die with the satisfying knowledge that I was hard at it to the end. . . .'³

Civil strife broke out even before the war was at an end. In Paris the Reds were threatening. Sand, who counted among them several friends of long standing, such as Félix Pyat who had been a professional revolutionary ever since the days of 1830, refused to panic. She was far more frightened of the monarchists, of the bonapartists, of the likelihood of a dictatorship. Gambetta's 'purges' shocked her. 'I see with regret the enormous proportions which all these sackings of civil servants and magistrates are

---

¹ GEORGE SAND: 'Journal d'un Voyageur pendant la guerre', in *Revue des Deux Mondes,* March 1st, 1871.

² Ibid., March 15th, 1871, p. 214.

³ Unpublished. Bibliothèque nationale: Department of Manuscripts.

assuming . . .'[1] Especially illegal and dangerous did it seem
to her that no elections had yet been held. The Paris
extremists, no less than the Bordeaux Government, claimed
to base their authority on 'active minorities'. Forgetting that
she herself had taken up the same position in 1848, she was
now loud in condemning it. 'Distrust of the Masses, that is
the crime of the moment.' When the bombardment of Paris
placed her friends in danger—Juliette Adam, Edmond
Plauchut, Eugène and Esther Lambert, Edouard Rodrigues—she waxed furious against Gambetta; 'The tragic
mistake has been to believe that courage was enough when
what was needed was practical good sense . . . Poor France!
. . . your eyes must be opened so that what remains of
you may be saved!'[2] She held the view that Gambetta was
honest and sincere, but deplored his complete lack of
judgment: 'It is a great misfortune to think oneself capable
of carrying through to success a task which is beyond one's
strength . . .'[3] She was especially critical of his speeches all
of which ended with the same invariable refrain, *'Patience!
Courage! Discipline!* When Monsieur Gambetta has affixed
a sufficient number of exclamation marks to his dispatches,
he thinks that he has saved the country! . . .'[4]

When the armistice allowed the Paris Government to
take a tighter hold on the national situation, she got the
impression that Gambetta was deliberately delaying the
holding of elections in order to prolong the Bordeaux
dictatorship and maintain a strong opposition to the
conclusion of a peace. She was heart and soul for Paris. 'I
would give a great deal to be sure that the dictator has
handed in his resignation. I was beginning to hate him for
having caused so much useless suffering and death. His
adorers irritated me with their constant talk about his
having saved our honour. Our honour would have been
saved without him. France is not such a poltroon that she
needs a schoolmaster to teach her courage and devotion in
the face of the enemy. Every party has had its heroes in this
war: every contingent has supplied its quota of martyrs. We
have every right to call down curses on the head of a man
who claimed to be able to lead us to victory and has, in fact,

[1] GEORGE SAND: 'Journal d'un Voyageur pendant la
guerre', in *Revue des Deux Mondes*, March 15th, 1871, p. 231.

[2] Ibid., April 1st, 1871, p. 418.

[3] Ibid., p. 422.

[4] Ibid., p. 432.

led us only to despair. We were entitled to demand of him some touch of genius, and he has proved incapable of supplying so much as an iota of common sense.' But to this she added, 'May God forgive him!'[1]

> *George Sand's Journal, Sunday, January 29th, 1871:*
> 'Ah! . . . thank God!—at last, at last an armistice has been signed, to continue in force for twenty-one days. An Assembly has been summoned to meet in Bordeaux. A member of the Paris Government is to be present. That is all we know so far. It seems that Gambetta is furious. He will find the dictatorship going bad on him . . . Will food be sent into Paris? . . . Will this pause in hostilities lead to a final peace? . . . Shall we be able to communicate with Paris? . . . The Sub-Prefect who came along at two o'clock to show us the telegram is of the opinion that Gambetta will put up a fight. Does that mean there will be civil war? He is quite capable of wishing it, if the only alternative is for him to surrender his authority!'[2]

As in 1848, the Elections produced an enormous number of votes. Except in Paris the peace-party carried the day. *George Sand's Journal, February 15th, 1871:* 'The national hero in Paris is Louis Blanc. In 1848 he was the best hated, the most unpopular, man in all the country. What changes we see in human affairs! In the country districts M. Thiers has triumphed, having been returned at the head of the poll in twenty Departments. Both are contemporary historians: both are dwarfs. But physical size goes for nothing. Here are two men of high intelligence who may hit it off if they are not too jealous of one another.'[3] Though Sand was depressed at the harshness of the peace terms, she did not weaken in her view that the war must be brought to an end.

> *George Sand to Edmond Plauchut, February 2nd, 1871:*
> Neither you nor your friends must be downcast. You have all of you done your duty. There is nothing shameful in misfortune. France may be drenched in blood, but she has not been smothered in dirt . . . The

[1] GEORGE SAND: 'Journal d'un Voyageur pendant la guerre', in *Revue des Deux Mondes*, April 1st, 1871.
[2] Unpublished. Bibliothèque nationale: Department of Manuscripts.
[3] Ibid.

time has come to make peace—to get the best peace possible, to be sure, but not to go on fighting in blind fury and seek revenge for our miseries. . . .[1]

She knew that France would recover rapidly. As a countrywoman of Berry she was aware of the infinite resources of the land and its prodigious powers of recuperation. Often, in the course of her life, she had stood on the very verge of suicide, and on each occasion had weathered the crisis. She was now, in her own person, a symbol of the Nation.

Thiers, of whom once she had felt so mistrustful, seemed to her the least of many evils. Called to lead the country, he had accepted the Republic. It was, he thought, the one system of government which 'would cause the least amount of division in France as a whole'. The task to be achieved was enormous—liberation, rehabilitation, and the drafting of a new Constitution. Thiers believed himself to be capable of carrying the work to a successful issue. But patriotic Paris refused to accept the peace. Socialist Paris refused to accept a reactionary Assembly. Paris, the Capital, refused to recognize a Government sitting at Versailles. Sand watched with anxiety the beginning of disturbances on the outer fringes of the city.

George Sand's Journal, March 5th, 1871: On the morning of March 1st the Prussians marched in by way of the Champs Elysées. On the morning of the 3rd they marched out again without having made any contact with the inhabitants. Paris behaved with good sense and dignity. But there is reason to fear, especially now that the Prussians have gone, something like the 'days of June'. There is a mood of despair in all parties. Shall we manage to avoid a crisis? . . . *March 8th, 1871:* Harrisse writes that the city is recovering its elegant appearance. The gas is working, and the cocottes are again in evidence. He thinks, however, that there will be some sort of an outbreak pretty soon. I do not as yet share his opinion . . . *March 19th, 1871:* The times more than ever disturbed. Paris is in the eddies and rapids of unthinking passions. An attempt was made last night to move guns from Montmartre. A contingent of troops was sent, and

[1] GEORGE SAND: *Correspondance.* Volume VI, pp. 73-4.

these after surrounding the 'Aventine Mount'—as it is now being called—found themselves, in their turn, surrounded by armed mobs from Belleville, and surrendered. There was, I am told, a certain amount of shooting, but that this soon came to an end because the soldiers refused to fire on the people . . . In the course of the day, the Government issued a statement to the effect that it is now in full session at Versailles, and that orders emanating from any other source are to be ignored. This would seem to show that the Hôtel de Ville has been occupied, and that the revolution, riot or conspiracy, has got the upper hand in Paris. Are we to have the old June troubles over again? I feel sick at heart. Antoine[1] and de Vasson[2] came to dinner. We were all very much down in the mouth. . . .[3]

Then came the Commune. Paris burst into a rash of barricades, cannon, and multiple-barrelled guns. Sand, on this occasion, was opposed to the insurgents. *George Sand's Journal, March 22nd, 1871:* 'The mob which follows them is composed in part of dupes and fools, in part of the most degraded and criminal elements of the population. . . .'

Thursday, March 23rd, 1871: The horrible adventure goes on. The insurgents are holding people to ransom, uttering threats, making arrests, staging trials. They are preventing the regular Courts from functioning. They have demanded a million from the Bank, and five hundred thousand from Rotchild [*sic*]. People are too frightened to do anything but yield. There has already been some street-fighting. In the Place Vendôme they opened fire and killed a number of persons belonging to a hostile demonstration. All the *Mairies* are in their hands, and all the public buildings. They are looting ammunition and food. Their *Official Gazette* is a disgusting sheet. They are nothing but a lot of coarse clowns, and it is pretty obvious that they have no idea what to do with

[1] Antoine Ludre-Gabillaud, the son of George Sand's lawyer.
[2] Paulin de Vasson, whose wife was related to the Perigois, to Gustave Papet, and to the Nérauds. The couple lived at the Château de Varennes, not far from Nohant.
[3] Unpublished. Bibliothèque nationale: Department of Manuscripts.

their success. The Versailles Assembly is stupidly reactionary, and won't have anything to do with reconciliation. Jules Favre is even more reactionary. Thiers is cleverer, and more master of himself, though he is quite clearly suffering from a sense of injury. The Assembly is very much opposed to him, and refuses to listen when he speaks. . . .[1]

She blamed her friends, the Paris republicans, for letting the insurgents overturn the Government. 'Letter from Plauchut. He is one of those whom I compare to a tenant letting his house burn, and himself with it, just so as to score off the landlord. . . .'[2]

Things continued in this way from March until June. Then Thiers triumphed.

George Sand's Journal, June 1st, 1871: It is all over in Paris. They are pulling down the barricades and burying the dead, this latter because there have been a number of summary shootings. People are being arrested by the cartload. A great many innocent, or only half-guilty, persons are going to pay with their lives for the genuinely guilty, who will get off scot-free. Alexandre[3] says that he has saved any number of prisoners on the strength of that science of physiognomy taught by Dr. Favre. His letter is all very odd, and I can't, for the life of me, imagine how he gets the Courts-Martial to listen to the results of his experiments. Hugo seems really to have a screw loose. He has published a deal of wild nonsense, and there have been manifestations against him in Brussels . . . *June 7th, 1871:* Just heard details of the damage done in Paris. Destruction has been on an immense scale, and it is quite clear that they had planned to burn down the whole city. What's going on now is a real reign of Tamango.[4] Very little news is reaching us, but it seems that the cowardly bourgeois who put up no sort of resistance during the trouble now want to indulge in an orgy of killing. Are

[1] Unpublished. Bibliothèque nationale: Department of Manuscripts.

[2] Ibid.

[3] Dumas the younger.

[4] The bloodthirsty negro tyrant, Tamango, is a character in one of Prosper Mérimée's novels.

people still being shot without trial? I am very much afraid so. . . .[1]

The excesses of the repression were no less cruel than those of the Commune had been. Consequently, as so often happens in the case of the honest-minded, Sand found herself at odds with everybody. Her political friends reproached her for no longer realizing that barricades were necessary. Her enemies accused her of a lack of firmness. She remained loyal to that doctrine which she called—'The teaching of the Gospel according to St. John'.

No need for me to ask where my friends are, where my enemies. They are where the storm has flung them. Those who have deserved my love, but do not see with my eyes, are not for that reason any less dear to me. The thoughtless censure of those who have broken away from me does not make me look on them as enemies. Friendship unjustly withdrawn stays still unsullied in the heart which has not deserved so cruel an outrage. That heart is far above the promptings of self-love, and knows how to await the return of justice and affection. . . .[2]

The party-champions in both camps, with their cowardice and their violence, brought grist to Flaubert's pessimistic mill. 'The Romantics, with their immoral sentimentality, will have a heavy bill to foot: so much tenderness for mad dogs, so little consideration for those who have been bitten . . .[3]'

George Sand to Gustave Flaubert, 1872: This is no time to be sick, old troubadour, no time to grumble. What we've got to do is cough, wipe our noses, get well, and declare that France is mad, humanity stupid, and we ourselves no more than a lot of badly designed and half-bungled animals . . . That's all true enough; still, we have got to go on being in love with ourselves, the species to

---

[1] Unpublished. Bibliothèque nationale: Department of Manuscripts.

[2] GEORGE SAND: 'Réponses à un ami', articles published in *Le Temps*.

[3] GUSTAVE FLAUBERT: *Correspondance*. Volume VI, pp. 296-7.

which we belong, and, most of all, our friends . . . Maybe this chronic state of indignation is one of the necessary conditions of your continued existence: I know that it would be the death of *me*! . . . Is it possible, you ask, to live in peace when the human race is so absurd? Speaking for myself, I am prepared to submit to the conditions, reflecting the while that I, perhaps, am no less absurd, and that it is about time I began to think how to improve myself. . . .[1]

No attitude could well contain more of distilled wisdom. If, instead of blaming the times, everyone would sweep his own doorstep, the street would be much cleaner. The months passed, but Flaubert's anger continued. The Assembly was now oscillating between Monarchy and Republic.

Flaubert to Sand: The sense of the Public seems to me to sink progressively lower and lower. To what depths of idiocy shall we fall? France is settling like a worm-eaten ship, and any hope of safety, even among the most level-headed, would seem to be little more than chimerical . . . I see no more hope of establishing new principles than of being able to respect the old . . . Meanwhile, I repeat to myself something which Littré once said to me: 'dear friend, mankind is an ill-balanced amalgam, and the earth a most inferior planet. . . .'[2]

This was not, really, a very intelligent remark. An inferior planet?—inferior to what? Are things better ordered on Saturn or on Mars? Sand was at one with Renan in hoping to find relative salvation in a moderate Republic. 'It will be extremely bourgeois, and miles distant from the ideal, but we have got to begin at the beginning. We artists suffer from a lack of patience. We look for the immediate establishment of an Abbey of Thelema. Before, however, saying "Do what thou wilt" we must pass through the intermediate phase of saying "Do what thou canst" . . .' To return to authoritarian government in any form, would be, she thought, to court disaster.

[1] GEORGE SAND: *Correspondance*. Volume VI, pp. 192-4.
[2] GUSTAVE FLAUBERT: *Correspondance*.

Universal suffrage, that is to say the expression of the will of all, whether for good or ill, is a necessary safety-valve. Without it, you will get merely successive outbreaks of civil violence. This wonderful guarantee of security is there to our hands. It is the best social counterweight so far discovered, and yet you wish to restrain and hamstring its activities. . . .[1]

This was no longer the revolutionary spirit of 1848. Rather was it the dawning wisdom of the Third Republic, and there was much good in it.

V

NUNC DIMITTIS . . .

George Sand to Gustave Flaubert: Why don't you get married? To live a solitary existence is odious: it is death and destruction for you, and for those who love you it is cruel. Your letters are full of misery and tear at my heart. Is there no woman whom you love, or by whom you could bear to be loved? Is there nowhere some brat you can believe yourself to have fathered? If there is, then devote yourself to his upbringing, make yourself his slave, forget yourself and think of him . . . Whether that is possible I do not know, but this I do know, that to live in and for yourself is bad. . . .[2]

SHE NOT only preached, but practised what she preached. In the years that followed the war, George Sand was, above all else, a passionately devoted grandmother. What happiness it was for this born governess to teach Titite how to read, to instruct Lolo in geography, history and literary composition! Aurore remained her favourite. 'She takes up much of my time. She grasps things too quickly, and needs

[1] GEORGE SAND: *Impressions et Souvenirs: Réponse à une Amie.*
[2] GEORGE SAND: *Correspondance.* Volume VI, p. 252.

to move forward at full gallop. Understanding is, with her, a passion. but mere factual knowledge she finds dull.'[1] The vision of the world shines with a new glory when it is seen, all bright and new, through the eyes of a child. The old lady was surrounded now by children, darting through the heather like so many rabbits. 'How good life is when all that one loves is aswarm with life!'

She had lost none of her delight in travelling, in sunshine, and in flowers, and now she could enjoy these things in the company of her granddaughters. What of her work as novelist? That she liked no more than she had ever done. She turned out her two or three stories a year because she had to fulfil the terms of her contract with Buloz, to which now another had been added, a Charles-Edmond agreement with *Le Temps,* and must do something to meet the demand for money coming from family and friends. The drudgery she could manage pretty well, for she had the professional's mastery of technique, but there tended to be a sameness about the themes—rural idyll *(Marianne Chevreuse),* kidnapped children *(Flamarande,* and its sequel, *Les Deux Frères).* Had she been free to choose for herself, she would have preferred to take her ease and get on with her wool-work. Flaubert urged her to read the younger writers, Emile Zola, Alphonse Daudet. She did not dislike their books, but found them depressing.

George Sand to Gustave Flaubert, March 25th, 1872: Life is not composed *only* of criminals and scoundrels. There is more than a mere handful of decent folk, because, after all, some sort of an ordered society *does* exist, and not all crimes go unpunished. It is true that fools form the majority, but there is a public conscience which weighs upon them, and forces them to observe decent standards of behaviour. That rogues should be exhibited and castigated is right, is even moral, but we should be told of, should be shown, the other side of the medal as well, otherwise the simple-minded reader—who is the common-or-garden reader—will react against such books, will grow depressed and fearful, and, ultimately, will deny the truth of the picture which their authors paint, because to do so is their only alternative to despair.[2]

[1] Ibid., Volume VI, p. 250.
[2] GEORGE SAND: *Correspondance.* Volume VI, p. 398.

For some time past the critics had ceased to pay any attention to her new novels. Even Hugo never devoted an article to her work, though she had, to his. In matters literary, she felt herself to be very much isolated. Nevertheless, a few men of the younger generation were beginning to praise her idealism. The world of literature, like the world of society, oscillates about a fixed point. *Itus et reditus*. The pendulum swings back as well as forwards. A certain Anatole France paid tribute to Madame Sand's considerable genius, to the many generous, the many confused, passions of this great and simple-minded lover of *things*.

Taine wrote: 'We have carried realism to extremes: we have stressed beyond measure the brutish part of man's nature and the most rotten aspects of society.'[1] He told Sand that she had more than ever a part to play, and that the French still expected much from her.

Hippolyte Taine to George Sand, March 30th, 1872: If only for our sakes, you must look after yourself for many years to come. Please give us, in addition to what you may be planning in head and heart, some such work as I once asked of you, more popular in tone, more vivid. It should be a sermon and an exhortation for men who have been bruised and wounded, but the tone of it must be that of a rousing call, of the encouragement for which all France is waiting. It is not a social thesis that her people demand, nor yet a moral one. In fact, it is not a thesis at all of which they stand in need, but the sound of frank and generous voices, the voices of maître Favilla, of Champi, of Villemer. They want to be persuaded that there *is* an heroic world still within their reach, and that the world in which they live could, if only they would stand on tip-toe, be made to resemble it. . . .[2]

In short, he praised her for being the saviour of faith, hope and charity. She was both delighted and surprised, 'for Flaubert, though he loves me truly as a person, certainly has not that amount of love for me as a writer. He does not believe that my feet are set on the right road, and he is not

[1] Letter published in the *Revue des Deux Mondes* for January 15th, 1933, p. 345.
[2] *Ibid.*, p. 346.

the only one of my friends to hold that I am not so much an artist as a woman who means well. . . .'[1]

Poor Flaubert could not cease from raging. Where politics were concerned he seemed to suffer from a species of mental incontinence. The thing had become a positive obsession with him. He was being persecuted by a 'sort of Holbach clique', and his two plays, *Le Candidat* and *Le Sexe Faible* had been 'flops of the first water'. There was no longer any room in the world for persons of taste. Yet he still believed, and would go on believing, in art for art's sake, in the precise and perfect word, in the rhythm of a phrase, in the high finish of a book. To him it did not matter what one said so long as one said it well. Sand gently scolded him. 'You seek only the well-constructed phrase. That is something, to be sure, but it is not the whole of art, it is not even the half.' She begged him to come to Nohant, to immerse himself once more in the gaiety and affection of a family gathering.

'What does it matter if one has a hundred thousand enemies, provided one can count on the love of two or three honest folk?'

But throughout 1872 he dug his toes in. Pauline Viardot, of whom he saw a great deal, tried hard to take him with her, but in vain. He let her start for Nohant without him, accompanied only by 'les Paulinettes', Marianne and Claudie Viardot. The visit was short but delightful. As in the time of Liszt, as in the time of Chopin, music reigned supreme.

George Sand's Journal, September 26th, 1872: What a day! What emotions! what a complete submersion in music! Pauline sang, both during the day and in the evening . . . Each time she sings she surpasses herself. She is incomparable. I cried my eyes out . . . Lolo sat with her eyes wide open, positively *drinking in* the music. The little Viardot girls sang deliciously . . . their voices are crystal-clear. But Pauline!—what genius that woman has! . . . *October 1st, 1872:* Pauline made her small daughters sing with her in a version of *Fra Galina* which she has arranged as a trio. It was charming. Then she sang 'Divinités du Styx' from *Alceste*—quite lovely. It made me literally tremble with an almost unendurable

[1] Letter published in the *Revue des Deux Mondes* for January 15th, 1933, p. 349.

emotion. I felt quite drunk when it was over, and could think of nothing else . . . *October 2nd, 1872:* Pauline sang a little, and promised to sing again in the evening. After dinner we had charades, in which Lolo took part— as a dog. She is the sweetest little creature, and went off to bed in the middle without a murmur . . . The charades continued until ten, after which Pauline sang *Pancito,* five or six ravishing Spanish songs, and Schumann's *Printemps.* She followed these up with Verdi's *Lady Macbeth.* I'm not in love with it, but she does it wonderfully. Lastly, *La Sonnambula* and *Orphée*[1]— perfection in the two modes of joy and pain.[2]

At long last the reverend Father Cruchard[3] made an Easter pilgrimage to Nohant, where he was joined by Turgénieff. The latter was initiated into the usual Nohant nonsense. There were wild dances, in the course of which each of the participants changed clothes three times. Flaubert ended up as an Andalusian dancer, and performed a sketchy fandango. 'He certainly is very comic, but after five minutes he has no more breath left. He is a great deal older than I am! . . . Lives too much with his brain so his body suffers . . . Our boisterousness is too much for him. . . .'[4]

George Sand's Journal, April 17th, 1873: Leaping, dancing, singing, shouting—Flaubert thoroughly put out—kept on trying to stop the fun in order to talk literature! But we wouldn't let him. Turgénieff loves noise and gaiety: he is just as much a child as the rest of us. He dances and waltzes and is altogether a nice, jolly man of genius. Maurice read us *La Ballade de la Nuit*—could not have been done better. Great success. Flaubert finds him in every way staggering . . . *April 18th, 1873:* Flaubert talked a great deal—very animated and comic, but he would not give anybody else a chance, and

[1] The pieces here referred to were Bellini's *Sonnambula* and Glück's *Alceste* and *Orphée.*

[2] Unpublished. Bibliothèque nationale: Department of Manuscripts.

[3] This was what Flaubert called himself: 'Chaplain to the Ladies of Disillusion'.

[4] George Sand's unpublished Journal: April 13th, 1873. Bibliothèque nationale: Department of Manuscripts.

Turgénieff, who is much the more interesting of the two, could not get a word in edgeways. It was like being assaulted with a battering-ram, and went on until one in the morning. They leave early tomorrow . . . *April 19th, 1873:* It is character rather than intelligence or greatness that gives one a sense of *life*. As a result of being with my dear Flaubert I am completely worn out, and feel as though I had been *trampled on*. All the same, I am devoted to him—an admirable man, but with too exuberant a personality. He positively beats one down . . . We made a most terrific noise tonight, playing games and being deliciously silly . . . We all miss Turgénieff. I know him less, and love him less, but he is blessed with true simplicity, and has the charm that goes with genuine good nature. . . .[1]

But Flaubert, as soon as he reached home, sent her a letter of the warmest thanks.

Gustave Flaubert to George Sand, April 23rd, 1873: It is no more than five days since we parted, but I miss you quite idiotically. I miss Aurore and every member of the company, down to Fadet.[2] Yes, I mean it. It is so lovely being with you! You are all so good and kind and vital . . . Your two friends, Turgénieff and Cruchard, did a great deal of philosophizing on the subject between Nohant and Châteauroux, travelling most comfortably in your carriage, behind two fine trotting horses. Long live the postilions of La Châtre! But the rest of the journey was *most* unpleasant because of our train companions. I was, however, consoled with strong drink, since the good Muscovite had with him a flask of the most excellent brandy. . . .[3]

She planned to take her brood of little ones abroad that Summer, and suggested Switzerland. The children, however, wanted to go to the seaside. 'The seaside be it, then! —so long as we travel and bathe, I don't care where we go. I am mad with delight . . . I am not better than my

---

[1] Bibliothèque nationale: Department of Manuscripts.
[2] A small dog.
[3] GUSTAVE FLAUBERT: *Correspondance*. Volume VII, p. 13.

granddaughters, who are drunk on the mere expectation of the holidays, and don't know why . . .'[1] So long as she was at Nohant she remained faithful to fresh water. She bathed in the river with Plauchut, and would lie there evoking a long procession of vanished faces.

> *George Sand's Journal, July 21st, 1873:* Lying there in the water, I found myself thinking of all those who used to bathe with us in the old days: Pauline and her mother, Chopin, Delacroix, my brother . . . We would bathe sometimes at night, walking down to the river, and then walking back again. They are all of them dead, except Madame Viardot and me. This poor little corner of the countryside has seen many celebrities without realizing it. . . .[2]

With politics she now concerned herself scarcely at all, though sometimes the thought of Henry V frightened her. 'I catch a whiff of something very much like the sacristy creeping up on us.' The reason for that comment may perhaps be found in the fact that the Governor-General of Paris had recently forbidden a performance of *Mademoiselle La Quintinie*, on the grounds that it might provoke public disorder. To her friend, Prince Napoleon, she sent her good wishes for the New Year, but not for a Bonapartist restoration.

> *George Sand to Prince Napoleon-Jérôme, January 5th, 1874:* You say that even in politics we should agree. About that I know nothing, because I am ignorant of how you view the present situation, nor have I any idea what it is that you hope for France, and whether you wish us to seek the remedy for our present discontents in a child.[3] Surely you cannot want that? I should find it easier to understand a purely personal ambition. But though such an ambition would, in you, be justified by reason of your high intelligence, your foremost enemy would be the party of the widow and her son.[4] Finally, I

---

[1] GEORGE SAND: *Correspondance*. Volume VI, p. 217.

[2] Unpublished. Biblothèque nationale: Department of Manuscripts.

[3] The Prince Imperial.

[4] The Empress Eugénie.

cannot see, within any measurable distance of time, a chance of the country as a whole rallying to the Imperial standard. . . .[1]

She thought that salvation must come from a moderate republicanism. Only in 1875 was the Republic she hoped for established by a majority of one. That is France all over.

Since 1873 Solange had been living, not far from Nohant, at the Château de Montgivray, which she had bought with her dubiously acquired fortune from her cousin, Léontine Simonnet, Hippolyte Châtiron's daughter. As a consequence of the war she had, in 1871, become temporarily reconciled with her mother and Maurice. She had arrived one day as a suppliant and a refugee. The good-hearted Lina had pleaded for her, and Solange, disciplined by danger, had sheathed her claws. Since she had inherited some of Sophie-Victoire's skill, she made herself very useful by cutting out and sewing clothes for Lina and the children. But, with the return of peace, the situation again deteriorated. Sand had forbidden the purchase of Montgivray, not wishing, as she put it, to have that 'screech-owl' spying from the top of her tower. But Solange had ignored her mother's injunctions, 'and had bought the Château through an intermediary who rejoiced in the name of Madame Brétillot. As a result of this act of rebellion her allowance was discontinued, and Nohant became more or less closed to her, since she criticized everything that went on there. From time to time, of a morning, however, she would 'blow in'. The children, who had a holy horror of her, would be watching at their grandmother's door, in order to intercept Aunt Solange.

Old friends and old enemies alike, were all vanishing. The Princess Arabella died on March 5th, 1876. She had, towards the end, recovered both her reason and her pride. In her resurrected Salon she entertained the new generation of Republican statesmen. She had lived long enough to see Liszt an Abbé and Henri Lehmann President of the Académie des Beaux Arts.

Jules Sandeau was in a very bad way. Age had increased his girth and thinned his hair. Laziness and disappointment had made him dull-witted, but there still remained some visible traces of what he must have been like in his charming youth. On the wall of his study there hung a drawing which

[1] GEORGE SAND: *Correspondance*. Volume VI, pp. 305-6.

Aurore Dudevant had made of him in the old days. 'It's only we old bald-heads who could have had as much hair as that,' he would say. When he sat at the *Café de la Rotonde,* in the Palais-Royal, the passers by nudged one another, and murmured, 'Look, that's Sandeau, George Sand's first lover'. It was his sole claim to fame.

Marchal, the 'Mastodon', was the cause of much anxiety both to Sand and to Dumas. The years immediately following the war, had, it is true, brought him chances of success. One of his pictures, *Alsace,* gained a Salon prize, was engraved, and had a considerable circulation. As a result he was commissioned to illustrate the works of Erckmann-Chatrian, and asked to design the scenery for a patriotic play. But he was lazy, careless and unpunctual, never on time with his plates or his stage models, with the result that most of his commissions went by default. He had lost his two most powerful patrons, Prince Napoleon and the Princesse Mathilde, who had both been living outside France since the collapse of the Empire. Gradually he had slipped into a squalid Bohemian existence, and was now living a shiftless existence on loans and windfalls. 'Wine and women will be the death of me', he wrote to Sand, and the phrase must have had, for her, a familiar sound. Elsewhere, too, we seem to hear an echo from her letters on the subject of Musset. 'Ten years of maternal affection', she writes, 'have not succeeded in exorcizing those two cruel demons, Laziness and Debauchery'—so true it is that women change scarcely at all—or men.

Hortense Allart, cynical friend of the romantic George, was growing old beyond a doubt. She had written an extremely frank book about her experiences in love—*Les Enchantments de la Prudence*—and Sand had expressed herself as being 'enchanted by these *Enchantements.* I have just read your astonishing book. You are a very great woman.' Very great?—perhaps 'outspoken' would have been a more suitable adjective. But George, who was not herself outspoken, set a high value on such verbal audacities.

Hortense Allart's Journal, April 16th, 1873: I have just had a letter from the queen.[1] It was in reply to two of

---

[1] This nickname was given by Hortense to George Sand, after Béranger had called her the 'queen of our new generation of writers'.

mine, in the second of which I had argued against the idea that there are any such people as fallen women. She puts it admirably when she says that the fallen woman is bound up with the whole of the past which she repudiates—Hell, priests and hypocrites . . . She thinks all that will be changed. She says that I show no sign of old age, and that I shall be alive and kicking on the day of my death.[1]

George Sand at seventy-two did not feel that she was growing old, and began to believe that she would live to a great age. She finished one perfectly empty book, *La Tour de Percemont,* and started another, *Albine Fiori,* a novel in the form of letters, which was the story of the natural daughter of a great lord and an actress. Once again the Saxe and Rinteau ancestors were going to be turned to account. But what chiefly occupied her was the writing of fairy-tales for Lolo.

George Sand's Diary, Shrove Tuesday, February 20th, 1876: Intended to work but could not get down to it . . . Went round the garden which is full of flowers—violets, snowdrops, crocuses and anemones—everything is coming up. The apricot near the greenhouse is in flower. Made a dress for myself, then the little girls came along to be seen and admired: Titite as a fairy, Lolo in a Velasquez dress, looking very sweet, René in a pierrot's get-up,[2] Maurice as a Chinaman, Lina as an Indian woman . . . They danced, and I sat at the piano playing until the children went to bed at nine. Then the others got back into their ordinary clothes, except Plauchut, who put on a smock and a false nose and went off to a ball in the village. . . .[3]

Early in the Spring of 1876 she began to complain of intermittent pains. All her life she had had trouble with her liver and a tiresome intestine. She resigned herself to these attacks, and was infinitely more worried by Maurice's neuralgia.

[1] Quoted by Léon Séché in *Hortense Allart de Mértens,* p. 23.
[2] René Simonnet.
[3] Unpublished. Bibliothèque nationale: Department of Manuscripts.

George Sand's Diary, May 19th, 1876: Maurice had a bad attack at five which lasted until half-past seven. Aurore kept him company, and waited dinner for him. They dined together in a gay mood, and the evening passed without any sign of a relapse . . . I had a good deal of pain all day. I gave Lolo her lesson, wrote some letters, and read. I finished Renan's *Dialogues et Fragments philosphiques.* . . .[1]

On May 20th Doctor Marc Chabenat of La Châtre was called in by Maurice and Lina, ostensibly to advise about 'Bouli's' neuralgia, but really because their mother's pains were causing general anxiety. Sand told the doctor that she had been suffering 'for the past fortnight from an obstinate attack of constipation, but that her brain was as clear as ever, and her appetite good'. She added that 'since my condition is an embarrassment rather than an illness', she had not bothered much about it. On May 23rd she wrote to her medical adviser in Paris, Doctor Favre:

In spite of my age (rising seventy-two) I am quite unconscious of the approach of senility. There is nothing wrong with my legs, my eyes are better than they have been for twenty years past, I sleep soundly, and my hands are as steady and as nimble as they were in the days of my youth. In the intervals between my terribly sharp attacks of pain, I feel stronger and generally less encumbered . . . I was slightly asthmatic but am so no longer. I go upstairs as briskly as my dogs. But, seeing that *one part of my vital functions is almost wholly suppressed,* I rather wonder what is going to happen to me, and whether I ought not to be prepared to go off quite suddenly one of these mornings. . . .[2]

Death is a humble and discreet visitor. It enters a house without noise. The last words that George Sand ever wrote contain nothing of fear.

May 29th, 1876: Weather delicious. No great pain. I took a nice walk round the garden and gave Lolo her lesson.

[1] Unpublished. Bibliothèque nationale: Department of Manuscripts.
[2] Letter quoted by Wladimir Karénine in *George Sand.* Volume IV, pp. 598-9.

Re-read one of Maurice's plays. After dinner, Lina went in to the theatre at La Châtre, I played at bésig [*sic*] with Sagnier.[1] Did some drawing. Lina got back at midnight.[2]

This is the final entry in George Sand's Journal. The following account is from the pen of her neighbour, Nannecy de Vasson.

On Sunday, May 28th—wrote Madame de Vasson—I had been to Nohant to spend the day with Ninie,[3] while Paulin was at Coudray with his parents. We had lunch without Madame Sand. As usual she was somewhat ailing, but nothing out of the ordinary. For some time she had been suffering a good deal of pain, but those about her had almost ceased to worry. After luncheon Lina and I went for a stroll in the kitchen-garden, where we spent some considerable time talking about all sorts of things . . . A little later, Madame Sand came down. We spent some time walking with her, admiring the various wild flowers of which she was so fond. The lawn was thick with them. She took us to a spot in a small copse where many paths meet, to look at a very rare orchis. After this we went back and sat down near the house. Madame Sand talked about a projected trip to Paris. The conversation languished. It was never very lively with Madame Sand, who always had a thousand and one things to think about. Something she said did, however, strike me. She was admiring a bird strutting on the ground in front of her. 'It is a very odd thing', she suddenly remarked, 'but I really believe I am recovering my sight. I can see today better without my spectacles than with them. . . .'[4]

[1] Charles Sagnier was one of the visitors at that time staying in the house. In *Sur la Maladie et la Mort de George Sand*, Paulin de Vasson says that this Sagnier was 'a young man from Nîmes who often stayed at Nohant . . .' The unpublished Journal informs us that he had been introduced to Sand on January 27th, 1871, by Jules and Paul Boucoiran, the nephews of Maurice's one-time tutor.

[2] Unpublished. Bibliothèque nationale: Department of Manuscripts.

[3] Jenny de Vasson, the daughter of Paulin and Nannecy.

[4] NANNECY DE VASSON: *Notes et Impressions*. Quoted by Wladimir Karénine in *George Sand*. Volume IV, pp. 599-600.

During the next few days Madame Sand was in a good deal of pain. 'I've got a devil clawing at my inside,' she said. She had an internal stoppage which was so agonizing that she could not keep from crying out. Her friend Doctor Papet said to Maurice, 'She is beyond our help.' Only an immediate operation could have saved her. But Sand wanted to send to Paris for Doctor Favre, in whom she had complete confidence, though in fact he was something of a quack, a great talker, and without any regular medical experience. He was asked to bring one of the great consultants with him. He arrived alone, and said, even before he had seen the patient, 'It is a hernia; I shall treat it with massage.' Aurore Dupin's first success as an actress had been at the English Convent, where, at the age of seventeen, she had appeared in an adaptation of *Le Malade imaginaire,* and now, here she was dying, surrounded by doctors *à la* Molière, all of them determined that if it were to be a question between her and their professional pride, she should be the one to succumb.

Finally the local descendants of 'Diafoirus' decided to call in a surgeon, Jules Péan by name, who judged it impossible to perform an internal operation, and would do no more than give her an abdominal puncture. For another six days, Madame Sand lay in great pain, praying for death, and humiliated by the nature of her illness. On June 7th she asked to see her granddaughters. 'My darlings, how I love you!' she said: 'give me a kiss, and be good girls.' During the night of the 7th-8th, she called out many times, 'Let me die, dear God! let me die!' Both Solange and Lina were now with her. Maurice had sent a note over to Montgivray: 'Our mother is ill, and her condition grave . . . Come if you wish to.' Solange was in Paris. Notified by a telegram which the servants had immediately dispatched, she came, first humbly requesting that she should be told when it would be convenient for her to arrive.

Solange and Lina were watching by the bed when they heard the words: 'Farewell, farewell, I am going to die,' then an unintelligible phrase, ending with—'leave grass' (laissez verdure). There was something in her gaze, and in the way she grasped their hands, which seemed to express great tenderness and good-will, but she lay there in her bed, silent, her mind seemingly elsewhere. Her last words were: 'Goodbye Lina, goodbye Maurice, goodbye Lolo, good . . .' She died at six o'clock in the morning. At the midday meal

Solange occupied her mother's place at the table, and issued orders to all and sundry. Maurice was speechless with misery.

George Sand was buried at Nohant, in the little graveyard in the Park, next to her grandmother, her parents, and her grandchild, Nini. A thin, cold rain was falling. The wind, moaning through the gnarled yews and the box-hedges, mingled with the mutterings of the aged Precentor. All the peasant-women of the neighbourhood kneeled on the wet grass, telling their beads. Much to the surprise of Sand's friends, the service was Catholic. Solange had insisted, and Maurice had given way. The Abbé Villemont, curé of Vic had asked permission of the Archbishop of Bourges, and this the latter, Monsignor de la Tour d'Auvergne, had un-hesitatingly granted. 'He did, right,' said Renan: 'it would have been wrong to trouble the simple minds of the women who came to pray for her with their hoods pulled over their faces and their rosaries in their hands. I, personally, should have been filled with regret had I passed the church porch under the shadow of its great trees without entering.'

Fifteen or so intimate friends had come from Paris. Prince Napoleon, permitted in 1872 to live once more in France, Flaubert, Renan, the younger Dumas, Lambert, Victor Borie, Edouard Cadol, Henry Harrisse, and Calmann Lévy. It was noticed that the giant Marchal was absent. He had always been markedly egotistical. Paul Meurice, representing Victor Hugo, read out a message from the poet:

> I weep for the dead and I salute the deathless . . . Can it be said that we have lost her? No. Great figures such as she may disappear—they do not vanish. Far from it. One might almost say that they take on a new reality. By becoming invisible in one form, they become visible in another. Sublime transfiguration. The human form eclipses what is within, masking the true, the divine visage, which is the 'idea'. George Sand was an 'idea'. She has been released from the flesh and now is free. She is dead and now is living. *Patuit dea.* . . .[1]

No man of letters can listen to the reading of a piece of prose, even at the graveside, without appraising it by

[1] VICTOR HUGO: *Depuis l'Exil.* Volume II, pp. 151-2.

technical standards. Flaubert considered Victor Hugo's
oration decidedly good. Renan remarked that it was a tissue
of clichés. Both were right, for Victor Hugo's clichés go to
the making of what is good in Victor Hugo. Suddenly a
nightingale started to sing with so sweet a voice that several
of those present said to themselves: 'Ah, that is the only sort
of speech the occasion needs!'

> *Flaubert to Turgénieff, June 25th, 1876:* The death of
> our poor mother Sand has caused me infinite pain. I cried
> my eyes out at the funeral, and not once but on two
> separate occasions: the first, when I embraced her little
> granddaughter, Aurore (whose eyes looked so like hers
> that it was as though she had risen from the grave), the
> second, when the coffin was borne past me . . . Poor,
> dear, great woman! Only those who knew her as I did can
> realize just how much of the feminine there was in that
> great man, how deep the tenderness which was so integral
> a part of her genius . . . She will remain one of the
> splendours of France, and her glory will be unrivalled.
> . . .[1]

VI

> 'Consuelo—what a strange name,' said the Count.
> 'A beautiful name, Your Highness,' replied Anzoleto. 'It
> means *consolation.*'   *George Sand*

'THAT HUGO was himself far below the level of his own
Bishop Bienvenu, I am well aware. But from the muddle of
his passions the child of earth could breathe life into a saint
who was more than a man. Similarly, George Sand, though
her personal life was mediocre, warped, frustrated, as are all
human lives, could create the supreme figure of Consuelo in
whom all women can find something to imitate, all men
something to understand in all women.'[2]

Like every woman, George Sand was a child of earth. She

[1] GUSTAVE FLAUBERT: *Correspondance.* Volume VII, p.
311.

[2] ALAIN: *Propos de Littérature.*

was more so than most, by reason of her discordant childhood, of the struggle within her between two social classes and two periods of history, of her precocious freedom, and of the painful experience forced upon her by a marriage which had never so much as approached the level on which her genius lived. Beyond all doubt, her life had been frustrated, as all lives are, but on a grand scale.

She attached but small importance to her work, because the true object of her search had always been the Absolute, at first in human love, later in love of the 'People', finally in love of her grandchildren, of nature, and of God. All the same, speak though she might with humility of her books, much that she achieved is still a living reality. 'George Sand has become immortal as the author of *Consuelo,* a work which strikes the true Pascalian note.' That is true enough, but the same may be said of her *Journal intime,* of her *Lettres d'un Voyageur,* of the immense accumulation of her Correspondence, so moderate in tone, so intellectually solid; of the lasting truth of her ideas. Many of the theses which she defended to the astonishment of unimaginative readers in her own day have now been absorbed into the political thought common to all the better elements of our contemporary societies. She demanded equality for women —they are well on the way to obtaining it. She demanded for the 'People' an equality, finding its expression in universal suffrage and a more just distribution of material wealth—things that are now a commonplace of all honest thought.

There have been many to blame her adventures in love: but the breathless, desperate nature of her search can be explained by the perfection—beyond all human power to find—which she pursued. George Sand's life brings to mind those novels by Graham Greene in which, through three hundred pages, a tormented hero commits every imaginable sin, and the reader discovers in the very last paragraph that it is the sinner, not the pharisee, who is marked out for salvation. Those fiery souls, the raw material of saintliness, have, more often than not, suffered much storm and stress in youth.

The life of every one of us rests upon a latent metaphysic. Sand's philosophy was simple. She believed that the world has been created by a good God, and that such powers of love as we possess proceed from Him. The only sin for which there can be no forgiveness is the sullying, by lies and reticencies, of the love which should be complete and

absolute communion. I do not say that Sand's own life was
always on the level of her principles. None of us remains
true to his ideas at every moment of existence. But human
beings should be judged rather in the light of their
occasional success in rising above themselves than by the
measure of that more common weakness which consists in
falling below their self-enjoined standards.

Posterity has not been deceived. Round about 1830,
public opinion in the little Berry township dealt hardly with
Aurore Dudevant. Today, there stands in La Châtre a
statue of George Sand. The outcast and the sinner has
become the patron saint of the district. Those who were
her friends—Néraud, Papet, Duvernet, Fleury—live on,
because their names are bracketed with hers in memory.
But where are the judges who condemned her? Who, now,
remembers their titles or their negative virtues?

When the centenary of Chopin's death was celebrated in
1949, all Berry met at Nohant. Admirers of George Sand
travelled there from distant countries. In a mood of simple
piety, the guests of a day looked with wondering eyes at the
fantastic puppets which had danced for Flaubert and for
Dumas; at the studio where Delacroix had worked; at the
lawns on which Marie d'Agoult's white shawl had fluttered
in the darkness. Then they went into the gloomy funereal
copse to meditate upon the tombstones which relate, with
that masterly concision which only death can compass, her
strange and lovely story.

*Marie Aurore de Saxe, Comtesse de Horn, Widow of
Dupin de Francueil, 1748-1821 . . . Maurice Dupin,
Lieutenant-General in the 1st Regiment of Hussars, 1778-
1808 . . . Antoinette-Sophie-Victoire Delaborde* (with an
epitaph now moss encrusted and illegible) . . . *Amantine-
Lucille-Aurore Dupin, Baronne Dudevant, GEORGE
SAND, born in Paris, 1st July 1804, died at Nohant, 8th
June 1876 . . .* And, side by side with this great succession,
still other names: *Marc-Antoine Dudevant* (Cocoton):
Jeanne-Gabrielle (Nini, though this name, so much hated
by Clésinger, is not mentioned on the stone); then: *Maurice
Sand, Baron Dudevant (1823-1889); Lina Sand, born
Calamatta (1842-1901); Solange Clésinger Sand, mother of
Jeanne (1828-1899);* and, finally, *Gabrielle Sand, wife of
Palazzi (1858-1909)*—who once, this last, had been Titite.

As to Lolo, who became Madame Lauth-Sand, active and
limber for all her eighty-three years, she tripped, that day,
along the garden paths, ran up the flight of old stone steps,

pointed out the great oval table made by the carpenter Pierre-Bonnin, the tiny desk at which *Indiana* had been written, the piano on which Liszt and Chopin had played, turning the while upon the crowd of reverent visitors those velvety black eyes which were her grandmother's legacy to her. When darkness fell, those present sat upon the terrace in the moonlight, gazing at the black cedars and the weeping willows. The scent of the rose trees which George Sand had planted drifted about the ardent pilgrims. Through the windows of the blue drawing-room, wide open on the Park, came the notes of those *Preludes* and *Nocturnes* which Chopin had composed within those walls, with his dear friend's hand upon his shoulder as he played. The sound was like the murmur of vague and melancholy confidences whispered on the light breath of a sigh. Those listening remembered the gentle sorrows of their own unhappiness. Then the blue note soared, and with it now came hope. Twin voices of the vanished great seemed to be speaking to the assembled visitors: 'Have trust, ye men of little faith. Lovers' quarrels die, the works inspired by love remain. There is room still in this world for tenderness and beauty.' Consuelo had triumphed over Lélia. Such is the unspoken judgment of the generations.

A NOTE ON THE BIRTH OF SOLANGE DUDEVANT-SAND

THERE ARE two theories about Solange's birth. Madame Aurore Lauth-Sand believes that Solange was the legitimate daughter of Casimir Dudevant. This view would seem to be supported by the fact that when Solange grew up she was well received, and generously sheltered, at Guillery. It was there that she gave birth to the two daughters of her marriage with Clésinger. The Baron never showed any especial preference for Maurice. 'It is certain', says Madame Aurore Lauth-Sand, 'that in the years 1827 and 1828 my grandmother made one last effort to be reconciled with her husband.'

The present Comte de Grandsagne, author of *Une His-*

toire Sommaire des Grandsagne, holds a diametrically opposite view. He draws attention to the striking resemblance which exists between his own daughter, La Victomtesse du Manior, and the portrait of Solange by Charpentier. In his volume of genealogical research, after making mention of the legitimate son of Stéphane (Paul-Emile-Trancrède Ajasson de Grandsagne, who died in 1902) he adds: 'Stéphane had had by George Sand a natural daughter who later became Madame Clésinger, and left no descendants.'

Paul-Emile Ajasson de Grandsagne (1842-1902), the son of Stéphane, was a Professor of Mathematics at the Collège Chaptal, and, later, editor-in-chief of the *Moniteur de la Guerre.* In 1876 he became Director of the *Moniteur général,* the official organ of the 'Service des Travaux de la Ville de Paris'. This publication contained a regular feature of *Correspondence,* and *Answers to Questions.* In the issue dated January 6th, 1900, the following reply to an earlier question was printed.

'As has been previously mentioned, there are in our possession 123 unpublished letters written by George Sand between the years 1820 and 1838. These letters are addressed to the man who was everything to her, and to whom she owed a considerable part of her knowledge, and of her immense talent as a writer. In the Province of Berry it is commonly held as true that from the age of sixteen or seventeen onwards, Aurore Dupin was on terms of extreme intimacy with Stéphane Ajasson de Grandsagne, the founder of the system of Public Libraries. (. . .). The letters in question are deeply interesting, but too curious to admit of publication. Were their contents known, they would completely overturn the generally accepted views on the life of the distinguished woman who was one of the glories of the nineteenth century. (. . .). We can, however, say that, in the course of this correspondence, there are frequent mentions of *Solange,* George Sand's daughter, who married the sculptor Clésinger. . . .'

It seems clear that this note was supplied by Paul-Emile de Grandsagne, the editor of the periodical in which it appeared. He had been introduced to George Sand in 1858. During the course of a stay in Berry, he had been taken to Nohant by his uncle, Jules de Grandsagne (his age at that time being sixteen). He met Sand again in Paris, and even during her time at Palaiseau. 'She more than once expressed a desire that her correspondence with Stéphane should never be made public'—adds the note in the *Moniteur général.*

I give below a few more facts which throw some light upon the problem.

On December 13th, 1827, that is, nine months to a day before the birth of Solange (which took place on September 13th, 1828) Aurore Dudevant was in Paris, whence she addressed a letter to Casimir, who had remained alone at Nohant:

Paris: December 13th, 1827: 'I am to see Broussais tomorrow if Stéphane is as good as his word. (. . .) Stéphane is coming this morning. Should he find it possible to leave on Monday, I might, perhaps, cancel the rest of my engagements. . . .

'*Noon* . . . Stéphane is compelled to spend Monday here, and has begged me most urgently not to leave before Tuesday. So, I must put off my departure. . .'[1]

Nine years later, when the action for separation was pending, Casimir drew up a Memorandum (cf. Spoelberch de Lovenjoul Collection, Group E. 948) which contains the following suggestive sentence: *November 1827:* Journey to Paris with Stéphane Ajasson de Grandsagne—pretext health.

We have also another piece of information supplied by Louise Vincent in her Doctoral Thesis (p. 122). 'It is still remembered in Nérac that, in 1837, when George Sand went to Guillery to fetch back Solange, who had been kidnapped by Dudevant, she said, "the oddest part of the whole business is that he is laying claim to a child who does not belong to him".'

It seems that Hippolyte Châtiron, too, had heard it said in Berry that Solange was the child of adultery. In a letter to his brother-in-law he alludes to this. The document is now at Chantilly. *Hippolyte to Casimir, June 28th, 1836:* 'As to the custody of Solange, 'pon my word, it's impossible not to take sides with you. *I'll only say this, that, from what I have heard, you should have no great difficulty about winning your case!*'

Finally, though Louise Vincent was not allowed to see Sand's letters to Stéphane, she seems to have had access to other documents bearing on their relationship. She wrote: 'There are letters which do not form part of the Spoelberch

---

[1] Spoelberch de Lovenjoul Collection: Group E. 868.

Collection . . . After her breach with Musset, Sand indulged
in a good deal of moaning over her misfortunes . . . *Before
ever Jules Sandeau came on the scene, she had had a lover
of whom Jules knew nothing.* There is another letter, also unpublished, in which she asks Madame Grandsagne's
forgiveness *for having caused her pain, for having had a
love affair with her husband.* She hopes and believes that
Madame de Grandsagne will be generous enough to pardon
her for the wrong she has committed. . . .'[1]

[1] LOUISE DE VINCENT: *George Sand et le Berry*, p. 125.

BIBLIOGRAPHY

MANUSCRIPT SOURCES

N.a.f. (fonds Aurore Sand): Diaries of George Sand, 1852-76: Unpublished Journal: Unpublished letters of Alexandre Dumas the younger to George Sand. Letters, in part unpublished, from George Sand to Dr. Emile Regnault. *Sketches and Hints*, manuscript in Sand's own hand, of a youthful journal. Letters from Chopin to George Sand.

Cote 24639 (fonds Balachowsky-Petit): Unpublished letters from George Sand to Alexandre Dumas the younger.

SPOELBERCH DE LOVENJOUL COLLECTION

E. 868. Correspondence, in part unpublished, between Aurore and Casimir Dudevant: Confession addressed by Aurore Dudevant to her husband. Letters from Hippolyte Châtiron to Casimir Dudevant.

E. 872. Unpublished Correspondence between George Sand, Marie d'Agoult and Carlotta Marliani.

E. 675, E. 876, E. 877. Unpublished letters from George Sand to Emile Aucante.

E. 879. Letters to Pierre Bocage.

E. 881. Letters, mostly unpublished, from George Sand to Michel de Bourges.

E. 881. *bis* and 881 *ter:* Unpublished letters from George Sand to Marie Dorval.

E. 883. Unpublished letters from George Sand to Alexis Dutheil.

E. 902. Journal addressed by Aurore Dudevant to Aurélien de Sèze: Letters of Aurélien de Sèze to Aurore Dudevant: Correspondence between Aurore Dudevant and Zoé Leroy.

E. 917. Unpublished letters from George Sand to Eliza Tourangin.

E. 920. Unpublished letters from George Sand to Jules Boucoiran, and other correspondents.

E. 921. Unpublished letters from George Sand to Théodore Rousseau, Gustabe Chaix d'Est-Ange and Charles Poncy. Letters, in part unpublished, from George Sand to her son Maurice.

E. 948. File of the Suit for Separation between the Dudevant husband and wife.

E. 953. Unpublished letters from Eugène Lambert to Emile Aucante.

E. 954. Letters from the Comte Ajasson de Grandsagne to Madame Varvara Komarow (Wladimir Karénine): Letters from Comte Ajasson de Grandsagne to the Vicomte Spoelberch de Lovenjoul.

PRIVATE COLLECTIONS

Madame Aurore Lauth-Sand's Collection

Unpublished Journal kept by Aurore Dupin when she was a young girl at the Convent of the English Ladies: Unpublished letters from Hippolyte Châtiron to Aurore Dudevant: Correspondence between George Sand and her daughter Solange: Unpublished letters from Prince Charles Radziwill to Solange Clésinger, etc.

Madame Bonnier de la Chapelle's Collection.

Unpublished Correspondence between George Sand and Jules Hetzel (P.-J. Stahl).

Monsieur Henri Goüin's Collection

Letters from George Sand to Edouard Rodrigues.

Monsieur Alfred Dupont's Collection

Unpublished letters from Lamennais to various correspondents.

Monsieur Jacques Suffel's Collection

Unpublished letters from George Sand to Duris-Dufresne.

Simone André-Maurois' Collection

Unpublished letters from Marie Dorval to George Sand: Unpublished letters from George Sand to Augustiné de Bertholdi, Charles Marchal, Edouard Charton and général Ferri-Pisani: Unpublished letters from Sainte-Beuve to Jeanne de Tourbey and Solange Clésinger: Letters from Marie Dorval to Félicie Sandeau.

PRINTED SOURCES

Adam (Juliette Lamber, Madame Edmond): *Mes Premières Armes Littéraires et politiques* (Paris: Lemeree, 1904): *Mes Sentiments et nos Idées avant 1870* (Paris, Lemerre, 1905).

Aderer (Adolphe): *Souvenirs inédits de Chopin* (*Le Temps*, January 28th, 1903): *George Sand et Marie Dorval* (*Le Temps*, February 19th and 21st, 1903).

Ageorges (Joseph): *L'Enclos de George Sand* (Paris, Bernard Grasset, 1910).

Albert-Petit (A.): *George Sand avant George Sand* (*Journal des Débats*, March 27th, 1896).

Amic (Henri): *George Sand. Mes Souvenirs* (Paris, Calmann-Lévy 1893): *La Défense de George Sand* (*Le Figaro*, November 2nd, 1896).

Anonymous: *Compte rendu de la procédure qui a eu lieu les 10 et 11 mai 1836 à La Châtre* (*Le Droit*, May 18th, 1896).

Anonymous: *Procès de Séparation de corps de Madame Dudevant, auteur des ouvrages publiés sous le nom de George Sand: arrêt de partage (Gazette des Tribuneaux,* July 31st and August 1st, 1836).

Balzac (Honoré de): *Lettres à l' Etrangère,* Volume I (Paris, Calmann-Lévy, 1899), Volume II (id. 1906), Volume III (id. 1933), Volume IV (id. 1950), Volume V (still unpublished in 1952). The originals are in the Spoelberch de Lovenjoul Collection: *Correspondance avec Lulma Carraud,* revised and enlarged edition published by Marcel Bouteron (Paris, Gallimard, 1951): *Lettres à sa Famille* (Paris, Albin Michel, 1951): *Béatrix* (Paris, Souverain, 1839): *Mémories de deux Jeunes Mariées,* dedication to George Sand (Paris, Souverain, 1842).

Barbès (Armand): *Lettres à Georges Sand (Revue de Paris,* July 1st, 1896).

Barbey d'Aurévilly (Jules): *Les Oeuvres et les Hommes au XIXme Siècle,* V: *Les Bas-Bleus* (Paris, Societé générale de Librairie catholique, 1878).

Barine (Arvède): *Alfred de Musset* (Paris, Hachette, 1893).

Barrett Browning (Elizabeth): *Letters,* edited by Frederick G. Kenyon, 2 volumes (London, Smith, Elder & Co., 1898).

Baudelaire (Charles): *Oeuvres posthumes et Correspondances inédites,* edited by Eugène Crépet (Paris, Quantin, 1887).

Baudelaire (Charles): *Journeaux intimes* (Paris, *Mercure de France,* 1908): *Mon Coeurmis a nu; Ecrits intimes,* with a Preface by Jean-Paul Sartre (Paris, éditions du Point du Jour, 1946).

Béranger: *Correspondance,* edited by Paul Boiteau, 4 volumes (Paris, Perrotin, 1860).

Bertaut (Jules): *George Sand devant la critique (l'Opinion,* January 16th, 1909): *Une Amitié romantique: George Sand et François Rollinat (Revue de Paris,* June 1st, 1914).

Bidou (Henri): *La Chartreuse de Valdemosa* (Supplement to *Le Journal des Débats,* July 1st, 1904).

Billy (André): *Balzac,* 2 volumes (Paris, Flammarion, 1944-47).

Blaze de Bury (Henri): *Episode de l'Histoire du Hanovre: Les Koenigsmark* (Paris, Michel Lévy, 1855): *Les Amours de Chopin et de George Sand (Mercure de France,* June 1900).

Brault: *Une Contemporaine: Biographie et Intrigues de George Sand* (Brochure issued without a publisher's name, Paris, 1848).

Brisson (Adolphe): *Les Amours de George Sand (Le Temps,* October 25th, 1896): *George Sand et Alfred de Musset (Le Temps,* December 23rd, 1896): *Gabrielle Sand* (Les Annales politiques et littéraires, July 18th, 1904).

Brunetière (Ferdinand): *Historie et Littérature,* Volume V, II: *George Sand et Flaubert* (Paris, Calmann-Lévy, 1891).

Cabanès (Docteur): *Un Roman vécu a trois personnages: Alfred de Musset, George Sand, Pagello (La Revue hebdomadaire,* October 24th, 1896).

Cadol (Edouard): *Une Visite à Nohant. La Bête noire* (Paris, Lévy: 1875).

Capo de Feuillide: *Lélia, par George Sand (l'Europe littéraire,* August 22nd, 1833).

Caro (Edmé): *George Sand* (Paris, Hachette, 1887).

Castellane (Maréchal de): *Journal,* 5 volumes (Paris, Plon, 1896), cf. Volume IV, 1847-53.

Catalogue de la Bibliothèque de Madame George Sand et de M. Maurice Sand—offered for sale, February 24th—March 3rd, 1890 (Paris, Ferroud, Librairie des Amateurs, 1890).

Chambon (Félix): *Notessur Prosper Mérimée* (Paris, Dorbon ainé, 1904).

Charpentier (John): *George Sand* (Paris, Tallandier, 1936). *Alfred de Musset* (Paris, Tallandier, 1938).

Chateaubriand: *Mémoires d'outre-tombe:* Edition du Centenaire edited by Maurice Levaillant, 4 volumes (Paris, Flammarion, 1948), cf. Volumes III and IV.

Chopin (*Souvenirs inédits de Frédéric*) edited by Misczyslaw Karlowicz. Translated by Laure Disière (Paris, H. Walter, 1904),

Claretie (Jules): *La Vie à Paris, 1880-83* (Paris, Harvard, 1881-84): *Jules Sandeau* (Paris, Quantin, 1883); *Madame Dorval (Le Temps,* April 1st, 1904).

Clément (Abbé S.): *George Sand: Souvenirs d'un curé de campagne* (Bourges, Sire, 1901).

Clouard (Maurice): *Alfred de Musset et George Sand (Revue de Paris,* August 15th, 1896): *Alfred de Musset: documents inédits* (Paris, Chaix, 1896): *Alfred de Musset: lauréat de l'Académie (Nouvelle Revue,* 1899).

Colet (Louise): *Lui* (Paris, Calmann-Lévy, 1880).

Cornuault (Charles-Pierre): *Une Grande Passion d'un grand Ecrivain* (Aix-en-Provence, Editions de la Victoire).

Coupy (Etienne): *Marie Dorval* (Paris, Albert Lacroix, Librairie Internationale, 1868).

Davray (Jean): *George Sand et ses Amants* (Paris, Albin-Michel, 1935).

Delacroix (Eugène) *Journal,* 3 volumes (Paris, Plon, 1932): *Correspondance générale,* edited by André Joubin, 5 volumes (Paris, Plon, 1936-38).

Donnay (Maurice): *Alfred de Musset* (Paris, Hachette, 1914).

Dorval (Marie): *Lettres à Alfred de Vigny,* edited by Charles Gaudier (Paris, Gallimard, 1942).

Dostoievsky (Fédor): *Journal d'un Ecrivain,* translated from the Russian by J-W. Bienstock and J-A. Nau (Paris, Charpentier, 1904), cf. *La Mort de George Sand,* pp. 225-36.

Doumic (René: *George Sand* (Paris, Perrin, 1908): *l'Amie de Michel de Bourges. Mauprat (Revue hebdomadaire*, March 1909): *Dix Années de la Vie de George Sand (Revue des Deux Mondes*, April 15th, 1912).

Duquesnel (Félix): *Les Diners Magny* (Le Gaulois, June 30th, 1904): *George Sand intime (Le Temps*, September 30th, 1912 and January 4th, 1913): *Comment écrivait George Sand (Le Temps*, October 10th, 1912): *Nohant (Le Temps*, January 7th, 1913).

Escholier (Raymond): *Delacroix, 3 volumes (Paris, Floury, 1926-29).*

Faguet (Emile): *XIXe Siècle. Etudes littéraires. George Sand; Amours d'Hommes de Lettres: George Sand et Musset* (Paris, Societé française d'Imprimerie et de Librairie); *Michel de Bourges (Revue des Deux Mondes*, November 1st, 1909).

Fidao (J-E.): *Pierre Leroux (Revue des Deux Mondes*, May 15th, 1906).

Foemina (Madame Bulteau): *Les Koenigsmark* (Literary Supplement of the *Figaro*, March 7th and 14th, 1914).

Fontaney (Antoine): *Journal intime*, edited by René Jasinski (Paris, Les Presses Françaises, 1925).

Forgues (E.): *Correspondance inédite entre Lamennais et la Baron de Vitrolles* (Paris, Charpentier, 1886).

France (Anatole): *Le vie littéraire*, Volume I (Paris, Calmann-Lévy, 1892).

Gailly de Taurines (Ch.): *Aventuriers et Femmes de qualité*: cf. *Le Fille du Maréchal de Saxe* (Paris, Hachette, 1907).

Galzy (Jeanne): *George Sand* (Paris, Julliard, 1950).

Ganche (Edouard): *Frédéric Chopin, sa vie et ses oeuvres* (Paris, Mercure de France, 1913).

Gestat (Pierre): *La Vie mouvementée et passionnée d'un grand avocat. Michel de Bourges* (Bourges, Societé historique et littéraire du Cher, 1949).

Ginisty (Paul): *Le Baron Haussmann et Geoge Sand (Journal des Débats*, March 31st, 1909): *Bocage* (Paris, Felix Alcan, 1932).

Goncourt (Edmond et Jules de): *Journal des Goncourts*, Volume III (Paris, Charpentier, 1888).

Grandsagne (Paul-Emile Ajasson de): *Correspondance et Qüestions posees* (Le Moniteur général January 6th, 1900).

Grenier (Edouard): *Souvenirs littéraires* (Paris, Lemerre, 1894).

Greville (Henry): *Maurice Sand* (Versailles, Cerf et fils, 1889).

Halpérine-Kaminsky (Ely): *Lettres d'Ivan Tourgueneff à Madame Viardot (Revue hebdomadaire*, October 1st, 1898): *Ivan Tourgueneff d'apres sa correspondance avec ses amis français* (Paris, Eugène Fasquella, 1901).

Haussmann (Baron): Mémoires (Paris, V. Havard, 1890), cf.
Volume II, pp. 129-36.

Haussonville (Othenin, vicomte d'); *Etudes biographiques et
littéraires: George Sand.* (Paris, Calmann-Levy, 1879).

Heine (Heinrich) *Sämmtliche Werke* (Hamburg, Hoffmann und
Campe, 1874): *Briefe von Heinrich Heine,* edited by Eugen
Wolff (Bereslau, Schottländer, 1893).

Hevesy (André de): *Liszt et les Romantiques (Revue de Paris,*
November 1st, 1911).

Heylli (Georges d'): (Edmond Poinsot): *La Fille de George
Sand* (Paris, without publisher's imprint, 1900. Limited to
200 copies).

Histoire de Maurice, comte de Saxe, 2 volumes, author unnamed
(Dresden, Walther, 1770).

Houssaye (Arsène): *Confessions. Souvenirs d'un demi-siècle*
(1830-90) (Paris, Dentu, 1891), cf. Volumes V and VI.

Isaac (Le Bibliophile), (Charles, vicomte de Spoelberch de
Louvenjoul): *Etude Bibliographique sur les oeuvres de
George Sand* (Brussels, 1868). Only 100 copies printed. See
also under Lovenjoul.

Janin (Jules): *Biographies de Femmes auteurs: George Sand*
(Paris, Alfred de Montferrand, 1836).

Jasinski (Rene): *Les années romantiques de Théophile Gautier*
(Paris, Vuibert, 1929).

Jaubert (Caroline): *Souvenirs, Lettres et Correspondances*
(Paris, Hetzel, 1881).

Karénine (Wladimir), (Varvara Komarow): *George Sand, sa
vie et ses oeuvres,* 4 volumes. Volume I (1804-33) and
Volume II (1833-38) (Paris, Ollendorff, 1899), Volume
III (1838-48) (Paris, Plon-Nourrit, 1912), Volume IV
(1848-1876) (Paris, Plon, 1926).

Karlowicz (Mieczylaw): *Lettres inédites de Chopin et Souvenirs
de Chopin (La Revue hebdomadaire,* January to September
1903).

Kératry (Comte de): *Lettres inédites de George Sand (Figaro,*
September 28th, 1888).

Knosp (Gaston): *Journal de Chopin (Le Guide musical,*
September 8th and 15th, 1907).

Laisnel de la Salle (A.): *Anciennes Moeurs, Scènes et Tableaux
de la vie provinciale* (La Châtre, Montu, 1900).

La Rochefoucauld (Sosthène, vicomte de): *Mémories* (Paris,
Allardin), cf. pp. 353-383. Ten letters from George Sand.

La Salle (Bertrand de): *Alfred de Vigny* (Paris, Arthème
Fayard, 1939).

Latouche (Hyacinthe Thabaud de Latouche, known as Henri
de): *Léo* (Paris, Michael Lévy, 1840).

Lauvrière (Em.): *Alfred de Vigny, sa vie et son oeuvre.* Expanded edition in 2 volumes (Paris, Grasset, 1946). Original edition, in one volume (Armand Colin, 1909).

Lecomte du Nouy (Hermine Oudinot, Madame), and Henri Amic: *En regardant passer la vie . . .* (Paris, Ollendorff, 1903): *Jours passés* (Paris, Calmann-Lévy, 1908).

Lemaitre (Jules): *Les Contemporains,* 7 volumes (Paris, Lecène et Oudin, 1886-99), cf. Volume IV, pp. 159-68: *George Sand; Impressions de théâtre,* 10 volumes (Paris, Lecène et Oudin, 1888-98), cf. Volume I, pp. 141-57 and Volume IV, pp. 123-35.

Levallois (Jules): *Sainte-Beuve, Gustave Planche et George Sand (Revue bleue,* January 19th, 1895): *Souvenirs littéraires. Visite chez George Sand (Revue bleue,* March 16th, 1895).

Liszt (Franz): *Lettre d'un Voyageur à monsieur George Sand (Revue et Gazette musicale,* December 6th, 1835: *Frédéric Chopin* (Paris, Escudier, 1852): *Correspondance de Liszt et de Madame d'Agoult,* edited by Daniel Ollivier, 2 volumes (Paris, Grasset, 1933-34): *Correspondance de Liszt et de sa Fille,* Madame Emile Olivier (Paris, Grasset, 1936).

Lorenz (Paul): *Aurore de Koenigsmark* (Paris, Editions de Quatre Vents, 1945).

Lovenjoul (Charles, vicomte de Spoelberch de): *Etudes balzaciennes: Un Roman d'Amour* (Paris, Calmann-Lévy, 1896): *A propos de lettres inédites (Le Figaro,* February 15th and 22nd, 1893): *La Véritable Histoire de "Elle et Lui"* (Paris, Calmann-Lévy, 1897): *Histoire des OEuvres de H. de Balzac.* Third edition, completely revised and corrected (Paris, Calmann-Lévy, 1888): *George Sand. Etude bibliographique sur ses Oeuvres,* published posthumously in an edition of 120 copies. This is a considerably augmented reprint of the bibliography published in Brussels in 1868. The author was working on it up to his death (Paris, Henri Leclerc, 1914).

Magon-Barbaroux: *Michel de Bourges* (Marseilles, Flammarion, Aubertin et Rolle, 1897).

Marbouty (Caroline): known as Claire Brunne: *Une Fausse Position,* 2 volumes (Paris, Amyot, 1844).

Mariéton (Paul): *Une Histoire d'Amour: George Sand et Alfred de Musset* (Paris, Harvard fils, 1897): *Les Amants de Venise* (Paris, Ollendorff, 1903).

Maugras (Gaston): *Les Demiselles de Verrières* (Paris, Calmann-Lévy, 1890).

Maupassant (Guy de): *Préface à l'Edition originale des Lettres de Gustave Flaubert à George Sand* (G. Charpentier, Paris, 1884).

Maurras (Charles): *Les Amants de Venise* (Paris, Albert Fontemoing, 1903).

Maynial (Edouard): *Le Procès en Séparation de George Sand (Mercure de France,* December 1st, 1906).

Mischaut (Dr.): *Une Observation d'Incompatibilité sexuelle (Chronique médicale,* July 1st, 1904): *George Sand et Dumas fils (Chronique médicale,* September 1st, 1904).

Mille (Pierre): *Frédéric Chopin d'après quelques lettres inédites (Revue bleue,* January 7th, 1899).

Monin (Hippolyte): *George Sand et la République de février 1848 (La Révolution française,* November 14th and December 14th, 1899, January 14th and February 14th, 1900).

Moser (Françoise): *Marie Dorval* (Paris, Plon, 1947).

Mourot (Eugène): *Un oublié: Ajasson de Grandsagne* (Paris, Imprimerie Chaix, undated).

Musset (Alfred de): *Confession d'un Enfant du Siècle* (Paris, 1836).

Musset (Paul de): *Lui et Elle* (Paris, Charpentier, 1860).
    Alfred de Musset, Biographe (Paris, Charpentier, 1860).

Nicolas (Auguste): *Aurélien de Seze* (Ch. Douniol, 1870).

Nozières (Fernand): *Marie Dorval* (Félix Alcan, 1928): *Elle et Lui (Le Temps,* June 11th, 1904).

Pailleron (Marie-Louise): *George Sand,* 2 volumes (Paris, Grasset, 1938-42): *François Buloz, et ses Amis.* I. *La Vie littéraire sous Louis-Philippe:* II. *La Revue des Deux Mondes et La Comédie Française* (Paris, Firmin-Didot, 1930): *Le Paradis perdu. Souvenirs d'enfance* (Paris, Albin-Michel, 1947): *Une Petite-Fille de George Sand (Revue des Deux Mondes,* October 15th, 1950).

Parturier (Maurice): *Une Expérience de Lélia ou le Fiasco du comte Gazul* (Paris, Le Divan, 1934): *Deux Lettres de Prosper Mérimée à George Sand* (Paris, Le Divan, 1935).

Pictet (Adolphe): *Une Course à Chamonix* (Paris, Benjamin Duprat, 1838).

Planche (Gustabe): *Portraits littéraires,* 2 volumes (Paris, 1848).

Plauchut (Edmond): *Autour de Nohant (Paris, Calmann-Lévy, 1898): George Sand à Gargilesse (Le Temps,* August 13th, 1901).

Pourtalès (Guy de): *Liszt* (Paris, Gallimard, 1926): *Chopin ou le Poète* (Paris, Gallimard, 1936).

Pyat (Félix): *Comment j'ai connu George Sand (Grande Revue de Paris et de Saint-Petersbourg,* February 15th, 1888).

Ramann (Lina): *Franz Liszt als Kunstler und Mensch,* 3 volumes (Leipzig, Breitkopf und Härtel, 1880-87).

Renan (Ernest): *Feuilles detachées* (Paris, Calmann-Lévy, 1894).

Rocheblave (Samuel): *Une Amitié romanesque: George Sand et Madame d'Agoult (Revue de Paris,* December 15th, 1894): *George Sand avant George Sand (Revue de Paris,* March 15th, 1896): *Préface à l'édition original des Lettres de*

George Sand à Alfred de Musset et à Sainte-Beuve (Paris, Calmann-Lévy, 1897): *George Sand et sa Fille* (Paris, Calmann-Lévy, 1905): *Lettres de George Sand à Charles Poncy (Revue des Deux Mondes,* August 1st and 15th, 1909).

Rollinat (Charles): *Liszt et Chopin (Le Temps,* September 1st, 1874).

Sainte-Beuve (Charles-Augustin): *Correspondance générale,* edited, classified and annotated by Jean Bonnerot, 1818-46 Six volumes (as seven) have already appeared (Paris, Stock, 1935-49).

Sainte-Beuve (Charles Augustin): *Causeries du Lundi,* édition Garnier frères, s.d., 15 volumes. Cf. Volumes I, II, III, IV, IX, X, XI, XII, XIII et XV: *Portraits de Femmes* (Paris, Garnier frères, s.d.). Cf. pp. 103, 163 et 447: *Premier Ludis,* 3 volumes (Paris, Calmann-Lévy, 1886-94). Cf. Volumes II et III: *Portraits contemporains,* 5 volumes (Paris, Calmann-Lévy). Cf. I, II, III et IV: *Nouveaux Lundis,* 13 volumes (Paris, Calmann-Lévy, 1870-94). Cf. I, II, III, V, VI, VIII, IX, X, XI, XII et XIII.

Sand (Aurore): *Souvenirs de Nohant (Revue de Paris,* September 1st, 1916): *Le Berry de George Sand* (Paris, Albert Morance, 1927).

Sand (Maurice): *Masques et Bouffons (Comédie italienne)* (Paris, Michel Lévy, 1860): *Le Monde des Papillons* (Paris, Rothschild, 1866): *Raoul de La Châtre* (Paris, Michel Lévy, 1865).

Sandeau (Jules): *Marianna* (Paris, Werdet, 1832).

Saxe (Maurice, comte de): *Lettres et Documents inédits,* edited by le comte d'Eckstaadt (Leipzig, Denicka, 1867).

Saxe (Maurice, maréchal de): *Mes Rêveries* (Paris, Durand, 1757).

Séché (Alphonse): *Alfred de Musset anecdotique* (Paris, Sansot, 1907).

Séché (Alphonse) et Bertaut (Jules): *La Vie anecdotique et pittoresque des grands Ecrivains: George Sand* (Grand-Montrouge, Louis Michaud, 1909).

Séché (Léon): *Sainte-Beuve, son esprit, ses idées, ses moeurs,* 2 volumes *(Mercure de France,* 1904): *Correspondance inédite de Sainte-Beuve avec M. et Mme Juste Olivier* (Paris, *Mercure de France,* 1904): *Hortense Allart de Méritens, dans ses rapports avec Chateaubriand, Béranger, Lamennais, Sainte-Beuve, George Sand, Madame d'Agoult* (Paris, *Mercure de France,* 1908): *Lettres inédites d'Hortense Allart de Méritens à Sainte-Beuve* (1841-48), with an Introduction and notes by Léon Séché.

Ségu (Frédéric): *Henri de Latouche, 1785-1851* (Paris, Société d'édition 'Les Belles Lettres', 1931). *Le Premier Figaro,*

1826-1833 (Paris, Société d'édition 'Les Belles Lettres',
1932).

Seillière (Baron Ernest): *George Sand, mystique de la passion*
(Paris, Félix-Alcan, 1920). *Nouveaux Portraits de Femmes*
(Paris, Emile-Paul, 1923).

Sellards (John): *Charles Didier, 1805-1864* Paris, Honoré
Champion, 1904).

Silver (Mabel): *Jules Sandeau, l'homme et la vie* (Paris, Boivin et
Cie, L'Entente Linotypiste, 1936).

Stern (Daniel), Marie de Flavigny, comtesse d'Agoult: *Historie
de la Révolution de 1848*, 3 volumes (Paris, G. Sandre,
1851). Cf. Volume II, *Nélida* (Paris, d'Amyot, 1846).
Souvenirs (Paris, Calmann-Lévy, 1877). *Mémoires* (Calmann-Lévy, 1927). *Autour de Madame d'Agoult et Liszt
(Paris, Bernard Frasset, 1941). Letters edited by Daniel
Ollivier.*

Taine (Hippolyte): *Derniers Essais de Critique et d'Histoire*
(Paris, Hachette, 1894).

Tocqueville (Alexis de): *Souvenirs* (Paris, Calmann-Lévy, 1893).

Toesca (Maurice): *Une Autre George Sand* (Paris, Plon, 1945).

Troubat (Jules): *Souvenirs du dernier Secrétaire de Sainte-Beuve*
(Paris, Calmann-Lévy, 1890).

Vicaire (Georges): *Manuel de l'Amateur de Livres au XIXe
siècle*, 8 volumes (Paris, P. Rouquette, 1894-1920).

Viel-Castel (Comte Horace de): *Mémorires sur le temps de
Napoléon III, 1851-1864*. Six volumes (Berne, Imprimerie
Haller, 1883).

Vincent (Louise): *George Sand et le Berry* (Paris, Edouard
Champion, 1919): *George Sand et l'Amour* (Paris,
Champion, 1917): *La Langue et le Style de George Sand
dans les Romans champêtres* (Paris, Edouard Champion,
1919).

Vivent (Jacques): *La Vie privée de George Sand* (Paris,
Hachette, 1949).

Vuillermoz (Emile): *Vie amoureuse de Chopin* (Paris,
Flammarion, 1927).

Wodzinski (Comte): *Les Trois Romans de Frédéric Chopin*
(Paris, Calmann-Lévy, 1886): ch. pp. 259-323: *George Sand.*

Zola (Emile): *Documents littéraires, Etudes et Portraits: George
Sand* (Paris, G. Charpentier, 1881).

Zweig (Stefan): *Balzac* (Paris, Albin Michel, 1950).

[While the present work was in the press, the author
received, in December 1951, the book by M. Edouard
Dolléans, entitled: *Féminisme et Mouvement ouvrier,
George Sand* (Les Editions Ouvrières, collection 'Masses et
Militants', Paris, 1951), and, also, the special number of the

Revue de Sciences Humaines, devoted to *Les Problêmes du Romantisme.* This particular issue contained an article by Mme Thérèse Marix-Spire: 'Bataille de Dames, George Sand et Madame d'Agoult'.]

INDEX